D1530734

SCHOOLING IN THE CULTURAL CONTEXT

Anthropological Studies of Education

EDUCATIONAL POLICY, PLANNING AND THEORY
Series Editor: Don Adams, University of Pittsburgh

SCHOOLING

IN

THE

CULTURAL

CONTEXT

Anthropological Studies of Education

JOAN I. ROBERTS

SHERRIE K. AKINSANYA

DAVID McKAY COMPANY, INC./NEW YORK

SCHOOLING IN THE CULTURAL CONTEXT:
ANTHROPOLOGICAL STUDIES OF EDUCATION

Copyright © 1976 by David McKay Company, Inc.

Manufactured in the United States of America

Developmental Editor: Nicole Benevento
Interior Design: Angela Foote
Cover Design: Jane Sterrett
Production and Manufacturing Supervisor: Donald W. Strauss
Composition: Automated Composition Service, Inc.
Printing and Binding: Hamilton Printing Company

Library of Congress Cataloging in Publication Data

Main entry under title:

Schooling in the cultural context.

(Educational policy, planning, and theory)
Bibliography: p.
1. Educational anthropology—Addresses, essays,
lectures. I. Roberts, Joan I. II. Akinsanya,
Sherrie K.
LB45.S36   301.2'1   75-42022
ISBN 0-679-30290-5

11/21/77 Aul. 8.95

For Yemi and Kemi

Acknowledgments

"Criteria for an Ethnographic Approach to Research in Schools" by Harry Wolcott is reprinted by permission of the Society for Applied Anthropology from *Human Organization*, Vol. 34, No. 2 (Summer 1975).

"Explicit and Implicit Culture in Puerto Rico: A Case Study in Educational Anthropology" by Theodore Brameld is reprinted from *Harvard Educational Review*, Vol. 28 (Summer 1958), 197–213. Copyright © 1958 by President and Fellows of Harvard College.

"Culture and Education in the Midwestern Highlands of Guatemala" by Robert Redfield is reprinted from *American Journal of Sociology*, Vol. 48 (1943) by permission of *American Journal of Sociology*, copyright 1943 by the University of Chicago Press.

"Alternative Attempts at Instruction in Atchalán" by G. Alexander Moore is reprinted from *Life Cycles in Atchalán: The Diverse Careers of Certain Guatemalans* (New York: Teachers College Press, copyright 1973 by Teachers College, Columbia University), pp. 156–193.

"The School at Vaucluse: Educating the French Child" by Laurence Wylie is reprinted from *Village in the Vaucluse*, 3rd ed., pp. 64–97. Copyright © 1957, 1964, 1974 by Harvard University Press. Reprinted by permission of Harvard University Press.

"The School: Authority, Its Sources and Uses" by Richard L. Warren is reprinted from *Education in Rebhausen, A German Village* by Richard L. Warren. Copyright © 1967 by Holt, Rinehart and Winston, Inc. Reprinted by permission of Holt, Rinehart and Winston, Inc.

"Village or City? Identity, Choice and Cultural Change" by George D. Spindler is reprinted from *Burgbach: Urbanization and Identity in a German Village* by George D. Spindler. Copyright © 1973 by Holt, Rinehart and Winston, Inc. Reprinted by permission of Holt, Rinehart and Winston, Inc.

"The Rebirth of a Grandfather's Spirit: Shumba's Two Worlds" by Clive Kileff is reprinted by permission of the Society for Applied Anthropology from *Human Organization*, Vol. 34, No. 2 (Summer 1975), 129–137.

"Instruction and Affect in Hopi Cultural Continuity" by Dorothy Eggan is reprinted from *Journal of Anthropological Research* (formerly *Southwestern Journal of Anthropology*), Vol. 12, No. 4 (1956). Copyright © 1956 by *Journal of Anthropological Research*.

"Educational Innovation and Desegregation: A Case Study of Symbolic Realignment" by Elizabeth M. Eddy is reprinted by permission of the Society for Applied Anthropology from *Human Organization*, Vol. 34, No. 2 (Summer 1975), 163–172.

"Attitude Organization in Elementary School Classrooms" by Jules Henry is reprinted from the *American Journal of Orthopsychiatry*, Vol. 27, No. 1 (January 1957), 117–133. Copyright © the American Orthopsychiatric Association, Inc. Reproduced by permission.

"Spontaneity, Initiative, and Creativity in Suburban Classrooms" by Jules Henry is reprinted from the *American Journal of Orthopsychiatry*, Vol. 29, No. 2 (1959), 266–279. Copyright © the American Orthopsychiatric Association, Inc. Reproduced by permission.

"The Amish Elementary School Teacher and Students" by John A. Hostetler and Gertrude Enders Huntington is reprinted from *Children in Amish Society* by John A. Hostetler and Gertrude Enders. Copyright © 1971 by Holt, Rinehart and Winston, Inc. Reprinted by permission of Holt, Rinehart and Winston, Inc.

"Cherokee School Society and the Intercultural Classroom" by Robert V. Dumont, Jr., and Murray L. Wax is reproduced by permission of the Society for Applied Anthropology from *Human Organization*, Vol. 23, No. 3 (Fall 1969).

"Oglala Sioux Dropouts and Their Problems with Educators" by Rosalie H. Wax is reprinted from *Education and School Crisis: Perspectives on Teaching Disadvantaged Youth*, edited by Everett T. Keach, R. Fulton, and W. E. Gardner. Copyright © 1967 by John Wiley & Sons, Inc. Reprinted by permission of John Wiley & Sons, Inc.

"Shut Those Thick Lips! Can't You Behave Like a Human Being?" by Gerry Rosenfeld is reprinted from *"Shut Those Thick Lips!" A Study of Slum School Failure* by Gerry Rosenfeld. Copyright © 1971 by Holt, Rinehart and Winston, Inc. Reprinted by permission of Holt, Rinehart and Winston, Inc.

"Realities of the Urban Classroom" by G. Alexander Moore, Jr., is reprinted from *Realities of the Urban Classroom* by G. Alexander Moore, Jr. Copyright © 1964, 1967, by G. Alexander Moore, Jr. Reprinted by permission of Doubleday & Company, Inc.

"The Transmission of Culture" by Solon T. Kimball is reprinted from *Educational Horizons*, Vol. 43 (1965). Copyright © 1965 by *Educational Horizons*. Reproduced by permission of the Author and Publisher.

"Lineal and Nonlineal Codifications of Reality" by Dorothy Lee is reprinted from *Psychosomatic Medicine*, Vol. 12 (1950). Reproduced by permission of the Author and Publisher.

"Autonomous Motivation" by Dorothy Lee is reprinted from *Anthropology and Education*, ed. Frederick C. Gruber (Philadelphia: University of Pennsylvania Press, 1961). Reprinted by permission of the publishers.

"Conceptual Styles, Culture Conflict, and Nonverbal Tests of Intelligence" by Rosalie A. Cohen is reproduced by permission of the American Anthropological Association from the *American Anthropologist*, Vol. 71 (1969).

"Culture and Memory" by Michael Cole and John Gay is reproduced by permission of the American Anthropological Association from the *American Anthropologist*, Vol. 74, No. 5 (1972).

"Language and Socialization" by J. A. Cook is reprinted from *Class, Codes and Control: Applied Studies Toward a Sociology of Language*, ed. Basil Bernstein (London and Boston: Routledge and Kegan Paul, 1973). Reprinted by permission of the author and publishers.

"Dialect Differences and Bilingualism" by Courtney B. Cazden is reprinted from *Child Language and Education* by Courtney B. Cazden. Copyright © 1972 by Holt, Rinehart and Winston, Inc. Reprinted by permission of Holt, Rinehart and Winston, Inc.

"'Teaching' Them Children to Talk" by Martha Coonfield Ward is reprinted from *Them Children: A Study in Language Learning* by Martha Coonfield Ward. Copyright © 1971 by Holt, Rinehart and Winston, Inc. Reprinted by permission of Holt, Rinehart and Winston, Inc.

"Teachers and Their Family Cultures" by Ruth Landes is reprinted from *Culture in American Education: Anthropological Approaches to Minority and Dominant Groups in Schools*. Copyright © 1965 by John Wiley & Sons, Inc. Reprinted by permission of John Wiley & Sons, Inc.

"The Concept of Culture and Its Significance for School Counselors" by Eleanor Leacock is reprinted from *Personnel and Guidance* Journal (May 1968).

"Teachers in Transition" by Elizabeth M. Eddy is reprinted from Elizabeth M. Eddy, *Becoming a Teacher* (New York: Teachers College Press, copyright 1969 by Teachers College, Columbia University), pp. 8-24.

"Schools and Teachers Union Interaction" by John Singleton is reprinted from *Nichū: A Japanese School* by John Singleton. Copyright © 1967 by Holt, Rinehart and Winston, Inc. Reprinted by permission of Holt, Rinehart and Winston, Inc.

"Maintaining the System: The Socialization of a Principal" by Harry Wolcott is reprinted from *The Man in the Principal's Office* by Harry Wolcott. Copyright © 1973 by Holt, Rinehart and Winston, Inc. Reprinted by permission of Holt, Rinehart and Winston, Inc.

Contributors

Sherrie K. Akinsanya is a professor of anthropology and education at the University of Maryland, Eastern Shore.

Theodore Brameld is a visiting distinguished professor at Hunter College of the City University of New York.

Courtney B. Cazden is a professor of education in the Graduate School of Education, Harvard University, Cambridge.

Rosalie A. Cohen is a professor in the Sociology Department at Temple University, Philadelphia.

Michael Cole is a professor of anthropology and head of the Laboratory of Comparative Human Cognition at Rockefeller University, New York.

J. A. Cook (Jenny Cook-Gomperz) is associated with the Institute of Human Learning at the University of California, Berkeley.

Robert V. Dumont, Jr., is currently working on a research project on the Fort Peck Reservation in Montana.

Elizabeth M. Eddy is a professor of sociology and anthropology at the University of Florida, Gainesville.

Dorothy Eggan is now deceased. She started making major contributions to knowledge and understanding of the psycho-cultural aspects of behavior in 1943. She became particularly interested in the significance of dreams for an understanding of the psycho-social aspects of Hopi behavior.

John Gay is currently associated with the United Nations Development Program in Lesotho, South Africa.

Jules Henry is now deceased. He was a professor of anthropology at Washington University, St. Louis.

John A. Hostetler is a professor in the Department of Anthropology at Temple University, Philadelphia.

Gertrude Enders Huntington is a research associate at Temple University, Philadelphia.

Clive Kileff is a professor in the Department of Sociology and Anthropology at the University of Tennessee.

Solon T. Kimball is a graduate resident professor of anthropology at the University of Florida, Gainesville.

Ruth Landes is a professor in the Department of Anthropology at City College of the City University of New York.

Eleanor Leacock is a professor of anthropology at City College of the City University of New York.

Dorothy Lee is now deceased. After receiving her Ph.D. in anthropology from the University of California, Berkeley, she taught at Vassar College, was associated with the Harvard University Health Center, and held numerous teaching positions throughout the country.

G. Alexander Moore is a professor in the Department of Anthropology at the University of Florida, Gainesville.

Robert Redfield is now deceased. He was the Robert M. Hutchins Distinguished Service Professor of Anthropology at the University of Chicago.

Joan I. Roberts, a specialist in anthropology and social psychology of education, was formerly at the University of Wisconsin, Madison.

Gerry Rosenfeld is a professor in the Department of Anthropology at the State University of New York at Buffalo.

John Singleton is a professor in the Department of Anthropology and in the International and Developmental Education Program at the University of Pittsburgh.

George D. Spindler is a professor in the Department of Anthropology at Stanford University, California.

Martha Coonfield Ward is a professor in the Department of Anthropology at the University of New Orleans.

Richard L. Warren is a professor in the College of Education at the University of Kentucky, Lexington.

Murray L. Wax is a professor in the Department of Sociology at Washington University, St. Louis.

Rosalie H. Wax is a professor in the Department of Anthropology at Washington University, St. Louis.

Harry Wolcott is a professor in the Center for the Advanced Study of Educational Administration, University of Oregon, Eugene.

Laurence Wylie is the C. Douglas Dillion Professor of the Civilization of France at Harvard University, Cambridge.

Preface

For many years, anthropologists have studied the kinship systems and patterns of enculturation of the young; but the specialized field of anthropology and education began to flourish only recently. The two books presented here—volume 1 on the anthropology of education and volume 2 on anthropological studies of education— together form an overview of the critical work done in this field.

The two volumes derive from bibliographic research that extended over a five-year period of time. Major bibliographic sources consulted include the *Education Index*, the *International Bibliography of Social and Cultural Anthropology*, the *Psychological Abstracts*, the *Review of Educational Research*, the *Sociological Abstracts and Index*, and the *Social Science and Humanities Review*.

In addition, the *Review of Anthropology* and all pertinent individual bibliographies appended to major works were examined. From these sources thousands of references were located and reviewed. Out of this large collection, only about seven hundred fifty met our criteria for inclusion in the final bibliography. This sharply defined collection is part 6 of the first volume. In it, all references are listed in chronological order, extending from the first statement in 1898 to those in 1975. The references for 1974-75 although incomplete, are included as they became available during the stages of preparation of this book for publication. The first draft of the bibliography, now revised for publication, was informally distributed by the Council on Anthropology and Education.

From the works chosen, we selected an initial set of those considered most important to represent the field as it has emerged over time. More importantly, we wanted the selection and organization of these materials to define the major parameters of the discipline. The first and all subsequent reorganizations of articles proved too long for publication in even two volumes, but the books that have been produced, although considerably shortened, should prove useful in clarifying the field of anthropology and education.

For those familiar with this area of research, some older studies will be quickly recognized. Our decision was to choose the best, not necessarily the most recent work. For those who are accustomed to an organization by cultural world areas, articles may seem unevenly distributed. We can only say that such organization yielded a useless product because the research itself is extensive in some areas and negligible in others. We would have preferred an organization around major cultural processes. This, given the state of the field, proved to be a premature organizational scheme.

The work of several competent scholars could not be included because of space limitations and organizational strictures. Although we cannot name the many authors we considered, we refer the reader to the bibliography for the publications of the following scholars: Wilfred Bailey, Roger Barker, Ruth Benedict, Howard Becker, Lyman Bryson, John Collier, Malcolm Collier, Yehudi Cohen, Lambros Comitas, Loren Eisley, Fred Eggan, Meyer Fortes, Estelle Fuchs, Herbert Gans, Marcus Goldstein, Nancy Gonzalez, Ward Goodenough, Bruce Grindal, Melville Herskovits, Philip Jackson, Landa Jocano, Vera John, Felix Keesing, George Kneller, Bud Kleif, Anthony Leeds, Philip Leis, Thomas Leemon, Oscar Lewis, Rhoda Metraux, Nancy Modiano, Ashley Montagu, Marie Montessori, Grace

Nicholson, Morris Opler, Alan Peshkin, George Pettit, Annette Rosenstiel, Seymour Sarason, Herbert Thelen, Charles Valentine, Anthony Wallace, Thomas Williams. In all cases, the bibliographic references and the articles chosen for inclusion were selected on the basis of the following criteria: first, the extent to which culture was the organizing concept; second, the degree of reliance on fieldwork methodology; third, the use of anthropological concepts in analyses; fourth, the inclusion of formalized education systems in relation to culture; fifth, the involvement of the author in the discipline of anthropology or in the concepts and methods basic to the field.

Neither book incorporates the literature on informal learning, or more broadly, on enculturation. The extensive literature in this area requires a separate volume. Although some of the finest work in the field of anthropology and education has been done on enculturation, we have confined ourselves to the works directly concerned with some aspect of formalized education. For a representative collection of the ethnographic studies of enculturation, we have compiled a Chronological Bibliography in the first volume of the critical studies conducted by anthropologists who have described the actual processes of growing up in different cultures throughout the world.

An examination of these and other anthropological studies will be incorporated in a textbook, *The Ethos of Learning*, to be published by David McKay Company, Inc., in the near future. It is hoped that this text, when combined with *Educational Patterns and Cultural Configurations* and with *Schooling in the Cultural Context*, will offer the overview necessary for an understanding of the fundamentals of the newly emerging field, anthropology of education. A field in which we would not have been involved were it not for the generous support of Solon Kimball, Elizabeth Eddy, Alexander Moore, Beatrice and Robert Miller, and Louise Sweet.

Contents

Part 1
Cultural Patternings of Education

Introduction
Joan I. Roberts

Patterns of meaning make possible the distinctive human experience. Culture, the total way of life developed and lived by a group of people, encircles the separate and idiosyncratic meanings of persons, defining the bounds of collective understanding.* To become human, the young are socialized, taught how to behave; more importantly, they are enculturated, given a world view that, hopefully, makes sense out of the pieces of life. To belong to the human species as it is known throughout the world, the way of life expressed in a world view of existence must be transmitted to the next generation. This process of continuing and enlarging the cumulative heritage is *the* unique characteristic of humankind†—it is found only in a species distinguished by the capacity to symbolize, to encode learning into meaningful configurations that can be passed on to the young.

To an anthropologist, learning embraces the whole of cultural acquisition: modes of thinking, acting, and feeling, symbol systems that separate experience into identifiable parts, customs that express standards of conduct, legal, political, religious, and economic institutions that perpetuate special statuses; artifacts and material products that distinguish particular forms of houses, clothes, tools, and the processes used to produce them. In contrast to the educator, who is too often trained to see learning as an individual act performed out of societal context, the anthropologist examines the acquistion of *total* patterns of education used to bring the learner into a particular system of shared meaning. In common with the educator, the anthropologist stresses the priority of learning but sees it as cultural acquisition. Without this cultural learning, there can be no anthropologist and no educator since these roles depend on the transmission of a way of life and a world view that provide the meaning inherent in the work of both professionals.

In volume 1, *Educational Patterns and Cultural Configurations*, we considered the field of anthropology and education, tracing its historical lineage, detailing relational linkages, defining methodological approaches, and discussing practical applications. In this volume, we are primarily concerned with actual field studies of education conceived in the broader sense of enculturation. Although the focus of each book is different, the assumptions central to anthropology remain consistent: the concern for complex configurations of all elements of human life, the concern for comparative insights into variegated socialization procedures, and the concern and respect for the multiple solutions devised to form human societies.

---

*In this brief introduction, debates on the meaning of anthropological concepts cannot be presented. The reader is urged to consult other sources such as Paul Bohannon, "Rethinking Culture: A Project for Current Anthropologists," *Current Anthropology* 14, no. 4 (October 1973).

†The word *man* as a generic term for the human species is an unacceptable usage to the editors. Because the materials presented here are quoted from other sources, however, the term, when used, cannot be modified.

These concerns form the basic outline of this book. Thus, the school is seen as only one form of cultural transmission, leading to studies of formal education as embedded in community. Similarly, learning groups, often located in classrooms, can be understood only within the cultural groups that provide the learners and the institutions in which the learning takes place. Even in confining bureaucratic structures the learner remains, to an anthropologist, a complex being. The key characteristics of the learner, intentionality and complicated patterning of stimuli, preclude a behaviorist analysis of only observable acts arranged in a linear sequence of stimulus-response bonds dependent on the presence of pleasure or pain. Both those who are educated and those who educate are seen as individuals who live within peer groups in which socialization for future or current occupational roles occurs with unrelenting regularity. Moreover, their functioning is seen as consistently contextual, with ethnic backgrounds of critical importance.

Cutting across the topical sections of the book are two central concepts that pertain to cultural stability. Since culture is thought to be an open system, cultural change is inherent in the flow of human life. The processes by which a culture is significantly modified are counterbalanced by those that maintain cultural continuity. The maintenance of a stable way of life and a corresponding world-view, in the face of sweeping changes that have occurred in this century, is more than an idle curiosity to anthropologists who respect cultural integration and understand the need for an ordered perspective. Of equal importance, however, is the growth flowing from culture contacts between groups holding distinctive ways of life. *Acculturation*, the process of adopting characteristics of another group, and *assimilation*, the incorporation into another culture, are concepts historically used to denote the interplay involved in change. These terms are still useful, if the prior tendency to obfuscate the *reciprocal* borrowing that actually occurs is avoided. Under conditions of multiple, sustained contacts, bi- or multiculturation will probably be the more likely terms in future discussions.

Not all parts of a system change at the same rate. The term *cultural lag* indicates the differential rate of change in one part relative to others, and often implies a maladjustment resulting from a rapid shift in material culture that is not accompanied by an equally quick change in nonmaterial culture. Despite worldwide upheavals, the human need for an ordered world view sustains constantly altered cultural patterns—those sets of interrelated ideas and activities that together provide meaningful configurations. Cultural complexes, those groups of interconnected characteristics dominated by a broader concept, seem to reflect changes yet often retain some of their original vitality as organizing themes. Continuity can also be observed across cultures in the major cultural areas of the world, in those regions identified by anthropologists as containing several groups of people who share at least some parts of a common pattern of life.

The stability of cultural patterns of life, however, seems increasingly subject to strain in complex cultures, those societies marked by advanced industrialization characterized by a high degree of labor specialization and by the capacity to control material sources of energy. In some complex cultures, pluralism of ethnic inhabitants is evident when such persons form subcultures out of national, racial, or religious identities. These subcultures are separate but share certain aspects of the broader culture. The ethnocentrism commonly found in many cultures becomes problematic in complex plural societies. Belief in the inherent rightness or superiority of one's own group and a tendency to view other groups in terms of one's own are attitudes that can only serve to foster cultural inconsistency. As the world becomes "one tribal village," ethnocentrism is increasingly a luxury, inappropriate even in remote and simpler societies as these are drawn into the global community.

Whether education acts as an innovating or a stabilizing influence on culture under world conditions of unprecedented change is a critical but unanswered question. Some anthropologists, such as Margaret Mead, question whether cultures can change rapidly enough to incorporate new conditions as they arise. She suggests that the younger generation may end up enculturating the older because the experiences and knowledge needed to cope with rapidly changing cultural realities may be generated by the young. Under these conditions, the educators' roles become even more confused. If schools are to transmit a patterned sense of wholeness, then the capacity to adapt rapidly to change in community and culture is a prerequisite of education. In the American culture, demands for profound educational changes have been accompanied by superficial alterations. Perhaps anthropologists with their unique cross-cultural perspective can shift the ways we look at the commonplace and open more original routes to the formulation and solution of problems.

CULTURE, COMMUNITY, AND SCHOOL

We begin with an article by Harry Wolcott, whose criteria for ethnographic research in schools provide a useful introduction to all subsequent studies presented in the book. Wolcott summarizes the key characteristics of anthropological research and analyzes the critical problems that arise in ethnographic studies of schools. The anthropologist engages in the very practical business of learning what one needs to know to be a member of a particular social system. From the very ordinary details of daily life, the researcher paints an ethnography, literally a picture of the way of life of an interacting group. The cultural patterns and forms of life are inferred from people's understanding of how things are and how they ought to be. Although theoretical assumptions are inherent in the researcher's prior training and in the choice of group and situation to be studied, the ethnographer will often be guided by a foreshadowed problem area which will take form only as the investigation proceeds. By the nature of the research, the anthropologist is likely to learn much that cannot be stated prior to the study nor controlled by administrative approval of a set of hypotheses or a questionnaire or a narrowly defined experiment. On-site research about real people in their actual situations can be a welcome relief from externally imposed experiments. It can also cause feelings of threat for those in power who cannot control the outcome of what is to be studied.

Given these circumstances, Wolcott questions whether the problem is appropriate to ethnographic research and then asks if the ethnographer is appropriate to the problem. In anthropological studies, the investigator is the main research instrument. It is reasonable to expect that he or she should have detached perspectives gained from training in other cultures. The cross-cultural perspective should foster a comparative view of the ordinary which is difficult to achieve if one has never experienced a different culture: "It would hardly be fish who discovered the existence of water." The sensitive, curious, perceptive researcher must also possess writing skills and a sound conceptual basis in cultural anthropology. To convey how it feels to walk in another's shoes requires literary competence. To systemize a mass of details into a consistent pattern that holds theoretical significance necessitates a solid understanding of how cultures function.

Assuming that the problem and ethnographer are appropriate, another question remains: Is the research climate appropriate to ethnographic inquiry? The scope of the situation must be narrow enough to allow for personal involvement in observation. Moreover, observation of people in their own environments is a time-consuming activity that results in voluminous field notes. During long periods of time, administrators may not see tables of numbers or other specific products. During the research period, the personal involvement of the researcher may create resistance, fear of someone's knowing what the situation is *really* all about. Throughout this process, the fieldworker must also record the changes in himself or herself. At the same time, professional autonomy must be maintained in order to protect the confidentiality of sensitive information.

All these factors suggest a fourth question: Are there appropriate expectations of the completed study? Wolcott lists elements commonly found in varying proportions in standard ethnographies. These may include: the allocation and distribution of resources, environmental supports and constraints, material culture/ technology, personal adaptations (in both words and action), ritual behavior, and social networks. More comprehensive categories include: economic organization, ethos or world view, ideational systems, languages, life-cycle customs, political organization, projective systems (religion, art, folklore), social control, and social organization. Beyond descriptive elements are particular theoretical concerns such as culture and personality, enculturation, culture and cognition, and linguistic patterns.

These aspects of human life are studied with a *variety* of techniques, but participant observation, key-informant interviewing, and life histories are major tools of the fieldworker who is immersed in the lives of the people being studied. Throughout this volume, the criteria presented by Wolcott can be used to consider the results of the ethnographic approach. The first research study is a report on a segment of a much larger study conducted by Theodore Brameld who questions whether the school provides a place in which incongruent cultural values are altered toward greater consistency or whether it simply reflects incongruencies in the community and culture. Researching Puerto Rican culture, he studied key cultural themes that serve as organizers of the societal pattern. Brameld distinguishes between explicit culture, that which is formally stated by its members; and implicit culture, assumptions so basic that they are considered "natural" and thus not formally articulated. Brameld describes these assumptions as the attitudes and beliefs "absorbed into the 'bloodstream' of the people with little awareness that the absorption is occurring steadily from the earliest to the latest years of every normal person." He searches for the configuration, the underlying patterns that order or disorder the deepest meaning of culture, and then compares the ideology with the actuality of daily life.

Analyzing religion, democracy, and morality, Brameld finds that the ideological separation of church and state is *not* apparent in the daily community or in school life. Although his conception of democracy is marked by his own cultural bias and is therefore somewhat limited, he does show that the ideology of democracy is disjunctive with the *personalismo* attributed to leaders, who are often idolized. This incongruity is also reflected in the schools: administrative imposition of authority over teachers and students sharply contradicts the shared decision making expressed in educational ideology. The conception of morality, again, is inconsistent: a single sexual standard explicitly requires the same behavior for women and men, yet the implicitly accepted behavior is reflected in the "virginity cult" for women and in widespread concubinage practiced by men. In schools, Brameld contends that the young are taught inharmonious relations between men and women, often marked by secrecy and suspicion.

Although Brameld's larger research study leads to a deeper analysis, his limited findings indicate that the schools do not serve to change culture through an integration of inconsistent cultural themes. Rather, education simply reflects the fragmented splits between ideal and real.

In the third article in part 2, Robert Redfield also looks at the relative impact of education on cultural continuity and change. In his classic study of education in the highlands of Guatemala, Redfield contrasts the influence on learning exerted by formal educational structures with informal processes in the community. Essentially, Redfield concludes that formal education does not have as much influence as informal learning in the community: "The educational process is not greatly dependent upon institutions organized for pedagogical practice or upon the organization of deliberate instruction in the family but on the multitude of daily situations in which through words and gestures some part of the traditional community is imparted without the pressure of any formal institution." Redfield qualifies his conclusion, however, as he points to the differential effects of social change on two ethnic groups within the community, Ladinos and Indians. Thus we find that cultural change is again dependent on the subcultures involved, even within a rural community in the highlands of a "developing" country.

Almost four decades have passed since Redfield reported his findings. During the intervening years, Guatemala has conducted massive literacy campaigns, stressing the importance of education to the populace. How successful are these efforts in bringing together formal and informal educational networks? In the next article, Alexander Moore discusses three attempts to bypass the rigidities of the national school system. In his recent study of the inhabitants of Atchalán, Moore finds that the peasants have come to accept the national goal of minimal literacy, at least for males. However, they have added the role of volunteer school master to the repertory of accepted and respected roles for adult males in keeping with their tradition that men initiate other men. The home classes conducted by indigenous teachers are oriented to and incorporated into the town life. In contrast, the state's effort to reach the illiterate by demanding the "volunteer" overtime of the national teaching corps has been, in Moore's estimation, ill advised. The Catholic church has probably been most successful. In their catechism classes, they combine formal and informal educational systems, using Indian peasants as initiators of the young, while retaining control by the clergy.

The inclusion of the closed, corporate community into the institutions of nation-states remains a problem in Guatemala and in many "developing" countries. We turn now to a nation already industrialized to observe the interconnections between education bureaucracy, community, and pedagogical practices. Laurence Wylie, studying a rural French village in the Vaucluse, provides a detailed analysis of both community and school as enculturating agents. Social change in a rural area of an industrialized society is experienced, but Wylie does not treat it as the central organizing theme. Nevertheless, the role of a bureaucratized national school system in complex culture is subjected to scrutiny: "Even the games to be played in the nursery school are determined by the decree of July 15, 1921." But French culture functions to mitigate against these ironclad regulations: "After all, the teachers are French and consequently recognize the gap that usually separates laws and regulations on the one hand from actual practice on the other." Thus the district supervisor elicits no great anxiety when he pays a visit to the school.

In general, Wylie portrays a community in which the cultural values of the home and school are congruent. Explicit cultural values are clearly upheld by teachers and parents, both groups expecting a continuity of cultural themes. One of these is the heavy emphasis on cultivated communication, in French of course. Language is the most important subject taught in the school—an emphasis mutually acceptable and explicitly stated by both teachers and parents.

Implicit cultural learnings are also apparent. Wylie notes that children are not encouraged to formulate principles independently. They are taught to recognize principles that seem "to exist autonomously," to accept them, and to solve problems by recognizing abstractions and concrete facts in order to establish the relationship between them. A second implicit assumption is that all learning fits into a framework of the part to the whole; every fact is an integral part of a larger unit—fragmented facts are useless. But facts, even in a sensible framework, make no sense unless clearly connected to human life. Thus a third cultural characteristic is implicit in daily life although never explicated formally in texts.

To the American reader, it may be difficult to reconcile this last cultural theme with the surprisingly frank and open judgments on French children's intelligence that are expressed by both teachers and parents. For example, the teacher, tapping her head with her finger, says in the presence of the child, "Poor Marie. She tries, but—I think all is not right." Wylie is never able to adjust to this practice; he notes that his lack of judgmental appraisal would not be considered "tact" but simply the inability to judge intelligence.

District examinations provide further evidence of open and, in American terms, brutally direct evaluations of French schoolchildren. More importantly, they indicate the interconnectedness of school and community as they exhibit a common response to national directives in a bureaucratized, complex culture. If a child fails, it is not the fault of the system, or the teachers, or the parents—it is the child's fault. From Wylie's analysis, the interlocking system of adults joins together to form a consistent pressure to perform according to the culturally shared values and beliefs.

Richard Warren's more recent study of education in Rebhausen, a German community, is an interesting parallel to Wylie's work in France. In both ethnographies, the enculturation process in school and community is subjected to careful examination. Warren begins: "The school building belongs to the community; the teacher belongs to the state." As in France, the bureaucratized national Ministry of Education controls schooling, but with quite different results.

Teachers are not chosen by the community; they are approved by the state and assigned to a school after a three-year probation period, the writing of a major paper, and an examination of classroom performance. In contrast to the French, the Germans appear to have few cultural processes that protect the individual from excessive institutionalized control. In fact, the examiner who judges classroom performance is greatly feared. In the example given, the examiner is described as the "true embodiment of the stereotyped German bureaucrat" who "exploits all the authority and prestige of his office" and exhibits "a raw, almost merciless use of power." Warren concludes: "The thrust of the power is never blunted; it flows through the educational system and comes to rest in the classroom, where the student stands vulnerable, obligated to adjust to it, faced with no alternative."

The control of education is both political and religious, with state and church interconnected on both national and local levels. There are two types of schools, Catholic and Protestant. Religious instruction is given by teachers, none of whom refuse the task even when they are disinterested in the topic. The principal is expected to be of the same religion as the majority in the town. Thus, in both formal and informal ways, institutional control over the young is extended.

The family seems in no position to exert independent control, and little is evident. A parent council was imported by Americans after the Second World War but seems to function in a traditional way, with officers chosen by acclamation from among community authorities. Parents have access to teachers only during the five-minute intervals between classes when students are milling around. Most conflicts between school and community are resolved by the principal and mayor through the blunt use of real or symbolic power. In short, there appears to be an almost crushing integration of political, religious, and social groupings that press down on the child and teacher in the classroom. Implicit learnings about power and authority, whether or not these are explicated, are obvious in Warren's analysis.

Contrast this account of German education with George Spindler's study of urbanization and education in the next article. Spindler studied the schools in Burbach and Schönhausen at approximately the same time Warren was conducting fieldwork in Rebhausen. While the surroundings in both towns reflect tradition, revision of the elementary curriculum is underway. Under pressure from the regional administration of education, the traditional emphasis on local geography, history, and culture is considered inappropriate to the modern world and reminiscent of the land, folk, and blood pattern of the Hitler period. From a content analysis of curricular materials, Spindler notes that changes are not as extensive as they would appear to be.

What is apparent is that traditional elementary schooling has historically provided students with the means for forming identities related to the town and the surrounding area. Spindler asks: Can children expand their frames of reference to make them relevant to an urbanized environment? Does traditional schooling place limits on the recognition and choice of alternatives in urban society? Does traditional education provide the basis for assimilation of divergent populations?

Spindler develops a theory and a technique, the instrumental activities inventory, to obtain and order the answers. To him, a cultural system operates so long as acceptable behaviors produce anticipated ends. Beliefs support the relationship between activities and goals, making the connections credible. The essential contribution of schooling is to create credibility in the relational linkages between activities and goals. Education is the means employed by established members of the cultural system to inform new members of sanctioned instrumental linkages; to communicate how they are ranked, integrated, and organized; to commit new members to the support and continuance of these linkages and to the belief system that supports them. Educational institutions serve to reaffirm linkages and recruit new members by creating individual cognitive structures that are predicated on the capacity to maintain working models of relevant and productive linkages. Supporting values justify preferences and identity is formed out of individual commitment to a given configuration of linkages. In rapid cultural change, established relations are challenged by new information; credibility is weakened; operational viability declines; and new alternatives arise. As the range of alternatives increase, cognitive control decreases.

To study the impact of urbanization on German children, Spindler analyzed the ordering of linkages to see if students from different backgrounds chose similar or dissimilar options, to identify the influence of the school on their choices, and to determine the kinds of identity fostered by the school. His research suggests that the children have an idealistic bias toward life in the small village, a bias that is not differentiated by regional, linguistic, or religious backgrounds. When *forced* to choose between alternatives, the students are more likely to select urbanized options while their teachers tend to remain more tradition-oriented. Essentially, Spindler discovered an idealized identity with supporting values; a pragmatic instrumental preference system with its supporting values; and a romanticized nonpragmatic set of preferences and values. Clearly, inconsistencies are inherent with the responses of German children to a changing environment.

The roots of industrialization and urbanization grow from within the German culture. If inconsistent cultural themes can be found in German children, what will be observed in non-Western children who live in cultures in which technological changes are imported? Consider next the impact of cultural change arising out of imposed cultural contact on the life of one child, Shumba, of the Shona people in Rhodesia. Clive Kileff details the two worlds of a young boy who is believed to be possessed by the spirit of his deceased grandfather. Shumba's behavior is acceptable in the traditional cultural setting where it conforms to the Shona religious beliefs. In the school, his behavior makes little sense to those who do not understand his cultural group.

Shumba's parents hold traditional religious beliefs; but at the same time they see school, the imported institution, as a way of increasing their son's earning potential. Kileff shows the manner in which the child holds on to conflicting instrumental linkages, incapable of letting go of the grandfather identity, insisting on the incorporation of his dual selves into the nontraditional world of the school. In this situation, the teacher comes to act as a cultural broker between two world views. She modifies her behavior by treating the young boy with the respect due an old man. Although she is inconsistent, she lowers the price paid by the parents, who give their son to a new world, and by the boy, who must eventually give way to the alternative linkages in order to survive within another version of reality.

We turn next to a group located within a complex culture, to a "conquered" people, the Hopi, who form a strong subculture in the presumed pluralistic society of the United States. Dorothy Eggan's classical study of cultural continuity among these Native Americans is a fascinating contrast to the research on other cultural groups.

Eggan examines a culture noted for its emphasis on cooperative values and studied by numerous anthropologists who were struck by the Hopi capacity to sustain their peaceful world view in the face of heavy pressures to become "Americanized." In studying their remarkable resistance to cultural contact, Eggan avoids stimulus-response learning theory because from her perspective it negates attachments and attitudes, replacing these with painful or pleasurable external stimuli. In contrast, Eggan believes that the shaping factors of affect or emotion lead to a need to belong which provides a strong impetus to incorporate culture and to resist the imposition of cultural change, which would shatter the unified and ordered world view.

Early affective learning internalized in infancy and childhood is, in Eggan's estimation, most resistant to cultural change. Eggan traces the effective use of affect in Hopi enculturation as expressed in deliberate instruction which emphasized kinship and community obligations and interconnected with religious observances to accentuate Hopi history through mythology. Through these processes, the young received the concept of "good heart," a mutually consistent idea of what a good Hopi is.

In white schools, Hopi children preserve an inner freedom and an independence of thought. Even when forced to stay in an alien environment, they lived in a Hopi world within themselves. To the Hopi student, Western education was an accessory that did not change their basic values. The traditional emphasis on cooperation for the well-being of the clan, not the individual, the time-honored rules for living with "good heart," the survival of the group through supernatural sanctions— these cultural themes remained intact. One Hopi expressed it this way: "You know then that you are Hopi. It is one thing whites cannot have, cannot take from us. It is our way of life given to us when the world began."

In reflecting on Hopi dignity when confronted with indignity, one can only speculate on who is conquered and by what means of social control? What remains unquestionable is the all-pervasive influence of culture that sustains, against all odds, a continuity even under extensive pressures arising from enforced cultural contact.

Legally enforced cultural contact in America centers on education. Elizabeth M. Eddy considers desegregation of schools in the next article, tracing educational changes intended to reorganize schools so that both black students and white students can receive an education of equal quality. Eddy presents a case study of an educational "innovation" introduced into a school at the time of desegregation in southern institutions. From her research it is clear that the innovation was essentially a rite of intensification in which whites and blacks established interaction patterns within a single school system by reinforcing the customary relationships among administrators, teachers, and pupils and the subordinate role of blacks within each of these groups. The development of a presumably new structural form, the middle school, was a simple reworking of traditional practices on a limited scale. The change was used as a rite of intensification, a ritual performed in response to a crisis that arises from changes affecting all the members of a cultural group.

The redefinition of the previously black school altered territorial rights of blacks. For them, the advent of whites meant the loss of the only school in the black community, a place of community assembly needed by them. For the whites, the change triggered images of inferior education. Through a sequence of symbolic acts, the information communicated to all was that the school was no longer one in which blacks would play major roles in the initiation of educational activities. The appointment of a white principal, the assignment of twenty white teachers as a form of punishment for participation in a teacher walkout, the assignment of black teachers to other schools and their reassignment back after a year of separation, the building of a fence around the school, the change of the school entrance so that it no longer faced the black community, the renaming of the school—all these acts reaffirmed the dominant status of whites within the school and community.

Cultural change, when reciprocal, may enhance the lives of persons in all groups affected. Under conditions of imposed contact or colonialism, the disintegration of cultural patterns may simply leave the people stranded between two worlds, to neither of which they belong. Even in a relatively stable situation, incongruities between explicit and implicit values, between formal and informal patterns, and between forms of institutionalized control may exist. With increasing institutional control of the individual in "advanced" societies we can contrast the internalized and personalized control in "primitive" societies and, perhaps, speculate on the direction of future cultural changes in store for all of us in a constantly shrinking world. One Hopi saw the American complex, pluralistic culture this way: "You have more goods than we have, but you don't have peace ever; it is better to die in famine than in war."

ANTHROPOLOGICAL ANALYSES OF CLASSROOMS

To obtain a closer look at the enculturation processes in a society that has "no peace," we turn now to microethnographies of the classroom, where children are taught the patterns of their culture. This section focusus only on learning groups in American culture in an attempt to obtain comparisons among subcultural groups.

Jules Henry, in the first article in part 3, describes the organization of attitudes of white elementary school children in an urban setting. According to this well-known study, most of us believe that an adult is supposed to organize emotions, attitudes, and activities to serve overall social goals; the child is seen as lacking this order. Given this assumption, "the prime effort of the adult world is to make the child's attitudes look organized to adults." Searching back into American history, Henry finds the witch-hunt: This historical blend of American characteristics seems to him to be one cultural means of organizing and controlling intragroup hostility through processes that involve the destructive criticism of others, feelings of vulnerability, fear of group hostility, confession of evil deeds, boredom, and emptiness.

Noting the presence of this syndrome, Henry begins to analyze his field notes around these processes. The carping criticism, in most extreme form, takes expression in a vigilance club. In a less structured manner, it is more commonly seen in tearing to pieces another's work on the basis of small and insignificant items. The competitive struggle for authority approval to ward off feelings of vulnerability leads to the learning of docility and to the covert understanding that the failure of peers makes success possible for the individual child. Fear of group hostility recurs in the analysis of children's stories in which Henry finds that "the child sends out his cloud of fears, and it returns with the leaden rain of hostility." This vulnerability sends the child searching for right answers to obtain the security of teacher approval, but the search itself simply reinforces docility.

In confession, children often present themselves as giving up their evil ways, in a profusion of nicely faked stories in which real emotions are subordinated to the desire to please the teacher. Boredom, according to Henry, is the price paid for this intellectual and emotional separation from the environment. Independence and courage are in these circumstances minimized.

In his second article in part 3, Henry searches for the ordering of spontaneity, initiative, and creativity in suburban white classes. He finds the teacher caught in a paradox, urging creativity while enforcing conformity to school requirements.

Female teachers may often play the role of the tired, entreating, overburdened mother who controls genuine spontaneity by the manipulation of guilt. Male teachers may assume the role of buddy-daddy, who commands silence (which does not last long) and who serves as a love object. In these white middle-class schools, Henry concludes that the teacher, principal, student, and community are one continuous cultural system expressing the false personalization in American institutions.

We turn now to the Amish, a group that has consistently rejected false personalization. It is no easy accomplishment to survive as a distinct, continuous system within a pluralistic society. The Amish have done just that. They have maintained a rural culture in the middle of twentieth-century America. Their fight to retain control over the education of their young is recurrent news. Just how they incorporate children into the values of a century ago is less widely reported. In the next article, John A. Hostetler and Gertrude Enders Huntington describe the means by which the Amish sustain the rural values of their group as it existed more than a hundred years ago.

In Amish schools, the teacher does not disappear from the lives of students at the end of each day. Hired to teach wisdom, not technology, the teacher is expected to teach with her or his whole life, to be integrated within the self and within the community, to be completely committed to the Amish way of life. Qualified teachers are not those certified by the state. Teaching is a calling rather than a job. The relationship between the teacher and the school board is personal and does not begin to resemble a business agreement.

By excluding radio, television, and movies, and by rejecting much of the printed material available, the Amish are able to maintain an oral tradition and an orientation to life that is relational rather than analytical. In the classroom, no one pretends that children make the decisions. Although their opinions are respected, obedience and order are basic to a good school. Cooperation is expected and competition allowed only in support of the group. Talents are God-given, so differences in learning capacities are expected and not concealed. Learning is not disguised as a game and memorization is frequent and consistent with the oral traditions of the community. Few rules exist but these are consistently reinforced. Older children help younger ones. The school has the atmosphere of a well-ordered family with a woman usually in charge. Respect is not based on titles.

In Amish culture, truth need not be searched out; it has already been revealed in the Bible. The Amish are taught *what* and *where* but not *why* or *how*. Unlike the teacher in American schools, who is not to teach attitudes or beliefs except a belief in the scientific method and a belief in the "democratic" form of government, the Amish teacher is to convey the full meaning of the Amish way of life. In Amish communities, life is a whole with education used to transmit the wisdom of that whole so that each new generation fits smoothly into a continuous cultural system.

One could scarcely regard the next classes under study to be part of a "continuous cultural system." To the contrary, the Cherokee students described by Robert Dumont and Murray Wax are portrayed as members of a lower caste or subordinated ethnic group whose education is unidirectional. In a schizophrenic cultural clash, the Native Americans are asked "to adapt to us, learn from us while we learn nothing from them, ignoring their customs, language and cultures."

Ethnically, racially, and linguistically alien, teachers live with the illusion that no discipline is necessary: "Silence is interpreted as timidity or shyness, control and restraint as docility." In short, elements of the witch-hunt syndrome are used to explain behavior in a culture in which the syndrome itself has no meaning. To the observers, the correct interpretation of such behavior is found in the Cherokee School Society in which "the students have wrought a reversal of roles, so that *their* standards of precision and *their* notion of social intercourse emerge as normative." The teacher notes only the outer form of the class, but "the student with gesture, or voice inflection, or eye contact reorders, builds, eventually, a wall of silence impenetrable to the outsider." The cold war is not a part of Cherokee society in which social conflict is deplored. The students resort to conflict to establish their cultural identity and to sustain their cultural integrity. When teachers try to adapt, students work with them in "cultural interaction on the frontiers of contact."

Rosalie Wax, in the next article in this section, observes among the Oglala Sioux a "peer group withdrawal so uncompromising that no voice might be heard in the classroom for hours but that of the teacher plantively asking questions or giving instructions to which nobody responded." The price students pay for cultural contact in the schools is high, however. About half the young men who had dropped out "found their high school experience so painful they could scarcely talk about it." For others, physical recklessness, deeds of risk taking and athletic prowess expected of Sioux males, were valued cultural behaviors incongruent with the narrow respect for school regulation and government property. For many, the capacity to make short-term, superficial social adjustments with strangers was in sharp contrast to Sioux values of powerful and deep loyalties to peers. For others who left school, ways of making their values consistent were achieved only on the periphery of an alien system. For many, dropping out was the natural consequence of "their own vitality and independence which were too positive to allow them to remain within a monotonous, alien, and dehumanizing situation." In short, cultural conflict led the Sioux to see themselves as crippled were they to stay in school.

That crippling process is detailed in black schools with the young children described by Gerald Rosenfeld in his article. Combining the roles of teacher and researcher, Rosenfeld attempts to balance his reactions as educator and anthropologist to the dehumanizing conditions he observed. The punitive behavior of teachers is perhaps most graphically detailed in the incident in which a teacher locks a child in a metal closet and then bangs loudly on the closet's outside walls. The question arising from Rosenfeld's work is: How does the enculturation process become distorted into behaviors that are so alien to the perpetuation of the species? We are thus directed to a study of the cultural history of childhood, particularly under conditions of rapid social change and of intense cultural contact, to determine how enculturation comes to take on the characteristics of socialization of inmates in an insane asylum. And we must ask two basic questions: What are the rights of children in the world's cultures; and how far can a human society, in an effort to sustain a presumed cultural continuity, define the young as essentially without rights?

In "civilized" states, ironically, one may find that the rights of children, especially children who are poor and black, are most likely to be dramatically denied. The process of institutionalization itself appears to provide the occasion for a form of cultural continuity that excludes the human rights of the growing cultural members. This paradox seems most closely associated with the control of space and time, most commonly called "discipline." Such control becomes exaggerated in literate societies where, for example, disruptions of institutional space and time are codified in anecdotal records. The life of one member of a culture may be labeled and extend as a symbol of that life over time. But, contrary to most cultural histories, it is kept secret from the person living it. Thus, the generation of a mythology of an individual or of the subculture to which he or she belongs is maintained. This is in opposition to fundamental scientific procedure in anthropology where investigators constantly check their perceptions of events with those living them.

Another paradox of cultural continuity in a complex culture such as the United States is the tendency for the school organization to conceal rather than reveal the realities of the broader culture. Rosenfeld points to the fake names given tracked groups, the Sharks and Flounders, as one example of the attempt to hide cultural realities. Another institutional characteristic that reflects cultural values is the supermarket conception of time. Although ostensibly in the process of intellectual training, students actually learn not to learn, knowing that deep involvement in any subject will be cut short by a bell pushing them to a new topic. They learn to "play it cool," with no intense interaction. Henry's depersonalized affect and Wax's superficial, short-term social adjustments both coincide with Rosenfeld's view of American shallowness in the control of time.

As many anthropologists before him, Rosenfeld asserts that children are evaluated not on an intellectual basis but on a behavioral one. Those in control appear more fearful of uncontrolled emotion than concerned with disciplined intellect. Cultural continuity depends on the full incorporation of whole human beings from each new generation. When institutional forms take precedence over individual enculturation, learning is precluded. Within pluralistic cultures, those excluded from learning are frequently members of a subcultural group whose way of life is viewed as aberrant. The abysmal lack of knowledge about the cultures of children can only exaggerate enculturative problems. Under these conditions, the major goal is pacification, not understanding. The children of minority groups are subhuman, "animals" with "prehensile lips." Rosenfeld concludes, "As I continued to look at what was happening at Harlem School, I came to think that it may be possible that a social system can survive and perpetuate itself even though it does not serve to support individual members."

When individual members are seen as subhuman, in Alexander Moore's research, then this repetitive perception and behavior can only lead to the conclusion that the system *is* functional—it prepares "animals" for an "animal" existence. We do not expect dogs and cats to share the full human capacity of complex learning; although part of our culture, they never participate in a fully human way. The job is to control and use these creatures. Similarly, if the poor or the racially different are seen as subhuman, then control is critical. In Moore's observations, control is never achieved, although it is constantly attempted. While Native Americans use silence to assert their human integrity, blacks may use noise to demand their rights. Both refuse to be treated as "the same but inferior" or as "different and subhuman." In both situations questions are asked, but answers are either withheld or are purposely presented as meaningless.

To avoid the question of how to sustain cultural continuity while respecting distinctive subcultures, American whites resort to labeling. In a highly verbal culture the categories used for "deviant" behavior cloak the cultural clash that exists. The dominant group does not get upset by what it does not see. Words screen out what is seen. A label such as "emotionally disturbed" or "mentally retarded" relies on an approach that is fundamentally different from, for example, the French direct honesty by which a child is described. Note the difference in two teacher's comments: "Now this girl, she is slow but she writes very nicely" and "Vera is a CRMD child." In each case the words can be used punitively, but in the latter statement the Puerto Rican girl who hears them is presumed not to know that the label means she is unintelligent.

As Moore points out, cultural transmission always depends on shared values. One must determine what, of the thousands of bits of stimuli, should be transmitted. This is accomplished through the gradual sharpening of specifics that take on a special significance. The affective affiliation of specific parts of culture cluster together around key images that come to be highly valued. The values are central to decisions about what is to be taught. Presumably, highly valued information is also high in survival value for the culture. The procedures used to impart the valued information should be, presumably, consistent with it. While the middle-class mothering figure in Henry's class forms a continuity with the parent at home, the child in Moore's class who sucks her thumb is called "a baby who clings all the time." Mothering a "subhuman" is not the norm—in this way, cultural continuity is broken. Labels replace love: "His father killed his mother. The home back-ground—terrible. They are all *emotionally disturbed*." (Italics added)

Moore explains teachers' behavior through the use of the concept *culture shock*, an idea originally developed by Oberg to denote the processes of adaptation to an alien culture. The teacher attempts to reorder reality through social control, to make it look familiar to her or him. When the children do not change, punishment is used to force a common reality.

Using Erving Goffman's theories, Moore shows that the polite or ceremonial behaviors expected in any culture are repeatedly violated. Avoidance rituals specify what is not to be done; presentational rituals specify what is to be done. The teacher, untrained in an analysis of cultures, continually violates *both* ritualized behaviors. The children respond with ceremonial profanation, defying the person in such a way that he or she can act as though the message has not been received.

Moore suggests two models to help teachers extricate themselves from their failures to transmit culture in circumstances of shock. He feels that cultural shock may shake educators out of the ideological interpretation of the school system, and *if recognized* for what it is, the new perceptions can impel teachers to observe the cultural assumptions on which they and their students interact. The anthropologist is suggested as a model because the search for cultural assumptions is the *usual* process of anthropologists in their field work. A second model, the revitalization prophet, is a radical recommendation. Such a person appears after periods of rapid cultural change in which traditional ways of life are destroyed. Acting with great creativity, the individual takes elements of all cultures in the contact situation and reforms them to create new patterns. Teachers who consciously rework educational ceremonies and rituals might be able to effect cultural change in transmission. The problem, of course, is the destruction or exclusion of such charismatic leaders by a system that feels threatened by their forceful originality.

CULTURE, EDUCATION, AND THE INDIVIDUAL

To generate systemic changes, the depth of cultural shaping of the individual must be understood. To Solon Kimball, in the opening article in part 4, we are far from knowing the individual processes in cultural transmission. The static data that tests and measurements produce do not reveal the intricate interdependencies between individual and environment: "Orderliness cannot be obtained in the categorization of the atomistic bits and pieces that are gathered . . . further, most studies have focused on the *consequences* and not the processes of learning, relying on an external entity such as God or society or on internal instincts, such as the acquisitiveness of Adam Smith or the libido of Freud." To Kimball, motivation as a concept is too glibly accepted as explaining the direction of behavior without understanding the stimuli evoking it. Moreover, the attribution of pleasure or pain to stimuli as basic motivators does not, in his thinking, provide a theory that includes the full range of human experience. Finally, the transfer of experimental findings from rats or pigeons stimulated to produce responses simply does not account for cognition or inventive and original combinations of ideas: "The experimental animal can never become the experimenter."

To deal with human beings as tool-making, social-grouping, abstract-symbolizing creatures requires a focus on the relationship and process of the individual and his or her environment to learning. In the prolonged period of time during which the young are intensely dependent, cognitive patterns are acquired within a cultural perspective that provides a screen through which existence is experienced. The world view, the system of thought and feeling that explains the operation of the universe, provides the rationale for explaining tragedy and joy, identifies things and their attributes, makes possible an existence that has meaning. This system contains *unstated premises* that order thoughts and feelings as well as the criteria by which events are analyzed and judged. It is these rule-sets by which human learning procedes.

Kimball distinguishes three universals of cognition: categories of knowledge, canons of discrimination, and process as a function of the relation between variables. The categories of knowledge permit a person to distinguish and classify individuals, things, qualities, events, and processes. Kimball specifies six universal categories: order, class, number, shape, time, and space. But these can be learned only according to the criteria which make identification possible. The key by which the categories and criteria are transmitted is process—the change in variable relationships.

One of the most fascinating analyses of the world view in cognitive functioning is Dorothy Lee's study of the nonlineal codification of reality among the Trobriand islanders who do not organize experience in terms of Western lineal phasing. A Trobriand word, according to Lee, refers to a self-contained concept. What Americans see as an attribute, Trobrianders name as an ingredient. Objects and events are self-contained points with no temporal connection and no arrangement into means-ends. There is evidently no causal relation in a sequence of events; each event is an ingredient of a patterned whole. Lee says of American culture: "The line is so basic that we take it for granted, as given in reality . . . we follow a line of thought, a course of action, or the direction of an argument, bridge a gap in conversation, speak of the span of life, lament an interrupted career." In contrast, Trobrianders see patterned activity as truth; acts and being derive value from the embedding patterns. Lineality involved in, for example, bartering to give and to get back, is despicable; it is without value.

In another contrast, the line in Western culture not only connects but it also moves. The line as a guide is necessary to a people who feel they must arrange events in a chronological order. Furthermore, the arrangement of objects and events must move toward a climax in the sequence presented. Trobrianders categorize according to the fitness in the repetition of an established unit. Climax in history is a denial of all good because it implies change and suggests that change increases good. Stimulus-response learning, given this nonlineal world view, makes little sense because lineality in learning bonds is assumed. Furthermore, the Western concept of achievement motivation with an upward and ascending line of accomplishment would make even less sense to a Trobriander, who would not be devastated if a career line were broken.

Lee's original analysis of the categories and criteria for cognition are paralleled by her inventive analysis of motivation, which appears in her second article in this section. Reflecting on the concept as defined in Western culture, she notes, "I have had to describe that which is without limit, in terms which imply limit." Rejecting social scientific versions of motivation, she turns away from the world view that sees people as motivated to satisfy basic needs, to reduce tension, to respond to an externally applied stimulus, or to be propelled by some inner drive. To Lee, all these theories view the person as inert, driven or prodded or dependent on a furnished motivated power. In comparison, Lee's cross-cultural analysis leads her to see behavior as often non- or even antiutilitarian. Why, she asks, do Eskimos continue to eat until all food is consumed, even when starvation may presently threaten? Why do Trobrianders engage in dangerous expeditions to perform magic that does not directly affect biological needs? Why do we often invite obstacles that demand extreme efforts which may or may not result in food, shelter, or status? She concludes, "It seemed as if the exertion itself, when expended within a meaningful situation, was sufficient in itself." Lee sees human beings as moving rather than motivated, as thrusting forward, striving, aspiring. The organism is not a responding machine but a primary activity, producing behavior that is often exuberant, even prodigal, and unlimited in reach.

To Lee, educational institutions set requirements, motivating falsely by competitive success, and thus protecting students from their own enormous appetites for knowledge and exploration, for a world that would engage the whole being in full commitment. Officially, educators ask for the calculable, the graspable; the young are asked to aspire to a ceiling. In contrast, Lee sees the *lack* of limit as a necessary dimension of what she calls "propriate striving."

To her, each culture contains its own definitions of what it is to be fully human and furnishes the situations which call forth exertion. Propriate striving cannot occur in isolation. To the Eskimo, collaboration with the universe is necessary because, without the efforts of people, the universe cannot exist—cannot come into being. Using this cultural world view, Eskimo exertion is a collaboration in building the world of existence. In American culture, "We failed to see achievement as the end product of spontaneously entered exertion and discipline as the enjoyed performance of carefully learned skills." In short, the implicit premises underlying the American conception of cognition and motivation lead, in Lee's two essays, to deeply unsettling questions about cultural transmission of categories and criteria to the young.

The study of culture and cognition, with its emphasis on the underlying patterns that shape thought, will probably continue to force new perceptions of previous research. In the next article, Rosalie Cohen, after reviewing the literature on "disadvantaged" children, recognizes the paucity of cultural analysis and the superficiality of studies that presume to relate intellect and environment. Working with tests that are used to define the "culturally disadvantaged" child, Cohen seeks to discover the covert categories and criteria threading through the overt content of these instruments. She seeks the generic requirements of these tests and finds three categories which, in Lee's terms, all require lineal thinking in varying degrees: the breadth and depth of general information, analytical abstraction, and field articulation or the ability to extract salient information from an embedded context. Cohen finds that students differ in their classification by what they see as salient because they process information according to styles of cognition—some split and some lump incoming stimuli. But, as Cohen states, the school requires one specific approach—analysis; thus those who "split" are acceptable and those who synthesize or "lump" are, too often, unacceptable. The analytic style, associated more commonly with middle-income students, and the relational style, found more frequently in lower-income children, are correlated with social and psychological behaviors. If the cognitive style is incongruent with that officially promulgated, the student is also likely to experience difficulties with school personnel.

Since social-class categories were only partially correlated with cognitive style, Cohen began to search for the social concomitants conducive to the development of each form of thought. Tracing patterns of enculturation, she discovered families in which critical functions were not assigned by status. These shared-function groups, when *both* familial and peer, seemed to transmit a polar-relational thought pattern. Other students, who had experienced a shift from status- to nonstatus-defined groups, appeared capable also of shifting cognitive styles as situationally appropriate. For students living in a mix of both groups, conflicts in cognitive style were apparent, evidently resulting from incongruous reality organization. This was particularly apparent with girls, who in American culture receive, regardless of social class, contradictory cues to the organization of their intellectual reality.

Perhaps the most fascinating finding is the fact that there were two distributions of achievement, *not* a single continuum. In other words, cognitive competence must be considered within the context of a particular socially transmitted cognitive organization of reality. Cohen states flatly that it is no longer appropriate to speak of "disadvantage." Instead, the selection and classification of rule-sets, not information content, must govern the ways in which learners are perceived. The implications of her work are clearly in support of Kimball, whose concern for criteria in judgments of classification is substantiated in Cohen's research. From a pragmatic angle, the implications are equally obvious: a massive change in the training of teachers and a complete reorganization of schools to enable them to accommodate more than one form of cognitive organizational style and more than one world view.

Cohen's research, although still tied to tests, represents the more complex approach to cognition taken by anthropologists during the last decade. It is in striking contrast to the half century of cross-cultural comparisons by psychologists who used instruments of Western origin, often not adapted or poorly modified, to "measure" intellectual capacities. As early as the 1940s, Allison Davis and other anthropologists attacked the irrelevance of test content to lower-income and ethnically diverse children.

A distinct improvement in this initial research is found in the cross-cultural comparisons of the *processes* of intellectual development expressed in Jean Piaget's theories. Ethnocentrism dies hard, however, so this research has at times been flawed by the assumption that Western development is the norm; thus, differences become deviations. The progress of cultural studies of cognition has been discussed by Michael Cole and John Gay and their associates in *The Cultural Context of Learning and Thinking* and by Cole and Sylvia Scribner in *Culture and Thought.* The next article exemplifies their field experimental approach to the study of one cognitive process. Combining psychological and anthropological approaches, the researchers ask the ancient question: Do the bearers of different cultures think differently? To them, previous research has not answered this question because it has been concerned with *what* people think rather than *how* they think. Eskimos and Bushmen think about different things because of their different environments. They also think about similar things, such as families, in different ways because of their divergent kinship systems. But *how* do they think the contents of their thoughts?

Memory is a cognitive process of particular interest because it has been reported as highly developed among some "primitive" people. Moreover, memorization in rote learning found in imported schools in "developing" countries has also been repeatedly noted. Cole and Gay studied memory by eliciting free recall of items from lists of commonly known objects in the Kpelle culture in Liberia. In general, they found that the Kpelle exhibited poorer recall with little use of clustering, a technique of organization used by the Americans to whom they were compared. The discovery of this difference adds little to a knowledge of how it occurs. The method of free recall is not particularly well suited to answer questions about processes; but with experimental modifications, it is possible to obtain some answers. The researchers then engaged in a series of standard experimental variations to detect the Kpelle mode of organization. They began these by asking if the items could be clustered from the Kpelle point of view.

Their further research showed that the Kpelle universe is divided into town things and forest things, which are subdivided into subclasses determined by their relation to human life. Although the processes underlying these categories are not reported, the researchers, on rechecking their lists, found that the objects could be clustered into Kpelle categories.

They then asked: Are the experimental conditions insufficient? If items within the lists were already clustered in the presentation would recall improve? The Americans improved less than the Kpelle, but the pattern of recall remained different. Americans were more likely to learn by rote on the first trial, but not on subsequent trials. Americans remembered last items, then beginning, and finally middle items. This pattern was not evident among the Kpelle. Instead of checking out Lee's hypothesis on the use of the line in Western thought or other possible principles of organization, the researchers turned to the question of concrete learning. Would the Kpelle do better if actual objects were presented? Previous observations have suggested that Africans may think concretely. The findings indicate that the educated Americans performed even better when objects were presented. Again the researchers did not test the formation of spatial Gestalts, but questioned the motivation of the persons tested. Extending the number of trials or the amounts of money failed to influence the major pattern of their findings.

The research was then shifted to the cues used. Was concreteness associated with the cueing process and not with the objects? The concrete cueing procedure produced greater recall among the Kpelle, but the means of their organization remained obscure. Locating objects in spatial dimensions by placing them over chairs began to produce similar levels of recall for both Kpelle and Americans.

Although this research tells us interesting things about cognitive ordering, the significance of the work will eventually be determined when the results can be used to learn about the forms of reality organization as these relate to conceptual rule sets within a particular world view. Because the *processes* of Kpelle cultural clustering on the societal level were not detailed with the same precision as those involved in cognitive clustering on the individual level, we are not able to interconnect both levels with sufficient clarity at this time. We consider next the formulation of rule sets from a linguistic perspective.

LANGUAGE AND CULTURAL LEARNING

The extent to which languages are the carriers of different kinds of thought is still a hotly debated question. There is, however, no controversy over the fact that cultural transmission depends on communication. Therefore, it is somewhat surprising that child socialization studies have largely neglected the linguistic transmission of cultural knowledge. In the first article in this section, J. A. Cook suggests that the acquisition of syntactic rules may provide a parallel model to the acquisition of the rules of social structure. The way language is used in giving social rules could provide more information about the rules themselves. The study of speech in interaction could show how rules of linguistic usage guide and constrain actual social performances. On the basis of these assumptions, Cook advocates research on the development of linguistic competence and of communicative competence.

All children in all cultures apparently gain control of the grammatical systems of their own native languages by the age of four or five. The stages of language development during which linguistic rules are acquired seem to be universal. Current theory postulates innate generative models by which children develop for themselves rules about language derived from their communication experiences. Children can comprehend more than they can produce and initially use single words which stand for whole utterances. The problem for parents and researchers is to decide which of several alternatives is the appropriate expansion of the child's "telegram." Many utterances can be interpreted only in terms of the context of events or the personal knowledge of a particular child. Rules for children's linguistic development cannot be written unless the meaning of their utterances is taken into account; and this meaning depends on the context, a part of which is the adult's own conception of language. Furthermore, rules in communicative competence depend on the requirements inherent in the child's life style. From this Cook concludes that the generative model has situational embeddedness. We cannot simply study words and sentences but interaction sequences seen as exchanges between speakers.

Cook turns to ethnographies to learn what it is that parents make clear to children about the conditions of cultural membership. To him, adult descriptions of the *why* of everyday life to children provide a rich source of information on adult notions of simplified social structures. To get at rulelike structures, the researcher may leave out the "confusing details" which may be those the members actually rely upon to make the rules work. To Cook, rule following is a "situated accomplishment" because all communications are dependent on the contexts in which they occur. Socialization is not a matter of learning the rules and applying them, but of developing a set of interpretive procedures, a set of taken-for-granted assumptions that enable the child to see the rules in the first place.

To complicate the task even further, no language is spoken in exactly the same way by all its speakers. The most neutral, nonjudgmental label for the different ways in which a language is spoken is variety, the verbal repertoire of a member of a speech community—regional, ethnic, religious, functional, social, occupational, and so on. As a term, dialect is reserved for varieties that initially and basically represent divergent geographic origins. In the next article, Courtney B. Cazden reviews the research on black English as a dialect and adds a shorter discussion on bilingualism. Black English exhibits both differences in deep meanings and in superficial forms. The black use of the verb "be" is not simply a random variation or a series of grammatical mistakes. Rather the deletion or appearance of "be" in any particular sentence is derived from a logical linguistic rule set within the dialect. Obviously, black dialect should not be confused with earlier childhood forms of standard English; the rule sets for verb usage are different in each linguistic form.

Cazden points to the asymmetry in comprehension and production. The child does not merely repeat a verbal stimulus but decodes and reencodes it in the forms of nonstandard and standard English, but may not produce the forms of the standard language. Members of many language groups use standard and nonstandard language in different contexts. Cazden states that teachers appear to switch from formal to informal style (you-ya, them-em, etc.) to lessen psychological distance between themselves and students. Dialect switching appears to operate below the level of consciousness and to be independent of the speaker's overt intentions in a variety of situations.

People tend to speak according to the values held within a particular community. To maintain a separate group in a pluralistic urban society, dialect differences will occur not simply out of isolation or ignorance, but because of the need for self-identification with a particular subgroup. Monitoring, or the attention a speaker pays to her or his own speech, will depend on the impression the speaker wishes to convey.

To Cazden, linguistic chauvinism is anachronistic. In a contracting world, bilingual and bidialectical education should be the normal experience of students in schools. Although there is insufficient research to establish the variables involved in learning more than one language, Cazden points to situational factors, i.e., whether the instruction is coercive, whether the learning environment is formal, whether the language is socially dominant, and so forth. These and many other aspects of context will determine the readiness to learn the rule sets of two or more linguistic systems.

In the last article in this section, Martha Coonfield Ward presents her research on the language learning of black children in one southern town. Among white adults, expansions of a child's language fill in incomplete sentences to expand them into the nearest properly formed complete sentences commonly used by adults. Ward found few of these reciprocal expansions in black parents' talk with their children. It appears that adults in this community do not engage in dialogue with young children. If the child has something important to say, the mother listens. However, black children in this study did not learn how to initiate and monopolize a conversation with an adult on a topic of their own choosing.

Although the adults did not expand the speech of children, they did expand their *own* speech *to* children. Ward found a pattern in which the same sentence was repeated, usually three times; in fact, the findings suggest that rhyme schemes could be used to describe the systematic repetition of the adult's sentences. The corrections used by parents centered on the standard of behavior and not on the standards of language. Requests for information were based on behavioral need, not linguistic conpetence. Much teaching was conducted by older children whose information was often inaccurate.

According to Ward, the adult's speech to a child is administrative, the speech necessary to conduct the business of the day. How do children learn their language and its rules in the absence of deliberate instruction? If Ward's research is correct, children in this black community imitate adults far less than adults imitate themselves to the children. Yet this pattern seems to produce youngsters who master black dialect at an early age, understanding the rules of the grammatical structure and expressing themselves within the speech patterns of their own group. Ward concludes that linguistically deprived children do not exist. The mistake is to confuse a set of verbal skills with a collection of correct responses to tests of grammar.

EDUCATORS FROM AN ANTHROPOLOGICAL PERSPECTIVE

When we turn from studies of children to those of educators in school systems, there are no equivalent studies of intellectual functioning. This peculiar omission is particularly problematic because professional socialization probably creates distinctive categories of thought and establishes the primacy of certain canons of discrimination. What is found, instead, are research studies of classrooms in which teachers and students are observed in interaction. Omitting these works, anthropological studies centered squarely on the educator are few, and those of administrators are practically nonexistent. It is, after all, much easier to study the powerless than the powerful.

The overabundance of articles *claiming* to be studies of lower-income nonwhite children is in startling contrast to ethnically based research on teachers. From the literature, one would assume an almost complete cultural homogeneity among teachers. Ruth Landes, in the article that leads off part 5, presents research which is the exception. Studying teacher's ethnicity within a larger undertaking, she asked teachers to reconstruct three generations of ancestral backgrounds; these exhibited an enormous social variety, despite the usual middle-class and professional appearances. Landes reversed the usual demand for adherence to a single, uniform perception of white Americans. A practical result of this was validation of diversity experienced by the teachers themselves. Many were privately ashamed of their "differences": "This is the first time I have ever discussed my background outside the immediate family circle. I guess there are many things one wishes to repress consciously or unconsciously."

Landes was delighted with the detailed genealogies, many of which traced the effects of culture contact and described the difficult problems inherent in acculturation to a single norm. The repression of difference in part explains the refection or pseudo acceptance of racial and ethnic variability in their students. One cannot validate, on any deep level, that which one does not wish to perceive in the self.

Repeatedly, throughout the genealogies, the social changes experienced most personally were changes in sex roles: "My father long held rather autocratic control over his wife and me, his only child. As a child I feared my father's anger." A Franco-American teacher: "The girls found it more difficult to rebel. Hence the men's rebellion greatly reduced the girl's chances of marriage." A teacher of Swedish origin: "Grandfather was a man more of deeds than of words; his most effective tool was silence." A German-American teacher: "My wife and I will carry out the duties of punishment less severely than in my childhood, for I still resent authority that has not approved itself, such as my father exercised."

Whether evolution or revolution, social change cannot occur without a basic shift in sex roles and kinship structure. One Greek-American teacher describes the interaction of societal and familial change this way: "The marriage barrier crumbles slowly, a few of the elders accept American in-laws. The degree of acceptance seems to depend on the Americans' understanding and tolerance of traditional Greek society, customs, and authoritative elders."

The importance of knowing one's cultural antecedents seems obvious, but the lack of such knowledge makes the article by Eleanor Leacock necessary. It is ironic that a nation considered tolerant of cultural diversity should suppress the most fundamental facts about culture to the point that adults, in this case school counselors, require a primer of essentials. Leacock, looking at the function of counselors, tries to give some relevant cultural insight that would enable them to see behind "superficial, socially patterned differences to the full integrity of an individual." To her, knowledge of culture might prevent counselors from misinterpreting behavior that is different from that which is seen as customary. A voguish awareness of differences has, as she correctly points out, led to an exaggeration and misinterpretation of the concept of culture, simply providing a new stereotype behind which "the individual is not revealed more fully, but masked even more insidiously." Citing the work of Estelle Fuchs and Helen Randolph, she describes a situation in which a principal drew a profile of the "deprived," stating that they would be poor financially, academically, and socially, and then continuing to document specific behaviors and actions for dealing with them. Ignoring the variations in the black community around him and relying instead on an assortment of negative characteristics drawn from nonanthropological research, he succeeded in enraging black parents. All this in the name of "culture" as misinterpreted by "experts" and misused by "administrators." Leacock stresses: "The culture concept should be used only to understand, not bury, the individual." To her, it is a tool to help counselors understand unquestioned assumptions.

Both counselors and teachers face difficult, and in urban schools almost insurmountable, problems in trying to relate humanly to the diversity of students. The systems within which they work are hardly conducive to deep probing about unquestioned assumptions. In her essay Elizabeth M. Eddy, drawing on Van Gennep's theory of rites of passage, describes the transition from student to teacher in a case study of professional socialization. The transitional changes in the life cycle that give rise to new functions and status are often accompanied by ritualistic behavior. The separation from an old status, the transition between old and new, and incorporation into a new role are the usual phases in ritualistic passage, the transition phase being the most difficult because uncertainty characterizes it. To be incorporated one must be accepted by established personnel, who are unlikely to claim someone who does not behave in approved ways. In these situations, beginning teachers, even those expressing a desire to change the status quo, are likely to revert to the "old ways," imitating older teachers or teachers they have had when they were students. In dealing with children from subcultures that differ from their own, these teachers will most assuredly experience cultural shock: "I am appalled and can't even conceive of the actions that these kids participate in and the language that they use . . . I keep remembering when I was in school . . . how I was respectful." Experimental programs to prepare prospective teachers by training them in poor neighborhoods do not necessarily produce a smooth transition. Professional incorporation is accomplished by older teachers who claim the younger when they have passed through the expected ritualistic behaviors. The children may have little to do with who is and who is not incorporated. Thus the system perpetuates itself, even if it does not serve the individuals for whom it exists.

With the rise of teacher unions, professional identity is an even more fascinating problem. John Singleton in the next article in this part studies the blend of two cultural forms in teachers unions in Japan. With the importation of a conflict model from the West, the questions of power become interesting. The unions, originally incorporating principals, now face pressure from the national Ministry of Education to exclude principals from the union; at the same time, teachers question the principals' right to leadership positions.

Direct confrontation, however, is mitigated in Japanese ways within the actual operation of unions. Singleton describes one meeting in which a chairman, ostensibly chosen from the group without prior notice, has the agenda already planned. The vote taken at one point, although unclear, is never subsequently clarified. Singleton says, "The formal selection [for officers], though done by ballot, is merely a part of the form that since the war has come to be regarded as democratic procedure." In another meeting, Singleton observes that rather than enter a second slate of officers in direct opposition to the first, the initial slate is rejected and a committee appointed; it returns with a slate approved of long in advance of the meeting. This slate is elected by acclamation.

Japanese unions have a special division for women; in contrast women teachers in the United States are almost totally excluded from top administrative positions in unions. Harry Wolcott's article, the last in the volume, is taken from his book *The Man in the Principal's Office.* Unintentionally, Wolcott has named the book aptly. In fact, his data could be reanalyzed as a case study in male culture, so complete is the domination of education by men. Within this culture, the socialization of the principal is traced by Wolcott in the networks of contacts and processes of promotion within the typical mobility pattern of the "success" ladder for men in American culture. Wolcott distinguishes between sponsored and contest mobility, stating that the first process is dominant in educational institutions. In the acquisition of power, elite status is *given* by those in authority rather than *taken* through effort and strategy. The sponsorship of one man by another is seldom publicly acknowledged, even though it is understood privately.

For power to be bestowed, a tacit demonstration of acceptance of the authority system must be expressed; the man then maneuvers himself into visibility by getting the attention of his superiors or by *gassing*, in inimical American jargon. This syndrome is quite familiar to men in the system and involves them in a cautious balancing act between actively seeking power and pretending they are not. In these dominance politics, formal academic preparation is primarily a means of obtaining needed credentials. The principal's role is defined as basically political, not intellectual. In fact, the principal studied by Wolcott had a total of thirty-three books, pamphlets, and journals on his bookshelf, most of them outdated and none consulted by him during the time period of the study. "Ed. admin." courses are held in low esteem *privately*; public negation is inappropriate because male professors form part of the sponsorship network.

In general, men in positions of educational power rely on oral tradition to train, to incorporate, and to replace one another. The effect of this dominance network is the maintenance of the system. We started this volume by questioning the ability of education to effect cultural change through the transmission process. Our conclusion is likely to be negative. Socialization for power, by the very processes involved, produces cultural continuity without any heightened capacity to incorporate changes or to create new cultural conditions. With increased institutional control associated with advances in material culture, the future viability of complex cultures and of those trying to imitate them seems subject to serious question.

PART II

Culture, Community, and School

1 / Criteria for an Ethnographic Approach to Research in Schools

Harry Wolcott

Along with increased interest in an ethnographic approach to research in schools, to the extent of including an ethnographic dimension in a number of grand-scale projects in educational research, has come a need for greater clarity regarding precisely what this approach really entails. Both the terminology and the approach are relatively unfamiliar in school research. What is ethnographic description? Are the terms "ethnography" and "case study" interchangeable? What prerequisites in training and experience should one expect from a would-be ethnographer? What can one expect from the ethnographer's presence on a research project? How can one distinguish an adequate job from an inadequate one?

It is to such questions of *criteria for an ethnographic approach* that this article is directed as a position paper. It presents the viewpoint of one individual, and of a rather "traditional" or "humanistic" ethnographer at that. I hope that the case I present will serve as an impetus for those who may wish to argue on behalf of different points of view or to discuss alternative roles such as that of the applied anthropologist in formal education.

WHAT IS ETHNOGRAPHY?

The term ethnography belongs to anthropology; ethnography provides the basic descriptive data on which cultural anthropology is founded. An ethnography is, literally, an anthropologist's "picture" of the way of life of some interacting human group; or, viewed as process, ethnography is the science of cultural description. One sometimes hears the term "ethnology" used interchangeably with ethnography, but it seems preferable to emphasize their distinguishing features, restricting ethnography to refer to basic descriptive work and taking ethnology to indicate more theoretically oriented statements about relationships and meanings either within one group or among a number of societies.[1]

Due at least in part to the impact over the last fifteen years of the "Case Studies in Cultural Anthropology" edited by George and Louise Spindler, one also hears anthropologists using the term "case study," although "ethnography" remains the preferred label. To the extent that the terms are used discretely, "case study" provides a handy and unassuming label, while the term ethnography suggests both a more comprehensive and detailed report *and* the perhaps unattainable ideal of a complete and perfect account. Any anthropological case study is more or less an ethnography, and most accounts labeled as ethnography are really contributions *toward* the ethnography of some culture-sharing human group. In my own work, for example, I rather presumptuously subtitled a monograph focused on one elementary school principal as "an ethnography" (Wolcott 1973). Clearly a study of one school principal is not a study of them all; by the second paragraph of the Preface I make that point quite explicit. Furthermore, the study is a tiny part of a growing literature that only collectively will constitute the ethnography of American schooling. My use of the subtitle is intended to signal to a potential reader the manner in which the research was conducted and the framework in which the completed account appears.

Obviously, not everything anthropologists write is ethnography, but I would insist that one can take an ethnographic *approach* to studying virtually any aspect of human social life. A deceptively simple test for judging the adequacy of an ethnographic account is to ask whether a person reading it could subsequently behave appropriately as a member of the society or social group about which he has been reading, or, more modestly, whether he can anticipate and interpret what occurs in the group as appropriately as its own members can. I do not wish to belabor a precise definition for ethnography. The term is a generic one, and it is in the interests of preserving the utility of its general nature that these comments are offered. I should also point out that this discussion is not concerned with ethnographic techniques; how one actually proceeds through fieldwork is a topic of extended scope.[2] Before turning to the discussion of criteria, let me address the question of what an ethnographic account provides that distinguishes it from other research approaches, looking first at ethnography in general and then at ethnography in educational settings.

"Culture" is the major concept and point of departure for most American anthropologists, and ethnography is the anthropologist's descriptive account of what he has observed and understood of another culture. The anthropologist is duty-bound to look for cultural patterns and cultural forms shared by members of a social system or subsystem; it is hardly surprising that he always finds them. Yet anthropologists actually use the term "culture" rather infrequently, especially when referring to behavior patterns shared by specific peoples.[3]

The anthropologist views culture as process, recognizing that it is ongoing, elusive, and always being modified. Paradoxically, it is the ethnographer himself who attempts, at least figuratively, to stay that process, to "hold it still" long enough to make a sketch of it. The perplexity of this task is handled through a linguistic ploy: most anthropologists report their studies of events already observed in a tense which they uneasily call the "ethnographic present."

It is his view of culture as process, and his interest in the nexus between the ethereal notion of culture and the very practical and immediate business of learning what one needs to know to be a member of a particular social system, that give the anthropologist a special slant on education. Unlike the professional educator whose interests lie largely within the domain of the school, the anthropologist is interested in the broad cultural context of teaching and, especially, learning. The anthropologist's frame of reference is "holistic."

The term holistic has recently found its way into educator jargon, and it has seemed to produce even more ambiguity in this new arena than in its anthropological one, so I am hesitant to employ the word itself at the same time that I want to emphasize the importance of the concept underlying it. Perhaps the term "context" is equally suited to make the point that the ethnographer is committed to look at people and events in a total milieu rather than only at bits and pieces. He sees the teacher as well as the pupil as a person who is also a son or daughter, probably a sibling, possibly a mate or parent, a person who plays out a multiplicity of roles and who is both learning and transmitting a set of values. He is more inclined to look at the educators he is studying as men or women who happen to be teachers than as teachers who happen to be men and women. Where the typical educational researcher may want to know where teachers took their training and how long they have taught, the anthropologist may also want to inquire where their grandmothers came from and what is remembered about them. The ethnographer wants to record and report not only the interaction he observes, but something of the setting and, especially, the meaning the actors themselves assign to events in which they engage. Even the applied anthropologist employed expressly to help some agency attain its goals in directed change feels a professional obligation to turn his attention not only to examining the cultural system of the recipient group toward whom the developmental efforts are directed but to the cultural system of the donor group as well.

The ethnographer's unique contribution is his commitment to understand and convey how it is to "walk in someone else's shoes" and to "tell it like it is." However, he must also attend to how the participants themselves say it *ought to be*, typically investigating actions and beliefs in a number of categories of human behavior. Therein, I believe, lies the fine line between good ethnography and good journalism (and I'll take good journalism over poor ethnography any time).

The ethnographer doing research in schools is quite likely to be interested in social behavior outside as well as inside them. The commitment to education as cultural process necessitates a broader perspective than that obtained by confining one's attention to events within the walls of the school building. Quite right: the ethnographer will want to look at (and contrast) what is learned in schools and what is learned outside them, at what is taught formally and what is learned informally, at unintended as well as intended consequences of formal instruction. And that brings us to the first of the four criteria to be examined here, the "problem" problem.

CRITERION I: APPROPRIATENESS OF THE PROBLEM

Anthropologists are not a particularly ornery bunch (some of my best friends are anthropologists), but they do have a stubborn streak about research: they do not like other people to define research problems for them. This quirk can prove an unfortunate handicap in pursuing an interdisciplinary endeavor like anthropology and education. I am sure that many anthropologists have been approached with invitations to join educational research projects and subsequently made a hasty exit when their anticipated role was fully explained. On the other hand, the fact that the anthropologist is interested in learning what problems exist in a research setting also gives him a fresh and relatively uncommitted approach for independent investigation.

I do not mean to suggest that anthropologists are unwilling to help other people look at their problems or that anthropologists insist on the privilege of only or always doing "irrelevant" research. But anthropologists join other social scientists in cautioning that no one knows exactly what research may become relevant (cf. Pelto 1970:322). I think there is a potential conflict of interest when people from an applied field like education employ professionals from the social science disciplines and all parties do not carefully spell out their expectations.

I would hold that ethnography is best served when the researcher feels free to "muddle about" in the field setting and to pursue hunches or to address himself to problems that he deems interesting and worthy of sustained attention. Citing Malinowski for chapter and verse, many anthropologists are content to embark upon new fieldwork guided only by a "foreshadowed notion" of problem areas that may prove interesting. One of the most satisfying aspects of this traditional approach is that one is free to *discover what the problem is* rather than obliged to pursue inquiry into a predetermined problem that may in fact exist only in the mind of the investigator.

The strictures of proposal-writing and funding at times restrict the freedom of problem identification that can be extended to ethnographers, especially when they are members of a project that includes an ethnographic facet rather than an ethnographic intent. Many project proposals that I have seen are much too highly focused to allow a fieldworker the luxury of a broad look around to assess for himself the problems that could be studied. In that regard, my feeling is that anytime someone has decided exactly what the problem is or exactly what he wants to know, he no longer needs the style of exploratory ethnographic research that I am advocating here. Nor is an ethnographic approach appropriate where time is of the essence, when new perspectives or new hypotheses are no longer welcome, or when justification is perceived as the only pure form of scientific endeavor, for ethnography is a high risk, low-yield venture in terms of the time that must be committed to it and the fact that it is more suited to generating than to verifying hunches or hypotheses.

Perhaps because it fits so well with my personal style, I am inclined to view fieldwork as essentially an individual undertaking. Sometimes one finds a team, usually a husband and wife, and often there are assistants present at particular stages during the data gathering, but in the final written report one person, or at most a pair of coauthors who have shared the fieldwork experience, must assume responsibility for writing it up. I have seen proposals for projects engaging many people, and I am aware that there are training sites and projects through which pass a virtual parade of trainees or assistants, but the authorship of completed accounts leaves me convinced that fieldwork is essentially a small-scale, and most often a one-person operation. A sociologically-oriented colleague in Africa sent me a quote that probably amused him: "It is estimated that about 1.5 anthropologists can properly study a community with a population no larger than 300 adults." As I have thought more about it, I wonder if "1.5 anthropologists" can really manage a study of even that magnitude.

In any case, ethnography is enhanced when the researcher works within reasonable bounds, and those bounds have most often been dictated by the scope of what one fieldworker—or a closely working team—can accomplish. Ambitious and overfunded projects beckon the grantsman into fantasies of ethnographic grandeur, and I assume that many an immodest ethnographer who promised to mount a massive ethnographic study eventually discovered that he was only acting as an administrator and ultimately withdrew from his position or abandoned his project altogether. It is certainly true that large-scale projects allow for a number of independent or interdependent pieces of fieldwork and reporting (Perlman 1970), and that subsequent to these accounts some fascinating cross-site comparison and analysis can be achieved, but it is essential to realize the order of this sequence, that ethnographic description remains the basic building block for it, and that ethnography is a human task with human limitations.

Let met get right to the guideline that emerges. I draw upon Rosalie Wax's excellent discussion of fieldwork for the rule and explication, "Do not make or let other people do your fieldwork":

> No matter how many research assistants are available, the head researcher, the person who is going to analyze the material and write the major report, should himself do as much of the interviewing and observation as he possibly can. (Wax 1971:266–67)

My own fieldwork has usually been limited to small numbers of people (e.g., one village of 13 households [1967b]; one elementary school principal [1973]), although clearly I had to become more focused in attempting to understand something about urban African life in a Rhodesian community where the presence of 200,000 blacks was coupled with the extreme likelihood that I would never know anything about even one of them (1974).

I have sometimes argued that my approach is largely unfocused and atheoretical, but I am coming more and more to recognize the necessity of some degree of problem orientation and of the influence of some underlying assumptions even in the most basic descriptive work, swayed by arguments such as Morton Fried's insistence that "there is no such entity as a theoretically unbiased work" (1972:111). I accept that the fieldworker needs to grapple with his own "underlying assumptions" and to recognize the kinds of evidence he is most attracted to in building his account. I acknowledge that many, or perhaps most, anthropologists state the relationship between theory and ethnography far less equivocally than I do (cf. Gerald Berreman's position that "good theory is essential to good ethnography" [1968:399]). But I am also sympathetic to a statement in a review written by Paul Kutsche:

> This reviewer takes the old fashioned view that good ethnography is good reporting, and that ethnographic facts clearly and accurately presented are likely to survive the theoretical frame of reference of the man who recorded them. (1971:957)

Summary of Criterion I

The research problems most intriguing to anthropologists are those problems that they themselves identify. If a research proposal contains provision for a broad descriptive dimension, there is probably no special stress for the "resident anthropologist." To the extent that the research project itself is narrowly focused, it would appear that either a longer period of time may be required to locate a qualified ethnographer with compatible interests or else compromises will have to be made between allowing the ethnographer to pursue his own interests and insisting that he pursue problems of interest to others. In any case, there needs to be an agreed-upon recognition that an independent descriptive study, broadly conceived, and with a focus that may be somewhat tangential to the project as perceived by insiders, will be a satisfactory, valuable, and welcome addition to the total research output.

Before the anthropologist silvers his "mirror for man" (Kluckhohn 1949), he and his clients need to review implications concerning who might look in that mirror and what might be seen there. Educational innovators, for example, seem eager to have ethnographers turn their attention to sources of resistance to change in school districts. Are they equally receptive to inquiry into why they themselves are so compulsive about producing change? Are grantsmen going to be as willing to forward their staff anthropologists' detailed and "detached" analyses if their projects prove to be failures rather than successes?

CRITERION II: APPROPRIATENESS OF THE ETHNOGRAPHER

For all his efforts at getting and verifying information through a variety of techniques, the fieldworker's essential research instrument has always been himself. In a text on research stressing the variety of techniques by which the fieldworker gets his data, anthropologist Pertti Pelto emphasizes the centrality of the individual researcher as instrument:

> Compared with many other sciences, methods of observation in anthropological work generally require very little in the way of specialized measuring and observing devices. The anthropologist himself is the main instrument of observation. (Pelto 1970:140)

In an approach that identifies the researcher himself as the "main instrument," establishing criteria for judging the adequacy of a candidate for the role of ethnographer becomes a critical issue. A credential-conscious society like our own gives great credence to processes of formal certification. What might we ordinarily expect a researcher to provide in validation of a claim that he can "do" ethnography?

In the "culture" of cultural anthropologists, the completion of a successful period of fieldwork remains the sine qua non of proof of one's having come of age, and in spite of increasing difficulties for achieving it, a strong belief holds that such experience should be in a cross-cultural setting. This is not to deny that a number of prominent anthropologists either were unsuccessful as fieldworkers or never did real fieldwork at all (cf. Fried 1972:123). Nor is it to deny that anthropology students are turning their attention increasingly to completing their initiation into fieldwork within their own society.[4]

Nevertheless, the bias remains in favor of cross-cultural experience. Anthropology is essentially a cross-cultural and comparative discipline, and the argument persists that only in the cross-cultural setting can the potential of observation and comparison be fully realized. Fried states the case explicitly:

> Anthropology requires a cross-cultural setting for its most basic theoretical operations. Rather than urging anthropologists to dwell within their own cultures, the needs of the discipline are best served by encouraging all anthropologists to maximize their experiences outside their own cultures. (Fried 1972:239)

Anthropologist Clyde Kluckhohn stated the case even more succinctly: "It would hardly be fish who discovered the existence of water" (1949:16).

The tyro fieldworker conducting a study in a cross-cultural setting has the very thing going for him that anthropologists hold to be so critical—he is surrounded by people and customs that he does not take for granted. Educators intrigued by the ethnographic method are suspect when they declare their intention to employ this approach to help them "see" the very schools with which they have probably been in more-or-less continuous contact since the age of six. A number of anthropologists interested in education have suggested that prior cross-cultural fieldwork is an important prerequisite to doing fieldwork in schools. For the schoolman turning attention to the schools of his own society, they argue, there might be cause for dismay or even for shock, but there is no possibility for experiencing "culture shock." Some anthropologists, like George Spindler, hold cross-cultural experience to be absolutely essential:

> It would be a grievous error to think that a generation of educational anthropologists could be trained without a solid exposure to this kind of [cross-cultural] experience. I suggest that no anthropologist-of-education-to-be should start with his or her first significant piece of empirical research in a school in our own society. It is essential for him or her to get turned around by seeing and experiencing differently. (Spindler 1973:16)

There are some other essential ingredients that one can expect among the credentials of the ethnographer. Foremost among them is a *thorough* grounding in cultural anthropology: a familiarity and basic compatibility with anthropology's perspective and terminology, a certain ease in knowing the "proper footnotes," and a sense of the development of the discipline and the relationships among its major subfields. There are other less tangible skills needed, skills which obviously can be sharpened by training and practice but which also depend on personal qualities not evenly distributed in the talent pool from which researchers emerge. One such set of skills includes those of the sensitive and perceptive observer, at once sympathetic, skeptical, objective, and inordinately curious (Berreman 1968:341–43). Another set provides physical stamina, emotional stability, and personal flexibility. A third set requires the skills of the story-teller and writer, a person who can transform a morass of notes and impressions into an account of sufficient merit that others will feel compelled to read and led to understand.

Although I ally with those who hold cross-cultural fieldwork as a customary prerequisite to doing ethnography in schools, let me hedge my position to the extent that I do not regard it as an absolute necessity, especially if most of these other attributes are present. For example, if the ethnographer does not transform his notes into a completed account, then there is no account, and so I place writing skill high among the essentials for validation. It is probably unfortunate that more anthropologists have not either recognized the importance of the skill of writing in their careers or teamed up with capable writers. Further, and cross-cultural experience notwithstanding, I would be suspicious of a candidate whom I felt lacked sensitivity as an observer, although I am at a loss to explicate exactly how I would assess this shortcoming on any basis other than a purely intuitive one. Perhaps ethnographers who have recognized shortcomings in their own sensitivity have occasionally been able to surround themselves with colleagues, assistants, or informants to compensate for their "blind spots"; complaints about having been "used" are not unknown in these ranks.

Just as one might conceivably compensate for a lack of observer sensitivity through a judicious selection of assistants, or, perhaps somewhat less satisfactorily, link personal qualities that enhance fieldwork with the skills of others who can help with the writing, one might conceivably compensate for the absence of cross-cultural experience by offering some reasonable substitutes. If I am skeptical about it being done often, at least I think it is possible of attainment. For example, one might complement a thorough background in cultural anthropology with extensive reading about one or two societies so that, at least vicariously, the reading could provide a comparative basis. Alternatively, one might develop skills in microethnography, focusing on specific, educationally-relevant events and settings along the lines described by Jacquetta Burnett (1973) or Louis M. Smith (1967). As yet another strategy one might take the standard topics found in ethnographies, introductory texts, or field guides as a basis for developing a systematic description, running the risk of following a cookbook approach but at the same time drawing on anthropological custom in identifying useful rubrics for the examination of human social behavior.

In fact, I think that every effort should be made to encourage researchers who are not of anthropological persuasion to draw upon facets of the ethnographic approach (cf. Sieber 1973, where he argued for integrating fieldwork and survey methods) without feeling that they must make all the commitments and meet all the prerequisites of the professional anthropologist. I assume that there is a bit of ethnographic talent in each of us. My impression is that, irrespective of formal training, evidence of such talent is likely to be admired (and, among promising students, encouraged). Professional boundaries are defended only against those whose claims exceed their talent. Simply assuming the role of observer does not perforce allow an individual to advertise himself as a professional ethnographer.

Educators-cum-novelists occasionally turn out "ethnographically correct" accounts in their stories about schools. A number of scholars in professional education have made impressive contributions to the descriptive literature without requiring validation as ethnographers and without attempting to satisfy all the usual criteria of ethnography.[5] Further, it should be noted that the literature of education is replete with "field studies" that provide the educational researcher with another tradition and label for descriptive efforts derived primarily from sociology but consisting of a set of research procedures similar to those of the anthropologist (cf. Zelditch 1962). Indeed, *except among anthropologists themselves*, the argument is sometimes heard that there is no fundamental distinction between sociology and anthropology, especially when it comes to conducting fieldwork in public schools (Khleif 1971:153). I hope this paper suggests that there are important distinctions, but I will not take up the argument here, especially since the discussion tends to be "in-house" and detracts from the critical point: one does not have to be an ethnographer to avail himself of elements of an ethnographic approach in his research.

Need I emphasize the point that ethnographic method is not the answer to educational research, any more than is any other approach? Observers who have been waiting for the anthropology of education to produce what it seemed to promise are growing impatient and critical[6] at the very time when a respectable body of ethnographic literature about schools is finally accumulating.[7]

Summary of Criterion II

In seeking a qualified ethnographer, one is not employing a method—or a methodologist—but an individual who will himself be the main instrument of research. Attention rightly should be directed to the qualities that the ethnographer can bring to the task. Thorough grounding in anthropology is essential. Prior cross-cultural fieldwork seems highly desirable, but a number of other qualities have been mentioned that need to be considered and might at times provide a compelling basis for making exceptions.

I recall an occasion when I had drafted a research proposal for an ethnographic study and decided to "try it out" on an anthropologist who has often been a valuable critic for me. I sent the proposal to him with the question, "Is this going to be good anthropology?" He replied, "Does it really matter if it's good anthropology? Aren't you really more concerned that it is a good study?" His point was well made. The criteria discussed throughout this paper, and particularly in this section on individual qualifications, are narrowly focused on standards that satisfy the conditions of professional ethnography, not the conditions of research. On numerous occasions I have read or reviewed research proposals supposedly including anthropological or ethnographic dimensions. Not infrequently the proposals were solid and relevant to the problem at hand; they simply did not happen to be anthropological in conception. How much easier it would have been if the proposal writers had exercised some constraint and identified their approaches as ones that borrowed generously from ethnographic techniques rather than insisted (and argued) that the studies were anthropological.

Although few institutions offer formal graduate programs in anthropology and education, a number of universities offer courses in this area of study or encourage students to pursue systematic study across departmental lines. At the graduate level, rather expectedly, this has brought more education students into anthropology than anthropology students into education. The consequence is that many people interested in doing educational ethnography are better grounded in education than in anthropology. For this reason I have spelled out some critical aspects for rendering judgments in individual cases so that educators (like myself) who have made a serious commitment to anthropology will continue to compete on favorable terms with anthropologists who express an interest in working in educational settings.

CRITERION III: APPROPRIATENESS OF THE RESEARCH CLIMATE

How one perceives the discussion of this third criterion may depend on the extent of his involvement or interest in the ethnographic approach. Colleagues familiar with fieldwork may welcome the airing of some of its inherent problems. Others unfamiliar with the approach may find themselves questioning whether its potential benefits warrant meeting a number of special conditions.

Two conditions necessary to nurture ethnography have already been noted. One is the problem of scope. The ethnographer is not so much in need of forty assistants helping him to gather data as he is in need of a problem one-fortieth as large so that he personally can conduct a substantial portion of the fieldwork. This is not to deny that field assistants can be valuable, but rather to suggest that as the number or complexity of sites increases, the anthropologist is more likely to need fellow ethnographers assuming responsibility for developing their own materials about facets of the setting than he is to need an army of assistants writing and forwarding field notes to him. In my opinion, fieldwork assignments ought always to entail both responsibility for recording initial observations and responsibility for preparing summary accounts.

The second condition is time. A bit more needs to be said about time from the fieldworker's point of view. Ethnography demands time. I usually feel a sense of dismay when doctoral students in education (other than those making a commitment to anthropology and education) declare that they are going to follow an ethnographic approach or conduct a field study to meet the dissertation requirement. Their estimates of time are seldom realistic. Typically they allow too little time for fieldwork and virtually no time at all for the writeup. As much as I wish to encourage the accumulation of ethnographic material about schools, I initially try to discourage doctoral candidates from pursuing this approach. (Of course, I would never discourage doctoral candidates in anthropology on those grounds, but they are generally younger and more patient, and they are fulfilling career requirements as well as graduation requirements. I should add that doctoral students in education who are not dissuaded by my admonitions have forged ahead to conduct and complete studies that are a substantial contribution to the ethnographic literature on schools.)

My preference is that school ethnography be conducted by people who are free of the constraints of graduate programs and who have time in their daily lives as well as in their career plans for fieldwork and for writing. I would not argue that fieldwork necessarily requires a full-time assignment, but I find it exceedingly difficult to conduct even modest studies while teaching on a continuing basis and meeting customary university and professional commitments. I have had to learn to write my field notes as extensively as possible during brief research forays, based on the (usually correct) assumption that I will not have time to review or expand them for weeks or even months. I cannot recommend this practice—nor am I seemingly able to find time to conduct new research under any other arrangement, except for the infrequent respite of academic leave.

As experienced fieldworkers know, time in the field is "just the beginning." I allowed one uninterrupted academic year for dissertation writing following a calendar year of fieldwork among the Kwakiutl Indians of British Columbia. Converting the dissertation to a publishable monograph extended through two more years. I anticipated one interrupted year for writing my ethnography of the school principal, following a year of intensive fieldwork, but I did not complete an adequately edited draft until two additional years had passed. It took more than a year after completing research in Africa to complete my final account even though I was able to finish a second draft while still in the field. Yet I failed to appreciate my own practice in apportioning time to write for time in the field until I read Rosalie Wax's straightforward recommendation:

> It is a horrid but inescapable fact that it usually takes *more* time to organize, write, and present material well than it takes to gather it. The notion that one can work in the field for a year and then write a good report while one is carrying a full- or part-time load is idiotic. (People do write in this fashion, but this is one reason why so many monographs are uninspired.) The sensible researcher will allow as much free time to write his report as he spent in the field. If he is really astute and can get away with it, he will allow himself more. (Wax 1971:45)[8]

Wax's book on fieldwork carries the subtitle "Warnings and Advice," but since this paper seeks to establish criteria, let me restate her advice in the strongest possible terms: at least as much time should be allowed for organizing and writing material as is allowed for gathering it. Coupled with the customary (but not inviolable) preference for extending one's fieldwork over a period of twelve months, a general guideline is to allow a two-year minimum for seeing ethnographic work to completion. For a briefer period of fieldwork I would recommend as an absolutely rigid minimum that one day be reserved for organizing and writing for every day in the field. No time? No ethnographic approach!

An interesting twist has recently developed regarding this issue of the time available for conducting and writing a study, a problem that I believe is unique to the educational research setting. Within the last few years, and related to the policy of funding federally supported projects for increasingly long periods of research, a new practice has been instigated, one of employing ethnographers for uninterrupted terms that may prove too long for productive fieldwork. A young anthropology student who had just completed fieldwork in northern Canada related that as he was preparing to leave the village where he had lived and studied for a year someone commented, "A year isn't long enough to learn about this community." The anthropologist replied forthrightly, "Maybe not, but it's long enough for me." The physical and emotional strains of the year and the psychological isolation of fieldwork had begun to wear, and he recognized the need to get away from the village and to begin sorting out experiences and data already at hand but not yet analyzed. There will be times when he wishes he was back in the field, and there may be opportunities for him to visit the village in the future, but he also recognized that there are advantages to having too little time when that likelihood is weighed against the prospect of having too much of it.

This problem of ethnographic fatigue has not yet fully materialized, but a number of people working in long-term assignments are concerned about it. Professional isolation and lack of variation are among the concomitants of ethnographic fatigue. I think that steps can be taken to alleviate such problems through careful attention to the research climate. Face to face interaction with other fieldworkers; periods for pursuing esoteric research interests of one's own choosing; extended periods away from the site for analysis, writeup, or further study; or even taking on another occupational role for a few months, all pose good opportunities for introducing variety. One way of introducing variety would be to encourage ethnographers to take part-time teaching assignments at nearby universities or to take occasional leave for full-time teaching. I share the dismay of a fieldworker on a long-term project who was denied a brief special leave which, coupled with several weeks of accumulated leave, would have allowed him to accept a summer-school position as a visiting lecturer. His request was perceived as a conflict of interest—with a five-year study. It seems to me that someone was confusing quality with quantity in fieldwork.

Too much rather than too little time has produced another source of strain, the insistence of sponsors and/or administrators that they must satisfy themselves that the ethnographer is "on the job" and competently pursuing a "significant" study while the fieldwork is in process. During projects of long duration, somebody somewhere in the administrative hierarchy inevitably exerts more pressure than anthropologists are accustomed to, in a thickly or thinly veiled effort to find out what the ethnographer is finding out. It seems likely that ethnographers—and the descriptive nature of ethnography itself—stand the risk of occasionally being compromised if they do not become adroit at simultaneously buying time and collecting their pay on long-term projects that are designed to be "purely descriptive" but that nonetheless have evaluative consequences somewhere in the bureaucratic hierarchy.

Fieldwork ordinarily calls for a degree of personal involvement far in excess of other research approaches. If the anticipation of having a real, live researcher "nosing about" for an extended period of time is not a matter of rejoicing for both the research-sponsoring organization and the people on-site, then the effort will surely be hampered and may not be successful. A reluctant acceptance is, of course, preferable to not being accepted at all; formal reluctance has occasionally been anticipated by collecting a promise of cooperation as a condition for initiating a developmental project or awarding funds. Over time, however, sponsoring agencies can become increasingly anxious as they realize that a fieldworker has been successful in gaining acceptance among members of the community being studied. Offhand comments advising that the researcher should not spend his time "always talking to the same people" usually hint at some influential's concern that his own views are getting less of a hearing than he had expected.

Personal involvement has another dimension: the fieldworker's own experience and reactions are likely to form part of the ethnographic account. Years ago Robert Redfield advised anthropologists not to hide behind a mask of neutrality in preparing their accounts but to present something of themselves and of how they felt personally toward people and events they were studying (Redfield 1953:156). Anthropologists have recognized that how they proceed during their fieldwork, how their presence in the field affects both what they learn and how they write about it, how personal and professional commitments necessitate compromises—in short, how each ethnographer makes his own field situation—are a proper topic for collective review (Freilich 1970, Spindler 1971). Now Rosalie Wax has gone still further and asked the fieldworker to report how he himself has been changed by the fieldwork experience (1971:363 ff.) The underlying theme here is that fieldwork is a research approach which not only tolerates but invites and, to an extent, is predicated on personal involvement. If there is neither the call for such involvement, the possibility of achieving it, nor a sense of urgency on the part of the fieldworker to engage in the activity as a human experience, then the likelihood of achieving ethnography seems quite diminished.

Ethnography also thrives under conditions favoring professional autonomy. Even the basic strategy concerning the degree and kind of personal involvement ought to be the prerogative of the individual fieldworker, and in the course of the research a number of decisions regarding strategies, ethics, and choices will have to be made. Experienced fieldworkers are quick to point out that since they have to live with the consequences of these decisions, and since their work is directly affected by them, they should ordinarily have a major voice in reaching them. Agencies and anthropological elders can lay down broad guidelines. But no one can or should attempt to anticipate for the fieldworker precisely how to handle all the problems of personal vulnerability and reciprocal obligation he will incur as he assumes the role of a person who has come to take something away and therefore will inevitably be required to give something in return. The critical business of maintaining rapport throughout fieldwork necessitates leaving the responsibility for tactical decision-making right where the action is.

The question of how "native" to go in fieldwork always prompts lively discussion. I have found as a useful guide anthropologist Arthur Vidich's pragmatic answer that you go as native as necessary to get the information you want (Vidich 1960). However, there are extenuating circumstances. One is the personality of the fieldworker and his attraction to and compatibility with members of the group he is studying.[9] Another is the fieldworker's own response to a vocal minority of anthropologists who urge each colleague to serve as an advocate who willingly "plunges into the trouble spots of his society" (Fried 1972:48 ff.).

My tactic has customarily been to avoid an advocacy position during fieldwork but to take a position in my subsequent writing. As I have learned and practiced the art and science of my craft over the years, I have also become less intimidated by its canons. If I have access to information or expertise that might help people in whom I have become professionally interested to improve their human condition, I look for ways to provide that help. If those ways seem to interfere with the purity of the research, then I take pains to report what I have done—cf. Wolcott 1967a:130). The critical point is that I have felt free to make these decisions myself.

There is one very tangible facet of this issue of autonomy. It deals with the problem of the ownership of materials gathered or prepared in the field. Project funding can lead to some confusion on this point, and I would like to take a clear position on it. Materials gathered expressly at the bidding of someone else clearly seem to belong to the individual who ordered that they be collected. Quite likely a field-worker would also gather other materials that he might well elect to forward at the termination of a project. But the primary accounts that he has collected (e.g., transcriptions of interviews he conducted, completed copies of questionnaires he devised), and, especially, his own written journals and/or field notes, are *private documents that belong to the researcher.* An anthropologist almost invariably gets more information, and information of a far more personal and confidential nature, than he necessarily intends or even wants to get. The notes he makes about other people and events, as much as the notes he makes of his own reactions and impressions, are private. They belong only to him.

Alexander Leighton, writing in 1945 about the studies conducted at one of the Japanese Relocation Centers, talks directly to this problem and raises some interesting issues about the ownership of field data. Each staff member on the project was encouraged to keep a journal "absolutely private and personal" that enabled him to "put things down as he saw and felt them and then decide later about how and when to contribute them" (Leighton 1945:392). Fieldwork in that sensitive setting proceeded with the understanding that "only the reports and general conclusions were to be considered government property" (1945:393) while the ultimate disposition of raw field notes was a matter to be decided among the anthropologists and their assistants. Leighton reports: "It was understood that eventually the data would be given to some institution of research and learning" (1945:393). On the latter point I would take issue. The option to release notes must always remain with the fieldworker who made them; although he might bestow an important favor to posterity, he owes science no necessary obligation to release his personal journals. It is interesting to note Leighton's observation that the extent to which the research staff felt free to discuss or contribute from their journals seemed to provide a tacit measure of the morale of the research unit:

> The tendency to hold back decreased progressively as the spirit of the group increased and they became more clear as to what it was they were doing, how the material would be used, and aware of the reality of ethical consideration for confidence. (1945:392)

When an ethnographer accepts a position to work on a project, rather than seeks independent funding for work of his own, he also accepts an obligation to prepare reports based on his notes. Presumably the reports he forwards will be treated as project rather than personal property—under conditions that should be carefully discussed in advance. Optimally, I would think that the ethnographer might retain a major say about how widely any particular report will be distributed or how a series of field reports might ultimately be brought together and reworked into a case study. But it must also be recognized that research projects are product oriented and that funding agencies will seek evidence that they are getting something for their money. Rather than gamble on the completion of a magnum opus, I would think that ethnographer and project director alike would find it preferable to press for the accumulation of a series of papers contributing *toward* an ethnography. Especially where there is no explicit and shared notion of what an ethnographic report looks like, or where there is a possibility that the fieldwork will be conducted by a succession of researchers rather than by one person, it seems more realistic for all parties concerned to see a final document accumulating in small but tangible units rather than anxiously to await the appearance of a full-blown ethnography. At the same time, it should be noted that the problem of how often and what kind in terms of reports can be expected to aggravate that inevitable tension between fieldworkers and project managers.

In terms of individual careers, I would think that ethnographers would always wish to be working toward publication of their accounts in whole or in parts, in some readily available form, and under their own name. The purposes of ethnography remain largely unfulfilled for anyone whose work remains inaccessible for review and study. Secret, restricted, or merely "filed-away" reports advance neither science nor professional careers; people who accept positions which require any of these alternatives as a condition of employment apparently meet their needs for professional gratification from what I assume must be exorbitantly high salaries. I must confess to a different kind of satisfaction that I get because I know that my accounts are read and that material I write is clearly identified. I have had a sponsoring organization wrest away my modest royalties, but it did not lay claim to the work itself. I feel that I have been unusually fortunate to work in institutional settings where both policy and individual encouragement have aided in seeing my accounts made available through publication or informal dissemination.

Summary of Criterion III

If one thinks of ethnography in pragmatic American terms as an investment of time, money, and human resources (in much the same way that formal education is regarded), the discussion of this section might be seen as a guide to protecting and "maximizing" that investment. From another perspective, the issues raised point to problems that have to be addressed in making a decision about the costs of ethnography in terms of possible problems and compromises for a research project. The most critical factor here is protecting the autonomy of the fieldworker. If project constraints or personal styles are not conducive to providing autonomy, then it would seem that ethnography is not a realistic research alternative. Perhaps the solution in such cases, as suggested earlier, is to draw selectively from an ethnographic approach without going so far as to make the total commitment.

CRITERION IV: APPROPRIATENESS OF EXPECTATIONS FOR THE COMPLETED STUDY

The final criterion deals with characteristics of competent ethnography as evidenced in both the process of research and the content of the completed account. At the risk of offending experienced ethnographers I will propose a list of *techniques* one might ordinarily expect a fieldworker to use as well as a list of the kinds of *topics* one might expect to find discussed in an ethnography. I propose these lists not as a guide for fieldworkers but with the intent of establishing some appropriate expectations for those who have only a vague notion of what an ethnographic approach entails and who might make more appropriate decisions if they knew more.

I will touch upon the issue of "adequacy," although I am not going to address the larger issue that anthropologist Charles Frake has termed ethnographic *theory*, the task of devising criteria for *evaluating* ethnography (Frake 1964:111). Explicating such criteria, both in general and for the special circumstances of the educational setting, is a problem with which anthropologists will continue to concern themselves in their professional dialogues. At the same time, I can and will suggest some guidelines for what one might expect from an investment in ethnography.

The methodological approach to be outlined in this section reveals a critical underlying aspect of ethnography—the use of varied modes of gathering information. The list of topics around which ethnographic accounts are typically organized serves as a basis for examining completed accounts as well as for anticipating the contents of new ones. It is entirely conceivable that an ethnographic account might be focused around only one of the topics to be identified here. It is conceivable (but just barely) that only one research technique among those listed might be employed. An account narrowly limited in scope and technique might indeed be an excellent piece of anthropology, but it is unlikely that it would be ethnographic. Thus the many facets described here together are characteristic of ethnography, and one's skepticism might be warranted in inverse ratio to the multiplicity of techniques or categories employed, especially in describing aspects of formal education in a complex society.

Frake has wrestled with the problem of judging descriptive adequacy and I find his comments instructive:

> To describe a culture, then, is not to recount the events of a society but to specify what one must know to make those events maximally probable. The problem is not to state what someone did but to specify the conditions under which it is culturally appropriate to anticipate that he, or persons occupying his role, will render an equivalent performance. This conception of a cultural description implies that ethnography should be a theory of cultural behavior in a particular society, the adequacy of which is to be evaluated by the ability of a stranger to the culture (who may be the ethnographer) to use the ethnography's statements as instructions for appropriately anticipating the scenes of the society. I say "appropriately anticipate" rather than "predict" because a failure of an ethnographic statement to predict correctly does not necessarily imply descriptive inadequacy as long as the members of the described society are as surprised by the failure as is the ethnographer. The test of descriptive adequacy must always refer to informants' interpretations of events, not simply to the occurrence of events. (Frake 1964:112)[10]

The procedures an ethnographer follows in research are a special hallmark of his work and their effect permeates his final report. Under most circumstances the anthropologist goes to the place and among the people about whom he wishes to learn. But his actual presence in the research setting is not his sole stock in trade. Once the hurdles of gaining entree and establishing initial rapport have been overcome, the fieldworker consciously endeavors to find different ways to get information just as he endeavors to find a variety of settings in which to learn how "his people" confront the problems of being human. The fieldworker rests his claims for validity on his use of a number of information-gathering devices. Anthropologists have contrasted how other social scientists *gather data* on some specialized topic, using specially-developed instruments (e.g., a questionnaire, a structured interview), with the fact that the ethnographer *does fieldwork*, generally by immersing himself in the setting that he wants to understand (cf. Foster 1969:60). A colleague succinctly defines fieldwork as the task of "living one's way into another culture."

At least one anthropologist, Pertti Pelto, has suggested that anthropological research is characterized by its multi-instrument approach. Let me illustrate the variety of techniques used by drawing on Pelto's text, *Anthropological Research, The Structure of Inquiry* (1970). In a chapter entitled "Tools of Research" Pelto offers the following list:

Participant Observation
Key-Informant Interviewing
Collection of Life Histories
Structured Interviews
Questionnaires
Ratings and Rankings
The Semantic Differential Technique

Projective Techniques
Other Psychological Research Instruments
Unobtrusive Measures
Technical Equipment in Field Work

The list is not intended to be a complete inventory of ethnographic techniques. The list itself is somewhat uneven. For example, it gives the appearance of equating either participant observation or interviewing, the two mainstays in most ethnographic fieldwork, with highly specialized (and not so widely used) techniques like Osgood's "Semantic Differential." More recent generations of anthropology students might be inclined to lump all the psychological research instruments together (and perhaps be equally inclined not to employ any of them in their fieldwork) while they might want to add eliciting techniques from the "New Ethnography" (which Pelto discusses in a separate chapter).

Pelto's chapter (and book) is well worth reading. Although I will not attempt a comprehensive review of the techniques as he lists them, the list does provide a point of departure for further comment. For example, it is no coincidence that *participant-observation* and *interviewing* are mentioned first among the tools of research. However, it is important to understand that neither of these methods is peculiar to anthropology and that some anthropologists employ the term participant observation not only to refer to *a* technique of research but also as a comprehensive term that includes *all* the techniques of fieldwork (cf. Berreman 1968:365). The third item on Pelto's list, the *collection of life histories*, occurs frequently in anthropological accounts, but case histories that include life history data abound in a number of fields ranging from the offices of collection agencies or welfare workers to education, psychiatry, public administration, and the FBI. The notion of *key-informant interviewing*, referring to extended interviews with one or a few members of a group rather than brief interviews with numerous "subjects," is a characteristic of anthropological fieldwork, but inquiries via *structured interviews* or *questionnaires* are no special hallmark. The *unobtrusive measures* of the anthropologist, especially when they include such everyday data as official documents, library collections, or children's schoolwork, are equally part of the research base of the economist, historian, or educator.

Indeed, only when we develop a list such as Pelto's and ask whether any group of social scientists might consistently use a combination of many or most of these techniques do we become aware of the ethnographer's commitment to being present in person on the scene over an extended period of time as well as to utilizing a number of approaches for gathering information. As Pelto himself concludes, "Examining cultural behavior with a *variety of different approaches* greatly enhances the credibility of research results" (Pelto 1970:145). It is also part of the ethnographer's customary "style" and a reasonable expectation to hold for him.

It is important to recognize an element of appropriateness in selecting among the variety of research techniques, an appropriateness related to individual style, training, resources, and the nature of the problem and the field setting. In doing research in schools, the widely used technique of participant-observation runs afoul of that organization's own tradition (cf. Khleif 1974). There are relatively few formal roles in schools, and the roles available are not necessarily attractive for accomplishing research that must be based on limited rather than on total involvement. Schools do entertain hordes of "observers," but anthropologists customarily expect to be more than just members in a passing parade. Yet unless one places himself behind a podium (cf. King 1974), a typewriter, a broom, or the principal's desk, there simply are no other roles (unless one really is a "Narc" [narcotics agent] as students these days are apt to assume). The only alternative in the school setting appears simply to resign oneself to becoming an observer. So—be an observer! Perhaps in time one can find additional avenues for enlarging one's perspective. For example, researchers and teachers alike have reported that high school students respond to training in ethnographic techniques and, as proto-ethnographers, have access to student groups and to a point of view that adults are not ordinarily able to tap.

The fact that the fieldworker in schools may find himself relegated to the role of a formal observer can be viewed as a blessing in disguise. I once heard an interesting paper presented by a sociologically oriented researcher who accepted a teaching position in the same school in which she was doing a field study. She later acknowledged a lingering concern that teachers in the school often forgot her research purposes and confided to her as a colleague, and she expressed the hope that she had not violated any confidences because of her dual role. Every fieldworker experiences that agony about personal confidences, but I feel that the extent of my agony over the problem must surely be less than hers, for I have found it more useful to dramatize my role as a researcher than attempt to hide it. I am inclined to carry my notebook everywhere and to write in it constantly, even intrusively, while people are talking to me or in my presence. This does not always endear me, and I have often been told, "Now don't put this down in your notes . . ." but my conscience is relatively clear about my presentation of self when I am "observing" in schools. The appropriate strategy in school research seems to be to seek diligently to uncover alternative techniques and sources for collecting information. My experience has been that teachers are usually quite willing to respond to a personal invitation for an interview even though they may be rather hostile to a request to complete "another damn questionnaire."

Let me express some reservations in providing the following list of topics that one might expect to find in accounts of ethnographic research conducted in an educational setting. For a number of reasons I would not expect to see every one of these elaborated in any one ethnography. First, some of these constructs are a matter of overall perspective rather than a specific subheading, and thus they might pervade the account without receiving much explicit attention. Second, if the reader accepts the view that most accounts contribute *toward* ethnography rather than achieve it, then adequate attention to an aspect of a culture is an acceptable ethnographic accomplishment. It has been observed in this regard that the anthropologist writing exclusively for his peers is more likely to prepare technical analyses of matters of quite limited focus, while the anthropologist writing for a patron audience is likely to strive for a broader focus in order to achieve a more esthetically satisfying portrayal (cf. Smith 1964).

It is also true that even the conceptual terms most closely associated with anthropology are used by professionals in other fields and therefore the mere presence of these headings is no guarantee of ethnography. Further, when the research focus is narrowed (as it frequently is in educational studies) to a school system, school, or possibly even a single role or group in a school, then certain of the concepts identified seem not to lend themselves to attention, at least in a customary manner. Yet here, perhaps, is a caution for the ethnographer, for he may discover that he is being commissioned to look at too small a part of the system for him to actually study "man," and that violates his commitment to be "holistic."

Let me begin with some relatively straightforward topics which one might expect to find:

> Allocation and distribution of resources
> Environment
> Material culture/technology
> Personal adaptations (in both words and action)
> Ritual behavior
> Social networks

The fact that any of these headings is likely to be found in the opening section of an ethnographic account suggests that these are the kinds of topics that provide a useful "starting point" both in fieldwork and in writing. The pursuit of such topics can lead to modest but useful insights (as, for example, when it occurred to me that in schools where pass keys are regarded as a scarce resource their allocation to only certain teachers may provide tangible evidence of subtle differences in teacher status [1973:169–701]); they can also provide a point of departure for extended study. The examination of ritual has proven to be an especially useful basis for organizing ethnographic accounts in educational settings (Burnett 1969, Eddy 1969, Leemon 1972).

Growing out of topics such as those listed above are a number of more comprehensive categories which ethnographers customarily use in presenting their materials, either by sorting their information among the most appropriate categories (or dutifully saying something about them all) or focusing on one or two in both fieldwork and writing:[11]

Economic organization
Ethos or world view/ideational systems
Language
Life-cycle customs
Political organization
Projective systems (religion, art, folklore)
Social control
Social organization

As the list is expanded still further the topics added extend the possibilities for analysis and nudge the ethnographer toward cross-cultural comparison, and we see how ethnography leads naturally into areas of interest that are more broadly "anthropological" than purely ethnographic. I will suggest only three more topics, all of particular importance in the anthropology of education:

Culture and personality
Cultural stability and change
Cultural transmission/enculturation

A colleague reading an earlier draft reacted strongly to my attempt to prepare this list, chiding that he did not for one minute believe that I use such an outline to guide my own fieldwork. Well, let me set the record straight. I do keep these very concepts in mind, not to reorder the field situation or structure day-to-day observations but to provide a sort of checklist as the work proceeds. Pausing to take stock of my notes, I might systematically examine the kinds of questions I would be asking if I were particularly interested in each of the facets mentioned.

I do not insist that all the categories are of equal importance in the study of education or in the dialogue between anthropologists and educators. For the very practical reason that educators particularly like to hear about it, for example, I make frequent reference to the topic of culture change, although my own observation is that schools reveal far more remarkable qualities when studied for their success in maintaining cultural stability than when studied for evidence of change. Personally I am most excited about the contribution that can be made by attention to two of the categories or to a combination of them: (1) the means by which people organize themselves into interacting social systems, what the anthropologist studies as *social organization*, and (2) the shared systems of beliefs and attitudes, the "ideational systems," that the anthropologist examines as *ethos* or *world view*. Spindler's concern that those involved with the anthropology of education recognize how important it is to "separate out culture as an ideational organization from social behavior and interaction" (1971:1) calls attention to a uniquely anthropological dimension for looking at what human beings do in schools.

Exactly how each ethnographer gets a toehold into his account is, of course, dependent on the special combination of his own talents and interests and the special features of the cultural scene that he is describing. Yet even under idiosyncratic circumstances there are some recurring and useful procedures. One of these is to describe apparent paradoxes or contrasts. An example of an educational paradox appeared in a site review report describing a research organization independently contracted to monitor the efforts of a school district to produce self-directed and self-conscious educational change. Turmoil and staff change in the research organization had seriously handicapped its efforts, and the report noted that the research organization was going to require more internal stability in order to successfully "track" change in the school district. Meanwhile, the school district attempting to undergo massive transformation had achieved only modest changes in its program. The paradox of a school district committed to but accomplishing little in the way of change, and of a monitoring research team so beset by personnel changes that it had not developed any continuity in its procedures for studying the schools, provided a point for entry and analysis on the part of a sensitive observer who recognized that there was change where there should have been continuity and continuity where there should have been change.

The study of contrasts includes not only comparison among different groups but also the differences noted within a culture-sharing group between "real" and "ideal" culture—differences between what people actually do and what they say they (should) do, frequently with a further distinction made to account for what they believe they do (Drucker and Heizer 1967:2) or what they believe others do (Richards 1969:1115). Such contrasts are sometimes easily apparent to an outsider, and they may signal points of weak linkage or stress within a cultural system. Ethnographic accounts frequently are focused on problems of contrast and stress. The problem of personnel evaluation in schools as observed in my study of the principalship is an example of an area of stress that generates anxious behavior among teachers and principals alike. In that study and elsewhere in my own writing (1969, 1972b, 1972c) I have often drawn attention to contrasts between real and ideal behavior, following the precedent set by several pioneers in the anthropology of schools (e.g., Jules Henry, Dorothy Lee, George Spindler) for noting discrepancies in our processes of formal education.

Regardless of how he proceeds in his analysis, even if he uncovers rather glaring inconsistencies or discrepancies between ideal and actual behavior, we expect the ethnographer to maintain sufficient objectivity and perspective that all who come within the locus of his account are recognized as behaving in cultural systems and that these systems are more or less integrated in terms of the particular setting. Like other humans, ethnographers sometimes fail to maintain their objectivity. They seem particularly susceptible to evoking more sympathy for certain groups they study—e.g., ethnically different pupils and the poor—than for other groups—e.g., white, middle-class teachers, administrators or bureaucratic functionaries (cf. Wolcott 1971). We have already noted that the ethnographer is advised to make his own feelings and attitudes clear so that the reader is able to take that perspective into account. The utility of ethnography is not enhanced by would-be ethnographers who cannot distinguish the need for objectivity from the option of neutrality.

Finally, I would insist that any ethnographic account should contain a wealth of primary data: actual quotes from informants, related in their own words from comments and written documents; stories, myths, and songs, as they are relevant; maps, photographs, sketches, and pictures (provided that they help tell the story without interfering with the protection of confidentiality); and examples of relevant artifacts if one has access to their art, their essays, their crafts, their skills and recipes. Regardless of whether or not the ethnographer attempts to explain his data, to suggest alternative interpretations, or perhaps even to weave his account into a tight theoretical framework, I feel that coupled with the obligation on him to order and make sense out of his material he is duty-bound to present sufficient primary data so that his readers have an adequate basis for rendering their own judgments concerning the analysis.

In my ethnographic work I have occasionally been criticized for under-analyzing my data and for providing too much descriptive detail, particularly from taped protocols. Probably these criticisms are warranted. At the same time, there is nothing so exciting or flattering to me as to have a colleague read my work and either disagree with my interpretation or, better still, find that he has been presented with sufficient data that he can come to a new interpretation on his own. I am satisfied with my efforts as an ethnographer when a student or colleague finds one of my accounts sufficiently interesting and credible that he is willing to use it in an attempt to create some larger scientific superstructure. That's what these bricks are for.

Summary of Criterion IV

Appropriate expectations for a completed account derive from two major traditions in ethnography, one dealing with the way information is acquired, the other with the way it is transmitted. Whether or not the ethnographer explicates the techniques which collectively comprise his fieldwork approach in a particular setting (and there is a growing preference for insisting that he should), we can expect that his account will be based on information from a number of sources gleaned through a variety of techniques, including his own presence on the scene as a "live" observer. Alternatively, where true participation is difficult or significant variation is extremely complex, the ethnographer may attempt to sample a number of different points of view concerning the meaning that individuals in different statuses attribute to some particular class of events, what Frake refers to as the "scenes" of a society. The ethnographic account is a set of instructions for "appropriately anticipating" these scenes. It is appropriate to expect that the account will be rendered both objectively and sensitively, and it is customary that the account include a wealth of primary data so that we feel that we are on the scene with the ethnographer rather than kept conveniently out of hearing through intrusive interpretation and explanation. One of the perennial issues on which misunderstandings occur between anthropologists and nonanthropologists is in expectations regarding the proper ratio between description and commentary. There is a professional bias among anthropologists favoring a high ratio of information to explanation (cf. Smith 1964).

Ethnographic accounts focus on the way particular groups of people confront the problems facing them. Programmatic research tends to define problems narrowly, and ethnographers are obliged to invest more than passing attention to such problems if they accept positions on funded projects. Regardless of the problem that may be of immediate attention and attraction to the vagaries of funding, however, the ethnographer's compelling interest is his continuing inquiry into human social life and to the ways that human beings confront their humanness. Thus it is appropriate to expect the ethnographer to look for connections between little problems and big ones, and for him to organize his account so as to show some comparability between a problem immediately at hand and the recurring themes among problems shared by humans in all times and places.

NOTES

1. Consistent with this distinction, editorial policy of the new journal *American Ethnologist* specifically excludes consideration of manuscripts that are "purely descriptive."

2. From my own work I can refer the reader to a bibliography developed especially for applying ethnographic techniques to research in schools (1972a) as well as to a number of articles in which I have discussed methodological issues and identified further references (1967a; 1970; 1971; 1973; 1975; see also Sindell 1969; Burnett 1974).

3. In spite of my commitment to creating a sense of "cultural awareness" among teachers, I always feel I help them achieve greater awareness when I can get them to stop using the term culture to refer in sweeping fashion to the behavior of all the people in some group, especially an ethnic minority represented in the schools.

4. See, for example, Agar's *Ripping and Running: A Formal Ethnography of Urban Heroin Addicts* (1973), Partridge's *Hippie Ghetto* (1973), or Pilcher's *Portland Longshoremen* (1972).

5. Three notable examples are professor/principal Philip Jackson (1968), who modestly refers to himself as a "classroom sitter"; educational psychologist Louis M. Smith (1968, 1971), who draws heavily on anthropological techniques but admits to having been trained in the tradition of "dust-bowl empiricism"; and Philip Cusick, author of *Inside High School*, who talks briefly about participant observation but makes no claim for any kind of disciplinary validation or affiliation except with "those like myself, teachers and administrators, who make the business of public education their professional career" (1973:vi).

6. See, for example, the review and critique by Philip Foster (1972).

7. See the comprehensive annotated bibliography *Anthropology and Education*, prepared by Jacquetta Burnett (1974), as well as the wealth of ethnographic description provided in Spindler (1974), as well as the gradually expanding offerings in two complementary series, Holt, Rinehart and Winston's *Case Studies in Education and Culture* and the *Anthropology and Education* series from Teachers College Press.

8. From *Doing Fieldwork: Warnings and Advice* by Rosalie H. Wax. Used with permission of the University of Chicago Press and the author.

9. Compare, for example, Colin Turnbull's *Mountain People* (1972) with Kenneth Read's *High Valley* (1965) or even with another of Turnbull's own studies like *The Forest People* (1961) to see contrasts in the personal sympathy evoked in the anthropologist by the people studied.

10. This quote is from "A Structural Description of Subanum 'Religious Behavior' " by Charles O. Frake, in *Explorations in Cultural Anthropology*. Used with permission of McGraw-Hill Book Company and the author.

11. Fred Erickson has suggested a somewhat comparable list in an article entitled, "What Makes School Ethnography 'Ethnographic'?" (1973). The contents page of each introductory text in cultural anthropology usually reveals the essence of the field as that author perceives it. Kaplan and Manners identify four major subsystems generally distinguished by anthropologists for examining the total structure of a society and, consistent with their theoretical orientation, propose what they feel to be their order of importance in the search for causal impact: technoeconomics, ideology, social structure, and personality (1972:chap. 3).

REFERENCES

Agar, M. *Ripping and Running: A Formal Ethnography of Urban Heroin Addicts.* New York: Seminar Press, 1973.

Berreman, G. D. "Ethnography: Method and Product." In *Introduction to Cultural Anthropology*, J. A. Clifton, ed. Boston: Houghton Mifflin, 1968.

Burnett, J. H. "Ceremony, Rites, and Economy in the Student System of an American High School." *Human Organization* 28(1969):1–10.

———. "Event Description and Analysis in the Microethnography of Urban Classrooms. In *Cultural Relevance and Educational Issues*, F. J. Ianni and E. Storey, eds. Boston: Little, Brown, 1973.

———. *Anthropology and Education: An Annotated Bibliographic Guide.* New Haven, Conn.: HRAF Press, 1974.

Drucker, P., and R. F. Heizer. *To Make My Name Good.* Berkeley: University of California Press, 1967.

Eddy, E. *Becoming a Teacher.* Columbia University: Teachers College Press, 1969.

Erickson, F., with A. Katz. "What Makes School Ethnography 'Ethnographic?'" *Council on Anthropology and Education Newsletter* 4(2)(1973):10–19.

Foster, G. M. *Applied Anthropology*. Boston: Little Brown, 1969.

Foster, P. A. "Review of *Anthropological Perspectives on Education*," M. Wax et al., eds. *American Journal of Sociology* 78(1973):439–92.

Frake, C. O. "A Structural Description of Subanun 'Religious Behavior.'" In *Explorations in Cultural Anthropology*, W. H. Goodenough, ed. New York: McGraw-Hill, 1964.

Freilich, M., ed. *Marginal Natives: Anthropologists at Work*. New York: Harper and Row, 1970.

Fried, M. H. *The Study of Anthropology*. New York: Thomas Y. Crowell, 1972.

Jackson, P. *Life in Classrooms*. New York: Holt, Rinehart and Winston, 1968.

Kaplan, D., and R. A. Manners. *Culture Theory*. Englewood Cliffs: Prentice-Hall, 1972.

Khleif, B. B. "The School as a Small Society." In *Anthropological Perspectives on Education*, M. Wax, et al., eds. New York: Basic Books, 1971.

———. "Issues in Anthropological Fieldwork in Schools." In *Education and Cultural Process*, G. D. Spindler, ed. New York: Holt, Rinehart and Winston, 1974.

King, A. R. "The Teacher as a Participant-Observer: A Case Study." In *Education and Cultural Process*, G. D. Spindler, ed. New York: Holt, Rinehart and Winston, 1974.

Kluckhohn, C. *Mirror for Man*. New York: McGraw-Hill (Premier Books 1959 edition), 1949.

Kutsche, P. "Review of *Tijerina and the Courthouse Raid; La Raza; and Chicano*." *American Anthropologist* 73(1971):957–58.

Leemon, T. A. *The Rites of Passage in a Student Culture*. New York: Teachers College Press, 1972.

Leighton, A. H. *The Governing of Men*. Princeton: Princeton University Press (Princeton Paperback Edition 1968), 1945.

Partridge, W. L. *The Hippie Ghetto*. New York: Holt, Rinehart and Winston, 1973.

Pelto, P. J. *Anthropological Research, The Structure of Inquiry*. New York: Harper and Row, 1970.

Perlman, M. L. "The Comparative Method: The Single Investigator and the Team Approach." In *A Handbook of Method in Cultural Anthropology*, R. Naroll and R. Cohen, eds. New York: Natural History Press, 1970.

Pilcher, W. W. *The Portland Longshoremen*. New York: Holt, Rinehart and Winston, 1972.

Read, K. E. *The High Valley*. New York: Charles Scribner's Sons, 1965.

Redfield, R. *The Primitive World and Its Transformation*. Ithaca: Cornell University Press (Great Seal Book edition 1959), 1953.

Richards, C. E. "Presumed Behavior: Modification of the Ideal-Real Dichotomy." *American Anthropologist* 71(6)(1969):1115–16.

Sieber, S. D. "The Integration of Fieldwork and Survey Methods." *American Journal of Sociology* 78(6)(1973):1335–59.

Sindell, P. S. "Anthropological Approaches to the Study of Education." *Review of Educational Research* 39(1969):593–605.

Smith, A. G. "The Dionysian Innovation." *American Anthropologist* 66(1964):251–65.

Smith, L. M. "The Micro-Ethnography of the Classroom." *Psychology in the Schools* 4(1967):216–21.

Smith, L. M., and W. Geoffrey, *The Complexities of an Urban Classroom*. New York: Holt, Rinehart and Winston, 1968.

Smith, L. M., and P. Keith. *Anatomy of Educational Innovation*. New York: Wiley, 1971.

Spindler, G. D. "Anthropology and Education." *Council on Anthropology and Education Newsletter* 2(1)(1971):1–2.

———. "An Anthropology of Education?" *Council on Anthropology and Education Newsletter* 4(1)(1973):14–16.

Spindler, G. D., ed. *Being an Anthropologist: Fieldwork in Eleven Cultures*. New York: Holt, Rinehart and Winston, 1970.

———. *Education and Cultural Process: Toward an Anthropology of Education*. New York: Holt, Rinehart and Winston, 1974.

Turnbull, C. M. *The Forest People*. New York: Simon and Schuster, 1961.

———. *The Mountain People*. New York: Simon and Schuster, 1972.

Vidich, A. J. "Participant Observation and the Collection and Interpretation of Data." *American Journal of Sociology* 60(1960):354–60.

Wax, R. H. *Doing Fieldwork: Warnings and Advice.* Chicago: University of Chicago Press, 1971.

Wolcott, H. F. "Anthropology and Education." *Review of Educational Research* 37(1967a):82–95.

——. *A Kwakiutl Village and School.* New York: Holt, Rinehart and Winston, 1967b.

——. "Concomitant Learning: An Anthropological Perspective on the Utilization of Media." In *Educational Media: Theory into Practice,* R. Wiman and W. Meierhenry, eds. Columbus: Charles E. Merrill, 1969.

——. "An Ethnographic Approach to the Study of School Administrators." *Human Organization* 29(1970):115–22.

——. "Handle with Care: Necessary Precautions in the Anthropology of Schools." In *Anthropological Perspectives on Education,* M. L. Wax et al., eds. New York: Basic Books, 1971.

——. "*Field Study Methods for Educational Researchers: A Bibliography.* Exchange Bibliography 300, Monticello, Illinois (P.O. Box 229), Council of Planning Librarians, 1972a.

——. *The Ideal and the Real World of Reading: An Anthropological Perspective.* ERIC Clearinghouse on Reading. ED 060 393, 1972b.

——. "Too True to Be Good: The Subculture of American Missionaries in Urban Africa." *Practical Anthropology* 19(1972c):241–58.

——. *The Man in the Principal's Office: An Ethnography.* New York: Holt, Rinehart and Winston, 1973.

——. *The African Beer Gardens of Bulawayo: Integrated Drinking in a Segregated Society.* Newark: Rutgers Center of Alcohol Studies Monograph No. 10, 1974.

——. "Feedback Influences on Fieldwork, or, a Funny Thing Happened on the Way to the Beergarden." In *Urban Man in Southern Africa,* C. Kileff and W. Pendleton, eds. Gwelo, Rhodesia: Mambo Press, 1975.

Zelditch, M., Jr. "Some Methodological Problems of Field Studies. *American Journal of Sociology* 67(1962):566–76.

2 / Explicit and Implicit Culture in Puerto Rico: A Case Study in Educational Anthropology

Theodore Brameld

No less than any in the world, Puerto Rican culture is saturated with a vast array of attitudes and beliefs about its own way of life. These attitudes and beliefs are sometimes called *metacultural* because, much of the time, they lie beneath the surface of daily experience. They are absorbed into the "blood-stream" of the people with little awareness that the absorption is occurring steadily from the earliest to the latest years of every normal person.

Theorists have various terms to describe this elusive level of culture, but the one we shall adopt is *configuration,* the underlying pattern of order that harmonizes—and sometimes disharmonizes—the deepest meanings of the culture. The few anthropologists who have paid careful attention to this phenomenon have had extreme difficulty in delineating any configuration they might investigate precisely because, by definition, it is never fully or accurately expressed in the formal or official language of government, religion, education, or other institutions.

To put the matter in a different way, metacultural beliefs are seldom if ever exactly equated with the *ideology* of a culture—that is, its symbolic self-portrait as conveyed through such typical agents as journalists, politicians, priests, and teachers. Yet, despite the difficulty of comparing an ideology with a configuration, no culture can be understood until the metacultural level is probed and interpreted. For here, more than anywhere else, the pervasive philosophy of a people living together in a society is to be discovered. In a genuine sense, it is the key to cultural order.

In this article, we propose to highlight the question by asking how far the *explicit* or ideological level on which Puerto Ricans, like all people, publicly communicate their attitudes, policies, and doctrines to one another is or is not compatible with their *implicit* or configurational level of experience. We shall not, of course, begin to exhaust the question. We hope only to become more conscious both of its significance and of its ubiquity by considering three important areas of belief encompassed by the terms *democracy*, *religion*, and *morality*, and what such consciousness may mean for Puerto Rican education.

METHODOLOGY

Our methodology has required field work in three subcultures of Puerto Rico: one, a sugar-cane community on the south coast; two, a coffee community in the mountainous interior; three, a middle-class urban community on the north coast; and, in addition, prolonged interviews with sixteen national leaders selected by a jury of their peers.*

In the three subcultures, attention centered in a total of twenty respondents, most of whom were democratically chosen by the groups they represented of teachers, students, parents, and school administrators. Many of the subcultural or grass roots respondents had lived in their respective subcultures all their lives, and they were chosen only after careful explanation to their respective groups of the purposes of the study, and of the kind of respondents desired in terms of those purposes. They represented a wide variety of backgrounds: Catholic and Protestant, rural and urban, lower and middle class, colored and white. Although such a method of selection was surely unorthodox, it proved to be fruitful when evaluated by the quality of the material they provided.

National-level respondents included the governor of Puerto Rico, leaders of the two opposition parties (one a millionaire industrialist, the other a lawyer), a college president, two university deans, two novelists, top government officials, and others. The themes of the interviews were the same for these respondents as for those in the three subcultures, but the level of communication varied. The leader panel was addressed in a fairly theoretical way, though examples were often used. In the grassroots panel an effort was made to dramatize each problem by couching it in terms familiar to the respondents' experience. Both sets of interviews were, however, flexible and open-ended. And in both, the issues raised were invariably placed in the setting of the Puerto Rican culture itself.

To illustrate the approach, a national leader might have been asked directly: "Is there any considerable discrepancy among Puerto Ricans between their explicitly accepted religious beliefs and their actual acceptance as revealed by, say, devotion to religious practices?" One of the hypotheses we were interested in testing (within severe limits, of course) was that the national panel was sufficiently sophisticated and habituated to abstract thinking to be able to respond significantly to a question of this sort. Looking back at the sixteen interviews (all of which, incidentally, required more than one session), our conclusion is that on the whole the degree of meaningful communication was high. This is not too surprising. While of course there were misunderstandings (the fact that all but one of the interviews were conducted in English would itself assure that), nevertheless the questions asked, as well

*All the respondents on both levels, with the exception of two leaders, were born in Puerto Rico and have lived there, except for brief periods, since birth.

as the many ramifications and applications encouraged by informal conversation, were close to their deepest interests. They had apparently thought about most if not all of these matters in some fashion before, and often theoretically.

On the grass roots panel the approach was less direct and more concrete. One of the favorite techniques was imaginary role playing. The respondent was asked to imagine two or three friends with familiar names sitting in the room. One of the friends would be quoted: "I am sure that . . ." Then, in vigorous tones and usually in colloquial Spanish, he would expound his view-point on the topic under discussion, pointing it up with an instance drawn from the respective subculture. Another friend would next, with equal vigor, express a sharply different viewpoint. Sometimes a third or even fourth imaginary friend would take issue with the others. The respondent would then be asked whether he agreed with any of the friends or whether, instead, he believed something quite different. His answer would often be followed by an effort to discover his reasons. Not infrequently he would give very emphatic ones, revealing that he, too, had previously thought about the matter.

Here is a somewhat abbreviated instance related to the same question asked the national panel in another way:

> *Senor Rodríguez* (the first friend): I go to church in San José at Easter and Christmas. The rest of the time I leave it to my wife to go.
> *Senor Sánchez* (the second friend): I think that's wrong. Everybody should go to church once a week and take confession.
> *Senor Quinones* (the third friend): I don't believe the things they tell you in church, so I never go.
> *Senor Rivera* (the fourth friend): I don't go to church either, but I believe in God and the afterlife.
> *Interviewer:* Now, do you think any one of these four friends here is right, or do you think all of them are wrong?
> *Interviewee:* Oh, I'm like Senor Rodríguez. I go the church in San José about twice a year. But I think the way Senor Rivera does too.

This line of conversation may have continued for some time. The technique of imaginary role playing was not invariably utilized, however. Some of the topics did not lend themselves to it as much as others. Also, it seemed more effective if not repeated too frequently. Nevertheless, it proved successful, if judged by rapport, indications of interest, and the capacity of respondents to grasp meanings which might otherwise have been more greatly distorted or missed entirely.

The Puerto Rican study as a whole is systematically built upon a theory of culture developed in the author's *Cultural Foundations of Education—An Interdisciplinary Exploration* (New York: Harper & Brothers, 1957). One of the many assumptions is that education can be regarded as a kind of institutional binoculars through which to focus upon the several dimensions of culture, such as order, process, and goals (the three major categories, aided by numerous subcategories, of the theoretical study). Equally, it is possible to turn around and focus upon education through the lens of culture. To some extent, both approaches were utilized: the first, through our grass roots respondents, all of whom were in some way connected with the schools; the second, through our national leaders who symbolized more of the attitudes, beliefs, and practices of the total culture. Or, to epitomize our methodology in still a different way, we wished to look at Puerto Rico in various perspectives—from the bottom up, as it were, but also from the top down—using education as a kind of fulcrum.

The total time devoted specifically to grass roots interviews totaled about two hundred hours—to national-level interviews, about one hundred hours. In addition, the author has devoted approximately two and one half years to direct immersion in the culture, including many visits to schools of all types and all levels, among other institutions.

While the study could claim to be primarily anthropological (its findings are therefore essentially qualitative, with all its advantages and disadvantages), we should point out that the methodology as a whole is interdisciplinary. So, too, are its objectives. The aim is to experiment with a fusion of three disciplines—philosophy (most familiar to the author), education, and anthropology. Another assumption of the study, indeed, is that traditional academic divisions are no longer adequate if one is to study the interworkings of human behavior.

The following discussion constitutes only one small part of the total project. Even this selection, however, should be sufficient to indicate to the critical reader that the study has many limitations. To mention but three: the data are derived primarily from very small and far from perfectly representative panels of informants; the data are clustered somewhat toward the middle strata of the culture; and they do not succeed in penetrating to the metacultural level by any means as deeply as might have been possible had more time and more skill been available. It is most important to emphasize, therefore, that this article claims nothing more than our limited evidence permits. It is one partial profile of culture-and-education in one small, but in revealing ways microcosmic, dot on the global map.

DEMOCRACY

Puerto Rico is a democracy-conscious culture. Its people—excepting a handful of extreme nationalists, a portion of those who support the dwindling Independentista party, and a still smaller number of Spanish expatriates—are publicly proud of their six decades of association with a nation which, since the eighteenth century, has been regarded by the world as one of the greatest of democratic nations. The Commonwealth Constitution is a model of democratic principles. The government formally operates according to these principles, and constantly expounds them in its pronouncements. All religions are free to worship. Race discrimination is unlawful. The public schools are modeled upon the North American pattern far more than any other (the doctrine of separation of church and state is one example), and children are taught the rights and duties of citizens living in a democratic country. Finally, other instruments that shape the citizen's mind, such as newspapers, radio and television stations, enunciate this ideology as loudly as they repudiate all alternatives. The syndicated columnists in *El Mundo*, for example, are for the most part the same ones that are read in continental newspapers, while the magazines most widely circulated are also continental—most notably, the Spanish and English editions of *Time* and the *Reader's Digest*. Explicitly, Puerto Rican culture is overwhelmingly devoted to the slogans of democracy, and all our respondents professed this ideology themselves.

Is it equally so on the implicit level? The answer here, as it would be in the parent democracy, is far more equivocal. According to most of our respondents, the bulk of the people have not yet learned the meaning of such devotion nearly as completely as they should in at least one major respect—namely, in their tendency to idolize their present leaders (particularly one, the governor), and to leave too much by way of policy and implementation to those they have elected.

Many voices were heard at the grass roots to the effect that Puerto Ricans trust their top-level leaders too abjectly for the good of their democracy. Only a small minority, one a respondent habituated to the pseudo-feudal life of a coffee hacienda, felt that it was a proper habit to encourage. The majority held that other types of leaders—notably, labor and religious—are also accepted too abjectly.

The degree and kind of acceptance varies, however. Two respondents pointed to the landslide election as senator of a well-known Protestant who had been publicly opposed by the Catholic church; this illustrated, they said, that political leaders have a stronger grip on the people than do religious leaders. A comparable point was made by a leader respondent who reported that the bishop of Ponce has repeatedly shown his hostility to the party in power, with little effect. Labor leaders were also said to have greater influence than religious leaders, but they, of course, have been closely affiliated with the dominant political leadership. Even local mayors, if a militant Catholic respondent was correct, are usually "listened to" much more than are local priests.

National-level respondents, although they usually supported this general opinion, were more inclined to qualify it. Whether or not they were influenced by the fact of their own positions of sometimes high authority, several pointed out that respect by the people for strong political leadership is not necessarily inconsistent with democracy. The real question is whether such leadership represents the genuine wishes of the people—also, whether they have sufficient opportunity to criticize and, if they so choose, to repudiate those they have elected.

Stated this way, no respondent on any level contended that the present government leaders are unrepresentative of what the great majority have thus far considered to be their best interests, and no one questioned the integrity of the top leadership. The point was also made that this leadership has performed a legitimate democratic function in motivating the people, in helping them to understand their own problems, needs, and rights. In this sense, even though it has often had to move more slowly than it might have wished or might have attempted if less democratic, the government in power has played a tremendous educational role as well as a strictly political one.

Nevertheless, even at the national level considerable concern was manifested by the gap between ideological and underlying attitudes concerning the leadership issue. The habit of relying heavily on leaders, several pointed out, derives from a mixture of Hispanic, religious, and colonial traditions, a habit symbolized by the term, *personalismo*, and connoting deep respect for persons in authority. Thus, while a larger proportion of adults were said to go to the polls every four years than in any state of the union, they tend to assume that their duty is then over and that it is up to the chosen leaders to work out a program for their benefit until the next election. One subcultural respondent estimated that 80 percent of the citizens—the least educated majority—think the leader should decide all crucial questions once they have approved him.

Some concern arose also over the question of minority dissent to majority rule—another fundamental democratic principle. Several leaders were convinced that Puerto Ricans already respect this principle, as indicated by their tolerance of unpopular ideas. One, for example, mentioned that it is difficult to keep nationalists in prison for extended periods, not because of widespread approval of their views, but because of respect for their right to oppose the majority. For the same reason, it would be more difficult to imprison communists convicted under the Smith Act than in many North American states. Likewise, if another leader is correct, most Puerto Ricans unlike most mainlanders are not frightened by "socialist" or equally unorthodox economic and political proposals; indeed, they often accept them not only in words but in housing, agricultural, and other practices. The reasonableness and tolerance of ideas even suggested to one leader that the *personalismo* tradition, with its spirit of arbitrary and sometimes violent authority, is nowhere nearly as influential as some have tried to argue.

The fact that the American Civil Liberties Union was engaged by the government to study minority rights in Puerto Rico and to recommend means of strengthening them—a quite unprecedented step among democratic countries—would support further the explicit acceptance of the majority-minority principle. It would not, however, prove that no incompatibility with the implicit level prevails. Censorship by the Department of Education of certain of its publications was cited as one deviation. Several respondents mentioned the refusal of majority-party mayors, despite the governor's plea, to grant minority parties an official voice in municipal affairs. Repeatedly, too, comments were made at the grass roots to the effect that dissenters are "afraid" to make themselves conspicuous, especially if they hold jobs that depend on the goodwill of party officers or government bureaucrats. Finally, according to one leader, government agencies set up to serve the people are too often staffed by persons who have feeble understanding of such methods of democracy as criticism and participation.

But respondents sharply disagreed as to where the greatest compatibility or incompatibility between democratic ideology and configuration lies in terms of class and region. Some were certain that the lower socioeconomic strata manifest the most compatibility—their argument being that, because ideological beliefs are of minor concern to people with little education and little guided opportunity to reflect about so profound a concept, their tendency is to be democratic simply because it is their "way of life." One leader made an intriguing distinction: lower-strata groups especially in the rural areas are more democratic in their individual relations (for example, their respect for one another as persons, which is partly the effect of their Christianity) than in their institutional behavior (for example, their careless regard for traffic rules).

A few, however, maintained that the middle urban strata are, on the whole, more consistently democratic than the lower: the former have thought more than the latter about democracy, and so they try harder to equate practice with professed belief, even in the face of insecurities and conflicts that sometimes result from such conscious effort. The fact that in the last election they were more critical than other classes, judging by the size of their vote against the party in power, could be offered in support of this contention. No respondent argued that the greatest compatibility is to be found in the highest social stratum.

Comment is also required with regard to the problem of race relations, viewed in the context of democratic beliefs. Equality among races is not only supported by law but is widely accepted both ideologically and in overt conduct. Respondents did not deny, however, that a limited kind of segregation occurs in restaurants, hotels, swimming pools and other places where tourists and the well-to-do gather. Any remaining segregation does not result, it was claimed, from official rules established by the management (such rules would be illegal) but rather from the fact that the average colored Puerto Rican cannot afford luxury prices. That he might also feel uncomfortable for fear of being unwelcome in such surroundings may likewise be an intangible factor, as it would be in many northern cities of the Continent. At the same time, a few colored people do appear in the most expensive establishments. More serious in terms of our problem is the fact that they were reported to be excluded by membership qualifications from most if not all upper-class casinos, from certain businessmen's clubs, and from such religious organizations as the Catholic Daughters of America.

Still more serious were the discrepancies between ideology and configuration that appeared in the responses of some resource persons. As anyone knows who has looked into the matter, one of the most revealing tests of such feelings is that of attitudes toward marriage between races. Only one white respondent on the subcultural level would have no serious objection to racial intermarriage for his own children, and three light-skinned fathers insisted they would do all they could to prevent it. Reasons were diverse: one respondent said that it would "lower the race"; another said that "white is for white" and "black for black"; still another feared that his daughter would be boycotted by her friends and that his grandchildren would suffer if they went to the United States. The question was not asked of all leader respondents, but it was possible to infer from related questions that their attitude was typically more liberal. Among all respondents, moreover, only one revealed the kind of extreme inconsistency that is chronic on the Continent: while unusually vocal in professing the egalitarian ideology and insisting that he was not "against" Negroes, he was hostile not only toward miscegenation but toward interracial dancing in high school; he spoke of the "trash," largely colored, that inhabited nearby slums; he thought that Negroes should be excluded from hotel swimming pools; he wanted them to "keep their distance" in social affairs.

The fact that Puerto Ricans who migrate to the States often experience discrimination would lead one to suppose that insular concern over the problem might increase, particularly since so many travel back and forth. The two army veterans among our respondents both admitted they had experienced discrimination, one at the hands of a private, the second from a Negro officer! Three others at the grass roots said they had heard of prejudiced treatment against Puerto Ricans. Yet no respondent, even among leaders, voluntarily expressed much concern over this problem.

Nor was anti-Semitism, which often develops in North American cities especially among lower-class people who are seeking a "scapegoat" for their troubles, discernible in the interviews. This is interesting in view of the fact, not only that many thousands of Puerto Ricans are employed in the New York garment industry which is manned predominantly by Jewish workers and managers, but that they live in Harlem tenements where anti-Semitism is often rife because of alleged Jewish landlords. The only evidence of anti-Semitism observed in Puerto Rico was the word "kike" splashed on two walls of the metropolis, and symptoms in some university students during class discussions.

Let us draw together our conclusions and inferences from this brief examination of beliefs toward democracy. As would be true of all cultures, even the most democratic, inconsistency prevails between the ideological and metacultural levels. The widest gap was partly attributed to the stubborn persistence of the *personalismo* tradition, although inadequate appreciation of the principle of minority dissent as the polar principle to majority rule was considered by two leaders as, in long range, even more serious a deficiency. Grass roots respondents were more incensed at their fellow citizens for relinquishing too much authority and responsibility to leadership than they were at leaders for accepting it. Also, they seemed less concerned with the problem of minority dissent than were most national-level respondents who, interestingly enough, seemed less concerned in turn with the problem of overconcentrated leadership.

In race relations, something of a gap between the explicit principle of equality and implicit attitudes was also discernible. Perhaps because the problem of race relations does not loom large on the island, little indignation was revealed toward discriminatory treatment even on the Continent. When tested by questions that touched personal sensitivities, however, discriminatory feelings toward colored persons were found to be acute. Whether these could be attributed entirely to the phenomenon that color is explicitly associated in Puerto Rico with lower status rather than with inferior race, or whether (as a minority of leaders insisted) strong ingredients of race prejudice can also be detected in such feelings, was not determined clearly enough to warrant generalization. It would be important to know whether, if racial prejudice does prevail to a markedly greater degree than most respondents were prepared to admit, this would not help to account for perpetuation of the generally lower status of colored people at the same time that the generally lower status of these people helps to perpetuate any remaining prejudice.

Looked at together, both groups of respondents were, nevertheless, convinced that democracy, racially as well as politically, is far from a mere shibboleth to the people of Puerto Rico, hence that an impressive compatibility is already revealed between their explicit allegiance to its principles and their implicit acceptance of them. Moreover, compatibility has increased rapidly in less than twenty years, although understanding of some aspects of democracy is still to be achieved. While strata and regions were considered unlike in the extent to which they have achieved a democratic configuration that harmonizes with their political ideology, it is a commentary on the unsettled nature of the problem that respondents also differed as to which groups have attained the greatest harmony thus far. They did imply that the upper stratum is the least compatible both in its political beliefs and in its racial attitudes. And they would probably hold that the degree of synthesis between the two levels is already greater, certainly in democratic political beliefs if not also racial ones, than in any other country south of the United States.

RELIGION

One of the paradoxes of Puerto Rican culture is the disparity between formal affiliation with the Catholic church—between 80 and 85 percent of the population, according to most estimates—and meager concern for its religious ceremonials and dogmas. The fact that services of the Catholic church are attended regularly by a much larger proportion of women than men—one leader was sure this was largely due to the tradition that it is unmasculine to be seen too often in church—and that the most ardent Catholics, class-wise, are members of the upper stratum, helps further to sharpen the paradox.

Its significance for our problem is obvious. If the religious ideology is predominantly Catholic, and yet if only a fraction (10 to 15 percent, according to some informants) are sufficiently devout to follow the mandates and rituals of Catholicism with any regularity, can it not then be said that another type of incompatibility appears between the explicit and implicit levels of belief?

Respondents were largely agreed upon a pronounced degree of incompatibility, but they were equally agreed upon the importance of distinguishing between the theological routines of the Catholic church, on the one hand, and the core tenets of Christianity, on the other hand. If one leader was right, only a tiny handful of Puerto Ricans could be considered free-thinkers. Virtually all believe in God; probably as many believe in immortality. Yet, several others placed the Christian belief in human brotherhood and sanctity of personality even higher in importance for most Puerto Ricans. And it is worthy of note that two leaders contended that the lower strata are more harmonious religiously than the upper strata, their reason being the same as in the case of democratic beliefs: though there is the least ideological sophistication on the lower levels, there is consequently the greatest implicit sincerity.

Another distinction was stressed by both groups of respondents, including Catholics themselves. The degree of incompatibility between ideological creed and deeper religious attitudes is strikingly less among Protestants in Puerto Rico. In other words, the 15 to 20 percent of the population belonging to one or another of their numerous denominations (the Baptist, to mention but one, was said to maintain about 50 churches on the island with a membership of about 150,000) are more successful in relating creed to behavior than is the Catholic majority. This is demonstrated not only in a higher ratio of church attendance by both Protestant men and women, not only in the greater zeal with which they participate in ceremonials, but especially in their development of social services such as rural hospitals and agricultural projects. These were said to dramatize the nonsectarian, nontheological, and democratic aspects of the Christian faith.

Several explanations were given for the greater gap between the two kinds of belief among Catholics. One was the reputation of "clericalism," meaning the affiliation of a politically minded hierarchy with the colonial rule of earlier centuries, a fact true of other Hispanic cultures. Such a reputation has lingered long and helps to explain the continued support of the church by the top status level of the population. (Families on this level are often fervently Spanish in their customs and loyalties.) Also, it at least partially accounts for a certain half-conscious suspicion if not outright hostility with which many people of lower and even middle status tend to look upon the Catholic clergy. These attitudes, which were noted in several subcultural respondents, have been reinforced by its reputed indifference to the personal and social welfare of the common people, an indifference related again to the "clerical" habits of a priesthood imported hitherto largely from Spain itself. But the situation is now changing, it was reported—indeed, one Protestant informant went so far as to assert that Catholics are already surpassing Protestant programs of social welfare.

Traditionally, at any rate, the use of Latin rather than the Spanish vernacular in Catholic rituals, the remoteness from churches of many rural settlements, the expense of ceremonials such as church marriages, and the great difficulty of living up to the stern principles of Catholicism (most notably, in sex relations)—all have been further contributing factors to the disparity.

This last point is underscored by the growing numbers of Puerto Ricans who practice birth control despite bitter opposition of the Catholic hierarchy; by the thousands of women, who, though they may attend church regularly, have also visited one of the many birth-control clinics established by the Department of Health; and by the fact that both sterilization and divorce are on the increase. Only one of the fifteen subcultural respondents who were Catholics expressed opposition to all forms of birth control as well as divorce (except for infidelity). This same respondent, a lifelong rural resident, was also the only one who expressed a wish that only Catholics would live in his *barrio* (township). But even this lone wish was countered by another Catholic respondent in the same *barrio* who said he would welcome Protestants as friends equally with Catholics.

We sum up our evidence concerning the second example chosen to focus upon cultural configuration by inferring that incompatibility between ideological and metacultural beliefs is wider in the case of religion than in that of democracy. As two respondents put it, Puerto Ricans may be deeply religious in certain attitudes, but this does not mean that most of them are ecclesiastical about these attitudes. If, however, one means by explicit religious beliefs the kind that would be accepted by earnest Christians everywhere, even though they may seldom be clothed in the doctrines of ritual or articulated as dogmatic creeds, then in this sense the degree of compatibility is regarded by our respondents as extremely high.

MORALITY

The problem of morality, which was confined in our research mainly to standards of sex conduct, is closely related to religion for the obvious reason that the ideological code is influenced by Christian doctrine, especially the Sixth Commandment. This problem is complicated by the traditional practices of concubinage and the double standard. Although both practices were said to be decreasing (most rapidly in the urban class), no one contended that they have become negligible.

Here, then, a conflict even in explicit beliefs inevitably occurs. The Christian ideology completely repudiates both premarital and extramarital sex relations; the secular cultural ideology tolerates, if it does not openly condone, these relations. Moreover, while it could not be argued that most women approve, it did not appear evident from several responses that even they tend to regard the double standard with markedly greater forbearance, albeit a reluctant one, than would be true in cultures such as the United States. To cite an example: one woman respondent reported that upper-class mothers of illegitimate children in her community were fully accepted socially by others of her class, and that she herself did so with little reservation.

We must, however, recall that the privilege of the double standard is limited to the male sex. Because of the so-called virginity cult, which is largely unmodified thus far even by the impact of more flexible continental standards, respondents would surely agree that a much higher compatibility prevails between explicitly approved virginity for unmarried women and implicit patterns of belief and conduct than it does for unmarried men. Because this compatibility is strongly reinforced by the explicit religious ideology, the degree of consistency between the latter and the wider cultural ideology is also much higher in the case of moral standards for women than for those of men.

Among our subcultural respondents, only one was emphatic in her opinion that women ought to have the same rights as men, and that if men are entitled to know several women intimately before marriage, women should have the same privilege. Yet she, too, concurred in the virtually unanimous opinion of her peers that though the double standard is ideologically wrong, either extramarital or premarital relations are "worse" for women than for men. Whether by "worse" was meant that the man's reputation is less easily damaged or that it is religiously more sinful for the woman remained unclear. Possibly one participant came closest to expressing the implicit belief of the majority when he confessed that his real reason for looking upon relations out of wedlock as "worse" for women than for men was that the "norms" of the culture compelled him to think so.

One leader respondent, however, offered the striking argument that within many families a serious disparity may prevail in another way. Since neither the average husband nor average wife admits, much less freely discusses, the husband's extramarital experiences, the results of trying on both sides to maintain the appearance of complete monogamy are a good deal of secrecy on the part of the husband and a good deal of silent suspicion on the part of the wife. Often, of course, the husband's relations, especially in the lower rural classes, become an "open secret," not only because he likes to share his experiences and perhaps boast among his friends about his virile powers, but because his illegitimate children and his responsibilities to them quickly become known to the neighborhood. By comparison, the operation of a double standard was said to be oftener concealed effectively, for several reasons, in upper-class groups. Concubines are more easily hidden in the large cities where these groups are concentrated; more discretion is likely to be exercised in conversation among friends; and birth control is more frequently and skillfully practiced. One concomitant effect of such concealment by upper-class husbands combined with often unconfirmed but unspoken suspicions by upper-class wives could be (although the hypothesis remains to be tested) a greater degree of intrafamilial tensions than in the lower classes where covert relations are harder to maintain and where consciousness of inconsistency may also be less severe.

Despite these various gaps, several leader respondents were inclined to the opinion that, in matters of morality, Puerto Ricans are on the whole more successful in harmonizing their explicit and implicit attitudes than are continentals. Their argument was, of course, that at least the nonreligious aspects of their moral tradition are widely tolerant toward the double standard. Thus there tends to be less hypocrisy than in cultures where, though they too may practice the double standard very widely, no comparably powerful sanction is available from custom. The widespread acceptance of consensual or common-law marriage is another instance: moral stigmatization of either partners or offspring because of earlier failure to perform a religious or civil ceremony is difficult to discern, certainly in the rural if not also the urban subcultures. To punctuate the argument, one respondent drew an analogy with gambling: here, too, there is less hypocrisy than in a country such as the United States where, though it is usually illegal as well as ideologically immoral, its implicit acceptance as measured by gambling practices was alleged to be even wider on a "per capita" basis than in Puerto Rico itself.

Whether the argument that moral hypocrisy tends to be less for these reasons than on the Continent is, however, open to further inspection. No respondent raised the question of why, if respect for female virginity and monogamous relations for the wife is as universal as the ideology would have us believe, such respect is violated as often as it apparently is by the polygynous inclinations and activities of the Puerto Rican male. Nevertheless, one leader perhaps came close to encapsulating the moral configuration when he pointed out that the Puerto Rican culture is somewhat "better off" than certain others because it is more modest in its claims. Therefore in the long run it achieves more compatibility between ideology and conduct than if it claimed too much.

EDUCATION'S ROLE: THE EXAMPLE OF DEMOCRACY

In the opinion of a respected leader, one of the most important tasks of Puerto Rican education is to narrow the gap between the explicit and implicit culture, a task which cannot, of course, be left only to formal institutions of learning but must be undertaken by all types of institutions concerned with building a unified culture—economic, religious, political, and others.

Can such a complex undertaking "get off the ground" in any deliberate, organized way? To begin again with democracy, the most far-reaching of all recommendations was that the schools and colleges learn how to become democratic by *experiencing* its principles, by teachers and administrators learning the difference between autocratic and democratic leadership in their own performance, and by students discovering in their classrooms that the right to participate in criticizing and planning is just as important as the duty to accept the plans that are made.

The official ideology of Puerto Rican education would endorse these proposals. At the same time, its own leadership would probably admit that they have not as yet been implemented in everyday practice except to a limited extent. The centralized system with its line-staff administrative structure has not been conducive to wide democratic sharing in the formulation or operation of policies. Curricula, teaching methods, and most rules have been established primarily in the central office for island-wide adoption. The personnel of local schools have been habituated, in turn, to following prescribed routines with minimum deviation.

Few grass roots respondents were unduly disturbed, however. The majority, on the contrary, seemed to accept this situation as a matter of course. It had not occurred to most parents, for example, that in their parent-teacher associations they might seriously consider matters such as the curriculum of their own schools. When the question was raised, some admitted that cooperative study and recommendations by parents might be beneficial, but others held that all such matters should be left entirely to officials of the school system. Nor was the question of whether teachers and students might also participate in curriculum planning, in formulating rules of discipline, and in offering constructive criticisms, apparently one which had received much previous consideration by subcultural respondents. Thus when they were asked to make their own recommendations for the improvement of education, only a small minority thought to include the strengthening of democratic processes in their own institutions.

This minority did suggest, however, that more decentralization in policies and programs ought now to be attempted. It objected to the frequency with which syllabi, for example, are prepared at the top with little help or guidance from teachers at the base. Particularly, it criticized some supervisors for imposing their own will rather arbitrarily upon principals and teachers who had deviated from their own directives.

Principles and teachers were also criticized by the same minority for deficient concern with democratic principles on the plane of daily practice. In the estimate of one administrator respondent, considerably less than half of the principals in charge of local public schools attempt in any significant way to encourage such practice, a habit that would tend to be reinforced by their own subjection to rules imposed from above. The more common orientation was thus perhaps expressed by another administrator respondent who, though emphatic in explicitly opposing "traditional methods," also opposed student councils with authority to make any rules except for parties, who felt that students ought not to criticize, who was content to have curricula made entirely at "headquarters," and who would insist on the right to "veto" any suggestions that parents might make.

The same estimate was roughly applied to the body of teachers, although in their case the fact that they are in charge of abnormally large classes of children (more than sixty per class were counted in several of the schools we visited) could help to account for their frequently rather authoritarian roles. It would hardly account entirely, however: considerable insecurity and fear of "higher ups"; the teacher's strongly traditional "matriarchal" role; youthful habits of passivity acquired in family relations; the still chronic practice (despite an official ban) of mild corporal punishment by elementary teachers; finally, on the university level, the hierarchical structure of administrative authority and the European-influenced custom of professorial dignity—these were noted by various respondents as other contributing though controversial factors.

Such examples by no means imply, however, that democracy in Puerto Rican education remains up to now wholly an affair of words. While the gap is still a wide one, it is slowly narrowing, a fact supported by the sensitivity of at least a subcultural minority to such incompatibilities as we have just listed. Also, in the opinion of some leaders, the gap is already closing rapidly in two fields, both of them concerned primarily with informal and functional rather than formal instruction: first, in the program of community education on the adult level; second, in the consumer cooperative movement. The latter, moreover, is reaching into some public schools where cooperative savings clubs and supply stores are being organized and run primarly by students themselves.

Nor should it be forgotten that individual schools and individual teachers vary markedly in their application of the democratic ideology. Thus, in one of the three subcultures, participation by teachers in limited curriculum planning, the operation of a high school student council with some authority, as well as group methods of learning, were becoming accepted, if still unevenly practiced, in schools of the municipality. Also, the fact that many grass roots respondents were willing when asked to endorse more participation and other democratic processes for parents, for teachers, and even for children, might indicate a potential readiness that has not yet found opportunity for actual expression. The fact, too, that several of these same respondents, including teachers, were unsure whether to admire or to condemn Franco as a leader might indicate lack of sophistication in democratic political principles rather than reasoned opposition to them.

Perhaps most revealing, the explicit concept of equality of races has moved far in education toward complete achievement as an implicit cultural pattern. Colored teachers are as commonly observed in charge of classes of predominantly white children as white teachers are observed in the converse situation. A great preponderance of all public schools contain some mixture of colored and white students as well as teachers—a phenomenon so taken for granted that school people showed surprise when it was called to their attention.

Many respondents would probably consider a more serious discrepancy between ideology and configuration to be the divisions that arise between classes due to the rapid growth of private schools—divisions that have the effect also of tending to separate racial stocks insofar as white children in larger proportion than dark children belong to the upper classes that can afford private school tuitions. Whether or not another limiting factor is, as one respondent contended, that qualified personnel who are conspicuously Negroid are less frequently promoted in administrative positions by the Department of Education than are Caucasoid personnel, the racial situation when appraised by democratic standards probably reveals as little discrepancy as in any comparably sized area under the American flag. No respondent on any level expressed the slightest opposition to racial integration in the public school system. Rather, it was wholeheartedly accepted.

Much of the evidence presented thus far concerning education as a configurational expression of democracy in Puerto Rico has been derived from the three subcultures. National-level respondents agreed with many of the same points, but they both limited and enriched them. One leader, particularly, insisted that a wider gap exists between the explicit and implicit levels in formal education than it does in most other institutions, a weakness he attributed more to ververbalization and middle-class biases operating in professional teacher-training programs than to any other cause.

Two other leaders differed almost diametrically from each other on the proposal that one way to narrow the gap would be to remake classrooms into miniature laboratories of democratic living and learning, with special regard for experience in majority rule–minority dissent. The one who opposed was afraid that children would learn the meaning of democracy in a naive and superficial manner. Maturity, he argued, must be attained first—especially the capacity to reason—an argument he supported by reference to classic thinkers in political philosophy, of whom Plato might have been one. The respondent who as strongly favored the proposal would avoid superficiality by giving teachers and children daily opportunity to learn democratic principles through practice.

We shall not here examine the issues for learning and teaching that arise from our second and third examples—religion and morality—except to assert that incompatibilities between explicit and implicit beliefs were equally discernible. They were most conspicuous in religion where the ideological principle of separation of church and state is neither strictly manifested in daily school activities nor supported on the implicit level by the beliefs of many respondents. As for morality, the fact that sex instruction is only slightly touched upon by most curricula, hence that sex morality is not as yet widely regarded as a fit subject for formal learning, makes it doubtful whether the gaps between ideological and metacultural beliefs that we have observed in the broader culture would be less pronounced in education.

One leader did insist that cheating is widespread on the college level and that this is symptomatic of a deeper moral challenge than the evils of the practice itself. It is due, he contended, to the "artificiality" of much Puerto Rican education, to the stress upon paper work, verbalization, and grades, and hence to the separation between those and the real interests of typical learners. Cheating will cease to be a problem, he predicted, when students become excited by the intrinsic importance and worth of what they are learning—a prediction that would be equally relevant to education in other cultures.

His point, however, is germane to the problem of sex morality as well. If the failure of many students to respect in conduct a code of honesty which they accept as ideology is much less of a reflection upon the code itself than upon the lack of functional relationship between it and the educations they continue to receive, then perhaps the deceits and other effects of customary sex morality are traceable to relationships that are equally dichotomous. One implication surely is that education should afford no less opportunity for scrupulous examination of disruptions caused at least partly by incompatibilities between explicit sex codes and implicit sex attitudes and conduct than it affords for any other cultural behavior—the political, say. Just as cheating will diminish, this leader believed, when Puerto Rican education is vitalized in terms of such behavior, so will the tragic effects of inharmonious relations between men and women also diminish.

Looking, finally, at our theme as a whole and recalling that its purpose has been to sample rather than to exhaust the difficult issues it has raised, we may nevertheless contend that the overall configuration of Puerto Rican culture-and-education can now be perceived in both negative and positive terms. Negatively, this configuration according to our evidence is decidedly less democratic, less religious, and less moral than we should expect were we to be guided by typical ideological formulations such as those taught by the schools. Positively, it appears according to our evidence to be more implicitly democratic than other Central American or South American cultures; it is manifestly more religious in basic Christian attitudes than in ecclesiastic allegiances; and it is more consistently moral according to its secular traditions than its religious ones. In important respects, moreover, there is perhaps a higher positive relationship between its metacultural democratic and religious attitudes than there is between these and its moral attitudes, although the contention could be argued further. At any rate, we may be reasonably sure that much the same congruities and incongruities that prevail in the Puerto Rican cultural configuration prevail also in education.

3 / Culture and Education in the Midwestern Highlands of Guatemala

Robert Redfield

When education is considered as it occurs in a modern society, we think first of the school. In a primitive society there are neither schools nor pedagogues; yet we speak of the "education" of the primitive child. In so doing we are, of course, recognizing a conception of education much wider than the domain of the school; we are thinking of it as "the process of cultural transmission and renewal"—a process present in all societies and, indeed, indistinguishable from that process by which societies persist and change.

When we describe education in such school-less and bookless societies, we are likely to fix attention upon other institutions which obviously and formally express and communicate the local tradition. Such are ceremony, myth, tribal and familial symbols and stories, initiation ceremonies, and men's houses. In these we recognize a certain fixity and emphasis of major elements of culture, and we see that in their perpetuation and repetition these elements receive restatement and are communicated to the young. Indeed, we have come to think of primitive societies as providing a well-organized and self-consistent system of institutions by which children are brought up to think and act as did their fathers. In such societies we connect education with traditional forms expressive of a rich content. In comparison with the educational effect of a katchina dance upon a Hopi child, a chapter in a civics textbook seems pretty thin, educationally speaking.

To the invitation to give an account of the educational process, I respond from a point of view of certain rural communities in the midwestern highlands of Guatemala which are neither modern nor primitive but in many respects intermediate between a simple tribe and a modern city. Educational institutions among these rural mountain dwellers do not quite conform to either the primitive or civilized type. These people have schools, but the schools are of small importance. They have ceremonies and legends but these forms do not have so much content as one might suppose. In these Guatemalan societies schooling is far from accomplishing what our educational experts claim generally for schools. On the other hand, ceremony and myth do not come up to the standard set by many primitive societies. In this part of the world there are no central and powerful educational institutions around which an essay can conveniently be written.

The situation is not without value, however, for students of the cultural process. In recognizing in this part of Guatemala the limited educational influence of schools, on the one hand, and of traditional forms, on the other, one is brought to see aspects of education which underlie all formal institutions. People in Guatemala do get educated (in the sense that the heritage is transmitted) with adjustments to meet changing circumstances, even though many of them never go to school and even though there are no great puberty ceremonies, with revelations of the sacred *alcheringa* and narrations of totemic myths, such as occur among Australian aborigines. In this paper I shall make some observations on certain features of these highlands societies in so far as the educational process is concerned; and I shall, in particular, call attention to aspects of that process which are probably to be encountered in every society. I call attention to them because education is ordinarily studied without much reference to them.

As I look at the school in the little village where I once was resident, it appears to me to play a greater part in changing the culture of the people than in handing it on from one generation to the next, although its influence in the direction of change is indirect. Nearly all the time in the school is given to learning to read and to write and to calculate. Some children acquire a fair command of these arts; others do not. The arts of literacy have many practical uses, and their possession carries some prestige. They improve the opportunities for gainful employment, and their possession disposes the individual to seek his fortune in the town or in the city. In some cases success in school leads to higher education in the city and so to participation in urban civilization.

The majority of people of this community are Indians; a minority are a Spanish-speaking people of mixed ancestry known as Ladinos. The cultures of the two groups are identical in many areas of experience; in others they are still notably different. Where both kinds of people live in the same settlement, both attend the same school. The school makes more change for the Indian than for the Ladino, because through association with the Ladinos in the school he learns Spanish and in not a few cases is disposed to put off Indian dress, to live in the manner of the Ladinos, and so to become a Ladino. There is here no obstacle of prejudice or law to prevent this not infrequent occurrence. The school is one important institution, therefore, through which the Indian societies tend to lose members to the Ladino society and so ultimately to disappear.

As such an instrument of acculturation and culture change, the school is only one among a number of effective institutions. The penitentiary deserves mention, for, although its liberalizing influence is less widely distributed than in the case of the school, not a few individuals profit by this form of widened experience and return to the village with a new song, a new trade, and a less parochial view of life. The common custom of bringing up other people's children is also effective, as when the child is an Indian brought up in a Ladino household. Of such individuals it may later be said that "that Ladino is really an Indian," but the ethnic origin of the individual carries little or no social disadvantage and is quickly forgotten.

Considered as an institution helping to preserve the local culture, the role of the school is small. I venture the assertion that the abolition of schools in these highlands would leave the culture much as it is. Except for the texts of prayers recited on many occasions, little of the rural Ladino heritage depends on literacy. And, furthermore, it is only necessary that a few individuals in each society be literate so as to preserve access to written or printed sources. Indeed, for generations the Indian cultures in the more isolated societies have got along with a semiprofessionalization of literacy. A few individuals in each village or group of villages were trained to read the Mass; the central government sent from the city a literate person to deal with the written communications of formal government. The more pagan religious ritual was, and still is, stored, unwritten, in the memories of a small number of professionals. Their knowledge is highly specialized and is little understood by the layman.

The village school in this area devotes little time to instruction other than the purely technical; and the little "cultural" instruction which it gives has small support in other branches of the village life. Some instruction is given in Guatemalan history and geography. What is taught is not reinforced by books in the homes, because there are almost no books in the homes. Nor is the instruction closely related to the content of oral tradition. The knowledge that Columbus discovered America is perpetuated in the school and is possessed by most Ladinos as an item of information, but few people whom I interrogated were able to tell me that that discovery was the event commemorated by the little celebration which the government orders to occur each year in the village municipal building on October 12. (Of course the more sophisticated townsman understands the meaning of the occasion.) At any rate, Columbus is no tribal or village legendary hero.

As not a great deal is accomplished by formal instruction in the school, one might suppose the lack to be made up by a great deal of deliberate inculcation and discipline in the home. At least with regard to the rural Ladino society, I am sure that this is not the case. Children are taught to do what they are expected to do chiefly as an aspect of coming to perform the tasks of adults. Moments of instruction are not segregated from moments of action. Boys are taught to farm and girls to cook as they help their elders do these things. Along with instruction in the practical arts, parents comment on conduct, saying what is "good" and what is "bad." The word *pecado* is applied to innumerable interdicted acts, from those which are regarded as mildly unlucky to those to which some real moral opprobrium attaches. Some parents will select a serious and special moment in which to convey sex instruction, and sometimes other subjects will be somewhat formally inculcated; but on the whole I should say that instruction in the home is casual and unsystematized.

Certainly it is not characteristic of this Ladino culture that the young gather around the knees of the old to listen reverently to a solemn exposition of the holy traditions and sacred memories of the people. Indeed, in this society, as in our own, it is hard to find the holy traditions, let alone to get anyone to listen while they are expounded. Most instruction that occurs in the home or outside it is connected with the practical arts of life.

It seems to me interesting that, while few of these Ladinos are today teaching their children the prayers of their Catholic tradition, they do take pains to teach them the traditional forms of address and salutation, which in these cultures are complicated and elaborate. It is characteristic of this people that requests and other communications are not abruptly and directly presented but are wrapped in highly conventional preliminary and terminal utterances; also, in general, among them polite language is regarded as seemly conduct.

It also seems to me that this formal language is a way in which people preserve their personal lives from too easy invasion and that it is therefore a useful art. It is, moreover, one which every man must practice for himself. The case is different with the prayers. Apparently it is not thought sufficiently important that every child have formal language in which to talk with God. It is, however, thought important that the prayers be recited by someone on the occasions of novenas for the saints and following a death. But all that is necessary is that one or a few persons be available to recite the prayers. It would not greatly surprise me if in these villages the reciting of Catholic prayers became a paid profession, as are now the reciting of a Mass by priest or layman, the teaching of the spoken text of a dance-drama, or the playing of the little flageolet which accompanies processions bearing images of the saints.

This observation about the teaching of prayers and of mannerly speech may be generalized into two wider characterizations of these Guatemalan cultures. The point of view on life is practical and secular rather than religious or mystical; and formal activity is more than usually large, it seems to me, in proportion to the content of symbolic meaning which underlies it. This statement I am disposed to make about both the Indian and the Ladino cultures, although there are differences of degree or kind in these respects between the two.

For the rural Ladinos it may be safely asserted that religious pageantry and mythology do not play a large part in the education of the individual. The Christian epic is known very incompletely; it exists in the form of many uncoordinated fragments of lore, and it is not vividly presented in any coherent or impressive way. These country people read very little sacred literature; they very rarely hear sermons; and there is no important traditional ceremony or drama in which it might be expressed. An exception in part must be made for the ninefold repetition at Christmas time of the journey of Mary and Joseph and for the little enactment of the birth of the child. The effigies of and stories about Christ, and in less degree and importance of and about the saints, do constitute a body of lore in which significant traditional conceptions are perpetuated. But these ceremonials occupy a very small part of the time and interests of the Ladinos, and the element of mere entertainment in them is very large.

For the Indian, more is to be said as to the contribution of ceremony and myth to the educational and cultural process. The cult of the saints is more elaborate, and ritual observances are more extensive. Justification for the statement that the culture of the Ladinos is more shallow or less integrated than that of the Indians is in part to be found, it seems to me, in the fact that most stories told among Ladinos—and they like to tell and to hear stories—deal chiefly with fairies, witches, talking animals, and the adventures of picaresque personages, and that these stories are not regarded as true and are not thought of as describing the world in which the individual lives. They are recognized as fanciful creations that serve to entertain. The Indian, on the other hand, is disposed to regard the stories which he tells as true. Taken as a whole, the Indian's stories deal with men and animals and supernatural beings that he believes to exist about him, and their telling helps to define and redefine the conventional world in which the Indian lives.

A story well known in the Indian village of San Antonio tells how Saint Anthony was once a man who dwelt in that village as other men, and how, counseled by his friend, Christ, whom he sought to rescue when our Lord's enemies were after him, he took the form of a saint so as to help the village where he lived and worked. The story offers an explanation for the origin of every significant element of costume and accouterment in the effigy of Saint Anthony as customarily fashioned and as it exists in the village church; and it explains and justifies by reference to the saint's divine will many of the elements in the cult now customary: the marimba, the masked dancers, the fireworks, incense, and candles. Indeed, except that the content of the story is of Old World origin, the story in feeling and form is quite like many origin or hero myths that are told among non-Europeanized Indians.

A study of the educational process among these Indians would certainly have to take into account the existence of these stories and the circumstances under which they are told. It is plain that their telling helps to communicate and perpetuate the tradition of the group. It is significant that in the Indian villages every man passes through a series of public services; that in the course of many of these employments he spends long hours sitting in company with his age mates and his elders, and that the elders at such times tell stories and relate episodes. The Ladino society is almost entirely without such an institution.

The existence of such a story as the one about Saint Anthony is another evidence of the power within a culture to make itself; if such an expression may be employed. We may be sure that no priest set out to teach just this story to the Indians of the village. The story has grown in the course of generations of speculation upon an effigy and a ritual already sanctified and mysterious. Indeed, we catch glimpses of this process today when we hear of Indians who have found new explanations for some element of decorative design in church, or when an ethnologist's informant begins to offer speculations of his own.

Yet I am struck with the fact that even in the case of the Indian cultures there is more form than content in their collective life. In this same village of San Antonio there is performed every year in Holy Week a series of ceremonies occupying several days. It is generally understood that these ceremonies are a representation of the Passion of our Lord, and a general air of gravity attends them. But in my notes is a list of elements of the ritual for which none of my informants has been able to offer any explanation at all. Structures are erected and taken down, and effigies are used to which no meaning is assigned other than mere custom. One could fill many hundreds of pages with a detailed account of the goings and comings, the processions, the handing-over of effigies, the ritual drinking and bowing and the like, which custom provides must be carried on each year in one of these Indian villages among the groups of men in whose custody rest the images of the saints. On the other hand, even making liberal allowance for the relative difficulty of getting trustworthy information on the meanings of these acts, I feel sure that little could be said about the symbolic connections these acts have with the content of tradition. Yet, even in so far as these rituals have no symbolic meaning, they do maintain traditional ways within which behavior is regulated, and, therefore, they have their place in a broad investigation of the educational process in these communities.

The relatively formal or external aspect of much of the Guatemalan cultures is conspicuously illustrated in the dance-dramas. These are performed by Indians at most Indian festivals and very infrequently are performed by Ladinos at Ladino festivals. The observer sees a score of men dressed in brilliant and fantastic costumes, carrying highly specialized objects in their hands, and dancing, gesturing, and reciting long lines of set speech. The performance might be an enactment of some centrally important holy myth. It is, as a matter of fact, nothing of the sort. There are about a dozen dance-dramas known in Guatemala. Most of these have spoken text. Specialists possess these texts and at festival time are hired to teach groups of Indians to speak them and to perform the accompanying dances. The texts are in oratorical Spanish, and it is rare that an Indian understands well what he is saying. The general theme of the drama is known: if the dance called "The Conquest" is danced, the combat between Alvarado, the Spanish invader, and the pagan Indians is understood. But the tradition means little to the dancers; they will just as well enact Cortes' triumph over Montezuma, if that dance is cheaper to put on or provides a better show. The dance is performed, indeed, because a group of men is willing to put money and time into doing something lively for the festival. It may be compared to putting on a minstrel show in another culture, or hiring a merry-go-round. The comparison is not quite fair, but it suggests the truth.

In these societies of which I write, then, the educational process is not greatly dependent upon institutions organized for pedagogical purposes or upon organized and deliberate instruction within the family or other primary group. The ceremonial and other expressive customs which we find in every society are significant educationally here in Guatemala, too; but at least this one observer finds that, compared with some other societies, there is a great amount of formal machinery for the regulation of activities without corresponding symbolic content. To a marked extent the transmission of culture takes place within a complex of regulations: the traditional machinery of government and of ritual observances, the superimposed police control of the Guatemalan national government, the general traditional emphasis upon forms of utterance and conduct.

Nevertheless, an investigation of the educational process in these communities would be far from complete if it were to consider only institutions, pedagogic or ceremonial, as elements in that process. Here, as elsewhere, the heritage of the group is communicated and modified in situations much less clearly defined than any of which mention has so far been made in this paper. I refer to that multitude of daily situations in which, by word and gesture, some part of the tradition is communicated from one individual to another without the presence of any formal institution and without any deliberate inculcation. This class of situations corresponds in a general way with what Spencer called the "primary forms of social control."

Let us imagine that we are standing unseen outside a house in the village where I am living. Within the house some Ladino women are praying a novena, and outside it six men and two boys stand around a little fire and talk. Someone compares the heaping-up of pine cones made ready for this fire to the heaping-up of twigs by Indians at certain places on hilltops where, by Indian custom, the traveler strokes away the fatigue from his legs with a twig and then adds the twig to a growing pile. As soon as the comparison has been made, one man of those beside the fire expresses derision at this Indian belief, which is well known to all present. Others briefly indicate similar disbelief in the custom. Another man then makes a remark to the effect that what does in fact serve to relieve tired legs is to rub rum on the ankle bones. A younger man—apparently unfamiliar with this remedy—asks how this can be effective, and the older man explains that the rum heats the nerves that run near the ankle bone and that the heat passes up the body along the nerves and so restores strength. The explanation is accepted; the apparent physiological mechanism provides a warrant for accepting the worth of rum as a remedy.

After a short period of silence, conversation begins about snakes, one man having recently killed a large snake. A young boy, apparently wishing to make an effective contribution to a conversation in which he has as yet played no part, remarks that the coral snake joins itself together when cut apart. The man who laughed at the Indian belief about tired legs scornfully denies the truth of the statement about coral snakes. Another older man in the group comes to the support of the boy and in a tentative way supports the truth of the belief as to coral snakes. A younger man says that it is not true, because he cut apart such a snake without unusual result. The skeptical man appeals to the company; another witness offers testimony unfavorable to the belief. The boy has not spoken again; the other man who ventured to support him withdraws from the argument. But this man wishes, it seems, to restore his damaged prestige. With more confidence he offers the statement that some animals *can* do unusual things: the monkey, when shot by a gun, takes a leaf from the tree in which he is sitting and with it plugs the wound. The smaller of the two boys, who has not yet spoken, adds that the jaguar can do this also. Discussion breaks out, several persons speaking at once; the trend of the remarks is to the effect that, although undoubtedly the monkey can do as described, the jaguar is unable to do so. The quick statements of opinion break out almost simultaneously, and very quickly thereafter the matter is dropped. The bystander recognizes that there is substantial consensus on the points raised; the boy is apparently convinced.

We may safely assume that in such a situation as this the states of mind of the participants in the conversation with reference to the points at issue differ from one another less at the conclusion of the conversation than they did at the beginning. The matter is not ended for any one of them, of course; subsequent experiences and conversations about fatigue, snakes, and monkeys will again modify their conceptions, or at least redeclare them. We may suppose also that the outcome of this particular conversation—an apparent consensus in favor of rum and against twigs, supporting the belief about monkeys and unfavorable to the beliefs about coral snakes and jaguars—will not be duplicated exactly in the next conversation that occurs among similar men on these subjects. We are not so simple as to suppose that by attending to this little talk we have discovered "the belief" of the Ladinos on these points. The personalities of the influential men, the accidents of recent experiences had with monkeys or snakes, and, indeed, probably also the general tone of the moment, which may or may not have been favorable to the serious reception of a marvelous story, are among the factors that have entered into the situation. They have brought about, not a conclusive conviction, but a sort of temporary resting place of more or less common understanding. We may think of the outcome of such little exchanges of viewpoint as the component of many forces. Because each man's state of mind at the time of the conversation is itself the component of many such forces, most of which have been exerted within the same community of long-intercommunicating men and women, it is likely to be not greatly different from that of his neighbors. Still, there are always individual differences; and it is largely in such little happenings as that which took place around the pine-cone fire that these differences are made influential and that they come to be adjusted one to another.

The episode may be recognized as one of that multitude by which the heritage is transmitted. It was a tiny event in the education of the people. Some part of the heritage with reference to the treatment of fatigue and with reference to the behavior of certain animals passed from older people to younger people—and, indeed, it passed also from younger people to older people, for oral education is a stream that flows through all contemporaries, whatever their ages.

At the same time it was a small event in which the culture of the group underwent a change. Some old people in the community tell me that when they were young they heard about the ability of the coral snake to join itself together and did not doubt its truth.

Perhaps the boy who advanced the belief received his first knowledge of it from such a grandfather. After this evening around the pine-cone fire he will treat grandfather's remarks with a new grain of skepticism. Some of the men who took part in this conversation have traveled and have lived in the city among men whose tradition disposed them more readily to laugh at the story of the coral snake, and the effects of such experiences were also registered in the outcome of the evening's conversation. The result of these various influences was to shift, though ever so slightly, the center of gravity of the community beliefs on these points.

Furthermore, the trifling occurrence was also an event in the transmission of tradition from one group to another. No Indian took part in the conversation, but one man, who was born an Indian but had lived long among Ladinos, stood silent in the dark edges of the group. As an ethnologist who has talked with Indians, I know that the belief about getting rid of fatigue by brushing the legs with twigs is by them generally accepted, and great credence is given to beliefs as to the ability of injured animals to treat themselves. Now there has impinged upon that silent Indian a set of forces tending to shift the center of his belief; and now, when he takes part in a similar discussion among Indians, he is more likely to be on the skeptical side of the center of consensus than if he had not been here this evening. It is largely by the accumulating effect of innumerable such occurrences that the culture of the Indians and that of the Ladinos are becoming more and more alike.

We are not to suppose that it is always the Indian who is disposed to change his mind so that it becomes more like that of the Ladino. For certain reasons the predominating trend tends to substitute Ladino tradition for that of the Indians. But the Ladino has in four hundred years taken on a great deal from the Indians—the techniques of maize farming and the use of the sweat bath, to mention just two elements—and he still learns from the Indian. The episode around the pine-cone fire could be matched by an episode in which Indians, showing Ladinos the nicked ears of wild animals, by this evidence tended to persuade the Ladinos that these animals were indeed under the domestication of a supernatural protector inhabiting the woods.

It is a fair guess that in any society the process of education depends more on such events as represented in the conversation I have reported than it does upon all the formal pedagogical devices which exist in the society. In the speech and gestures which take place in the home, in the play and work groups, and wherever people talk naturally about matters that are interesting to them, the tradition is reasserted and redefined. In these situations the culture is not merely spoken about; it is acted out, it happens before the eyes and even through the persons of children, who by this means, in large degree, are educated. This basic part of the educational process takes place in every society and probably to such an extent that societies are greatly alike in this respect. Upon the flow of such experiences are erected those more clearly defined institutions of the folk traditions, as well as the deliberate enterprises of pedagogy and propaganda. As to these, societies will be found greatly to differ.

Comparing these particular Guatemalan societies with—let us say, that of the French-Canadian villages—I should say that here education is more secular and more casual. These Guatemalan societies seem to me relatively meager with respect to organized moral convictions and sacred traditions. What the Indians tell me about the times of their grandfathers suggests strongly that the Indian societies have lost in ceremonial richness, as I suspect they have lost in the moral value and the integration of their local traditions. Because I have observed the influence of priests in other communities in maintaining a sacred tradition and in explaining symbolic significance of traditional rituals, I think it likely that, if, indeed, these societies have been becoming more casual and more secular, the lessened influence of the Catholic priests has been one factor in this change. The Guatemala of today is well regulated by secular government in the interests of public order and hygiene. My guess—which is to be tested by historical investigation—is that secular external regulation (important probably even in pre-Columbian times) has grown in later years, while that control dependent upon moral conviction and instruction and upon local tradition has declined. The school, for these rural people, is another form of external regulation rather than an expression of local tradition.

Whatever study of the history of this part of rural Guatemala may in fact show, the present situation in these societies suggests the question of whether a rich culture is compatible with a society in which the mechanisms for education consist chiefly of formal regulations and of casual conversation. The comparison between Indian and Ladino societies—alike though they are in their generally secular character—indicates a correspondence between certain characteristics of culture and certain characteristics of education. The Indian beliefs and tales have relation to current life, and more of them have moral content or depth than is the case with Ladino beliefs and tales. And, second, in the Indian societies there is a social-political-religious organization—a system of progressive public services through which all males pass—that is largely native to the community, that is a force in social control, and that involves relatively sacred things. This organization is largely lacking in the Ladino societies. These differences may be stated in terms of differences in the educational institutions of the two peoples: To a greater degree than is the case with the Ladinos, the Indians hear and tell stories that express and justify traditional beliefs; and by passing through the hierarchy of services the individual learns the ritual that is the inner and relatively sacred side of the formal civic organization. Emphasizing characteristics of those Guatemalan societies which are more evident in the case of the Ladinos than of the Indians, this paper concludes, then, with the suggestion that an education which is made up, on the one side, of practical regulation and instruction without reference to tradition and, on the other, has nothing much more compulsive and expressive in which to exert its influence than the casual contacts of everyday life is not likely to educate with reference to any greatly significant moral values.

4 / Alternative Attempts at Instruction in Atchalán

G. Alexander Moore

This chapter examines three attempts in Atchalán to bypass the formal rigidities of the national school system. The attempts are all efforts to reach people the schools have not reached, or have reached without effect: the preschool child, the out-of-school-child, and the dropout of whatever age. These alternative attempts use daily and yearly time more flexibly than the ordinary school program does, fitting their lesson times to the more pressing schedules of the pupils. The attempts are also more flexible in use of space than the ordinary school program, often turning individual households into classrooms.

The first attempt I consider, that of the nation-state through its literacy campaigns, has also redefined the minimal national educational goal to be the possession of literacy, not the successful completion of six years of schooling. The second attempt I consider is that of the newly militant Roman Catholic church to reach and incorporate all of its baptized flock, at an early age, through participation in the sacraments. Unlike the state, the church has freed itself from the demands of an urban-oriented corps of civil servants, and uses peasants as initiators with signal success. Finally, I show how the Indian peasants themselves have accepted the redefined national goal, minimal literacy, as something to be desired at least for males. To achieve wider-spread literacy, they have added the role of volunteer school-master to the repertory of acceptable and respected roles for adult Indian males, a role that complements their traditional demand that all men initiate other men. The church and peasant attempts provide rich suggestions for ways to strengthen the nation's lagging attempt to reach all its educationally needy citizens. . . . There can be no question that the Guatemalan nation-state is facing an educational problem of enormous magnitude. In terms of absolute numbers of illiterates in the total population, the problem increases every year. The Guatemalan population is expanding at a tremendous rate; and the expansion of primary schools is not keeping up with the population growth. Each year, greater numbers of illiterates pass from the school-age population into the "adult" population. It was inevitable that sooner or later the state would consider, if not actually implement, alternatives to the primary school system, particularly alternatives concerning adult education. Such has been the case. Since 1945—with the second resurgence of a "revolutionary" movement to unify and uplift the nation—Guatemala has attempted, haltingly and not always well advisedly, to carry schooling to all the people by means of national literacy campaigns. . . .

A LITERACY CLASS

The only official literacy effort, conducted by a schoolteacher, which was going on in Atchalán in 1968, was the vigorous night school of Julián Otzoy, the bachelor teacher at the plantation school at El Rincón.

Of all the schoolteachers in Atchalán, Otzoy is the most enthusiastic nationalist. His career demonstrates that a peasant may join the nation in Guatemala. His behavior shows that he considers teaching to be a kind of proselytization among peasants.

Moreover Otzoy has time on his hands at the plantation. Far from being an imposition for him, the night school classes and the recreational activity he organizes after them are, instead, a diversion. Otzoy has none of the impediments to literacy campaign volunteering listed by the AID report on the Jutiapa project, which notes that teachers residing in towns are not likely to teach evening classes in the countryside. Nor are teachers already burdened with a hundred or more pupils in the daytime likely to embark on teaching experiments at night. Otzoy, in contrast, is a bachelor living alone in strange and rustic surrounding. Night classes make up for the lack of family and urban diversions.

Otzoy's interpretation of the literacy campaign is interesting. When he arrived to take his job on the finca he inherited a literacy evening class for older men. There were some fourteen of them, and all had passed their national literacy exam shortly before Otzoy arrived and were hanging on to finish the books they had started to read. The next year Otzoy decided to try something different. He considered but rejected the idea of teaching women in afternoon classes. (Good judgment, considering he is a young, single man and a women's class could mean all sorts of difficulties with the male plantation workers.) He also rejected the idea of forming another class under the title of "nocturnal followup center." He got the permission of the school district supervisor in Burgos, who visited several of his classes. The supervisor also gave him some books which were especially designed for adult education. Following that, the female literacy supervisor for the area arrived and visited a class. She too volunteered to bring materials for adults.

Then Otzoy found himself in the midst of a bureaucratic dispute between the two supervisors. In late July he discovered that the plantation work cycle began to pick up. The coffee harvest was starting on the coast. Plantation workers were increasingly having to work overtime to meet the demands of the harvest. Absenteeism occurred in the night class. Otzoy felt that his group was sufficiently far along to sustain a regular third-grade final examination. But he could not get both supervisors to agree to it. The literacy supervisor wanted him to hold a special midterm exam, and then hold the final exam in October at the proper time for such exams. Otzoy replied that the students would not be ready for an exam in October after three months without studying. Otzoy won, with the support of the regular district supervisor. His exam was an unqualified success by Guatemalan standards. All twenty-four of those who showed up to take the exam passed it. The only casualties were four youths enrolled in the class who failed to take the exam.

All the students in this class were males. Their ages ranged widely—from eleven to forty-five—but the great majority (22) were teen-agers, as shown in the table. One, at the same time he was taking this night school class, was also enrolled in the

Age	Number
11	1
13	3
14	7
15	3
16	3
17	1
18	3
19	2
22	1
26	2
40	1
45	1

fourth grade in the town school. The rest, however, had never finished more than the second grade. In this class Otzoy has established that it is possible for adolescents and adults to complete the Guatemalan third-grade curriculum in much less time than the official calendar requires. That is, these men successfully completed the course three months ahead of schedule. Moreover they put in much less class time than the school day requires. The class met from 7:00 to 9:00 in the evening, usually four or five times a week. Otzoy's class, then, has been a successful addition to the careers of second-grade graduates. It has not seriously attacked the problem of completely illiterate out-of-schoolers, or of early dropouts.

I now report a visit to Otzoy's night class, the evening before its official final examination. His brief school year is about to end.

It is 8:00 P.M. A hard August rain is falling. The teacher has just distributed a pamphlet on citizenship entitled *Vida Ciudadana* ("Citizenly Life"). The pamphlet is official material for adult education.

Pamphlets, Otzoy is telling the class, can serve as an example for us when we do not remember things. If we do not remember how to write a letter we can look it up in our pamphlet on the Spanish language. Now, this pamphlet on citizenship can teach us how to be men. It is not enough just to know how to read and write. Reading and writing is not enough to be a man. A man has to fulfill certain obligations.

We must know what we must fulfill in order to be Guatemalans. We must know this before we can be men. Now no one in this class is really young. There is no one here under thirteen. (That is a mistake if the class roll is correct.) When we reach the mature age of eighteen years we might have thought we were to become free men. On the contrary, we have more obligation than ever toward others.

Our parents have brought us up and we have always been in their care. At eighteen we think we are free of them. We might plan to get married, because our father cannot command us. When we are married we might stay away from home for a week. But pretty soon we come back. The next thing we know, one's father has a double weight of obligation pressing on him.

To really become a man, you need three things: responsibility, work, and honesty. It's not money, it is these three things it really takes to become a man.

(Many in the class look bored. Some have their heads on their desks. Many do not appear to be listening.)

Thus you must know your responsibility when you reach eighteen years of age. The first thing you must do is go and get your residency card. You must get that from your municipality. That card authorizes us to be citizens. It is also useful at voting time. Many women do not bother to use it for this important purpose. (Women are not obliged to vote under the Guatemalan constitution.) They leave everything up to men, saying that they are just women. But when other things more immediate come along they don't claim just to be women.

But we should all vote in the elections, particularly those for the presidency. If we do not fulfill our obligation to vote, we might not like the government that comes along afterwards. And whose fault would that be? We lost the opportunity to vote for good government. Since voting is secret, many people do the wrong thing. If there are two people on the list they might vote for both of them. This leaves a null vote. And that's not right. Because for one null vote the right man might lose office. And whose fault would that be?

(The class seems to be a bit more interested now.)

Another duty of a citizen is to pay his taxes. Everyone has to pay their one-dollar head tax. With this, we know, our municipality will keep our streets clean. Now of course if the officials steal the money, as some people say, then that is not one's own fault. That is on the conscience of the officials. The citizen's conscience is clean, since he paid his tax.

The teacher continues to talk, touching on the Independence Day celebration. He finally ends by assuring the students they need not be frightened of the exam. He knows that all of them know what the exam will cover. The only thing that could possibly let them fail would be their own fear.

Otzoy has elected, it turns out, not to teach a lesson on this occasion (the night before the exam), but to present only the patriotic exhortation we have just heard.

Evidently this method was efficacious; in any case all those who took the exam passed it.

I now describe Otzoy's encounter with the same group after they have passed the exam.

The school term is over, but the group continues to meet regularly in the school-room to prepare for the celebration of Independence Day on the plantation. These meetings continue the recreational periods that at 9:00 P.M. had followed Otzoy's night classes. The youths continue to do what they did then: play Ping-Pong, peruse magazines (gifts from the big house), or even type letters to relatives in the city or on the coast on the old typewriter in Otzoy's custody. They also discuss plans for their celebration of Independence Day on September 15. For this celebration Otzoy has organized two soccer teams, one from among his third-grade pupils in the day school, the other from among his youths at the night school. The planter has graciously supplied both groups with uniforms and a ball. The teams will play groups from town on Independence Day. Between matches, however, they will engage in an elaborate ceremonial. A "sweetheart" will be invested in her role. To honor her and to honor the nation the youths will present a short play. The play resembles nothing so much as the flowery verse dramas Atchaleños put on during their saints' festivals. Now we will observe its rehearsal.

First the boys recite the play with their parts in front of them. They often have to refer to the script. Next Otzoy has them rehearse it in action. The play is entitled *The Prayer of a Bootblack*. Written by Juan O. Rivera, it appeared in September of 1966 in a magazine entitled *El Maestro: Revista de Orientación Pedagógica*. This is a teachers' professional magazine published in Guatemala.

The principal part, that of the bootblack, is played by an eleven-year-old boy from the night course. The play starts out with the bootblack alone, bewailing his fate. He is unable to find anyone to give him work. His mother is sick and he needs money. A clown comes by and taunts him derisively: would the boy shine his bare feet? Then a beggar comes by. The bootblack makes it clear that he is better than the beggar because he works for a living. A priest comes along to tell the boy that he should be grateful to God for making him suffer. At that, the boy, disconsolate, is approached by a person who tells him he is his guardian angel. The boy replies that he does not believe in guardian angels. Turning away, he kneels and prays directly to God for help. He begs for a miracle to save his sick mother. Just as he finishes his prayer, the guardian angel tells him that a miracle is about to occur. At that moment a policeman enters to take the boy with him to the stationhouse. The boy cries that he has committed no crime. Of course not, says the policeman, but tomorrow is Independence Day. Consequently all policemen need to have their shoes shined for the parade. The angel laughs joyfully in the background. His miracle has happened.

It is a curious little drama: anti-clerical but pro-religious. Many of its lines are in favor of schools and schooling. It is anti-begging. Clearly it is partisan toward the police force, representatives of the nation.

All told, Otzoy seems to have organized nothing so much as his own version of certain new religious brotherhoods in town. But his is a cult of the nation, expressed through sport, examinations, and Independence Day ceremony. And, like the new and militant religious groups, which I will discuss next, Otzoy's organization depends upon the volunteering activity of one person. There is no assurance that future schoolteachers will continue with his kind of work. It is highly unlikely that a man of his talents and energy will long remain in a plantation school, at a low salary. Rather, his efforts are most likely to bring him to the attention of the national school authorities. His promotion will probably follow. Otzoy's is an interesting effort, but one that few of the teachers who will inevitably replace him are likely to imitate; for they, like most other Guatemalan teachers, will resent demands made on their private time.

The Chantry Catechism Classes

This section examines the Roman Catholic Church's attempt to extend all its sacraments—not exclusively those of baptism and marriage—to all the Guatemalan peasantry. The church's efforts to reach each parishioner parallel the state's efforts to reach each citizen. Like the state, the church treats individuals in terms of age-grades. Unlike the state, the church makes slight demand on children's time: an hour or so from time to time—for six months, a year, or at most a year and a half—in a chantry instruction class, to learn a corpus of sacred material by chanting it from memory. Instruction ends upon passing of a trial which shows the individual can chant briefly from the material at demand. His status is then changed by formal passage through the rite of first communion. Here I examine the church's rationale of age-grading, its use of the first-communion ritual, and the nature of its chantry classes. Finally I try to describe and account for the social workings of this movement in Atchalán.

We have seen how the new nation-state ideally would take each individual national and turn him into a citizen, incorporated into the wider citizenry as a voter at elections with an appropriate written credential, as a fluent and literate speaker of the national language, and as someone who has at least been screened as a possible candidate to become a practicing civil servant in the new national bureaucracy. Similarly, the church militant ideally would take every peasant and turn him into a parishioner, a fully conscious and believing participant in the Mass.

Sacraments and Age-grades: The Career of a Catholic

In the early church an explicit age-grading structure did not exist; infants were admitted to the Lord's Supper immediately after baptism. By the twelfth century these two sacraments had been separated in a person's lifetime. Children were to be admitted to the Lord's Supper only after they had reached the "age of reason." There was some dispute, in the centuries that followed, as to what this meant. In some cases, particularly in bourgeois Europe after 1800, first communion was delayed until the age of twelve or even fourteen. A papal bull of 1910 settled the question. A child could be admitted to the Eucharist as soon as he could distinguish between eucharistic bread and ordinary bread. Most parishes declared this ability to be present after age seven. Thus communicants were officially distinguished from young children.

But most European countries were not satisfied with this single distinction. Another was at least equally important in bourgeois culture: the distinction between adolescence and childhood. This has been emphasized, in many parishes of Europe, through associating the onset of adolescence, at about age twelve, with the rite of confirmation, a ritual symbolizing rebirth of the communicant in the Holy Spirit. In the early church, this rite was part of baptism. It is still so today in Atchalán, and indeed throughout much of Latin America.[1] Atchaleño peasants are included at the Lord's Supper through the mechanism of formal instruction upon reaching the age of reason, usually between seven and nine years of age. No age-grade rite distinguishes the adolescent from first-communicants.

A Catholic career in Atchalán today comprises the following statuses: unbaptized infant, baptized child, first-communicant, married communicant, and lapsed communicant (usually, someone who lives in concubinage, not having taken advantage of the rite of marriage). Ideally such a career would include the status of last-communicant, the moribund who receives extreme unction shortly before death. However, since their priest resides in Burgos, very few Atchaleños achieve this status.

---

1. The *New Catholic Encyclopedia* (1967) has full information on the history and current theological interpretation of these rites.

First-communicants and "Children of Mary"

During the year after a child first starts receiving instruction at chantry classes, both before and after he becomes a first-communicant, he is in great demand as a ritualist in Atchalán.

Groups of white-clad children receive first communion, providing a decorative component in sacred and festive proceedings, on three dates in the year. The first is the Sunday in February on which the Royal Street Ladinos celebrate their own fiesta in honor of the Virgin of Concepción. This is almost exclusively a first-communion date for children of these Ladinos.

More children receive first communion the last Sunday in May, the "Month of Mary," when the same Ladinos parade their image of the Virgin in a procession. To accompany the statue they invite all the town's "children of Mary" (as the children studying Catholic doctrine are called) to join the procession in first-communion dress.

The great majority of Atchalán's children make their first communion in mid-October, at the Feast of Christ the King, sponsored by the voluntary Indian brotherhood of the Sacred Heart of Jesus.[2]

In June, on San Juan's Day, all the "children of Mary," as well as all the children who have made their first communion in February or May, are asked to make an appearance in costume. This Day of San Juan (Saint John), the patron saint of the town, is the ritual climax of the year. In Atchalán this day has something of the special quality that Christmas Day has in the United States.

By afternoon everything has happened. The evening before, the brotherhood of San Juan, and then the municipal corporation, have toured, each in their turn, a set of four gaudy makeshift altars that mark the four corners of the town. At dawn all the images of the saints of official brotherhoods have accompanied the image of San Juan himself to the church. The Atchaleños, for such an impressive convocation, do the only thing possible to go one step further. They demand that the priest put God on parade.

A Corpus Christi is a procession of the body of Christ. A wafer from the consecrated Host is taken and placed by the priest in a monstrance, a glass vessel elevated in the form of a sunburst. The priest will hold the monstrance high as he goes forth from the church under a canopy.

San Juan's Day Mass has ended. The parishioners have emptied the church ahead of the priest. Among these go a small group of children. The girls are all wearing white dresses and white gauze veils; the boys, white shirts. They are being shepherded by a tall Indian carrying a missal (it is the only such book in evidence in the church). He is Clemencio Tsul, chief steward of the traditional brotherhood of San Francisco. Clemencio is also a "zealot," a spiritual supervisor of a group of Franciscans, members of the Third Order of Saint Francis, an apostolic group new to the area. These children are being trained by members of the order to receive first communion. Some may have recently received first communion at the end of May.

The padre has not yet appeared at the door with the monstrance. The pageant is not ready. For one thing, a number of giants—great framed structures covered with gingham and sporting high masks—have not departed the plaza. Traditionally they always dance ahead of a Corpus. This is a custom the padre does not like, although he can see that it is of European origin and not "pagan" Indian. He suffers

2. This is one of several self-recruiting groups that have appeared in Atchalán in the last two generations to hold fiestas honoring saints or deities who, it is claimed, inspired the founders. Another relatively new brotherhood—that of Jesús Nazareno, which celebrates Holy Week—has been incorporated into the official roster: its cargo, like the traditional ones, is now rotated by the elders. The voluntary groups make some attempt to rotate the cargo among a large number of semipermanent devotees. The Royal Street Ladinos, for example, rotate the sponsorship of their annual fiesta for the Virgin.

the giants only on condition that they dance out of sight of the Most Holy Sacrament. But another symbolic embellishment is entirely to the padre's pleasing: the little children dressed in white, the symbol of purity. There is not yet, however, the full complement. The handful shepherded out by Clemencio does not begin to fill the long avenue of green pacaya boughs in front of the church. But presently the others appear, coming rapidly up the hill, led by José Tsin, their doctrine master.

Over a hundred children come, in two files, the first section composed exclusively of girls. Older girls, generally taller, come first. Many of them are wearing white dresses. All wear white gauze veils, although many, particularly the younger ones, wear the ordinary Indian dresses. Shuffling behind the girls, doing all she can do to keep up, is a tall, gaunt old woman wrapped in a black veil. She is Escolástica Torres, a poor Ladina of more than seventy years. Escolástica is famed throughout the county for her devotion to instruction in the faith. Behind her come the boys. Again the older and taller ones lead the way. There are not as many older boys as there are older girls. Many of the boys wear white shirts. All are wearing diagonal sashes of crepe paper emblazoned with gold paper sunbursts, representing the Host. Each is carrying a little paper banner as well.

All together the children make a charming retinue to greet the padre as he appears at the door of the church, holding the monstrance high. The band blares the hymn of the church, just as it does when any sacred image sallies forth. Everyone kneels. The commercial carnival and the county market on the other side of the plaza momentarily suspend activities and noise. Silence continues until the procession is out of sight.

The leadership of the traditional closed, corporate village is in full attendance. One past steward of a brotherhood goes ahead of the Host carrying the silver banner of the Lamb of God. Around him are the stewards and past stewards of the official brotherhoods. Alongside the Host walk the elders, carrying lighted tapers.

The padre will find his duties tiring, for he must make a circuit of the town, stopping at all four special altars. He wears dark glasses to protect himself against the tropical glare, but he must suffer the dust and heat of the hot June day. Consequently, particularly as the procession draws to a close, he hurries somewhat to enter the church again.

A Chantry Class

I present an afternoon class in mid-June, two weeks before the Day of San Juan. This, however, is shortly after the celebration at the end of the Month of Mary, when children from this particular chantry class have already taken their first communion and thus graduated from it. Today is midway between two festivals of importance for the pupils.

I go to the compound of the foremost doctrine master in the town, José Tsin. He had told me that his classes generally begin every afternoon around 4:00. I arrive almost exactly at this hour, under a light drizzle. The compound is a particularly lush one, being on low ground near the river. Outside, it has richly foliaged fences of stubby aloes. Inside, it has many trees grouped around a large black sand courtyard, swept clean, above a small terraced wall.

I call out "Ave María," the proper greeting when a stranger enters a household in Guatemala. A man's voice tells me to come forward. Over to the right, José can be seen standing on the porch of his large rancho shaded in the trees.

The rancho is one of the very largest in Atchalán; it once housed the image of San Juan himself, in the days of José's father. Now its old thatch is grown over with moss. To the left are two smaller ranchos used as a kitchen and storehouse. In front of them is an old steel drum filled with water, and round about are the various large stones used for washing and drying. To one side of the compound are the ruins of yet another large rancho, a few desolate decaying houseposts.

I go to the porch of the house where José, a man in his fifties, is talking to a man in a dark brown suit, introduced to me as Chano Awachó, one of the other cathechizers in the town, who has come to discuss with José preparations for the children's part in the procession of Corpus Christi. They are at this moment deciding upon the children's costumes. They have just finished making a sunburst of the type they will put on the boys' sashes. Chano, who is in his mid-thirties, is a junior catechist. He took on the role some four years ago at the padre's insistence. There are simply too many children for José and the few other catechizers in town to handle. The padre recruited four men to the job at that time. They became members of Acción Católica, and attended a short course in doctrine, given by the padre. Chano, however, does not have many students. His classes seldom have as many as 15 in attendance, while José may have 70.

Today the children are slow in coming. Those who are attending the public school were dismissed at 4:00. On drizzly days like this, José observes, attendance is always low. He doubts that old Escolástica, who comes by often to help him in the afternoon, will come out in the wet. Indeed she does not. At 4:21 the first children appear. Four little girls come in from the back gate and are suddenly alongside the porch. They call out, "Good afternoon, Senor José!" They also shout a greeting to José's wife, who is out of sight in the kitchen. Upon seeing me they giggle and run across the courtyard to the other gate, where two other little girls have appeared. All huddle together. Then one produces a rope at least eighteen feet long. Two of them twirl it while the others jump. There seems to be a complete disorganization. Three girls are jumping at once. But after a while, turns are organized. The first girl who misses a jump has to wait her turn after all the others, and so on.

All these girls can be seen to be Indian from their dress. Some of them, however, have been at the public school. They are carrying their notebooks in little plastic bags tucked inside their shawls, which they are wearing tied around their waists.

At 4:26 six little boys appear at the main gate. They too call a greeting, but stay at one side of the courtyard, busy with a game of marbles. Within the next few minutes more children appear. A boy and a girl, probably siblings, come in through the interior gate from another compound belonging to relatives. These little kinsmen go straight to the kitchen to converse with the master's wife. More children appear. Boys and girls separate and run to take part in the games of their groups.

José is still in conversation with his colleague, Chano. But he is also trying to get the children to come inside. He bids them do so. Some of the boys run in right away, but a group of five girls is timid in the presence of the anthropologist. Finally five of them gather up courage and go running past, giggling. Others hang back and make a game of it until the master—who is now over in the kitchen talking to his wife—calls out and more firmly bids them enter. The children do so, but the class still does not begin. Inside, three taller girls announce that this class is for beginners. They come out and start jumping rope by the entrance of the rancho. All the children who are entering the compound gate now go directly inside. All call out a greeting to José.

I leave my seat on the porch and enter the large gloomy room. It measures about 15 by 24 feet, and the entry is in the middle of one of the longer walls. Furniture is arranged in total disregard of conventional classroom uses. Left of the entry, along the front wall, is an oblong household table with its bench. Facing the entry, but near the back of the room, is a small blackboard on an easel. Behind it and extending to the right, along the rear wall, is a long line of benches reserved to the boys. The girls' three benches are at right angles to these—one in front of the blackboard, another left of that, a third along the left wall. The master's chair is between the first and second of the girls' benches, not far from the blackboard.

The children are left to themselves for the moment. The boys seem to be doing nothing except poking and giggling. They sit in squirming interaction on one long bench at the rear. Their bodies all touch. The girls, in similar close colloquy on their first two benches, are busy reciting parts of the catechism. One child, Tomasa, seems quite small to be in a classroom, but she has glittering bright eyes and a lively face. She leads. She starts off saying a line and the others pick it up in chorus with her. They are reciting in high sing-song voices: "The commandments of the Holy Catholic Church are four. . . ." They go on to recite the commandments.

The master enters and takes control. From his chair in their midst, he directs the children to rearrange themselves. The boys spread out to occupy more space along their line of benches. Two girls are asked to move to the empty bench along the left wall; the other girls distribute themselves more evenly on their other benches. All this time, the master addresses only one child, Tomasa, by name. He places her in the exact center of the girls. Soon everyone is settled. Chano, the other master, is busy on the porch, clipping out gold paper sunbursts for Corpus Christi costumes.

The master tells the girls that he is first going to work with the boys. He turns to the boys, without moving his seat, and begins to conduct their chanted choruses of responses in the newly promulgated liturgy in the Spanish language. (The class is conducted entirely in Spanish.) Just as the child Tomasa has done with her friends, he begins a response and the boys join in when they can as he goes along.

The girls, left to themselves, continue with a sort of impromptu recitation of other texts. One of these is the Lord's prayer.

At 4:59 the master feels it is time to conduct the entire class together. He does so by calling out the questions of the catechism. The children reply in unison in high-pitched voices. The first question is "Where is God?" The master is holding a printed copy of the catechism but does not consult it. He knows it by heart. None of the children has a copy of the catechism; in fact many of them have their arms folded as they chant the responses.

Often the responses begin slowly. Only a few of the children say the first few words. Once these have been repeated, almost everyone else joins in, and the last words of the response are recited by everyone. Indeed the last three words in all the responses are literally shouted, with an upbeat intonation.

Although some children, particularly Tomasa, know almost all the responses seemingly to perfection, obviously not all the children are so well versed. It is also clear that some parts of the catechism are much better known than others. The sections having to do with the passion of Jesus Christ have very good responses. This no doubt is because the local celebration of Holy Week, grown to be a great pageant, is dramatically instructive to all children.

But not all points meet with such success. Indeed, a few questions even stump the leading pupils.

For example, when the master calls out, "How was God made man?" there is a long silence.

Finally one boy says, "Nailed upon the cross."

"Impossible!" says José, quietly but indignantly.

At no point, however, does the master expatiate on the text. To correct the error we have just seen, for example, he simply recites the correct response. It is apparent that he jumps from one part of the catechism to another and does not keep directly to the order of the text. He does so in spite of the fact that the Guatemalan catechism is written strictly according to the canons of scholastic logic. All the questions and answers are internally consistent and logically related. For example, the question "Is Jesus Christ the true God?" must receive an affirmative answer, since the text has already stated that Jesus is one of the Holy Trinity, and that consists of the true God.

The recitations are proceeding rapidly. By 5:08 at least twenty questions have been covered. At 5:10 there is a sudden shower. Many children turn their heads, still reciting, to inspect the rain. A little boy and a little girl, siblings, come running in, calling out their greetings to the master. They run to sit with their respective sexes. A moment later another little girl comes running in to take a seat with the girls who are behind the master. She too calls out a greeting. Now all the children are very restless. Although there is still fairly good response, there is also much whispering. At all times the children, who have now moved into body contact on the benches, are jostling and squirming even as they continue to recite.

At 5:20, the master, who is apparently dissatisfied with his pupils' showing in front of a visitor, calls a halt. They had been reviewing the nature and the history of the papacy. Following that, the master had jumped briefly from the catechism to review some of the responses in the new Spanish Mass. Now he asks me what time it is. Then he gets up and goes out.

The children, left to their own devices, do not now recite on their own, but jostle and fidget. None, however, gets up. Shortly the master returns, holding a cookie tin. This he opens and passes around. Each child draws from the tin a small card stamped with the seal of the Holy Asylum in Antigua. The cards are lots. At the time of their first communion, the sisters from Antigua will hold a lottery and pass out prizes to the winners. But the children must attend chantry class from time to time to get their lots.

Once everyone has his card, José tells the children they may leave. The dismissal is done in strict order. The little girls in the front of the room, on the first two benches, stand up one by one, starting with the one nearest to the door. They genuflect toward an altar that stands in the rear wall behind the blackboard. Then they call out their farewells to the master and go running off. The children who had been seated along the walls now form a line moving counterclockwise toward the door. That is, the girls who had been sitting along the left wall are the first of this group to leave, followed by the boys. The children shove each other as they bunch up to the spot, near the entry, where each must kneel to the altar. However, no one shoves the child who is actually kneeling.

Such, then, is one chantry class. Every afternoon of the year very similar events take place.

Function and Origin of the Classes

The classes are formal only in that they are groups, loosely age-graded, gathered together and engaged constantly in the memorization of the same material. Children may join the classes at any time. Their attendance may be highly sporadic. They may drop out for weeks at a time if they are needed at home. All they must do is learn the sacred text by heart, so that they may be examined, in passages chosen at random by a nun or priest, before taking their first communion. All must study at least six months; some dally through the course for a year's time or more.

Yet when children enter a chantry class they take on the status of a "child of Mary," expressed ritually by their processions in special costume several times a year, and culminating—usually in October—in first communion, although some children continue in the processions a while longer.

A child's entry into such classes is also sure sign that his parents have granted him the status of street child and judged his physical maturity worthy of that status. Accordingly, "children of Mary" are anywhere from seven to nine years old. Some parents prefer that a child take first communion in October before entering public school in February. Thus they may put off entry into the national school until the child has first entered the church.

Such classes are a new institution in the township, dating from around 1920. Before 1920 it is probable that most Indians of the township never took communion. Many went from birth to death with only the sacrament of baptism to sustain their

Christian souls. Bunzel reports that this was entirely the case of Chichicastenango in the early 1930s. Some Atchaleños before 1930 received instruction in the catechism from an individual tutor, usually someone regarded as almost compadre of the new communicant's parents. But this rudimentary tutorial system has now blossomed into a formal classroom system, albeit still a voluntary one, not recruited by the elders.

The first such formal classes, although an attempt to extend ultramontane Catholicism to the villagers, ended in the formation of another Indian peasant brotherhood. Accordingly the peasantry had in one generation reincorporated the church.

Around 1917 a circle of devout Ladino ladies, wives of local merchants or plantation staff men, gathered some 30 Indian boys together. The ladies cooperated with the priest. Together they got two poor but devout Ladino men to instruct the boys. Both Ladinos were outsiders. One, Julio López, was a very poor cottager, a day laborer who made his meager living by making charcoal. At times he was reduced to living off the charity of the principal lady among the founders. His memory is still revered in the town today for his exceptional holiness and his exemplary life.

But this group of Indian boys did not disband upon receiving first communion. Instead they became something of an educational society. Under their sainted leader, the boys managed to buy an image of the Sacred Heart of Jesus, which they still revere on the feast day of the Sacred Heart, in June, and again during their October celebration of Christ the King, when most Indian children take first communion today.

When these young men reached maturity in the early 1930s, that is to say when they were already serving as ministriles, they began to recruit their own pupils. Each became a *celador*, or apostle, leading some 30 pupils. Although the exact number of these celadors is obscure, several of them continue with some sort of chantry activities today. For a number of years the activities were fully supported by the priest. Among other things, they were supposed to pay for two masses a month! Eventually the study groups ceased to be instructional chantries and became merely devotional groups. One of them is almost exclusively composed of Indian women under the direction of a kinsman. Such groups are much in demand for both private and public festivals. They chant a number of Catholic text responses at the household celebrations of particular saints, or at funerals and wakes. New groups of this kind have continued to be formed.

By the early 1940s, then, the original apostolic movement had transformed itself into a private brotherhood celebrating the image of a saint, much as the traditional Atchaleño brotherhoods do. It lent orthodox ultramontane ritual to the celebration of other saints' images. But instruction in the faith lagged.

A second attempt at chantry classes came when a number of nuns in Antigua set out, together with the local priest, to remedy the situation in 1945, a year of revolutionary activity in Guatemala, by trying to recruit other doctrine masters. They recruited the recently widowed José Tsin. Thus it was under the tutelage of a nun that José began his teaching career every afternoon in the town friary. After his second marriage a few years later José began to hold his classes in his home. Shortly thereafter he also founded a private brotherhood, this one in honor of the Virgin of the Rosario. The people he has recruited to help him in this brotherhood, however, have not become doctrine masters.

Nevertheless José serves with the blessing of the nuns and of the padre as the dean of the local catechizers. Thus it is no accident that we saw young Chano Awachó— recruited by the padre into the role of catechizer— at José's house.

In the mid-1950s, yet another apostolic group appeared in Atchalán in the presence of the Third Order of Saint Francis. This was founded directly by zealots from Guatemala City, including a well-educated city lawyer. This group has been busy repeating almost exactly the activities of the earlier group formed in the

1920s. However, they have not bought an image, not even one of Saint Francis. They meet for Saturday study sessions under the leadership of their various celadores. They have become something of an ultramontane sect within the town. Thus they are unable to attract more than a few children of outsiders to their classes, which are filled mainly by their own children. They maintain these classes strictly separate from those given by other catechizers, as we have seen during their participation in the Corpus.

The ultramontane church militant runs the very-present danger of creating, not numbers of proper Catholics indistinguishable from Catholics anywhere, but groups of parochial Catholics whose allegiance to cargo saints and their local religious officers is stronger than their bond to the Pope or the Mass. However, as long as the priest and the nuns themselves recruit catechizers and examine "children of Mary," they maintain their own initiatory structure in which the priest and the nuns are the initiators, the catechizers are the initiate/initiators, and the "children of Mary" are the initiates. Should the priest lose interest in the chantry groups, an unlikely possibility, there is danger that they will die out. Unlike the official saints' brotherhoods, the chantry groups do not have a group of aged zealots, in the persons of the elders, to insure that the burden of maintaining them is passed on equally among those who are capable of it. But certainly as long as the current catechizers are alive, chantry groups will remain in Atchalán.

Chantry classes, then, remain under the direct supervision of the church hierarchy. In contrast, the national school bureaucracy does not really control the activities of another group of local initiators: the peasant schoolmasters. Their labors represent "stimulus diffusion," in that they have imitated the institution of the school; but in doing so they have converted it into a new institution, which I examine next.

THE PEASANT SCHOOLMASTERS

Birth of an Educational Innovation

We have seen that the Guatemalan national state has, since 1945, set great store by universal literacy. The literacy movement in Guatemala has all the earmarks of a metropolitan movement attempting to proselytize the countryside. Thus it was with considerable surprise that I discovered that the literacy movement in Atchalán itself is far more deeply rooted and more viable among the peasants than any metropolitan import would seem likely to be. There exists a native, entirely peasant, literacy movement within the community that was originated and sustained without national help, and indeed in spite of obstacles that have been put before it by the local school.

This native literacy movement is in large part the creation of one man, Modesto Tactíc. Yet I do not claim that his work, meritorious as it was, resulted only from his genius. There was something else in the social and intellectual climate of Atchalán in 1934 that enabled the "genius," Modesto, to found his private school.

Let us look at the background behind Modesto's innovation, both in his life history and in the community experience at the time. In 1934 Modesto was twenty-four years old, unmarried, living in the large extended household of his father. Not many years before, Modesto's father had received the image of San Juan into his house, and had thus passed through the highest of the town's religious brotherhood offices. Modesto in 1934 was serving as ministril, probably for a second or third time. In the 1920's he had attended the Atchalán public school for three years, during which time he had been a star pupil. National schooling was an essential, but not sufficient, prerequisite to the innovation Modesto was about to institute.

Modesto was also one of the first Atchaleños to be swept up into the new Catholic orthodoxy. At the age of seven he had been entrusted to the town's first doctrine class (1917-18). This class, the reader will recall, was under the leadership of a poor Ladino holy man sponsored by a number of elite Ladino ladies. The original doctrine class continued to meet sporadically during the decade of the 1920's under the magnetic direction of its teacher. Together the group undertook doctrinal exercises and devotions in honor of the Sacred Heart of Jesus. As soon as the boys reached maturity—in 1929—they turned themselves into a brotherhood, the Society of the Sacred Heart of Jesus. That is to say, the year following their induction into the town corps of ministriles, they then expressed their social maturity in the religious sphere as well.

Within a year or two of their incorporation as a religious society, some of the more active of their group went forth to proselytize. They established catechism classes or they brought together groups for devotional exercises. Such groups continue today to sing responses in Spanish at life-crisis rites. Several of Modesto's first cousins were very active in establishing such devotional groups.

Another item in Modesto's social and intellectual background in 1934 consisted of his experience as a temporary construction laborer in the capital. For brief periods when Modesto was eighteen and nineteen, he was employed in the city. A cousin had already migrated to the capital, where he found Modesto a job and provided him lodging. On the job Modesto discovered that the adult, licensed masons were illiterate. Several times he offered his services to them to make calculations concerning measurements. He used a piece of charcoal and a bare slab to find solutions for their problems. His efforts excited gratitude and admiration; moreover they were immediately turned to good use in the progress of the construction. Thus did Modesto discover that literacy could be useful and could bring its own social reward.

In 1934, when Modesto was called home to serve another term as ministril, he impressed his home town companions with his written calculations. But new results followed. Fellow ministriles begged Modesto to instruct them in the valuable art of arithmetic, and in "letters" as well. They began to meet with him in a loosely structured group tutorial session each evening in the thatched dwelling of Modesto's father. The dwelling was a large one, since it had housed San Juan. There Modesto drilled them in the same schoolbooks he had used a decade before in the public school. While most of the pupils were his own age, one or two were considerably older. Modesto's pupils, although drawn from one status, that of ministril, had other statuses in terms of national schooling. They were all former out-of-schoolers or dropouts.

The class was considered a success. The original group kept at it for several years, until one by one they felt themselves "graduated." But in the meantime their numbers had been replenished by new arrivals, youths like themselves, garnered from the afternoon street-corner gatherings of Atchalán.

By 1936, then, there was a new, voluntary classroom going strong in Atchalán. Its success came quite without the direct intervention of the school. Moreover within two years it no longer depended upon the company of ministriles for its recruitment. Lastly the class had been created and was inducting pupils quite without benefit of any literacy campaigns, since these were not to arise in Guatemala for another nine years.

Modesto's voluntary classes have never ceased since 1934. They were threatened only once, in 1966. In 1968 I saw a great deal of Modesto; he was greatly embittered. True, Modesto had twice been much celebrated during literacy campaign years. He was, in 1968, the dean of the local alphabetizers. Although it is certain that no literacy official realized that Modesto himself had founded the local volunteer classes long before the literacy bureau was founded, all the Atchaleño volunteers were aware of his prior distinction. But in 1966 Don David, the school director, throwing off the burden of evening literacy classes imposed by the bureau on the school, brought suit in the local court, charging that Modesto was illegally registering school-age children for literacy training. Indeed Modesto was.

Modesto, outraged, mustered all his many diplomas from the Ministry of Education and took them to court, where they were impounded as evidence and never returned. The leftist mayor was in a quandary. Modesto had long been a leading member of the opposing faction. Yet Modesto's labor was much esteemed by everyone. Moreover, many of the sons of the leftist faction had availed themselves of his instruction. The director was legally right, however, even though his school did not have room to accommodate all the school-age children. The mayor ended by enjoining Modesto in writing not to teach any more school-age children. Modesto, for the first time in three decades, suspended his classes.

But not for long. The Atchaleño peasants slowly subjected Modesto to inexorable pressure. By the start of the next school year Modesto was quietly taking in pupils again.

Voluntary Schooling

It was during this twilight, almost *sub rosa*, time that I knew Modesto's efforts best. I visited his classes first during March of 1968, and then again during August of that year. In March, Modesto was quietly holding one class for seven pupils from 4:00 to 6:00 in the afternoon. By August, attendance had swelled so that he was back to his more usual habit of conducting two classes, one in the afternoon from 4:00 to 6:00, and the other in the evening from 6:00 to 8:00. The classes were roughly age-graded; young children were supposed to come to the early class, and older boys, roughly supposedly the same age as the ministriles, were supposed to come to the evening class. In fact, ages and experiences were mixed most promiscuously in the two classes. As always in Modesto's practice, those few female pupils who attended did so only in the afternoon, not in the evening.

It was difficult for me to grasp the character and constituency of Modesto's classes. That is so because he was essentially running a nongraded free school during the time I observed it. His practice has resulted from his own efforts, not from literacy bureau guidelines. I have the official roll, obtained in Guatemala City, for Modesto's last officially registered class, in 1966. The ages of those listed roughly correspond to the ages of local ministriles. There were 13 males registered. Two were under eighteen (one sixteen and the other seventeen). The rest ranged in age from 19 to 28 years old, almost exactly the ministril age range in Atchalán. However, the official roll omitted information about the previous school experience of the pupils. It is here that Modesto has been left to his own devices quite completely, and it is here that he has departed most adventurously, if probably quite unwittingly, from the public school model. His pupils proceed almost entirely at their own pace, and not according to the time they have "served" studying.

Modesto's classes are very different constructs in time and space from the national classes. This is so in spite of the curriculum Modesto uses: three books that were his own school primers in 1920. (However, he also invents quite freely—ad libs, that is—when it comes to arithmetic problems.) Unlike the national schoolteachers, Modesto does not marshal the groups in any rigid yearly calendar on any particular daily lesson plan. He is much freer than the school in his use of time. It is true, as Modesto claims, that he follows the official school year: meaning that he allows himself a vacation from November through January. Otherwise his classes bear little resemblance to the official ones.

In their daily structure the classes look like nothing so much as a collection of tutorials. All activity depends upon an initial contract with the schoolmaster. Thus there is great elasticity in the use of time, both during the day and through the year. Pupils enter at any point in the year and leave at any point, often to enter again at the next convenient moment. For two weeks in late August of 1968, the master himself found it very difficult to meet his afternoon class for more than a few minutes each day. One day Modesto was caught in a sudden torrential downpour in his fields before he could return to town. Another day he had to attend to civic duties at the electoral commission meeting. And for nine days running he had to attend the novena (mourning prayers) after the death of his father-in-law. During this time, however, Modesto still met faithfully with his evening group. The afternoon group, left to its own devices, spent some time studying on its own, but just about as much in roughhousing.

On one such day, when the afternoon group was waiting for the appearance of the master, I took a count of it. Nine pupils had come. (Two boys were absent because their little brother had died the day before. Like the schoolmaster, they would be out for a nine-day prayer period.) One pupil was a twelve-year-old girl, clad in Indian costume. She always sat by herself at one of the two household-type tables in the room. There had been two other, older girls in the class, but they had left some weeks before to take employment as domestics in the capital. Possibly their prospective employment had been one reason they were studying to begin with. The remaining pupils were boys. One was ten years old. Another was twelve. Two were fourteen and two were fifteen. All had been studying for some months before. At this particular time, most were at the same place in their studies.

On this one afternoon the boys were sitting around the table singing Mexican popular songs from one of their notebooks. This notebook, belonging to a fifteen-year-old boy, had a large number of songs written in it. The boy claimed that he had copied them from a printed songbook which he had purchased for twenty cents in Antigua and sold, after he copied it, for twenty-five cents. This might have been. But I feel sure that some of the songs must have been copied by ear from the radio, since their spelling—although phonetic—was most unorthodox.

The song copier was the son of a member of the militant order of Saint Francis. His parents would expect him to learn to read in order to study sacred texts in any case. He was using his new talents in other directions. He was a boy, Modesto later assured me, who had been a very slow beginner. He spent months simply learning the alphabet and syllables before he went on—as is Modesto's method—to learn words. Once he passed that point, however, he took off into fairly rapid and successful reading. Many of his pupils, Modesto claims, are late bloomers.

An Evening Class

I now visit Modesto's evening class, also held in this difficult time in August, 1968. Modesto's house is on Royal Street. He is one of the very few Atchaleño Indians whose dwellings are completely on the Ladino formal model, being flush to the street and having a cement floor, masonry foundation, frame walls, and tin roof. A window opens onto the street. There many children and passers-by stop in the afternoon to observe the class proceeding within. At night, however, that window is closed up tight.

From the street, I enter the yard through a gate at one side of the house and go around to the dirt porch to enter the door there. I come into the main domicile of the family, also the quarters that once received and housed the image of San Juan, in 1957. To the left of the door is a bedstead. Beside it is a cabinet, on top of which are a great variety of household articles in no apparent order. There is also a household altar there. In front of the bed stands an easel holding a blackboard. Directly in front of the door is a table, with chairs around it. To the door's right is another table with chairs, and against the right or south wall is a long bench. On the night I am observing, there are four male pupils sitting at the table to the right. Modesto, the master, is standing over them. All are barefoot, although Modesto is wearing a warm wool jacket. I greet them and take a place on the bench.

Other details of the room include an old and faded map of Guatemala, and a similar old and faded portrait of the "Liberation" strongman, Carlos Castillo Armas. Several old calendars decorate the walls as well. The room is illuminated by a single candle, in an old brass candlestick on the study table. The pupils have brought a supply of candles, which are kept in a drawer of that table.

I can hear Modesto's newborn baby crying in the kitchen, a thatch structure behind this dwelling. Down the street a marimba practice is going on. The boys have left their hats on the ledge formed by the masonry behind the table. The streets outside are crowded; I can hear men in conversation. There is a brilliant full moon outside.

One boy, named Ermenegildo, is reading aloud. He is using the old-style primer that Modesto used in the 1920's. He reads sentences very laboriously. Later I find out that he is sixteen years old and has studied a year with Modesto. The next week Modesto is to decide that the boy already knows well enough how to read and henceforth must concentrate on doing arithmetic problems. The boy has copied a series of sentences from the primer into his copybook. This was his homework problem. He is now going over these sentences. The next to the last statement, for example, is, in translation, "The world is a vale of tears." At the bottom of his copybook the boy had written *Atchalán*, the date, and his name. I asked to see his copybook. The sentences are well executed in script, not printed as in the public school, and done letter-perfect.

Modesto has moved on to the next pupil on the left of the first pupil. This boy, Rigoberto, is thirteen years old and has been studying with Modesto for two months. He is still learning the alphabet and syllables. He is reading from his primer a series of letters and the syllables they can form. Right now the consonant is the letter X. He is forming syllables by combining X with vowels. For example, X, U, then the syllable XU.

Modesto's two sons, ages nine and eleven, are busy in conversation at the other table.

Rigoberto continues with his exercises. When he falters, the boy across the table from him, named Segundo, who is fourteen years old and has also been studying two months, leans across the table to help him.

When Modesto has finished these exercises he moves over to Segundo. Segundo also reads a syllabary, but this time from his own copybook. Modesto corrects him from time to time, absently, without even looking at the book. At one point the master pauses, coughs, and then spits on the cement floor. Modesto finishes with Segundo, closes his book, and compliments him.

Now the master moves on to the fourth boy. Joaquín is seventeen years old and in his second year of study with Modesto, but he is very little more advanced than the other boys. That is to say, he is still poring over ABC's and syllabaries. Modesto was later to tell me that he has despaired of Joaquín's learning but that the boy insists on coming. Modesto is cautious. Perhaps sometime Joaquín will suddenly catch on. This has happened before. The boy is working on syllables of three letters. He is working on L and vowels. For example:

L	O	LO	
L	E	E	LEE
L	A	LA	
L	O	L	LOL
L	A	M	LAM
L	E	N	LEN
L	U	Z	LUZ

Joaquín makes mistakes which Modesto corrects loudly. The boy mumbles and can hardly be heard. He protests at first that he has not done this lesson and cannot recite it. But Modesto insists, knowing full well that he has covered this ground before, and the boy manages to do fairly well.

Then Modesto goes over the exercises for the morrow. These concern the letter M as an initial letter for a number of syllables. The other boys have put their books down and are watching with folded arms.

When this is over Modesto tells them he is going to give them a problem in addition for their homework. He goes and writes numbers on the board. This is the problem:

$$468$$
$$873$$
$$754$$
$$628$$
$$537$$
$$\underline{483}$$

Modesto then asks Segundo, the boy who has been studying for two months, to read the numbers aloud. Several times Segundo has difficulty reading them. Ermenegildo, the boy in his second year, who already knows how to read, chimes in and finishes them for him.

Modesto, anxious to chat with me, dismisses the class. The boys get up and retrieve their hats and, in marked contrast to the less formal group in the afternoon, shake hands with both the observer and the master as they leave.

This class is noteworthy also in that two of Modesto's sons, ages nine and eleven, who already know how to read, often engage the pupils in exercises on the syllabary. Doing so, they act just like their father. And they are doing what children ordinarily do in Indian homes. They initiate peers.

Schoolmaster as Compadre

Although Modesto times his classes according to the school year, his actual method of induction and graduation is that of the individual contract involving himself and the pupil's father, primarily, and the pupil himself, secondarily. Thus the class personnel is constantly changing, although the classes do end at a certain date. Characteristically the classes form slowly; they begin with three or four pupils and then more join. Modesto holds that the ideal minimum class size is six pupils. Each pupil joins through individual agreement with the master.

The reciprocal mechanism behind these informal teaching contracts is very much like the old model of godfatherhood, or ritual sponsorship. In a sense Modesto is a "godfather of letters" to hundreds of Atchaleños today. They do not call him by that title; but pupils, past pupils, and their parents act just as if he were some sort of godfather. Indian Atchalán has many kinds of godfathers or ritual sponsors. At a wedding alone, as we have seen, there are no less than five classes of sponsors. All these are rewarded with gifts of food and drink by the "owner of the wedding." In the case of the formal godfather the debt lasts a lifetime. The groom's father sends the godfather yearly gifts of food and drink on the day of San Juan, the town's patron saint, for the rest of his life. Gifts to the other sponsors seldom continue past the wedding itself.

Another kind of ritual sponsor is the "gospel godfather," the man who pays for and conducts a curing ceremony over a sick child. Gift-giving to this man seldom goes on for more than a year or so after the ceremony itself.

Atchaleño parents treat Modesto as if he were their child's godfather. During the time the child is receiving instruction, his parents send unsolicited monthly gifts of cash to Modesto: twenty cents or twenty-five cents, according to their means and spirit. Pupils in the night school also bring the candles for their own illumination. Adult male pupils, or fathers of younger pupils, usually gather at Modesto's house at the end of the "school year," bringing liquor with them to toast their master in a modest celebration. On the day of San Juan, Modesto is showered with gifts. Adult "graduates," or as we term them "godsons," in particular are likely to remember him on that day.

This godfather model of teaching provides us with a partial explanation of Modesto's motivation in continuing to teach, in spite of the trouble stirred up by the school director and in spite of the lapsing of the national literacy efforts locally. When Modesto tells us of his voluntary career, he is eager to stress the achievements of some of his former pupils. These "graduates" themselves publicly and annually acknowledge their debt to Modesto. One of them has a supervisory job in the capital. When he arrives in town for a visit, he wears a city suit and tie. He pays a respect call on Modesto. Another such "graduate" is a Protestant pastor in the capital. He too pays a courtesy call on Modesto, when he visit Atchalán. A number of others, still living in town, are employed as foremen on coffee plantations or on road crews working for the Ministry of Public Works. Foremen must keep work rolls and be able to perform other paperwork. These men too make public display of their gratitude to Modesto, often in front of their own children.

The achievements of these men, in turn, must very well influence the decision of other youths or their fathers to seek Modesto out. Some of these others are motivated also to make up for past deficiencies in the school, to really set themselves the task of using literacy and arithmetical skills after a year or more of futile school attendance.

To illustrate such a case, there is the Ladino youth, a third-grade graduate, who had been cheated in a written contract on the coast. Bothered by this business deal, he went to Modesto, who sat down and figured out his losses. Shocked, the youth immediately contracted for fifteen days of arithmetic instruction for a fifty-cent fee. It is only a Ladino such as this, who holds himself to be socially superior to Modesto, who would treat Modesto's tutoring as a commercial service to be purchased, rather than a social favor to be reciprocated with other favors.

Others of Modesto's "graduates" have used their new skills for the paperwork that the religious brotherhoods require. And still others are among the ranks of newly orthodox Catholic militants of the town. All of these join groups to study sacred texts.

In short there are many motives that bring men, boys, and girls to Modesto with the desire to learn how to read, write, and do calculations. All, however, come with the expectation that Modesto can teach them. Most go away having learned something. All were out-of-schoolers, dropouts, or perhaps "graduates" of the local school who felt themselves insufficiently schooled in reading, writing, and arithmetic. Often they hoped to hold a more formal job than most peasants hold, and sometimes one that would take them to an urban center.

Modesto of course has had long experience with literacy campaign officials. From them he has picked up a great deal of nationalist rhetoric. I find it hard to believe that the nationalistic ideals expressed in this rhetoric are themselves as much of a motive as the actual social pressures I have mentioned above. Still, Modesto will assert solemnly: "To alphabetize someone is to aggrandize our beloved fatherland." In the next breath he hastens to add: "To lead someone out of ignorance is an act of piety." Nationalist and religious motives, then, are mixed when he explains and validates his conduct.

It was inevitable that the Literacy Bureau would involve Modesto in their campaigns. Thus in 1946 when the Literacy Bureau formed a committee in Atchalán to carry out its work, Modesto received the post of secretary. The committee structure was modeled on that of a religious brotherhood: president, four assistants, and a larger group of followers (in this case, alphabetizers). But what Modesto found most memorable about those years was the happy fact of examinations with cash prizes. Once, his own pupils were examined in Antigua, and each one who passed gained the master a prize of three dollars in cash.

When the campaigns reappeared in 1961 in Atchalán, Modesto was involved once again. However, in these later years no local committee was formed. Modesto simply came to the general meetings and was listened to with respect. His house was adorned with a sign calling it "Alphabetizing Center Number 1." Each year until 1966 literacy officials awarded Modesto a diploma for his efforts.

Yet in spite of all these "modernizing" efforts, Modesto remains a pillar of the traditional community. His life has been one of fervent service in the old religious structure. Thus in the years 1940, 1941, and 1942 Modesto served as the second steward of the brotherhood of San Juan, the patron saint of the town. Indeed during those years he defended the popular tradition of the fiestas against the criticism of the priest. Modesto's father had served as director of the new society of the Sacred Heart of Jesus from its foundation in 1929 until he died in 1941. In 1947 Modesto took on that office as well, keeping it until 1961 when he passed it on to a cousin. He received in turn the post of secretary of that society. What is more, Modesto had the first stewardship of San Juan—that is, the direction of the greatest festival of the year—in the years 1957 and 1958. Thus at forty-eight years of age he was eligible to the highest post in the town, that of elder. Modesto has thus repeatedly, in the festivals, attained the status of initiator. I believe he has carried on his classes with enough autonomy, often without any direct contact with literacy officials, to merit the classification of initiator in terms of the voluntary classes as well. . . .

THE THREE ATTEMPTS COMPARED

Of the three attempts at instructional alternatives, the home classes of Modesto have become the most parochial, the most particularistically local. The state's effort to reach the illiterate by demanding the "volunteer" overtime of the national teaching corps is probably ill advised. The literacy campaign's attempt to recruit peasant volunteers is much better advised, but it lacks permanent supervision or a stable mechanism of recruitment and rotation of task. The church's catechism classes, judged by their attendance and their coverage of their age-grade, are the single most successful attempt at formal instruction today in Atchalán. The conduct of the chantry classes has two advantages over the conduct of both the national literacy classes and those of the autonomous schoolmasters. First, the yearly examination of the "children of Mary" by the priest insures final supervision over the classes by outside authority. Second, the priest's constant proselytizing visits to the town provide a sure means of recruiting new catechizers (initiate/initiators); so the chantry classes are in no danger of dying out with their current teachers, although they might disappear should the Catholic clergy itself disappear or relax its supervision.

All three attempts are flexible in their use of time and space. The church age-grades its efforts in loose agreement with the parents. It is not adamant about attendance and tardiness. The literacy campaign redefines the daily time it brings to pupils, and calls up pupils at any point in their life cycle after school age. The peasant classes have the same flexibility about daily time. They are also flexible about life cycle time, taking pupils of any age, including school age. Of the three attempts, the chantry classes and the volunteer letters classes seem more viable than those of the national state. We cannot know, however, if new peasant schoolmasters will continue to arise spontaneously in the generations to come. . . .

Today the national schoolhouse has preempted half of the formerly spacious plaza. Here, even more than in the courthouse with its frequently leftist mayors, resides the Atchalán of the nation-state, represented in the careers of the schoolteachers. Two schoolteachers in the municipio were born Indian peasants. They have embraced the nation and no doubt will move up into higher-paying and probably urban posts. Most other schoolteachers are quite content to use Atchalán as the workplace that allows them to reside in Burgos or Antigua. In this their orientation resembles that traditional to Guatemalan Ladinos. Their careers have reinforced traditional objectives: securing themselves a place in the urban lower middle class. The school for them exists less to transform the peasantry than to validate their own security.

The drama continues. No world view—no daily, yearly, or lifetime script—has won. Atchaleños—Indians, Royal Street Ladinos, gentry, and schoolteachers—are all actors moving on the same stage but acting under different direction. They speak to each other, but the lines they speak were learned from different scripts. And in these strange encounters, where rhetoric often confuses earnest attempts at communication, the drama of changing Atchalán is rewritten every day.

REFERENCES

Valverde, Victor Manuel. El analfabetismo en Guatemala. *Guatemala Indígena* 2:3, 21–112 (julio-septiembre). Guatamala: Instituto Indigenista Nacional, 1962.
Wright, Peter C. Una evaluación del plan Jutiapa, programa piloto de alfabetización. (Mimeographed technical report). U.S. Agency for International Development, Guatemala, 1964.

5 / The School at Vaucluse: Educating the French Child

Laurence Wylie

The schoolyard starts to fill up at eight o'clock in the morning. The children who live the farthest away from school arrive first. Villagers sleep later than country people. The village children drift down to school only a few minutes before the eight-thirty deadline. Even five or ten minutes after school has started one may hear a door bang up the street, then the thumping of a child's heavy boots as Yves Biron or Colette Favre runs down the street, late as usual but hoping to avoid in some way the usual scolding.

At eight thirty Madame Vernet blows her whistle, and lines form in front of the three entries to the classrooms. There is some jostling in the ranks of the four, five, and six-year-olds among those who want to be first in line, but Madame Girard with a sharp word and clap of her hands stops the confusion at once. The children seven to nine years old in front of Madame Druetta's door, and those ten to fourteen in front of Madame Vernet's door stand in a dignified manner and look at the scuffling younger children with an air of amusement and superiority. When order has been completely established the teachers open the doors and the children file in, hang their wraps on the proper pegs, sit down at their desks and start arranging materials from their briefcases.

The school day begins with a fifteen-minute *leçon de morale*. The teacher reads a short story or tells an incident from which she draws a moral lesson which may be summed up in a sentence, repeated in chorus and learned by heart by the children. Officially, the purpose of the *leçon de morale* is to teach the children to practice "the principal individual and social virtues (temperance, sincerity, modesty, kindness, courage, tolerance), to inspire in them the love for work, the taste for cooperation, the spirit of teamwork, the respect for one's word of honor, the understanding of other people, the love of one's native soil, the obligations toward one's family and toward France." [1]

Most of the teacher's moral tales are taken from ready-made texts like Souché's *New Moral Lessons* or *On the Straight Road* by Leterrier and Bonnet, and when she can she tries to relate them directly to the life of the children. This is an easy matter if, for instance, it concerns family obligations. It is harder if the moral lessons concern cooperation and teamwork, which are not characteristic virtues of the people of Peyrane. A few lessons are so completely in conflict with the customs of Peyrane that it seems futile to teach them.

One morning Mrs. Wylie was at school when Madame Girard was giving a moral lesson designed to increase the children's love and respect for nature. The anecdote, from Souché's *New Moral Lessons*, concerned "Two Poor Little Birds," and the sentence which the children repeated and learned by heart was, "Let us be the friends and protectors of the little birds." In a region where a favorite dish is roasted little birds, where a husky man boasts of consuming fifty or sixty warblers at a sitting, there is little likelihood that this lesson will have much effect.

When the *leçon de morale* is finished, work is begun in earnest on the subjects in the curriculum. At ten o'clock the children file out to the school yard for a recess of fifteen minutes. Sometimes, especially at the beginning of the year, the teachers organize singing games for the girls and younger children, but usually the children are left to their own devices. They may run and yell and play at will so long as they do not attack each other physically, get wet or dirty, or expose themselves to danger. The children break up into groups spontaneously, the younger children playing with friends of either sex and the older children playing only with friends of their own sex. The boys play tag or may organize a game of soccer if one of them has brought a ball to school. There is no play equipment of any kind in the school yard except for a climbing rope which children must learn to climb in order to get their *brevet sportif scolaire* (athletic certificate). The older girls sit in a sunny corner of the yard gossiping and petting one or two of the youngest children who turn instinctively to them when they need affection. The younger boys and girls run about madly in groups of two or three or four, often chasing and verbally tormenting a current scapegoat. The three teachers stroll about the yard, chatting and vaguely keeping an eye on the whole situation. Play is stopped only in case a child gets hurt or is punished. Then all the children crowd about the victim. If the child is hurt, faces of the other children are filled with sympathy, and there are murmurs that "he shouldn't have been doing that; he was sure to get hurt." If he is being punished, there is a mocking expression on their faces. Usually, of course, the play continues uneventfully until Madame Vernet blows her whistle and the children line up to march back into the school.

At a few minutes past eleven thirty Madame Vernet sends a child out in the school yard to look at the town clock. When he runs back to report that the time is up, there is a scuffle to put away books. The two older classes are excused, and the children leave the classroom at will. The little ones in Madame Girard's class must line up outside the classroom and wait until all are ready to leave. They line up by twos, with boys and girls paired up and holding hands. When all is ready they march to the break in the wall between the school yard and the street where they stand poised for a moment. Madame Girard has them wait until they are all calm and until she makes sure no cars are coming down the street. Then she calls: "Avancez!" The children answer in one voice, "'voir, Madame," and they start down the street, running and yelling, temporarily freed from the restrictive weight of discipline.

Most of the village children hurry straight home, for they have errands to do before lunch. Jacques Leporatti must carry a bucket and a pitcher of water home from the public fountain, for there is no running water in the Leporatti house. George Vincent has to bring bread from the bakery for his father's restaurant.

Tatave Pouget has to run to the store to get a bottle of wine. Colette Favre has to take care of her little brother while her mother is finishing preparations for lunch, and when lunch is ready she has to go call her father at the café.

Back at school, lunch is being served to the children who live too far away from school to return home and to a few village children whose mothers are working and cannot prepare a proper lunch for them. Now and then children who could return home persuade their parents to let them eat at the canteen, for the children all enjoy eating there. They like eating together, and they say that the food which old Madame Bardin prepares is very good. It consists of three courses—two substantial dishes (stew, thick soup, spaghetti, or something of the kind) and dessert (usually jam or stewed fruit). Each child brings his own big piece of bread to school with him. This meal costs twenty-five francs, about eight cents.

Discipline at the canteen is strict. The children must sit up straight, keep their wrists on the edge of the table, and finish everything on their plates. There is a double purpose in requiring the children to clean up their plates. It teaches them not to waste food, and it also reduces the number of dishes which have to be washed. At the canteen, as in most homes, when the main course is finished and each child's dish is wiped clean with a piece of bread, the dish is turned over so that dessert may be served on the back of it. The spoon is also inverted so that jam may be eaten from the handle.

During the meal absolute silence is maintained. A child may speak only if he receives permission from the teacher in charge. The teachers justify this rule of silence by saying that the acoustics in the canteen are such that the place would be a bedlam if the children were allowed to talk. They also say that lunch would last forever if the children were allowed to distract each other. As it is, lunch is so disciplined that it lasts no longer than fifteen or twenty minutes. Then the children are turned loose on the playground and play as they do during recess until class begins at one o'clock.

The afternoon session differs little from the morning session. It lasts three hours with a recess of fifteen minutes in the middle of the period. The children are dismissed at four o'clock in the same way as at eleven thirty, with this difference, that at the end of the morning all the children leave the school. At four o'clock, five or six children are required to remain in their seats for any time from a few minutes to an hour in order to make up work that they have done improperly or as a punishment for misbehavior.

By five o'clock the school is cleared, and the cleaning woman comes to scrub and sweep. After she leaves the school is ready for the next day, and the shutters and doors are locked until morning.

When the village children leave school they run directly home for their *goûter*, or mid-afternoon snack. Since supper will not be served for three or four hours the *goûter* is important, and if a child does not return home directly after school his mother will send someone out to look for him. Some children sit down at the table for a fairly substantial meal, but most of them are impatient to get outdoors. They are given their large hunk of bread and a piece of chocolate or cheese and go out in the street to eat it in the company of other children.

After the *goûter* the younger children may play, but the older ones have work to do. Water must be carried from the public fountain. Armloads of wood must be carried from the basement room down the street where wood is stored. Trips must be made to the edge of the village to gather fresh grass for the chickens and rabbits or to pick mulberry leaves for the silkworms. When these chores are finished there is homework to be done. Finally at six or six thirty the older children may go out in the streets to play, but even then the older girls have the responsibility of keeping an eye on their little sisters and brothers.

When the country children leave school they start their long walk toward home. Some of them live as far as two miles from the village. In winter when it gets dark early and the mistral is blowing, this walk is accomplished as fast as possible.

In nice weather, however, groups of five or six children dawdle all the way home. This is the only time of the day when they are free from adult surveillance. They learn how to get along with other children without the pressure of adult authority but with the severe social pressure that can be exercised by other children of their group.

The groups grow smaller and smaller as children reach home and drop out. In the last few hundred meters there is usually a sudden rush to get home, for the children remember that they will be scolded if they have lingered too long. They may be late for the *goûter*, which is always a more formal, more substantial meal in the country than in the village. The men come in from the fields and the whole family sits down to a heavy snack of bread, cheese, sausage, jam, and wine.

After the *goûter*, all but the smallest children have their chores, more numerous and more important than the chores of the village children. They have the problem of carrying wood and water and getting grass for the rabbits and chickens, and when this work is finished they have to help work in the field or in the garden. They have to take their turn watching the sheep or goats, bringing them into the fold when it starts to get dark, and milking the ewes and nannies that are fresh. If there is time to spare between chores and supper it must be devoted to school-work. There is no time for homework after supper, for supper is not served until the men have stopped working, usually well after dark. By the time supper is finished it is time to go to bed. The next morning they must get up early to get to school on time, and in the cold early morning one has neither time nor inclination to dawdle or play. The walk home from school in the afternoon gives the country children their only playtime.

The four-year-old child who has just started to school soon falls into this routine. He has no homework. He has no chores. The routine is hard, however, and he must accept it without complaining. He knows that complaining would not relieve him of the pressure, for no one would listen to him. He has already learned that there are unpleasant aspects of life that must be faced. He is told that he is old enough to face the school routine, and he does so stoically. He is partially re-warded by his feeling of pride in being considered old enough, reasonable enough to accept the inevitable with resignation.

For ten years, until the child is fourteen, the school routine is the most important part of his life. His parents, his teachers, his friends constantly remind him of its importance. Confronted by this unbroken social pressure, he accepts the school routine as a serious responsibility to which he must measure up.

The educational program of the school of Peyrane is the same as that of every other public primary school in France. It is formulated by the Department of National Education which sends out precise and detailed instructions concerning educational goals, subjects to be taught, methods to be followed, distribution of class time, and all other aspects of the functioning of the school. As one reads page after page of these instructions, one gets the impression that the officials of the Department of National Education do not recognize the special needs of different communities and leave nothing to the imagination of the teachers. Even the games to be played in the nursery school are "determined by the decree of July 15, 1921."

In practice, of course, the program is far from being as rigid and impersonal as it seems. The teachers know that these official instructions are intended as a guide and should not be taken too literally. After all, the teachers are French and consequently recognize the gap that usually separates laws and regulations on the one hand from actual practice on the other. They know that they need not follow the daily program blindly so long as over a period of time they observe the relative proportions for the important subjects indicated in the program. They know that for everyone in Peyrane it is more important for a child to be able to read well than to take part effectively in choral singing. If they take the time allocated for singing and devote it to drill in reading no one will object.

Monsieur Valentini, the primary inspector from Avignon, who supervises the primary schools of the district, shares this flexible, reasonable attitude. The teachers speak as though they were in constant fear of his annual inspection visit and of the unexpected visits he pays now and then, but confidentially they admit that this anxiety is superficial, for Monsieur Valentini is a genial, tolerant person who expects teachers to carry out the spirit of the official program as best they can in their own specific, local situation. He calls the teachers of the district together for a meeting once or twice a year to discuss with them the program and their problems and to go over the new regulations sent out by the Department of Education. At one of the meetings I attended he explained at length a new ruling which some of the teachers had not understood. He concluded his remarks by saying, "That's what the regulation says, and I hope you all understand it now. Unofficially, of course, I might add that no one is going to object if you follow your own judgment in this matter."

Although the official curriculum prescribed by the Department of National Education is long and complicated,[2] it may be described in simple terms as it is put in practice in the school in Peyrane. The children of the school are divided into five classes: *Classes enfantines* (Nursery Group) with children from four to six, *Section préparatoire* (Preparatory Section) with children from six to seven, *Cours élémentaire* (Elementary Course) with children from seven to nine, *Cours moyen* (Intermediate Course) with children from nine to eleven, and the *Classe de Fin d'Etudes* (Concluding Course) with children from twelve to fourteen. Of course, the age division is by no means rigorous. A bright five-year-old may be placed with the six-year-old group, and a dull twelve-year-old may be kept with the seven-year-old group. Paul Jouvaud, who is mentally defective, remained in the room with the smallest children until he was thirteen years old and the biggest, strongest child in school. He was "graduated" from the Nursery Group and dropped from school, according to Madame Girard, when the stirrings of puberty made him too difficult for her to handle.

Madame Girard has charge of both the Nursery Group and the Preparatory Section. We have already seen how the Nursery Group spends its time. The Preparatory Section, to which Madame Girard devotes the major portion of her energy, concentrates on learning to read, write, and do simple problems in arithmetic. In an average six-hour school day about two hours are devoted to reading, a half hour to writing, a half hour to grammar, and an hour to arithmetic. The use of the remaining two hours depends on the mood of the teacher and of the children and on a variety of other human factors. Usually the time is split up into brief periods which are given over to singing, drawing, paper and scissor work, the *leçon morale*, short talks on such subjects as divisions of the year, points of the compass, parts of the body, hygiene, and so on. Recess, of course, takes up a half hour.

There is no radical difference between this program and that of the children in the Elementary Course, which is Madame Druetta's sole concern. The same time is spent on reading and writing, but the emphasis is slightly shifted. Less time is devoted to reading and more to the formal study of grammar. Two new subjects are introduced, but in moderate amounts: history and geography take up about fifteen minutes of the school day.

In Madame Vernet's room are both the Intermediate Course and the Concluding Course, and it takes a teacher as skillful as Madame Vernet to handle these two quite different sections in the same schoolroom. The Intermediate Course is a continuation of the Elementary Course, and one sees in its program the same tendencies. Half the school time is still devoted to reading and writing, but the emphasis is shifted somewhat further: the study of formal grammar replaces reading as the primary concern of the class. No new subjects are introduced at this level, but the time devoted to arithmetic, geography, and history is doubled. Together these three subjects take up a third of the class time. Arithmetic alone takes up an hour a day. We noted that in the Preparatory Section, Madame Girard now and then gave brief talks on practical subjects such as divisions of time. By the time the children have reached the Intermediate Section these talks have become a formal subject to which a half hour a day is devoted and which is called *leçons de choses*. This might be translated "lessons in things" or "exercises in observation," but it may be best understood as a kind of practical approach to the study of science.

The program of the Concluding Course is rather different from the programs of the other courses. The study of French is still the primary consideration of the class, but the time devoted to it is reduced to an hour or so a day, the same time that is now given over to the study of arithmetic and science. History and geography take up about a half hour, and what used to be called the *leçon morale* has now become civics which the class studies for a half hour daily. This makes for a more balanced program than that of the other courses, but of course the balance may not be evident from day to day. If the class is especially weak in one subject, most of the time may be spent on drill in that subject until the students perform adequately. This is especially true with the study of French, which is recognized by everyone as the most important subject taught in the school. Any other subject may be slighted or sacrificed in order to increase the time for drill in reading (silent or aloud) and writing (penmanship, spelling, grammar, composition).

The program is frequently interrupted. The visit of the inspector or some other official, the illness of a teacher, preparations for the Primary Certificate Examination, a teachers' meeting which the teachers must attend in Apt, a visit to the ochre mine, the annual excursion to Marseille, and many other events frequently interrupt the routine. And then there is always the preparation for the two public performances—the Christmas Party and the Prize Awarding Ceremony—to which a substantial part of two months of the school year is devoted.

In spite of these interruptions and in spite of the rigidity, more illusory than real, of the official curriculum, when a child leaves school at the age of fourteen he has learned approximately what his parents expected him to learn in school. He can read with ease. He can write without making too many grammatical errors. He can solve most of the practical problems in arithmetic with which he is confronted in daily life. He knows enough of history, government, geography, and science to make him aware of his relationship to his environment; he is aware of the moral and ethical values professed by society.

To an observer who studies school life in Peyrane over a period of time it is apparent that the children learn much that is not explicitly stated in the curriculum. From the attitude of the teachers, from the way in which the school work is presented, from the textbooks, the children learn to make basic assumptions concerning the nature of reality and their relationship to it. These assumptions are not mentioned in the directives of the Department of Education. They are not prescribed by the primary inspector. If the teachers are conscious of them they never discuss them directly in class. Yet these assumptions are so important that they will determine to a large extent the frame of mind and the manner in which a child will approach the problems with which he is confronted throughout his life.

In teaching morals, grammar, arithmetic, and science the teacher always follows the same method. She first introduces a principle or rule that each pupil is supposed to memorize so thoroughly that it can be repeated on any occasion without the slightest faltering. Then a concrete illustration or problem is presented and studied or solved in the light of the principle. More problems or examples are given until the children can recognize the abstract principle implicit in the concrete circumstances and the set of circumstances implicit in the principle. When this relationship is sufficiently established in the minds of the children, the teacher moves on to another principle and set of related facts.

The principle itself is not questioned and is hardly discussed. Children are not encouraged to formulate principles independently on the basis of an examination of concrete cases. They are given the impression that principles exist autonomously. They are always there: immutable and constant. One can only learn to recognize them, and accept them. The same is true of concrete facts and circumstances. They exist, real and inalterable. Nothing can be done to change them. One has only to recognize them and accept them. The solution of any problem lies in one's ability to recognize abstract principles and concrete facts and to establish the relationship between them.

Another basic assumption is most clearly seen in the way history, civics, geography, and literature are studied, but it is important in all subjects. In learning history the children are first presented with a general framework which they are asked to memorize. Studying history consists partially in filling in this framework, that is, in learning how the facts of history fit into the framework. An isolated fact is unimportant in itself. It assumes importance only when one recognizes its relationship to other facts and above all its relationship to the whole framework. In learning geography a child first studies his own countryside, then the surrounding region, then France, then the world. Heavy stress is placed on the relationship of each geographical unit to a larger whole. In the study of morals and civics the children learn the proper relationship and reciprocal obligations of the individual to the family, to the community, to France, and to humanity.

This emphasis on the relationship of the part to the whole is also seen in the rather rudimentary study of literature that is carried out in the higher grades. No attempt is made to understand or to appreciate the text which is presented to the class until it has been thoroughly dissected and analyzed. It is broken down into its logical divisions, and the author's purpose in each division is explained. Difficult or obscure words and expressions are explained. Only when each of the component parts of a passage is understood and when the relationship of each part to the whole is made clear is the passage put back together and appraised as a unit.

Thus a child comes to believe that every fact, every phenomenon, every individual is an integral part of a larger unit. As in a jigsaw puzzle each part has its own clearly defined and proper position. They make sense only if their proper relationship is recognized.

Finally, it is assumed that knowledge is important only as it is related to human beings. There is no stress on learning simply for the sake of learning, no stress on the accumulation of facts without regard for their usefulness. This is most evident in the study of arithmetic and geometry. The principles studied and the problems solved are chosen exclusively on the basis of their usefulness in teaching the students to solve the problems which they will be confronted with after they leave school.

The purpose of the rudimentary instruction they receive in science is equally related to the children as human beings. No effort is made to have the children collect butterflies, learn to recognize different kinds of birds, study rocks simply for the purpose of being able to classify them. A bird offers no interest in itself. It is interesting because it is good to eat, or because it is harmful to the crops or eats harmful insects, or because it has beautiful plumage or a beautiful song. In the same way the study of geography does not consist in memorizing the capitals of all the departments of France; its purpose is rather to show the relationship of the people of Peyrane to their surroundings.

The learning of grammatical rules is so emphasized that at times it appears that the rules are considered important in themselves. This impression is false, however. The rules are considered important because it is believed that a person cannot express himself properly unless he knows them thoroughly. It is difficult for an Anglo-Saxon to comprehend how essential this language study is to the French. The French judge a person to a far greater degree than we do on the basis of his ability to speak and write correctly. Even in a rural community like Peyrane the way a person speaks and writes is considered an important indication of his social status. The study of grammar is thus strongly emphasized in school, not because of its intrinsic value but because it will be important to the children throughout their life.

The history course shows the same orientation. The framework of dates and facts must be memorized, it is true, but is important because it lends perspective to the two aspects of historical study which are emphsized in the course: the life of the French people at different periods of history and the study of the lives of great men.

In 1938, Monsieur Jean Zay, then minister of education, sent out a circular which Madame Vernet and Madame Girard told me they consider the most authoritative statement of purpose and method in primary education. Concerning the study of history the statement says:

> In teaching history the teachers should emphasize the role played by those men who have helped bring about progress. Today we no longer believe that history can provide a means to foretell the future; we no longer believe that the study of history can provide us with solutions for present-day problems. It does teach us, however, to meet events in their unfolding with a more impassive attitude, and that is a valuable contribution. It teaches us the value of honest labor, the value of great example, the comfort to be derived from healthy admiration. Children should be told of the effective role played by those men and women whom we consider the benefactors of humanity. If they retain only a genuine feeling for such people we shall have accomplished much. For they will have learned that this material progress of which we are so proud was accomplished at the cost of great effort, that it is the ever-threatened result of an immense collaboration, that in enjoying it we are responsible to the great men who created it.[3]

Not dates or facts alone then, but human beings in relationship to dates and facts, should constitute the study of history.

So in their study of arithmetic, science, geography, grammar, and history, children learn that man is the measure of all things. Facts are important only as they may be related to human beings, and especially to the human beings living in the commune of Peyrane.

The most successful child in the school of Peyrane is the child who goes beyond the subject matter to grasp these basic assumptions. Without consciously realizing that he does so, he learns to recognize the relationship between abstract principle and concrete fact, the relationship between the part and the whole, and the relationship of knowledge and experience to himself as a human being.

Even the average child, who certainly has only a partial grasp of these relationships, is sufficiently imbued with their importance that they will help determine the manner in which he seeks a solution to any problem—in human relations, in politics, in mechanics. He will approach the problem as he was taught to approach all problems in school. In every problem he knows there is a principle involved, and it is important for him to recognize the principle. In every problem lurk practical, concrete difficulties which make the application of the principle difficult. There is no isolated problem; every problem is related to a larger problem. The only problems worth worrying about are those which affect people. To approach problems with these assumptions is to approach them sensibly, reasonably, logically, and therefore, it is assumed, correctly.

Of course, these assumptions are not new to the schoolchild, for they are also implicit in most of the home training he has received. One day Madame Favre was sitting in front of her house sewing. Three-year-old Dédou, who was playing in

the street, went too near the gutter and was about to get muddy. His mother
looked up and called sharply to him:

"Dédou, you'll get yourself dirty. Get away from there!" Dédou was usually a
docile child, but this time a naughty urge got the better of him. He looked up
impudently and shouted:

"Why?"

His mother gave him a glance that he would remember and said through her
teeth:

"Because I tell you to be good ("sage"). Because you're the child and I'm the
mother. Because we're not animals. That's the way it is! So!"

Madame Favre was not merely exerting her authority. She was unwittingly
explaining that there was a principle involved in this situation over which Dédou
had no control. He could only recognize it and accept it. She was explaining that
both she and he were part of a family and that each had a role that must be
maintained. She was emphasizing the importance of human dignity. She was
saying that those were the facts, pleasant or unpleasant, and that his only reasonable course of action was to conform.

There is no conflict between the principles of thought and action taught in the
home and those taught in the school. The only difference is that in school they
are taught formally. The basic assumptions are fundamentally the same.

Three afternoons a week a group of older children stayed at school from four to
four thirty to study English in the special course which the teachers and the
primary inspector had authorized me to teach. One day, not long after I began to
teach this course, I was talking to Henri Favre, the father of one of my pupils.

"How's Jacqueline doing in the English class?" he asked.

I was embarrassed because Jacqueline was the worst student in the class. Physically mature for her thirteen years, she was merely putting in time in school until
her fourteenth birthday. She was attending the English class only because of its
prestige value. However, I did not want to hurt her father's feelings, so I commented as favorably as I could:

"Oh, she's making progress."

Henri Favre looked pleased but surprised. "I'm glad," he said, "but, you know, it
astonishes me because she's lazy and she's not very intelligent."

It took time for me to become accustomed to the honest, objective manner in
which parents openly appraised the intelligence of their children. They recognize
the fact that some people are more intelligent than others, and since it is a fact it
must be recognized, faced, and accepted like all other facts. They see no point in
hiding it, or denying it, or even in minimizing it. One cannot hide what is perfectly
evident to everyone, and little purpose would be served by minimizing it. It is
better to accept such facts as they exist and to try to make the most of them.
Consequently, parents, teachers and children discuss differences in intelligence
with relative frankness. When a parent says, "My child is not so intelligent as
yours," he is not fishing for a compliment; he is stating a fact.

The first day I attended Madame Girard's class I was shocked at the way in which
she insisted on discussing her pupils with me in front of them. After each child
in the Preparatory Course recited she stopped the recitation to give me an analysis
of his capacity.

"There's an intelligent little one," she said after Jeanne Reynard had answered
a question. "She works hard, too. It's a pleasure to teach a child like that."

Renée Chanon failed to answer her question. "There's Renée. Not stupid, but
lazy. She sits there distracted with her mouth open all day. And untidy! You
can't expect much of that kind of girl."

Marie Père tried painfully to give some kind of answer to her question but
Madame Girard cut her off and gave me a look of despair. "Poor Marie. She
tries, but—I think all is not right." She tapped her forehead significantly with her

forefinger. Marie squirmed in her seat and looked as unhappy as I felt over the situation, but the recitation and the commentary moved on until all the children had had their turn.

Eventually I became accustomed to hearing teachers and parents discuss the children in front of them, although I was never able to force myself to speak with frankness in the presence of the children. I am sure that my lack of forthrightness was not considered an indication of tact, however. It was taken simply as an indication that I was no judge of intelligence.

Since children differ in the degree of their intelligence and since there is no point in hiding this no one expects them all to achieve the same standard of performance. Each one is expected simply to do his best, depending on his own individual capacity. This means that there is a different standard of intellectual performance for each child in the school. Of course, no formal recognition is given to the existence of different standards. The system is simpler than that. The teacher, as she gets to know a child, inevitably makes a judgment concerning his intellectual potentialities, and once this judgment is made she expects the child to live up to her conception of his potentialities. The goal she unconsciously sets for each child is high, probably too high for the child to reach, but she exerts constant pressure on him to make an effort to live up to it.

Only the child who makes an extraordinary effort to fulfill his individual potentialities escapes punishment. Georges Vincent, one of the brightest boys in the school, does far better in his lessons than most of the children, but he receives the most sarcastic criticism of which Madame Vernet is capable because she believes his performance could be even better than it is. On the other hand, Marie Père receives very little criticism because it is recognized that she does the best she can with her limited capacity for learning. After her class had been learning how to write the alphabet Madame Girard said to her mother one day:

"Marie is doing very well. She has learned how to make only three letters, but she makes them quite neatly."

The judgment a teacher makes concerning the potentialities of a child is based entirely on her common-sense observations. She knows about objective intelligence tests, for she has studied testing in Normal School, but she is skeptical of the usefulness and validity of objective tests. She is timid about expressing this skepticism —which, incidentally, is shared by her superior, the primary inspector—because she knows that "modern" education lays heavy stress on objective tests, and she does not like to be considered backward. However, she has confidence in her own judgment of a child's capacity, which almost always coincides with the judgment made by the child's parents and friends.

"Why," asked Monsieur Valentini, "should the teachers take the time and trouble to give these tests to their children only to find out what is already obvious?"

Differences in intelligence are recognized, and a multiple standard is set up for intellectual performance. Differences in personality and home training are also recognized, but there is a rigorous, single standard for social behavior. The teachers may understand the reasons for a child's misbehavior. They are not surprised that Joseph Mariano, the motherless child of a migrant laborer, is naughtier than Henri-Paul Favre, whose parents are benevolently strict in the matter of home training. To understand these differences is not to accept them, however. They refuse to tolerate misbehavior for any reason. Deviation from the standard set for all children brings immediate and stern punishment.

The code of social behavior which the teachers enforce is essentially the same that most parents have tried to maintain at home. The function of the teachers is to carry on this home discipline and to make up for omissions of lax parents. Since most parents are lax in some respect, this means that for most children the discipline is harsher at school than at home.

Whenever I went to Madame Vernet's classroom all the children would rise at once and say in chorus, "*Bonjour, Monsieur.*" They would remain standing until Madame Vernet told them to sit down. In Madame Girard's room the six-year-olds would stand up, but the younger ones had to be prompted by Madame Girard who said to them harshly:

"Well! What does one do when a grownup enters the room? One stands up straight and says '*Bonjour, Monsieur.*' " Then the little children would rise and the class would perform as directed.

It disturbed me that I should disrupt the class activities when I really wanted to slip in unobserved, so I asked Madame Vernet if this rite could be omitted when I came in. She refused.

"We're glad when you come in," she said. "It gives the children a chance to practice their lesson in politeness which they need so badly."

It is as important for the children to be polite in school as it is for them to learn their lessons. They must never speak to a teacher or to any adult without addressing her or him directly as "*Mademoiselle*" or "*Madame*" or "*Monsieur.*" If an adult stops and greets them they must extend their right hand in a forthright manner. A boy must, of course, remove his hat when he is greeting someone; simply touching one's finger to a hat is insufficient. Children must never dispute the word of the teacher. Whatever she says must be accepted respectfully, absolutely and without other comment than "*Oui, Madame*" or "*Non, Madame.*" If the teacher is in error, it is up to her to discover the fact. A child must never contradict.

In all circumstances a child must *parler comme il faut*, that is, he must speak clearly and directly. He must not talk to another child in the classroom without the teacher's permission. If he wants to speak to the teacher he should hold up one finger and wait patiently for her to recognize him. He should not at the same time wave his finger and call out in a loud whisper, "'*dame, 'dame!*"

Children must also be careful *se tenir comme il faut* at all times. This means that they must sit up straight and keep their hands no lower than the level of the desk top. They must not slouch or drape themselves over their desk. When they stand they must stand erect, squarely on both feet, without leaning on the desk in front of them.

Neatness is another virtue that is stressed. Children have already learned to play without getting dirty; now they must learn to work neatly. They must not get ink on their hands or clothing or books. The papers they write must be free of blots and smudges. An arithmetic paper with the correct answers is unacceptable if the problems are not written neatly. Finger prints and careless writing are an infraction almost as serious as a wrong answer.

The teachers try to maintain a high standard of personal cleanliness among the children, but home conditions beyond their control sometimes frustrate their efforts. If a child is always dirty they do what they can to teach him to keep himself clean, taking care not to criticize his parents. Only if the dirt is a menace to the health of the other children will they remonstrate with the parents. Of course, if a child is ill he is sent home at once. Running noses and coughs, however, are accepted as part of the normal winter condition.

The children are taught that needless daring is not a virtue. Physical danger must be faced only when it cannot be avoided. The teachers stress this lesson not only because it is part of the code but also because they feel the weight of responsibility for the safety of the children at school. They enforce the safety rules rigorously. Children must not climb on walls or jump from high banks. They must not bring knives to school. They must not expose other children to danger. Rough games are avoided. If two children start to fight they are separated, and both of them are punished, regardless of who started the fight and regardless of who was "in the right." Complete tolerance is shown to verbal attacks, but physical aggression is taboo.

If a child is hurt he tries to hide the pain. At recess one afternoon Jules Marchal jumped from a wall and hurt his arm. Everyone crowded around, but little pity was shown in spite of the fact that Jules was obviously in pain. He was used, rather, as an object lesson to remind the other children that they often get hurt when they disobey the rules. To minimize the criticism he was receiving from both teachers and children, Jules pretended he was not really hurt. He smiled and started to play, but his face was white and he was unsteady on his feet. He stayed at school the rest of the afternoon and discovered only that evening when his parents took him to the doctor, that his arm was broken. A child in Jules' predicament learns to keep his feelings to himself. Expressing them only exposes him to criticism. I do not mean to imply that Madame Vernet felt no personal sympathy for Jules, in this case, incidentally. Her pity was simply overshadowed by her desire to clear herself of the responsibility for this mishap.

The worst sin of all—that is, the worst sin that could conceivably be committed by a schoolchild—is dishonesty in the form of either lying or stealing. For both these offenses a child is severely punished. If it is proven that a child has knowingly and maliciously taken an object which does not belong to him, he is even more severely punished.

I observed and heard of very few cases of dishonesty among the children, however. Two of the children were said to be habitual cheaters at school, and they were frequently punished. The only sensational case of dishonesty I knew of was that of one of the youngest girls, whose father came to school one day and told Madame Girard that she had taken forty francs from his purse. When she was questioned she denied having done it. The father then went to the store and asked Monsieur Reynard if she had been there. Monsieur Reynard said that she had come in that morning to buy forty francs' worth of chewing gum. This girl received the most severe punishment given at the school during the year. No doubt her punishment at home was even more severe.

This instance of collaboration between home and school in the enforcement of the social code is typical. The parents welcome the cooperation of the teachers and complain only if the teachers are insufficiently harsh. In general, they say that the teachers are more successful in disciplining the children than they, the parents, are. Times have changed, they say. When *they* were children they feared their parents and would not dare to offend them. Now, they say, children are impolite. They disobey their parents and insult them with impunity. Only the teachers can discipline them.

To an American, however, the children of Peyrane seem incredibly well behaved. They are courteous, docile, gentle, cooperative, respectful. They seem deficient in daring, but on the other hand there is no malicious destruction of property by gangs of children. They are cruel-tongued to their equals, but they are gentle and patient with children younger than they. Above all they have a sense of dignity and social poise. Regardless of what complaining parents say, the children of Peyrane appear to accept the social yoke that is placed on them. The teachers rarely have to punish a serious infraction. Their principal disciplinary efforts are directed toward insisting on courtesy and neatness, and toward repressing restlessness and talking out of turn.

The directives of the Department of National Education expressly forbid the infliction of physical pain as a punishment of children. There is no conflict between this injunction and the attitudes of the teachers, or even of the parents, of Peyrane, for they seem to find physical punishment neither desirable nor effective. Madame Girard, when she is pushed to the limit of her patience, may give a spank on the buttocks or she may tug a child's hair or tweak his ear, but this is only incidental to the official punishment she is about to give.

Usually there is an attempt to make the punishment appropriate to the offense. If a child's fault lies in insufficient work, he is made to do extra work. If his work is careless he has to do it over again until it is done properly. This usually means that he has to make up work outside of regular school hours—during recess, after school, or on Thursday when the school is closed. A child may even be asked to go to the teacher's house to make up work on Sunday. This punishment means, of course, that the child is deprived of playtime or that he is unable to do chores expected of him at home. This, in turn, means that he will receive another punishment at home.

The punishment for restlessness in class might also be called appropriate. One afternoon when I went to school during recess I saw only the four-year-olds and the older children in the playground. When I asked Madame Girard where her five- and six-year-olds were, she said, "They were naughty after lunch. They fidgeted so much that I kept them in at recess." I looked in the classroom and saw the "little ones" all sitting at their desks with their hands folded in front of them. They were having no recess, and it was an hour and a half before school would be dismissed. However, they grasped at a straw. When they saw me they jumped to their feet and chorused, "*Bonjour, Monsieur*" so politely that Madame Girard relented and let them go out on the playground for the remaining few minutes. Perhaps she, too, welcomed this way out, for it is against the regulations to deprive children of recess.

The most unusual punishment and apparently the most effective one lies in shaming a child by isolating him and pitting the rest of his society against him. Every effort is made to make him feel ridiculous or guilty in the eyes of others. Minor infractions bring forth a stream of mocking criticism from the teacher as she calls on the rest of the class to bear witness to the misbehavior. If a visitor is present the teacher includes him in the jury.

Since I was at school so frequently I was pressed into jury service more often than I wished. A scene that took place in Madame Vernet's room one day after she had given a dictation was typical. I arrived just as she was going over the children's papers.

"Ah, *Monsieur*, you arrive just at the right moment," she said, "Just look at this dictation of Laure Voisin. Have you ever seen anything so careless, so untidy? Six mistakes in three lines, and an ink smudge to end it with!"

She was speaking to me, but her eyes were flashing at Laure who sat staring at her desk.

"Just look, *Monsieur*," she went on. "She wrote *ses* instead of *c'est*, so the sentence has no meaning at all. Stupid! It's only stupidity—and I used to think she was fairly intelligent."

She paused for these remarks to sink in.

"And lazy. Maybe she could do good work if she wants to. But, no, she prefers to sit there and dream! And to think that this girl insists on presenting herself for the *certificat primaire*! I wouldn't shame the school or her parents by letting her try. What candidate could pass who writes *ses* instead of *c'est* on a dictation?"

The other children laughed mockingly. I would have preferred to be elsewhere. Laure winced and tears came.

"That's right. Now you cry. As though that would help you. It's not by crying that you'll learn to write a dictation. No, you will stay in after school and we shall do that dictation over until you do it right."

A child is also effectively ashamed if his performance, which should be good but is not, is compared with the performance of another child which is better than might be expected. Madame Druetta's class was practicing the multiplication tables one day. Marie Bourgues was one of the good pupils in the class, but she was weak on the multiplication tables.

"What is seven times nine, Marie?"

"I don't know, *Madame*."

"Ah! She doesn't know seven times nine. Everyone in this class knows that. Class, what is seven times nine?"

The class roared the answer.

"You see, Marie, everyone in the room knew but you. Do you know seven times eight?"

". . ."

"No, of course she doesn't. Aren't you ashamed? Even Alain Jouvaud knows seven times eight, and he's been out of school sick for a month. What is seven times eight, Alain?"

"Fifty-six, *Madame*."

"You see, Marie. Even Alain knew, and he's not as intelligent as you, either. You haven't worked on this or you'd know it. Have you?"

"*Non, Madame*."

"Well, you stay in here during recess and learn the table of sevens, and if you don't learn it then you can stay in after school. Do you understand?"

"*Oui, Madame*."

Since Johany Wylie knew no French when he entered Madame Girard's class she found him a convenient shaming instrument. When another child failed to learn something which Johany had learned she could always say: "You see, even Johany knows that, and only a few months ago he didn't even know French!" (The name "Johany" was Madame Girard's own version of Jonathan.)

A child's shame may be increased by exposing his guilt to a larger group. Madame Vernet may go to the door and call Madame Girard into her classroom to witness a particularly deplorable recitation. The situation may be extended even beyond the school. One day Alphonse Peretti turned in a *copie* which was full of errors, carelessly written, and covered with smudges. Later in the day he was sent with a group of children to catechism at the church. The church is at the top of the hill; the school is at the bottom, so the children had to go through the whole village to reach the church. Before Alphonse left the school, Madame Vernet pinned the *copie* to his back so that his guilt would be exposed to the attention and mockery of everyone who saw him on the street. The villagers can be counted on to cooperate.

The little girl who took forty francs from her father's purse to buy chewing gum was punished by having pinned on her back a big sign saying VOLEUSE. During recess she was forced to walk in a circle around the playground while the other children were encouraged to run after her taunting her and crying "Thief! Thief!" This was the most severe case of shaming which I observed.

For minor infractions a child is usually put *au piquet*, a punishment which combines mild social ridicule with immobilization in an awkward position. The child kneels a few inches away from the wall at the front of the room, places his forehead against the wall and remains there with his hands folded on top of his head until the punishment is ended. The children consider the *piquet* punishment more severe when, instead of kneeling, the child is asked to stand with his forehead against the wall and with his hands on his head. To increase the ridicule and shame of punishment the teacher may have the culprit spend the recess quarter-hour walking around a small circle on the schoolground with his hands folded on his head. It is not unusual during recess to see six or eight children being punished together, walking round and round in a circle with the hands atop their heads, stoically accepting the taunts that other children may shout at them from time to time.

Being put *au piquet* is a punishment primarily for the four-, five-, and six-year-old children. The prevalence of this punishment in Madame Girard's classroom may to a degree be attributed to the personality of Madame Girard, but it may also be attributed to the fact that the younger children are naturally more restless and less accustomed to discipline than the older children in Madame Vernet's and Madame Druetta's classrooms. By the time the children have been promoted to higher grades they have accepted the discipline imposed on them.

If, however, an older child forgets his dignity and reverts to misbehavior more typical of smaller children, he is shamed by being punished as though he were still a small child. One day in Madame Vernet's class Odette and Alphonse Peretti seemed unable to keep from talking to each other. Madame Vernet reprimanded them several times, but they persisted. Finally she told them they were acting like babies, and she sent them to Madame Girard's classroom where they were put *au piquet* beside five-year-old Léon Pascal, who was being punished.

A child being punished can expect no pity from any quarter. Neither tears nor a face twisted in distress arouse sympathy. To the contrary, tears may release a new torrent of sarcastic remarks from the teacher and mocking epithets from the children. The underdog arouses no pity if he is being justly punished. Even his parents participate in the recrimination unless, as we have seen, the child can show that the teacher has unjustly accused him or discriminated against him. If a punishment is equitably inflicted, the child stands completely alone. What solace he can find he must find within himself.

Outside of school and away from adult supervision the children as a group appear to accept the responsibility of maintaining the social code. Joseph Mariano has been mentioned several times because he seems to reject almost every point in the code and is consequently the child most punished in school. Outside of class when the children are playing in the streets they continue to shame Joseph Mariano and to outlaw him as the teacher does in school.

They obviously enjoy singling out an individual and shaming him when his behavior is unacceptable, even in the slightest degree. A child who forgets to wipe his running nose will find his playmates howling at him: "*Uuuuuuuu, Uuuuuuuu, Uuuuuuuu, la chandelle, la chandelle!*" and taunting him with their forefinger and middle finger crooked to imitate the stream pouring from his nose. (*La chandelle* means candle. The child's nose is dripping like a candle.)

When the teacher is forced to leave the schoolroom she often appoints a child to police the room. On her return the observer faithfully makes his report, and she punishes culprits without hesitating. The other children, even the culprits, accept this procedure and seem to harbor no resentment against the informer. The child who informs spontaneously on his fellows, however, without having had the responsibility placed on him by the teacher, is subject to the disapproval of the other children. One of the most infuriating insults a child can fling at another during a quarrel is *mouchard* (stoolpigeon). The teacher also discourages the telltale as a matter of principle and because sometimes the telltale forces her to punish misbehavior which she would prefer to ignore. The self-appointed informer who receives as thanks only the most barbed remarks of the teacher learns that it is better not to get involved with those in authority.

The child who is asked by the teacher to proctor the room during her absence is usually one of the teacher's pets. The teachers say they avoid favoring any child, but the children and the children's parents to whom I talked were surprised that I should even ask if the teachers had pets. Of course teachers have pets, they said! Teachers always have pets! Teachers have natural likes and dislikes as everyone else does. It would be silly to expect them to treat all the children exactly alike.

Because it seems inevitable that some children should be favored, little resentment is harbored against the teachers' pets. So long as a teacher distributes punishments justly and impartially, no one objects if she singles out a few pupils to whom she grants special favors. Favors are not necessarily a part of the official system of punishments and rewards. They may or may not be related to virtue and justice. They are often granted simply on the basis of indefinable and rather mysterious personal tastes. Instead of showing resentment toward a favored child, the other children may even join with the teacher in favoring him.

During the year that he was a pupil in the school of Peyrane, Johany Wylie was granted preferential treatment to an unusual degree. We pleaded with the teachers to treat him exactly as they treated all the children, but our pleas accomplished nothing. He was allowed to roam around the school at will. If he got bored sitting at his desk in Madame Girard's room, he went into Madame Vernet's room to sit next to Odette Peretti, the older girl he had adopted as his foster mother in the school. Madame Vernet allowed her to interrupt her lessons "to amuse Johany." Madame Girard usually chose him to check on the behavior of the other children while she was out of the room. The other children did what they could to increase his preferential treatment. They let him take their place at the head of the line. They brought him chewing gum and candy. The older boys let him join their games, and they played with him gently. The older girls mothered him and cuddled him as much as he would allow.

This case of favoritism was extreme, of course. No child of Peyrane could ever have hoped to receive this treatment. Johany was outside the system, and the rules did not apply to him. He was not expected to grow up in Peyrane so there was no need to force him into the pattern. The teachers felt no responsibility for the future of Johany as a citizen of the village. The children did not see in him a competitor. Their parents did not see in his freedom from discipline an insult to their family dignity. All felt that they could, without qualms and without criticism, follow their strong but usually frustrated inclination to spoil little children.

This feeling was intensified by the fact that Johany was considered a guest in Peyrane and must therefore be accorded privileges which the inhabitants deny themselves. As an American child, he was an exotic guest who aroused unusual interest. Finally, as a foreign child, he aroused the missionary zeal of the teachers. When I complained to Madame Vernet about his preferential treatment, she always said:

"Oh, *Monsieur*, he's with us only a few months. That's not long for us to teach him to speak French. If he doesn't have a good time in school he might not come. And we want him to love France and have good memories of it."

Johany was obviously a very special case. No amount of insistence on the part of his parents could make him fit into the regular framework of school discipline. To accomplish this we should have had to settle in Peyrane as permanent residents.

Children who are not teachers' pets may receive recognition and privileges by earning them through the official system of rewards, called the *système des bons points*. A *bon point* is usually a little colored print of some object—a flower, an animal, a provincial costume, etc.—of the type traditionally called *image d'Epinal*. Chocolate-candy manufacturers often package these prints as prizes, and they are printed in series so that children may be induced to collect complete series to paste in an album. The teachers may buy the prints in wholesale lots from an *imagerie*, a printing house specializing in these pictures.

According to this system of rewards, a child is presented a *bon point* for each meritorious act. He saves his *bons points*, and when he has received twenty of them he is entitled to receive a special prize. For the younger children the prize is usually a piece of candy, but by the time children are six years old they are considered big enough to be awarded "something more serious." Then they are allowed to go check the time by the town clock, to carry a message to one of the teachers, to distribute papers for the day. They may have their name written in a special notebook in which Madame Girard records unusual rewards of merit. In Madame Vernet's room the virtuous child's name is recorded on the weekly Honor List posted on the board.

The teachers say that the *système des bons points* effectively motivates children to do their best to surpass their comrades in both intellectual and social behavior.

To the observer, however, it seems that there are two rewards which are still more effective in motivating the children to attain the high intellectual and social standards set for them.

The unusually intelligent and ambitious child is rewarded by his feeling of pride. A higher level of performance is expected of him, and the teacher devotes more time and effort to teaching him individually than to the other children. He receives no softer words and no more praise than they, because the level of the teacher's expectation is always fixed a little higher than the level of his actual performance. He receives no more extra favors than other children. He even has to spend more time studying than they, because more is expected of him. He is set apart from other children. The teachers, his parents, and the children tell him that he is more intelligent than they, and they place more responsibility on him. In family council it has been formally decided that if he lives up to expectations he will be sent away to learn a trade or prepare to enter a profession or government work. To accomplish this ambition the familiy must make financial sacrifices of which the child is made keenly aware. Responsibility has been placed on him in such a way that there is no escaping it, and he is constantly reminded of it by the teachers and his parents. This pressure supplies ample motivation for him to do his best to succeed in school.

This sort of motivation is completely lacking to the other children, of course. They have no lofty ambitions. The average child knows that he is not especially intelligent; he has been told so often enough by his teachers and by his parents. It would not occur to him to envy the brightest pupil, for it would not be *raisonnable* to entertain ambitions which obviously could not be realized. On the other hand, he knows he is not stupid and that he can get along in life.

Jacques Leporatti was considered an average student, just intelligent enough so that with great effort he passed the Primary Certificate exams. When I asked him why he worked so hard at his lessons his reply was prompt and forthright:

"Pour qu'on me laisse tranquille!" ("So people will leave me alone!")

For Jacques and for most of the children of the school the most substantial reward for good behavior and hard work lies in *not* bringing shame to themselves and to their family, in *not* being punished, in *not* being saddled with avoidable responsibilities. They know that if their performace is satisfactory they will be left to themselves to enjoy the normal routine of life with a minimum of interference from authority of any kind. This may seem a negative, uncreative kind of gratification, but to the average child it is sufficient.

The best pupils, like Georges Vincent, leave Peyrane when they are twelve years old to continue their studies in a more advanced school in the city. The poor pupils, like Jacqueline Favre, drop out of school without formalities on their fourteenth birthday. If a child is sufficiently intelligent, however, and if he is willing to work hard he is groomed to become a candidate for the *certificat d'études primaires*. This certificate, framed and hung in the *salle* (the kitchen–living room), will bring honor to his family and will be a source of pride for him the rest of his life. Its possession brings practical advantages, too, for it is the minimum educational requirement for any kind of government position and for many other types of employment. A child of fourteen may not be interested in the kind of work requiring the Primary Certificate, but who knows? Perhaps some day for some reason he may want to qualify for the position of postman. If the certificate can be obtained with only extra hard work it is better to try for it as a hedge against the future.

For Madame Vernet, the Primary Certificate Examination is professionally the most important event of the year. The villagers and to a certain degree her colleagues and superiors judge her ability as a teacher on the performance of her candidates at the examination. It is given at Gordes, the *chef-lieu* of the canton seven miles from Peyrane. It is administered by Monsieur Valentini, the primary inspector, with the aid of primary school teachers called in from other cantons.

Thus the candidates from Peyrane are placed in competition with candidates from all the other primary schools of the canton, and their work is evaluated by judges living outside the canton. The whole situation is beyond the control of the local teachers. Whether the candidates will bring shame or honor to Madame Vernet depends entirely on the candidates themselves.

Consequently Madame Vernet, like all the teachers of the Concluding Course of Primary Schools, is preoccupied with the question of which students to sponsor as candidates. Her sponsorship is not essential. A student may present himself as a candidate independently, but if Madame Vernet believes that he is likely to disgrace himself and her at the examination it is unlikely that he will persist in the face of her opposition.

In the spring of 1951 Madame Vernet chose as students likely to succeed Jules Marchal, Félix Raboul, and Jacques Leporatti. Laure Voisin also insisted on being a candidate, and although Madame Vernet told her she had no chance of passing the examination Laure could not be dissuaded. Madame Vernet grudgingly included her in the group, insisting that there was no hope but offering to help her as best she could.

The examination was to take place at the end of May, and during April and May, Madame Vernet devoted most of her time and effort to tutoring her three candidates and Laure Voisin. They were assigned extra lessons. Jules and Jacques stopped coming to my English class. The group stayed on at school after four o'clock almost every day for an hour or more. They went to Madame Vernet's apartment for tutoring sessions on Thursday and on Sunday. They were excused from chores at home so that they might spend all their free time studying.

The nature of the examination is specifically defined by the Department of National Education. It consists of a four-hour written examination in the morning followed by a two-hour oral examination in the afternoon. The subject matters and grading system are specified as follows:

WRITTEN EXAMINATION

Subject	To pass, a candidate must get a grade of at least:

I. Dictation, followed by questions on:
  1. General understanding of the text
  2. Grammar
  3. Explanation of difficult words
	10 out of a possible perfect grade of 20

II. Mathematics
  1. Geometry
  2. Arithmetic
  3. Metric system
	10 out of 20

III. Composition
  1. A letter on a given subject
  2. A free subject
	5 out of 10 on composition
	2½ out of 5 on penmanship

ORAL EXAMINATION

Subject	To pass, a candidate must get a grade of at least:	
I. Geography	2½ out of 5	The candidate must
II. History	2½ out of 5	get a total of 10
III. Sciences	5 out of 10	points in this group
IV. Mental calculation	No points given, but must be acceptable	
V. Drawing (for boys) Sewing (for girls)	No points given, but must be acceptable	
VI. Reading aloud, recitation, or singing	No points given, but must be acceptable	

To pass the examination the candidate must receive a total of at least forty points, so that he may get a low grade in one subject and catch up in another—provided, of course, that he receives at least the minimum grade in each subject. The examiners have the right to waive the rules and make a special decision in extraordinary cases, but such exceptions are rarely made. All the people I questioned about the examination—teachers, parents, and children—agree that the examiners and examination are severe but fair. There is no need to make special exceptions; a child who fails to pass does not deserve to pass.

Madame Vernet does not, of course, know the exact questions which are to be asked on the examination, but from her experience as teacher and examiner (since she is called to proctor exams in other cantons) she knows the kind of question which is usually asked. She knows the usual mistakes that are made. She knows which mistakes are passed over tolerantly and which ones are catastrophic to the chances of a candidate. She knows, for instance, that to write *ses* for *c'est* on a dictation may mean failure, whereas other mistakes may not even be counted. There are other peculiarities she is aware of. She knows that a student strong in arithmetic but weak in composition has a better chance of passing than a student weak in arithmetic and strong in composition, because a perfect grade may be given in arithmetic, but a composition is never given a perfect grade. She knows that a child who does well in French and mathematics is almost never failed regardless of his performance in the oral examination.

It is with all these points in mind that Madame Vernet drills her candidates for the last few weeks before the examination. Each child has weaknesses peculiar to him, some of which do not matter and some of which are particularly vulnerable. If the weakness is too great to overcome, then the child must be drilled in his strong subjects so that he may pick up enough points in them to make up for his deficiencies.

On the morning of the examination two carloads of people left Peyrane at seven o'clock and went down the hill on the little road toward Gordes. Jules Marchal was riding with his parents in their 1923 Renault. In my car were Madame Vernet, Jacques Leporatti, Laure Voisin, and her mother. A few kilometers from Peyrane we stopped and picked up the Raboul family who were accompanying Félix. I was surprised that so many parents make the effort to go with their children to the examination, for in most cases it is a serious economic sacrifice to give up a day's work. Yet, of the parents of our four candidates only the Leporattis, the poorest of all, stayed at home. When I asked Monsieur Marchal why so many parents came he said:

"*Qu'est-ce que vous voulez?* Jules asked us to come. He said he'd feel more sure of himself if we were there. And even if I had stayed at home I'd have been too upset to work."

The ordeal of the child is the ordeal of the family. Each child knows this. He bears the weight of the family dignity on his shoulders.

When we stopped to pick up the Rabouls we rearranged ourselves in the cars so that all the parents were in Monsieur Marchal's car and the four candidates were with Madame Vernet in my car. She wanted to get them together with her for the last few minutes so that she could go over the situation again with them. As we drove along she talked with each child, warning him against the mistakes he usually made, and drilling them all on points which were sure, she felt, to be included in any examination.

When we arrive at Gordes, the *place* was full of cars, and the schoolyard was filled with parents, teachers, and children standing quietly in little groups, too tense to carry on a normal conversation. Finally, at eight o'clock Monsieur Valentini clapped his hands, and the candidates and examiners filed into the classrooms. The parents drifted out of the school yard. The mothers sat down in little groups on steps in the *place* and brought out their handwork. Some of the fathers took advantage of the trip to Gordes to carry out business; others gathered in the café. The teachers who were not serving as examiners remained in the school yard and sat talking in little groups.

A few minutes before ten o'clock the parents were all back in the school yard waiting for the children to emerge for their fifteen-minute recess. The bell rang, and they came out, blinking their eyes in the mid-morning sun. Their mothers gave them bread and chocolate, and Madame Vernet gathered the children around her to find out what questions they had been asked and how they had answered. She tried to evaluate the work of each child so that he might know if he had made enough points to give him a safe margin or if he had done so poorly that he would have to be particularly careful in the rest of the test. As the children left to go back to the examination she reminded them of pitfalls they should avoid the rest of the morning.

At twelve o'clock the parents were back again to take their children off for a picnic lunch and a rest until the oral examination began at two o'clock. I went with the teachers and examiners to the special lunch that had been prepared at the village inn. Monsieur Valentini did not come with us. When I asked one of the teachers why he was not included, she said:

"We like each other, but we don't feel comfortable together."

The situation at the lunch was already somewhat awkward because the examiners and the teachers of the candidates were thrown together. There was banter and professional gossip during the meal, but several of the teachers also talked quietly and earnestly with the examiners sitting next to them. Before lunch Madame Vernet had apologized for not sitting next to me, for she said that she wanted to take advantage of the opportunity to speak to a friend of hers. Later she explained that the friend was a teacher from a neighboring canton who was serving as examiner in that canton. During the lunch she had tried to find out how the candidates from Peyrane were faring, but she did not try to probe too indiscreetly, for she knew that the next week the roles would be reversed.

At two o'clock everyone assembled in the school yard again, and the oral examination began. By four o'clock the written examinations had all been graded and the oral examinations had ended. The parents and children and teachers waited nervously outside while Monsieur Valentini met with the examiners. Finally he emerged, carrying under his arm the certificates, each bearing his signature and the name of a successful candidate. He stood in the middle of the school yard and called off the names. One at a time the children came forward and were given their certificates. There was no applause, no word of congratulation, no handshake. When Monsieur Valentini had finished I could recognize the successful candidates and their families only by the smiles on their faces.

There was a smile on the face of the children who had failed, too, but it was a frozen smile that did not conceal the tears in their eyes. Of the candidates from Peyrane only Laure Voisin had failed, just as Madame Vernet had predicted for several weeks. Madame Voisin was standing near Laure, but neither she nor anyone else made any effort to console the girl. When I moved over toward her, patted her on the shoulder, and tried to say a few consoling words, she looked at me in so bewildered a manner that I felt awkward and left her alone with her disappointment.

On the way back to Peyrane, Madame Vernet, Jacques Leporatti, Madame Voisin, and Laure were in my car. Madame Vernet and Jacques scarcely spoke a word. Madame Voisin talked most of the time. Her eyes were filled with tears as were Laure's. She was as disappointed as her daughter, but the emotions that she felt were turned against Laure. Laure had failed, said Madame Voisin, only because she had not worked hard enough. When her mother and father had tried to get her to study she had sat at a back table in her father's café dreaming with Jacqueline Favre and playing "Babyfoot" with the older boys. It was not the fault of her parents. And it was not the fault of Madame Vernet, who had certainly done her best to keep Laure from disgracing herself. It was Laure's fault and she was getting only what she deserved. It was only too bad that through her laziness she had disgraced her parents. Laure made no attempt to reply to her mother.

The month of June is one of the busiest months in the village and on the farm. The children who have taken the Primary Certificate Examination, now that they have in effect finished their schooling, could usefully be put to work at home. Nevertheless, they continue to go to school until the classes end on the Fourteenth of July. The hard work at school is finished, but the Prize Day Program is approaching. The three teachers spend most of the time in the *Salle des Fêtes* with the children of the school practicing songs, recitations and skits for the program. Laure Voisin did not come back to school after the examination, but Jules Marchal, Jacques Leporatti, and Félix Raboul were there every day. Their families were willing to sacrifice a worker needed at home in order to have their child—a child who had received his Primary Certificate—represent them in the Prize Day Program.

NOTES

1. *Le Livre des Instituteurs* (19th ed., Paris: Le Soudier, 1948), p. 161.
2. Ibid., pp. 150 ff.
3. Jean Zay, "Enseignement du Premier Degré. Instructions relatives à l'application des arrêtés du 23 mars 1938 et du 11 juillet 1938," *Journal officiel*, *Annexe*, 24 September 1938.

6 / The School: Authority, Its Sources and Uses

Richard L. Warren

The role the school in Rebhausen develops in transmitting the traditional culture and mediating cultural change is affected not only by the enduring life of the village and by impelling forces for change such as the factory but also by individuals, groups, and institutions whose established authority impinges on the life of the school. It is clear that an active response by the school to the kind of change Rebhausen is experiencing requires versatility and maneuverability on the part of the faculty. To assess the response the faculty is manifesting, it is necessary to consider the sources and uses of authority which have their origin outside the school.

THE FACULTY AND THE STATE

The school building belongs to the community; the teacher belongs to the state. Neither village officials nor the school principal are involved in the selection of new teachers for their community. In the teaching profession the process of closure and promotion is controlled by the state, a fact which helps to explain the local independence a teacher enjoys.

Undergraduate education for those who decide to become teachers is varied, but all candidates for elementary and junior high school teaching must eventually complete a three-year program at a teachers' college. The program is thorough, requiring work in educational theory, philosophy, theology, psychology, sociology, and all the subjects normally taught in the elementary school, as well as in the activities supervised: music, art, physical education, and handicrafts. The academic preparation is supplemented by practical experience. At the end of each of the first two semesters, student teachers spend between eight to fourteen days in a city school and are given short teaching assignments. During the third, fourth, and fifth semesters, they are to spend at least one day a week in practice teaching under the supervision of the regular teacher. Between the fourth and fifth semesters a month's experience in a rural school is required. Until recently, graduates have been required to be proficient in at least two musical instruments—now only one is required.

At the conclusion of the program, state exams must be passed to establish eligibility for a probationary teaching assignment. The standard format is a five-hour written exam in psychology and a three-hour written exam on methodology. A short oral exam completes the test program. If the student is successful, he is designated as *Beamier auf Wiederruf* (a civil servant with a provisional certification).

The college registers all prospective teachers with the *Oberschulamt* (a regional office of the Ministry of Education), and this office distributes the names to county offices designated by the candidate. The latter has some choice of assignment if his grades are good enough. It has been traditional that beginning teachers be assigned to rural schools, the rationale being that it is a valuable pedagogical experience. Furthermore, it is always harder to recruit teachers for these areas because of the attractions of the city. However, in making the assignment, the county office gives some consideration to the grades on the exams. A "1" may enable a candidate to avoid a rural position.

Three years of probation are required, after which a second examination is administered. In the second of these three years, the teacher reestablishes contact with a professor at the teachers' college and solicits advice in choosing a theme for a lengthy paper on some aspect of teaching. The professor is to read and grade the paper and send the grade to the *Oberschulamt*. In the first year of probation the teacher is also required to write a report on some teaching experience, and at the end of the third year, there is a short oral exam.

The climax of the probationary period is the examination by the *Oberschulrat* (county superintendent—but a state official) of the teacher's classroom performance. This teacher evaluation technique is central to understanding the teacher-pupil and teacher-community relationship. During the three years of probation the *Oberschulrat* visits the teacher at least once each year, to spend time observing, counseling, and directing. (The supervisory role of the principal remains very informal.) Since the school's schedule is on file at the county office, the *Oberschulrat* can decide in advance what classes he will observe. His arrival is not prearranged.

These interim visits are primarily for counseling, although the teacher does receive a grade. But the final visit, a formal evaluation, is perhaps the most important part of the whole process. Teachers at Rebhausen feel that the grade one receives on this examination is crucial. Although a "3" or even a "4" is considered acceptable and passing, a "2" is necessary if one wishes to teach in the city, where the competition for positions is more intense, or if one aspires to become a principal.

In addition to these considerations of subsequent job opportunities, there are many considerations relative to achieving a permanent status in the teaching profession. If, at the end of the probationary period, the teacher's total performance on tests and teaching is satisfactory, he is given a classification of *Beamter auf Lebenzeit* (permanent civil service classification). The prerequisites are considerable:

1. *Job security.* A teacher cannot be fired except for criminal behavior, moral turpitude, or gross neglect of duty. He cannot be transferred to another position without his consent (unless as a punishment established at a trial by Ministry officials). If for some reason his position is eliminated, the state is obligated to find him another position of comparable status.

2. *Remuneration.* The salary scale for teachers, once very poor, has been climbing steadily in the past decade, especially for elementary school teachers, of which there is a shortage. The beginning salary is approximately 800 DM, better than average for wages and fixed salaries throughout the state. The pension plan permits at retirement a pension equal to 75 percent of the last salary. Medical insurance, usually a combination of state and private plans, provides almost complete coverage at reasonable rates. Depending on the size of the town, teachers receive a housing allowance, averaging perhaps 100 DM per month. The community is obligated to locate inexpensive housing for the teachers.

The stakes are high. Herr Könecke was finishing his probationary status and preparing for the final requirements. While I was there, he completed his written exam and his research paper and was subjected to an evaluation of his teaching. The process began when he notified the *Kreisschulamt* (county office of education) that he was ready for the evaluation. It is generally assumed that after this registration a candidate can expect as many as five months to elapse before the evaluation. In Herr Könecke's case, a month was given to make general preparations. Eight days prior to the evaluation he was sent notification of the classes and subjects he was to teach. In his case it was arithmetic to the seventh grade, civics to the fourth grade, and German to the third grade, his own class.

The examining committee consisted of the *Oberschulrat*, an experienced teacher from a nearby village, and Herr Doering, as principal. The combined vote of the three determines the final standing, but Herr Doering explained that the position and prestige of the *Oberschulrat* gives added weight to his evaluation. Herr Doering usually reviews the record of the teacher with the other two. He wants to protect the chances of a promising but erratic teacher and also make it a little easier to get rid of a candidate who is patently incompetent.

On the morning of the evaluation there was an undercurrent of excitement within the faculty. They commiserated with Herr Könecke, talked of their own anxieties and experiences, and described the personalities of the *Oberschulräte* who had examined them. The following is an account of the first period, with the seventh grade class in arithmetic.

8:35   Könecke waits for the three to stop talking and then begins. *Oberschulrat* gets up after a few minutes and walks to the front to ask a girl something. Könecke continues teaching. *Oberschulrat* wanders slowly down the aisle, stops, looks out the window, stands a few minutes by his seat, and then sits down.

8:45   The three start talking about the class. Some children look over at them. They talk louder as Könecke writes on the board.

8:46   *Oberschulrat* gets up again, asks girl for her arithmetic notebook, sits down to look at it. Doering leans over to talk to him.

8:48   *Oberschulrat* gives notebook back to girl.

8:50   Doering says something to *Oberschulrat*.

8:53   *Oberschulrat* gets up again and wanders around, looks at pictures on the wall, then stands in middle of aisle and watches Könecke teach. *Oberschulrat* walks down toward the front, crosses between Könecke and students, and comes back to seat.

8:58   The three are talking again, in voices loud enough to bring glances from students.

9:00   Könecke asks student in front something. Student answers rather softly. *Oberschulrat* says sharply from back, *"Laut, laut"* (loud, loud).

9:01   Doering speaks to *Oberschulrat.*

9:02   Könecke studies his teaching plan before continuing.

9:03   Könecke tells students to get out arithmetic text. *Oberschulrat* gets up and goes to student to look at one.

9:04   *Oberschulrat* wanders down the aisle. With his foot he nudges feet of student which aren't directly under the student. Tells him to straighten up and use good posture. Tells another the same. Könecke goes on teaching. *Oberschulrat* tells another student to use blotter when writing.

9:06   Könecke asks girl a question. She starts to stand up. *Oberschulrat* says, "Sit down; you don't have to stand up during arithmetic."

9:08   Confusion about the books. Könecke has been using one book and the students have another so he has to write the problem on the board. A tense moment. Könecke starts to write. *Oberschulrat* says sharply, "Abbreviate so that the kids can get to work on the problem." *Oberschulrat* tells Könecke some words he can abbreviate.

9:09   *Oberschulrat* talks rather loudly with other two in back.

9:12   *Oberschulrat* gets up and opens window. Doering also opens one.

9:13   *Oberschulrat* starts down the aisle again. Corrects a girl's arithmetic along the way. Stands at board by Könecke. A student answers a question using DM. *Oberschulrat* shakes his head in disgust and says, "You still say DM in the village; you should simply say Mark and write DM."

9:14   *Oberschulrat* walks back up the aisle and talks to Doering. Complains about warm room. Doering opens more windows.

9:15   *Oberschulrat* looks at another notebook as Könecke goes to another problem.

9:16   All three are writing.

9:20   Doering leans back to tell *Oberschulrat* something; the three talk.

9:23   Könecke begins to sum up.

9:25   *Oberschulrat* says something to Doering and then gets up and goes to front and tells Könecke he will take over. There are history dates on the board that the seventh-grade teacher has put there. *Oberschulrat* asks students about them.

9:30   *Oberschulrat* excuses Könecke and tells kids to leave the room for recess.

Of all the activities, problems, and interpersonal relations I observed in the school the events of that morning incorporated most dramatically the forces and cultural directives that create the pressures and constraints characteristic of school life. The *Oberschulrat* was in his early sixties and close to retirement age. He was by reputation and demeanor a crusty, demanding person, who exploited all the authority and prestige of his office—the true embodiment of the stereotyped German bureaucrat. There was little disagreement among the teachers concerning their feelings about him. His presence on the school grounds, practically always unannounced, created an anxiety that permeated the atmosphere.

The teachers have encountered *Oberschulräte* who were more understanding and less imperious, but they have all been subjected to the same evaluation system, which is more overpowering than any single personality acting in an instrumental role. The *Oberschulrat* subjected Herr Könecke to the raw, almost merciless use of power; it was Herr Könecke's climatic experience with closure on his chosen profession. If one distills from these events the *Oberschulrat's* personality and mode of operation, there still remains a concentration of power, the dynamics of which, I am led to conclude, infuse the whole life of the school. It might be said that teachers really earn the job security they acquire with a successful completion of probation. But the psychological and cultural cost accounting required to protect an individual and an institution from the debilitating effects of such power must be measured in something other than mere financial units. The thrust of the power is never really blunted; it flows through the educational system and comes to rest in the classroom, where the student stands vulnerable, obligated to adjust to it, faced with no alternative.

Herr Könecke passed, but just barely. The judgment was that in all three classes he did not encourage the children to participate enough and did too much of the talking himself. His grade, Herr Doering felt, would make it difficult for him ever to become a principal, unless it were to happen late in his career. Furthermore, the chances of his locating a teaching position in Waldstadt (where he lived) were greatly damaged. What seemed to me to be especially tragic was that the whole matrix of power and human relationships provided little support for Herr Könecke in this crucial moment. As was his custom, he prepared thoroughly for the evaluation. His lesson plans (which he had to file with the county office) were worked out in minute detail, including the questions he intended to ask his pupils and the points at which he intened to ask them. But the authority exercised by the state in the system of teacher evaluation is decisive. The system at this point tends to isolate the candidate since there are few, if any, supportive forces at the local level. Teachers view this experience as a confrontation between the individual and the state. For Herr Könecke, it was a kind of isolation he could not afford.

THE FACULTY AND THE CHURCH

The first day of school begins in church. Before the first class, students report to the school grounds and move by classes down Herrenstrasse to the two churches, located three or four blocks apart. Regular worship services are held; the sermons usually concern the religious implications of a new school year.

In his comprehensive 1963 report to higher church authorities, Pfarrer Riedel of the Evangelical Church reported that in the past seven years no parent had refused religious instruction for his child, and no teacher had refused to give religious instruction. These conditions are characteristic of the church-school relationship. Religious instruction is mandatory, at least two to three hours each week in all elementary and secondary schools. The content of instruction is carefully outlined in the syllabus. The checks that the state exercises to insure conformity to the syllabus are imposed on religious instruction as well. The teacher is required to submit an outline covering the year's work, maintain the *Wochenbuch* (a weekly advance outline for each subject), and at the end of the year turn in a detailed report with titles of themes written and of songs and poems memorized.

The extent to which the church's presence pervades the life of the school and the community is no proof that this presence is not somewhat controversial—although less so in Rebhausen than other parts of the state. Two types of schools exist in the state, the *Christliche Gemeinschaft*—or *Simultanschule*, and the *Konfessionsschule*. The latter is found largely in areas which are predominantly Catholic. In the *Konfessionsschule*, religious instruction is given in only one denomination, either Protestant or Catholic. Parents who wish a different content in the instruction for their children must arrange a transfer to another community. The region in which Rebhausen is located has only *Simultan* schools, which is appropriate for Rebhausen with a church affiliation two-thirds Protestant and one-third Catholic. Under this arrangement, both affiliations have equal time in the schools.

Church control over the administration of religious instruction is considerable, based on a Concordat signed with the state. Teachers' performances in religious instruction are evaluated by church authorities. At least once every three years, both teachers and the clergy are observed in the classroom. In the lower grades the teachers generally teach religion; in the upper grades the clergy teach two of the three hours assigned to the subject. The responsibility is, among Rebhausen teachers, somewhat controversial. Teaching religion is not mandatory. A teacher can, when attending a teacher's college, exclude from his program the appropriate courses. But the pressures to take the normal route are considerable; refusal narrows job opportunities. Elementary school teachers are expected to teach all subjects, including religion. If they cannot, they are not as valuable to a school, and if the missing subject is religion, they are less acceptable to the community. All the Rebhausen teachers give religious instruction—some with little enthusiasm.

The church can expect from the Ministry of Education a balance of religious affiliations among faculty members that reflects the balance in the village. The church has also come to expect that the principal will always be of the same religious affiliation as the majority in the village. Herr Doering is Catholic and therefore a notable exception to this arrangement. When the position was vacated four years ago, Herr Doering decided, to the surprise of the community, to compete for it. He registered his intention with the county office.

Although the community has no control over teachers assigned to it, it does exercise some control over the selection of a principal. The county office sends the names of three candidates to the mayor who, along with the *Gemeinderat*, makes the selection. Herr Doering's name was among the three, and the debate was underway. He was a popular individual with teachers, parents, and local officials, but a Catholic in a predominantly Protestant village. The Evangelical Church Council, under the leadership of Pfarrer Riedel, supported his candidacy. There was, however, considerable opposition from church officials at the regional and state levels. They thought it a questionable exception to a workable arrangement. The wishes of the community prevailed and Herr Doering received the appointment—the best measure of the respect and affection he commands in Rebhausen.

Pfarrer Riedel and Pfarrer Kurtz are not only official members of the faculty but also channels of mediation between parents and the school, particularly with regard to issues involving religious instruction. Along with the principal and the mayor, they hear protests from parents who are either too shy to approach teachers directly or who want to build support for some change. Protests are minimal and usually involve an offense to the parent's religious belief system.

From the first day of the first grade, children experience the influence of the church on the life of the school and are constantly reminded of the religious division in the village. The schedule must be adjusted to this fact. When Evangelical children start the day with religious instruction, Catholic children come an hour later. When first graders are being accustomed to the schedule, there are almost daily announcements by teachers, such as "Evangelical children report tomorrow at 7:45 A.M.; Catholic children at 8:45." It is an administrative procedure that gives them an early lesson on the character of the community.

FACULTY AND PARENTS

Within the first few months of a new school year, each teacher is responsible for calling a meeting of parents and seeing that two representatives to the parents' council are elected. When the process is completed, the principal calls a meeting of the council to elect officers and to consider the role of the council and the needs of the school. Rektor Doering convened the meeting in early June; Herr Bergmann, the bank president, was reelected president and Herr Schroder, the town clerk, reelected vice-president. No vote was taken; by informal acclamation the group was happy to have the two men continue in their offices.

Herr Bergmann, representing the council to the principal, reiterated his statement of graduation night that the function of the council is to intervene in the affairs of the school when a problem that requires outside mediation arises between parents and school personnel. He considered the leadership of the school to be in excellent hands and the faculty to be competent. There was, therefore, no need for the council to be active. Herr Doering acquiesced and suggested that members of the council could help the school by bringing parental complaints to him.

The narrow interpretation of the council's interests reflect certain historical and social developments. The council itself is new to the life of the village, a product of a constitutional promulgation following World War II. Second, the traditional social structure of the village has dictated a distinct social distance between teachers and parents. Teachers, along with the mayor and clergy, have occupied the apex in village society. They are *Respektpersonen*, a classification which assigns to them the whole catalog of social amenities the traditional culture has created for ranking members. Since the determination of educational policies and directives is the domain of the state, the operating space of such a council is narrowly constrained.

Third, parents are also generally satisfied with the relationships between teachers and pupils. Most parents experienced a more severe discipline in their school days than that to which their children are exposed. What they observe now is a more comradely relationship, a development they welcome, at least as it manifests itself in the immediate, daily life of the school. However, the trend is also suggestive of a weakening in the discipline and order of the traditional folk life. When parents observe that the children no longer always give teachers their due respect (such as crossing the street to greet them), they feel a tinge of regret. A few parents view this "degeneration" with disgust.

A final factor is the attitude of the faculty. They view the council with mixed emotions. A friendly, cooperative relationship with parents is considered desirable. At the same time, the whole matrix of relationships is, teachers know, relatively unexplored, and therefore unpredictable. They suspect that the council, as an institution, might lead to a habit of parental intervention which, unrestrained, could challenge the professional and personal authority of the teacher. The only control device available to them is a kind of cautious indifference. They prefer to organize the one parent meeting required of them and call additional meetings only when parents are needed to act on a problem the teachers want to solve. The uncertainty of teachers about the council is aggravated by the growing presence of a constituency over which they exercise less influence. Factory parents are not integrated into the life of the community and are not, therefore, subject to the traditional constraints which the folk culture imposes. For them, in this setting at least, teachers are not necessarily *Respektpersonen*.

Confronting the centers of power and prestige in the community, of which the school is one, is for the average Rebhausen native an unwieldy experience. Consequently, when an excited parent shows up at the school to lodge a complaint or submit the same in writing, the whole process is characterized by an awkward, brittle, unpredictable quality. By general understanding, parents are to seek out the teacher during the school day, at any one of the recesses. There are no conference periods set up after school, when a parent can talk quietly and privately. Sometimes this kind of exchange takes place, but it is generally accidental and does not usually involve a redress of grievances. Parents locate a teacher and have five minutes to reach an understanding, while they stand outside the classroom with students milling about as the recess begins and ends. Whatever sense of urgency the parent comes with is usually compounded by conditions forcing a hurried, excited exchange.

On a morning late in February, two parents appeared at the school with particularly vehement protests about low grades their children had received and disciplinary action they had experienced. The mother and grandfather who accosted Frau Schenke became excited, almost abusive. Teachers crowded around to "protect" her. Herr Doering said afterward that, should this sort of thing happen again, he would ring the school bell three times, a signal for the teachers to gather. He thinks it important that the faculty present a united front in the face of criticism. Herr Doering and the faculty feel that this kind of parental behavior is more characteristic of rootless, working-class families attracted to Rebhausen by the factory. They are sure they have an understanding relationship with the natives.

The possible threat of legal action is often present in parent-teacher conflict. Teachers are conscious enough of their legal vulnerability to feel, with some seriousness, that *"Ein Lehrer steht mit einen Fuss in einem Gefängnis"* ("A teacher stands with one foot in prison"). The teacher is, of course, responsible for whatever happens under his supervision, on the school grounds, in the classroom, on a field trip. The kind of incident that can produce legal action was described to me by one of the teachers. A child bumped her head in the classroom, at a time when the teacher had stepped out of the room to speak to a parent. The supervision was not there; the child had headaches for a week following the incident. A suit did not develop only because the faculty was able to persuade the parents not to file one.

Certain legal cases in the state have had such disastrous results for the teachers involved that much has been published by educational organizations to remind teachers of the precautions they should take. The norms for the use of corporal punishment that teachers are expected to follow and that reflect state policy can be summarized as follows:

1. Corporal punishment of girls and of children in the first and second grades is forbidden.
2. In the education of boys, corporal punishment is to be eliminated. It is permitted to be used only in very rare cases.
3. Teachers still on probation are absolutely forbidden to use corporal punishment.
4. In each school there is to be a punishment log or record set up and each act of corporal punishment entered, with a short explanation for its necessity.
5. The teacher must understand that it is a denial of his dignity when he uses corporal punishment.
6. If it must be done, use a stick on the rear end—nothing else.
7. The best advice is just do not use corporal punishment.

The policy of the state is in obvious conflict with the practice of corporal punishment in the Rebhausen school. It is clear that, despite the power the Ministry of Education exercises over the professional advancement of teachers, the latter do not accept the policy as binding, and state authorities do not choose to enforce the policy. They appear willing to wait until legal action, instituted by a parent, forces state intervention. This ambiguity leaves Rebhausen teachers uncertain as to the course such intervention will take. Consequently they are beginning to be more cautious in their use of physical punishment. They agree that native parents consider a teacher weak if he does not use force when appropriate, but that factory parents will be more likely to intervene on behalf of the child when force is used. They conclude it behooves a teacher to know the parent whose child he is about to punish.

THE PRINCIPAL AND THE MAYOR

The relationship between the school and local government depends on the personalities of the two major protagonists, the mayor and the principal, and on the tenacity and specificity with which the mayor carries out his responsibilities. The principal possesses no administrative interest in village government. His domain of authority is limited to the school. However, although faculty salaries are paid by the state, the construction, furnishing, and repair of school buildings are financial obligations of the village, along with the cost of textbooks and other instructional materials. In addition, because the mayor is involved in the selection of the principal, he has a definite administrative interest in the educational system.

The mayor and Herr Doering have a common commitment to help the community and the school adjust to and participate constructively in the urban, industrial culture, which is spreading out from the population centers and engulfing the folk life of their village. They are both deeply and energetically involved in implementing this commitment: the mayor with his long range plan for the expansion of community facilities, and Herr Doering with his interests in an orientation program, driver education, and English instruction. At the same time, their routine administrative duties tend to maintain separate spheres of action.

It is obvious the mayor has considerable respect for Herr Doering's ability as principal and his standing in the community. Otherwise, he would not have supported his appointment as principal. However, the mayor is moved periodically to remind the principal that he is the ranking official in the village. The pretense is usually an inspection of the school, a detail which is technically his responsibility but which he could leave to Herr Doering. When, for example, he showed up one winter day and expressed displeasure with the appearance of the hall (jackets piled high, general disarray), he was reminding Herr Doering of the relationship between the two. It is the kind of maneuver that might be expected where there exists areas of overlapping interests. The protocol traditional among village officials makes it inevitable that the resolution of such a conflict be affected through the blunt exercise of power.

THE FACULTY AS A GROUP

Rebhausen teachers are a friendly, open group of individuals. I spent hours with most of them discussing school life and related subjects, and visited them in their homes for long evenings of conversation and wine. I attended the coffee klatsch, a weekly gathering in the early afternoon of some of the younger teachers, and went bowling with them each month in a dilapidated, but *gemütlich*, old bowling alley in a nearby village.

Faculty interpersonal relationships are often delightfully informal. During "open house" at the new school building, while parents were inspecting and the older teachers were greeting them and answering questions, the younger teachers gathered in the faculty room. With the help of the janitor who located some wine, the cleaning lady who had brought some cake, and Herr Kost who had his guitar, the building got a real dedication.

Yet, however well they come to know each other, the formal social amenities so characteristic of village life are not ignored. Several of the younger women teachers, especially the two who room together, use the informal *Du* with each other and first names. Most of the teachers use formal address and seldom if ever first names, regardless of age and standing. They always shake hands with each other in the morning and are careful to make certain they have not missed anyone, even if the process continues into the second or third period. The custom is warm and friendly, and when they are all together and about to depart—after a bowling evening, for example—the handshaking tradition has all the complexities of an intricate dance routine.

The internal administration of the school creates no appreciable pressure for a teacher unless his performance is patently incompetent and disruptive of the school program. Teachers operate quite independently of the principal. The administrative decisions he has to make concerning such matters as teaching assignments and disciplinary cases among the students are accepted as integral to his position. When a case of dereliction of duty does occur, Herr Doering involves the faculty in the initiatory aspects of the process. During the year we were there a young man, assigned to the school as a physical education instructor on a part-time basis, was erratic in attendance and slipshod in supervising the children. He had been warned often by the principal without results, and because the end of the year was near, Herr Doering felt moved to take official action. He called the faculty together, in the faculty room during the fifteen-minute recess, and had, in Herr Volker's presence, charges of dereliction read and entered in the faculty log book. Herr Volker offered a few lame excuses, and the meeting was dismissed. Herr Doering said it was the first case he had ever carried so far. It meant, he said, that Herr Volker would not be assigned to Rebhausen the next year.

Most decisions over which the faculty holds autonomy are made democratically in faculty meetings. Under Herr Doering's leadership the group works well together. There are normal interpersonal strains, provoked, for example, by the distribution of teaching assignments or by conflicting points of view about appropriate classroom procedures. But the authority exercised by the Ministry of Education eliminates many potential sources of internal conflict.

FACULTY-STUDENT RELATIONS IN RETROSPECT

The methods of discipline used in the school have been described in detail. The attention given to this aspect of school life is not meant to suggest that it is the key to the character of Rebhausen life, but that it is certainly basic to assessing the forceful, definitive enculturation process, which the school structures. Within the framework of the total disciplinary pattern and the general tenor of teacher-student relationships, the specific kind of punishment utilized has less significance. It is one strand in an intricately woven fabric.

Most elements in the teacher-pupil exchange establish and reinforce an unbending relationship, in which the pupil learns to find the important cues to successful behavior and general school performance in the teacher's words and actions. The content of the student's learning experiences is almost always rigidly controlled by the teacher. Opportunities for manifesting and expressing individualistic renditions of this content are constrained within narrow limits. The recitation process is, in this respect, particularly significant. Lines of communication run almost exclusively between individual students and the teacher, with the latter controlling and directing the content of the communication. Only in a few instances does any meaningful exchange occur, in which students examine each other's ideas. In one sense students are, in the classroom, isolated from each other intellectually and therefore more vulnerable to and dependent on the dictates of the teacher.

The almost limitless power of the teacher seems to affect the kind of respect he displays toward students. One has the feeling that the respect must be earned either through academic performance or through appropriate behavior. There is little psychological protection in the classroom for those who have difficulty measuring up to acceptable standards. Their exposure is constant, with few avenues of relief available.

The more informal teacher-student contacts during the school day tend to reinforce the dominant relationship. Any relaxed interchange, before or after class, about the academic content is almost totally absent. Teachers prefer to gather together, smoke, and talk during the recesses. Pupils grow up learning to be ready to perform personal favors for the teachers during these free minutes. They may be asked to buy cigarettes across the street at the drugstore, hurry to the bakery for a teacher's mid-morning snack, get a quart of milk at the dairy, or carry the teacher's briefcase to the classroom when he arrives in the building. They do these things gladly and cheerfully (at least the younger children). The errands present an excuse to leave the building or the playground and are certainly far less onerous than pruning tomato plants or feeding the pigs—which was what their parents sometimes had to do in an era when limited finances forced teachers to engage in such enterprises.

When teachers and students are together there is seldom any release from this highly directive, intense relationship. When the setting is the countryside during a hike or the dormitory at a youth hostel, instead of the school building, the teacher as chaperone has to exercise careful direction of student activities. In spite of such constraints, these shared experiences are meaningful for both teachers and students. It seems that what is required, to affect some kind of release is a third, mediating influence—nature or song.

The mayor had told the eighth graders that he always hoped the village would elect *anständige Leute* to the *Gemeinderat*. During interviews teachers consistently identified *anständig* as the personal trait they considered most important for students to develop. Basically the word means *decent* and *respectable*, but it is undoubtedly invested with cultural significance that can never be completely delineated. In Rebhausen, when parents and teacher admonished children to be *anständig*, I understood them to be demanding behavior that displays in interpersonal relations a respect for traditional social amenities and distinctions and that reflects positively on home and school.

The importance to teachers of this behavior cannot be explained simply in terms of the norms of village life. It has been the purpose of this chapter to provide a broader setting in which to place school life, particularly the performance of teachers. This setting illustrates the importance in a folk culture of the organic relationship between the village and the urban environment. It is from and through such a relationship with institutions and power centers outside the school that teachers also accumulate valuable evidence concerning the cultural directives they are to implement and the set toward students that is most appropriate.

It is clear that Rebhausen teachers themselves experience within the structure and operation of the state school system an authority comparable to that which they exercise in the classroom. However well established a teacher is as *König im Klassenzimmer*, the state Ministry of Education is the real king. The ministry is linked to a teacher in an isolated village through a well-organized bureaucratic structure in which each level is invested with ample power to act effectively toward the next subordinate level. Furthermore, the culture of this bureaucracy appears to lack cushioning attributes—in terms of interpersonal relations—which render a subordinate position more tolerable. Thus it is fair to say that the kind of respect Rebhausen teachers show students is in part the result of the kind of respect shown them by their superiors.

7 / Village or City? Identity, Choice, and Cultural Change

George D. Spindler

Cultural systems are maintained through the cultivation of certain attitudes, values, and beliefs in the young, as well as certain skills and knowledge. In complex modern societies this cultivation takes place within the family, in the formal school, in churches, business and industrial establishments, in peer groups, and through mass media. In this chapter we will be mainly concerned with the school, since it is charged with responsibility for mediating change.

Of the various kinds of schools present in the Remstal, we will concentrate on the Grundschule, the basic four-year elementary school to which all German children go irrespective of what educational-occupational route they take after these four years through the Hauptschule, Realschule, or Gymnasium.

The structure of the school system in western Germany seems extremely complicated to the American observer. After four years of Grundschule and at about age ten, children go to one of the above-mentioned three schools.[1] The Hauptschule leads to occupations relatively low in the prestige and income hierarchy and lasts through the ninth year. Most students who graduate from a Hauptschule will also go on to one or another kind of apprenticeship training or vocational education. Children going to the Realschule (or *Mittelschule*) continue through the tenth grade and then usually go on to three years of specialized training in engineering, or to a *Fachschule* or *Berufsfachschule* that gives them advanced vocational training, or in a few cases to a *Wirtschafts-Gymnasium* which stresses economics and business training. The third type of school is the Gymnasium, the "highest" school before the university level, with a curriculum emphasizing natural sciences, ancient languages, or modern languages. The professions in their advanced forms are open only to those who have passed the *Abitur*, the final examination given at the end of the thirteenth grade of the Gymnasium, since only individuals who have passed the Abitur are eligible to study at an institution of higher education.

Until recently, these three branches of secondary education have been almost hermetically sealed off from one another. Current attempts are being made to make it possible for children to move from one to another branch by taking special examinations. This attempt has been only partially successful, since each of the branches tends to constitute a self-confirming system in regard to who attends from what economic level and with what cultural and educational background.

A Gymnasium education has recently been made available to more students by the building of more Gymnasien and by encouraging children to enter these schools after finishing the Grundschule. The result has been a considerable increase in attendance at the Gymnasium which has resulted in a further glutting of the higher education facilities of West Germany.

There are other complications in the formal structure of the German educational system, but they are not particularly relevant to our discussion. Our concern is with the elemental processes of cultural maintenance and adaptation, and they take place as far as schooling is concerned mainly in the Grundschule. Further on, however, we will be concerned with the ways in which the Grundschule experience influences the way in which children think about their environment, how it forms their identities and shapes their futures, as they make choices that will affect decisively their styles of life. We will also be interested in the extent to which the Grundschule experience aids in the assimilation of children from divergent cultural backgrounds.

DIE GRUNDSCHULEN

Two Grundschulen will be described. One is in Burgbach, and the other is in nearby Schönhausen. These two villages are different from each other in that Schönhausen is in its own little valley connecting to the Remstal, whereas Burgbach is more centrally located in the Remstal itself. Their locations have affected the pace of urbanization. Burgbach has expanded more rapidly and is today more than twice as large as Schönhausen. Burgbach also looks more modern and is losing its Fachwerkhäuser, replacing them with modern apartment houses or business establishments. It has already undergone a radical renovation of its central area, and

---

1. The structure of the educational system is somewhat different in other parts of Germany. The description applies to Baden-Württemberg.

planning for the future is based upon the assumption that Burgbach will become at least a town and join with other population nuclei in the immediate area of the Remstal, as a part of an organized metropolitan area. Schönhausen, will always be a little bit off to the side and may be able to preserve more of the amenities of semirural life that now are so apparent. Nevertheless, Schönhausen, too, has been caught up in the urbanization process. Its population has doubled since World War II; its brook has also been canalized and covered over with asphalt. Some of its beautiful old Fachwerkhäuser are likewise being replaced by more crass commercial structures, even on its main street. And as in Burgbach, only a small minority of the people still work the land and live in Bauernhäuser with their livestock and farming equipment. Most of the people in Schönhausen, as in Burgbach, work in factories or business establishments, and about half of them commute to work.

The two communities have much in common, not only because they stem from the same local culture and have the same ecological orientation, but also because they are urbanizing and industrializing. Though their outward appearances are quite different, the Grundschulen are alike in many respects, and the children are sent to the same advanced schools in the immediate area.

The Burgbach school sits well above the Marktplatz. Down the gently sloping hill below it are several old Bauernhäuser. Across the street is the village cemetery. Modern duplexes, apartment buildings, and some single-family dwellings have been built on the slope above the school. The view from the Grundschule is truly beautiful, looking out across the ancient Stiftskirche, over the roofs of the old part of Burgbach to the Weinberge on the hills rising from the other side of the Remstal.

On the Marktplatz side of the school there is a black-top playing area about 50 by 120 feet, completely without recreation equipment or even painted lines for different games. The recesses there are almost wholly unorganized, since all equipment is located in the *Gymnastikraum*, a recreation hall nearby. All games played during the recess period are, therefore, individual or group efforts requiring considerable imagination as well as gross physical activity. There is always jumping, skipping, hopping, wrestling, piggy-backing, tag, and racing. Often a guessing game is played where two people tangle up their arms and legs in very complicated patterns, with the guesser trying to figure out how to undo them—lifting a leg over an arm, here, unwrapping a leg from a neck, there. Another game uses a giant rubber band stretched between the legs of two children in a changing pattern, manipulated by children at each end of the band, while the players attempt to jump in and out of it without touching it.

On the wall by the front door of the very modern schoolhouse in Burgbach is a giant mosaic, extremely modern in style and message, presenting a man and woman very close to each other and distinguishable only by hair length, with fish, animals and landscape, and the rising sun in the background casting its rays over them. Inside, the walls of the hall offer samples of each class's art, often quite unusual to the perception of the American visitor. On the wall by the stairway leading up to the main floor, certain sayings are framed: "Serve everyone in reaching the best of his capabilities," and "He who does not regard God as the truth does not believe in his fellow man."

Upstairs, the long hall is split into two levels. Entering any classroom one is first struck by the large windows in the far side of the room. They reveal much of Burgbach, including the Stiftskirche, as well as a large section of the Remstal and the vineyard-covered slopes and forested ridges on the valley side across from the school. The view from the classroom itself seems to be a constant reinforcement of much that goes on within the classroom.

The Schönhausen Grundschule is much older, built at the turn of the century, in the ponderous German public-building style of that period. It is surrounded by a cemented and asphalted area which, in front, serves as a parking lot for teachers' cars, and along the sides, as a playground. As in the Burgbach Grundschule, there is no play equipment and children play the same self-created games or simply run about during the short recesses. In back of the school there is a large area composed of about equal parts of garden and turf maintained by an *Oberlehrer* (senior teacher) and his family who live in the back part of the school building.

As one enters the Schönhausen school, one is reminded immediately of the old-style grade schools in middlewestern towns in America with their creaking wooden floors, rooms that are either too hot or too cold, windows set in massive walls above eye level, and walls distinguished by brown stained and varnished wood and more-or-less cream-colored plaster, with light globes suspended from the ceilings. Children's drawings enliven the walls here and there, as do an occasional natural science exhibit or map, but the overall impression is rather drab.

Directly adjacent to the school is the Schönhausen church which is much older and very distinguished in appearance. Within it are the beautiful fourteenth- and fifteenth-century frescos that were uncovered and restored in the recent renovation of the church. In the tower, that part of the church closest to the school, are four massive bells that ring periodically and are heard very clearly in the classrooms. Across from the school and up the street as far as the eye can reach are Fachwerk-häuser, and down the street is the Rathaus, built in the fourteenth century and carefully maintained into the present. The children in the Schönhausen Grund-schule cannot escape the visual and sensory impact of tradition. Nor as they walk down the street or look out of the windows of the school can they escape the impression, given the vineyard-covered slopes totally surrounding Schönhausen, that this village is still a Weinort. The traffic down the street in front of the school, the new and very modernistic post office, the new bank being built in a place vacated by a Bauernhaus, the modern building for gymnastics and other indoor sports, the public swimming pool, and the new factories springing up in the flatter land in the valley below Schönhausen (as the valley opens into the Remstal) also remind the children that things are changing. . . .

Criticism and Revision of Curriculum

Revision of the elementary curriculum, textbooks and other materials, and presumably of educational philosophy is at present underway, stemming mainly from the centralized administration of schooling in Baden-Württemberg and prompted by increasing consensus on the part of professional intellectuals and some politicians that the German educational system is antiquated. The Heimatkunde curriculum is an object of special concern in this revision. Many German educators have felt that the emphasis upon local geography, history, and culture is inappropriate to the expanding participation of German citizens in the modern world and that in some ways it smacks of the land, folk, and blood pattern of the Hitler period. Many of the older teachers, particularly those from Swabia, resent this change. They point out that many of the higher officials in the Ministry of Education are not Schwäbisch themselves and have little interest in or regard for the local area and its history. The older teachers feel that children should start by learning about things familiar to them, that they themselves can see and experience, that they can learn better about the outside world if they have learned about the immediate world to which they can more easily relate. We will touch upon this controversy later and apply some research results to it.

Whatever controversies there may be about Heimatkunde or whatever changes may have occurred or be occurring, at the time that we studied the Burgbach and Schönhausen schools, Heimatkunde, Naturkunde, and Erdkunde were taught in the style that we are describing. It is appropriate that we should concentrate upon this style, since it was the one that the adults of the populations of Burgbach and Schönhausen themselves experienced as children, and one that their own children in turn have experienced. We think this educational experience has had a significant influence on the course of events in the Remstal villages as urbanization has taken

place. Heimatkunde and its associated emphases in related subject areas, we hy-
pothesize, has provided a common identity for children in the heterogeneous Remstal communities, though the commitment to this identity may not run very deep
for many children. This orientation may act in later years as a constraint on the
ability of children to make an adjustment to the urban scene. For the moment this
is an open question. However, Heimatkunde is certainly not all that is taught in the
Grundschule, and within the framework of Heimatkunde, the urbanizing environment is taken into consideration.

Materials of Instruction

Besides classroom and extra-classroom experiences, one must consider the materials of instruction if the purpose is to describe the school as a culture-transmitting
process. Examples of all the various categories of the published books, manuals,
lesson guides, etc., used by the teachers in the Schönhausen School were collected.
Most of the same books and manuals are used in the Burgbach School. Following
are examples from two textbooks, both for the third school year and both "reading
books" (Lesebücher). The first is one published in 1957, Haus in der Heimat, and
used in 1968 when the study was done. The other, Schwarz auf Weis, was published in 1967, and was still being used in 1971. It should be noted that neither
of these books are directly associated with either Heimatkunde or Naturkunde;
they are prepared for the teaching of reading.

A selection from the 1957 book titled Frühling in der Grosstadt (Spring in the
Big City, p. 5), is paraphrased below:

> In the middle of the great city, among tall, gray houses, the autos, streetcars,
> and people, stood a woman with a basket of spring blossoms. They had only
> this morning come in from the country on the early train and they were very
> lonesome. In the country the sky is so wide and blue, the air so fresh, and
> the earth so wonderfully green. One hears nothing there but singing birds,
> the brook, and now and then a murmur from the village. One sees only the
> sky, the forest, the paths, and the garden with its many, many colorful
> blooms.
> "I am dizzy, and I've got dust in my eyes," said the violet and sank her
> head.
> "And not a butterfly is there to see or to fly over my yellow dress," the
> Narcissus complained.
> The bushroses were not satisfied either, "Here there is no wind to flutter
> our white skirts," they said.

The story goes on, each of the flowers with a specific complaint directed at conditions in the great city. The woman keeps trying to sell the flowers, but everyone
hurries past, intent upon their business. Only a little girl stops. A bouquet would
make her mother happy, so she chooses some of the blossoms that would please her
the most and takes them home.

> Oh! how happy the little flowers were, as they stood on the table, explaining
> about the forests and meadows, the stars and the sky. They described every-
> thing so beautifully that everyone in the room believed they sat outside in the
> lovely spring. Instead, they sat in the huge city.

The book contains fairy tales, little stories, poems, descriptions of nature, short
essays on the garden, the first Maikäfer (a plant-eating beetle that occupies a special
place in the literature of the Grundschule), the zoo, the fire station, annual seasons,
and ceremonies. Frequently presented themes include:

Personification of plants and animals

Magical events, people, places, animals

Nature, land, garden, village, are clean, friendly, fun, and warm; the city is the converse of these

God protects us all. He made everything beautiful, particularly nature

Mother and father take care of us and ask nothing in return

There is a secret, wonderful world of childhood where adult realities need not intrude

In general there is considerable sentimentality centering upon mother love, home, God, comrades, animals, and plants, and the beauties of the country, nature, and gardens. There is only one story set in the city "Die Stadt erwacht" ("The City Awakens"), and one poem about the railroad station. The book is beautifully illustrated with tasteful, imaginative watercolor paintings.

The orientation of reading books for the lower grades has been the subject of commentary by German educationists and social scientists. As concluded in *Das Bild der Heimat in Schullesebuch* (Ehni 1967:241), "The Heimat as the essence of cultivated feelings, of the internalization of the world, and of retrospective sentimentality has become questionable, and is no longer useful as a pedagogical goal." But this conclusion is modified to the effect that values the Heimat orientation was designed to communicate should not be overlooked (by implication) in the reorganization of schoolbooks and curriculum. It is the heavy sentimentality and the unreality to which there are objections, and the 1957 reading book is really a mild example.

In fairness to the teachers of Heimatkunde, Naturkunde, and Erdkunde at the Schönhausen and Burgbach schools, it must be emphasized that the total range of lessons and experiences covering these subjects moves far beyond the rather heavy sentimentality of some of the readings. When Herr Steinhardt demonstrates the geography, demography, and ecology of the Remstal by taking his pupils to the top of a tower overlooking the valley and points out things they have already learned about in the classroom, he is not merely perpetuating the picture of the Heimat represented in school reading books. When Frau Müller takes the children to see the bells in the church and contextualizes this event in a solid presentation of local history and a functional analysis of the community and its demands upon its members she is not merely transmitting sentimentality. She (and Herr Steinhardt) use *sentiment* to communicate the content of the lesson units, as all educators must, if children are to accept the credibility of the content.

The current movement against Heimatkunde and its associations may destroy or seriously weaken the implicit values of this subject matter and the learning process associated with it. This could have unfortunate consequences, since the configuration that has been described may have been a significant factor in the development of a common identity among children from diverse backgrounds. This may, in turn, have been influential in the assimilation of the great influx of new population, and in the relatively smooth ongoing transition from an essentially folk community to an essentially urban way of life.

A Changing Curriculum

The changes in the curriculum and teaching methods following upon recent educational reforms have only begun to be an influence in Burgbach and Schönhausen schooling at the Grundschule level.[2] We may pick up some clues as to their

2. We remind those readers familiar with German that we are not following case endings in the use of German words in the context of English sentences. The endings are dropped in order to avoid confusing the reader who does not know German.

probable direction by looking briefly at a story from one of the new reading books, *Schwarz auf Weiss* (1967). Though published in 1967, this book was not used until the fall of 1968 in either of the communities. The scene is China (paraphrased from p. 10).

> Little Pear stands by the river that goes past his village. His mother has told him to be very careful and not fall in. But he does, just as a houseboat, with a family, including three children, goes past. He almost drowns, but is saved. They go downstream to the next dock, perhaps a mile or two. Little Pear talks to the children while they drift along. They ask him about his village, family, fields, animals, etc. All their lives they have been on the boat. He gets out at the dock, finally, and runs and runs toward his village and home. He is so glad to see it in the distance, and even happier when he is embraced by his mother, father, grandparents, and siblings.

Perhaps the change in emphasis between the old and new reading books is not so great as it at first seems. The village and its associations (family, fields, animals) are still presented in desirable terms. But as one Schönhausen teacher said, "Why do we have to start with strange and far-off places? Why can't the children be taught to value their own surroundings first, and then be led to an understanding of the rest of the world?" Indeed, the educational theory standing behind Heimatkunde is familiar to American elementary school teachers—it is sometimes called the "concentric ring" theory—that experience should begin with the familiar and widen out to the unknown. *Schwarz auf Weiss*, however, appears to have changed the scene, but not, in this story, the theme. The consequences of this are indeed difficult to foresee, but one sympathizes with the teachers who know their local area well, and who regard it as a resource in the transmission of a unified view of reality.

However, to be fair to the "new wave" it must be pointed out that *Schwarz auf Weiss* is less heavily sentimental, there is less emphasis on the small village and cosy valley, less personification of plants and animals, fewer explicit moral lessons, and more straightforward descriptions of places and events. The locale shifts about from China to Italy, to Siberia, to India, to Eskimoland, and often to generalized Germanic locales. There are also some classic fairy tales, thirty-five poems (of which eighteen are about nature or animals). And there are some very flat-footed descriptions of events, such as the abrupt death of a migrant worker in the city who tried to cross a busy street against a red light and is run down, that would probably not be included in a third-grade reading book in the United States. The reading books for the third grade described in this chapter seem more advanced than comparable materials from American schools. The sentences are long and complicated, the vocabulary large, the ideas quite sophisticated, the illustrations superb, and the material is very imaginative.

It seems probable that there will be a shift in emphasis in the Grundschule, but that there will be enough continuity so that the major conclusions of the study reported in this chapter will remain viable for that part of the Remstal represented by Schönhausen, and for some time, even Burgbach, though the area itself becomes *de facto* urbanized. . . .

Identity and Choice

It seems clear that schooling at the basic elementary level in Burgbach and Schönhausen provides children with a means for forming an identity related to the village and its local area. The question we are left with for the Remstal children is whether, given this identity and its localization, children are able to expand their frame of reference sufficiently as they grow up to make relevant choices in an increasingly urbanized environment. The question for children in the United States is almost the reverse. American elementary schools in communities of roughly comparable economic standing, with their elaborate teaching aids, stress on the relationship of learning problems and teaching procedures to individuals, general richness of material educational environment, as well as in the organization of the curriculum itself, seem to be oriented toward a complex, internally differentiated, open, urbanized society. But it is difficult to see how American school children can achieve any sort of identity within this experience. With what can they identify? The supermarket (usually a part of the social studies curriculum)? The profit motive? Capitalism? Set theory (the new math)? With the teacher? With the Eskimos (a part of the social studies curriculum in some elementary schools)? Perhaps a clear-cut identity would be inappropriate, even dysfunctional in United States society, and yet the lack of one is lamented by youth, teachers, and intellectuals.

The intended identity in the two German schools we have described is clear, and curriculum content and teaching methods are appropriate to it. The present constituency of Burgbach and Schönhausen is from many different parts of Germany and its former outlying populations, and is diverse in religious, linguistic and regional cultural background. Do these two schools provide common identity for children from this diverse population?

INSTRUMENTAL PERCEPTIONS AND CHOICES

We can now consider the effects of the Grundschule experience more precisely. These are our questions: Does this experience place limits on the recognition and choosing of alternatives in later life related to the urban society? Does this experience provide the basis for the assimilation of divergent populations to a common cultural standard? What evidence is there of identity formation and if so, what is it? Some of our research was directed specifically at these questions. As a part of the research strategy, we adapted the Instrumental Activities Inventory developed by the Spindlers for research on other sites, and applied it in both the Grundschulen and in more advanced schools. The technique as developed for research in Germany consisted of a total of thirty-seven line drawings of thirty-seven activities that are instrumental to the attainment of goals considered appropriate in the Remstal area. Activities instrumental in the traditional as well as the urbanizing, industrializing Remstal are included. The technique is designed to elicit from respondents their preferences for certain instrumental activities and goals and their rationale for these preferences. The activities are not only occupations such as working in a factory, being a chemist, or being a Weingärtner, but also such things as having a dinner for friends at home, or going to a lively party in a public place of entertainment, going to church, living in a particular kind of house, going to school, and commuting to work. The goals are to be thought of not only as specific attainments such as a certain income or possession of a certain object, but as life styles or conditions of being which may subsume a number of specific preferences and instrumental activity-goal linkages. Rather than being a personality test, the Instrumental Activities Inventory (IAI) is a technique for eliciting responses relevant to the perception of social reality and the alternative possibilities contained within it (Spindler and Spindler 1965).

Every research technique should be related to a theoretical model. We use a model of a cultural system upon which we must expand a little. It is possible to understand the results obtained by using the IAI at one level, without understanding the theoretical model. A statement of it is included for those whose interests extend beyond the data relevant to this particular case study. The statements following are applicable to all complete cultural systems.

A THEORETICAL MODEL

A cultural system operates so long as acceptable behaviors usually produce anticipatable and desired results, and unacceptable behaviors usually produce anticipatable and undesired results. These behaviors can be thought of as *instrumental activities*, and the results as goals, or satisfactions. Beliefs that are part of the cultural tradition support the accepted relationships between activities and satisfactions. The relationships are *credible*. The credibility of the instrumental relationships is an essential attribute of the system and one that schooling is designed to support. Both goals and the activities instrumental to them are socially sanctioned. These sanctions may not involve a consensus of all the members of a cultural system, for various subgroups, classes, and cliques within the whole system have their own goals, instrumental activities, and sanctions. The relationship between given activities and the goals or end-states to which they are instrumental may be thought of as *instrumental linkages*. Activities may also become goals in themselves in that they may become so satisfying that the original goal to which they are linked becomes of secondary importance. The linkages are dynamic. *Social control* may be defined as sanctioned intervention in the operation of the instrumental linkages for members of a cultural system, by other members. *Social organization* is the organization of personnel and their roles in relation to each other, and of the necessary materiel, so that the linkages can function. Education as *cultural transmission* may be defined as means employed by established members of the cultural system to inform new members coming into the system of the sanctioned instrumental linkages, to communicate how they are ranked, integrated, and in general, organized, and also to commit these new members to the support and continuance of these linkages and the belief system that gives them credibility. (In this sense educational institutions serve mainly functions of reaffirmation and recruitment.) The *cognitive structure* in individual minds that results from this education consists partly of this organization and related commitments, insofar as cognitive structure is relevant to perceived social reality. *Cognitive control* as socially relevant is the ability of an individual to maintain a working model, in his mind, of relevant and at least potentially productive instrumental linkages and their organization. When IAI data are analyzed, we will refer to *supporting values*. Supporting values are situations, events, or states of being that are used by respondents to justify expressed instrumental preferences. All acceptable activities and end-products have "value," but some have more than others. Unacceptable or negatively sanctioned activities and goals may be said to have "negative value." *Identity* may be defined as individual commitment, often at an ideal level, to a given configuration of instrumental linkages and supporting values, and to symbols representing them. This commitment is at least partly verbalizable.

This system model is open-ended and provides for adaptive change. During rapid culture change established instrumental linkages are challenged by new information and behavior models. Their credibility is weakened. Their operational viability declines. Alternative linkages are recognized, acquire credibility, and become operable. The range of alternative instrumental linkages from which individuals may choose increases. The total range will include a number that conflict. Cognitive control becomes more difficult.[3] In studies of culture change one may be concerned with either the culture system processes (economic, technological, political) that result in new instrumental linkages, or with the perception, selection, and cognitive ordering of alternative linkages by individuals.

THE RESEARCH PROCEDURE

We can now convert our questions to the frame of reference described above. We want to find out whether children from different backgrounds choose the same, or

---

3. Attempts to maintain cognitive control under conditions of radical cultural confrontation may result in expulsion of conflicting instrumental linkages, reaffirmation of some synthesis of selected elements, or segmentalized adaptation.

different, instrumental activities, anticipate the same ends, and rationalize their choices similarly (or differently). We want to identify the influence of the school on these choices, and, particularly, in the ways the school may act as a constraint upon urban-oriented instrumental perceptions and choices. We are also interested in changes that occur as children mature, and in sex differences. And we want to discover whether there is a common identity fostered by the school experience.

Though we could, and did, use all thirty-seven IAI drawings in individual administrations, it was necessary to select a smaller number for administration to classroom groups. After we had administered thirty interviews on an individual basis and used the line drawings in their original form with one Gymnasium class, we selected seventeen, for which we had 35-mm. slides made. These seventeen were selected as particularly diagnostic of different orientations with respect to the process of urbanization, "folk" to urban, and as relevant to our particular sample. By using two 35-mm. slide projectors simultaneously, we were able to show in classrooms seven pairs of pictures from which children were asked to make choices as well as three pictures shown singly that they were asked to evaluate. A simple data sheet filled out by each child included such items as birth date, father's occupation, birth place, birth place of parent, etc., as well as two essay questions.

The drawings include a contrast between the traditional Fachwerkhaus and a modern single-family dwelling; A Weingärtner versus a white-collar office worker; factory workers versus an independent owner of a small shop; a farmer and family working on a flatland plot versus a machinist working at a lathe; the Grundschule with children going into it, a traditional church as compared to a rectangular, very modernistic church; a large-scale farmer with his helper working with a very large tractor plow versus a technical draftsman; a large and modern Bauernhaus with stalls for stock, lofts for hay, machinery, etc., combined with a family home; a dinner table with party-style settings but clearly in the home, versus a very lively party in a public place; the grape harvest showing a wagon and several people, including children, pouring grapes into it.

These drawings were shown with two 35-mm. projectors to 282 children in the Grundschule in Schönhausen and in a nearby Hauptschule which is attended by children from both Schönhausen and Burgbach. They were also shown, in the same manner, to the teachers in the Schönhausen Grundschule and to a sample of 31 parents of children attending this school. As stated, the technique was also administered, using somewhat different procedures, to one Gymnasium class and to 30 individuals representing various schools in the area. Besides the responses elicited by pictures, we asked for short essays stating agreement or disagreement with two statements, one supportive of city as against village life, and one supportive of being a Weingärtner as against being a factory worker. The essay questions were included to elicit global, generalized orientations toward rural-village versus city life, rather than responses to specific instrumental linkages relevant to village versus city life. The details of the results are presented elsewhere (Spindler 1973), and we will summarize only the most relevant parts.[4]

THE RESULTS

In the essay responses the children in the sample as a whole show an idealistic bias toward life in the small village. These responses are not differentiated by regional, linguistic, religious background, urbanization, or origin of parents. There is a common outlook. Specific values offered in support of village life include: fresh air; less traffic; quietness; nearness to nature; friendliness; and availability of fresh

4. The sample of 282 pupil respondents was computer programmed for every conceivable combination of urban-rural, regional, occupational, sex and age factors, and statistical tests run in distribution of IAI responses in relation to these differences. I am grateful to Erika Lueders-Salmon for her help on this and other aspects of the data analysis.

foods. City life is seen as: noisy and dangerous; there is no place to play or walk; the air is bad; life is impersonal.

The same general bias operates in the essay responses in favor of the life of the Weingärtner, without significant variation as related to any background factors excepting sex and age. Supporting values for the Weingärtner life style include: self-determination and independence; being near nature; breathing fresh air; having healthier work; being owner of one's land.

These choices of Weingärtner and village are supported at a highly idealized level. The configuration of choice and supporting values seems to be virtually a replication of what children are taught in school in the Heimatkunde lessons. The bias is persistent at the older grade level, although there are significant statistical differences between older and younger children, and also between girls and boys. Girls tend to be more urban-oriented in most of their responses than the boys, and older children more than the younger.

The teachers in the Schönhausen Grundschule, from whom responses to the essay questions and the IAI were also collected, share these idealized biases toward the Weingärtner-village way of life. They are consistent, too, in the supporting values with which they rationalize their choices. The parents are like the teachers.

However, when the specifics of pragmatic choice are presented to the children in the form of the paired instrumental activities expressed by IAI pictures, the children tend, with certain exceptions that will be noted, to choose in an urbanized direction. For instance, when they are asked to choose between a traditional Fachwerkhaus and a very modern single-family dwelling, they choose the modern dwelling more often. And they support their choices with such values as: convenience; luxuries; practicality; a better life; more comfortable; easier to keep up; warmer; more valuable. Girls tend to choose the modern house more frequently than the boys and there is a tendency for the younger children to prefer the traditional house.

When presented with a choice between white-collar office work and Weingärtner, white-collar office work is preferred. Specific values supporting the white-collar positions are: regular hours of work and free time; more regular pay; cleaner work; not such hard work; more pay per hour; and independence from the weather. Younger children choose Weingärtner more frequently, and girls choose white-collar work more frequently. In both instances, the teachers are more tradition-oriented than the children in their choices, choosing most frequently the traditional house and the Weingärtner occupation.

In the choice between being a factory worker or the independent owner of a small shop of some sort, more of the children prefer the latter. Supporting values include: being one's own boss; making better money; owning one's own shop and equipment; being surrounded by less noise; and having fewer people to deal with. Independence of rules, hours, and goals set by others was the most frequently cited value. But again, girls preferred factory work more frequently because of its security and regularity.

In choosing between farmer and machine worker, there was a moderate preference among the children for the latter. Parents and teachers were strongly divergent from the children, choosing farmer much more frequently. The children supported the choices of *Maschinenarbeiter* with: secure and regular job and pay, physically easier work and cleaner work.

When shown the picture of the school and asked to express their liking or dislike for it, most of the children liked it, and parents and teachers agreed. Supporting values for school include: specific subjects and teachers that were especially enjoyed; the necessity of schooling for the future; and just plain "like it." Many responses were qualified in what we have come to regard as the typical "Swabian" way: "almost all, but not all, go gladly"; "many are enthusiastic, some not." Older children tend to dislike school more frequently.

Between the old and the new church, the majority of the children prefer the old church. Parents and teachers are consistent with them. Supporting values include references to age, history, tradition, and beauty.

Between the large-scale farmer and the technical draftsman, the majority of the children in all grades choose the latter. Supporting values for the draftsman cited by children include: good pay; pleasant kind of work; independence of weather; clean work; not such hard physical labor (as the farmer); evenings free; regular vacations. The teachers choose the farmer.

When shown the picture of the modern Bauernhaus and asked whether they would like to live in it, a bare majority of the children (51 percent) said they would. They supported their choice with: lots of space; modern; better for children to live near animals; outdoor space; interesting things going on; would like to work as a farmer; living in fresh air; living in the village or out in the country.

When asked to choose between a party at home versus a party in a public place, the children tended to choose the affair at home, but there was a clear difference between the older and younger respondents, with the former choosing more frequently the party outside of the home. Girls choose the party outside more frequently at all ages. Supporting values for the affair at home include: quieter, more control over what happens; less expensive; more gemütlich; family-oriented; and not so wild.

The last picture, that of the grape harvest, was supported very strongly by all grade levels. Values evoked in support of enthusiasm for the grape harvest include: it is just fun; one can eat grapes; it's a good kind of work; one can enjoy the nice, early fall weather and be out in the sun; one can be with friends and relations; one can be out in nature.

In all choices, not just those where teacher choices were mentioned above, teachers tend to be more village tradition-oriented than the children. Parents are more like the teachers than their children are, but are less conservative than teachers. And the children's responses are significantly differentiated by age and sex, but not by regional origin or any other background factors. Younger children choose village-land-nature more frequently than do older ones, and girls make urban-oriented choices more frequently than do boys.

INTERPRETATION

The choices with which respondents are faced in the essay questions do not require finite pragmatic judgements of an instrumental nature. Respondents express their generalized, idealized, value orientations. The pattern of responses to these two statements suggests a sentimental identification with the village and its associated supporting values.

But what is the depth of this identity? The responses to the IAI pictures do not seem to be constrained by it.[5] Pragmatic considerations become important when respondents are faced with finite instrumental choices. The village-land-nature identity therefore may be regarded as idealized, perhaps even, in a sense, as "spurious," in that it is not possible to apply it consistently to the real choices presented in an urbanizing environment.

That this idealized identity is consistent with the emphases in the school curriculum, teaching materials, classroom and outside of classroom experience, and the

---

5. One of the more interesting writings on identity processes is by Treinen (1965), whose research indicates that identification with a given place is the consequence of membership (at some time) in a social system that is closely bound to that place, and that is symbolized by place-names capable of eliciting complex emotional reactions—feelings of "identity," or place-reference. Something of this kind may be operating in the identification by respondents of themselves as "villagers" even though they express various urban-oriented instrumental preferences.

teachers' explicit biases does not prove that the Schönhausen school produced it. The majority of the parents also share this identity, despite diverse origins. School and home are consistent with each other, so far as our present sample of parents indicates and insofar as we are concerned with the idealized identity configuration. They both apparently transmit the same messages. Perhaps parents who live in small villages like them, or must believe they do. Or perhaps only people who like village life stay there. These are variables that we have no way of controlling with the scope of our data at present. But the fact remains, the school appears to transmit an idealized identity and supporting values that are oriented in a certain way. The children appear to have accepted these values and this identity at one level of cognitive organization.

However, when the children are faced with finite choices, during the presentation of IAI pictures, that force them to express a preference for a more village-nature-land or a more urban-linked instrumentality, they tend to choose the latter, though the proportion doing so varies by age and to some extent by sex. The majority prefer modern apartment houses to live in, white-collar office work, working as a machinist, or as a technical draftsman, to alternatives that are clearly village and land oriented. The supporting values for these choices are very pragmatic: better pay, more security, regular hours, independence of the caprices of nature, guaranteed vacations, cleaner and less physically exhausting work.

When "romantic" instrumentalities, uncomplicated by pragmatic realities, are presented to the children—the old versus the new church, and the Weinlese—the majority express preferences in a traditional, village, land-oriented direction—the beautiful old church and enthusiastic interest in the grape harvest. Possibly the school is also supported as a part of this configuration. These choices do not challenge pragmatic orientation and are a logical extension of the idealized identity revealed in preferences for small village life and the Weingärtner occupation expressed in the essay responses. This identity survives where it does not conflict with practical considerations.

The cognitive organization of the majority of children in our sample, insofar as relevant to our research problem, is therefore comprised of three parts: (1) the idealized identity—villager and Weingärtner, with supporting values: independence, quiet, friendliness, love of nature, etc.; (2) the pragmatic instrumental preference system (modern house, white-collar work, etc.), together with supporting values such as regular income and hours, security, less hardship, etc.; and (3) the romanticized, nonpragmatic instrumental preferences (traditional church, Weinlese, village life) and their supporting values such as beauty, freedom, health, etc. The majority of the children appear to maintain cognitive control over these three potentially conflicting dimensions, perhaps because pragmatism has priority in critical areas of choice. Also, a compromise is, in reality, possible since one can live in a small village, and commute to a nearby city to work.

The interpretations stated above are given general support by the fact that the older children closer to full instrumental participation in society tend to choose more pragmatically, and consequently are more urban oriented. Conversely, the young children are more village and nature oriented in their choices. As the time of entry into the adult instrumental structure nears, the choices become of greater pragmatic significance.

It is of considerable interest that the teachers definitely, and the parents somewhat less so, are more oriented toward village-land-nature, and are more "romantic" in their view, than are the children, particularly the older ones. The teachers are not faced with the necessity of making the same practical instrumental choices as the older children. They can allow the idealized identity that is present somewhere in the responses of almost everyone in the sample to dominate their cognitive organization. The fact that the children seem capable of making pragmatic choices that are divergent from those of their teachers (and often their parents), particularly as they grow older, suggests that the school as a culture transmitting agency does not act as a powerful constraint. Possibly the Heimat and Natur lessons in the Schönhausen school are broad and realistic enough to provide means by which children can come to grips with the practicalities of life in the urbanizing Remstral.

It is important that the children's responses are differentiated by age and sex, but not by the regional origin of parents, or even by the size of population aggregate (city, town, or village) in which the parents (or child if from outside Schönhausen) were born. Although we cannot prove decisively that the school assimilates this population of diverse background (about one half of the school population is derived from a recently immigrant, Zugezogenen population) to a common standard, the probability that it has some significant influence in this direction seems high. The Grundschule has apparently acted both as a stabilizer of culture and as a mediator of a changing culture.

The school helps provide an idealized identity that is not a barrier to full participation in a changing cultural system. This identity may serve useful functions. If identity is as significant as many social scientists claim, then the result has been positive. A common framework of communication is created and sustained for a diverse population. That the identity is, in the absolutely practical sense, spurious, is unimportant. Keeping a village-land-nature identity intact in the midst of an expanding urban complex may have helped the Remstal avoid the disasters that seem inevitable in analogous situations in the United States. Most importantly for the future, the children educated in the Grundschulen do not seem to have been crippled by this identity. Though they idealize village and land, they can make instrumental choices, and provide relevant support for them, that are oriented toward the urbanized future of the Remstal. They have already moved beyond their teachers and parents in their understanding of the contemporary world, but share with them some significant aspects of a common identity.

The Deviants

Not all the children of either native or migrant parents in the Remstal grow up with a conflict-free village-oriented identity, "spurious" or not. The situation as we have described it is most relevant to the two villages, Burgbach and Schönhausen, that we have studied. Our description should be more or less adequate for other communities of comparable size, equidistant from urban centers and with the same ecological orientation. It is less applicable to youth in more urban centers, and changes are taking place everywhere.

An increasing number of young people in the Remstal area dress in clothing that seen through adult eyes has a "hippie" aura. Some dress in "mod" fashion. Many boys affect long hair, though more Gymnasium students wear their hair longer than do students in other schools. A few engage in demonstrations against the Establishment, or openly reject their parents and their way of life.

There is also a drug subculture developing. There is a high degree of communication within what we can call a "hard core" aggregate of drug users. "Hash" (hashish), similar to American "pot," or "grass" (marijuana) but probably more predictable in its effects due to impurities frequently found in marijuana as it is purveyed in the American market, is universal. These youths also experiment with "acid" (L.S.D.), mescaline, heroin, "speed" (amphetamines), cocaine, and various commercial drugs. This hard core aggregate offers various forms of aid and support to its participants, including offers of places to sleep, food, and psychic reinforcement. Within it attitudes of antagonism to all forms of adult authority and scorn for established norms of conduct governing sexual behavior are held in common. And of course the drug experience and the sharing and purveying of drugs are an important part of the life style. In general, the way of life, the shared identity, within this aggregate of hard-core drug users is a direct confrontation with the basic values and identities of the einheimisch Remstal culture.

The basic supporting ideology of the hard core aggregate is confrontation and dropout. The participants in this hard core seem to express the same ennui and disenchantment with modern society as does the proportionately larger group of young people in the United States. Some of these attitudes, in milder form, appear to be developing in a wider population of the young in the Remstal. They may increase in intensity and extent as the urbanization of the Remstal increases, though there is nothing inevitable about this relationship.

What is probably more important for the future of the Remstal is that most of the young are opting for a way of life and for instrumental opportunities that were not available to their parents. Weingärtner complain that their sons are not interested in "taking over the land." Young people complain that there is "nothing to do" in the smaller communities, and increasing numbers opt for a more urbanized environment. The idealized, romanticized values centering on land and village do not govern instrumental choices for them.

CONCLUSION

We have studied the Burgbach and Schönhausen Grundschulen and their influence upon children who, as young adults, must make character-defining choices of occupations and life styles in an urbanizing environment. Those schools must serve the same general purposes as do similar institutions in urbanizing America. The Remstal schools provide the basis for communication between children from culturally divergent groups, and their assimilation into a shared cultural framework of meanings and values. This sharing of a common identification with village, land, nature, and folk in the earlier years of childhood and in the form of romantic idealization in later years does not appear to inhibit a wide and pragmatic range of adaptations relevant to an urbanizing environment.

An until now divergent subculture of drugs, relaxed sexual mores, and confrontation is developing among Remstal youth. It may not expand to the proportions that similar subcultures have in the urban portions of the United States, but it is symptomatic of some of the same underlying conditions. The credibility of the established instrumental linkages and old identities is being eroded by radical changes in the conditions of existence. That some aspects of the old culture and identity have persisted, is an indication of the strength of the family and basic school as socializing institutions, and the forces for continuity.

Spurious identities, though useful in providing some common ground for diverse elements, are unlikely to serve for long when the cultural system and the conditions of its existence are undergoing transformative change. Burgbach and Schönhausen are just entering the age of transformation. What new images that will guide commitment and shape behavior will emerge? Perhaps none will, and the Remstal will decline into the state of goallessness and low morale that often accompanies rapid urbanization, industrialization, and rationalization where the credibility of established identities is decisively challenged. On the other hand, the combination of romanticism and pragmatism that is deeply characteristic of the Swabian world view and the interaction of natives and newcomers in the dynamic Remstal population seem likely to produce new and viable identities and supporting values. It also seems probable that although these identities and values will be a sharp departure from the old ones, they will exhibit some continuity with the past.

TO COME

Whatever continuity of identities there may be, the changes taking place during the decade to come will transform the Remstal from a still recognizable landscape of small communities, farmland, vineyard, and forest to a great metropolitan area. Freeways will cut ruthlessly through forest-covered ridges. Population will increase to more than twice its present size. Consolidated municipal governments will replace separate administrations, including Burgbach's. Community identities will be blurred. Already the marks of individuality and tradition upon the Weinberge have been obliterated by Flurbereinigung. The relationship of man and animals to land is already drastically altered.

The new cultural system with its rationalized technology is very different from that which has persisted for so long. It is different in principle. It consumes air, water, and other precious resources and replaces little. It groups and moves people in anonymous relationships. It is less constrictive, more exciting, and less reassuring. It may also be less enduring than its predecessors.

REFERENCES

Ehni, Jörg, 1967, *Das Bild der Heimat im Schullesebuch*, Volksleben, Vol. 16. Tübingen: Tübinger Vereinigung für Volkskunde.

"Haus in der Heimat," Lesebuch für das dritte Schujahr der Volksschulen in Baden-Württemberg, 1957, Karlsruhe: Gemeinschaftsverlag.

"Schwarz auf Weiss": Ein neues Lesebuch für Baden-Württemberg, Drittes Schuljahr, 1967, Darmstadt-Hanover: Herman Schroedel Verlag KG.

Spindler, George D., 1973, "Schooling in Schönhausen: A Study of Cultural Transmission and Instrumental Adaptation in an Urbanizing German Village," in *Education and Cultural Process: Toward an Anthropology of Education*, ed. by G. Spindler. New York: Holt, Rinehart and Winston, Inc.

Spindler, George, and Louise Spindler, 1965, "The Instrumental Activities Inventory: A Technique for the Study of the Psychology of Aculturation," *Southwestern Journal of Anthropology*, 21 (No. 1):1-23.

Treinen, Heiner, 1965, *Symbolische Ortsbezogenheit: Eine soziologische Untersuchung zum Heimatproblem*, Inaugural Dissertation Köln and Opladen: Westdeutscher Verlag. (Also published in the Kölner Zeitschrift für Soziologie und Sozialpsychologie, Heft 1/2, 1965).

Warren, Richard L., 1967, *Education in Rebhausen: A German Village* (Case Study in Education and Culture). New York: Holt, Rinehart and Winston, Inc.

8 / The Rebirth of a Grandfather's Spirit: Shumba's Two Worlds

Clive Kileff

African parents in Rhodesia make great financial sacrifices to send their children to school. Yet it is school which often creates barriers between the generations. In school a new culture is transmitted to the young and discontinuity with the past exists. Upon entering the "world" of school, Shumba,[1] a young boy who is in harmony with his ancestors and family, now faces a new set of demands, values, and expectations.[2]

Spirit possession and spirit mediumship are found among most rural Shona people (Bourdillon 1973:16). A famous tribal spirit or a family spirit can possess a living person and shows its presence by causing the host to become ill (Bourdillon 1973:17). At this stage, Zvarevashe (1970:45) writes, the host "may go to the hospital only to be told there is no sign of disease. Then a true Shona would go to a *Nganga* (diviner). The *Nganga* may tell him that a *mudzimu* (ancestor) or *shave* (wandering spirit) wants to possess him."

Shumba's spirit possession followed the same pattern. After he fell ill his parents took Shumba to a *Nganga*. The *Nganga* diagnosed the complaint as spirit possession and instructed Shumba's parents to name Shumba after his grandfather and to give him the foods that his deceased grandfather preferred when he was alive.

The dominant force in Shumba's life is his possession by his grandfather's spirit; hence he is expected to behave as a grandfather would. In addition, others are expected to treat Shumba with the respect due a grandfather. For a summary of Shumba's web of relationships, see table 8.1.

Shumba's behavior is acceptable in the traditional cultural setting where it conforms to the Shona religious beliefs, yet this same behavior is unacceptable in the school setting where the goal is classroom learning. Shumba's parents hold traditional religious beliefs but at the same time they see school, a nontraditional institution, as a way of increasing their son's earning potential.

This article shows how Shumba's teacher, Miss Chamba, mediates between the traditional and modern as a kind of cultural broker. The task of mediator is made simpler in her case because she herself has been possessed by an ancestral spirit. Miss Chamba does not publicize her possession, however, because she teaches in a mission school and fears that the church authorities might dismiss her for believing in ancestral spirits and in spirit possession.

Miss Chamba modified her classroom behavior in the face of Shumba's traditional demands. As soon as she realized that he was his grandfather, she proceeded to call him by the proper term of address for a grandfather, *Sekuru*. When Shumba was treated with respect by his teacher and called by the name, *Sekuru*, he responded enthusiastically because he felt he was being treated the same way as at home. Not only Miss Chamba, but also the headmaster and the school manager addressed Shumba as *Sekuru* as soon as they appreciated the situation. Whenever so addressed, Shumba was eager to carry out any request.

An hypothesis emerging from this study is that where the social and cultural worlds of the teacher and the pupil overlap extramurally, the pupil will be treated

TABLE 8.1. THE MAIN CHARACTERS IN SHUMBA'S TWO WORLDS

Shumba	Eight-year-old school pupil and ninety-year-old deceased grandfather
Dzavo	Ninety-year-old deceased grandfather and eight-year-old school pupil
Tichafa	Shumba's father
Rufaro	Shumba's mother
Godfrey	Shumba's fourteen-year-old brother
Egfa	Shumba's sixteen-year-old sister
Runganayi	Shumba's eleven-year-old sister
Paradzayi	Shumba's six-year-old brother
Rasikayi	Shumba's two-year-old sister
Miss Chamba	Shumba's teacher
Stephen and George	Shumba's village friends and classmates

more favorably in the classroom. Hence a middle-class teacher might respond more positively to a middle-class pupil and a teacher with a background of spirit possession may respond positively to a pupil of similar circumstances.

The following case history illustrates the respective influences upon Shumba and how his teacher Miss Chamba mediates between his two worlds.[3]

TICHAFA

Tichafa, Shumba's father, is a man in his early forties who was born in the Nyamutumba Village of the Seki Tribal Trust Land. He excels at hunting, running, and singing and his explanation for this is simple: "the *shavi* spirits of hunting, running, and singing have possessed me." He is tall, with a light complexion; heavy furrows appear on his forehead when he is deep in thought or listening intently to someone.

The first-born of five, Tichafa grew up in a village surrounded by his paternal kinsmen. The clan name is Hungoro. His name, Tichafa, means "we shall die" and was given to him by his parents to remind conceited people that death is for everyone.

Tichafa recalls that his favorite boyhood pastimes were making toy cars out of bits of wire and playing *mahumbwe* (house). When he was six and seven years old, Tichafa and his friends would pose as children of the older boys and girls during play. When the younger children were left on their own they often mixed sand and water in old tins and broken pumpkin shells. They served these ingredients to each other as *sadza* (crushed corn meal).

When Tichafa grew older he accompanied his father, Dzavo, on hunting expeditions to the other side of the Nyatsime River. Here, with the help of dogs, they hunted wild pig, deer, antelope, and rabbits. Tichafa said, "Dzavo was possessed with the hunting spirit; he could run very fast after an animal and touch its hind legs. His dogs would come to help him by biting the animal to the ground."

At the age of seventeen, Tichafa started school.[4] Dzavo was anxious for his son to learn to speak English. Dzavo had been astonished to see a young clerk act as an interpreter for older people in the District Commissioner's office in Salisbury and was impressed by the power this young man had because of his ability to speak English.

While at school, Tichafa became known for his deep singing voice and his classmates called him *munhu vebesi* (the person with a bass voice) and *munhu anodzvova* (the person who roars). He said, "As one of the oldest boys at school I sang bass. My voice was popular wherever our school sang. My friend and I were often made to sing for villagers who visited the school. In interschool singing competitions my school came out on top."

Tichafa is also proud of the extraordinary results of his agricultural work and his running abilities at school. He claims that the maize and vegetables which he planted and cared for in the school garden always looked the best. Referring to his running ability, Tichafa said, "No one left me in the running events."

At nineteen, Tichafa, then in Grade 2, grew restless. He saw others who were younger than himself returning from their jobs in Salisbury wearing "smart" suits. These young men laughed at their friends who were still at school wearing khaki shorts and shirts. Tichafa did not like being laughed at, and he left school to seek work in Salisbury. In retrospect, Tichafa regrets this decision. He says, "Please tell those who are learning to continue. Ignorance does not help."

In December 1948, Tichafa got a job in Salisbury as an office messenger. From his meager earnings he saved enough money to buy a suit which he proudly wore for his former schoolmates to see. He continued working in the city, commuting back and forth each day by bus. Since Tichafa's home village is close to Salisbury, working in the city did not involve dislocation from home and family.

In 1950, Tichafa married Rufaro, a girl from his village. She is the daughter of the village headman and third-born in her family. Tichafa's father and brother helped him acquire the bride price. This consisted of two head of cattle, a suit for her father, and a *chari* (shawl) for her mother. The marriage was accompanied by traditional celebrations and feasting. It was an important occasion for Tichafa's parents as he was their first-born.

Tichafa began to grow tired of his work as a messenger; and in 1952, he got a job as a dispatcher in a mattress factory. His salary was $5 per week. Although he was unhappy with this small income, Tichafa remained in this job for two years before deciding to return to farming. He said, "It is better to grow maize and vegetables and have enough food than to earn poor wages in the city."

When Tichafa left his job, he was returning to follow the ways of his father, Dzavo, who was an excellent farmer and was said to be possessed by the spirit of farming. With his wife, Rufaro, Tichafa planted a garden in the rich, wet soils along the Nyatsime River. They grew cabbages, rape (a spinach-like vegetable), squash, onions, pumpkins, beans, peas, tomatoes, and beets. It was far more than their family could eat and Tichafa found ready markets at nearby mission boarding schools. He also sold some of his produce to stores in Salisbury. The income from his garden was often $100 a month.

He was now able to lend money to others; something he could never have done when he earned only $5 per week working in town. Tichafa was very proud that as a villager he had money left over to lend to those who were working in town earning wages. He was able to buy a large delivery bicycle which he used to carry vegetables to customers. Like his father before him, Tichafa soon earned the reputation of being industrious.

In 1971, Tichafa's vegetable enterprise suffered a severe setback. He had been farming along the banks of the Nyatsime River. Chief Seki sold this land to a company to build a factory. Tichafa could no longer farm the rich, wet soil on the river bank. He was bitter that the land had been sold to Europeans. Tichafa was forced to move his garden to a small plot beside a stream that flows into the Nyatsime River. It is closer to his home, but he is no longer able to produce enough to sell; his garden only feeds his family.

In other fields near his homestead, he and his wife and children work hard cultivating maize, but the income from the vegetables is gone. On another small plot, Rufaro has her own crop of groundnuts. From the maize, Tichafa earns $100 to $160 in a good year. This is spent on school fees and clothing for the family. From the groundnuts Rufaro earns about $50 which she keeps for household supplies like sugar, tea, bread, and meat.

Rufaro has borne Tichafa eight children in their twenty-three years of marriage. The oldest two, both girls, died about eighteen years ago. They were ill and the treatment given them by an herbalist failed to save them. The surviving children include a sixteen-year-old daughter, Egfa, who left school after five years because she was unable to learn. She now stays at home and assists her mother with household duties like collecting firewood, washing clothes, and taking maize to the grinding mill three miles away. Egfa is very quiet and seldom speaks to her brothers and sisters.

Godfrey is fourteen. He completed primary school, but his results were not good enough to gain a place for him at secondary school. Runganayi is eleven and in Grade 4. She accompanies her eight-year-old brother, Shumba, to school each day. Shumba is in Grade 1. Paradzai, a six-year-old boy, and Rasikayi, a two-year-old girl, remain at home with their mother because they are too young for school. Tichafa is very fond of all his children, especially his sons Godfrey and Shumba. He buys the boys clothes like his own and allows them to use his bicycles. They often accompany their father on hunting and fishing expeditions. The three of them are fond of telling jokes about hunting, recalling the behavior of their three dogs, or the excitement of chasing an animal until they are close enough to spear it.

In November 1972, Tichafa began as usual to prepare his maize field for the rains that were due to come soon ending the long dry season. But the rains did not come and the young maize plants withered and died. Tichafa became worried about how he would look after his family. He needed money, but even a good farmer earns nothing in a drought. Since the factory had been built near Tichafa's village there had been much talk among the men of money to be earned in the factory. Tichafa was eager to get money for school fees and food so he took a job in one of the nearby factories. He finds the work exhausting and hard, but until he can return to farming he is likely to continue. Since he began working he rises very early in the morning, before the rest of the family, so that he may work in his vegetable garden before going to work. When he returns to the homestead an hour later, he finds that Rufaro has boiled water for him to wash. He changes his clothes, drinks a cup of tea and sets off for the factory wearing a shirt, a pair of cotton shorts, and a pair of rubber sandals he has made out of old automobile tires.

RUFARO

Rufaro is not yet forty but she has been married for twenty-three years. She has spent her whole life in the same village. The daughter of the village headman, she married Tichafa, whose family also live in the village. She is the third-born and eldest daughter in a family of seven children. All her brothers and sisters live in the village, except a sister, Tsitsi, who was very clever at school and continued her education to become a State Registered Nurse. The family observe traditional obligations to one another. Rufaro sometimes visits Tsitsi in Salisbury. Because of her good income, Tsitsi is very generous with her family and often buys clothing and other gifts for them.

When Rufaro and Tichafa married, they established their own homestead at one end of the village. Today, this homestead consists of three round thatched huts which Tichafa built. The walls are made of sun-baked bricks and each of the huts has a strong, wooden door which can be padlocked on those rare occasions when everyone leaves the homestead together. The largest hut is used as a kitchen where Rufaro spends most of her time. It is here that she keeps all of her cooking utensils and dishes. In the center of the hut is a hearth and running across the center at the height of the wall is a pole where meat is hung to dry. At night the older girls sleep in the kitchen. A second, smaller hut is used by Rufaro and Tichafa as a bedroom. At night they spread sleeping mats on the floor. The three younger children sleep with them, but Shumba is nearing the age when he will be sent to sleep in the storage hut with Godfrey. Hanging from the thatched roof of the bedroom hut are a table and four chairs. These are seldom used and are hung here out of the way.

The family's clothing is also hung from a pole at one side of the hut. Each member of the family has several articles of clothing and these are hung neatly together on the wall. Other clothing is kept inside several cardboard suitcases which are stacked against one wall. Nearby is a small, hand-operated sewing machine.

The storage hut where Godfrey sleeps is elevated about a foot off the ground to protect the grain stored inside from dampness and insects. Here too are kept the traditional *badza* (hoes for cultivating the fields), pots for brewing beer, two large watering cans, tins for drawing water from the shallow well in the vegetable garden, and a large zinc tub which is used for bathing and washing clothes. The family's four bicycles are also stored in this hut. One of the bicycles has no tires.

Rufaro rises very early in the morning before any of the children are awake, but after Tichafa has left for his garden. She puts on an old cotton dress and a sweater because the early mornings are cold. She gathers firewood and heats water in an old tin so that her husband and children may wash before they eat breakfast. When she hears the baker's bell, she runs to buy bread from a passing deliveryman. The fact that she is able to feed her family fresh bread every day is an indication of the dramatic changes which have taken place in this area of Seki. The effects of industrial development and urban influence are felt in the advent of conveniences such as bread delivered to the homestead. Rufaro remembers as a little girl the novelty of bread in the family's diet. Since her son Shumba has been possessed with the spirit of his paternal grandfather, he no longer eats *sadza*. She feeds him bread instead. She prepares tea and *sadza* and then milks the cows. She wakes Shumba and Runganayi so that they will be on time for school. The others are fed later.

Rufaro spends her days looking after her two youngest children, cleaning the homestead, and working in the maize and groundnut fields. Egfa assists her mother. The family are together for lunch and dinner. Lunch usually consists of meat, *sadza*, and vegetables from the garden. The meat is purchased at a nearby store. Godfrey spends a great deal of his time fishing now that he is not attending school and his fish are often served instead of meat. The evening meal is similar to lunch. The family eat in three groups seated on the dirt floor of the kitchen hut. Rufaro and Tichafa eat together on a straw mat. Their food is in separate dishes. As the father and head of the house, Tichafa has special traditional dishes, two wooden bowls and a clay saucer. On a goat skin nearby, the girls eat together and the boys sit on a burlap sack. The children eat with their hands out of the same dishes. When Tichafa was a boy it was common for the men of his village to eat together seated outside. They were served by the women and girls. Children from neighboring families also ate together. Today this has changed.

SHUMBA AT HOME

Tichafa's sixth-born was given the name Shumba at his birth eight years ago. Since then he has acquired three other names. "Motoro" is a nickname given to him by his village playmates. They call him Motoro because as a small child he was short and chubby and liked to run about. This reminded them of an automobile and they called him Motoro. Since the death of Dzavo, his grandfather, in 1968, Shumba has been given the name Dzavo, and it is believed that the boy is possessed by Dzavo's *mudzimu* (spirit). Hungoro is a clan name used by members of Shumba's extended family. Shumba uses it too.

After his grandfather Dzavo died and had been buried near the family homestead, Shumba became ill, began to cry a lot, and was seen imitating the behavior and gestures of the deceased Dzavo. His parents were concerned by this and took him to a *nganga* (diviner) in the Chiota District. This man told them that Shumba's strange behavior was caused by the spirit of the grandfather manifesting itself in the boy. They were instructed to give Shumba the name Dzavo.

Shumba follows the same diet as his grandfather; he eats no meat or *sadza*. His head is shaved like his grandfather's. He wears a *zangu* (charm) given to him by the *nganga*. It consists of some medicine wrapped in cloth and hung around his neck on a fiber of *msasa* tree bark. He sometimes speaks in a deep voice and copies the gestures and mannerisms of the old man.

It is said by the villagers that Shumba is like Dzavo. As a boy Dzavo preferred his own company and would wander along the banks of the Nyatsime River, sometimes stopping to swim or fish. Today, Dzavo is a legend among the villagers. They enjoy telling stories of how, even as an old man, he would "drown himself" in the pools of the Nyatsime River, only to emerge minutes later with a fish in his hand. Dzavo was a spirit-guided hunter who never returned home empty-handed. His spirits forbade him to eat meat and *sadza* and he sustained himself on vegetables, fish and bread. Dzavo is also said to have been very industrious and energetic. The ant heap where he is buried is in the maize field that Shumba helps his parents to cultivate.

SHUMBA AT SCHOOL

In January 1973, Shumba was enrolled in Grade 1 at St. John's Primary School four miles from the village. His first day at school was an unusual one. Miss Chamba, Shumba's teacher, was asking the children their names. The boys and girls eagerly identified themselves. However, when she came to Shumba he refused to answer. She repeated the question in Shona. "What is your name?" Shumba remained silent. Stephen and George, Shumba's cousins and classmates began to laugh.

MISS CHAMBA:	What is wrong?
GEORGE (*pointing to Shumba*):	He is Motoro.
SHUMBA:	I am Motoro Dzavo.
MISS CHAMBA:	Is Dzavo your surname?
SHUMBA:	I am Motoro Dzavo Hungoro.
MISS CHAMBA:	Where do you come from?
SHUMBA (*angrily*):	I am Dzavo and I am possessed. I am an old man and I don't want to be troubled. Chief Seki knows me. This year he is going to die because he sold our land to the Europeans for factories. Yesterday I was in the pool in the Nyatsime River. I want to play the *mbira* [a traditional musical instrument].

Miss Chamba and Shumba's classmates were mystified. She asked a senior female teacher to help her clear up the matter. This teacher also questioned Shumba and received similar responses. Finally Shumba said, "Go to Gogo."[5] Miss Chamba asked, "Where is Gogo?" Shumba did not answer, but pointed in the direction of the Grade 4 classroom. Miss Chamba and the other teacher went to the Grade 4 classroom and asked the teacher if there was a pupil named Gogo in his class. Shumba's sister, Runganayi, came forward and Miss Chamba asked her, "Are you Motoro's sister?" Runganayi replied that she was. Miss Chamba then asked, "What is your brother's other name?" Runganayi replied, "He is Motoro Dzavo Hungoro." However, when Miss Chamba asked Runganayi where she came from, Runganayi remained silent. Miss Chamba did not persist as she was beginning to accept Shumba's behavior. She knew from her own experience how difficult it was to deal with spirit possession within the grounds of a Christian educational institution. After this incident, Miss Chamba often addressed Shumba as *Sekuru*, the title appropriate for an elder or grandfather.

As the days went by Shumba slowly began to adapt to school but he continues to behave like an old man and expects others to accord him the status of an elder. He shows resentment when female teachers, excluding Miss Chamba, greet him first, as tradition prescribes that an old man must greet younger people and females first.

Once in school, Shumba begins his day by joining the other children in informal play at the discovery shelf. Miss Chamba has left a small toy piano, a guitar, and a drum on the shelf. The children's curiosity leads them to handle the instruments and to discover what they are. The children love to go to this shelf as soon as they arrive at school to see what interesting and mysterious objects Miss Chamba has left for them to find. Shumba shows interest in the small drum, but ignores the other instruments. When they have played with the piano and guitar and drum for a few minutes Miss Chamba enters and asks, "What are these things?" Several hands are thrust into the air. Most of the village pupils say that the toy piano is a *mbira*, whereas several of the township pupils insist that it is a typewriter saying that the sounds of the keys are like typewriter keys clicking. The bell rings and the pupils leave the room and run to assemble in the school yard. Grade 1 pupils stand in the front line. Shumba positions himself between George and Stephen.

GEORGE:	Shumba, stand up straight like a policeman.
MISS CHAMBA:	George, stop talking and leave Shumba alone.

Miss Chamba approaches Shumba and speaks in English, "Good morning, Shumba." Shumba looks puzzled and does not speak.

MISS CHAMBA: Good morning, Shumba.
SHUMBA: Good morning, Shumba.

George and Stephen burst into laughter. Miss Chamba speaks then in Shona: "I don't want any child to laugh at others. You are all learning. I will punish you if you laugh. Come on, Shumba, relax and greet me correctly."

Shumba also speaks in Shona, "But I have replied. What more do you want?" At this point Miss Chamba calls Shumba by his traditional name, *Sekuru*, and instructs him in the correct responses to English greetings. At this time the assembly is silenced and prayers begin. Assembly consists of morning prayers, inspection of pupils' dress and cleanliness, and announcements. The headmaster asks the children to bring a hoe or a sickle to school the next day to cut the grass around the school. He also tells pupils to hurry home after school because parents complain that children arrive home as late as 7. School officially ends at 12:30.

After the assembly, Shumba and his classmates march in a line back to the door of their classroom. It is then that someone spots Frazzer, one of their classmates, inside the room. He has remained behind and not gone to assembly. Instantly three girls and two boys pounce on him and begin dragging him out of the room toward the teacher. She scolds Frazzer and makes him stand in front of the class like a "cock."

Miss Chamba uses three methods of punishment. Each one is designed to make the pupil feel ashamed of himself for a few moments by making him look ridiculous in front of his classmates. These punishments are called: (1) *Hwejongwe* (the cock); the pupil stands in front of the class on one leg with the other half-raised and bent and his arms stretched outwards. This is the manner in which a cock sometimes stands. (2) *Hweshiri* (the bird); the pupil stands with his feet together and his arms stretched out on either side. (3) *Hwetebu* (the table); the pupil stands on the teacher's table with his arms stretched out sideways.

Shumba sits next to George and Andrew. On the opposite side of the table are three girls. George often tells Shumba the answers to questions, much to Miss Chamba's annoyance. When Miss Chamba tries to separate George and Shumba, Shumba says, "I will go home if you tell George to sit somewhere else." Shumba's other friend, Andrew, also tries to whisper answers to him. In addition to Shumba's table there are eight other tables in the class, each seating six pupils. Children are seated around tables so that it is easier for them to engage in group activities and learn from each other.

Miss Chamba enters the classroom and says, "Stand up, boys and girls." Half of the class stand. Miss Chamba repeats herself and the rest of the pupils stand up except for a small boy who has fallen asleep and Shumba who looks puzzled. The pupils laugh at Shumba and finally Miss Chamba loses patience and shouts. "Shumba, *simuka*" (Shumba, stand up). Shumba stands up quickly and looks angrily around as if to chastize his noisy classmates. Meanwhile, the other boy wakes up at the sound of the children's laughter and jumps to his feet.

"Good morning, boys and girls," says Miss Chamba. "Good morning, mistress," the class replies in unison. Shumba does not join in, but stands watching the teacher. Miss Chamba sees that he has not greeted her with the others and commands, "Shumba, say good morning, mistress." He remains silent and continues watching the teacher. She repeats, "Shumba, say good morning, mistress." Suddenly he replies in a loud voice, "Shumba, say good morning, mistress." This pronouncement is greeted by laughter from the other children. Miss Chamba, not wishing to embarrass Shumba, withdraws, and says, "That is very good, Shumba." She directs the class to sit down.

The first lesson of the day is music. The children enjoy the songs Miss Chamba teaches them. They sit outside on the ground in a circle under a big tree and sing. Shumba and two boys accompany the others with small drums. The children have a repertoire of songs in Shona and English, many including parts which are acted out. They often can be heard singing these songs when they are away from school.

From 8:15 to 8:30, still outside, the class has a scripture lesson. To introduce the lesson, Miss Chamba holds up a branch from a wild tree and asks in Shona, the name of the tree. There is a show of hands.

MISS CHAMBA (*in Shona*):	Shumba, tell us.
SHUMBA:	It is called *musvusvu*.
MISS CHAMBA:	Is that so, class?
PUPILS:	Yes, it is called *musvusvu*.
MISS CHAMBA:	Very good, Shumba, please sit down. Who makes trees? Yes, Stephen?
STEPHEN:	God made trees.
MISS CHAMBA:	Yes, very good, Stephen. Now class, please stand up and sing, We thank our Lord Jesus for the trees.

After the children have sung the song, Miss Chamba asks the children to tell her the uses of trees. There is a show of hands and she calls on Shumba.

SHUMBA:	What about if the trees are graded by the bulldozer? Trees near my home were graded. [Other pupils begin to laugh.] Don't laugh at me. You don't know the graded trees. I will hit some of you now.
MISS CHAMBA:	No, no, *Sekuru*, please sit down. You have answered your question. If anyone laughs at Shumba or the others I shall punish you.

Miss Chamba singles out several noisy ones and makes them stand on one leg with arms outstretched in front of the group. The lesson continues and the children give many uses for trees including building huts, firewood, fruits, and shelter. Shumba states that trees are used for medicine to cure stomach troubles and headaches.

From 8:30 to 9:00 Miss Chamba stands at the front of the group and shows the children how to draw a circle and a square. She asks the children to make imaginary circles in the air with their fingers. All obey except Shumba who is singled out for a second instruction. Then shyly Shumba tries to comply. Some of the better pupils demonstrate. The others practice drawing circles in the sandy ground with their fingers. Shumba's attempts are very poor. The teacher goes through the same procedure to teach a square. Again Shumba's work is the poorest. One boy cries because he has broken his fingernail. Miss Chamba comforts him.

As soon as the group returns to the classroom, several children ask to be dismissed to go to the toilet. About a dozen more quickly follow when they realize that permission has been granted. Miss Chamba feels that the children's break period is too late in the morning for Grade 1 pupils. They are too young to sit until 10:15 without a break.

When the children are all present again, Miss Chamba begins the English lesson. She asks a boy and a girl to stand at the front of the class. The children take turns pointing to the boy and saying, "This is a boy," and then to the girl and saying, "This is a girl." When Shumba's turn comes, he stands and says, "I am a boy." Everyone laughs. The teacher corrects him and brings him to the front of the room and asks him to point first to the boy and then to the girl repeating the proper sentences in each case. Shumba looks at the teacher and then says, "I am a boy, boy! boy! am boy!" Everyone laughs and Shumba says in Shona, "I will beat some of you now." The teacher takes Shumba's hand and leads him to the boy and explains to him in Shona what is required. At this time she addresses him as *Sekuru* and this time he is successful. She then notices that the boy has his hands in his pockets. This is an offense in the classroom so she requires him to stand on one leg with arms outstretched in front of the class.

Next, the teacher gives each child a card with their name printed on it in big letters. They examine their cards and look around at the names of their friends. Miss Chamba also holds a card with her own name on it. She asks the children to say in English, "The name of our teacher is Miss Chamba." They do this one at a time and say their own name too. George takes Shumba's card. Miss Chamba hears Shumba protest and makes George serve his punishment in front of the class. When he returns to his seat beside his friend, Shumba attempts to hide behind George so he can avoid being called on. Miss Chamba spies him and says, "Shumba, don't hide. I can see you and I will give you a question. What is your name?" Shumba stands up, but remains silent. Stephen whispers to Shumba, "Say, my name is Shumba." The teacher repeats her instruction and at last Shumba says, "Shumba, Shumba! I am sitting down now." The children begin to laugh. Choosing not to disrupt the class further, Miss Chamba ignores this and continues with the lesson.

At 10:15 there is a fifteen-minute break when the pupils may do as they please. Many of them spend the time eating maize cobs and bread they have brought from home. Some buy mangoes from a village vendor who passes by. Shumba and his friends, George and Stephen, approach the vendor. They are busy trying to untie the bits of cloth in which their few cents are wrapped. A few minutes later they are sitting under a big tree in the school yard eating mangoes. Children who have no money and bring no food from home spend their break time playing.

From 10:30 to 11:00 the class has a Shona lesson. Part of the time is spent singing a traditional Shona song in two parts with a leader and a chorus. The song must be sung very rapidly and each time the leader must substitute the name of a different child. The children are all holding the cards bearing their names.

From 11:00 to 11:30 the teacher conducts a handwriting lesson. She writes the letters "a, e, i, o, u" on the blackboard. The children practice moving their fingers in the air to form the letters. Miss Chamba explains the importance of the loops. During this time Shumba is hiding behind George and does not attempt the exercise. Various children are asked to come one at a time and practice making the letters on the blackboard. Shumba is chosen and reluctantly attempts to write the letters. Only his "o" is recognizable. The children go outside to practice tracing the letters in the sand with their fingers. The teacher moves among them offering help to those having difficulty. She holds Shumba's hand with hers and moves it to form the "a, e, i," and "u." Shumba protests that the work is too hard and Miss Chamba scolds him saying, "You came here to learn. You must try with the others or I will hit you with a stick." Here Miss Chamba shows some ambivalence toward Shumba. Her role as a teacher sometimes conflicts with her empathy for his individuality.

Between 11:30 and 12:00 noon, Miss Chamba takes her class for a walk in the bush near the school. The children collect seeds and wild plants. Shumba and his companions, George and Stephen, are sent back to the classroom to fetch tins for collecting seeds.

At 12:30 the children are dismissed for the day. The upper grades often remain after school to work in the garden or to perform manual work for the teachers. Shumba and his village mates hurry back along the four-mile route which brought them to school in the morning. They are eager to get home and can be seen laughing and talking along the way.

AFTER SCHOOL

When Shumba arrives home he greets his mother and brothers and sisters and then goes into the hut to change into his old clothes. Rufaro is busy preparing lunch for her family. Since Tichafa began working in the factory he no longer returns at lunch time. Rufaro feeds her children *sadza*, meat, and vegetables. Shumba eats bread instead of *sadza* and after the meal the older children drink tea with their mother.

While Rufaro, Egfa, and Runganayi clean up the lunch dishes, Shumba and Godfrey sit outside near the kitchen hut. They are busy making toy cars out of pieces of wire. The wire is bent carefully to the proper shape and then attached. The boys connect a long piece of wire from the front axle to a steering wheel which they hold in their hands. In this way they can steer the car as they push it along in front of them. Shumba and Godfrey also spend time playing with their three dogs. Later they join other boys from their village on a fishing-swimming expedition of the Nyatsime River.

In the late afternoon when it is much cooler, all the older children in the family, including Shumba, take *badzas* and go to work in the maize fields. Godfrey is sent to fetch the family's cattle from the communal herd. Just as it is getting dark, Shumba goes to collect the chickens from the homestead. He chases them into a fowl-run for the night. When he is finished he joins Godfrey at the cattle kraal and helps him secure the gate for the night.

Tichafa is returning from his work at the factory and he sits with his two sons in the hut of his brother-in-law for a chat about the day's happenings. At seven Shumba and his family are once again seated on the floor of the kitchen hut eating a supper of *sadza*, meat, and vegetables. After dinner the family sits around the fire talking and telling folk tales. At about eight Shumba goes to bed.

CONCLUSION

Shumba lives in two worlds—his school is one, his home another. The extent to which the two are different creates conflict and change. However, Shumba's problems are not unique to children growing up within alien educational systems, but are present to some degree in school systems where cultural continuity is often presumed to exist.

The above ethnographic account of Shumba and his family illustrates the way in which Miss Chamba mediates in the school situation. Shumba's behavior is accepted and reinforced at home. However, at school the behavior of acting like his deceased grandfather, Dzavo, is defined as rebellious. He either refuses to answer the teacher or answers inappropriately and authoritatively. It is only Miss Chamba's mediating role, exemplified by her addressing him as *Sekuru*, which serves to soften the contrast. Thus, Miss Chamba's informal role as mediator is more important for Shumba than her formally designated role as transmitter of knowledge.

NOTES

1. The names have been changed to provide anonymity for the people in the study.
2. Certain traditional values are taught in African schools in addition to alien values. This is because the teachers are Africans with considerable knowledge of traditional Shona culture. Examples of traditional values perpetuated in the school are forms of greeting and respect for authority. Boys clap their hands before speaking to the teacher and girls genuflect before speaking. The *ngano*, or traditional story, is told in certain class periods. Time is scheduled in the

school syllabus for instruction in Shona language and customs. However, in Rhodesia, by contrast with South Africa, English is the medium of instruction in African schools from the first grade.

3. Students in three primary schools were studied in the classroom and in the home. The research methods used were observation, interviews, and questionnaires. Six pupils and their families were studied intensively by spending several days with each pupil. An attempt was made to select case studies of both traditional and acculturated pupils.

4. Until 1956 there were no restrictions on school enrollment age in Rhodesia. Hence it was possible for Tichafa to begin school at 17 years of age.

5. Gogo is the name of Shumba's grandmother, the wife of Dzavo. The name was given to Runganayi because she is believed to be possessed by her deceased grandmother's spirit.

REFERENCES

Bourdillon, M. F. D. "Traditional Religion in Shona Society." In *Christianity South of the Zambezi*, J. A. Dachs, ed. Gwelo: Mambo Press, 1973.

Zvarevashe, I. M. "Shona Religion." In *Shona Customs: Essays by African Writers*, C. Kileff and Kileff, eds. Gwelo: Mambo Press, 1970.

9 / Instruction and Affect in Hopi Cultural Continuity[1]

Dorothy Eggan

Education and anthropology have proved in recent years that each has much of interest to say to the other[2] for both are concerned with the transmission of cultural heritage from one generation to another—and with the means by which that transmission is accomplished. And although anthropology has tended to be preoccupied with the processes of cultural *change*, and the conditions under which it takes place, rather than with cultural continuity, it would seem, as Herskovits has said, that cultural change can be best understood when considered in relation to cultural stability (Herskovits 1950:20).

Both education and anthropology are concerned with learned behavior, and the opinion that early learning is of vital significance for the later development of personality, and that emotional factors are important in the learning process, while sometimes implicit rather than explicit, is often found in anthropological literature, particularly in that dealing with "socialization," "ethos" (Redfield 1953), and "values." From Mead's consistent work, for instance, has come a clearer picture of the socialization process in a wide variety of cultures, including our own, and she examines early "identification" as one of the problems central to all of them (Mead 1953). Hallowell, too, speaking of the learning situation in which an individual must acquire a personality pattern, points out that "there are important affective components involved" (Hallowell 1953: 610), and elsewhere he emphasizes a "need for further investigation of relations between learning process and affective experience" (Hallowell 1955: 251). Kluckhohn, writing on values and value-orientation, says that "one of the severest limitations of the classical theory of learning is its neglect of attachments and attitudes in favor of reward and punishment" (Kluckhohn 1951:430). And DuBois states explicitly that, "Institutions which may be invested with high emotional value because of patterns in child training are not ones which can be lightly legislated out of existence" (Du-Bois 1941: 281).

In fact, increasing interaction between anthropology and psychiatry (which has long held as established the connection between emotion, learning, and resistance to change in individuals) has in the last decade introduced a theme into anthropology which reminds one of Sapir's statement that "the more fully one tries to understand a culture, the more it takes on the characteristics of a personality organization" (Sapir 1949: 594).

Psychologists, while perhaps more cautious in their approach to these problems, since human emotional commitments—particularly as regards permanency—are difficult if not impossible to examine in the laboratory, emphasize their importance in the learning situation, and frequently express dissatisfaction with many existing methods and formulations in the psychology of personality. The shaping factors of emotion—learned as well as innate—are stressed by Asch (1952: 29) in his *Social Psychology*, and focus particularly on man's "need to belong." He feels that the "psychology of man needs basic research and a fresh theoretical approach." Allport speaks of past "addiction to machines, rats, or infants" in experimental psychology, and hopes for a "design for personality and social psychology" which will become "better tempered to our subject matter" as we "cease borrowing false notes—whether squeaks, squeals, or squalls" and "read the score of human personality more accurately" (Allport 1951: 168–69). And Murphy, starting with the biological foundations of human learning, particularly the individual form this "energy system" immediately assumes, examines man as psychologically structured by early canalizations in which personality is rooted, to which are added an organized symbol system and deeply ingrained habits of perception, and suggests that the structure thus built is highly resistant to change. He says that, "The task of the psychology of personality today is to apply ruthlessly, and to the limit, every promising suggestion of today, but always with the spice of healthy skepticism," while recognizing "the fundamental limitations of the whole present system of conceptions" as a preparation for "rebirth of knowledge" (Murphy 1947: 926–27).

Anthropologists as well as psychologists are aware that any hypotheses in an area so complex must be regarded as tenuous, but since the situations cannot be taken into the laboratory, there is some value in taking the laboratory to the situation. Progress in these amorphous areas can only come about, as Redfield has said, by the mental instrument which he has called a "controlled conversation" (Redfield 1955: 148)—this discussion, then, must be considered a conversation between the writer and others who have brought varied interest and techniques to the problem of resistance to cultural change[3] (DuBois 1955). It begins logically with a recent paper on "Cultural Transmission and Cultural Change" in which Bruner discusses two surveys (SSRC 1954: 973–1002, Keesing 1953; also Spiro 1955: 1240–51) of the literature on acculturation and adds to the hypotheses presented in them another which he finds relevant to the situation among the Mandan-Hidatsa Indians. As stated in his summary paragraph we find the proposition: "That which is learned and internalized in infancy and early childhood is most resistant to contact situations. The hypothesis directs our attention to the age in the individual life career at which each aspect of culture is transmitted, as well as to the full context of the learning situation and the position of the agents of socialization in the larger social system" (Bruner 1956a: 197).

This proposition will be further extended by a consideration of the *emotional* commitment involved in the socialization process among the Hopi Indians: here the "conversation" will be directed to emotion in both teaching and learning, and will center around resistance to cultural change which has been remarkably consistent in Hopi society throughout recorded history *until the Second World War brought enforced and drastic changes.*[4]   At that time the young men, although legitimately conscientious objectors, were drafted into the army.   Leaving the isolation of their reservation, where physical violence between adults was rare, they were rapidly introduced to the stark brutality of modern warfare.   In army camps alcoholic intoxication, an experience which was the antithesis of the quiet, controlled behavior normally demanded of adult Hopi on their reservation, frequently brought relief from tension and a sense of comradeship with fellow soldiers.   Deprived of the young men's work in the fields, many older people and young women were in turn forced to earn a living in railroad and munition centers off the reservation. Thus the gaps in the Hopi "communal walls" were, for the first time, large enough in numbers and long enough in time—and the experiences to which individuals had to adapt were revolutionary enough in character—so that the sturdy structure was damaged.   It is emphasized, therefore, that in this discussion *Hopi* refers to those members of the tribe who reached *adulthood* and were thoroughly committed to their own world view before 1941.   Much of it would not apply as forcefully to the children of these people, and would be even less applicable to their grandchildren.

The major hypotheses suggested here, then, are:

1. That the Hopi, as contrasted with ourselves, were experts in the use of *affect* in their educational system, and that this element continued to operate throughout the entire life span of each individual as a *reconditioning* factor (Herskovits 1950: 325–26, 491, 627).

2. That this exercise of emotion in teaching and learning was an efficient means of social control which functioned in the absence of other forms of policing and restraint, and also in the maintenance of stability both in the personality structure of the individual and the structure of the society.

These hypotheses may be explored through a consideration of (a) the early and continued conditioning of the individual in the Hopi maternal extended family, which was on every level an inculcation of *interdependence* as contrasted with our training for *independence*; and (b) an early and continuing emphasis on religious observances and beliefs (also emphasizing interdependence), the most important facet of which—for the purposes of this paper—was the central concept of the Hopi "good heart."[5]

If we examine the educational system by which a Hopi acquired the personal entity which made him so consistently and determinedly Hopi, we find that it was deliberate and systematic (Pettit 1946, Hough 1915: 218).   Students of Hopi are unanimous on this point but perhaps it can be best illustrated by quoting one of my informants who had spent much time away from the reservation, including many years in a boarding school, and who was considered by herself and other Hopi to be an extremely "acculturated" individual.   In 1938 when she made this statement she was about thirty years old and had brought her children back to the reservation to be "educated."   Said she:

It is very hard to know what to do. In the old days I might have had more babies for I should have married early. Probably some of them would have died. But my comfort would have been both in numbers and in knowing that all women lost babies. Now when I let my little son live on top [a conservative village on top of the mesa] with my mothers, I worry all the time. If he dies with dysentery I will feel like I killed him. Yet he *must* stay on top so the old people can teach him the *important* things. It is his only chance of becoming Hopi, for he would never be a *bahana* (white).

The education which she considered so vital included careful, deliberate instruction in kinship and community obligations, and in Hopi history as it is seen in mythology and as remembered by the old people during their own lifetimes. The Hopi taught youngsters fear as a means of personal and social control and for the purposes of personal and group protection; and they were taught techniques for the displacement of anxiety, as well as procedures which the adults believed would prolong life. Children were instructed in religious lore, in how to work and play, in sexual matters, even in how to deal with a *bahana*. Good manners were emphasized, for they were a part of the controlled, orderly conduct necessary to a Hopi good heart.

Constantly one heard during work or play, running through all activity like a connecting thread: "Listen to the old people—they are wise"; or, "Our old uncles taught us that way—it is the *right* way." Around the communal bowl, in the kiva, everywhere this instruction went on; stories, dream adventures, and actual experiences such as journeys away from the reservation were told and retold. And children, in the warmth and security of this intimate extended family clan group, with no intruding outside experiences to modify the impact until they were forced to go to an alien school, learned what it meant to be a good Hopi from a wide variety of determined teachers who had very definite—and *mutually consistent*—ideas of what a good Hopi is. And they learned all of this in the Hopi language, which, as Whorf has made so clear, has no words with which to express many of our concepts, but which, working together with "a different set of cultural and environmental influences . . . interacted with Hopi linguistic patterns to mould them, to be moulded again by them, and so little by little to shape the world outlook" (Whorf 1941: 92).

Eventually these children disappeared into government schools for a time, and in the youth of most of these older Hopi it was a boarding school off the reservation where Indian children from various reservations were sent, often against their own and their parents' wishes.[6] Here white teachers were given the task of "civilizing" and "Christianizing" these wards of the government, but by that time a Hopi child's view of the world and his place in it was very strong. Moreover, trying to transpose our concepts into their language was often very nearly impossible for them, since only Hopi had been spoken at home. Examining Hopi memory for such a method of education we quote a male informant who said:

> I went to school about four years. . . . We worked like slaves for our meals and keep. . . . We didn't learn much. . . . I didn't understand and it was hard to learn. . . . At that time you do what you are told or you get punished. . . . You just wait till you can go home.

And a woman said:

> Policemen gathered us up like sheep. I was scared to death. My mother tried to hide me. I tried to stay away but the police always won. . . . Then we were sent up to Sherman [in California]. . . . It was far away; we were afraid on the train. . . I didn't like it when I couldn't learn and neither did the teachers. . . . They never punished me, I always got 100 in Deportment. . . . I was there three years. . . . I was so glad to get home that I cried and cried . . . , glad to have Hopi food again, and fun again.

As children, the Hopi usually solved this dilemma of enforced education by means of a surface accomodation to the situation until such time as they were able to return to their own meaningful world. For, as Park has said, man can "make his manners a cloak and his face a mask, behind which he is able to preserve . . . inner freedom . . . and independence of thought, even when unable to maintain independence of action."[7] In other words, because the inner core of Hopi identification was already so strong, these children were able to *stay* in a white world, while still *living* in the Hopi world within themselves.[8] And while for some there was a measure of temptation in many of the things learned in white schools so that they "became friendly with whites and accepted their gifts,"[9] the majority of these older Hopi acquired a white education simply as a "necessary accessory";[10] they incorporated parts of our material culture, and learned to deal with Whites astutely, but their values were largely unaffected.

If we now examine more closely the pattern of integration through which the Hopi erected a communal wall[11] around their children we find in their kinship system the framework of the wall, but interwoven through it and contributing greatly to its strength was a never-ending composition which gave color and form, their religious ceremonies and beliefs.

Let us first contrast briefly the affect implicit in the way a Hopi born into this kinship system experienced relationships and the way in which Western children experience them. In the old days it was rare for a growing primary family to live outside the maternal residence. Normally each lived within it until the birth of several children crowded them out. And in this household each child was eagerly welcomed, for infant mortality was high and the clan was always in need of reinforcement. Thus, in spite of the physical burden on the biological mother, which she sometimes resented, the first strong *clan* sanction which we see in contrast to our own, was the absolute need for and desire for many children. From birth the young of the household were attended, pampered, and disciplined, although very mildly for the first several years, by a wide variety of relatives in addition to the mother. These attentions came both from the household members and from visitors in it. In no way was a baby ever as dependent upon his physical mother as are children in our culture. He was even given the breast of a mother's mother or sister if he cried for food in his mother's absence. True a Hopi saying states that a baby is made "sad" if another baby steals his milk, but it has been my experience that these women may risk making their own babies sad temporarily if another child needs food.

Weaning, of course, when discussed in personality contexts means more than a transition from milk to solid food. It is also a gradual process of achieving independence from the comfort of the mother's body and care, of transferring affections to other persons, and of finding satisfactions within oneself and in the outside world. Most people learn to eat solid food; many of us are never weaned, which has unfortunate consequences in a society where *individual* effort and independence are stressed. The Hopi child, on the other hand, from the day of his birth was being weaned from his biological mother. Many arms gave him comfort, many faces smiled at him, and from a very early age he was given bits of food which were chewed by various members of the family and placed in his mouth. So, for a Hopi, the outside world in which he needed to find satisfaction was never far away. He was not put in a room by himself and told to go to sleep; every room was crowded by sleepers of all ages. He was in no way *forced to find satisfaction within himself*; rather these were provided for him, if possible, by his household and clan group. His weaning, then, was from the breast only, and as he was being weaned from the biological mother, he was at the same time in a situation which *increased* his emotional orientation toward the intimate in-group of the extended family—which was consistent with the interests of Hopi social structure. Thus, considering weaning in its wider implications, a Hopi was never "weaned"; it was not intended that he should be. For these numerous caretakers contributed greatly to a small Hopi's faith in his intimate world—and conversely without question to a feeling of strangeness and *emotional insecurity* as adults in any world outside of this emotional sphere. The Hopi were often successful outside of the reservation, but they have shown a strong tendency to return frequently to the maternal household. Few ever left it permanently.

In addition to his extended family, while a Hopi belonged to one clan only, the clan into which he was born, he was a "child" of his father's clan, and this group took a lively interest in him. There were also numerous ceremonial and adoptive relationships which were close and warm, so that most of the persons in his familiar world had definite reciprocal relations with the child (Eggan 1950: chap. 2; Simmons 1942: chaps. 3, 4). Since all of these "relatives" lived in his own small village, or in villages nearby, his emotional and physical "boundaries" coincided, were quite definitely delimited, and were explored and perceived at the same time. It cannot be too strongly emphasized that the kinship terms which a Hopi child learned in this intimate atmosphere were not mere verbalizations—as, for instance, where the term "cousin" among ourselves is sometimes applied to someone we have never seen and never will see. On the contrary, each term carried with it definite mutual responsibilities and patterns of behavior, and, through these, definite emotional interaction as well. These affects were taught as proper responses, together with the terms which applied to each individual, as he entered the child's life. This process was deliberately and patiently, but unceasingly, worked at by every older individual in the child's surroundings, so by the time a Hopi was grown kinship reaction patterns were so deeply ingrained in his thinking and feeling, and in his workaday life, that they were as much a part of him as sleeping and eating. He was not merely told that Hopi rules of behavior were right or wise; he lived them as he grew and *in his total environment* (Henry 1955) (as contrasted to our separation of teaching at home, in school, and in Sunday school) until he was simply not conscious that there was any other way to react. Note that I say *conscious!* The unconscious level of feeling, as seen in dreams and life-history materials, and in indirect behavior manifestations (jealousy and gossip), often presents quite a different picture. But while ambivalence toward specific persons among the Hopi—as with mankind everywhere—is a personal burden, the long reinforced conditioned reaction of *interdependence* on both the emotional and overt behavior level was highly uniform and persistent (see Whorf 1941: 87; Aberle 1951: 93-94, 119-23). Perhaps the strength of kinship conditioning toward interdependence which was conveyed in a large but intimate group, living in close physical contact, can be best illustrated by quoting from an informant:

> My younger sister ——was born when I was about four or five, I guess. I used to watch my father's and mother's relatives fuss over her. She didn't look like much to me. I couldn't see why people wanted to go to so much trouble over a wrinkled little thing like that baby. I guess I didn't like babies as well as most girls did. . . . But I had to care for her pretty soon anyway. She got fat and was hard to carry around on my back, for I was pretty little myself. First I had to watch her and joggle the cradle board when she cried. She got too big and wiggled too much and then my mother said to me, "She is *your sister*—take her out in the plaza in your shawl."
> She made my back ache. Once I left her and ran off to play with the others for a while. I intended to go right back, but I didn't go so soon, I guess. Someone found her. I got punished for this. My mother's brother said: "You should not have a sister to help you out when you get older. What can a woman do without her sisters?[12] You are not one of us to leave your sister alone to die. If harm had come to her you would never have a clan, no relatives at all. No one would ever help you out or take care of you. Now you have another chance. You owe her more from now on. This is the worst thing that any of my sister's children has ever done. You are going to eat by yourself until you are fit to be one of us." That is what he said. That is the way he talked on and on and on. When meal time came they put a plate of food beside me and said, "Here is your food; eat your food." It was a long

time they did this way. It seemed a long time before they looked at me.
They were all sad and quiet. They put a pan beside me at meal time and said
nothing—nothing at all, not even to scold me.

My older sister carried ——now. I didn't try to go near her. But I looked at
my sisters and thought, "I need you—I will help you if you will help me." I
would rather have been beaten or smoked. I was so ashamed all the time.
Wherever I went people got sad [i.e., quiet]. After a while [in about ten days
as her mother remembered it] they seemed to forget it and I ate with people
again. During those awful days Tuvaye [a mother's sister] sometimes touched
my head sadly, while I was being punished, I mean. Once or twice she gave
me something to eat. But she didn't say much to me. Even she and my grandfather were ashamed and in sorrow over this awful thing I had done.

Sometimes now I dream I leave my children alone in the fields and I wake
up in a cold sweat. Sometimes I dream I am alone in a desert place with no
water and no one to help me. Then I think of this punishment when I dream
this way. It was the worst thing I ever did. It was the worst thing that ever
happened to me. No one ever mentioned it to me afterward but —— [older
male sibling], the mean one. I would hang my head with shame. Finally my
father told him sharply that he would be punished if he ever mentioned this
to me again. I was about six when this happened, I think.

This informant was about forty when she related this incident, but she cried, even
then, as she talked.

Nor was withdrawal of support the only means of punishment. There were bogey
Kachinas who "might kidnap" bad children, and who visited the mesas sometimes
when children were uncooperative; thus the "stranger" *joined effectively* with the
clan in inducing the "ideal" Hopi behavior. But children *shared* this fear, as they
also frequently shared other punishments. Dennis has called attention to the fact
that a whole group of children often shared the punishment for the wrongdoing of
one (Dennis 1941: 263). This method may not endear an individual to his agemates,
but it does reinforce the central theme of Hopi belief that each person in the group
is responsible for what happens to all, however angry or jealous one may feel toward
siblings.

Before we examine the religious composition of the Hopi "communal walls," we
might contrast more explicitly the emotional implications of early Hopi conditioning to those experienced in our society. From the day of *our* birth the training toward *independence*—as contrasted to *interdependence*—starts. We sleep alone; we
are immediately and increasingly in a world of comparative strangers. A variety of
nurses, doctors, relatives, sitters, and teachers march through our lives in a never-
ending procession. A few become friends, but *compared with a Hopi child's experiences*, the impersonality and lack of emotional relatedness to so many kinds of
people with such widely different backgrounds is startling. Indeed the disparity of
the relationships as such is so great that continuity of emotional response is impossible, and so we learn to look for emotional satisfaction in change, which in itself
becomes a value (Kluckhohn and Kluckhohn 1947: 109). In addition, we grow up
aware that there are many ways of life within the American class system; we know
that there are many choices which we must make as to profession, behavior, moral
code, even religion; and we know that the values of our parents' generation are not
necessarily ours. If the permissive intimacy in the primary family in our society—
from which both nature and circumstance demand a break in adulthood—is too
strong, the individual cannot mature so that he can function efficiently in response to the always changing personalities in his life, and the always changing demands of the society (Riesman 1955, Mead 1948: 518). He becomes a dependent
neurotic "tentative between extreme polarities" (Erikson 1948: 198, Murphy 1947:
714-33). But precisely because the permissive intimacy, as well as the punishing

agencies, in a Hopi child's life were so far and so effectively extended in his formative years he became *interdependent* with a larger but still definitely delimited group, and tended always to be more comfortable and effective within it. His self-value quickly identified itself with the larger Hopi value (Hallowell 1955: chap. 4; Erikson 1948: 198, fn), and to the extent that he could continue throughout his life to identify with his group and function within it, he was secure in his place in the universe.

We have now sketched the situation which surrounded the young Hopi child in his first learning situations, and contrasted these with our own. For descriptive convenience this has been separated from religious instruction, but in the reality experience of the children—with the exception of formal initiation rites—no one facet of learning to be Hopi was separated from others. To understand the meaning his religion had for a Hopi one must first understand the harsh physical environment into which he was born. While it is agreed that it would not be possible to predict the character or the social structure of the Hopi from the circumstances of this physical environment,[13] it is self-evident that their organized social and ritual activities are largely a response to it. And such activities are at once a reflection of man's need to *be*, and his need to justify his existence to himself and others. If those who doubt that the forces of nature are powerful in shaping personality and culture were confined for one year on the Hopi reservation—even though their own economic dependence on "nature" would be negligible—they would still know by personal experience more convincing than scientific experiments the relentless pressure of the environment on their own reaction patterns. They would, for instance, stand, as all Hopis have forever stood, with aching eyes fastened on a blazing sky where thunderheads piled high in promise and were snatched away by "evil winds," and thus return to their homes knowing the tension, the acute bodily need for the "feel" of moisture. When rains do fall, there is the likelihood of a cloudburst which will ruin the fields. And there is a possibility of early frost which will destroy their crops, as well as the absolute certainty of sandstorms, rodents, and worms which will ruin many plants. These things on a less abstract level than "feeling" resolved themselves into a positive threat of famine and thirst which every Hopi knew had repeatedly ravaged his tribe. Is it possible that the effects of this silent battle between man and the elements left no mark on successive generations of individuals? It certainly was the reinforced concrete of Hopi social structure, since strongly conditioned interdependence was the only hope of survival.

Thus, the paramount problem for the Hopi was uncertain rain, and the outward expression of their deep need for divine aid was arranged in a cycle of ceremonies, the most impressive of which, at least among the exoteric rituals, were Kachina (Earle and Kennard 1938) dances. These were, for the observer, colorful pageants in which meticulously trained dancers performed from sunrise until sunset, with short intermissions for food and rest. Their bodies were ceremonially painted; brilliant costumes were worn, along with beautifully carved and painted masks which represented the particular gods who were taking part in the ceremony. The color, the singing, and the drums which accompanied the dance, the graceful rhythm and intense concentration of the dancers, all combine into superb artistry which is an hypnotic and impressive form of prayer. Ideally, the Hopi preceded every important act with prayer, and with these older Hopi the ideal was apt to be fact. A bag of sacred cornmeal was part of their daily equipment.

In the religious context also, we must remember the intimate atmosphere which surrounded a Hopi child in the learning situation. Here children were taught that if *all* Hopi behaved properly—i.e., kept good hearts—the Kachinas would send rain. It was easy for the children to believe this because from earliest babyhood these beautiful creatures had danced before them as they lolled comfortably in convenient laps. There was a happy, holiday atmosphere throughout a village on dance days, but while each dance was being performed, the quiet of profound reverence. Lying in the mother's lap, a baby's hands were often struck together in the rhythm of the dance; as soon as he would walk his feet were likewise directed in such rhythm, and everybody praised a child and laughed affectionately and encouragingly as it tried to dance. As the children grew older, carved likeness of these gods, as well as other presents, were given to them by the gods themselves. And as he grew in understanding, a child could not fail to realize that these dancers were part of a religious ceremony which was of utmost importance in his world—that the dancers were rain-bringing and thus life-giving gods.

When first initiation revealed that the gods were in reality men who danced in their stead, a *reorganization* of these emotions which had been directed toward them began, and there is much evidence in autobiographical materials of resentment, if not actual trauma, at this point. For some of them the initiation was a physical ordeal, but for those who entered this phase of their education by way of Powamu there was no whipping, although all initiates witnessed the whipping of those who were initiated into the Kachina cult (F. Eggan 1950: 47-50, Steward 1931: 59 ff).[14] However, the physical ordeal seems to be less fixed in adult memories than disillusion.

In Don Talayesva's account of initiation into Kachina we find:

> I had a great surprise. They were not spirits, but human beings. I recognized nearly every one of them and felt very unhappy because I had been told all my life that the Kachinas were Gods. I was especially shocked and angry when I saw my uncles, fathers, and own clanbrothers dancing as Kachinas. . . . [But] my fathers and uncles showed me ancestral masks and explained that long ago the Kachinas had come regularly to Oraibi and danced in the plaza. They explained that since the people had become so wicked . . . the Kachinas had stopped coming and sent their spirits to enter the masks on dance days. . . I thought of the flogging and the initiation as a turning point in my life, and I felt ready at last to listen to my elders and live right. (Simmons 1942: 84-87)

One of our informants said in part:

> I cried and cried into my sheepskin that night, feeling I had been made a fool of. How could I ever watch the Kachinas dance again? I hated my parents and thought I could never believe the old folks again, wondering if gods had ever danced for the Hopi as they now said and if people really lived after death. I hated to see the other children fooled and felt mad when they said I was a big girl now and should act like one. But I was afraid to tell the others the truth for they might whip me to death. I know now it was best and the *only way to teach* children, but it took me a long time to know that. I hope my children won't feel like that.

This informant was initiated into Powamu and not whipped. She was about thirty when she made this statement to the writer.

Another woman, from a different mesa, speaking of her initiation into the Kachina society, said to me:

> The Kachinas brought us children presents. I was very little when I remember getting my first Kachina doll. I sat in my mother's lap and was "ashamed" [these people often use ashamed for shy or somewhat fearful], but she held out my hand for the doll. I grabbed it and hid in her lap for a long time because the Kachina looked too big to me and I was partly scared. But my mother told me to say "asqualie" [thank you] and I did. The music put me

to sleep. I would wake up. The Kachinas would still be there. . . . I dreamed sometimes that the Kachinas were dancing and brought me lots of presents. . .

When I was initiated into Kachina society I was scared. I heard people whisper about it. . . . Children shook their heads and said it was hard to keep from crying. . . . My mother always put her shawl over my head when the Kachinas left the plaza. When she took it off they would be gone. So I knew they were gods and had gone back to the San Francisco mountains. . . . My ceremonial mother came for me when it was time to go to the kiva [for initiation] and she looked sad [i.e., serious]. She took most of the whipping on her own legs [a custom widely practiced among the Hopi]. But then I saw my father and my relatives were Kachinas. When they took their masks off this is what I saw. I was all mixed up. I was mad. I began to cry. I wondered how my father became a Kachina and if they [these men, including her father] would all go away when the Kachinas went back to the San Francisco mountains where the dead people live. Then when my father came home I cried again. I was mad at my parents and my ceremonial mother. "These people have made me silly," I said to myself, "and I thought they were supposed to like me so good." I said that to myself. But I was still crying, and the old people told me that only babies cry. They kept saying I would understand better when I got bigger. They said again that the Kachinas had to go away because the Hopi got bad hearts, and they [the Kachinas] couldn't stand quarreling, but they left their heads behind for the Hopis. I said why didn't they rot then like those skulls we found under that house? They said I was being bad and that I should have been whipped more. . . .

When children asked me what happened in the kiva I was afraid to tell them because something would happen to me. Anyway I felt smart because I knew more than those *little* children. It took me a long time to get over this sadness, though. Later I saw that the Kachinas were the most *important things in life* and that children can't understand these things. . . . It takes a while to see how wise the old people really are. You learn they are always right in the end.

Before we try to find our way with the Hopi to an "understanding of these things" we must examine their concept of the good heart which functions both in their kinship system and religion to maintain the effectiveness of the "wall of Hopiness." Of greatest significance in all activities among these people, and particularly in their religious ceremonies, is the fact that everything of importance is done communally. Thus each individual who has reached maturity is responsible *to* and *for* the whole community. The Hopi speak of this process as "uniting our hearts," which in itself is a form of prayer. A slight mistake in a ceremony can ruin it and thus defeat the community prayer for rain; so too can a trace of "badness" in one's heart, although it may not be visible to the observer. Thus their religion teaches that *all* distress—from illness to crop failure—is the result of bad hearts, or possibly of witchcraft (here the simple "bad heart" must not be confused with a "Two-heart," *powaka*, witch), an extreme form of personal wickedness in which an individual sacrifices others, particularly his own relatives, to save himself (Titiev 1942; Aberle 1951: 94).

This concept of a good heart in *conscious contradistinction* to a bad heart is of greatest importance not only in understanding Hopi philosophy but also in understanding their deep sense of cultural continuity and their resistance to fundamental change. A good heart is a positive thing, something which is never out of a Hopi's mind. It means a heart at peace with itself and one's fellows. There is no worry, unhappiness, envy, malice, nor any other disturbing emotion in a good heart. In this state, cooperation, whether in the extended household or in the fields and ceremonies, was selfless and easy. Unfortunately, such a conception of a good heart is also impossible of attainment. Yet if a Hopi did not keep a good heart he might fall ill and die, or the ceremonies—and thus the vital crops—might fail, for, as has been said, only those with good hearts were effective in prayer. Thus we see that the Hopi concept of a good heart included conformity to all rules of Hopi good conduct, both external and internal. To the extent that it was internalized—and all Hopi biographical material known to the writer suggests strongly that it was effectively internalized—it might reasonably be called a quite universal culturally patterned and culturally consistent Hopi "superego."[15]

There was, therefore, a constant probing of one's own heart, well illustrated by the anguished cry of a Hopi friend, "Dorothy, *did* my son die as the old folks said because my heart was not right? Do *you* believe this way, that if parents do not keep good hearts children will die?" And there was a constant examination of one's neighbors' hearts: "Movensie, it is those —— clan people who ruined this ceremony! They had bad hearts and they quarrel too much. That bad wind came up and now we will get no rain." Conversation among the Hopi is rarely censored, and the children heard both of these women's remarks, *feeling*, you may be sure, the *absolute belief* which these "teachers" had in the *danger* which a bad heart carries for everyone in the group.

In such situations, since human beings can bear only a certain amount of guilt,[16] there is a great game of blame-shifting among the Hopi, and this in turn adds a further burden of unconscious guilt, for it is difficult to love properly a neighbor or even a sister who has a bad heart. However, in the absence of political organization, civil and criminal laws, and a formal method of punishment for adults, this consistent "tribal superego" has maintained, throughout known history, a record almost devoid of crime and violence within the group,[17] and it has conditioned and ever *reconditioned* a Hopi to feel secure only in being a Hopi.

For through the great strength of the emotional orientations conveyed within the kinship framework and the interwoven religious beliefs, young Hopi learned their world from dedicated teachers whose emotions were involved in teaching what they believed intensely, and this in turn engaged the children's emotions in learning. These experiences early and increasingly made explicit in a very personal way the values implicit in the distinction between a good heart and a bad heart. For public opinion, if intensely felt and openly expressed in a closely knit and mutually dependent group—as in the case of the child who left her baby sister alone—can be more effective potential punishment than the electric chair. It is perhaps easier to die quickly than to live in loneliness in a small community in the face of contempt from one's fellows, and particularly from one's clan from whence, as we have seen, comes most of one's physical and emotional security. Small wonder that the children who experience this constant pressure to conform to clan dictates and needs, and at the same time this constant reinforcement of clan solidarity against outsiders, are reluctant as adults to stray too far from the clan's protective familiarity or to defy its wishes.

There was much bickering and tension within the clan and village, of course, and it was a source of constant uneasiness and ambivalence among the Hopi.[18] But tension and bickering, as I have indicated elsewhere, "are not exclusively Hopi"; the Hopi see it constantly among the Whites on and off the reservation. What they do *not* find elsewhere is the *emotional satisfaction* of belonging intensely, to which they have been conditioned and reconditioned. For, as Murphy says, "It is not only the 'desire to be accepted' ... that presses the ego into line. The basic psychology of perception is involved, the individual has learned to see himself as a member of the group, and the self has true 'membership character,' structurally integrated with the perception of group life" (Murphy 1947: 855; Asch 1952: 334-335, 605). Actually the Hopi clan, even with its in-group tensions and strife, but with all of the advantages emotional and physical it affords the individual, is one of the most successful and meaningful "boarding schools" ever devised for citizenship training.

In this situation, where belonging was so important, and a good heart so vital to the feeling of belonging, gossip is the potential and actual "social cancer" of the Hopi tribe. It is devastating to individual security and is often senselessly false and cruel, but in a country where cooperation was the only hope of survival, it was the *servant* as well as the policeman of the tribe. Not lightly would any Hopi voluntarily acquire the title Kahopi[19] "*not* Hopi," and therefore not good. Throughout the Hopi life span the word kahopi, *kahopi*, KAHOPI was heard, until it penetrated to the very core of one's mind. It was said softly and gently at first to tiny offenders, through "Kahopi tiyo" or "Kahopi mana" to older children, still quietly but with stern intent, until the word sometimes assumed a crescendo of feeling as a whole clan or even a whole community might condemn an individual as *Kahopi*.

It is true that we, too, are told we should keep good hearts and love our neighbors as ourselves. But we are not told that, if we do not, our babies will die, *now, this year!* Some children are told that if they do not obey the various "commandments" they learn in different churches they will eventually burn in a lake of hell fire, but they usually know that many of their world doubt this. In contrast, Hopi children constantly *saw* babies die because a parent's heart was not right; they *saw* evil winds come up and crops fail for the same reason; they *saw* adults sicken and die because of bad thoughts or witchcraft (to which bad thoughts rendered a person more vulnerable). Thus they learned to *fear* the results of a bad heart whether it belonged to themselves or to others. There were witches, bogey Kachinas, and in objective reality famine and thirst to fear. Along with these fears were taught mechanisms for the displacement of anxiety, including the services of medicine men, confession and exorcism to get rid of bad thoughts, and cooperative nonaggression with one's fellows, even those who were known to be witches. But the best technique was that which included all the values in the positive process of keeping a good heart, and of "uniting our hearts" in family, clan, and fraternal society—in short, the best protection was to be *Hopi* rather than *Kahopi*.

It is clear throughout the literature on the Hopi, as well as from the quotations given in this discussion, that in finding their way toward the goal of "belonging" Hopi children at first initiation had to deal with religious disenchantment, resentment, and with ever increasing demands made by their elders for more mature behavior. These factors were undoubtedly important catalyzing agents in Hopi personality formation and should be examined from the standpoint of Benedict's formulations on discontinuity (Benedict 1948: 423-24). Here we must remember that shock can operate either to destroy or to mobilize an organism's dormant potentialities. And if a child has been *consistently* conditioned to feel a part of his intimate world, and providing he still lives on in this same world; it seems reasonable to suppose that shock (unless it were so great as to completely disorganize personality, in which case the custom could not have persisted) would reinforce the individual's *need* to belong and thus would tend to reassemble many of his personality resources around this need.

If the world surrounding the Hopi child had changed from warmth to coldness, from all pleasure to all hardship, the discontinuity would have indeed been insupportable. But the new demands made on him, while more insistent, were not unfamiliar in *kind*; all adults, as well as his newly initiated age mates, faced the same ones. He had shared the shock as he had long since learned to share all else; and he now shared the rewards of "feeling big." He had the satisfaction of increased status along with the burden of increasing responsibility, as the adults continued to teach him "the important things," and conformity gradually became a value in itself— even as we value nonconformity and change. It was both the means *and* the goal. Conformity surrounded the Hopi—child or adult—with everything he could hope to have or to be; outside it there was only the feeling tone of rejection. Since there were no bewildering choices presented (as is the case in our socialization process), the "maturation drive"[20] could only function to produce an ego-ideal in accord with the cultural ideal,[21] however wide the discrepancy between ideal and reality on both levels.

And since the Kachinas played such a vital role in Hopi society throughout, we must consider specifically the way in which the altered faith expressed by informants gradually came about after the first initiation (Aberle 1951: 38–41). First, of course, was the need to find it, since in any environment one must have faith and hope. They also wanted to continue to believe in and to enjoy that which from earliest memory had induced a feeling of pleasure, excitement, and of solidarity within the group. A beginning was undoubtedly made in modifying resentment when the Kachinas whipped each other after first initiation; first, it was again sharing punishment, but this time not only with children but *with adults.* They had long known that suffering came from bad hearts; they also knew, as indicated above, that something must be done about bad hearts. The Kachinas whipped to cleanse the bad hearts implied by disobedience to the rules of Hopi good conduct and then whipped each other for the same reason; thus there was logic in an initiation which was actually an extension of an already established conception of masked gods who rewarded good behavior with presents but withheld rain if hearts were not right, and who sometimes threatened bad children (Goldfrank 1945: 516–39).

Another reorganizing factor explicitly stated in the quotations was "feeling big." They had shared pain with adults, had learned secrets which forever separated them from the world of children, and they were now included in situations from which they had previously been excluded, as their elders continued to teach intensely what they believed intensely: that for them there was only one alternative—Hopi as against Kahopi.

Consistent repetition is a powerful conditioning agent and, as the youngsters watched each initiation, they relived their own, and by again sharing the experience gradually worked out much of the bitter residue from their own memories of it, while also rationalizing and weaving the group emotions ever stronger into their own emotional core—"It takes a while to see how wise the old people really are." An initiated boy, in participating in the Kachina dances, learned to identify again with the Kachinas whom he now impersonated. To put on a mask is to "become a Kachina," and to cooperate actively in bringing about the major goals of Hopi life. And a girl came to know more fully the importance of her clan in its supportive role. These experiences were even more sharply conditioned and directed toward adult life in the tribal initiation ceremonies, of which we have as yet only fragmentary knowledge. Of this one man said to me: "I will not discuss this thing with you only to say that no one can forget it. It is the most wonderful thing any man can have to remember. You know then that you are Hopi. It is one thing Whites cannot have, cannot take from us. It is our way of life given to use when the world began."

And since children are, for all mankind, a restatement of one's hopes to be, when these Hopi in turn became teachers (and in a sense they had always been teachers of the younger children in the household from an early age), they continued the process of reliving and rationalizing, or "working out" their experiences with an intensity which is rarely known in our society except, perhaps, on the psychoanalytic couch. But the Hopi had no psychiatrists to guide them—no books which, as Riesman says, "like an invisible monitor, helps liberate the reader from his group and its emotions, and allows the contemplation of alternative responses and the trying on of new emotions" (Riesman 1955: 13). They had only the internalized "feeling measure" and "group measure" explicit in the concepts of Hopi versus Kahopi.

On the material level, the obvious advantages of, for instance, wagons versus backs were a temptation. And to the extent to which white influences at first penetrated to these older Hopi it was through this form of temptation. But outside experiences usually included some variation of hostility, scorn, or aggression, as well as a radically different moral code, and these were all viewed and reinterpreted through the Hopi-eye view of the world and in the Hopi language, so that a return to the familiarity of the Hopi world with its solidarity of world view and behavior patterns *was experienced as relief*, and increased the need to feel Hopi, *however great a burden "being Hopi"* implied.

In summary, the hypothesis here developed, that strong emotional conditioning during the learning process was an instrument in cultural continuity among the Hopi, is suggested as supplementary to that of early learning as being resistant to change. It further suggests that this conditioning was *constantly* as well as *consistently* instilled during the entire lifetime of an individual by a circular pattern of integration. For an individual was surrounded by a series of invisible, but none the less solid, barriers between himself and the outside world. To change him, influences had to breach the concentric walls of social process—as conveyed through the human entities which surrounded him and which were strengthened by his obligation to teach others—and then to recondition his early and ever increasing emotional involvement in Hopi religion, morals, and mutually dependent lineage and clan groups, as well as those attitudes toward white aggression which he shared with all Indians.

In 1938 one old Hopi, who in his youth had been taken away from his wife and children and kept in a boarding school for several years, said to me:

> I am full of curiosity; a great *bahana* [white] education would tell me many things I've wondered about like the stars and how a man's insides work. But I am afraid of it because I've seen what it does to folks. . . . If I raise a family, clothe and feed them well, do my ceremonial duties faithfully, I have succeeded—what do you call success? . . . [And again, while discussing fear in connection with a dream, his comment was] Well, yes, we are afraid of *po-wakas* [witches] but our medicine men can handle them. Neither your doctors nor your gods can control your governments so you have more to fear. Now you are dragging us into your quarrels. I pity you and I don't envy you. You have more goods than we have, but you don't have peace ever; *it is better to die in famine than in war.*

As the old man anticipated, enforced participation in modern warfare soon replaced instruction for Hopi citizenship, and the concentric walls were finally seriously breached. But for these older Hopi the walls still enclose "our way of life given to us when the world began."

NOTES

1. The substance of this paper was originally presented to the Society for Social Research of the University of Chicago in 1943, and subsequently enlarged in 1954 at the request of Edward Bruner for his class in Anthropology and Education. Disscussion with him has greatly clarified my thinking on the problems examined here. Some elimination and revision has been made in order to include references to recently published work and suggestions from Fred Eggan, David Aberle, Clyde Kluckhohn, David Riesman, and Milton Singer. But intimate association with the Hopi over a period of seventeen years has given me this perception of the Hopi world.

2. See, for example, Mead 1931: 669-87, Mead 1943: 633-39, Whiting and Child 1953, Spindler 1955.
3. Of particular interest in this problem is this paper of DuBois' and the discussion following it. See also Dozier's (1954) analysis of the interaction between the Hopi-Tewa and Hopi; compare Dozier 1955.
4. An evaluation of these changes has not been reported for the Hopi, although John Connelly is working on the problem; see Adair and Vogt 1949, and Vogt 1951 for discussions of Navajo and Zuñi reactions to the war and postwar situation.
5. The concept of the Hopi "good heart" as contrasted to a "bad heart" which is *Kahopi*, has been documented by every student of Hopi known to the writer, in references too numerous to mention, beginning with Stephen (written in the 1890s but published in 1940) and Hough in 1915. But the clearest understanding of this and other Hopi concepts may be had in Whorf 1941, especially pp. 30-32.
6. See Simmons 1942: 88-89 for an excellent description by Don Talayesva of the government's use of force in the educational policy of this period; and pp. 134, 178, 199, and 225 for some of the results of this policy. Cf. Aberle 1951, for an analysis of Talayesva's school years and his later reidentification with his people.
7. Park 1950: 361. Cf. Kluckhohn 1951: 388-433, who points out that values continue to influence even when they do not function realistically as providers of immediate goal reactions.
8. Cf. D. Eggan 1955 on the use of the Hopi myth in dreams as a means of "identification."
9. Simmons 1942: 88, and compare pp. 178, 180.
10. Bruner 1956b: 612 indicates that his Mandan-Hidatsa informants were quite conscious of this "lizard-like" quality of protective coloration in white contacts.
11. Stephen 1940a: 18 says that the Hopi "describe their fundamental organization as a people" by "designating their principal religious ceremonies as the concentric walls of a house." The concept is extended here to include the entire wall of "Hopiness" which they have built around their children.
12. In a matrilineal household and clan, coöperation with one's "sisters" is a necessity for the maintenance of both the social structure and the communal unit.
13. Redfield 1955: 31-32; cf. Titiev 1944: 177-78, Whorf 1941: 91, D. Eggan 1948, Thompson and Joseph 1944: 133.
14; The Powamu society is coordinate with the Kachina society and furnishes the "fathers" to the Kachinas on dance occasions. At first initiation parents may choose either of these societies for their children. It is reported that on First Mesa Powamu initiates were whipped, but my Powamu informants from both Second and Third Mesas were not whipped.
15. See Piers and Singer 1953: 6, where Dr. Piers defines "superego" as stemming from the internalization of the punishing, restrictive aspects of parental images, real or projected.
16. See Dr. Piers' definition of guilt and of shame (Piers and Singer 1953: 5, 16). Hopi reactions are not classified here either in terms of guilt or of shame, since, as Singer points out on p. 52, an attempt to do so can confuse rather than clarify. In my opinion, both shame and guilt are operative in the Hopi "good heart," but it is suggested that the reader compare the material discussed here with the hypotheses in *Shame and Guilt*, particularly with Singer's conclusions in Chap. 5.
17. Cf. Hallowell 1955: chap. 4, on the positive role anxiety may play in a society.
18. In a short paper it is impossible to discuss both sides of this question adequately, but these tensions, and a Hopi's final acceptance of them, are discussed in D. Eggan 1948, particularly pp. 232-34. Cf. Thompson and Joseph 1944: chap. 16, where Joseph speaks of fear born of the internally overdisciplined self in Hopi children, and its role both in adult discord and social integration. See also Thompson 1945 for hypotheses regarding the integration of ideal Hopi culture. Aberle (1951) discusses various tensions in Hopi society; see especially p. 94. All authors, however, call attention to the compensations as well as the burdens in Hopi society.
19. See Brandt 1954. In his study of Hopi ethical concepts, *Kahopi* is discussed on p. 92.
20. See Piers (in Piers and Singer 1953: 15) for a discussion of the maturation drive.

21. Erikson 1948: 198, fn: "The child derives a vitalizing sense of reality from the awareness that his individual way of mastering experience (his ego-synthesis) is a successful variant of a group identity and is in accord with its space-time and life plan."

REFERENCES

Aberle, David F. *The Psychosocial Analysis of a Hopi Life-History*. Comparative Psychology Monographs, 21:1-133. Berkeley and Los Angeles, Calif.: University of California Press, 1951.

Adair, John and Vogt, Evon Z. "Navaho and Zuni Veterans: a Study of Contrasting Modes of Culture Change." *American Anthropologist* 51 (1949): 547-61.

Allport, Gordon W. "The Personality Trait." In *Psychological Theory: Contemporary Readings*, edited by Melvin H. Marx, pp. 503-7. New York: Macmillan, 1951.

Asch, Solomon E. *Social Psychology*. Englewood Cliffs, N.J.: Prentice-Hall, Inc., 1952.

Benedict, Ruth. "Continuities and Discontinuities in Cultural Conditioning." In *Personality in Nature, Society, and Culture*, edited by Clyde Kluckhohn and Henry A. Murray, pp. 414-23. New York: Alfred A. Knopf, 1948.

Brandt, Richard B. *Hopi Ethics: a Theoretical Analysis*. Chicago: University of Chicago Press, 1954.

Bruner, Edward M. "Cultural Transmission and Cultural Change." *Southwestern Journal of Anthropology* 12 (1956a): 191-99.

Bruner, Edward M. "Primary Group Experience and the Process of Acculturation." *American Anthropologist* 58 (1956b): 605-23.

Dennis, Wayne. "The Socialization of the Hopi Child." In *Language, Culture, and Personality: Essays in Memory of Edward Sapir*, edited by Leslie Spier, A. Irving Hallowell, and Stanley S. Newman, pp. 259-71. Menasha, Wis.: Sapir Memorial Publication Fund, 1941.

Dozier, Edward P. *The Hopi-Tewa of Arizona*. University of California Publications in American Archaeology and Ethnology 44 (1954): 259-376. Berkeley and Los Angeles, Calif.: University of California Press, 1954.

Dozier, Edward P. "Forced and Permissive Acculturation." *American Anthropologist* 56 (1955): 973-1002.

DuBois, Cora. "Attitudes toward Food and Hunger in Alor." In *Language, Culture, and Personality: Essays in Memory of Edward Sapir*, edited by Leslie Spier, A. Irving Hallowell, and Stanley S. Newman, pp. 272-81. Menasha, Wis.: Sapir Memorial Publication Fund, 1941.

DuBois, Cora. "Some Notions on Learning Intercultural Understanding." In *Education and Anthropology*, edited by George D. Spindler, pp. 89-126. Stanford, Calif.: Stanford University Press, 1955.

Earle, Edwin, and Kennard, Edward A. *Hopi Kachinas*. New York: J. J. Augustin, 1938.

Eggan, Dorothy. "The General Problem of Hopi Adjustment." In *Personality in Nature, Society, and Culture*, edited by Clyde Kluckhohn and Henry A. Murray, pp. 220-35. New York: Alfred A. Knopf, 1948.

Eggan, Dorothy. "The Personal Use of Myth in Dreams," in "Myth: a Symposium," *Journal of American Folklore* 68 (1955): 445-53.

Eggan, Fred. *Social Organization of the Western Pueblos*. Chicago: University of Chicago Press, 1950.

Erikson, Erik Homburger. "Childhood and Tradition in Two American Indian Tribes, with Some Reflections on the Contemporary American Scene." In *Personality in Nature, Society, and Culture*, edited by Clyde Kluckhohn and Henry A. Murray, pp. 176-203. New York: Alfred A. Knopf, 1948.

Goldfrank, Esther. "Socialization, Personality, and the Structure of Pueblo Society." *American Anthropologist* 47 (1945): 516-39.

Hallowell, A. Irving. "Culture, Personality, and Society." In *Anthropology Today: an Encyclopedic Inventory*, edited by A. L. Kroeber and others, pp. 597-620. Chicago: University of Chicago Press, 1953.

Hallowell, A. Irving. *Culture and Experience*. Philadelphia: University of Pennsylvania Press, 1955.

Henry, Jules. "Culture, Education, and Communications Theory." In *Education and Anthropology*, edited by George D. Spindler, pp. 188-215. Stanford, Calif.: Stanford University Press, 1955.

Herskovits, Melville J. *Man and His Works: the Science of Cultural Anthropology*. New York: Alfred A. Knopf, 1950.

Hough, Walter. *The Hopi Indians*. Cedar Rapids, Iowa: Torch Press, 1915.

Keesing, Felix M. *Culture Change: an Analysis and Bibliography of Anthropological Sources to 1952*. Stanford, Calif.: Stanford University Press, 1953.

Kluckhohn, Clyde. "Values and Value-Orientations in the Theory of Action: an Exploration in Definition and Classification." In *Toward a General Theory of Action*, edited by Talcott Parsons and Edward A. Shils, pp. 388-433. Cambridge, Mass.: Harvard University Press, 1951.

Kluckhohn, Clyde and Kluckhohn, Florence R. "American Culture: Generalized Orientations and Class Patterns." In *Conflicts of Power in Modern Culture*. 1947 Symposium of Conference in Science, Philosophy, and Religion, chap. 9.

Mead, Margaret. "The Primitive Child." In *A Handbook of Child Psychology*, pp. 669-87. Worcester, Mass.: Clark University Press, 1931.

Mead, Margaret. "Our Education Emphases in Primitive Perspective." *American Journal of Sociology* 48 (1943): 633-39.

Mead, Margaret. "Social Change and Cultural Surrogates." In *Personality in Nature, Society, and Culture*, edited by Clyde Kluckhohn and Henry A. Murray, pp. 511-22. New York: Alfred A. Knopf, 1948.

Mead, Margaret. *Growing Up in New Guinea*. A Mentor Book published by The New American Library, New York, 1953; first publ., 1930, by William Morrow & Company.

Murphy, Gardner. *Personality: a Biosocial Approach to Origins and Structure*. New York: Harper & Row, 1947.

Park, Robert Ezra. *Race and Culture*. New York: Free Press of Glencoe, Inc., 1950.

Pettit, George A. *Primitive Education in North America*. University of California Publications in American Archaeology and Ethnology, 43 (1946): 1-182. Berkeley and Los Angeles: University of California Press, 1946.

Piers, Gerhart, and Singer, Milton B. *Shame and Guilt: a Psychoanalytic and a Cultural Study*. Springfield, Ill.: Charles C Thomas, 1953.

Redfield, Robert. *The Primitive World and Its Transformations*. Ithaca, N.Y.: Cornell University Press, 1953.

Redfield, Robert. *The Little Community: Viewpoints for the Study of a Human Whole*. Chicago: University of Chicago Press, 1955.

Riesman, David. *The Oral Tradition, The Written Word, and the Screen Image*. Founders Day Lecture, no. 1, Antioch College, 5 October 1955.

Riesman, David, in collaboration with Reuel Denney and Nathan Glazer. *The Lonely Crowd: a Study of the Changing American Character*. New Haven, Conn.: Yale University Press, 1950.

Sapir, Edward. "The Emergence of the Concept of Personality in a Study of Cultures." In *Selected Writings of Edward Sapir in Language, Culture, and Personality*, edited by David G. Mandelbaum, pp. 590-97. Berkeley and Los Angeles, Calif.: University of California Press, 1949.

Simmons, Leo W. *Sun Chief: the Autobiography of a Hopi Indian*. Published for The Institute of Human Relations by Yale University Press, New Haven, Conn., 1942.

[SSRC] Social Science Research Council Summer Seminar on Acculturation. "Acculturation: an Exploratory Formulation." *American Anthropologist* 56 (1954): 973-1002.

Spindler, George D., ed. *Education and Anthropology*. Stanford, Calif.: Stanford University Press, 1955.

Spiro, Melford E. "The Acculturation of American Ethnic Groups." *American Anthropologist* 57 (1955): 1240-52.

Stephen, Alexander MacGregor. *Hopi Indians of Arizona*. Southwest Museum Leaflets, no. 14. Highland Park, Los Angeles, Calif.: Southwest Museum, 1940.

Steward, Julian H. "Notes on Hopi Ceremonies in Their Initiatory Form in 1927-1928." *American Anthropologist* 33 (1931): 56-79.

Thompson, Laura. "Logico-Aesthetic Integration in Hopi Culture." *American Anthropologist* 47 (1945): 540-53.

Thompson, Laura, and Joseph, Alice. *The Hopi Way*. Indian Education Research Series, no. 1. Lawrence, Kan.: Haskell Institute, 1944.

Titiev, Mischa. *Notes on Hopi Witchcraft*. Papers of the Michigan Academy of Science, Arts, and Letters 28 (1942): 549-57.

Titiev, Mischa. *Old Oraibi: a Study of the Hopi Indians of Third Mesa*. Papers of the Peabody Museum of American Archaeology and Ethnology, Harvard University, vol. 22, no. 1 (1944).

Vogt, Evon Z. *Navaho Veterans, a Study of Changing Values*. Papers of the Peabody Museum of American Archaeology and Ethnology, Harvard University, vol. 41, no. 1 (1951).

Whiting, John W. M., and Child, Irvin L. *Child Training and Personality: a Cross-Cultural Study*. New Haven, Conn.: Yale University Press, 1953.

Whorf, B. L. "The Relation of Habitual Thought and Behavior to Language." In *Language, Culture, and Personality: Essays in Memory of Edward Sapir*, edited by Leslie Spier, A. Irving Hallowell, and Stanley S. Newman, pp. 75-93. Menasha, Wis.: Sapir Memorial Publication Fund, 1941.

10 / Educational Innovation and Desegregation: A Case Study of Symbolic Realignment

Elizabeth M. Eddy

American schools are currently engaged in a revolutionary educational experiment. The deliberately planned and legally enforced mixing of pupils of widely divergent racial and cultural backgrounds in all schools and the abandonment of the local neighborhood school to achieve this goal is an unprecedented step in the history of American education. The purpose is to reduce traditional inequalities between schools so that all children may receive an education of equal quality, but especially those who because of their skin color, ethnicity, or social-class status have been shortchanged in the distribution of educational resources.

The massive regrouping of pupils to achieve racial balance between schools has been accompanied by a number of innovations within them. These changes are broad in scope and encompass such concepts as the middle school, the open classroom, differentiated staffing, behavioral objectives, individualized instruction, flexible scheduling, accountability, educational vouchers, and team teaching. Each innovation has unique features which can have an important impact on the social organization of the instructional program and the entire structure of the public school system. Nearly all of these contemporary innovations have been discussed and even practiced in a few schools for many years, but their use in a large number of schools has been a development of the last decade.

Although the recent emphasis on educational innovations has been concurrent with a period of rapid change in the ethnic and racial composition of schools, only a few studies have been directed toward an understanding of the social processes whereby innovations are adopted, implemented, and modified in schools and school districts (Atwood 1964, Gross et al. 1971, Sarason 1971, Smith 1971). Even less attention has been given to the role of educational innovations in the desegregation process. The purpose of this paper is to contribute to our knowledge in these areas by giving an account of the use of a major educational innovation on the part of school board members, school administrators, teachers, and others in the adaptation of a local school system to meet the court ordered desegregation of the schools.

The focus of the data to be reported here is on one school in the district studied and the transition of the school from one all-black serving pupils in the first through twelfth grades into a middle school for white and black pupils in the sixth, seventh, and eighth grades.[1] The local setting and the major events that led to this change in the social organization of the school will be described before turning to the events that occurred when the middle school was opened and to the subsequent modification of the innovation over a three-year period. Emphasis will be given to the relationships between the changes in the school and the disturbance in the customary patterns of human activities and interaction between blacks and whites in the school system as a consequence of desegretation. Finally, there will be a discussion of the innovation as a rite of intensification whereby those affected by desegregation were enabled to reorganize the school system so that a new biracial system of human relations became possible. Before turning to the data, we will first summarize the philosophy and organizational patterns of middle schools as those have emerged during the past several years.

MIDDLE SCHOOL PHILOSOPHY AND ORGANIZATIONAL PATTERNS

When the middle school opened in the fall of 1969, it was one of more than 100 middle schools in the state and over 2,500 in the nation. The movement toward the middle school form of school organization is a recent development in American education and has been especially widespread since 1965. Teacher-training programs are currently in effect specifically to train personnel for middle schools, and state certification in middle school teaching is found in more than 40 states. All over the country old schools are being remodeled or new ones built to provide flexible physical plant facilities for middle school programs. What is a middle school and how does it differ from the traditional elementary and high school?

Essentially the middle school is a school between the elementary and high school for children who are in the "middle" of growing up and approaching adolescence. Middle schools represent a trend away from the traditional 6-3-3 plan of dividing the twelve grades and seek to replace it with some type of intermediate school different from the 7-9 junior high school. No one grade organization is found in all middle schools, but they typically include some combination of the fifth, sixth, seventh, and eighth grades. A trend toward four-year high schools which include the ninth grade has occurred with the growth of middle schools (Alexander et al. 1969).

Middle schools are intended to be more than merely a reorganized junior high school. Considerable impetus for the formation of middle schools comes from dissatisfaction with the program of the upper years of the elementary school. Middle school proponents believe that the 6-3-3 plan of school organization does not adequately provide for the older elementary school child. They argue that the human growth and development of these pupils warrant a different and more specialized type of teaching and learning than that which is found in the traditional self-contained classroom taught by a generalist elementary school teacher. At the other end of the spectrum, it is maintained that the junior high school is dominated by a rigid organizational model which mimics the high school because of the need for ninth graders to meet the requirements of the Carnegie Unit Schedule. As a consequence, younger pupils are forced into educational molds which are inappropriate to their "in-between" stage of development. (Alexander et al. 1969).

The middle schools that are emerging across the nation have several common elements. Their central purpose is to serve the educational needs of the "in-between-agers" in a school bridging the elementary school for childhood and the high school for adolescence. Three basic strategies are used to achieve this goal—the reorganization of academic work, a strong emphasis on the development of values, and the provision of activities and services for personal development.

The reorganization of academic work is perhaps the chief characteristic of middle schools. The traditional lockstep scheduling of teachers, pupils, and subject matter is superseded by interdisciplinary groups of teachers who plan together for a hundred or more students; by flexible groupings of pupils based on specific learning needs, abilities, and interests; and by an individualization of curriculum and instruction for a school population of great variability. Multimedia approaches, independent study programs, interdisciplinary studies, exploratory opportunities, an earlier introduction to organized academic knowledge, and the development of the skills of continued learning which will help students to learn better on their own are some of the pedagogical methods used. Diagnostic testing of pupils is encouraged so that the right academic content and methods may be prescribed in response to the individual child's needs.

A second major feature of middle schools is the increased responsibility of teachers for the development of values among students. Middle school teachers are defined as key persons in the guidance program, and the role of especially trained guidance counsellors is one of helping teachers to develop guidance skills. Often the middle school includes a home base program in which each teacher is assigned to twenty or twenty-five pupils for the explicit purpose of meeting with them daily so as to personally know and help them with their problems. Large group guidance programs supplement the small group efforts of individual teachers and provide additional opportunities for the child to acquire skills in group processes and an education in the values of school and society.

The third important way in which the middle school contributes to the personal development of the child is by the development of special activities programs which enhance the academic program. The content of these activities programs varies greatly, but they are usually related to crafts and hobbies, career education, health and family life education, study habits, grooming and dress, the writing of a school newspaper, sports, or whatever else the ingenuity and resources of teachers and students can provide. The activities program tends to be an elective one in which the pupil chooses the activity group he or she wishes to join.

The characteristics of middle schools described above are ideal ones from the point of view of those committed to the middle school program. Only a very few and perhaps no middle school would have all of these characteristics. In real life the philosophic and organizational achievements of the middle school are more modest than those proposed in the educational blueprint.[2] The unplanned modifications that occur when middle school blueprints are translated into action are well illustrated by the case of the middle school to be examined in this paper. The details are presented below.

THE SETTING

The school which is the focal point of this study is the Longview Middle School in the city of Royal Palm.

> The school has a dismal atmosphere. It is dirty and on the rundown side.
> The teachers' lounge has furniture in it which is old and worn. There is a
> stuffed chair in the corner with the stuffings spilling out of it. It is gloomy,
> not a very pretty school. In the front of the school, there is a concrete and
> brick sign. One third of it is broken away. The sign says "Washington High—
> Home of the Washington Bobcats, Adult Class, 1965."
> There is a chain link fence with barbed wire on top. It surrounds the
> school. Two iron gates mark the entrance and exit to a new driveway in the
> back of the school. This driveway has replaced an old one in the front of the
> school which is no longer used. The back of the school faces an open field;
> the front of the school faces Washington Street and a poor black
> neighborhood.[3]

Until 1969, the school was called the Booker T. Washington School. Its pupils ranged from the first through twelfth grades. It was a social, community, and educational center for the blacks of the city. One of the school buildings was brought years ago to Washington from out in the country where it used to be a one-room school house for grades one through eight. For years all the old furniture and books that the white schools no longer could use were sent to black Washington. When the faculty was integrated here in 1968, the white teachers found books they had used a decade or more ago.

Today the Booker T. Washington School is called the Longview Middle School. It was renamed by the school board in 1969 when the school became a desegregated middle school for black and white pupils in the sixth, seventh, and eighth grades. Longview is the name of the county in which the school is situated, and the school serves pupils from the county as well as Royal Palm, the county seat in which the school is located. Despite its new name, the school is low on the list of school board priorities for the investment required to meet the standards for regional accreditation.

By 1970 census definition, Longview is a rural county. Less than half of its nearly 15,000 residents live in urban areas. Royal Palm, the largest city, has a population of nearly 7,000. Somewhat less than one-quarter of the total county population is black. The median number of school years completed by Longview county residents is eight; only a third of them are high school graduates, and only 5 percent have finished four or more years of college.

Longview County is a leading producer of tobacco, corn, beef cattle, and poultry. Since the 1930s small family-operated farms have yielded to large machine-operated farms and the agribusiness which is the bedrock of the local economy. Parallel developments in the educational system have transformed the 30 schools that were found throughout the county in the 1930s into the 6 consolidated schools of the 1970s. Five of these schools are in Royal Palm, and one of them is a new vocational, technical, and adult center which is a source of local pride and increased state and federal support. The other four schools are the Longview Primary School, for kindergarten through the third grade, the Longview Elementary School, for the fourth and fifth grades, the Longview High School, for the ninth through twelfth grades, and finally the Longview Middle School, for those in the process of making the transition from the elementary to the high school.

How did it happen that in 1969 the all-black Washington School became the biracial Longview Middle School? What preceded this innovative event? What subsequent modifications have been made since it occurred? The answers to these questions are by no means simple. Like the modern highway system that now connects the city of Royal Palm to the external world, the answers lead to the nation's capitol, the state capitol, the nearby state university system and into the community of Royal Palm itself. Like all educational innovations, this one did not originate in a social vacuum. It originated, was implemented, and continues to be modified within a specific social setting and by specific persons who join together for the activities of formal education. The account of this innovation begins by describing the major events which led up to it. We will then describe the history of the innovation during its first four years.

THE TRANSITION OF A SCHOOL

In the fall of 1967, Clyde Manning became the principal of the Booker T. Washington School. He displaced the former black principal who became the assistant principal. Manning brought extensive administrative experience to his new position. From a beginning teacher in a one-room schoolhouse, he had risen in the educational ranks to become the appointed superintendent of schools in a community of the midwestern state in which he was born and raised. His professional career as an educator was helped by a graduate degree in vocational agriculture and a variety of jobs outside of the educational system which gave him new perspectives on the schools. The fact that he had worked in the Longview county system for several years made him attractive to the local school board for the assignment to Washington.

The selection of Clyde Manning as principal of Booker T. Washington was note-worthy. He was the first white man to serve the school in this role and the only white person on the staff of the school during 1967-68. His appointment fore-shadowed the greater changes to come to the school and to the county educa-tional system as a consequence of the court ordered desegregation of schools. These changes were even more evident in the building program which preoccupied school board members during the first year that Manning was principal at Washing-ton. In anticipation of the desegregation of pupils two years later, part of the old junior high school was remodelled for use by the kindergarten and primary grades. The high school was expanded to accommodate the ninth grade, and ground was broken for the construction of a new elementary school for the fourth and fifth grades.

The primary, elementary, and high schools were all located in the white residential areas of Royal Palm. Many of the 1,000 blacks who attended Booker T. Washing-ton in 1967-68 would attend these schools two years later. At the same time, the school board had determined that all sixth, seventh, and eighth grade pupils would attend Washington. The decision to place these grades at Washington was based on the best utilization of the physical facilities available. The new elementary school was too small to house the sixth grade; the high school was too large to be used solely for the tenth through twelfth grades.

An important part of Mr. Manning's task as principal of Washington was to make the school acceptable to the whites whose children would become pupils there. During the spring and summer of 1968, he began to give serious attention to this problem by discussing with others the idea of turning the Booker T. Washington School into a middle school. In particular, he had lengthy conversations with Celeste Allen, a respected guidance counsellor at the white high school who was strongly supportive of middle school philosophy and aims.

Faculty desegregation at Washington and in the other county schools began in the fall of 1968. Twenty white teachers were assigned to Washington, and twenty black teachers were sent from Washington to other schools. Nearly all the white teachers assigned to Washington had joined in a statewide walkout of teachers in the winter of 1968. Their placement in the black school was viewed by the school board and themselves as punishment for participation in this event. Nevertheless, they included some of the strongest teachers in the school system. "Weak" teachers who had walked out were fired by the school board whose members were glad for an excuse to get rid of them. Among the black teachers transferred out of Washing-ton in the fall of 1968, several of the secondary school teachers returned a year later when the desegregation of pupils occurred. Some of them had also joined in the walkout.

There were many faculty discussions about the middle school concept during the 1968-69 school year. A small group of teachers at Washington was sent to visit al-ready established middle schools in nearby communities. Clyde Manning and Celeste Allen conferred with a nationally known expert in middle schools at the state uni-versity and circulated copies of his book on the subject among the faculty. Principal Manning also solicited and received the support of the newly elected Longview county superintendent of schools. Federal funds available to the county were pro-vided for travel expenses and for the consulting fees of outside experts. A state university faculty member knowledgeable about guidance programs appropriate to middle schools was brought to Washington to train teachers in the philosophy and implementation of a guidance program. He helped to persuade the county school board to adopt the middle school idea.

The activities begun while school was in session continued throughout the summer of 1969. Clyde Manning, Celeste Allen, and a dozen or more teachers attended a summer workshop on the middle school sponsored by the state university. The county paid for the teachers' registration fees and transportation costs. After the workshop, several of the teachers and Mrs. Allen continued to work voluntarily with the principal in the development of the plans for the middle school. Toward the end of the summer, the principal and Mrs. Allen planned teacher and pupil assignments and the formal schedule of school activities for the coming year.

While the final organizational plans were being made for the middle school, changes were made in the physical plant of the Washington School. The school had already been painted during the school year in an effort to brighten its appearance. Although the school had no previous history of vandalism, a barbed-wire fence was now put up around the school grounds in order to protect school property. A new driveway was constructed at the back of the school so that teachers, pupils, and others would not have to drive through the black neighborhood to get to the school. There was talk of removing walls between the classrooms and making other structural alterations which would facilitate the implementation of the middle school philosophy. However, an engineering survey of the school plant revealed that major physical renovations of this type were not possible since the walls slated for removal were supporting ones.

The formal transition of the school from an all-black school to a biracial one was marked by changing the name of the school to the Longview Middle School. An intensive public relations campaign was undertaken during the summer months for the purpose of informing the community about the new middle school and helping local citizens to forget that it had ever had an identity as a black school.

The New School

When the Longview Middle School was opened in the fall of 1969, an innovative plan was introduced for the organization of educational activities. As indicated earlier, this plan had the strong support of Clyde Manning, the principal, and Celeste Allen, the guidance counsellor of the high school. Mrs. Allen's enthusiasm was so genuine that when the middle school was opened, she left the high school to take the position of guidance counsellor there. The careful preparation of teachers during the school year and summer resulted in a substantial group of faculty who were committed to the new plan. In addition, the plan had the backing of the county superintendent and the school board. Funds were allocated for teacher workshops during the 1969–70 school year so that teachers could continue to receive help as they encountered the problems during the first year of the middle school.

The new organizational model introduced into the Longview Middle School was comprised of six interrelated parts. These were the grouping of teachers and pupils into pods, the scheduling of class periods so that they rotated from day to day or week to week, the initiation of a home base program, the provision of an activities program, the election of a faculty chairman to represent the faculty to the school administration, and the establishment of a parent-teacher conference system whereby the parents met with all of the teachers in a pod rather than with an individual teacher. The plan did not include team teaching, but it was anticipated that the school would work toward achieving this goal over a three-year period despite the severe limitations on team teaching imposed by the physical plant. During the first year, primary efforts were given to the guidance program, as evidenced by the appointment of Mrs. Allen to the school, the county funded in-service workshops on guidance which were held every six weeks under the leadership of a state university professor, and the awarding of credit for certification purposes to teachers who attended these workshops.

The grouping of teachers and pupils into pods was an organizational arrangement whereby approximately 130 pupils were assigned to a pod of four teachers. Podding was adopted in order to change the emphasis of the school from subject matter to students, to gain maximum flexibility with a minimum number of teachers, to enable teachers to have more ability to communicate with parents, and to be able to work and plan together. Podding enabled the school to avoid the type of scheduling practiced at the high school: departmentalization and self-contained classrooms.

In order to comply with county school board policy, the student racial composition of each pod was 70 percent white and 30 percent black. Several of the pods were taught by both black and white teachers; others had only white teachers; none of them was taught exclusively by black teachers. The total number of students taught in a pod were divided into four racially balanced groups which traveled from one academic teacher to another throughout each day. Insofar as the arrangement of classrooms allowed, the classrooms of the four academic teachers were adjacent or close to each other.

The pods were allocated four-hour blocks of time during which the academic subjects of English, mathematics, social studies, and science were taught. The teachers were assigned to one subject area which they taught to all four pupil groups. Complete freedom was given to the pod teachers to determine how the four-hour blocks of time were to be used. Usually the teachers taught each class for fifty minutes to one hour. The periods for the academic subjects were regularly rotated so that students did not have the same academic subject at a set time each day. This rotation system allowed equal distribution of time for the several subjects so that no one subject always appeared in prime time.

The teachers within a pod were given the same free hour each day for planning and the coordination of activities and schedules. This hour was scheduled during physical education periods. Since all the pupils on a grade had physical education at the same time, the teachers of all the pods on a particular grade could join together for planning as necessary. The planning periods were also used for innovative parent-teacher conferences which were part of the middle school plan at Longview. Parents wishing (requesting) to consult with teachers about their children were expected to meet with all of the pod teachers and Mrs. Allen, the guidance counsellor, for a group conference. Teachers were discouraged from meeting individually with parents.

Podding, subject area rotation, and group conferences with parents were only three of the innovations introduced. They were accompanied by the initiation of a home base program and an elective activities program which were viewed and accepted by most teachers as an integral part of their responsibility. Twenty minutes at the beginning of the morning session and thirty-five minutes after the lunch period were allowed for the home base program. The program was an effort to overcome "the poor home environments" of many of the pupils. It was designed to give teachers more time with a group of pupils so that they could take primary responsibility for their welfare in the school. The time was to be used for individual student counselling and the general guidance of pupils in the development of social skills.

The elective activities program occurred for an hour each day. Once during the week large group guidance activities were scheduled. These were planned by several teachers on a pod or grade, and the teachers rotated the responsibility for these sessions. On the remaining four days, pupils met for teacher sponsored clubs or arts programs. They were free to select the activity they wished to join. At the end of specified periods of time, the activities and clubs changed, and students elected new ones.

The final innovation was that of having an elected chairman of the faculty. Clyde Manning was deeply committed to faculty participation in decisions and to faculty direction of the middle school program. For this reason he urged the faculty to choose a chairman, to call faculty meetings without his permission, and to govern themselves. In a close race with another highly respected white teacher and long time resident of Longview County, Mrs. Matthews, a native of the county and a former president of the county teachers' association, won the election for the 1969-70 year. There were many faculty meetings during the year as well as informal meetings of teachers in the principal's home.

THE TRANSITION OF THE PLAN

The 1969-70 school year at Longview Middle School was difficult for all concerned. The blacks were bitter about the loss of their school and alma mater. They especially resented the change of the school entrance so that it no longer faced the black community and the high barbed wire fence around the school grounds. The whites felt that the school was contaminated because of its long history as a black school.

The city of Royal Palm and the county were rife with rumors and gossip. It was alleged that the school smelled and was filthy. Some said that there was no proper sewage system and that sewage was simply dumped on the school grounds. The lack of air conditioning added insult to injury for those who had left temperature controlled classrooms behind. There were stories of youths who carried knives and reports of stabbings in the bathrooms. Tension was high, and many of the white pupils were afraid to walk down the halls. Some of them refused to use the lavatories and objected to sharing the shower rooms with blacks. Physical education classes were frequently canceled lest rioting break out on the school grounds.

Misunderstandings about the middle school program added fuel to the flames of parental discontent. The lack of homework assignments, the use of texts that were below grade level for some of the pupils, the grouping policies and the differential marking system for pupils in the same class were particular sore points among local parents. There were complaints too about the lack of school dicipline. Mr. Manning's philosophy of talking to children who were discipline problems instead of paddling them was a matter of controversy among parents and teachers alike. Within the classrooms, instructional problems arose because of the heterogeneity of abilities within the same class, the amount of preparation time required for the home base program, the inadequate organization of the activities program, the restrictions of the physical plant and the minimal resources provided for teaching.

At the end of a hectic school year, several teachers and the principal attended a special workshop held in Royal Palm to improve their skills in implementing the guidance program. The workshop was in mid-session when Mr. Manning suddenly announced his resignation and abruptly left the school and county for a new position. Although people did not elaborate on the matter, there are indications that his departure was not entirely voluntary. His successor was William Myers, a white assistant principal in the high school and the former principal of the old junior high school.

Mr. Myers was well known to most of the teachers in the school. He had been in the county school system for many years and had worked with several of the middle school teachers in the past. He was trained and experienced in the traditional junior high school. Upon assuming the role of principal in the fall of 1970, he quickly moved to reduce the home base program to a ten-minute period of taking attendance in the morning and to rescind the Manning policy of having an elected faculty chairman. He also restored the tradition of paddling in the principal's office and in other ways began to move the school away from the middle school philosophy.

Two years after Mr. Myers became principal, podding, the rotation of academic periods, group conferences with parents, and an elective activities program were still in effect in the school. Major differences other than those mentioned above included the following: a greater homogeneity based on standardized test scores within the four pupil groups of each pod; a consequent larger proportion of black pupils in the lower ability groups; the absence of a continuing inservice teacher training program; the centralization of the activities program under a director especially hired for the purpose; decreased financial support from the county for the middle school; the abandonment of plans to initiate team teaching; infrequent faculty meetings; marked discouragement on the part of teachers committed to middle school philosophy and new ideas; and a stronger orientation toward administration and discipline on the part of the school principal.

Race relations within the school continued to be tense although many of the unfounded rumors and anxieties of the first year had been dispelled. Black teachers remained uncomfortable in the school despite the fact that most of them had taught there for several years prior to desegregation. Increased political activity on the part of educated young black adults in Royal Palm contributed to the racial ferment which was just beneath the surface of human relations in both school and community. The overt hostility expressed toward blacks by some of the white teachers and other staff at Longview increased their feelings of being unwelcome. Both the blacks and the whites knew that Mr. Myers held less liberal views about race than his predecessor.

In summary, the new Longview Middle School which proposed to be a radical departure from the traditional schools of the past was in reality only a reworking of the traditional on a limited scale. It is believed by many of the teachers that the establishment of the middle school was primarily due to the leadership of Mr. Manning. Now that he has left the school, it is said that the school is moving further away from the middle school philosophy with each year that passes.

THE MIDDLE SCHOOL PLAN AS A RITE OF INTENSIFICATION

Thus far, we have described the major events that led to the establishment of the Longview Middle School as a response to the court ordered desegregation of schools in Longview County. We have also described the major modifications of the plan during the years immediately following the year of pupil desegregation. The remainder of this paper will present an analysis of the middle school plan in this situation as a rite of intensification.

Rites of intensification have been defined as "ritual performed in response to a crisis which arises from changes affecting all the members of a group in concert" (Chapple and Coon 1942:706). It was with a crisis of this kind that community and educational leaders had to deal when the courts ordered the desegregation of schools in Longview County. This was so because for several decades the Booker T. Washington School, "home of the Washington Bobcats," had been a symbol of a dual segregated school system which gave expression to the subordinate position of blacks in the white-dominated social system of the community. Indeed the construction of the Washington School originally was specifically intended to allay the possibility of school integration by providing blacks with "their own new school."

As a school located in the major black area of Royal Palm and serving approximately a thousand black pupils of all ages, the Washington School was a major social institution of the black community. Within its walls, blacks had become school principals, and black teachers had dominated the classroom. From its playing fields, black football teams had sallied forth to engage in competitive sports with black teams from other schools. The exclusive use of the school buildings by the black community for educational and other activities meant that the school was proudly claimed as black territory by students, teachers, school administrators, and community leaders. These territorial boundaries were accepted by the whites who had been instrumental in creating them so that the blacks would remain "in their place" in the educational and social system.

The court-ordered desegregation of schools necessitated a redefinition of the socially defined territorial rights to the school. With few exceptions, neither the blacks nor the whites welcomed the mandated change. Like other institutions in our society, particular schools are identified by the "kinds" of people who attend them. Thus, the characteristics of the pupils enrolled become a symbol of the school. For the blacks, the advent of whites into the school meant the loss of the only school in the black community and a place of community assembly which many of them cherished. For the whites whose children were assigned there, the school was a symbol of inferior education. In addition, these parents were the only ones who had to send their children into the black community for schooling. Hence many parents of both races were embittered by the transition of the school from an all-black to a biracial status. For these reasons the disturbance of the traditional patterns of educational activities and interaction was especially acute at Washington.

The response of the educational leaders to the crisis of meeting the legally required changes in the interaction patterns between blacks and whites in the Washington School was an elaborate one. As already noted it consisted of bringing whites and blacks together in a new middle school form of social organization for educational purposes. The details of the plan have been given above. Here we are concerned with the ways in which the Longview Middle School provided the educational context for a new form of interaction between blacks and whites and a dramatic representation of the habitual relationships between the significant aggregate groups of individuals in the school. The school not only reinforced the traditional patterns of interaction between school administrators, teachers, pupils, and parents, but it did so in a way which supported the traditional subordinate relationships of blacks to whites.

The transformation of the Washington School into the Longview Middle School represented a claiming of the school by the whites of Royal Palm. The assignment of a white principal to the school was the first in a sequence of symbolic acts which communicated to all concerned that the school was no longer one in which blacks would play major roles in the initiation of educational activities. The assignment of twenty white teachers to the school as a form of punishment for participation in a teacher walkout served to separate them from their customary relations in schools in white areas of the city while at the same time indicating the low status of the school in the community. Simultaneously twenty black teachers were assigned to other schools, including several secondary teachers who were reassigned to the school after a year of separation. Those symbolic acts were the second step in changing the roles of black teachers as the dominant initiators of pupil activities. The building of the fence around the school to shut it off from the black community, the change of the school entrance so that it no longer faced the black community, and the renaming of the school were additional symbolic acts which reaffirmed the dominant status of whites within the school. The realignment of race relations symbolized by these events was a significant one. It was greatly facilitated by the innovative organizational plan that went into effect when white pupils enrolled in the school.

As reported by many of those in the school, the clustering of teachers and pupils into a pod form of organization was not entirely a matter of educational philosophy. Some alleged that it was not a matter of educational philosophy at all. A primary reason for instituting podding was to deter pupils from transferring from one class to another because of racial and personality clashes with teachers. In order to transfer out of one teacher's class, a student had to transfer out of the pod entirely and enter a new one with four new teachers. Podding also allowed the distribution of black teachers throughout the school so that no child had only black teachers. The requirement that parents must simultaneously confer with all of the pod teachers and the guidance counsellor when they wished to discuss matters concerning their child was a further step in the effort to prevent conflict based on racial factors between individual teachers and parents. Similarly, many aspects of the guidance program were consciously planned to help pupils of different races to get along better in the school.

It is significant that all of the major organizational innovations introduced in 1969 strongly reaffirmed the traditional patterns of interaction between teachers, pupils, and parents in the school. While teachers now planned in groups, planning was largely confined to the scheduling of activities, the guidance program, and the handling of discipline problems. Nearly all teaching was done by a single teacher to successive groups of children as in the traditional junior high school. The fact that a child had to deal with a group of teachers organized into an administrative and teaching unit meant that the control of teachers over him was greater than in the traditional elementary and junior high school, and especially over any desires he or she might have to change teachers. Similarly parents now had to confer with four teachers and the guidance counsellor in a group meeting rather than with one teacher.

The subsequent modifications of the original plan introduced in 1969 were of a type which reinforced the traditional role of teachers while at the same time removing those innovative features of the original plan which threatened to alter traditional school relationships. Principal Manning's policies of heterogeneous grouping, faculty initiative in planning, an expanded guidance role for teachers, and a guidance approach to discipline on the part of the principal were supplanted as the school returned to homogeneous grouping based on test scores for academic work, the traditional faculty meeting, the centralization of the guidance program under the direction of specialists, and the use of the paddle by the principal. The restoration of traditional administrative relations to teachers and pupils made the school more acceptable to many in the community.

The realignment of blacks and whites for educational purposes in the desegregated Longview Middle School not only expressed the traditional patterns of interaction between those who occupied different positions as pupil, teacher, or administrator. It also expressed the traditional subordination of blacks in an educational system in which whites occupied the positions of status, authority, and control within the school as they turned it around to face the white community. The social organization of both the original and modified middle school plan was such that blacks occupied subordinate positions. The principal was white. His assistant was black. Black teachers were found in the sixth and seventh grade pods but not in the more prestigious eighth grade pods. None of the pod leaders was black. At the time the school was visited, only a handful of black students were in the top ability groups of the pods. With one exception, those pods that had black teachers had not fully incorporated them. Several of the white administrators and teachers were openly derogatory in their remarks about black members of the staff and pupils. There were few observed or reported social relationships between blacks and whites.

In conclusion, the Longview Middle School plan ended the traditional segregated interaction forms of the school and the relationships between community, school administrators, teachers, and pupils that had been built upon them. The innovative plan introduced for the organization of school activities was preceded by a series of symbolic acts whereby people began to visualize the school differently and became motivated to participate in its activities. The plan itself required the performance of new modes of interaction in which the desegregated group structure was made explicit and reinforced. This group structure is one which maintains the traditional dominance of administrators, teachers, and whites in directing the activities of blacks and pupils.

The Longview Middle School stands today as a symbol of a new type of race relations within Royal Palm, but the interaction forms which will allow the unification of blacks and whites in their institutional relationships so that they may "speak with one voice" have still to emerge. Whether or not they will do so is as yet unknown. What we do know is that there is no magic in symbols alone and that the new symbols and rites of intensification required will come only as the customary patterns of human interaction and activities change so as to fully incorporate blacks into the educational system and the nation of which it is a part.

NOTES

1. The data reported here were gathered as part of a series of case studies of educational innovations made in the winter and spring of 1973. They are based on an analysis of field reports obtained using extensive interview techniques of a partially structured but open-ended nature. A total of 35 people was interviewed by two researchers who each spent seven days in the school. Those interviewed included 28 teachers, one substitute teacher, four administrators and one university professor. The interviews were supplemented by written materials about the school and observations of school activities.
2. A survey of organizational patterns of reorganized middle schools made by Dr. William M. Alexander in 1968 reports that the program of studies is "generally comparable to that of these grades in predecessor organizations, with a relatively sparse offering of elective and other curriculum opportunities, especially for grades five and six. Instructional organization for grade five is most frequently similar to that of the elementary school, with the departmentalization patterns of the junior high school introduced even here and becoming the predominant organization in the other grades." Despite this typical pattern, Alexander reports developments in some schools that could be forerunners of a movement toward middle schools that are different from those prevailing in the traditional junior high and elementary schools (Alexander et al. 1969: 185–86).
3. The material quoted is from the field notes of the researchers. The name of the school has been changed. Throughout this paper all names of persons and places are pseudonyms.

REFERENCES

Alexander, W., E. Williams, M. Compton, V. Hines, D. Prescott, and R. Kealy. *The Emergent Middle School.* 2nd ed. New York: Holt, Rinehart and Winston, 1969.

Atwood, M. "Small-Scale Administrative Change: Resistance to the Introduction of a High School Guidance Program." In *Innovation in Education*, M. Miles, ed. New York: Teachers College Press, 1964.

Chapple, E., and C. Coon. *Principles of Anthropology.* New York: Henry Holt, 1942.

Chapple, E. *Culture and Biological Man: Explorations in Behavioral Anthropology.* New York: Holt, Rinehart and Winston, 1970.

Gross, N., J. B. Gianquinta, and M. Bernstein, *Implementing Organizational Innovations.* New York: Basic Books, 1971.

Sarason, S. *The Culture of the School and The Problem of Change.* Boston: Allyn and Bacon, 1971.

Smith, L. *Anatomy of Educational Innovation.* New York: John Wiley, 1971.

Part III

Anthropological Analyses of Classrooms

11 / Attitude Organization in Elementary School Classrooms

Jules Henry

The word *organization* in this paper is used to stand for order and determinateness as distinguished from disorder and randomness. The emotions and attitudes of prepubertal children in our culture are not, on the whole, directed toward generalized social goals, but focused rather on the peer group and parents. From the point of view of an observer who has in mind the larger social goals, like the maintenance of stable economic relations, common front against the enemy, maintenance of positive attitudes toward popular national symbols, and so on, the emotions and attitudes of prepubertal children in our culture may be viewed as lacking order. The adult, on the other hand, is supposed to have so organized his tendencies to respond to the environment that his emotions, attitudes, and activities subserve overall social goals. While it is true that attitudes and feelings are bent toward social goals even from earliest infancy (Henry and Boggs 1952), many institutions combine to organize these attitudes and feelings so that ultimately a social steady state will be maintained. The elementary school classroom in our culture is one of the most powerful instruments in this effort, for it does not merely sustain attitudes that have been created in the home, but reinforces some, deemphasizes others, and makes its own contribution. In this way it prepares the conditions for and contributes toward the ultimate organization of peer- and parent-directed attitudes into a dynamically interrelated attitudinal structure supportive of the culture.

This organizing process is comparable to, though not identical with, the reorganization of attitudes and resources that takes place as a society shifts from a peacetime to a wartime footing. During a period of peace in our society, adult hostility and competitiveness may be aimed at overcoming competition in business or social mobility, while love and cooperation are directed toward family and friends, and toward achieving specific social economic ends *within* the society. With the coming of war the instruments of government seek to direct hostility and competitiveness toward the enemy, while love and cooperation are directed toward the armed forces, civilian instruments of war (price controls, rationing, civilian officials, etc.), and national symbols. From the point of view of an observer *within the war machine*, the civilian attitudes at first seem random and unorganized. He wants to change them so that from *his point of view* they will seem organized. The situation is similar, though not identical, with respect to the child: to an observer inside the head of even some psychotic children, attitudes and behavior may seem organized. But to the observer on the outside, whose focus is on social goals, the child seems *un-* or *dis*organized. The prime effort of the adult world is *to make child attitudes* *look organized to adults.* The emphasis in this paper is on the description of the process of organizing child attitudes as it can be observed in some middle-class urban American classrooms.

THE WITCH-HUNT SYNDROME

One of the most striking characteristics of American culture since the settlement has been the phenomenon of intragroup aggression, which finds its pathological purity of expression in witch-hunts (Starkey 1949). It comes as a frightening surprise to democratic people to find themselves suddenly in terror of their neighbors; to discover that they are surrounded by persons who carry tales about others while confessing evil of themselves; to perceive a sheeplike docility settling over those whom they considered strong and autonomous. The *witch-hunt syndrome* therefore, as constituting one of the key tragedies of democracy, is selected for the elucidation of the organization of attitudes in our culture. In this witch's brew *destructive criticism* of others is the toad's horns; *docility* the body of the worm; *feelings of vulnerability* the chicken heart; *fear of internal (intragroup) hostility* the snake's fang; *confession of evil deeds* the locust's leg; and *boredom and emptiness* the dead man's eye. The witch-hunt syndrome is thus stated to be a dynamically interrelated system of feelings and actions made up of destructive criticism of others, docility, feelings of vulnerability, fear of internal aggression, confession of evil deeds, and boredom.

The witch-hunt syndrome in full panoply was observed in but one of the dozen classrooms in four schools studied in the research which I discuss here. Thus it seems a relatively rare phenomenon. But the question I set myself to answer is, How could it occur at all? What are the attitudes, present in the children, that were organized by this teacher into the syndrome? How could she do it? With what materials did she work? She did not create out of nothing the attitudes she manipulated in her "Vigilance Club" in this fourth-grade classroom in a middle-class American community. She had to have something to start with. The argument of this paper will be that the feelings and tendencies to action which this teacher organized into the witch-hunt syndrome in her class are present in an *un*organized state in other classrooms. Given a certain type of teacher, he or she will be able to develop into a highly specialized, tightly integrated system in his classroom those attitudes which are present in differently organized states in the children in all classrooms. Let us now look at a meeting of the Vigilance Club.

> 1. In the extreme back of the room is a desk called the "isolation ward."
> A child has been placed there for disciplinary reasons. The Vigilance Club of the class is holding a meeting. . . . Officers are elected by the group. The purpose of the club is to teach children to be better citizens. The order of procedure is as follows: the president . . . bangs her gavel on the desk and . . . says, "The meeting of the Vigilance Club will come to order." Each child then takes from his or her desk a booklet whose title is *All About Me* . . . and places it on top of his desk. The vice-president calls the name of a child, gets the child's booklet, and places it on the teacher's desk. The president then calls on the child and asks, "——, have you been a good citizen this week?" The president says, "Name some of the good things you have done," and the child tries to recall some, like opening doors for people, running errands, etc. Next the president asks the class if it remembers any good things the child has done. Each point is written in the child's booklet by the teacher. The president then . . . says to the child, "Name the bad things you have done . . ." The child reports the wrongs he has committed during the week, and the class is asked to contribute information about his behavior. This too is written in the booklet by the teacher, who also reprimands the stu-

dent, registers horror, scolds, etc. . . . When one child reports a misdemeanor of another the teachers asks for witnesses, and numerous children sometimes volunteer. . . . The child in the "isolation ward" reported some good deeds he had done; the children reported some more, and the isolated child was told he would soon be released. . . . [During this meeting some children showed obvious pleasure in confessing undesirable behavior. One child, by volunteering only good things of the students, seemed to be using the situation to overcome what seemed to the observer to be her unpopularity with the class.] *

Before analyzing this protocol for the attitudes present in it, it will be well to look at some events that occurred in this classroom on another day.

2. During the game of "spelling baseball" a child raised her hand and reported that Alice and John had been talking to each other. This occurred when neither child was "at bat." The teacher asked Alice if this was so, and she replied that it was, but John denied having spoken to Alice. The teacher said that John must have listened to Alice, but he denied this too. Then the teacher asked whether there had been any witnesses, and many hands were raised. Some witnesses were seated on the far side of the room, and hence could not have seen Alice and John from their location in the room. All those testifying had "seen" Alice talking, but denied John's guilt. Alice was sent to the "bull pen," which meant that she had to sit on the floor behind the teacher's desk, and could no longer participate in the game. . . .

3. Mary raised her hand and said, "It hurts me to say this. I really wish I didn't have to do it, but I saw Linda talking." Linda was Mary's own teammate, had just spelled a word correctly, and had gone to first base. The teacher asked Linda if she had talked, and Linda said, "No, I just drew something in the air with my finger. . . ." She was sent to the "bull pen."

In these examples we see intragroup aggression; docility of the children in conforming, with no murmur of protest, to the teacher's wishes; and confession of "evil." In such a situation children develop feelings of vulnerability and fear of detection. Let us now look for these phenomena in classrooms presided over by teachers who seem to represent the more normal American type, in comfortable, middle-class, white communities: teachers who are conscientious and reasonably gentle, but creatures of their culture, and humanly weak. We begin not with internal aggression as expressed in spying and talebearing, but with the milder, though closely related phenomenon of carping, destructive criticism. While this occurs throughout the sample, I give here examples only from a fifth-grade classroom in the same school system.

4. Bill has given a report on tarantulas. As usual the teacher waits for volunteers to comment on the child's report.
Mike: The talk was well illustrated, well prepared. . . .
Bob: Bill had a piece of paper [for his notes], and teacher said he should have them on cards. . . .
Bill says he could not get any cards.
Teacher says then he should tear the paper next time if he has no cards.
Bob: He held the paper behind him. If he had had to look at it, it wouldn't have looked very nice.
5. Betty reports on Theodore Roosevelt.

*In order to prevent identification of teachers and children, the names of my student observers are not used.

A child comments that it was very good but she looked at her notes too much.

Teacher remarks that Betty had so *much* information.

Bob: She said "calvary" [instead of "cavalry"].

6. Charlie reads a story he made up himself: "The Unknown Guest." One dark, dreary night . . . on a hill a house stood. This house was forbidden territory for Bill and Joe, but they were going in anyway. The door creaked, squealed, slammed. A voice warned them to go home. Spider webs, dirty furniture . . . Bill wanted to go home. They went upstairs. A stair cracked. They entered a room. A voice said they might as well stay and find out now; and their father came out. He laughed and they laughed, but they never forgot their adventure together.

Teacher: Are there any words that give you the mood of the story? . . .

Lucy: He could have made the sentences a little better. . . .

Teacher: Let's come back to Lucy's comment. What about his sentences?

Gert: They were too short. . . .

Charlie and Jeanne are having a discussion about the position of the word "stood."

Teacher: Wait a minute, some people are forgetting their manners. . . .

Jeff: About the room: the boys went up the stairs and one "cracked"; then they were in the room. Did they fall through the stairs or what?

Teacher suggests Charlie make that a little clearer.

Lucy: If he fell through the step. . . .

Teacher: We still haven't decided about the short sentences. Perhaps they make the story more spooky and mysterious.

Gwynne: I wish he had read with more expression instead of all at one time.

Rachel: Not enough expression.

Teacher: Charlie, they want a little more expression from you. I guess we've given you enough suggestions for one time. (Charlie does not raise his head, which is bent over his desk as if studying a paper.) Charlie! I guess we've given you enough suggestions for one time, Charlie, haven't we? (Charlie half raises his head, seems to assent grudgingly.)

The striking thing about these examples is that the teacher supports the children in their carping criticism of their fellows. Her performance in this is not, however, consistent; but even where, as in example 6, she seems at one point to try to set herself against the tide of destruction, by calling attention to the possible artistry in Charlie's short sentences, she ends up supporting the class against him, and Charlie becomes upset. Thus teacher, by rewarding the children's tendencies to carp, reinforces them. Teachers, however, are able to make their own contributions to this tendency. The single example given below will serve as illustration:

7. Joan reads us a poem she has written about Helen Keller . . . which concludes with the couplet:

> "Helen Keller as a woman was very great
> She is really a credit to the United States."

Teacher (amusedly): Is "states" supposed to rhyme with "great"? When Joan murmurs that it is, the teacher says, "We'll call it poetic license."

From time to time one can see a teacher vigorously oppose tendencies in the children to tear each other to pieces. The following example is from the sixth grade:

8. The Parent-Teachers Association is sponsoring a school frolic, and the children have been asked to write jingles for the publicity. For many of the children the experience of writing a jingle seems painful. They are restless, bite their pencils, squirm around in their seats, speak to their neighbors, and

from time to time pop up with questions like, "Does it have to rhyme, Mr. Smith?" ... At last Mr. Smith says, "All right, let's read some of the jingles now." Child after child says he "couldn't get one"; but some have succeeded. One girl has written a very long jingle, *obviously the best in the class.* However, instead of using Friday as the frolic day she used Tuesday, and several protests were heard from the children. Mr. Smith defended her. "Well, so she made a mistake. But you are too prone to criticize. If *you* could only do so well!"

It will be observed that all the examples are taken from circumstances in which the child's self-system is most intensely involved; where his own poetry or prose is in question, or where he has worked hard to synthesize material into a report. It is precisely at the points where the ego is most exposed that the attack is most telling. The numerous instances in the sample, where the teachers, by a word of praise or a pat on the head, play a supportive role, indicate their awareness of the vulnerability of the children. Meanwhile, as I have pointed out, the teachers often fall into the trap of triggering or supporting destructive impulses in the children.

The carping criticism of one's peers is a form of intragroup aggression, which can be quite threatening and destructive. Tale-bearing, however, countenanced by some teachers more than by others, can be an overwhelming threat to autonomy. While telling on others can be organized into the patrol-monitor complex (prestige through controlling and telling), useful perhaps in maintaining order in large school populations, its operation within the classroom may have serious consequences. Let us look at a couple of examples.

9. Second grade. As teacher asked the children to clear their desks one boy raised his hand, and when called on said, "Jimmy just walked by and socked me on the head."
Teacher: Is this true?
Jimmy: He hit me first.
Teacher: Why don't you both take seats up here (in front of the room). I'm not sure people like you belong in the second grade.

10. Sixth-grade special class for bright students. The children are working on their special nature projects. Joseph passes where Ralph is working.
Ralph (to teacher): Joseph is writing too much on his birds.
Teacher: Joseph, you should write only a few things.

In our sample, telling on other children in the classroom is infrequent outside the class in which the Vigilance Club was formed. Destructive criticism is the preferred mode of attack in most classrooms. The ease with which tendencies to attack peers can be organized into telling on others, however, is illustrated by the monitor-patrol complex, and by the Vigilance Club (example 3).

Competition

Competition is an important element in the witch-hunt syndrome. Since witch-hunts involve so often obtaining the attention and approval of some powerful central figure, the examples of competitiveness that I shall cite illustrate how approval and attention seeking occur as the child attempts to beat out his peers for the nod of the teacher. It would be easy to cite examples from protocols of the merciless laughter of children at the failures or gaucheries of their classmates. I am interested, however, more in showing the all-pervading character of the phenomenon of competition, *even in its mildest forms.* The first example is from a fourth-grade music lesson:

11. The children are singing songs of Ireland and her neighbors from the book *Songs of Many Lands.* ... Teacher plays on piano while children sing. ... While children are singing some of them hunt in the index, find a

song belonging to one of the four countries, and raise their hands before the previous song is finished in order that they may be called on to name the next song. . . .

Here singing is subordinated, in the child, to the competitive wish to have the song he has hunted up in the index chosen by the teacher. It is merely a question of who gets to the next song in the index first, gets his hand up fast, and is called on by the teacher.

The following examples also illustrate the fact that almost any situation set by the teacher can be the occasion for release of competitive impulses:

> 12. The observer enters the fifth-grade classroom.
> Teacher: Which one of you nice polite boys would like to take [observer's] coat and hang it up? [Observer notes: From the waving hands it would seem that all would like to claim the title.] Teacher chooses one child . . . who takes observer's coat. . . .
> Teacher: Now children, who will tell [observer] what we have been doing? Usual forest of hands . . . and a girl is chosen to tell. . . .
> Teacher conducted the arithmetic lesson mostly by asking, "Who would like to tell . . . the answer to the next problem?"
> This question was usually followed by the appearance of a large and *agitated* forest of hands; apparently *much competition to answer.*

Thus the teacher is a powerful agent in reinforcing competition.

It has already been pointed out that carping criticism helps to settle in the child a feeling of vulnerability and threat. In this connection it is significant that *the failure of one child is repeatedly the occasion for the success of another.* I give one illustration below from the same class as the one from which I have taken example 12.

> 13. Boris had trouble reducing $^{12}/_{16}$ to lowest terms, and could get only as far as $^6/_8$. Much excitement. Teacher asked him quietly [note how basically decent this teacher is] if that was as far as he could reduce it. She suggested he "think." Much heaving up and down from the other children, all frantic to correct him. Boris pretty unhappy. Teacher, patient, quiet, ignoring others, and concentrating with look and voice on Boris. She says, "Is there a bigger number than 2 you can divide into the two parts of the fraction?" After a minute or two she becomes more urgent. No response from Boris. She then turns to the class and says, "Well, who can tell Boris what the number is?" Forest of hands. Teacher calls Peggy. Peggy gives 4 to be divided into $^{12}/_{16}$, numerator and denominator.

Where Boris has failed Peggy has been triumphant; *Boris's failure has made it possible for Peggy to succeed.*

This example and also Example 6 are ones in which the discomfort of the child was *visible*, and such instances may be multiplied. They illustrate how vulnerable the children feel in the presence of the attacks of the peer group in the classroom. But since these are children who face the world with serious anxiety to begin with, the classroom situation sustains it. Let us look at some stories created by these very children, and read by them to their classmates. We have already seen one, example 6, Charlie's story of "The Unknown Guest." Here are *all* the stories read to their classmates by these children during an observation period.

> 14. (a) Charlotte's story: "Mistaken Identity." One day last year my family and I went to the hospital to visit somebody. When we were coming out

and were walking along my father hit me. I came up behind him to hit him back, but just as I was about to do it I looked back and he was behind me! I was going to hit the wrong person!

(b) Tommy's story: "The Day Our House Was Robbed." [Observer has recorded this in the third person.] He was coming home from school one afternoon. He knew his Mom was away that afternoon. He started to go in the side door, but decided, he doesn't know why, to go round the back. He found the door open, went into the kitchen, looked into the front room where he saw a thief. Tommy "froze stiff" (chuckle of appreciation from the class), ran out, shouted, "Stop thief" as the man ran out after him. He went to a neighbor, rang the bell, called his mother at the store. The cops came, asked questions, but the man had gotten away with $99 and his mother's watch. If he had gone in the side door he would not have had a chance to see the man. Changing to the back door "may have saved my life." [Teacher's only remarks about this story were: (1) instead of having said "froze stiff," Tommy should have said, "froze stiff as something"; (2) he should have left out the word "then" in one place; (3) he could have made the story clearer; (4) he changed from the past to the present tense.]

(c) Polly's story: "Custard the Lion." Custard the Lion was the most timid animal in Animal Town. The doctors couldn't cure him. Then they found a new medicine. It had strange effects, but Custard wanted to try it. When he did he felt very queer. (Child gives details of queer feeling.) But he soon realized he wasn't afraid of anything. [Teacher's first remark: "You didn't let us hear the last sentence."]

(d) Dan's story: "The Boy Hero." Bill wanted to be a fireman, so he went to the firehouse. The Chief was telling him to go home when the bell clanged. While the Chief was getting into the engine, he didn't see Bill was getting on too. (Class or teacher picks up flaw in sentence and it is reread correctly.) The Chief said O.K. as long as Bill was aboard, "But you're not to get into no mischief." (Class choruses, "Any . . . .") Everyone was out of the fire except a little girl and her doll. The firemen cannot figure out what to do, but Bill, seeing a tree near the house, climbs it over the protests of the firemen. He misses the girl on his first try, but gets her on the second. While sliding down the tree she slips and almost falls, but grabs Bill's pants, and they make it to safety. . . . [Children's remarks center on position of "clang, clang, clang" in the story. Teacher talks about how to use direct quotations, which, it seems, Dan had not used properly.]

(e) Bertha's story: Title not recorded. The story is about Jim who was walking home past the Smith's house one night and heard a scream. Penny Smith came out and said there was a robber in the house. When the cops came they found a parrot flying around in there, and Penny's parents told her to shut the parrot up before she read mystery stories again. [This story was followed by much carping criticism, which was terminated by the teacher's telling Bertha to change the story to suit the class.]

These stories contain elements of anxiety and even of terror. As each child finishes, the carping criticism of students and teacher then reminds him of his vulnerability. As the child sends out his cloud of fear, it returns with the leaden rain of hostility.

Docility

It comes as a somewhat shocking surprise, perhaps, to middle-class parents, to find their children described as "docile." Yet we have already seen the perfection of docility in the Vigilance Club, and we shall presently see its manifold forms in more normal classrooms.

15. First grade. The children are to act out a story called "Pig Brother," which is about an untidy boy. The teacher is telling the story. One boy said he did not like the story, so the teacher said he could leave if he did not wish to hear it again, but the boy did not leave.

16. In gym the children began to tumble, but there was much restless activity in the lines, so the teacher had all the children run around the room until they were somewhat exhausted before she continued the tumbling.

17. Second grade. The children have been shown movies of birds. The first film ended with a picture of a baby bluebird.
Teacher: Did the last bird ever look as if he would be blue?
The children did not seem to understand the "slant" of the question, and answered somewhat hesitantly, yes.
Teacher: I think he looked more like a robin, didn't he?
Children, in chorus: Yes.

Item 17 is one of a large number of instances, distributed throughout all grades, in which the children exhibit their docility largely through giving the teacher what he wants. Thus in the elementary schools of the middle class the children get an intensive eight-year-long training in hunting for the right signals and giving the teacher the response wanted. The rest of the examples of docility document this assertion.

18. Fourth grade.
(a) An art lesson.
Teacher holds up a picture.
Teacher: Isn't Bob getting a nice effect of moss and trees?
Ecstatic Ohs and Ahs from the children. . . .
The art lesson is over.
Teacher: How many enjoyed this?
Many hands go up.
Teacher: How many learned something?
Quite a number of hands come down.
Teacher: How many will do better next time?
Many hands go up.
(b) Children have just finished reading the story "The Sun Moon and Stars Clock."
Teacher: What was the highest point of interest—the climax?
The children tell what they think it is. Teacher is aiming to get from them what *she* considers the point of climax, but the children seem to give everything else but.
Bobby: When they capture the thieves.
Teacher: How many agree with Bobby?
Hands, hands.

19. Fifth grade. This is a lesson on "healthy thoughts," for which the children have a special book depicting, with appropriate illustrations, specific conflictful incidents among children. The teacher is supposed to discuss each incident with the children in order to help them understand how to handle their emotions.
One of the pictures is as follows: A sibling *pair* is illustrated by *three* boys: (1) One has received a ball. (2) One is imagined to react with displeasure. (3) One is imagined to react benignly and philosophically, saying, "My brother couldn't help being given the football; we'll use it together."
Teacher: Do you believe it's easier to deal with your thoughts if you own up to them, Betty?
Betty: Yes it is, if you're not cross and angry.

Teacher: Have you any experience like this in the book, Alice?

Alice tells how her brother was given a watch and she envied him and wanted one too; but her mother said she wasn't to have one until she was fifteen, but now she has one anyway.

Teacher: How could you have helped—could you have changed your thinking? How could you have handled it? What could you do with mean feelings?

Alice seems stymied. Hems and haws.

Teacher: What did Susie (a character in the book) do?

Alice: She talked to her mother.

Teacher: If you talk to someone you often then feel that "it was foolish of me to feel that way. . . ."

Tommy: He had an experience like that, he says. His cousin was given a bike and he envied it. But he wasn't "ugly" about it. He asked if he might ride it, and his cousin let him, and then, "I got one myself; and I wasn't mean, or ugly or jealous."

Before continuing it will be well to note that since the teacher does not say Alice was wrong the children assume she was right and so copy her answer.

Two boys, the dialogue team, now come to the front of the class and dramatize the football incident.

Teacher (to the class): Which boy do you think handled the problem in a better way?

Rupert: Billy did, because he didn't get angry. . . . It was better to play together than to do nothing with the football.

Teacher: That's a good answer, Rupert. Has anything similar happened to you, Joan?

Joan can think of nothing.

Sylvester: I had an experience. My brother got a hat with his initials on it because he belongs to a fraternity, and I wanted one like it and couldn't have one; and his was too big for me to wear, and it ended up that I asked him if he could get me some letters with my initials, and he did.

Betty: My girl friend got a bike that was 26-inch, and mine was only 24; and I asked my sister what I should do. Then my girl friend came over and was real nice about it, and let me ride it.

Teacher approves of this, and says, Didn't it end up that they both had fun without unhappiness?

Here we note that the teacher herself has gone astray, for on the one hand her aim is to get instances from the children in which they have been yielding, and capable of resolving their own jealousy, etc.; yet, in the instance given by Betty, it was not Betty who yielded, but her friend. The child immediately following Betty imitated her since Betty had been praised by the teacher:

Matilde: My girl friend got a 26-inch bike and mine was only 24; but she only let me ride it once a month. But for my birthday my mother's getting me a new one, probably (proudly) a 28. (Many children rush in with the information that 28 doesn't exist.) Matilde replies that she'll probably have to raise the seat then, for she's too big for a 26.

As we go on with this lesson, we shall continue to see how the children's need for substitute gratification and their inability to accept frustration are the real issues, which even prevent them from getting the teacher's point. We shall see how, in spite of the teacher's driving insistence on her point, the children continue to inject their conflicts into the lesson, while at the same time they gropingly try to find a way to gratify the teacher. *They* cannot give the "right" answers because of their conflicts; teacher cannot handle their conflicts, even perceive them, because *her* underlying need is to be gratified by the children! The lesson goes on:

> Teacher: I notice that some of you are only happy when you get your own way. You're not thinking this through, and I want you to. Think of an experience when you didn't get what you want. Think it through.
>
> Charlie: His ma was going to the movies and he wanted to go with her, and she wouldn't let him; and she went off to the movies, and he was mad; but then he went outside and there were some kids playing baseball, so he played baseball.
>
> Teacher: But suppose you hadn't gotten to play baseball? You would have felt hurt, because you didn't get what you wanted. We can't help feeling hurt when we are disappointed. What could you have done; how could you have handled it?
>
> Charlie: So I can't go to the movies, so I can't play baseball, so I'll do something around the house.
>
> Teacher: Now you're beginning to think! It takes courage to take disappointments. (Turning to the class.) What did we learn? The helpful way . . .
>
> Class: Is the healthy way!

Before entering the final section of this paper, we need to ask: Why are these children, whose fantasies contain so many hostile elements, so docile in the classroom; and why do they struggle so hard to gratify the teacher and try in so many ways to bring themselves to her attention (the "forest of hands")? We might, of course, start with the idea of the teacher as a parent figure, and the children as siblings competing for the teacher's favor. We could refer to the unresolved dependency needs of children of this age, which make them seek support in the teacher, who manipulates this seeking and their sibling rivalry to pit the children against each other. Other important factors, however, that are inherent in the classroom situation itself, and particularly in middle-class classrooms, ought to be taken into consideration. We have observed the children's tendency to destructively criticize each other, and the teachers' often unwitting repeated reinforcement of this tendency. We have taken note of the anxiety in the children as illustrated by the stories they tell, and observed that these very stories are subjected to a carping criticism, whose ultimate consequence would be anything but alleviation of that anxiety. Hence the classroom is a place in which the child's underlying anxiety may be heightened. In an effort to alleviate this he seeks the approval of the teacher, by giving right answers and by doing what teacher wants him to do under most circumstances. Finally, we cannot omit the teacher's need to be gratified by the attention-hungry behavior of the children.

A word is necessary about these classrooms as middle class. The novel *Blackboard Jungle* describes schoolroom behavior of lower-class children. There we see the children *against the teacher*, as representative of the middle class. But in the classes I have described we see the *children against each other*, with the teacher abetting the process. Thus, as the teacher in the middle-class schools directs the hostility of the children toward one another and away from himself, he reinforces the competitive dynamics within the middle class itself. The teacher in lower-class schools, on the other hand, appears to become the organizing stimulus for behavior that integrates the lower class, as the children unite in expressing their hostility to the teacher (Hunter 1954).

Confession

The Vigilance Club would have been impossible without confession, and the children's pleasure in confession. But, as with the other parts of the syndrome, confessing occurs in other classrooms also; it can be elicited when the proper conditions are present, and the children can be seen to enjoy it—to vie with one another in confessing. Let us follow the lesson on "healthy thoughts" a little further. We will see how confession occurs as the children seek to give teacher *precisely* what she wants.

> 20. Teacher asks if anyone else has had experiences like that [of two children who have just recited], where they were mean and angry.
> Dick: He has a friend he plays baseball with, and sometimes they fight; but they get together again in a few minutes and apologize.

In this first example we note one of the important aspects of the confession element in the syndrome: the culprit must have given up his evil ways, and now be free of impurities.

> In response to Dick's story, teacher says: You handled it just right. Now let's hear about someone who had a similar experience and didn't handle it just right.
> Tom: His little brother asked for the loan of his knife, but it was lost, and he got angry with his little brother for asking. [This knife story follows a sequence of several stories about knives told by other children. The exuberance of knife stories following immediately on the teacher's approval of the first one suggests that some of them are made to order and served up piping hot for teacher's gratification.]
> Teacher: Now Tom, could you have worked it out any differently? [Observer notes that Tom seems to enjoy this confession; certainly he is not abashed or ashamed.]
> Tom: Later he asked me if he could help me find it. He found it in a wastebasket, and then I let him borrow it.
> Harry: Sometimes I get angry when my friends are waiting for me and . . . [observer missed some of this] and my little sister asked if she could borrow my auto-racing set, and I hit her once or twice. (Class laughs.)

Here we see another factor so important to the flourishing of the syndrome: the audience gets pleasure through the confessor's telling about deeds the audience wishes to commit: who among Harry's listeners would not like to have hit his sister, or anyone, "once or twice"?

> The teacher then goes on: What would you do now—would you hit her?
> Harry: Now I'd probably get mad at first, but let her have it later.

Thus Harry has mended his ways—in teacher-directed fantasy at least—and returned to the fold.

So far we have had confession of mean and angry thoughts and violence. We shall now see confession to unacceptable fear. In all cases the teacher says what type of confession she wishes to hear, and what the resolution should be of the unacceptable behavior; and the children vie with one another to tell commensurable tales, as they derive pleasure from the total situation—through approval of the teacher, expression of their own real or fantasied deviations, and the delight of their peers. In these situations the pleasure of the peer group is seen to derive not so much from the "happy ending" the children give their stories but rather from the content of the story itself. It is interesting that no carping criticism appears; rather the entire situation is a jolly one. It seems that within unspoken limits the children permit one another to boast of "evil" behavior because of the deep pleasure obtained from hearing it. Thus impulse expression becomes a device for role maintenance in the classroom.

The lesson proceeds:

> Two children enact a little skit in which they have to go to the principal to ask him something. One of them is afraid of the principal, the other is not. The moral is that the principal is the children's friend, and that one should not be shy.
>
> Gertrude: Well, anyway, the principal isn't a lion, he's your friend; he's not going to kill you.
>
> Teacher: That's right, the principal is a friend, he says hello and good morning to you. . . . Have you ever felt shy?
>
> Meriam: The first year I sold Girl Scout cookies I didn't know how to approach people; and the first house I went to I didn't know the lady; and I stuttered and stammered, and didn't sell any cookies. By the second house I had thought it all out before I rang the bell, and I sold two boxes. (Triumphantly.)
>
> Teacher: It helps to have self-confidence.
>
> Ben now tells a story, with a happy ending, of being afraid of a principal. Then Paul tells a story, amid gales of laughter, about his being scared on a roller coaster. By this time there is so much excitement among the children that the teacher says: Wait a minute—manners!
>
> John: He was scared to go on the Whip-the-Whirl (scornful laughter from the class); but after he went he liked it so much that he went eight times in a row. (This is well received.)
>
> Many hands go up. Teacher waits. . . .
>
> Michael: He was at Pleasure Park on the ferris wheel (scornful "Aw" from the class) and a girl kept rocking it, and I started to get green (roar of laughter).
>
> Teacher: Now we'll have to stop.

Certain phenomena not emphasized before appear in this section. Confession is used by the authoritative figure, the teacher, to strengthen attachment to significant but potentially terrifying figures like school principals, and to polish up cultural shibboleths like "self-confidence." For the child storytellers confession becomes an opportunity for bathing in the emotional currents of the peer group, as the child stimulates the group's approval through presentation of group standards, and awakens group pleasure as the peer group responds to its own anxiety about weakness, and experiences resolution of the anxiety through the happy ending. With a perfect instinct for what is right, each child provides catharsis for his peers. By presenting himself as weak, he enables his peers to identify with him; and then, as he overcomes his weakness, he enables his companions too to feel strong.

What this lesson on healthy thoughts may have accomplished by way of creating a permanent reservoir of "healthy thoughts" is difficult to say, but that it helped create solidarity among the students, and between them and the teacher is clear from the fact that when she suddenly shifted ground to say, "Do you think you are wide enough awake for a contest in subtraction of fractions?" the children responded with a unanimous roar of "Yes," as if she had asked them whether they were ready for cookies and ice cream!

Thus in this lesson, in which all have participated more with their *unconscious* than with their conscious emotions, solidarity has been achieved. Teacher thought she was teaching the children to have healthy thoughts, but she was showing them how to gratify her. The children sensed this and struggled to gratify her, while they sought acceptance by their peers also. The essential difference between this teacher and the one who perpetrated the Vigilance Club is that though the latter tended to demolish solidarity among the children while placing the teacher in supreme command, the lesson on healthy thoughts tended to a dubious solidarity among all. *Both teachers organize some of the same elements in the children, but into different configurations, of total feeling and behavior.*

Boredom

It seems unnecessary to document the fact that children become bored in class, for much of modern thinking and curriculum arrangement is aimed at eliminating it. The shifts at fifteen-minute intervals from one subject to the next in the elementary school classrooms is one example of this effort. Boredom, which means emotional and intellectual separation from the environment, is an insupportable agony, particularly if the emotional vacuum created by such separation is not filled by gratifying fantasies, or if it is filled by terrifying ones. To fill this vacuum people in our culture will throw themselves into a great variety of even relatively ungratifying activities. Since in this situation, bored children attack almost any novel classroom activity with initial vigor, the witch-hunt syndrome or any modification thereof helps to overcome boredom: better to hunt than be bored. In a full and satisfying life there is no place for witch hunts. The school system that can provide a rich program for children has no need of Vigilance Clubs, nor even of lessons on "healthy thoughts."

DISCUSSION AND CONCLUSIONS

In this paper I have used suggestions from communications theory in an effort to order the data obtained from direct observation of elementary school classrooms. Information, the central concept of communications theory, refers to measurable differences in states of organization. In human behavior, as seen in the classroom under discussion, we observe *qualitative shifts in state*, for *different teachers organize the same underlying emotional characteristics of the children to achieve different organizations of the emotions.* One teacher so organizes the children's emotions as to accomplish an intensification of the fear of intragroup aggression, while she turns the children's hostility toward one another. A different teacher may organize the emotions of the children so that a euphoria in which students and teacher are bathed in a wave of emotional gratification is achieved. The great skill in being a teacher would seem to be, therefore, a *learned* capacity to keep shifting states of order intelligently as the work demands. This does not mean the traditional classroom order, where you can hear a pin drop, but rather the kind of order in which the *emotions of the children are caught up and organized toward the achievement of a specific goal.* It is not necessary, perhaps, that even the most prominent emotions of the children, like competitiveness, for example, form part of the organized whole. Yet, on the other hand, it is difficult to see how, in the present state of our culture, competitiveness can be overlooked. It would seem, perhaps, that the important outcome to avoid is that the competitiveness should become destructive of peers, while reinforcing dependence on the teacher.

The phenomenon I have labeled "docility" occurs because of the absolute dependence for survival of the children on the teacher. That is to say success in school depends absolutely on the teacher, and self-respect, as a function of the opinion of others, in the home or among peers, is in part a function of success or failure in school. In these circumstances the child's capacity to respond automatically to the signals he gets from the teacher is bound to acquire somewhat the appearance of instinctive behavior. Although it occurs at a much higher level of integration than instinct, the child hunts for the proper signals from the teacher, and the child's responses take on instinctual quality. They *must*; otherwise, like the nestling who does not open its mouth when the mother arrives with a worm, he will never eat the ambrosia of teacher's approval, so necessary to his survival. In this situation both children and teacher easily become the instruments of their own unconscious processes, as they, like Joseph and his brethren, fall on each other's necks in a shared ectasy of exuberant dependence. Teacher and pupil will have gratified each other, but it remains an open question whether the children will have learned what the curriculum committee planned.

We see in the organization of the components of the witch-hunt syndrome an important phase in the formation of American national character, for tendencies to docility, competitiveness, confession, intragroup aggression, and feelings of vulnerability the children may bring with them to school, are reinforced in the classroom. This means that independence and courage to challenge are observably played *down* in these classrooms. It means, on the other hand, that tendencies to own up rather than to conceal are reinforced—a development which, in proper hands, might become a useful educational instrument. It means, further, that while many teachers do stress helping others they may inadvertently develop in the children the precise opposite, and thus undermine children's feelings of security. One could come from a very secure and accepting family and yet have one's feelings of security and acceptance threatened in these classrooms. On the other hand, what seems most in evidence from the stories they make up is that the children come to school with feelings of vulnerability which are intensified in the classroom.

Meanwhile we should try to understand that all the teachers in the sample were probably trying to be good teachers,* and all the children were trying to be good pupils. Their unconscious needs, however, naturally dominated their behavior. The teacher who organized the Vigilance Club probably thought she was teaching her children to be upright and honest, and to perform good deeds, but her unconscious tendencies caused these worthy inclinations to seek the wrong expression. All teachers need conformity in the classroom in order that the children shall absorb a respectable amount of academic knowledge. But the teacher's (often unconscious) need for acceptance by the children, and her fear (sometimes unconscious) of her inability to control free discussion, compel her to push the children into uncritical docility at times, while they seek her approval.

The creation of stories, and their discussion by the class, are accepted principles of progressive education. But the teacher's own (at times unconscious) need to carp and criticize gets in the way of her adequately developing the creative and supportive possibilities in her charges. Thus these are not "bad," "vicious," or "stupid" teachers, but human beings, who express in their classroom behavior the very weaknesses parents display in their dealings with their children. The solution to the problem of the contradiction between the requirements of a democratic education on the one hand, and the teachers' unconscious needs on the other, is not to carp at teachers, and thus repeat the schoolroom process, but to give them some insight into how they project their personal problems into the classroom situation.

REFERENCES

Henry, Jules, and Boggs, Joan Whitehorn. "Child Rearing, Culture, and the Natural World." *Psychiatry* 15 (1952): 261–71.
Hunter, Evan. *The Blackboard Jungle*. New York: Simon and Schuster, 1954.
Starkey, Marion L. *The Devil in Massachusetts*. New York: Alfred A. Knopf, 1949.

*I am indebted to B. Bettelheim for this suggestion.

12 / Spontaneity, Initiative, and Creativity in Suburban Classrooms

Jules Henry

Nowadays much of the preoccupation with creativity seems to stem not so much from interest in artistic and scientific originality as from anxiety about preserving any human impulse toward spontaneity and initiative. Fundamentally, our contemporary concern about creativity is a culturally acceptable rationalization of our own fear of loss of Self. In our expressed anxiety over creativity in our children, we are really saying that we are frightened that our culture has wrested our Selves from us and is selling them down the river. The present paper, reflecting the current fear, deals, therefore, with factors affecting initiative and spontaneity in elementary public school classrooms in middle-class suburbs.[1]

This paper is based on direct observations by my students and me over a three-year period.[2] We owe a debt of deepest gratitude to the teachers who voluntarily put up with our intrusions into their classrooms. There is no doubt that an objective description of anyone's behavior in our culture would have in it much that might appear on superficial examination to be strange or bizarre. Our observations show teachers as normal and dedicated human beings struggling with massive problems the culture has dropped in their lap, and if anything in these studies of them were to be construed as absurd or bizarre, it would be a gross injustice.

DIRECT OBSERVATIONS

The root of life is impulse; and its release in the proper amounts, at the proper time and place, and in culturally approved forms, is one of the primary concerns of culture. Day after day in the classroom, the public school teacher faces the surging impulses of the children and she resists them in order not to be overwhelmed; in order to do her duty as a cultural surrogate; and in order that the whelming impulse life of her charges—normal as well as sick—may not get in the way of their learning the materials prescribed in the curriculum. The contemporary public school teacher is thus faced with the following paradox: in line with current educational philosophy she must foster initiative and spontaneity in her children and at the same time maintain order and teach according to school requirements. In the middle-class suburban classrooms we have studied, however, the emphasis on initiative and spontaneity fosters a "permissiveness" which, in some rooms, sweeps the class to the brink of chaos. In these circumstances it became an empirical requirement of our research to develop a rough rating for noise; and it is still an unsolved problem as to whether such classrooms can be said at certain times to have any social structure at all. Indeed, it would almost appear as if the pivot of order were no longer, as under more traditional discipline, the teacher, but rather had become lodged in the egos of the children; as if responsibility for the maintenance of order had been shifted from the teacher to the children. Meanwhile, it is important to bear in mind that these are not delinquent children, tearing the social structure from its hinges by brute force, but nice, clean middle-class suburban boys and girls who are merely given their heads.

The impulses of the children are always a serious matter to teachers, and one of the most important problems of our day is to discover the variety of devices they use to control or evade them. Since, quite without our requesting it, principals have selected for us classrooms having what they consider outstanding teachers, the examples I give here of classroom control represent forms considered best by the principals. The first example is from a second-grade classroom in school A, with 37 children. Rather full excerpts are taken from one typical day, and very brief materials from one day a month later.

> The Observer arrives in the classroom at 12:45 and remarks, "As has been the case in past observations, the noise rating was 2."
> There are about seven children walking around, apparently doing nothing. There are about nine children sitting on the floor on the left side of the teacher's desk. Teacher is passing back some papers the children worked on yesterday. She says, "If you missed more than one of the questions on the board, it means that you either aren't reading carefully or that you aren't thinking enough. Betty, will you sit over here, please. Thank you."

This teacher, like most of the teachers in the area, uses "honey" and "dear" a great deal in interaction with the children. Some of the examples recorded on this day are:

1. Could you talk a little louder, Johnny dear?
2. I'll have to ask you to go to your seat, honey.
3. Honey, where were you supposed to go if you didn't have your paper?
4. Bill, I think George can do that by himself, honey.
5. Susie, honey, what's the name of it?
6. It's up here, dear.

The record continues:

> 1:10. The reading period is over. Children return to their seats. Teacher begins to write four words on the board. As she does this the talking and moving around the room increase to a mild uproar. Noise rating 3. Teacher says, "May I have your eyes this way, please? Bill, will you and Tommy please watch?"
> 1:20. "May I suggest that the people in John Burns' group, instead of doing this work with the vowels, read in *The Family Village*."
> 1:40. Teacher is sitting at desk. Children seem to be busy at work. Everyone seems to be doing something different. Noise rating has dropped to 2. Fifteen out of 34 of the children present are not doing the assigned work. Most of the children in this group are doing absolutely nothing in the line of schoolwork. Some are merely staring into space; some are playing with rubber bands, hankies, etc.
> 1:56. Presently there are ten children out of their regular seats and seated in the rockers at the bookcase, at the library table, or just aimlessly walking around the room. Two little girls in the back of the room are showing each other their scarves. There is a great deal of footshuffling; everyone looks as if he is preparing to go home. Teacher comments, "Boys and girls, we do not go home at two o'clock, so please continue with your work. Doug, may I talk to you a minute?" Doug goes up to Teacher, who says, "We're going to let you stay five minutes after school because of this talking."

A month later the record reads as follows:

> 12:40. When the teacher reprimands the children, her voice in all instances is soft, almost hesitant. She informed me [the Observer] later that when she scolds she wants the children to feel she is disappointed in them. I can see how the sad tone of her voice would convey this message.
> 12:50. Teacher says, "May I have you in your seats, please." During the collection of papers the noise rate had increased to 2, and 12 people were out of their seats.

A few minutes later the teacher left the room and the noise rate approached 3. Six children were walking around the room, most of them chatting with their neighbors. Roger says to Observer, "Kind of noisy, isn't it?"

1:04. Teacher returns and says, "Annie, would you sit down honey, and get busy. Whose feet are making so much noise?" One child says, "Pam's!" and the teacher says, "Pam, that's very annoying, please don't. Observer remarks, "It's odd that this small noise should bother Mrs. Olan. I didn't even hear it." Teacher says, "Doug, will you turn around, please? Billy, do you understand the process—how to do it? I thought maybe Jimmy was helping you. Stephen, are you finished? Murray and Mickey! Boys and girls, let's tend to our own work, please."

1:55. Five minutes before recess. Teacher says, "Put your work away quietly." She sits back and with a completely expressionless face waits for the five minutes to pass. The number of children out of their seats increased to 17. Three boys were bouncing balls on the floor; one was throwing his against the wall of the cloakroom; three children were killing each other with imaginary guns.

Regardless of their age, our observers became tired and irritated by the noise in this type of classroom. During any ninety-minute observation period, Mrs. Olan was in and out of the classroom several times, sometimes for as long as ten minutes. It will be observed that at one point she merely sat and stared into space. Meanwhile, her repeated withdrawal results in an intensification of the noise, which mounts toward the third level when she leaves, so that when she returns, an effort must be made to reestablish the previous lower noise level. Probably the reason why the social structure of the room does not disintegrate is that the teacher warms the atmosphere with "honey" and "dear" and by occasionally fondling a child; and because by saying she is "disappointed" in them she makes the children afraid of loss of love. Actually, Mrs. Olan plays the role of the tired, overburdened, entreating mother, who attempts to control her children by making them feel guilty. Her sweetness and elaborate politeness—she even says "honey" and "dear" when she reprimands a child—are really saying to the children, "Look how sweet and courteous *I* am; how could you be otherwise?"

In all of this the children's egos seem remarkably firm, and Mrs. Olan's capacity to do an all-but-impossible job is striking. Although the noise rating is never zero in this room, it is sometimes recorded as 1 or approaching 2, which suggests that the children have inner resources of control which are skillfully mobilized by the teacher. When one understands, however, the pressure toward "permissiveness" in these schools, the fact that the children do learn something is a tribute to Mrs. Olan's fortitude and to her dedication to teaching, as well as to to the ego strength of the children.

The contemporary American idea that good elementary school teachers should be accepting, giving parents has resulted, as we have seen, in the teachers' using affection as a defense against other impulses of the children: the teacher stimulates their love by calling them "honey" and "dear" and by fondling, while at the same time she awakens fear of loss of her love if they get out of line. Though in our sample, caressing is common, its full possibilities in the classroom can be evaluated best by studying minutely the behavior of one teacher who obtains deep pleasure from fondling the children. Mrs. Thorndyke is affectionate, sensitive, and alert, and, as usual, is considered one of the best by her principal. In the observation record we are present at a reading lesson in her third-grade class on a day when the children are asking each other questions about the story instead of being asked questions by her. There are twenty-five children in the class, but the group to be described is made up of the dozen or so best readers, and they are sitting facing each other in two rows of little chairs placed in front of the room. The rest of the children are working at their desks on their exercise books. This paper picks up the lesson when it has been in progress about fifteen minutes, during which excitement has mounted and the children tend to erupt in noisy argument. At 10:27 Mrs. Thorndyke is standing behind one row:

> She pats Alfred to restrain him and he shows a slight tendency to withdraw. There is a loud burst of noise. Mrs. Thorndyke's hand is on Alfred and he seems to wish to get out. Now her hand is on Arty, who makes no move. Teacher pats and strokes Matty, who also makes no move to withdraw. Now Teacher is standing behind Arty, lightly passing her finger tips over his neck. She goes back to Arty, puts a hand on Alfred to restrain him. He makes withdrawal signs. Alfred and Arty are now interlocking their hands in the air and Alfred is talking to Arty. At 10:32, Teacher stops behind Otto to restrain him. Her hands are on his cheeks; his tongue goes in the direction of his right cheek and pushes it out as he closes his eyes. When Mrs. Thorndyke withdraws her hands, his eyes pop open as if he had suddenly awakened. Mary, who previously was holding onto Mrs. Thorndyke as the teacher stroked the child's arm, has now slumped in her seat. Teacher goes to her, puts her arms around her and pulls her back. Mary takes Teacher's hand. Alfred is talking and Mrs. Thorndyke pats and strokes him. He does not withdraw this time. Alfred is now talking to Arty and Teacher is stroking Alfred. Again he does not withdraw. Now Alfred caresses Otto and Arty caresses Alfred. Malcolm asks questions now (10:38) and all the children say his questions have been asked. Mrs. Thorndyke says, "My only objection to that question is that it can be answered by either yes or no." She stroked Matty. All this time the questions are being asked and there is great excitement among the children. Sherry asks question and Teacher says, "We've gone over that." She strokes Matty and he does not resist. She touches Mary flutteringly with her finger tips.
>
> Now Mrs. Thorndyke terminates the lesson, and the papers with the questions are collected. Suddenly she becomes very grave and silent. She later told me that Mary had answered a snippety "no" to something Teacher had said. Now Mrs. Thorndkye says, *"My, I'm terribly disappointed."* There is absolute silence, and Mrs. Thorndyke says, "Matty, you're excused to go to your seat." She later told me it was because he's a general all-round talker and wouldn't quiet down. Matty goes to his seat looking very unhappy, his lips compressed. The room is silent now.
>
> Now Group 2, the poorer readers, occupy the seats deserted by Group 1. Teacher seems very tired now, and goes through the lesson mechanically. Her voice is weak and she leans against the blackboard. Time, approximately 10:50.

The interesting thing about erotization is that it *substitutes one impulse or one impulse pattern for another*: The children's excitement, whatever its effective components, is narcotized by releasing other, namely libidinal, emotional resources in the children. What is so striking in Mrs. Thorndyke is her skill in so stimulating these resources that contagion occurs: the affectivity of the teacher is spread by some children to others. Otto is a somewhat different case: he simply went into a regressive trance while enjoying the teacher's stroking.

Put in the broadest possible way, what we have seen here is Mrs. Thorndyke's effort to master, by means of narcotization, powerful *spontaneous* impulses of the children which had been placed at the service of their intellects. Thus, in the very act of releasing spontaneity, the teacher, in order not to be overwhelmed by it, narcotizes it. Obviously the effort was exhausting, for when the lesson was over, Mrs. Thorndyke was tired and listless and leaned against the blackboard for support.

While women teachers in our sample of middle-class suburban schools seem repeatedly to control the children's impulses by awakening affection and fear of loss of it, as would almost any normal middle-class mother, the question arises as to what the male teacher does in the same situation. Over the years we have been able to get good observations on only one man teacher, Mr. Jeffries, who teaches a sixth-grade class of thirty-five in the same school as Mrs. Thorndyke. In the classroom Mr. Jeffries takes the role of a type of contemporary middle-class American father: a Puckish imp-of-fun, buddy of the boys and sweetheart of the girls, he addresses the latter with endearments and uses nicknames and diminutives for the former as he pats them on the head or puts an arm around their shoulders. His room is a rough-and-tumble, happy-go-lucky, brink-of-chaos sort of place, much less controlled than Mrs. Thorndyke's and less overtly erotized. Mr. Jeffries calls it a "rat race" and says, "We get tired and ready to drop by the time it is over." Let us then have a look at Mr. Jeffries' room:

> 11:05. The class is having a reading lesson. Teacher says, "Galapagos means tortoise. Where are 300-pound turtles found?" A boy says, "In the zoo," and Teacher says, "Where are they native in this country?" A girl says, with a grimace of disgust, "We saw them in Marineland in Florida. They were slaughtered and used for meat. Ugh!" John has raised his hand and Teacher calls on him. "We saw one in Wisconsin about the size of Bob's head." Teacher says, "That's plenty big." and the class laughs.
>
> Teacher asks, "What was Douglas [a boy in the story] doing on the island? Have you ever been scared, John?" "Yes," replies John. "So have I," says the teacher, and the class laughs. Teacher says, *"That's what I like about buddies."*
>
> 11:25. Teacher says, "Let's read the story silently." He says to a girl. "Do you mind putting your beads away for the rest of the morning instead of tearing them apart?"
>
> The room is now very quiet. He walks around the aisles as the children read.

Mr. Jeffries obviously runs a "democratic" classroom, and his pupils are spontaneous and effervescent. He tells the children that he is their "buddy"; he is no aloof figure, pretending to invulnerability, but like them he is capable of fear; he is "scared" *with* them. He is right down there on the floor with the kids, so to speak: like a contemporary American *buddy-daddy*, he has leveled the distance between himself and the children. Yet by command he can suddenly get quiet when he wants it, though rarely for long. A sound curve of his class would have a relatively constant high noise plateau with occasional narrow valleys of relative quiet.

> 10:15. The class is discussing types of nouns. Teacher says, "If I had lots of Ritas, she'd be a type. Maybe we're lucky we have only one." Class laughs. A girl raises her hand and Teacher says, "What is it, honey?"
>
> 10:25. The room has grown noisy during the lesson and Teacher says, "Can't hear you, Shirley. You're not going to find out a thing by looking in that direction." His voice has risen, getting louder in order to be heard above the classroom noise.
>
> 10:40. Clatter is increasing. Eight or nine pupils are walking around the room. One boy throws a paper wad at another. Four pupils are at the pencil sharpener. Noise grows louder but *teacher ignores it.*
>
> 10:45. Teacher says, "It would seem to me that in the past five minutes you haven't accomplished a thing; you've been so busy wandering around." This creates complete silence. Then two boys stand to look at neighbor's

work. Another goes to Teacher's desk to get help. Teacher and he confer.
Noise is louder now.

10:55. Two boys raise hands. Two others stand next to Teacher. One girl
pats his back as he bends over. She giggles.

11:00. Teacher: "O.K., put language books away, please!" He giggles as a
girl asks him a question. Pupils put books in desks. Teacher: "Take a couple
of minutes here. Girl with the blue hair, get up. Stretch a bit." Loud
laughter from the class. Teacher: "Get up and stretch." Most of the class
stands. Two boys continue writing at their desks. A boy and girl push each
other. The smallest boy in the class stands alone and looks on as two girls
wrestle.

At the end of the observation period on this day the Observer wrote, "I feel that
the pupils are truly fond of Mr. Jeffries. They enjoy laughing together; not at somebody, but *with* each other." Of course, we might question the last in view of the
jokes about Rita and the earlier one about the size of Bob's head. At any rate,
there seems little doubt that, like Mrs. Thorndyke, Mr. Jeffries is a love object to
his children. In the present observation segment, one little girl strokes his back, and
he giggles with another one in a private joke during the lesson. Everybody, including
the teacher, has a wonderful time. Frequently, however, the noise gets so loud that
Mr. Jeffries has to shout and the students cannot hear. Suddenly at 10:45 he scolds
the children for not accomplishing anything, even though he has permitted the
disorder and noise to increase. At 11 o'clock the children are pushing and wrestling,
but Mr. Jeffries ignores it. The following week, during a particularly hilarious and
noisy arithmetic lesson, when the children can barely hear what is going on, a girl
takes a boy's paper, tears it up and throws it into the wastebasket; but the teacher
laughs, the class pays no attention, the paper is fished out and taped together, and
the lesson continues.

About five weeks later the Observer was in this classroom when Mr. Jeffries was
out sick and a substitute was on duty. The room was in its usual noisy state when
the principal walked in and stood in the back of the room for a few minutes. No
change took place in the class, but the principal bent over one of the little girls,
embraced her, whispered something to her, then turned to the Observer, said,
"Fine bunch of gals here," and left. Thus, in his behavior the principal reinforces
the emphasis on impulse release at deeply gratifying levels. *Teacher, principal,
children, and community are one continuous cultural system.*

As the school year entered the last month, evidence began to appear that impulse
release and noise had reached a point beyond the endurance of the *children*, for
the children, particularly the girls, began spontaneously to *shush* the class:

10:40. The children have just finished singing. Teacher says, "Get paper,
eraser, pencil." There is a loud buzz at this command, and a girl says, "What's
the paper for?" Teacher says, "Now don't go wild just because you sang.
Your pencils don't have to be so sharp." Observer notes that a bunch of
youngsters is storming the pencil sharpener as Teacher says this. *Someone
shushes the class.* Teacher says, "Fill this out the same as yesterday." He
passes the sheets out very carefully, dropping the correct number on the
first desk of each row. "Today's date is the eighth of May," says Teacher.
"Sorry you're so noisy. Don't open your books till I tell you. Just fill out the
first page. This is a reading test." The class reads in silent concentration.

11:01. The test is over. Teacher starts to issue instructions for the next
activity and a girl says to the class, *"Shush!"*

11:06. A girl goes to the teacher's desk for help in spelling. He spells a
word aloud as she writes, leaning on his desk for support. A girl walks by
John and smacks him playfully. He gets up, walks by her, smacks her on the

back soundly and sprints away. Teacher says, "I notice that most of you have finished your papers promptly. I'm very pleased. Now devote your time, the next fifteen minutes, to your spelling." A girl says, "*Shush!*" There is a loud buzz. Observer notes that this shushing has occurred several times today, *only from the pupils*.

These observations drive home the point made earlier, that responsibility for maintenance of order has shifted in such a way that the children determine when controls shall be set in motion. In the last observation, the children's efforts to hold the social structure together become overt; but throughout the term, the teacher's interest in order is so slight, he so often ignores the racket in his room that the conclusion is inescapable that the children have set their own limits because the teacher has abdicated.

INTERVIEWS WITH TEACHERS

The first section of this paper was devoted to direct observation and interpretation of teacher-pupil interaction. In the interpretation of observations, however, there is always the problem of whether the observer is "imposing his own ideas" on the data. Mindful of this difficulty, I interviewed the teachers on the subject of their ideas about classroom discipline two years after the original observations were made. The original observations of Mrs. Thorndyke were made by me; those of the other two teachers were made by my students. I give excerpts from Mrs. Olan's interview first. She says:

> In this day and age the children have more tensions and problems than when I first taught. In the one-room schoolhouse in which I first taught the children came from calm homes. There was no worry about war, and there was no TV or radio. They led a calm and serene life. They came to school with their syrup pails for lunch buckets. Children of today know more about what is going on; they are better informed. So you can't hold a strict rein on them. It is bad for children to come in and sit down with their feet under the seat: you have to have freedom to get up and move around. When they do this they are more rested and have a greater attention span. . . .
>   Children need to enjoy school and like it. They also need their work to be done; it's not all play. You must get them to accept responsibility and do work on their own.

Thus, Mrs. Olan feels that children have severe inner tensions that must not be held in close rein because it is not good for them. In answer to the question, "What would you say is your own particular way of keeping order in the classroom?" she explains simply and movingly how she manages her children:

> Well, I would say I try to get that at the beginning of the year by getting this bond of affection and a relationship between the children and me. And we do that with stories; and I play games *with* them—don't just teach them how to play. It's what you get from living together comfortably. We have share times—that's the time a child can share with the teacher; and he gives whatever he wants to share: a bird's nest he has found; a tadpole that he and his dad got. Sometimes he may simply tell about something in his life—that his grandmother fell down and broke a leg and is not at home. . . . These are the things that contribute toward this discipline. Another thing is discipline: it took me a long time to learn it, too—I thought I was the boss, but I learned that even with a child, if you speak to him as you would to a neighbor or a friend you get a better response than if you say, "Johnny, do this or

that." If you say, "Mary, will you please cooperate, you are disturbing us; we want to finish our reading," rather than just giving a command, they feel they are working with you and not just taking orders.

Mrs. Olan is aware of what she is doing: love is the path to discipline through permissiveness, and school is a continuation of family life in which the values of sharing and democracy lead to comfortable living and ultimately to (Mrs. Olan's own interpretation of) discipline.

> With primary children the teacher is a mother during the day; they have to be able to bring their problems to you. They get love and affection at home, and I see no reason not to give it in school.
>   If you have the right relationship between teacher and child or between parent and child he can take harsh words and the things you say in the right spirit; and if you don't have that bond of affection, he just doesn't take it.

To Mrs. Olan, mother of a twenty-one-year-old son, children are warm little pussy-cats, and you quiet them the way you do kittens. For example, in answer to the question, "Do you think children tend to be quieter if the teacher is affectionate?" she said:

> If a teacher has a well-modulated voice and a pleasing disposition her children are more relaxed and quiet. Children are like kittens: if kittens have a full stomach and lie in the sun, they purr. If the atmosphere is such that the children are more comfortable, they are quiet. It is comfortable living that makes the quiet child. When you are shouting at them and they're shouting back at you, it isn't comfortable living.

Two years before this interview, observation had made clear that Mrs. Olan was no "boss," but lodged much responsibility in the children. She clarifies the matter further:

> It means a great deal to them to give them their own direction. When problems do come up in the room, we talk them over and discuss what is the right thing to do when this or that happens. Usually you get pretty good answers. They are a lot harder on themselves than I would be; so if any punishment comes along, like not going to an assembly, you have group pressure.

As I was about to go, Mrs. Olan spontaneously remarked, "My children don't rate as high [on achievement tests] as other children; I don't push, and that's because I believe in comfortable living."

Mrs. Thorndyke's response to the interview was entirely different from Mrs. Olan's. Mrs. Thorndyke has no children of her own, and we have seen how outgoing she is to her little third graders, patting and stroking them. However, when I talked to her about how she ran her class, she sounded like a strict though benign disciplinarian, who hardly ever touched her pupils. The youngsters need "strong guidance," she said, and from the very first day have to be taught "who the leader is," meaning, of course, Mrs. Thorndyke. Demonstrative affection, in her opinion, is only for kindergarten and first grade; by the time the children get to her, Mrs. Thorndyke said, it should "level off." Thus, if we relied only on what she told us about herself, we would have no sound idea of what Mrs. Thorndyke was really like. If there were no direct observations of her with her children, we would think of her as a "schoolmarm" who, while laying down the law, was at the same time somewhat sensitive—rather at the mechanical "social skills" level—to children's emotional needs.

Since Mrs. Thorndyke's responses in the interview made me wonder whether her view of the teacher's role had changed or whether she was merely unaware of what she was doing, I decided to ask her permission to observe her again and she graciously consented. Her position as a teacher had changed in the intervening two years: according to new school regulations, superior students had been placed in special classes with special teachers, leaving Mrs. Thorndyke, among others, with only the slow children; and these had "a very short attention span," as she put it rather regretfully. As one watched her with these pupils, the most striking feature of her behavior was her *enormously increased mobility* in the classroom as she responded to the children's requests for help. Whereas previously, for example, as Mrs. Thorndyke walked around the room helping children in language skills, she had been able to spend more time with each child as she assisted him in his work, now she was in the midst of a constant silent clamor of hands as these children of lower IQ sought her help again and again. Whereas two years before she *sauntered* around the room, now she rushed, and though this did not prevent her from touching, tapping and stroking them in an affectionate way, her contacts were more ephemeral. There was also a pervasive air of irritation and fatigue in her behavior. However, a striking phenomenon had entered to change the situation in an even more dramatic way: this was David, a disturbed boy with a "hopeless" mother and a "no account" father. Mrs. Thorndyke said that as long as she kept David close to her, she could help him better and keep him under control. He sat close to the front of the room near her desk, and when the other children were sitting at their places reciting, she sometimes had David right beside her at her desk. Some extracts from the record of one observation period will show what the relation was between Mrs. Thorndyke and David:

> Her hand is on David's head. He takes her hand. Now her hand is on his head again.
>
> 1:35. Now she is over near David again; he takes her hand and puts his face against it. She puts her hand on the head of Bobby. Now she touches David again; he holds her hand.
>
> 1:45. David takes her hand, really her whole arm, and holds it for about 30 seconds as he puts his face against it. She calls on him to read and he does. He has her hand again.
>
> 1:50. She is near David again and gives him her hand. He kisses it, fondles it, nuzzles it.
>
> 2:40. David is sitting close to the teacher while the rest of the children are at their seats reciting in the language skills lesson. David is a very beautiful boy. Mrs. Thorndyke puts her hand on David's arm and pats it and he places his fingers on her arm. They are like mother and child. He reads rather well. She strokes and fondles his face like that of a beloved child.

Mrs. Thorndyke says that David "needs affection" and there is no doubt that he is getting it from her. I would be inclined to say that if David could only stick with Mrs. Thorndyke long enough, it would help him. Meanwhile, one becomes aware of the fact that this restless child is held in check by his teacher's affectivity. One would be inclined to say that where affectivity is not dictated by the heart as a way of controlling middle-class children, "common sense" might suggest it. Meanwhile, the problems involved in using this as an *overall* technique have already been pointed out.

Finally, with respect to the apparent discrepancy between what Mrs. Thorndyke does and what she says she does, I would say that she is unaware of her own behavior along the dimension of "physical contact with children."

Two years after he was observed for one semester in a sixth-grade class by one of my students, Mr. Jeffries was principal of the school in which he once was teacher.

His passionate involvement in teaching and in children easily won me. The following are some excerpts from a very long and thoughtful interview. He says,

> The very first day, I introduce myself to the children and tell them about myself. I use my family a great deal. I talk about my boy and about my daughter. I tell them about certain of my experiences, just to give them an understanding that "here is an individual."

In this way he begins to draw closer to the children. He becomes almost one with them. Speaking of himself, he says,

> They know the teacher's a friend with whom they can exchange jokes and banter. But if the teacher says, "Come on, we must get to this or that," they say to themselves "We must do it." Maybe they say, "He's a good Joe, a good guy, so let's get the job done."

Mr. Jeffries is like Mrs. Olan in that he sees himself as working out the "criteria" for classroom management and discipline with the children in a democratic way, and he lets the children set their own punishments when they get into serious trouble, like fighting in the school yard. Mr. Jeffries' long explanation of how he goes about letting the children set their own rules cannot be reproduced here, but, actually, what he does is guide the children in the course of a discussion to the acceptance of his own ideas of what the "criteria" for classroom management should be.

We have seen that Mr. Jeffries' own room is a buoyant, noisy milieu. "You can't hold children in a tight rein," he says, "no more than you can hold a racehorse in a tight rein. A racehorse needs freedom and so does a child." As a matter of fact, Mr. Jeffries fears that if you hold a child in during class he will somehow break loose and "stomp" on somebody, just like a racehorse that breaks out into the fans at a steeplechase, as he put it. Children are "God-given individuals" and have a right to get up and walk around whenever they please. He says that since in this way they may find their way to an encyclopedia or a map, mobility is closely related to creativity. To Mr. Jeffries, "a quiet classroom is a dead classroom" where "the children are not thinking or are afraid to think." A stranger walking into his room, he says, might think it a "riot" or that "mayhem was being committed," but he simply would not understand the basic thinking behind Mr. Jeffries' management. Furthermore, "A classroom with affection can be an awfully happy and joyous one. A quiet classroom may be an awfully fearful situation for someone."

Love, demonstrativeness, freedom, mobility, creativity, noise and thoughtfulness go together, as Mr. Jeffries sees it. He is literally afraid of quietness and restraint.

In reviewing these findings, it is important to bear in mind that *the first section of this paper was compiled before the interviewing was done, and has not been altered in any way since.* With this in mind, it can be seen that what Mrs. Olan and Mr. Jeffries *say* about what they do and why they do it confirms both observation and interpretation. In Mrs. Thorndyke, we are dealing with a person who is unaware of her affectional responses to the children.

SUMMARY AND CONCLUSIONS

Today our emphasis on creativity and spontaneity goes hand in hand with culture-weariness—a certain tiredness and disillusionment with impulse restraint, and a feeling that the Self has been sold down the river to the pirates of production, consumption and war. In these circumstances, permissiveness with children, an attitude that had been gaining strength before World War II, has invaded many phases of work with children, so that in some middle-class suburban public schools, there is a great relaxation of controls, and the teacher who is often most highly regarded is the one who lets the children be "free." These teachers are trying to be good teachers: like devoted public servants they are performing their duties as the community requires them to do. The surging impulses of the children whom they are "permitting," however, are threatening: when they are turned loose on a substitute or one of their fellows, they can be terribly destructive. In these circumstances the teachers handle the children in accordance with their own roles in the culture of contemporary America, and in response to their own inner needs. Women teachers in these schools often manage by making themselves love objects and by making the children feel guilty. The one man in our sample played the role of one type of American *buddy-daddy*, exercising what little control there was by making himself loved the way this kind of modern American daddy is loved, and by occasionally issuing, like any suburban daddy, a peremptory command for order, the effects of which rarely lasted more than a few minutes.

Though in the very act of being released, the children's impulses are narcotized, in most cases it is not enough: the children "climb the walls" anyway. A consequence of this is impairment of the efficiency of the teachers and fatigue and obstruction of learning; for in the midst of constant turmoil, the children's capacities to hear, to concentrate and to absorb are interfered with. This explains the interesting phenomenon of the sixth graders' assuming responsibility for order in the class by *shushing* when the teacher does nothing. As a matter of fact, it would appear that under the conditions of spontaneity, as understood in this portion of surburbia, noise and disorder destroy the very thing educators would foster.

In the broader cultural context the classroom is the children's first important experience with the administrative structure of the society. It is their first contact with what is fundamentally an impersonal mechanism for getting the culture's business done. But on the other hand, the children are prepared by the erotized atmosphere they encounter for the buddy-buddy, "false personalization" which Riesman has described for American institutions. The boys in particular will become an executive part of the impersonal structures—businesses, government bureaucracies—within which, in line with contemporary ethos, every effort is made to mix business with libido. From this point of view, life in public elementary middle-class schools of suburbia is a preparation for work in a libidinized social structure which is at the same time basically impersonal and which pivots on "social skills."

Because of its necessary brevity, this paper is scarcely even an introduction to a single dimension of the cultural dynamics of learning. In these schools there is a great variety of ways of managing, and I have discussed but three teachers. In a limited sense, however, they present a view of one important problem: how our teachers manage under the pressure of an ideology of permissiveness and spontaneity which makes their task difficult.

In some of these rooms we get the picture of the immature yet strong egos of children manipulating a social structure which has been practically handed over to them, yet never letting it disintegrate, never actually stepping into chaos. For them this is a training in what has become known in other aspects of our culture as the art of "brinkmanship": a training in holding together in a relatively shapeless social field.

In order to round out the picture somewhat, it seems necessary to point out that the urban public elementary schoolrooms we have studied are entirely different from those discussed here. In those schools, the children are held under rigid control by the teacher, there is little talking that is not specifically permitted, the children stay in their seats, and the rooms are quiet. On the other hand, the atmosphere is also more impersonal, more attention seems to be given to rote procedures, and spontaneity is at a minimum.

In conclusion I should like to reemphasize the fact that all the teachers I have known in surburbia are thoughtful, dedicated normal human beings, trying to find within themselves the resources to deal with a dictum handed down, while at the same time they have received little instruction in how to do it. This being the case it would be wrong to make teachers the scapegoats of any adverse feeling that might be generated by the spectacle of classroom turmoil, for teachers are the instruments of their culture, as we all are.

NOTES

1. To the teachers and principals who have so tolerantly accepted me and my students as observers in their classrooms I am most grateful. The need to protect the identity of teachers, principals, and children makes it impossible for me to thank them or my observers by name. Nevertheless, I can thank them all anonymously for their thoughtfulness and help, but above all for their contribution to this work.
2. Other publications on this research are J. Henry, "Culture, Education, and Communications Theory," in *Education and Anthropology*, ed. George D. Spindler (Stanford, Calif.: Stanford University Press, 1955); J. Henry, "Docility, or Giving Teacher What She Wants." *Journal of Social Issues* 11 (1955): 33–41; J. Henry, "Attitude Organization in Elementary School Classrooms," *American Journal of Orthopsychiatry* 27 (1957): 117–33; J. Henry, "Working Paper on Creativity," *Harvard Educational Review* 27 (1957): 148–55.

13 / The Amish Elementary School Teacher and Students

John A. Hostetler and Gertrude Enders Huntington

When county school superintendents initially learn that Amish teachers have no formal training beyond eighth grade, they are often appalled and doubt the teachers' qualifications. But to the Amish, qualifications for teaching have little relation to the acquisition of college degrees. Qualifications and suitability for teaching in Amish society are best understood by comparing the role of teacher in the two cultures, the Amish and the typical suburban school.

Today in many suburban schools, by the time children have reached fifth grade they know more about certain facts and even areas of knowledge than a teacher who must teach all subjects. The prevalence of television, ease of travel, and the availability of books stimulate children's curiosity and enable many of them to pursue their interests, at least in limited areas, to a remarkable degree. The American school system emphasizes the development of the students' rational powers. The amount of factual material that children are taught steadily increases as the total amount of knowledge increases and as society becomes more complex. For these reasons, it is essential that public school teachers be well trained.

Outside the classroom, the public school teacher disappears from the life of his pupils. They do not know how he spends his time, what he does, how he lives, or what he believes about religion or politics—and these may, in fact, have surprisingly little influence on the subject matter he teaches the children. The public school teacher must be competent in his subject and able in his teaching methods, for, at least superficially, he is hired to teach technology rather than wisdom. Most communities do not want him to teach attitudes or beliefs, other than belief in the scientific method and our form of government. They want him to stick to his subject: teach the children the material, but not how in a moral sense the material should be used. The teacher is an authority on subject matter; his authority comes from his training; and most of that comes from books. The printed word—the most recently printed word—is the final authority in most American classrooms.

The Amish, who have kept radio, television, and movies outside their experience, have been minimally affected by the communication revolution. They have limited the printed word, rejecting much of the more recent material that flows from the world's printing presses. In maintaining a primitive type of Christian church, they have kept an oral tradition and an orientation to life that is relational rather than analytical (Cohen 1969). By its very nature oral tradition is social; it is tied to the community. Where there is extreme reliance on the printed word, teacher and pupil need never meet. In contrast, the oral tradition requires personal interaction; teaching within this tradition is by example as well as by word.

In keeping with the oral tradition, the Amish teacher must teach with his whole life. He should be a person integrated within himself and integrated with the community, for every aspect of his behavior and of his personality is related to his teaching. He must be well grounded in his religious faith and completely committed to the Amish way of life, accepting the limits set by the *Ordnung* and exemplifying the Amish traits of humility, obedience, steadfastness, and love for his fellow man. In addition, he must be interested in education and have sufficient factual knowledge to provide a substantial margin between him and his students. In other words, the teachers should be capable and sound of character.

An elderly teacher explains the Amish attitude toward qualification and certification: "It is essential that we have qualified teachers. By that I do not mean certified ones, for state-certified teachers do not qualify for teaching in our schools." State certified teachers are not qualified because their approach is mainly cerebral (understanding-oriented) rather than visceral (identification-oriented), to use a distinction made by Saltzman (1963:323) in discussing successful community schools. Both qualities are essential to cultural integrity and continuity. Teachers who understand but do not identify with the community are at a serious disadvantage when they confront children and parents who differ from them in race, class, culture, or ethnicity. Trained middle-class teachers are too far removed from the oral tradition to identify with the Amish, and in most instances they are unsuitable as examples.

Because the Amish teachers' role is primarily that of Christian example rather than authority in subject matter or methodology, they are not likely to present themselves to the children as "gods, all-knowing, all-powerful, always rational, always just, always right" (Holt 1964:171). Instead they freely admit their human weaknesses and the need to turn to the "Master Teacher" for help and guidance.

The Amish regard teaching with such importance that it is beginning to be thought of as a calling rather than a job. Their ministers are called; that is, they do not themselves choose to be ministers, but are chosen by the congregation of God through the working of the lot. Similarly, an Amish person usually does not apply for his first teaching job; rather he is approached by the school board. One girl said they had "been after" her for about six years before she decided she was ready to teach. When she did decide, she spent several weeks with various good teachers in the area, observing and helping for a week in each school. If the prospective teacher is younger than twenty-one, the father is asked, rather than the girl or boy directly, since an Amishman is under the care of his father socially and financially until he is twenty-one. One young teacher who had enjoyed her year of teaching said she was trying to persuade her father to let her teach next year, "but I can bring so much more money home if I clean house and baby-sit and we don't have much money, so that maybe I'll have to do housework instead." In such a case the school board may try to remind the father how important it is to have good teachers in the Amish school. Teachers who have taught successfully are believed to have demonstrated that they have a calling, and if they wish to change jobs, they can apply to another school. However, the teachers' grapevine is sufficiently effective that the information is usually passed around informally, enabling the school board to make the initial move. A good teacher may receive as many as six or seven requests, even if she has not indicated an interest in changing schools. These requests are written in such a way that they are very difficult to turn down. The relationship between teacher and school board, both by letter and when the school board calls, is a very personal one and does not in any way resemble a business agreement.

Amish teachers are not motivated by monetary rewards. They do not have contracts, nor do they have tenure. Life is uncertain, and no one knows when it will change. Perhaps the teacher will be needed somewhere else. If her parents fall sick, for instance, she may have to stop teaching to care for them; or a young man who has been teaching may have to stop to take over his father's farm. The same principle applies if the teacher turns out to be unsuccessful. He or she is asked to leave. This is considered unfortunate, for it is hard on the children. If a teacher, however, cannot handle the work, it is obvious that God did not intend for him to teach and that it would be better for everyone for him to do something else. The Amishman who remains a teacher does so because he has demonstrated talent and because generally he wants to teach.

TEACHING METHODS AND SCHOOL MANAGEMENT

An Amish teacher's way of life and his teaching methods are in agreement. He teaches primarily by being an exemplary individual in close contact with the children. The teacher is a role model. But he is more than a role model, for he also imparts facts as well as his attitudes and his beliefs as to how these facts should be used and how they fit into an Amish world view. He creates the atmosphere of the school. He is the shepherd, the responsible adult, who is older and more experienced and knows better than the children what is good for them. The classroom runs smoothly, for he does not pretend that the children make the decisions. An Amish teacher quietly tells a child what to do and he does it. Obedience and order are basic to a good school not just part of the time but all of the time. A biblical phrase, "Let everything be done decently and in order" (I Corinthians 14:40), is a motto on the wall of some classrooms. "For God is not the author of confusion, but of peace" (I Corinthians 14:33) is recited by the pupils. Orderliness is believed to make for more security and less tension in the pupils' lives.

Amish teachers instruct their children to "Do unto others, as you would have others do unto you." This quotation "should be placed in front of the schoolroom where all children can see and study it, and the teacher should quite often point to it as a reminder that this Golden Rule should be followed at all times" (Byler 1969). The Golden Rule is not compatible with individualistic competition. The Amish teach a nonexploitive value system by emphasizing individual responsibility rather than self-assertiveness. The Amish schools avoid the contradiction that Jules Henry (1963:295-97) speaks of in many modern public schools, where the children are simultaneously taught to compete and to have love for one another. There is some competition in the Amish schools, but it is usually structured to support the group. The children will try to have better attendance this week than last week, better spelling scores this month than last month. They may even vie with another school for good attendance, or the teacher may post weekly spelling scores from a school where she taught some years ago and the children as a school, or as a class, try to do better than her former pupils. Under the teacher's guidance the peer group is used to enhance adult values. The children encourage one another's good performance in order that their whole class or their school may do well (Bronfenbrenner 1970:50).

The Amish believe that an individual's talents are God-given; therefore, no one should be praised if he is an easy learner nor condemned if he is a slow learner. These differences in talent are God's will, and there is a place for each person God created. The teachers and children are tolerant of such differences. All children are expected to work hard and use their time well; they are not all expected to master the same amount of material. Their differences are not concealed, for though slowness in intellectual learning makes for added difficulties, it is nothing to be ashamed of. A motto displayed in one Amish school says,

> Little children you should seek
> Rather to be good than wise;
> For the thoughts you do not speak
> Shine out in your cheeks and eyes.

This attitude is not too different from that of the Hopi Indian: "A man need not be ashamed of being poor, or of being dumb, so long as he was good to others" (Lee 1959:20). A quick mind is not an asset in itself, but only when used properly. Many Amish believe that what is learned slowly is remembered better. Abraham Lincoln is quoted as saying, "My mind is like a piece of steel—very hard to scratch anything on it, but almost impossible after you get it there, to rub it out." Another motto expresses it this way:

> If you would have your learning stay,
> Be patient, don't learn too fast;
> The man who travels a mile each day
> May get around the world at last.

Subject grades are given for achievement not effort. Daily and weekly grades are averaged mathematically with test grades to get the score that goes onto the report card. The children know what their daily grades are; in some schools they keep a record of their grades so they can also work out their own averages. A distribution curve that balances Bs and Ds and gives the majority of children Cs is never used by the Amish. Not only are the number of pupils too small but this would lead to an unacceptable type of competition in which one child's good grade would depend on another child's poor grade. They prefer an absolute grading system in which a given number corresponds to a given letter grade. Grades are not manipulated to motivate the student; rather students are taught to accept the level of work they are able to do, to always work hard to do better, to "try, try again," and to remember that "it isn't so bad when you have tried and can't succeed as when you start thinking of giving up before you have really tried." Students are told, "God does not ask for success but for effort." Differences in ability are assessed realistically and accepted matter-of-factly. A mother will say, in front of her children, "This child is an easy learner," and pointing to another, comment, "He learns hard," in much the same way she might comment, "Reuben has blue eyes, Paul's are brown."

Consistent with the oral tradition, Amish children commit a considerable amount of material to memory. They memorize poems the teacher selects and Bible verses. They memorize songs so they can sing while they work and will not be dependent on books. They sing and recite at their Christmas program. All eight grades in one school that tested unusually high in arithmetic recited in unison the multiplication tables from 2 through 12 and the tables of conversions of measurements, weights, and volumes. The children enjoyed it as they would enjoy choral reading, and it never failed to impress visitors. It was a pleasant way for the children to learn the arithmetic facts, for they did it as a group activity, protected from the embarassment of obvious error by the carrying capacity of forty voices. Just as the children memorize hymns and Bible verses before they really understand them, so these children knew their multiplication tables before they used or understood them.

The discussion method is not considered appropriate for academic subjects, for every child is expected to learn the facts and to be able to recite them. Instead of the children wildly waving hands and competing for the chance to answer, each child is questioned by the teacher, each is given his turn to answer, and each child answers the same number of questions. Learning is not disguised as a game. The children are taught that it is work, and although in the Amish culture work is something that must be done whether or not one likes it, whether or not it is convenient, the prevailing attitude is that people are fortunate to be able to work and that work is something to enjoy. "The spirit in happiness is not merely in doing what one likes to do, but to try to like what one has to do."

Discussion is used very effectively in areas where it applies. In many schools the children help to formulate the rules—although the teacher always has veto power—and these are openly and honestly discussed. Sometimes in the public schools the attempt to have a democratic classroom may blur the lines of decision making: the teacher "helps" the children democratically reach the "correct" decision (Jules Henry in Spindler 1963:230). This is not the case in Amish schools. If a decision is to be made by the teacher, the school board, or the parents, the decision is made without discussing it with the children and they are told what is acceptable. When the children are invited to participate in a decision, however, their opinions are respected and they are actually allowed to reach their own decision. Because Amish schools are homogeneous and there is an emphasis on sensitivity to the group and on the individual's working for the good of the group, this effective procedure is good preparation for future participation in church decisions. The larger boundaries are set by the teacher as representative of the community; within these boundaries the children are given freedom of choice. So it will be for the adult church member.

Control is relaxed during recess and the noon hour when the children play vigorously, freely, and noisily. "Play at recess and noon opens our mind for study," said one teacher. Most schools have relatively few rules. The belief is that there should be few rules but these should be consistently enforced.

The Amish stress humility, the elimination of self-pride, mutual encouragement, persistence, the willingness to attempt a difficult task, and love for one another. A perusal of mottoes on schoolroom walls, of verses memorized, and of teachers' sayings illustrates the consistency of these values. For the Amish, education is primarily social rather than individual. Its goal is not "the freedom which exalts the individual" (Educational Policies Commission 1962:3), but social cohesion. Teaching the children to get along together in work and play is as important as teaching the academic subjects—both are essential for the continued existence of the Amish community. Specific teaching techniques and hints are mentioned in numerous teachers' letters and articles in the *Blackboard Bulletin*. The book *School Bells Ringing*, by Uria Byler, discusses methods for teaching every subject from phonics to health and also gives suggestions on such things as playing games, keeping the schoolhouse clean, and dealing with "newspaper pests." Over eighty teachers contributed to a book *Tips for Teachers, A Handbook for Amish Teachers* (Pathway Publishers, 1970).

In the one- and two-teacher schools the number of pupils per teacher ranges from 13 to 47, with 27 as the average number. This number keeps the teachers busy. They have worked out a variety of ways for the children to help teach. In some schools the children exchange papers for checking. In other schools the older children help check the papers of the younger children. One teacher has the rule that grades five through eight may not read library books until the arithmetic papers for the lower grades have been corrected and that the third and fourth grades may not have library books until the first and second-grade workbooks and arithmetic papers have been corrected. In other schools certain of the oldest children may help with reading words, give flash cards to the younger children, or listen to them read. Children also are permitted to help each other. These practices not only reinforce the children's learning by having them go over earlier material, but they also encouarge concern and care for the younger children. Helping the teacher in specified ways is consistent with the Amish concept of sharing one another's burdens. However, the teacher must administer the program in such a way that she does not seem to the parents to shirk her leadership responsibility. Some teachers have a paid helper who answers hands. These are often girls who are recent graduates.

The Amish teacher is the recognized leader of the classroom, the one who is in charge and responsible. As would be expected, the Amish children identify closely with their teacher. Many of the mottos and sayings used in the school include the teacher with the pupils:

> As the bird's song is refreshing every morning,
> so *we* should refresh each other with friendliness.

> Do *we* wonder at times what use *our* little life may be?
> Well, all that is asked from *us* is to fill *our* little
> place in this world as best *we* can.
> This could be a place important or one that is
> unimportant in the eyes of men.

Many of the teachers enjoy playing with the children during recess and the noon hour, as much as the children enjoy having them play. The school has the atmosphere of a well-ordered family, in which the teacher represents a parent or an older sibling. The pupils and teacher call one another by their first names, as is done throughout the Amish communities, where even the youngest children call the oldest women, the ministers, and the bishops by their first names. Respect is not based on titles.

The teachers plan occasional surprises for their pupils: a picnic in the woods, popcorn at noon, or a special trip. They may even plan a trip for their pupils during the summer. Sometimes a teacher will invite the children to her house for dinner, which is the noon meal. The children in turn have surprises for the teacher, especially for the teacher's birthday, when the children may hide a cake and lunch to surprise their teacher during the noon hour or after school. Often the teacher is a relative of many of the children and very likely attends the same church, so the children know their teacher in many roles, as a person in the community as well as in the classroom.

The children, under the teacher's direction, put on Thanksgiving and Christmas programs for the parents and invite them for a picnic on the schoolgrounds at the end of the term. The programs vary considerably from one community to another. In one school the children put on small skits, but this would be frowned on in other regions, where they sing religious songs and recite memory work. These programs provide a great deal of pleasure for the students, the parents, and the teachers. The children are beside themselves with excitement and delight as they enjoy one another's performance. One teacher said of their Thanksgiving program, "It was a heaping success."

Experienced Amish teachers are resourceful in maintaining their pupils' interest and in creating a pleasant school. The children and the teachers make school decorations. They may wash, dry, and crush eggshells which they then glue onto black paper to make mottoes. During the winter they make their own games. One class made "Farmopoly," a board game based on *Monopoly* but with dairy farms and harness shops instead of Boardwalk and public utilities. Sometimes a school will have a project of making a book. The children will each write an original story and then copy it into their own books. Some of the stories are illustrated. The excitement comes when everyone's book has been turned in and the stories are read aloud (without authors' names) to the class.

To summarize Amish methods of teaching, it may be said that Amish teachers are as much concerned with the development of Christian character, including a proper relational orientation to others, as with teaching facts. They are more concerned with giving their students correct knowledge than with teaching them critical thinking. The primary method used to instill correct knowledge is memorization and drill. Only within the framework of the material presented are the children taught to think for themselves. They are taught "what" and "where" but not "why" (except in theistic terms) and usually not "how" (except in a moral sense). In a secular school with a scientific orientation, children's analytic powers are trained to enable them to solve the "riddles of life, space, and time" (Educational Policies Commission 1961:9). In the Amish school these are not believed to be riddles that need to be solved by man. Truth need not be searched for, it has already been revealed (in the Bible), and it is there for those ready to believe. Because the Amish and the public schools have such different concepts of what truth is and how it is to be obtained, it is not surprising that their teaching methods are different: the Amish stress believing while the public schools stress questioning. Twentieth-century America not only should have room for both approaches, it needs both. Even the most rational questioner needs a basis in belief—though not necessarily a theological basis—from which to ask his questions and by which to judge his answers. And religious zeal needs the tempering of rational thought.

DISCIPLINE

Experienced Amish teachers from three states were asked, "What, in your opinion, constitutes good control in the schoolroom?" One teacher from Pennsylvania answered, "Good control is wearing a smile, regardless of how you feel inside. Be firm. Have a strong backbone, but not too stiff that it doesn't want to bend when necessary. A teacher should be humble." Another, from Ohio, said, "Be firm, not stern. . . . Have respect for the pupils, be honest with yourself and admit your mistakes if in the wrong. Be cheerful and slow to anger." Others mentioned trusting the children, not having too many rules, and being careful that no one, including the teacher, breaks them.

This same group of teachers was asked about the methods of discipline they used. The most common form was speaking to the offending child, often in private. Some teachers have the children apologize, but mention that "a false or forced apology is worse than none." A common punishment for a fairly serious offense is keeping children in their seats during recess or the noon hour. Sometimes, in addition, they have to write sentences during this period. Finally, corporal punishment, either a strap across the palm or paddling, may be used. Some teachers never use it; those who do state that it should be used very infrequently and with love. One teacher observed that it is "very effective but should be used with caution and plenty of love. I use it only for lying, cheating, vulgar language, or smutty talk, which is rare." Another teacher said, "We teachers should always see to it that punishing is done out of love. If it isn't, I believe it causes more harm than good, only causing rebellion on the part of the child." Physical punishment is used for the infractions mentioned above, for open disobedience, and for activity that is physically dangerous, such as children running into the highway or teasing a nervous buggy horse. Parents approve of limited use of physical punishment to enforce their children's moral and physical safety, but they do not tolerate physical punishment as a substitute for respect or as a means of frightening children into obedience. The occasional teacher who resorts to these methods soon finds himself looking for a different kind of employment.

Teachers use encouragement and rewards much more than punishment. Children are given stars, stickers, even pencils and candy bars for good behavior, good grades, and abiding by the rules. Not all teachers, however, approve of this. One teacher writes, "In my humble opinion, it works better to reward or treat the children unexpectedly, whether at home or at school, for their efforts and good work, *after* the task is done, rather than to promise rewards if they do this or that thing according to our wishes." Another teacher says she always has a treat for her pupils at the end of the six-weeks test day, not just for those who received 100 percent, but for each child who did his best. "Needless to say, no one admits not having done his best," one teacher said. Each one gets a candy bar, a pack of lifesavers, or some popcorn.

Amish teachers aim never to belittle their pupils or to use sarcasm or ridicule as a means of controlling them. They try to make the children understand their transgressions and accept punishment willingly—because it is deserved. Amish teachers feel emotionally very close to their pupils, and the children in turn admire and want to please their teachers.

TEACHER TRAINING

Most Amish teachers receive no formal training beyond eighth grade; however, new teachers use all available means for self-education. The Amish school system is in the process of becoming institutionalized and means are developing for the training and professional support of the teachers. In regions with a number of schools, teachers' meetings are held regularly.

A national Amish teachers' meeting is held annually, a teachers' publication (*The Blackboard Bulletin*) is issued monthly, and supplemental teaching material is being printed, including texts and teachers' manuals. Teachers also support one another by circle letters, visits to one another's schools, and frequent informal gatherings.

A national meeting of Amish teachers has been held annually since 1954. On the average, one-third of the teachers attend each year, in addition to board members, ministers, beginning teachers, and retired teachers. A teacher who has attended the first meeting and almost every one since wrote, "I believe these meetings have done more to create a better understanding of school matters than anything else." The two days are very full, but are pleasant and rewarding. Teachers from all states where the Amish live have an opportunity to meet one another and to talk informally as well as to listen to formal presentations on topics of practical interest.

The regional teachers' meetings function to bring teachers together for the opportunity of discussing their problems both formally and informally. They help the teachers realize that others have similar problems and successes. They function as training seminars in which the teachers learn how to handle their role. The teachers leave these meetings encouraged and anticipating ways they can improve their teaching and their schools.

The Amish teachers' journal, *Blackboard Bulletin*, founded in 1957, is an important publication serving the Amish school movement. It has a circulation of about 5,000. In keeping with the Amish tradition, its format is simple. Each year a list of schools is published. As the Amish schools become more institutionalized and the number of teachers increases, a limited professionalism is developing. Another publication, *Family Life*, issued by the same publisher, Pathway Publishing Corporation of Aylmer, Ontario, has appeared monthly since January 1968. It is "dedicated to the promotion of Christian living among the plain people, with special emphasis on the appreciation of our heritage." Teachers read these periodicals for reinforcement of values, for news that affects them, for practical help in their classroom teaching, for help in their role as teacher, and for enjoyment of the stories and articles.

The contributors to the school journal are teachers, parents, and concerned Amish people, many of whom are widely read and value a good academic foundation. The editors have been careful to represent various Amish attitudes and have not been dogmatic in either their writings or their selections. The more conservative viewpoint is probably underrepresented from the perspective of the total Old Order Amish culture. The most conservative individuals are not as motivated to write and are not as committed to an excellent school program. They still regard the school as a peripheral rather than an integral part of the community. Sensitive leadership and selfless hard work have produced a journal and a movement within the Amish culture that is meaningful to Amish people of the twentieth century.

Teacher training among the Amish continues to be primarily informal and personal. Some of the teachers work as helpers for a year or two before they take charge of a school. The apprentice system works well for the younger teachers, who serve full-time under the direction of an experienced teacher. A helping teacher takes charge of the school for several days, which gives her an opportunity to learn how to manage a school while she still has the senior teacher available. Some of the teachers continue to take correspondence courses, although actual completion of high school is discouraged. The Amish feel that certain of the required courses are of no benefit to the Amish and that to work for a diploma is therefore a form of pride. The best preparation for teaching from the point of view of the Amish, in addition to the personal attributes of patience and a love of children and learning, is a firm grounding in the Amish faith. Informal means are used to train future teachers and to develop interest in teaching. Experienced teachers may talk to individual students who they think would make good teachers.

The informal support among Amish teachers constitutes a form of on-the-job teacher training. When they live near enough to one another, they may gather informally for supper and spend the evening with one another discussing school problems. The newer teachers visit the older teachers to ask about teaching methods and to learn such things as how to prepare a six-weeks test. Teachers compare parents and board members and problems and pleasures. They never meet without discussing aspects of school. Teachers may make friendship quilts for one another. Each teacher makes a square, the teacher whose quilt it is sets it up in a frame, and all the contributors gather for a quilting to finish the gift. Many teachers belong to one or more circle letters in which they discuss episodes and problems too personal or specific to be published in the teachers' journal.

Some professionalism is unavoidable, and in fact is desirable, even within this small, homogeneous subculture. As one Amishman put it, "It seems that after teaching school a while, a person gets a little hard to understand sometimes. And no wonder. Teaching is so far removed from farming or housekeeping that it takes just a little different kind of thinking, which is reflected in everyday living." Amish schools have a minimal bureaucracy that has no chance of growing into unworkable proportions. When the usual question is asked, "How can we improve our schools?," the answers are not those of the adminstrator or technician who thinks in terms of curriculum, buildings, or equipment. The Amish think in terms of character improvement, experience, knowing the pupils better, and bettering relations between teacher, pupils, parents, and board members.

RELATION TO PARENTS AND SCHOOL BOARD

There is some tension between the parents and the teacher. Teachers are sensitive to parental criticism and need their support. Because the teachers must be examples to the children as well as dispensers of information, they are especially vulnerable, for a teacher can be criticized not only for what or how she teaches, but how she dresses and spends her free time. The Amish believe very firmly that the training and conversion of children is the responsibility of the parents, not of the school—even an Amish school. The school teaches the child, and to that extent it is an extension of the parents, who have trained him well enough to make him receptive to the teaching he receives in school. The basis of classroom discipline is the respect of the children for the teacher and the teacher's respect for each child and each family. If the parents do not respect the teacher, the children feel this and the teacher soon has serious discipline problems.

The parents express their affection for the teacher in many ways. They bring her small gifts of food, they invite her to supper and to spend the night, and they may organize a birthday surprise for her. Sometimes the parents will get together and make a friendship quilt for her—perhaps with each child's signature embroidered on his family's square. In some of the schools the parents take turns bringing in a hot lunch once a month during the winter for the teacher and children. Unmarried teachers often try to spend at least one night a term in the home of every family in the school.

Parents are urged to visit their schools. Most schools leave it up to the parents' discretion when they should come, but their requests are persuasive. Parents are reminded that they don't put their steers out to pasture and never bother to check on them—and certainly their children are more valuable than cattle. Different schools have worked out various methods to get the parents to visit school regularly. In one school the parents drew dates out of a hat and then visited during their assigned week. In another school the parents decided to visit in order of the age of the father, with one couple coming each week. A teacher in Pennsylvania listed some of the advantages of parents' visiting school, and the disadvantages of their not visiting. Here are the advantages of regular parental visits:

1. Teacher gets an opportunity to visit with the parents.
2. Children get the feeling they (the parents) are a part of the school. It makes them feel important; they are being looked after.
3. The students have brushed up considerably in their lessons. They aren't going to be caught standing in class looking like a dumbbell.
4. Respect in many ways has greatly improved.
5. Teacher has the privilege to discuss discipline problems, if there are any, with the parents.

Here are the disadvantages if parents do not visit school:

1. Teacher has no fellowship with parents.
2. Children become careless; after all, no one is coming in to check on them except the teacher.
3. Children become rude.
4. Teacher has to work doubly hard to keep everyone happy and friendly.
5. Parents cannot understand low report card marks.
6. Discipline problems are hard to overcome.

Many teachers feel that parental visits support the teachers' authority and make the job easier and more pleasant.

Parents come to the school when it is not in session to participate in frolics and work bees, to get the school and yard ready for the new term, to cut and stack wood, to repaint the woodwork, or to refinish the desks.

Many schools have meetings for the parents and board members every month. They strive for 100 percent attendance, but this is of course not possible. Teachers rely on these meetings. Any problems they have can be brought up then to get some idea of community consensus on what should be done; even if there are no problems, the meetings still serve a worthy function. These are evenings the teachers look forward to and delight in. One teacher says that the fathers trudging through the snow carrying their lanterns "show interest. And an evening together discussing farm sales, wood cutting, manure hauling, and school work is helping to lay a foundation for the future generation."

The teachers look to their school boards for guidance, support, and direction. The school board acts as a buffer between the teacher and the parents, between the teacher and the wider community, when such a buffer is needed. Most teachers say that they take all their problems to the school board. "My board is a great help by seeing that there are plenty of supplies, books, workbooks, especially for the lower grades, paper, pencils, etc. as needed. Last but not least important is their visiting the school frequently. It is encouraging when I meet the board members and they have smiles on their faces. I realize their job is not always the most pleasant, for they have the task of trying to satisfy the [Amish] taxpayers, parents, teachers and probably their wives and themselves," one teacher explained.

Any problems of noncooperation by parents or children are taken to the board. Good school board members consider their teacher's happiness. They stop on the way to town to inquire if she needs anything; they often have her over for supper and to spend the night; they may take her to church with them. Members of the school board often function as family for women or single men who are teaching outside their home church district. As is characteristic of the Amish culture, the relationship between the school board members and the school teacher is a personal one.

The school board hires and fires the teacher, woos her, and accepts her resignation. Many teachers seem to feel that it is not good to teach too long in the same school, and some parents believe that it is better if the children have more than one teacher during their years of schooling. A good teacher-board relationship was described by two teachers who said that, though this is their fourth year of teaching in the same school, they are treated as though it were their first. The school board and parents are anxious to have them stay. A problem may arise when a school board says nothing to a teacher about whether or not they want her back in the fall, since it is not the teacher's position to broach the subject unless she plans to leave. Experienced teachers recommend changing schools at least for one year if the teacher feels at all undecided about continuing.

School boards, in conjunction with parents, also make and implement decisions that affect the teachers' personal comforts—decisions to build a house for the teacher, set up a trailer for her, or build outside stairs at the home where she rooms so she can have her own entrance and not have to go through the family kitchen every time she leaves and enters. They must be concerned with all aspects of running the school, and therefore, with their teacher's equipment, living arrangements, and general contentment.

Uria R. Byler (1969) points out that it takes a lot of time and energy to be a good school board member and that those who serve should be "pushers," always working to keep the school going, to improve it, and to help start a new school when needed.

REFERENCES

Bronfenbrenner, Urie, 1970, *Two Worlds of Childhood: U.S. and U.S.S.R.* New York: Russell Sage.
Byler, Uria R., 1963, *Our Better Country*. Gordonville, Pa.: Old Order Book Society.

———, 1969, *School Bells Ringing: A Manual for Amish Teachers and Parents.* Aylmer, Ontario: Pathway Publishing Corporation.

Cohen, Rosalie A., 1969, "Conceptual Styles, Culture Conflict, and Nonverbal Tests of Intelligence," *American Anthropologist* 71:828–856.

Educational Policies Commission, 1961, *The Central Purpose of Education.* Washington, D.C.: National Educational Association.

Henry, Jules, 1963, *Culture against Man.* New York: Random House.

———, 1963, "Spontaneity, Initiative, and Creativity in Suburban Classrooms," in *Education and Culture*, George D. Spindler, ed. New York: Holt, Rinehart and Winston, Inc., pp. 215–233.

Holt, John, 1964, *How Children Fail.* New York: Pittman.

Lee, Dorothy, 1959, *Freedom and Culture.* Englewood Cliffs, N.J.: Prentice-Hall.

Pathway Publishers, 1970, *Tips for Teachers, A Handbook for Amish Teachers.* Aylmer, Ontario, and Lagrange, Indiana.

Saltzman, Henry, 1963, "The Community School in an Urban Setting," in *Education in Depressed Areas*, A. Harry Passow, ed. New York: Teachers College Press, Columbia University.

14 / Cherokee School Society and the Intercultural Classroom[1]

Robert V. Dumont, Jr., and Murray L. Wax

Indian education is one of those phrases whose meaning is not the sum of its component words. Notoriously, "education" is an ambiguous word used to justify, idealize, or to criticize a variety of relationships. In the context where the pupils are members of a lower caste or ethnically subordinated group, education has come to denominate a unidirectional process by which missionaries—or others impelled by motives of duty, reform, charity, and self-sacrifice—attempt to uplift and civilize the disadvantaged and barbarian. Education then is a process imposed upon a target population in order to shape and stamp them into becoming dutiful citizens, responsible employees, or good Christians.[2]

In the modern federal and public school systems serving Indian children, there is less of the specifically religious quality; but the active presence of the missionizing tradition, however secularized, is still felt. To appreciate this fully, we must remind ourselves that the purpose of education presented to, and often enforced upon, the American Indians has been nothing less than the transformation of their traditional cultures and the total reorganization of their societies.[3] By denominating this as *unidirectional*, we mean to emphasize that the far-reaching transformations which have been occurring spontaneously among Indian peoples are neglected in the judgments of the reforming educators.[4] As a major contemporary instance, we need but turn to the first few pages of a recent book, representing the work of a committee of a high repute. The initial paragraph states that the goal of public policy should be "making the Indian a self-respecting and useful American citizen" and that this requires "restoring his pride of origin and faith in himself," while on the following page we find that very origin being derogated and distorted with the left-handed remark that, "It would be unwise to dismiss all that is in the traditional Indian culture as being necessarily a barrier to change."[5] The mythic image of an unchanging traditional Indian culture does not bear discussion here. Rather, we direct attention to the fact that such a remark could be advanced as the theme of a contemporary book about Indians, and that this book then received favorable reviews both from liberals involved in Indian affairs and from the national Indian interest organizations. Clearly, such reviewers take it for granted that Indian education should be unidirectional—e.g., none seemed to think it noteworthy that the last chapter of the book is on "Policies Which Impede Indian Assimilation," the implication of that title being that the necessary goal is total ethnic and cultural dissolution.

An alternate way of perceiving the unidirectionality which characterizes "Indian education" is to note the curious division of labor bifurcating the process of cultural exchange with Indian peoples. That is, missionaries and educators have devoted themselves to instructing the Indians but not to learning from or being influenced by them; whereas ethnographers have devoted themselves to learning from the Indians but not to teaching or influencing them. Thus, the ethnographers valued the learning of the native languages, while the schoolmasters and missionaries only seldom bothered to learn them, even when the native language was the primary tongue of their Indian pupils and the primary domestic and ceremonial medium of the community in which they were laboring.[6]

Because Indian educational programs have been unidirectionally organized, deliberately ignoring native languages and traditions, they have had to proceed more via duress than suasion. Today the duress is in the laws of compulsory attendance, as enforced by an appropriate officer; but the climax of traditional "Indian education" was the forcible seizing or kidnapping of Indian children by agents of the U.S. government. These children were then incarcerated in boarding establishments whose programs were designed to shape them within the molds of the conquering society. Yet the irony of this crude and brutal effort was that, while the mass of children underwent profound changes, their very aggregation provided them with the need and opportunity to cohere and resist. Like the inmates of any total institution, Indian pupils developed their own norms and values, which were neither those of their Indian elders nor those of their non-Indian instructors. This process of autonomous development has continued to distinguish much of Indian conduct in relation to modern programs and schools, including the classroom we will be reviewing.[7]

TRIBAL CHEROKEE COMMUNITIES

The consequence of the various reformative and educational programs aimed at the Indian peoples has been not to eliminate the target societies but, paradoxically, to encourage an evolution which has sheltered an ethnic and distinct identity, so that today there remain a relatively large number of persons, identified as Indians, and dwelling together in enclaved, ethnically, and culturally distinctive communities. The tribal Cherokee of contemporary northeastern Oklahoma are not untypical.[8] Like other Indian communities, they have lost to federal, state, and local agencies the greater measure of their political autonomy. Many contemporary Indian peoples do have "tribal governments," but these do not correspond to traditional modes of social organization or proceed by traditional modes of deliberation and action. In the specific case of the Oklahoma Cherokee, for instance, the tribal government is a nonelected, nonrepresentative, and self-perpetuating clique, headed by individuals of great wealth and political power, while the tribal Cherokee are among the poorest denizens of a depressed region, whose indigenous associations are denied recognition by the Bureau of Indian Affairs.

The Cherokee of Oklahoma once practiced an intensive and skilled subsistence agriculture, which has all but disappeared as the Indians have lost their lands and been denied the opportunity to practice traditional forms of land tenure. The rural lands are now used principally for cattle ranching (often practiced on a very large scale) and for tourism and a few local industries (e.g., plant nurseries, chicken processing), or crops such as strawberries, which require a cheap and docile labor supply. Until the recent building of dams and paved highways and the concomitant attempt to develop the region as a vacationland, the tribal Cherokee were able to supplement their diet with occasional game or fish, but they now find themselves harassed by state game and fish regulations, and subjected to the competition of weekend and vacation sportsmen.

Like the other Indian societies of North America, the Cherokee have been goaded along a continuum that led from being autonomous societies to being a "domestic dependent nation" and thence to being an ethnically subordinated people in a caste-like status. In Oklahoma there is a distinctive noncaste peculiarity, since a vast majority of the population proudly claim to be of "Indian descent" as this signifies a lineage deriving from the earliest settlers. To be "of Cherokee descent" is, therefore, a mark of distinction, particularly in the northeast of Oklahoma, where this connotes such historic events as "civilized tribes" and the "trail of tears."[9] Yet, paradoxically, there exist others whose claim to Indianness is undeniable, but whose mode of life is offensive to the middle class. The term "Indian" tends to be used to denote those who are considered idle, irresponsible, uneducated, and a burden to the decent and taxpaying element of the area. Within northeastern Oklahoma, these "Indians" are the tribal Cherokees, and their communities are marked by high rates of unemployment, pitifully low cash incomes, and a disproportionate representation on relief agency rolls. Perhaps the major respect in which the Cherokee Indians differ from groups like the Sioux of Pine Ridge is that the latter, being situated on a well-known federal reservation, are the recipients of myriads of programs from a multiplicity of federal, private, and local agencies, whereas the Cherokee are still mainly the targets of welfare workers, sheriffs, and aggressive entepreneurs.[10]

In this essay we wish to focus on the schools attended by Indian children in the cases where they are the preponderant element of the school population. This condition is realized not only on reservations, where the federal government operates a special school system under the administration of the Bureau of Indian Affairs, but also in other regions by virtue of covert systems of segregation. As in the case of Negro/white segregation, the basis is usually ecological. Thus, in northeastern Oklahoma the rural concentrations of tribal Cherokee along the stream beds in the hill country predispose toward a segregated system at the elementary levels. But the guiding principle is social, so that there is reverse busing of tribal Cherokee children living in towns and of middle-class white children living in the countryside. Within the rural elementary schools, the Indian children confront educators who are ethnically and linguistically alien, even when they appear to be neighbors (of Cherokee or non-Cherokee descent) from an adjacent or similar geographic area.

Such classrooms may be denominated as "cross-cultural," although the ingredients contributed by each party seem to be weighted against the Indian pupils. The nature and layout of the school campus, the structure and spatial divisions of the school buildings, the very chairs and their array, all these are products of the greater society and its culture—indeed, they may at first glance seem so conventional that they fail to register with the academic observer the significance of their presence within a cross-cultural transaction. Equally conventional, and almost more difficult to apprehend as significant, is the temporal structure: the school period; the school day; and the school calendar. The spatial and temporal grid by which the lives of the Indian pupils are organized is foreign to their native traditions, manifesting as it does the symbolic structure of the society which has encompassed them.

The observer thus anticipates that the classroom will be the arena for an unequal clash of cultures. Since the parental society is fenced out of the school, whatever distinctive traditions have been transmitted to their children will now be "taught out" of them; and the wealth, power, and technical supremacy of the greater society will smash and engulf these traditionalized folk. Forced to attend school, the Indian children there must face educators who derive their financial support, their training and ideology, their professional affiliation and bureaucratic status, from a complex of agencies and institutions based far outside the local Indian community. The process is designed to be unidirectional; the children are to be "educated" and the Indian communities thus to be transformed. Meanwhile, neither the educator nor the agencies for which he is a representative are presumed to be altered—at least by the learning process.

CHEROKEES IN THE CLASSROOM

The classrooms where Indian students and a white teacher create a complex and shifting sequence of interactions exhibit as many varieties of reality and illusion as there are possible observers. One such illusion—in the eyes of the white educator— is that the Cherokee are model pupils. Within their homes they have learned that restraint and caution is the proper mode of relating to others; therefore in the classroom the teacher finds it unnecessary to enforce discipline. As early as the second grade, the children sit with perfect posture, absorbed in their readers, rarely talking—and then only in the softest of tones—and never fidgeting. Even when they are marking time, unable to understand what is occurring within the classroom, or bored by what they are able to understand, they make themselves unobtrusive while keeping one ear attuned to the educational interchange. They respect competence in scholastic work, and their voluntary activities both in and out of school are organized surprisingly often and with great intensity about such skills. Eager to learn, they devote long periods of time to their assignments, while older and more experienced students instruct their siblings in the more advanced arithmetic they will be encountering at higher grade levels.

To the alien observer (whether local teacher or otherwise), the Cherokee children seem to love to "play school." The senior author, for example, recalls talking during one recess period with an elderly white woman who had devoted many years to teaching in a one-room school situated in an isolated rural Cherokee community and who now was responsible for the intermediate grades in a more consolidated enterprise that still was predominantly Cherokee. "You just have to watch these children," she said. "If you don't pay no mind, they'll stay in all recess. They like to play school." And, as if to illustrate her point, she excused herself, went back into the school building and returned with a straggle of children. "They told me they had work they wanted to do, but it is too nice for them to stay inside. . . . You know, I forgot how noisy students were until I went to [the County Seat] for a teacher's meeting. It's time for me to ring the bell now. If I don't, they will come around and remind me pretty soon."

Given the seeming dedication of her pupils, the naive observer might have judged this woman an exceedingly skilled and effective teacher. Yet in reality, she was a rather poor teacher, and at the time of graduation the pupils of her one-room school knew scarcely any English—a fact so well known that parents said of her, "She don't teach them anything!"

Like many of her white colleagues, this woman was interpreting Cherokee conduct from within her own culture, as is evident in her description of the intensive involvement of her pupils in learning tasks as "*playing* school." In kindred fashion, other teachers describe the silence of the students as timidity or shyness, and their control and restraint as docility. Most teachers are unable to perceive more than their own phase of the complex reality which occurs within their classrooms because they are too firmly set within their own traditions, being the products of rural towns and of small state teacher's colleges, and now working within and limited by a tightly-structured institutional context. Certainly, one benefit of teaching Indians in rural schools is that the educators are sheltered from observation and criticism. Except for their own consciences and professional ideologies, no one cares about, guides or supervises their performance, and little pressure is exerted to encourage them to enlarge their awareness of classroom realities.

Even for ourselves—who have had much experience in observing Indian classrooms—many hours of patient and careful watching were required, plus the development of some intimacy with the local community, before we began to appreciate the complexities of interaction within the Cherokee schoolroom. The shape assumed by the clash of cultures was a subtle one. At first, it could be appreciated most easily in the frustration of the teachers; the war within the classrooms was so cold that its daily battles were not evident, except at the close of the day as the teachers assessed their lack of pedagogical accomplishment. Those teachers who defined their mission as a "teaching out" of native traditions were failing to make any headway; and some of these good people had come to doubt their ability to work with such difficult and retiring children (actually, as we soon dicovered, their classes contained a fair share of youngsters who were eager, alert, intelligent, and industrious). A few teachers had resigned themselves to marking time, while surrendering all notions of genuine instruction.

As these phenomena began to impress themselves upon us, we began to discern in these classrooms an active social entity that we came to call "The Cherokee School Society." Later still, we were surprised to discover in other classrooms, which we came to call "intercultural classrooms," that this society remained latent and that instead the teacher and students were constructing intercultural bridges for communication and instruction (these will be discussed in the next section).

In order to comprehend the complexity of classroom interaction, we need to remind ourselves that the children who perform here as pupils have been socialized (or enculturated) within the world of the tribal Cherokee as fully and extensively as have any children of their age in other communities. In short, we must disregard the material poverty of the tribal Cherokee families and their lower-class status and avoid any of the cant about "cultural deprivation" or "cultural disadvantage." These children are culturally alien, and for the outsider (whether educator or social researcher) to enter into their universe is as demanding as the mastering of an utterly foreign tongue. In the compass of a brief article, we can do no more than indicate a few of the more striking evidences of this distinctive cultural background.

Even in the first grade, Cherokee children exhibit a remarkable propensity for precision and thoroughness. Asked to arrange a set of colored matchsticks into a pyramidal form, the children became so thoroughly involved in maintaining an impeccable vertical and horizontal alignment that they were oblivious to the number learning which they are supposed to acquire via this digital exercise. These six-year-olds do not resolve the task by leaving it at the level of achievement for which their physical dexterity would suffice, but continue to manipulate the sticks in a patient effort to create order beyond the limitations of the material and their own skills. As they mature, the Cherokee students continue this patient and determined ordering of the world, but as a congregate activity that is more often directed at social than physical relationships. At times, this orientation is manifested in an effort toward a precision in social affairs that is startling to witness in persons so young (here, sixth graders):

> The teacher has asked about the kinds of things which early pioneers would say to each other in the evening around the campfire as they were traveling.
> *Jane:* Save your food.
> *Teacher:* That's preaching.
> *Jane and Sally* (together): No.
> *Jane:* That is just to tell you. (The tone of voices makes her sound just like a teacher.)
> The teacher agrees, and his acquiescent tone makes him sound like the student. He continues, "They would get you in a room. . . ."
> *Jane interrupts:* Not in a room.
> *Teacher:* In around a campfire then. [He continues by asking if everyone would be given a chance to speak or just representatives.]

Dick: That would take all night; they might forget. (Jane and Sally agree that representatives would be the right way.)

The foregoing is as significant for the form of the interaction, as it is revealing of the students' concern for the precise reconstruction of a historical event. The students have wrought a reversal of roles, so that *their* standards of precision and *their* notions of social intercourse emerge as normative for the discussion.

Although this kind of exchange may be rare—normally it is typical only of the intercultural classroom—we have cited it here, as reflecting many of the norms of Cherokee students. As healthy children, they are oriented toward the world of their elders, and they see their adult goal as participating in the Cherokee community of their parents. In this sense, the art of relating to other persons so that learning, or other cooperative efforts, may proceed fruitfully and without friction becomes more important to them than the mastery of particular scholastic tasks, whose relevance in any case may be dubious. In the matrix of the classroom they learn to sustain, order, and control the relationships of a Cherokee community; in so doing they are proceeding toward adult maturity and responsibility. According to these norms, the educational exchange is voluntary for both students and teachers and is governed by a mutual respect.

In any educational transaction, the Cherokee School Society is actively judging the competence of the teacher and allowing him a corresponding function as leader. Their collective appraisal does not tolerate the authoritarian stance assumed by some educators ("You must learn this!") but rather facilitates the emergence of a situation in which the teacher leads because he knows ("I am teaching you this because you are indicating that you wish to learn"). A consequence of this configuration (or, in the eyes of an unsympathetic observer, a symptom) is that the Cherokee students may organize themselves to resist certain categories of knowledge that the school administration has formally chosen to require of them.

We must bear in mind that within the tribal Cherokee community, the reading or writing of English, calculating arithmetically, and even speaking English have minor employment and minimal utility. By the intermediate grades, the students perceive that, with no more than a marginal proficiency in spoken or written English, their elders are nonetheless leading satisfactory lives *as Cherokees.* Attempts to exhort them toward a high standard of English proficiency and a lengthy period of time-serving in school are likely to evoke a sophisticated negative reaction. After one such educational sermon, a ten-year-old-boy bluntly pointed out to his teacher that a Cherokee adult, greatly admired within the local community—and senior kin to many of the pupils present—had only a fifth-grade education. When the teacher attempted to evade this rebuttal by suggesting that the students would, as adults, feel inferior because they lacked a lengthy education and could not speak good English, the pupils were again able to rebut. To the teacher's challenge, "Who would you talk to?" the same boy responded, "To other Cherokee!"

Orienting themselves toward the community of their elders, the Cherokee students respond to the pressures of the alien educators by organizing themselves as The Cherokee School Society. As the teacher molds the outer forms of class procedure, the children exploit his obtuseness as a white alien to construct the terms on which they will act as students. But, while among the Oglala Sioux this transformation is effected with a wondrous boldness and insouciance,[11] here among the Cherokee it is with an exquisite social sensibility. A gesture, an inflection in voice, a movement of the eye is as meaningful as a large volume of words would be for their white peers. By the upper elementary grades, the result is a multiple reality according to which the adolescent Cherokee appear now as quiet and shy, or again as stoical and calm, or yet again (apparent only after prolonged observation) as engaged in the most intricate web of sociable interaction. Such delicacy of intercourse, so refined a sensibility, reflects and requires a precision of movement, a neat and exact ordering of the universe.

Interestingly, the Cherokee School Society does not reject the curricular tasks formulated by the alien educational administrators. In fact, the pupils proceed with their usual patient intensity to labor at assignments that can have no bearing on their tradition or experience. The fact that they are unable to relate these materials meaningfully to life within the Cherokee community acts as an increasing barrier to their mastery of them. In particular, the fact that most students have acquired no more than rudimentary proficiency in spoken English means that the involved patterns of the printed language in the advanced texts are beyond their most diligent endeavors; neither the language nor the topics can be deciphered.

So far, we have emphasized that the Cherokee students are interested in learning and that, from the viewpoint of the educator, they are docile pupils. Yet the cultural differences noted, and the basic social separateness and lack of communication, ensure that conflicts will develop and become more intensive as the students mature. The school cannot proceed along the trackways established by educational authority, nor can it be switched by the students into becoming an adjunct of the rural Cherokee community. Hence, as the children mature, the tension within the schoolroom becomes more extreme. Since the participants are one adult and many children, and since the latter are imbued with a cultural standard of nonviolence and passive resistance, open confrontations do not occur. Instead, what typically happens is that, by the seventh and eighth grades the students have surrounded themselves with a wall of silence impenetrable by the outsider, while sheltering a rich emotional communion among themselves. The silence is positive, not simply negative or withdrawing, and it shelters them so that, among other things, they can pursue their scholastic interests in their own style and pace. By their silence they exercise control over the teacher and maneuver him toward a mode of participation that meets their standards, as the following instance illustrates:

Teacher: Who was Dwight David Eisenhower?
Silence.
Teacher: Have you heard of him, Joan? (She moves her eyes from his stare and smiles briefly.)
Very quickly, the teacher jumps to the next person. There is something in his voice that is light and not deadly serious or moralistic in the way that is customary of him. He is just having fun, and this comes through so that the kids have picked up. They respond to the tone, not the question, "Alice?"
Alice leans back in her chair; her blank stare into space has disappeared, and her eyes are averted. She blushes. Now, she grins.
The teacher does not wait, "Wayne?"
Wayne is sitting straight, and his face wears a cockeyed smile that says he knows something. He says nothing.
Seeing the foxy grin, the teacher shifts again, "Wayne, you know?" This is a question and that makes all the difference. There is no challenge, no game-playing, and the interrogation mark challenges Wayne's competency. But Wayne maintains the foxy grin and shakes his head, negative.
Quickly, the teacher calls on another, "Jake?" He bends his head down and grins but says nothing.
Teacher (in authoritative tone): Nancy, tell me. [But she says nothing, keeping her head lowered, although usually she answers when called upon.]
The teacher switches tones again, so that what he is asking of Nancy has become a command. Perhaps he catches this, for he switches again to the lighter tone, and says; "Tell me, Debra."
The only one in the room who doesn't speak Cherokee, Debra answers in a flat voice: "President."
As soon as the answer is given, there are many covert smiles, and Alice blushes. They all knew who he was.

To most educators and observers, such an incident is perplexing. Who within that classroom really is exercising authority? Are the students deficient in their comprehension either of English or of the subject matter? Are they, perhaps, flexing their social muscles and mocking the teacher—because they don't like the lesson, they don't like him to act as he is acting, or why? For the Cherokee School Society has created within the formal confines of the institutional classroom another social edifice, their own "classroom," so that at times there appears to be not simply a clash of cultural traditions but a cold war between rival definitions of the classroom. Such tension is not proper within Cherokee tradition, since the tribal Cherokee value harmonious social relationships and frown upon social conflict.[12] Moderate disagreement is resolved by prolonged discussion interspersed, wherever possible, by joking and jesting, while severe disagreement leads to withdrawal from the conflict-inducing situation. Given the compulsory nature of school attendance, however, the students cannot withdraw from the classroom, much as they might wish to, and the teacher can withdraw only by losing his job and his income. Thus, an unmanageable tension may develop if the teacher is unable to recognize the Cherokee pupils as his peers who, through open discussion, may share with him in the decisions as to the organizing and operating of the school.

The unresolved conflict of cultural differences typifies these classrooms. Within them, there is little pedagogy, much silence, and an atmosphere that is apprehended by Indians (or observers of kindred sensibility) as ominous with tension. The following incident, participated in by Dumont, exhibits all these features in miniature:

> The classroom was small and the teacher had begun to relate a joke to Dumont. Not far away were seated four teenage Cherokee, and the teacher decided to include them within the range of his ebullience: "Boys, I want to tell you a joke. . . ." It was one of those that played upon the stoical endurance of Indians in adapting to the whimsical wishes of whites, and to narrate it in the classroom context was highly ironic. The plot and phrasing were simple, and easily apprehended by the students. But when the teacher had finished, they merely continued looking toward him, with their eyes focused, not upon him, but fixed at some point above or to the side of his eyes. As he awaited their laughter, their expressions did not alter but they continued to stare at the same fixed point and then gradually lowered their heads to their work.

The Cherokee School Society maintains a rigid law of balance that says, in effect, we will change when the teacher changes. If the teacher becomes involved in appreciating the ways of his students, then they will respond with an interest in his ways. Needless to say, the older the students become, the higher their grade level, the less is the likelihood that this reciprocity will be initiated by their educators. There is thus a deep tragedy, for it is the students who lose and suffer the most. Yet the School Society is their technique for protecting themselves in order to endure the alien intrusiveness of the teacher and the discourtesy and barbarity of the school. Occasionally, observer and students experience a happier interlude, for some teachers are able to enter into a real inter-cultural exchange. Unfortunately, they are as rare as they are remarkable. And they are sometimes unaware of their truly prodigious achievements in establishing what we term the intercultural classroom.

THE INTERCULTURAL CLASSROOM

Within the intercultural classroom, tribal Cherokee students do such remarkable things as engaging in lengthy conversations with the teacher about academic subjects. For this to occur, the teacher must be responsive to the distinctive norms and expectations of the students; but, strikingly, he need not abide by these nor accept norms as long as he is able to persuade the students of his willingness to learn about them and to accommodate to them. This attitude places the teacher on a plane of parity such that he must learn from his students the most rudimentary Cherokee cultural prescriptions. Naturally, both parties experience conflicts in this re-shuffling of teacher/learner roles. Certainly, such interaction is not what the teacher has been trained to sustain. Yet there arise structured devices for reducing these conflicts.

For instance, to bridge the social breaches that are always opening, the Cherokee students urge forward one of their members—not always the same person—to mediate and harmonize. Then if the teacher, by an unconscious presumption, disrupts the harmonious flow of class activity, it is the mediator whose deft maneuver reduces the intensity of the tension and relaxes the participants. In a sense, what the mediator does is to restore parity between teacher and students by removing the nimbus of authority from the teacher, thus allowing the students to work out with the teacher a compromise which redirects class activities and so permits them to regain their proper tempo. The teacher is freed to pursue the subject matter, but as scholastic assistant rather than classroom tyrant. With this in mind, let us examine the sequence of events which ended in a conversational repartee already quoted:

> They are reading about important men in history and have just finished with a section about adult educators.
> *Teacher* (referring to the observers): We have two distinguished educators here. Does this make you feel proud?
> It is quiet for the first time in the room. It is likely that the students are all thinking, how could we be proud of educators! As observer, I am uneasy and expectant; I wonder who will break the silence and how he will handle the delicate situation.
> *John:* I don't like schools myself. (!)
> *Teacher:* Would you quit school if you could? (He's asking for it!)
> *John (a firm answer):* Yes.
> *Teacher:* Suppose that your dad came and said you could quit, but he brought you a shovel and said, "Dig a ditch from here to Brown's house," since you weren't going to school.
> *John:* Okay.
> Another student: He might learn something.
> Everyone finds this humorous; the class is in good spirits and is moving along.
> John, too, is quick to reply: "Might strike gold." The topic has been dis-cussed earlier in class. (The interaction develops and others become involved, including the more reticent students.)

Here it is John who has played, and most successfully, the role of mediator. The teacher had ventured into a delicate area that had the potential of disrupting the classroom atmosphere. The responding silence was a token of the social peril, and John, who so often among his peers had assumed the mediating role, moved forward first, boldly countering with a declaration as strong as the teacher's. As a conse-quence, he redefined the structure of the interaction and became the initiator of the exchange, while the teacher merely sustained it. A cultural bridge was thereby constructed, accessible alike to students and teacher; and John's "Okay" is his con-sent to the conditions of the structure.

The mediating role becomes less necessary as the teacher grows more attuned to the interactional norms of Indian society; it becomes more difficult (if more essen-tial) if the teacher insists on maintaining a tyrannical control over the classroom. Yet, even as the teacher is attuned, some function is reserved for a mediator, for the teacher tends to proceed in terms of work to be done by an abstract student, while the mediator explores how the task can be redefined with the framework of the Cherokee student. His is a work of adaptation, and insofar as he is successful, the classroom becomes *intercultural*—a locus where persons of different cultural traditions can engage in mutually beneficial transactions without affront to either party.

What must the teacher do to foster the emergence of an intercultural classroom within the crosscultural situation? The answer would require another essay at least as long as the present one, but it may be helpful to quote the remarks of one teacher in the region:

> "I can't follow a lesson plan, and I just go along by ear. I've taught Cherokee students for six years in high school, and this is my first [year] in elementary school." Referring, then, to his experiences as a high school coach, he continued, "The thing you have to do, if you get a team, is that you got to get them to cooperate. . . ."

At first glance, this appears at odds with our earlier assertions about the spontaneous emergence of the Cherokee School Society, not to mention contradictory to the conventional notions that Indians will not compete with each other. But what he is explaining is that unless the teacher chooses to recognize the social nature of the classroom and to work toward integrating his teaching with that life, he will not be able to elicit active learning experiences from his pupils. Or, to put it negatively, if the teacher does not work with his Indian students as a social group, their union will be directed toward other goals. Yet the teacher can secure their response only if he "gets them" to cooperate; he cannot "make them" do so.

CONCLUSION

The foregoing report provides the basis for judgements and hypotheses on a variety of levels. On the practical level, it would seem that ethnic integration is not an essential precondition for satisfactory education of groups from a low socioeconomic background. The tribal Cherokee certainly are impoverished and poorly educated. Nevertheless, we would predict that the consolidation of rural schools into larger, better-staffed, and better-equipped schools in northeastern Oklahoma may actually lead to deterioration rather than improvement of the educational condition. Given the ethos of the tribal Cherokee, consolidation may mean the irremediable loss of many opportunities for assisting their children educationally.

On the methodological level, we are reminded of how sociologically valuable it is for researchers to focus on the frontier situation "where peoples meet."[13] The resulting accommodations, adaptations, and divisions of labor are an enlightening and fascinating phenomenon, which especially deserve to be studied as a corrective to those theoretical systems which regard the national society as an integrated social system. On the methodological level also, our study illustrates anew the value of ethnographic observations of classroom activities. Basic and simple as it may seem, and unpretentious in the face of modern testing procedures, direct observation still has much to teach us.[14]

Finally, on the substantive level, the research reported here cautions against the erosion of our conceptual armamentarium when researchers allow their research problems to be defined by educational administrators. When that happens, the educational situation of peoples such as the Indians tends to be conceived in terms of individual pupils and their "cultural deprivation." The researcher then is asked to assist the administration in raising these disadvantaged individuals to the point where they can compete in school in the same fashion as do white middle-class children. Our research is a reminder that such styles of conceptualization neglect the social nature of the classrooms and the social ties among the pupils. They also neglect the tension between teacher and pupils as a social group, and the struggles that occur when the teacher presses for individualistic achievement at the expense of group solidarity.[15]

NOTES

1. This study is a product of the Indian Education Research Project sponsored by the University of Kansas under contract with the U.S. Office of Education according to the provisions of the Cooperative Research Act. The principal investigator was Murray L. Wax, and the field research on rural schools was conducted by Robert V. Dumont and Mildred Dickeman, with assistance from Lucille Proctor, Elise Willingham, Kathryn RedCorn, Clyde and Della Warrior. Sole responsibility for this text rests with the authors.

   A paper entitled "The Intercultural Classroom," having much the same orientation but differing in details and in structure of the argument, was presented by Robert V. Dumont at a panel on Indian education at the annual meetings of the Society for Applied Anthropology, Washington, D.C., Spring 1967.
2. Cf. Rosalie H. Wax and Murray L. Wax (1965), reprinted in Levine and Lurie, (1968): 163-69.
3. For an enlightening account of the mission schools for American Indians, see the chapter "Nurseries of Morality," in Berkhofer (1965): 20-43.
4. Unfortunately, some of the anthropological textbooks on American Indians are guilty of the same static imagery, as they present particular tribes in "the ethnographic present." Conspicuous and happy exceptions are such books as Edward H. Spicer, *Cycles of Conquest* (Tuscon: University of Arizona Press, 1962); and Fred Eggan, *The American Indian* (Chicago: Aldine Press, 1966). Cf. Murray L. Wax, "The White Man's Burdensome 'Business': A Review Essay on the Change and Constancy of Literature on the American Indians," *Social Problems* 16, no. 1 (1968): pp. 106-13.
5. *The Indian: America's Unfinished Business*, comp. William A. Brophy and Sophie D. Aberle (Norman: University of Oklahoma Press, 1966), pp. 3-4.
6. While missionaries have always included a small number of individuals who have patiently tried to understand the language and culture of their alien flock, and while some few missionaries have been excellent ethnographers, the majority, particularly on the North American continent, have had quite the opposite attitude. Today, missionary activity on the world scene has become increasingly sophisticated and culturally humble (as evidenced by *Practical Anthropology*), yet it is noteworthy how slowly this has affected labors among American Indians. Despite a century (or even several!) of mission activity among some tribes, the church in many instances remains a mission, detached from tribal influence or control, and the clergyman continues to be a person who is culturally alien and socially isolated and who regards his task as preaching but not learning.
7. An excellent brief summary and bibliography of the history of research on Indian education is found in the presentation by Philleo Nash, *Proceedings of the National Research Conference on American Indian Education*, ed. Herbert A. Aurbach (Kalamazoo, Mich.: Society for the Study of Social Problems, 1967): 6-30. In order to discuss the history of Indian education research, Nash had to deal with some of the major changes of policy as well. The conference *Proceedings* also contained a summary review by William H. Kelly of current research on Indian education and other helpful discussions and bibliographies. See also Beatty (1956): 16-49, Adams (1946), Fey and McNickle 1959: chap. 12. And of course the Meriam Report included an intensive assessment of the goals and achievements of Indian education: Lewis Meriam and Associates (1928), especially pp. 346-429.
8. We take the term "tribal Cherokee" from the research reports of Albert Wahrhaftig, which, in addition to whatever information may be inferred from the tables of the U.S. Census, constitute the best recent source on the condition of the Cherokee of Oklahoma. See, e.g., his "Social and Economic Characteristics of the Cherokee Population of Eastern Oklahoma" and "The Tribal Cherokee Population of Eastern Oklahoma," both produced under sponsorship of the Carnegie Cross-cultural Education Project of the University of Chicago, 1965 (mimeographed); and "Community and the Caretakers," *New University*

Thought 4, no. 4 (1966/67): 54–76. See also Wax 1967 (mimeographed), and Debo 1951.

9. Responding to contact and intermarriage with the European invaders, the Cherokee were one of several tribes noteworthy during the eighteenth century for their adoption of foreign techniques. By 1827 they had organized themselves as a Cherokee nation, complete with an elective bicameral legislature and a national superior court. Meantime, Sequoyah had been perfecting his syllabary, and in 1828 there began the publication of the Cherokee Phoenix, a bilingual weekly. Developments of this character led to the Cherokee and several neighboring tribes of the southeastern U.S. being called, "the civilized tribes"; nevertheless, this did not protect them from the greed of the white settlers, particularly in Georgia. When the Indian nations would not cede their lands peaceably, Andrew Jackson employed federal troops to herd the Indian peoples westward into the region which subsequently was to become Oklahoma. There the survivors of the terrible journey ("the trail of tears") incorporated themselves once again as a Cherokee nation and remained such until dissolved by act of Congress early in the present century. Today, books, museums, and pageants commemorate these events and highlight for the tourists the high-cultural aspects of upper-status life in the Cherokee nation. Judged by that historical standard, the life of contemporary tribal Cherokee constitutes a blot on a record otherwise cherished by Oklahomans of Cherokee descent.

10. Cf. Wax and Wax 1968: 101–18.

11. Cf. Wax, Wax, and Dumont 1964: chap. 6.

12. See the discussions of "The Harmony Ethnic," in Gulick 1960: 135–39 et passim.

13. Hughes and Hughes 1952.

14. Consider for example, the impact and contribution of such recent books which rely either on direct observation or participation observation of classrooms as John Holt, *How Children Fail* (New York: Delta, 1964); Harry F. Wolcott, *A Kwakiutl Village and School* (New York: Holt, Rinehart and Winston, 1967); Wax, Wax, and Dumont 1964; Estelle Fuchs, *Pickets at the Gates* (New York: Free Press, 1966); G. Alexander Moore, *Realities of the Urban Classroom: Observations in Elementary Schools* (New York: Doubleday Anchor, 1967); Elizabeth M. Eddy, *Walk the White Line* (New York: Doubleday Anchor, 1967).

15. Such phenomena were clearly noted by Willard Waller in his *Sociology of Teaching*, first published in 1932, reprinted by Science Editions (New York: Wiley, 1965). It is unfortunate to see the neglect of such elementary sociological considerations in much of the more recent literature of the "sociology of education."

15 / Oglala Sioux Dropouts and Their Problems with Educators

Rosalie H. Wax

Neither the dropout nor the process of dropping out are well understood. Persons otherwise well informed, including educators themselves, assume on the basis of spurious evidence that dropouts dislike and voluntarily reject school, that they leave it for much the same reasons, and that they are as persons much alike. But, as Miller and Harrison[1] have discovered in the case of urban lower-class youth, dropouts leave high school under strikingly different situations and for quite different reasons. Many state explicitly that they do not wish to leave school and see themselves as "pushouts" or "kickouts" rather than "dropouts." As a Sioux youth in our sample put it, "I quit, but I never did *want* to quit!"

Perhaps the fact that educators perceive dropouts as similar tells us more about the educators and their schools than it does about the process of dropping out. Or to put it another way, an understanding of dropouts provides us with a mirror in which certain important but otherwise concealed aspects of our schools are reflected. In consequence, I shall more easily communicate this mirror image to the reader by beginning with a descriptive analysis of how Sioux boys[2] come to drop out of high school, and by then turning to a comparison between their experiences and those of urban lower-class youth.

PREADOLESCENT EXPERIENCES

The process that alienates many country Indian[3] boys from the particular kind of high school they are obliged to attend begins early in childhood and is related to the basic structure of the Sioux social system. Sioux boys are reared to be physically reckless and impetuous. If they are not capable of an occasional act of derring-do, their folks may accept them as "quiet" or "bashful," but they are not the ideal type of son, brother, or sweetheart. Sioux boys are also reared to be proud and feisty and they are expected to resent public reproof. While they have certain obligations to relatives, the major instrument of socialization after infancy is the local peer group. From about the age of seven or eight, boys may spend almost the whole day without adult supervision, running or riding about with age mates and returning home only for food and sleep. Even we, who had lived with Indian families from other tribal groups, were startled when we heard a responsible and respected Sioux matron dismiss a lad of six or seven for the entire day with the statement, "Go play with Larry and John." Similarly, at a ceremonial gathering involving a trip to a strange community and hundreds of people, boys of nine or ten might, as a matter of course, take off and stay away until late at night. These unsupervised activities do not cause elders much concern. There is a wide terrain of prairie and creek land for roaming and playing in ways that bother nobody. The only delinquencies about which we have heard Sioux elders complain are chasing stock, teasing bulls, or, occasionally, some petty theft.

Mark Twain, Jean Piaget, and other perceptive observers have noted that the kind of situation here described leads to socialization by the peer group. Among Sioux males it leads to a highly efficient yet unverbalized system of intragroup discipline and to powerful intragroup loyalties and dependencies. During our seventh month stay in a particular reservation community, we were impressed by how rarely the children of the community quarreled with each other. This pacific behavior was not imposed by elders but by the children themselves. As we remarked in our major report:

> Our office contained some things of great attractiveness to them, especially a typewriter, which [the Indian children] were allowed to use. . . . We were astonished to see how quietly they handled this prize that only one could enjoy at a time. A well-defined system of status existed such that when a superordinate child appeared at the side of the one typing, the latter at once gave way and left the machine to the other. A half-dozen of these shifts might take place within an hour, as children came or went, or were interested in typing or attracted to some other activity; yet, all this occurred without a blow or often even a word.[4]

Since we will have more to say later about the Sioux peer group's intense loyalties and dependencies, we add here only that Sioux boys almost never tattle on each other. Again, when boys are forced to take up residence with total strangers, they tend to become inarticulate, psychologically disorganized, or, as so many investigators have put it, "withdrawn."

In ordinary environments the school is where the peer group reaches the zenith of its power. In middle-class areas, the power is usually mitigated by the ability of independent children to seek and secure support from parents, teachers, or through them, from adult society as a whole. But when, as in an urban slum area or Indian reservation, the teachers keep aloof from the parents and the parents feel that it is not their place to approach the teachers, the power of the peer group may rise to the extent that the children literally take over the school. The classroom becomes the place where numerous group activities are carried on—jokes, notes, intrigues, teasing, mock-combat, comic-book reading, courtship—without the teacher's knowledge and often without grossly interfering with the process of learning. Competent and experienced teachers who have come to terms with the peer group still manage to teach their charges a fair amount of reading, writing, and arithmetic. But teachers who are incompetent, overwhelmed by large classes, or sometimes merely inexperienced, may be faced by groups of children who refuse even to listen. Indeed, as observers, we could not but marvel at the variety and efficiency of the devices developed by the Indian children to frustrate the standard process of formal learning: unanimous inattention, refusal to go to the board or writing on the board in letters less than an inch in height, mumbled and inarticulate responses, whispered or pantomimic teasing of victims called on to recite, and in some seventh- and eighth-grade classes, a withdrawal so uncomprising that no voice might be heard in the classroom for hours but that of the teacher, plaintively asking questions or giving instructions to which nobody responded.

Most Sioux children attending the day schools insist that they like school and most Sioux parents corroborate this. Once the power and depth of their social life within the school is appreciated, it is not difficult to see why they like it. Indeed, from the children's point of view, the only unpleasant aspects of school are the disciplinary regulations (which, as highly organized juveniles, they soon learn to tolerate or evade), an occasional "mean" teacher, bullies of either sex, or feuds with members of other peer groups. Significantly, we found that notorious truants had usually been rejected by their classmates and also had no older relatives in school to protect them from bullies. But the child who does have a few friends, or an older brother or sister to stand by him, or who "really likes to play basketball," almost always finds life in school more agreeable than truancy.

DAY-SCHOOL GRADUATES

By the time he has finished the eighth grade, the country Indian boy has many fine qualities: zest for life, curiosity, pride, physical courage, sensibility to human relationships, experiences with the elemental facts of life, and the loyalty and integrity that comes with intense internalized group identification. His experiences in day school have done nothing to diminish or tarnish his ideal: the physically reckless and impetuous youth, whose deeds of derring-do and athletic prowess are admired by all. On the other hand, the country Indian boy is almost completely lacking in the traits most highly valued by the school authorities: a narrow and absolute respect for "regulations," routine, discipline, diligence, and "government property."[5] He is also deficient in other skills which seem to be essential to a rapid and easy passage through high school and boarding school: the ability to make short-term superficial social adjustments with strangers[6] and come to terms with a system which demands, on the one hand, that he study competitively and as an individual and, on the other, that he live in barrack type dormitories where this kind of intellectual endeavor is impossible. Finally, his comprehension of English is inadequate for high school work. Despite eight or more years of exposure to formal training in reading and writing English, many day-school graduates cannot converse fluently in this language even among themselves.[7] In contrast, most of the students with whom the country Indian will be competing in high school have been brought up in town or have attended the boarding school and, in consequence, have spoken English with each other since childhood.

Leaving the familiar and relatively pleasant day-school situation for life as a boarding-school student in the distant and formidable high school is a prospect both fascinating and frightening. To many young country Indians the Agency town of Pine Ridge is the center of sophisitcation: there are blocks of "Bureau" homes with lawns and fences, a barber shop, big grocery stores, churches, gas stations, drive-in confectionary, and even a restaurant with a jukebox. While older siblings or cousins may have reported that at high school "they make you study harder," that "they just make you move every minute," or that the "mixedbloods" or "children of Bureau employees" are "mean" or "snotty," there are the compensatory attractions of high school movies, basketball games, and the social (white man's) dances that highlight the school year. For the young men there is the chance to play high school basketball, baseball, or football; for the young women there is the increased distance from overwatchful conservative parents; for both, there will be the opportunity to hitchhike or refuse to hitchhike to White Clay, with its beer joints, bowling hall, and archaic aura of Western wickedness. If, then, a young man's close friends or relatives decide to go to high school, he will usually prefer to share in the adventure rather than remain at home and live the circumscribed life of a fellow who must "live off his folks." A young man is also likely to be impelled into enrolling in high school by his elders, for most older Sioux are convinced that "nowadays only high school graduates get the good jobs." Every year, more elders coax, tease, bribe, or otherwise pressure the young men into "making a try at" high school.

THE STUDENT BODY

The student body of the Oglala Community High School is remarkably heterogeneous. First, there are the children of the town dwellers, ranging from well-paid white and Indian government employees who live in neat government housing developments to desperately poor people who live in tarpaper shacks. Second, there is a large aggregate of institutionalized children who have been attending the Oglala Community School as boarders for the greater part of their lives. Some of these boarders are orphans, others come from isolated parts of the reservation where there are no day schools, others come from different tribal areas. But whatever their differences, these town dwellers and the boarders share the advantage that entry into high school is little more than a shift from eighth to ninth grade, so that they possess an intimate knowledge of their classmates and a great deal of local knowhow. High school for them involves no more significant change than going to a new set of classes with new teachers. In marked contrast, the country Indian freshman enters an environment that is alien in almost all respects. Not only is he ignorant of the system for bucking the rules, he doesn't even know the rules. Nor does he know anybody who cares to put him wise.

In studying the adolescents on Pine Ridge we concentrated on two areas, the high school and a particular day-school community with a country or conservative Indian population of about one thousand. We interviewed somewhat less than half the young people then enrolled in the high school and, in addition, a random sample of forty-eight young people from the country Indian community. Subsequently, we obtained basic socioeconomic and educational data from all the young people who had graduated from a particular day school in 1961, 1962, and 1963. All in all, we obtained some 153 interviews from young people between the ages of 13 and 21; some 50 of these were high school dropouts. We used many approaches and several types of questionnaires; but our most illuminating and reliable data were obtained by semistructured and unstructured interviews administered by Indian college students who were able to associate with the Sioux adolescents and participate in some of their activities.

NINTH-GRADE DROPOUTS

Many of the country Indians drop out of high school before they have any clear idea of what high school is all about. In our universal sample, 35 percent dropped out before the end of the ninth grade and many of these left during the first semester.[8] Our first interviews were tantalizingly contradictory. About half the young men seemed to have found their high school experience so painful they could scarcely talk about it. The other half were also laconic, but insisted that they had liked school. In time, the young men who had found school unbearable confided that they had left school because they were lonely or because they were abused by the experienced boarders. Only rarely did they mention that they had trouble with their studies.

The following statement, made by a mild and pleasant-natured respondent from a traditional family, conveys some idea of the agony of loneliness, embarrassment, and inadequacy that a country Indian newcomer may suffer when he enters high school:

> At day school it was kind of easy for me. But high school was really hard, and I can't figure out even simple questions that they ask me. . . . Besides I'm so quiet [modest and unaggressive] that the boys really took advantage of me. They borrow money from me every Sunday night and they don't even care to pay it back. . . . I can't talk English very good, and I'm really bashful and shy, and I get scared when I talk to white people. I usually just stay quiet in the [day school] classroom, and the teachers will leave me alone. But at boarding school they wanted me to get up and talk or say something. . . . I quit and I never went back. . . . I can't seem to get along with different people, and I'm so shy I can't even make friends. (Translated from Lakota by interview.)

Most of the newcomers seem to have a difficult time getting along with the experienced boarders and claim that the latter not only strip them of essentials like soap, paper, and underwear, but also take the treasured gifts of proud and encouraging relatives, wrist watches and transistor radios.[9]

> Some of the kids—especially the boarders—are really mean. All they want to do is steal—and they don't want to study. They'll steal your schoolwork off you and they'll copy it. . . . Sometimes they'll break into our suitcase. Or if we have money in our pockets they'll take off our overalls and search our pockets and get our money. . . . So finally I just came home. If I could be a day scholar I think I'll stay in. But if they want me to board I don't want to go back. I think I'll just quit.

Interviews with the dropouts who asserted that school was "all right" and that they had not wished to quit, suggest that many of these had been almost as wretched during their first weeks at high school as the bashful young men who quit because "they couldn't make friends." But unlike the latter, they managed to find some friends and, with the support and protection of this new peer group, they were able to cope with and (probably) strike back at the other boarder peer groups. In any case, the painful and degrading aspects of school became endurable. As one lad put it: "Once you *learn* to be a boarder, it's not so bad."

But for these young men, an essential part of having friends was "raising Cain," that is, engaging in daring and defiant deeds forbidden by the school authorities. The spirit of these escapades is difficult to portray to members of a society where most people no longer seem capable of thinking about boys like Tom Sawyer, Huckleberry Finn, or Kim, except as juvenile delinquents. We ourselves, burdened by sober professional interest in dropouts, at first found it hard to recognize that these able and engaging young men were taking pride and joy in doing exactly what the school authorities thought most reprehensible and that they were not confessing but boasting to our interviewers as they related the exciting and humorous adventures that had propelled them out of school.

Some of the fun and the reckless adventure involved in "raising Cain" is reflected in the verbal account of a bright youth of fifteen who had ran away from the high school. Shortly after entering the ninth grade, he and his friends had appropriated a government car. (The usual pattern in such adventures is to drive off the reservation until the gas gives out.) For this offense (according to a respondent) he and his friends were restricted for the rest of the term; that is, they were forbidden to leave the high school campus or attend any of the school recreational events, games, dances, or movies. (In effect, this meant doing nothing but going to class, performing work chores, and sitting in the dormitory.) Even then our respondent seems to have kept up with his class work and did not play hookey except in reading class:

> It was after we stole that car. Mrs. Bluger [pseudonym for reading teacher] would keep asking who stole the car in class. So I just quit going there.

Then:

> One night we were the only ones up in the older boys' dorm. We said "Hell with this noise. We're not going to be the only ones here."
> So we snuck out and went over to the dining hall. I pried this one window open about this far and then it started to crack, so I let it go. . . . We heard someone so we took off. It was show that night I think. [A motion picture was being shown in the school auditorium.]
> All the rest of the guys was sneaking in and getting something. So I said I was going to get my share too. We had a case of apples and a case of oranges. Then I think it was the night watchman was coming, so we ran around and hid behind those steps. He shined that light on us. So I thought right then I was going to keep on going.
> That was around Christmas time. We walked back to Oglala [about 15 miles] and we were eating this stuff all the way back.

> [Interviewer:] You took those two cases?
> [Respondent:] Naw. We just took what we could carry in our coats.

This young man implied that after this escapade he simply did not have the nerve to try to return to the high school. He insisted, however, that he would like to try another high school:

> I'd like to finish [high school] and get a good job some place. If I don't I'll probably just be a bum around here or something.

Another young man told a similar story:

> Int: What year did you go to high school?
> Res: I quit three years ago after they kick me out of school.
> Int: What happened?
> Res: I and two other boys stole a government car and went to White Clay, Rushville, Gordon, and back.
> Int: What kind of car?
> Res: It was a 1948 model.
> Int: How come you are involved with these two other boys?

Res: I don't know. We just decided to steal the car and the other guy said [suggested] it.

Int: Then they kicked you out of school?

Res: No. They weren't going to kick me out, but the week before that, we broke into the bowling alley and took five boxes of candy.

Int: Why did you do that?

Res: I don't know.

Int: Are you willing to go back to school?

Res: I don't know. Since they kicked me out, they probably won't want me back.

(Translated from Lakota by interviewer.)

YOUNG MEN WHO STAY IN SCHOOL

If roughly half the young Sioux who leave high school very early in their career claim that they left because they were unable to conform to the school regulations, what happens to the country Indian boys who remain in school until the eleventh and twelfth grades? Do they "shape-up," obey the regulations, or perhaps, even internalize them? We found that most of these older and more experienced young men were, if anything, even more inclined to boast of their triumphs over the rules than were the younger fellows who had left school. Indeed, all but one older male respondent assured our interviewers that they were adept at hookey playing, food and car stealing, and that they were frequent participants at the surreptitious beer parties and the other enjoyments outlawed by the school authorities. Relying on these verbal accounts, we do not know whether, for example, star athletes actually disobey the school regulations as frequently and flagrantly as they claim. But that most Sioux young men between the ages of twelve and twenty (and older) wish to be regarded as hellions who seize every chance to play pranks on the school authorities there can be no doubt at all. To hold any other attitude would be unmanly.

An eleventh grader in good standing explained his private device for playing hookey and added proudly: "They never caught me yet." A twelfth grader and first-string basketball player told me how he and some other students "stole" a jeep from the high school machine shop and drove it all over town. When asked why he did this, he patiently explained: "To see if we can get away with it. It's for the enjoyment . . . to see if we can take the car without getting caught." Another senior assured our male staff worker: "You can always get out and booze it up." Still another senior and outstanding athlete remarked:

> Once a bunch of us were restricted—all the guys who work in the bathroom. I didn't care so I took off, went to Holy Rosary homecoming, to White Clay, and then to a dance over to Kyle. But I didn't get slicked. Other times when I try to sneak around, then I get slicked.

The impulse to boast of the virile achievements of youth seems to maintain itself into middle and even into old age. Country Indians with college training zestfully told (male) members of the study how they and a group of proctors had stolen large amounts of food from the high school kitchen and were never apprehended, or how they and their friends drank three fifths of whiskey in one night and did not pass out.

Clearly, the activities regarded as immature or delinquent by administrators and teachers are regarded as part of the world of youthful daring, excitement, agonistic play, and manly honor by the Sioux young men and by many of their elders. They are also, we suspect, an integral part of the world of competitive sports. "I like to play basketball" was one of the most frequent responses of young men to the question: "What do you like most about school?" Indeed, several ninth and tenth graders stated that the opportunity to play basketball was the main reason they kept going to school and one eighth grader who had run away from school several times as a juvenile stated:

> When I was in the seventh grade I made the B team on the basketball squad. And I made the A team when I was in the eighth grade. So I stayed and finished school without running away anymore.

The unself-conscious devotion and ardor with which many of these young men participate in sports must be witnessed to be even mildly appreciated. They cannot communicate their joy and pride in words, although one seventeen-year-old member of the team that won the state championship tried, by telling how a team member wearing a war bonnet "led us onto the playing floor and this really gave them a cheer."

ELEVENTH- AND TWELFTH-GRADE DROPOUTS

Our knowledge of dropouts at this level is limited, for many had left the reservation or entered the armed services. Those whom we reached gave various reasons for dropping out. One said that he was bored: "I was just sitting there doing anything to pass the time." Another said he didn't know what made him quit, "I just didn't fit in anymore. . . . I just wasn't like the other guys anymore." Another refused to attend a class in which he felt that the teacher had insulted Indians. When the principal told him that he must attend this class or be "restricted," he left school. Significantly, his best friend dropped out with him, even though he was on the way to becoming a first class basketball player. Different as they first appear, these statements have a common undertone; they are the expressions of relatively mature young men who find the atmosphere of the high school stultifying and childish.

THE DILEMMA OF SIOUX YOUTH

The intense study of any cross-cultural area is likely to reveal as many tragicomic situations as social scientific insights. Thus, on the Pine Ridge Reservation, a majority of the young men arrive at adolescence valuing élan, bravery, generosity, passion, and luck, and admiring outstanding talent in athletics, singing, and dancing. While capable of wider relations and reciprocities, they function at their social best as members of small groups of peers or relatives. Yet to obtain even modest employment in the greater society, they must graduate from high school. And in order to graduate from high school, they are told they must develop exactly opposite qualities to those they possess: a respect for humdrum diligence and routine, for "discipline," (in the sense of not smoking in toilets, not cutting classes, and not getting drunk), and for government property. In addition, they are expected to compete scholastically on a highly privatized and individualistic level, while living in large dormitories, surrounded by strangers who make privacy of any type impossible.[10]

The young men who remain in the high school until the eleventh or twelfth grade do not seem to have developed any of the qualities considered essential by the formulators of the school regulations. What they have learned is another and perhaps more efficient way of maintaining their identity and their values on the periphery of an alien social system.[11] They have also grown older, and as more mature youths, are less inclined to commit the extremely compulsive and explosive deeds characteristic of healthy boys in their early and mid-teens.[12]

If the educational scene were as it was a generation or two ago, then the situation might be bettered by democratizing the schools, involving the Sioux parents in their control. While this system of locally controlled schools was not perfect, it worked pretty well. Today, however, the problem is more complicated and tricky because educators have become professionalized and educational systems have become complex bureaucracies inextricably involved with universities, education associations, foundations, and federal crash programs. Even suburban middle-class parents, some of whom are highly educated and sophisticated, find it difficult to cope with the bureaucratic barriers and mazes of the schools which their children attend, and it is difficult to see how Sioux parents could accomplish much unless, in some way, their own school system were kept artificially small and isolated and accessible to their understanding and control.

THE DILEMMA OF WORKING-CLASS YOUTH

A specific comparison of the Sioux dropouts with dropouts from the urban working class—Negroes, Puerto Ricans, or whites—would, no doubt, reveal many salient differences in cultural background and world view. Nevertheless, investigations so far undertaken suggest that the attitudes held by these peoples toward *education and the schools* are startlingly similar. Both Sioux and working-class parents wish their children to continue in school because they believe that graduating from high school is a guarantee of employment. Again, many working-class dropouts, like the Sioux dropouts, express a generally favorable attitude toward school, stating that teachers are generally fair and that the worst thing about dropping out of school is missing one's friends. Even more important, many working-class dropouts assert that they were pushed out of school, and frequently add that the push was fairly direct.[13] The Sioux boys put the matter more delicately, implying that the school authorities would not really welcome them back.

Valuable as the recognition of these similarities may be, they should not be seized on as evidence that the offspring of all disprivileged peoples are alike and that, in consequence, they can all be counted on to respond as a unit to the one ideal educational policy for high school dropouts. Rather, many of the similarities in attitude and experience of working-class youth spring from the fact that they are in much the same situation vis-à-vis the monolithic greater society and its one-track educational escalator. It is the schools and their administrators that are so monotonously alike that the boy who is brought up in an ethnic or a little community can but regard and react to them in similar fashion.

A more important and relatively unrecognized point is that while the school poses a dilemma for the working-class or ethnic boy, the boy poses a dilemma for the school. In many traditional or urban ethnic cultures, boys are expected and permitted to have a virile adolescence and so become genuine men. Our schools try to deprive youth of adolescence and demand that high school students behave like "mature people" which, in our culture, means in a pretty dull and spiritless fashion. Those who submit to these demands and succeed in school are often able to meet the bureaucratic requirements of future employers, but they are also likely to be lacking in independence of thought and in creativity. The dropout of boys like the Sioux is a failure on their part to become what the school demands. On the other hand, the school has failed to offer them what the boys from the most "deprived" and "underdeveloped" peoples take as a matter of course—the opportunity to become whole men.

Miller and Harrison, studying working-class youth, assert that individuals who do poorly in school are handicapped or disfavored for the remainder of their lives, because "the schools have become the occupational gatekeepers" and "the level of education affects the kind and level of job that can be attained." On the other hand, the investigations of Friedenberg[14] and Henry[15] suggest that the youth who perform creditably in high school according to the views of the authorities and of their peers, are disfavored in that they emerge from this experience as permanently crippled persons or human beings. In a curious way our researches among the Sioux may be viewed as supporting both of these contentions, for they suggest that some people leave high school because they are too vital and independent to submit to a dehumanizing situation. In this respect, we note that the dean of a major school of engineering has recently asserted that the young men who drop out of his institution "include a major share of those with high potential creativity; and that our educational processes tend to destroy the creative potential of a large share of those who survive."[16]

NOTES AND REFERENCES

1. S. M. Miller and Ira E. Harrison, "Types of Dropouts: 'The Unemployables,'" in *Blue-Collar World: Studies of the American Worker*, ed. Arthur B. Shostak and William Gomberg (Englewood Cliffs, N.J.: Prentice-Hall, 1964), pp. 469–84.
2. For a more detailed report on the educational situation and attitudes of Oglala Sioux adolescents, see Rosalie H. Wax and Murray L. Wax, "Dropout of American Indians at the Secondary Level" (Final Report, Cooperative Research Project No. S-009, U.S. Office of Education, 1964), mimeographed. In addition to further materials on the boys who are the main subject of the present article, the report also discusses the Sioux girls and the large body of young people who do not even attempt to enroll in high school.
3. Although "country Sioux" or "country Indian" might loosely be considered as synonyms for "fullblood," I have avoided the latter term as connoting a traditional Indian culture which vanished long ago and whose unchanging qualities were a mythology of white observers rather than a social reality of Indian participants. In any case, I use "country Indian" to refer to the people raised and living "out on the reservation (prairie)" who participate in the social and ceremonial activities of their local rural communities, as opposed to those persons, also known as Indians, who live in Pine Ridge town and make a point of avoiding these backwoods activities. The questions of Indianness and the nature of Indian identity are complex. Those interested should consult Chapter 3 of *Formal Education in an American Indian Community* by Murray L. Wax, Rosalie H. Wax, and Robert V. Dumont, Jr. (Monograph #1, The Society for the Study of Social Problems, 1964), as well as Robert E. Daniels, "Cultural Identities among the Oglala Sioux" (M.A. thesis, Department of Anthropology, University of Chicago, 1964).
4. Wax, Wax, and Dumont, *Education in an American Indian Community*, p. 96.
5. These virtues were preached for many decades in the boarding schools operated by the Indian Service. Today those Indians who have graduated from those schools and who, having attained an official post within the Bureau of Indian Affairs, are considered successful by the standards of those ("white") virtues, in turn, preach them to their pupils. One of the administrators of the Oglala High School, an Indian by birth, stated that he had dedicated his life to uplifting his people toward these virtues; strangely, few of his people seemed to appreciate his sacrifices. Compare Murray Wax and Rosalie Wax, "Cultural Deprivation as an Eduational Ideology," *Journal of American Indian Education* (January, 1964): 15–18.
   The social dynamics of contemporary Indian communities are more complex than might appear and have not been discussed, even in anthropological literature. The richest discussions we know of are in as yet unpublished manuscripts of Robert K. Thomas and Albert H. Wahrhaftig of the Carnegie Cross-cultural Educational Project of the University of Chicago.
6. Ralph Turner, *The Social Context of Ambition* (San Francisco: Chandler, 1965).
7. For a discussion of this phenomenon and its causes, see Wax, Wax, and Dumont, *Education in an American Indian Community*, pp. 80–82; and Wax and Wax, "Eighth Grade Dropouts."
8. Also, it should be noted that some twenty percent of the youth in our sample who had finished the eighth grade did not attempt to enroll in high school.

9. Although the boarding students are given lockers, they are not permitted to lock them.
10. The conflict between congregate living and individuated achievement afflicts college students as well: see E. Jackson Baur, "Achievement and Role Definition of the College Student" (Final Report, Cooperative Research Project No. 2605, U.S. Office of Education, 1965), chap. 7.
11. See the manuscript of Thomas and Wahrhaftig.
12. S. M. Miller makes the same point with regard to lower class youth: their acts of delinquency decrease with age, rather than as a result of special programs or therapies. See his "The Outlook of Working-Class Youth," in *Blue-Collar World: Studies of the American Worker.*
13. Miller and Harrison, "Types of Dropouts," pp. 471f. Other investigators in Detroit and Kansas City, whose work is not yet published, report that working-class boys in these cities also feel that they are pushed out of school.
14. Edgar Z. Friedenberg, *The Vanishing Adolescent* (Boston: Beacon Press, 1953); idem, *Coming of Age in America* (New York: Random House, 1965).
15. Jules Henry, *Culture Against Man* (New York: Random House, 1963).
16. Quoted by Lawrence S. Kubie, *National Observer*, 27 September 1965.

16 / "Shut Those Thick Lips! Can't You Behave Like a Human Being?"

Gerry Rosenfeld

Harlem School, once you realize it is there, dominates the street on which it is located. Its looks are not substantially different from other schools like it and the descriptions given of them.

> A five-story, gray stone building surmounted by a . . . late Victorian mode, . . . its exterior is grimly institutional—though no more so than the sterile facades of its more modern sisters. . . .
>
> The interior of the school is also uninspiring at first glance. The narrow corridors are dim and deeply scarred and exude the unmistakable odor of that disinfectant that seems to be used in American public schools and nowhere else. . . . Besides being a "K-6" (kindergarten to the sixth grade), it is also a "special service" school, which means it is called upon to perform a whole range of functions over and above those assigned to public elementary schools in other neighborhoods. (Schickel 1964: 3)

Closer examination reveals an odor from children's having urinated on radiators and an occasional broken window resulting from children's playing ball against the walls after school each day. Through the open windows poured the thick gray-black smoke from tenement stacks adjacent to it. Harlem School is a "neighborhood school," which means that its children are from the immediate locale. More than its physical appearance is conveyed to those who attend school there and to those who work there. Once within its walls, enmeshed in its educational exploits, it becomes a place not easily forgotten. Its children are almost all black with an occasional white Puerto Rican child sometimes present in its classes. It is another school for which statistics of achievement have been collected.

> Harlem may not be absolutely typical of all the city's Negro ghettos, but
> there is little reason to suppose that its schools are much different from those
> of others. There are twenty elementary schools and four junior high schools
> in Central Harlem. On an average, the record of academic achievement in
> these schools shows a marked inferiority in the attainment of grade level; and
> what is worse, the children suffer a progressive deterioration with the passage
> of years. In reading comprehension, for example, from 13.2 to 39.6 per cent
> of the pupils in third grade are below grade level, while from 10 to 36.7 per
> cent are above, but by the sixth grade, from *60.4 to 93.5* per cent score below
> grade level. . . . The figures are much the same for word knowledge and
> arithmetic. (Decter 1964: 32)

Few may be acquainted with these statistics, and fewer still might be concerned
with them. But for the children who have attended Harlem School only to find
that they are unequipped with formal skills for better job employment or the
pursuit of further education, it has momentous meaning. For if it is indeed true
that "one of the most significant facts about human nature may be that we all
begin with the natural equipment to live a thousand kinds of lives and end having
lived only one" (Geertz 1966: 5-6), the kinds of lives Harlem School children will
live are in great measure determined within its walls. The teachers at Harlem
School are in more than one sense the keepers of hundreds of lives. Where a person
will live, whom he will marry, the kind of job he will hold, the well-being of his
children, indeed, where he will be buried, are closely connected with the kind
of formal education he receives.

Many of the children, as did Courtney and Kenny in Opportunity Class, deny
the relevance of schooling in their lives, perhaps because Harlem School has been
irrelevant. Rather than have their will submerged, children rebelled in a variety of
ways. Manuel's had been a silent rebellion. Kenny's was more overt. Courtney's
tactics were guile and manipulation. These were not strategies brought initially to
school by the children, but actions developed there. They were, in a sense, personality survival tactics. They were defensive maneuvers against the attacks of
teachers.

Mr. Dorf, for example, punished misbehaving children by putting them in his
metal teacher's closet and locking the door. He then banged on the sides creating
a deafening noise for the child, who cringed in the darkness. This would deter
the child from "talking out without raising his hand."

Other teachers punished children who left their seats "without permission" by
making them stand for the remainder of the day. Still others refused to allow children to go to the bathroom, as a punitive measure when they were disobedient,
apparently delighting in this "biological warfare." Often children urinated in
their clothing, facing embarrassment and ridicule. Another favorite method of
disciplining was ear tweaking, a rather painful application of learning.

Directives from the principal's office sometimes encouraged their practices,
however inadvertently. We were told, for example, to "check the 'out-of-room'
book periodically and compliment children who do not leave the room frequently.
(A positive approach is more effective in reducing the number of children leaving
the room.) Refer to the nurse those who go to the lavatory excessively."[1]

A barrage of directives was steadily issued by the school administration, usually
concerned with regulating children's behavior. Very few directives dealt with
more effective ways of handling subject material or suggestions on how to enhance
personal expression, nor did the orders received always make sense. We were given
suggestions, as in one instance, on "starting a rhythm band." This informed us how
children might be introduced to musical instruments to learn about the orchestra.
Yet, in the time I had spent at Harlem School, I had never seen a musical instrument other than a piano.

We were also encouraged to keep an "anecdotal record" on children who were troublesome. Items were to be checked off, such as: "uses bad language," "does not get along with teachers," "unresponsive," "extremely restless," and "bizarre behavior." These records were to "prove the case" against recalcitrant children and would help in having children removed from classes if teachers requested this. A child could thus be proved guilty without benefit of defense, for if the teacher does not speak for the child, who does?

Harlem School was not solely an agency of cultural transmission in an educational sense, but an agency of personality restriction. It did not serve to connect the child and the larger cultural world so that the child would eventually be passed into that world in confidence; it served more to tell the child that he was unacceptable as he was, and that he would have to be substantially changed in order to fit the images others had for him. Children, however, could be expected to object to this characterization of them, and they did. Perhaps it took the form of truancy, or urinating on walls and radiators, carving on desks, dropping blackboard erasers out windows, or "refusing" to learn. Whatever the tactic, it usually had its promptings.

> When you're a kid, everything has some kind of special meaning. I always could find something to do, even if it was doing nothing. But going to school was something else. School stunk. I hated school and all its teachers. I hated the crispy look of the teachers and the draggy-long hours they took out of my life from nine to three-thirty. I dug being outside no matter what kind of weather. Only chumps worked and studied. . . .
> Always it ended up the same way: I got up and went to school. But I didn't always stay there. . . . It was like escaping from some kind of prison. (Thomas 1967: 64)

The school was not a source of joy and exhilaration for many children, and it may well be true that children fail because "life outside the school is so much more compelling than life inside; that a student is psychologically absent during the hours he spends in class" (Jencks 1966: 147). Entanglements are avoided in school; they are reserved for neighborhood friends instead. Few, if any, children would consider Harlem School teachers as friends. Thus, the peer group and close siblings become for most children the primary agents of cultural transmission.

> My brother, Caleb, was seventeen when I was ten. We were very good friends. In fact, he was my best friend and, for a very long time, my only friend.
> I do not mean to say that he was always nice to me. I got on his nerves a lot, and he resented having to take me around with him and be responsible for me when there were so many other things he wanted to be doing. Therefore, his hand was often up against the side of my head, and my tears caused him to be punished many times. But I knew, somehow, anyway, that when he was being punished for my tears, he was not being punished for anything he had done to me; he was being punished because that was the way we lived; and his punishment, oddly, helped unite us. More oddly still, even as his great hand caused my head to stammer and dropped a flame-colored curtain before my eyes, I understood that he was not striking me. His hand leaped out because he could not help it, and I received the blow because I was there. And it happened, sometimes, before I could even catch my breath to howl, that the hand that had struck me grabbed me and held me, and it was difficult to know which of us was weeping. He was striking, striking out, striking out, striking out; the hand asked me to forgive him. I felt his bewilderment through the membrane of my own. I also felt that he was trying to teach me something. And I had, God knows, no other teachers. (Baldwin 1967: 118, 157)

So much of the children's lives and ways was derived in the community, but was found unacceptable in the school. When some could not find outlet for their feelings in the school, they found themselves more and more attracted to events in the neighborhood.

> I used to feel that I belonged on the Harlem Streets and that, regardless of what I did, nobody had any business to take me off the streets. . . .
> To me, home was the streets. I suppose there were many people who felt that. . . .
> When I was very young—about five years old, maybe younger—I would always be sitting out on the stoop. I remember Mama telling me . . . not to move away from in front of the door. Even when it was time to go up . . . I never wanted to go, because there was so much out there in that street . . .
> I could go out in the street for an afternoon, and I would see so much that, when I came in the house, I'd be talking and talking for what seemed like hours. Dad would say, "Boy, why don't you stop that lyin'? You know you didn't see all that. You know you didn't see nobody do that." But I knew I had. (C. Brown 1966: 415)

Harlem School was not only antagonistic to many of the children, but dull too; no relationship existed between class and what they had learned in family and neighborhood. Indeed, it was as if the school demanded of children that they relinquish all they knew and assume entirely new postures for themselves. And the reasons for this demand were never fully clear to them. For what purpose were they to be changed? Was it for some future benefit, or to ease the burden of teachers' school lives?

> When an anthropologist sees a person learning something in a primitive culture he asks himself, "What is he learning it for?" The answer is usually the obvious one—in order that the person may be able to survive in the culture. Thus, if a boy learns to hunt, it is in order that he may become a hunter and live by hunting; and if he learns gardening, it is to become a primitive farmer and live by farming. There is in such a culture a congruence or complementarity between what a child learns and what he will become. Of course, the whole process of becoming is also clear to a primitive child; for as soon as he is capable of objective knowing, he knows what he will become. . . . We also observe that . . . there is no separation between learning and life.
> Once we realize that in our society there is not only a lack of complementarity between what children learn and what they will become, but also that our elementary school . . . tends to conceal rather than to reveal the realities of our culture . . . then we get an idea of why, in many classrooms, the teaching . . . tends to become a problem, even a burden. (Henry 1963: 35, 36)

There are incongruities, then, in the education of children at Harlem School. They are not always apparent, however, nor are the reasons for their prevalence perceptible to teachers in every instance.

> Perhaps we should be more explicit about the pressures to which the child is subject. The cultural context within which these appear is, of course, that children cannot just be allowed to grow up; they must be wisely directed. . . . What is not made explicit to the child and is probably perceived by only a few . . . teachers is that their own role is dependent upon child accomplishment. (Kimball 1963: 280)

This fact is extremely important to realize: the failure of children at Harlem School is also the failure of the teachers, just as individual success may be related to teachers' efforts. Culture is a group phenomenon and even individual expressions of it are the result of group influences. If the child slips back in his educational achievement, it is likely that a cultural shove was provided in that direction. Learning not to learn is just as effective as learning to learn.

It was my own view that too much attention was likely paid to the "emotional" condition of children who did not achieve rather than to the social and cultural factors influencing the learning situation. I had realized early in my experience that children have different learning styles. Until now "little careful analysis is given how the child's learning might improve simply by concentrating on the way he works and learns, rather than on his affective reasons for not learning" (Riessman 1964: 51). And equal attention has to be paid to the differences in teaching styles. Learning style and teaching style combine through the medium of subject matter—in a specific cultural context—to effect educational transmission.

> The corpus of learning . . . is reciprocal. A culture in its very nature is a set of values, skills, and ways of life that no one member of the society masters. Knowledge in this sense is more like a rope, each strand of which extends no more than a few inches along its length, all being intertwined to give solidity to the whole. The conduct of our educational system has been curiously blind to this interdependent nature of knowledge. We have "teachers" and "pupils," "experts" and "laymen." But the community of learning is somehow overlooked. (Bruner 1966: 45)

LEARNING NOT TO LEARN

If one examined the average school day at Harlem School he would discover various educational procedures that are found in other schools. Some approaches seemed standard, even immutable. Yet, the implications of these procedures for learning were not as readily perceived. It seemed to me that the very format for the instructional sequence followed each day encouraged children to see subject presentation as tenuous and tentative. The children saw no connecting link among the fragments of material offered them. Rarely was a child permitted to bring his involvement in subject matter to an extensive probing. His passions were not brought to bear in any meaningful engagement in the content of learning. This can be illustrated by drawing out the events on an average school day.

Children flock to school each morning and line up outside the gates. They get to their classrooms shortly thereafter and become incorporated in the routines prescribed for them. Various norms, sometimes unstated, govern their actions. For example, it is not expected, nor permitted, that a child be immediately allowed to go to the bathroom upon arrival in the morning. Similarly school culture prescribes that when a boy has gone to the bathroom during the day, only a girl may go next—as if this were to "preserve democracy" in the classroom. These procedures are not seen as mysteries by teachers or children; they are carried out as "natural" and normal events. Thus, it seems altogether proper that reading and writing lessons predominate as these are seen as requirements for effective later participation in a literate culture.

Customarily the teacher attempts to capture the collective imagination of the children at the outset of each day with a group assignment—penmanship, let us say. While the children practice their letters, they are summoned in groups for reading. The groups may be given names to distinguish reading achievement levels and to help children derive a sense of common membership with others in the group. One teacher at Harlem School named the three reading groups in her class the "Sharks," the "Barracudas," and the "Flounders." These were, of course, allegorical for the

"Bright," the "Average," and the "Dull." The children interpreted the meaning of these labels quite easily, just as they had been able to understand the meaning of footprints on the bindings of books. Even the "Dull" knew they were so perceived, and some refused to read as an objection to their designation, often complaining, "We never get any interesting stories to read."

As each group is brought forth, a child may complain that he has not yet finished his penmanship assignment. The teacher, however, insists he join the group. During the reading this same child might not be called upon nor get actively involved over the procedings. It may not be "his turn" to read on this day, leaving him with only a peripheral interest in what is going on. Soon thereafter he and his classmates might be involved in a continuing variety of subject explorations, including arithmetic, social studies, art, science, music, and more. None of those is ever brought to completion, but is postponed until that subject time is rescheduled.

Mixed in with these wanderings may be an unplanned itinerary that would include messages from the school office, a dispute over a pencil, the collection of milk and cookie money, even an occasional fire drill. At other times during a day there are an assembly period, a gym period, recess, and so on. These repeated partial excursions into the nature of subject matter render the child only partially aware and almost wholly uncommitted to that subject matter. It is as if he is being told that the bits of learning he is presented with are after all only temporary, and that he must be ready to relinquish his accruing insights at any given time in order to go on to other involvements. He learns in this way to "play it cool," knowing that his feeling for his subjects cannot be intense or lasting.

This appraisal may be denied by some, but at Harlem School the proof of it was evident, just as it is evident in the junior and senior high school where the fragmenting of learning is built into a format of brief fifty-minute periods for the various subjects. The constant clanging of bells punctuates the day to reassert this arrangement. In college, continuing this accepted pattern, students and subject material become even more anonymous in oversize classes, where a student's grades often become the only proof of his existence. What made Harlem School a bit more unique was that these practices—and children's subsequent underachievement—were given a mythical rationale. Teachers had a common agreement that "those" children had to be presented with material in short bursts, as it were, because they "couldn't concentrate for long." It occurred to me, however, that the children's concentration was obviously shortened by the very procedures employed in teaching them. A commitment to subject content was not built up, but denied. "Lack of readiness," as it was alleged in behalf of children, was really a lack of reading among teachers. A child could not extensively pursue a topic to a satisfactory conclusion, perhaps because teachers' own knowledge of the topic was limited. Elementary school teachers are generalists who usually do not have a particular subject specialty for which they have prepared in formal training. They may indeed be jacks-of-all-trades, masters of none.

When such procedures prevail, one's success with children cannot be measured by the children's internalizations of knowledge or their personal investments in content fields, for these do not occur. Instead, children are evaluated and estimated for their worth on a behavioral basis. That is why discipline is so important in the slum school. One can excuse his ignorance of subject matter by translating this ignorance into some alleged dysfunction in children's conduct. I learned soon enough that the administrators at Harlem School would more likely evaluate my own teaching efforts, not by what children learned, but by my bulletin board display, my disciplinary techniques, or the class play we performed in the assembly during the year.

An example of this kind of thinking came at the end of my second year at Harlem School. None of the children in my "average" fifth-grade class read at grade level;

some of the children began the year reading at second- and third-grade reading levels. I had worked very hard with two children in particular, Ronald and Charlene, to bring them close to grade level. I felt myself successful with them at the end of the school year, though they had attained only fourth-grade reading level. They had begun the year reading just beyond the primer stage. This represented to me a distinct effort and capability on the part of the two children, and I was confident that they would subsequently reach expected attainment standards. Thus, I was very surprised when Mr. Green told me that Ronald and Charlene would not be promoted. When I asked why this had to be, I was told that it was undesirable to pass children on to the next grade if they were two years behind in reading. I protested that the work of Ronald and Charlene was satisfactory in other subject areas and that they had shown deliberate improvement in reading as well. It would be punishing them, I submitted, for their hard work and effort, and it would be penalizing me for the investment I made in their potential and demonstrated desire to improve. My arguments were fruitless. There was an established pattern at Harlem School: records counted more than feelings. If children were disappointed, one could understand why. They often lost conviction in their own desires and abilities and learned not to try too hard so that they would not be repeatedly denied in their efforts. If you are going to fail, you may as well not try hard to succeed.

In another effort to help Ronald and Charlene I was again overruled. I had learned who the children's teachers would be the next year after placements had already been made. It was customary to do it this way at Harlem School. When children were placed in new classes, it was not with any specific thought in mind that certain teachers can work better with certain children. In this instance I thought that Ronald would do better with Charlene's teacher and that Charlene would fare better with Ronald's assigned teacher. I spoke to the two teachers in question, and they agreed that we should switch the children for the next year. I told Mr. Green of the agreement and formally requested the change. Mr. Green told me it would be "too much trouble" to switch them because rosters had already been made out. When I pleaded on the basis of sound educational principle he told me, "You can switch a boy for a boy, or a girl for a girl, but never a boy for a girl."

I was stunned by this. He saw the children as statistics, not people. His explanation was that too much clerical revision would be necessitated. For example, if there were seventeen boys and fourteen girls in a class, the roster would read "17 + 14." One could switch a girl from another class in place of a girl and the roster would still indicate "17 + 14"; but if a girl were switched for the removal of a boy, the roster would have to read "16 + 15." The administrative upheaval would be too great. This is indeed hard to believe, but this is how the situation ended.

DISCRIMINATION WITH AND WITHOUT PREJUDICE

Many other practices at Harlem School were equally absurd, in the classroom and out. For example, it was generally thought that children who "can't learn" are "good with their hands." It is difficult to find objective evidence for this, yet almost all lessons would culminate by teachers telling children, "Now draw a picture of what you learned."[2] Crayons were often used as a substitute for more extensive knowledge of subject matter by teachers. They often replaced needed instruction.

"Very poor children need hope in order to achieve. So do those who work with them" (Henry 1965: 34). The policies adopted at Harlem School seemed designated to preclude hope for everyone. The incidents with Ronald and Charlene were, at the least, discouraging. They were not perhaps the result of direct prejudice, but of ignorance and too little concern for the feelings of children. They were matters not of the heart, but of routine. There were, however, other practices that were more overt and of even greater impact on the minds of the children.

Miss Matthew's subtle denigration of the children was a case in point. She was the leader of the fifth-grade assembly during my second year at Harlem School. When the children came in each week, she presided at the assembly and read a passage from the Bible during opening exercises. Several teachers noticed that Miss Matthew read the same passage each week. It turned out not that it was a favorite psalm of hers, but that she felt the "dopey kids didn't know the difference, anyhow." She told us that she objected to their "bowing their heads and praying, when they don't know what the hell it's all about." Perhaps she objected to the children sharing the same God with her.

In a similar type of encounter Mr. Hecht once approached me and remarked, "You're an anthropologist; why, when these kids are born so musical, can't they even sing the Star-Spangled Banner correctly?" At first I thought he was kidding, but he pressed the issue. He really believed that black children were innately possessed of a musical quality. When I offered that no one is "born musical," he suggested I was uninformed. Finally I asked Mr. Hecht why he didn't institute a well-developed music program at Harlem School in order to extend and make use of children's "inborn" musical ability, but he walked away, irritated, to join in the singing himself.

To me the most subtle, yet most openly outrageous form of derogation was employed by Mrs. Carp. Her class preceded ours down the stairway at dismissal time each day. Without fail, every afternoon, she turned to her children, halted them and shouted: "Shut those thick lips! Can't you behave like human beings?" Even had Mrs. Carp not realized what she was saying, it was altogether too clear to the children. At other times they were referred to as "wild," "crazy," "animals in a zoo."

Mr. Norman was another teacher who, though capable of being a fine teacher, undermined children at times. Like others after being at Harlem School for many years, he had adopted a variety of denigrating forms of behavior by which he vented his own discontent and frustration on the job. He stood in the hallway when children entered in the afternoon and mockingly addressed them in an assumed southern drawl. Some children simply dismissed his actions, while others gazed in anger at him. Mr. Norman had a favorite routine: he unbefittingly extended his hand to a child and mimicked him by drawling, "Gimme five, man." The child unknowingly smiled and "slapped skin" with Mr. Norman, who then called after the child as he left, "Prehensile lips!"

Perhaps the child at first did not understand the meaning of "prehensile lips," but sooner or later he understood and he did not remember Mr. Norman fondly.

I too realized how a prejudiced remark might even be made without intention when talking to children. Such an instance occurred in class one day. We were periodically required to check children's addresses, just as it was sometimes ordered that we take an ethnic count of children in the class. A teacher was to indicate how many children in the class were Negro or white. One was not supposed to speak to the children about this, but simply to make the appraisal casually. If one were "uncertain," he was to check the category "other" provided for on the form. This was an occasion for great mirth among some teachers, who delighted in categorizing Puerto Rican children as "other." Their hilarity was marked in lunchroom sessions on the days these "ethnic inventories" were made.

I was noting children's addresses on this particular occasion and had almost finished calling on all the children for verification when Marty, who sat just in front of my desk, asked: "Where do you live?" I did not think about my answer and simply repeated an address given by several of the children who lived in the same building. It simply had come to mind because so many of them had stated it.

I was merely being lighthearted. However, Marty literally fell from his chair, seemingly hurt. I jumped up to see what was wrong, when I noticed he was doubled up with laughter. It came to me immediately. Marty was laughing so hard because my response had placed me entirely out of cultural context. He, and I, knew that no white people lived on the street I had mentioned. If he ever saw me coming out of one of those old brownstone tenements on that block, it would be the most hilarious sight he had ever seen. My remark was really a mockery of his cultural life. Had it been a deliberate jibe, it would have deserved scorn, not merely laughter. It made me realize how often my own and other teachers' behavior, however innocent, might be interpreted as prejudiced, the fact that Marty found it amusing notwithstanding.

It is little wonder that children reject the school and teachers. In fact it is often necessary to do so in order to maintain an acceptable image of oneself.

> Any Negro born in this country who accepts American education at face value turns into a madman—*has* to. Because the standards that the country pretends to live by are not for him, and he knows that by the time he starts pledging allegiance to the flag. If I had believed, if any Negro on my block had really believed what the American Republic said about itself, he would have ended up in Bellevue. And those of us who did believe it *did* end up in Bellevue. If you are a Negro, you understand that somehow you have to operate outside the system and beat these people at their own game—which means that your real education essentially occurs outside of books.[3]

It is difficult to tell which actions against children are more objectionable than others; the examples proliferate. Several teachers at Harlem School delighted in threatening to summon a child's parent when they knew definitely that the child was an orphan or his parent was not living in the home. This embarrassed the child and made him feel to blame if he had been adopted or was living with relatives. It would be serious enough if only Harlem School provided the backdrop for such unforgivable treatment of children, but unfortunately such things occur in other schools as well. Mr. Gould spoke of his friends, also teachers, at other schools in Harlem who delighted in destroying the work of children in front of them. Mr. Gould himself referred to the work of children as "rubbish." Most often he did not even look at their assignments, but collected them and threw them in the trash. At other times he ripped work up, dropped it on the floor, and made the children clean it up. It is sad, to be sure, that Mr. Gould has his counterparts.

> If Stephen began to fiddle around during a lesson, the Art Teacher generally would not notice him at first. When she did, both he and the children around him would prepare for trouble. For she would go at his desk with something truly like a vengeance and would shriek at him in a way that carried terror. "Give me that! Your paints are all muddy! You've made it a mess. Look at what he's done! He's mixed up the colors! I don't know why we waste good paper on this child!" Then: "Garbage! Junk! He gives me garbage and junk! And garbage is one thing I will not have." Now I thought that that garbage and junk was very nearly the only real artwork in the class. I do not know very much about painting, but I know enough to know that the Art Teacher did not know much about it either and that, furthermore, she did not know or care anything at all about the way in which you can destroy a human being. Stephen, in many ways already dying, died a second and third and fourth and final death before her anger. (Kozol 1967: 3-4)

Why would any teacher behave this way toward children? One must assert that racial prejudice was at the root of much of this behavior. Teachers were themselves victims of the Harlem School social system. Some had long before lost sight of their original motivations for wanting to teach. They had adopted an arsenal of techniques and maneuvers over the years by which to subjugate and pacify children. Perhaps this was easier than developing new techniques of instruction. New teachers learned these restrictive techniques early in their experience. Indeed, the person who rejected these was thought of as an idealist or nonconformist. One need not be consciously committed to a social system in order to behave as if to support it (Kimball and McClellan 1962:219–323). And many teachers denied that it was their intention to be brutal or defamatory with children. They had found that their preparatory college work was not adequate to equip them for work at Harlem School. They came to see the children as obstacles to smooth educational practice. This is true for teachers in other places too.

> Some Chicago schoolteachers chose to remain in a lower-class school for the lengthy period necessary to reach the top of the list for a very desirable middle-class school. When the opportunity to make the move came, they found they no longer desired to move because they had so adjusted their style of teaching to the problems dealing with lower-class children that they could not contemplate the radical changes necessary to teach middle-class children. They had, for instance, learned to discipline children in ways objectionable to middle-class parents and become accustomed to teaching standards too low for a middle-class school. They had, in short, bet the ease of performance of their job on remaining where they were and in this sense were committed to stay. (Becker 1960: 37)

While teachers at Harlem School were quick to allege the deficiencies of children, I knew it was the attitude of the individual teacher that needed scrutiny (Zamoff 1966: 875). Every person, in the last analysis, must hold himself responsible for his own actions. Besides, that which teachers attributed to children was more often accurate attributions of themselves.

> I have seen teachers in ghetto schools resort to mechanical judgements as a means of protecting themselves from facing their own failures. They see in the environment, the family, the home, the native intelligence of the child, the reasons for the children's failures. It is always thought of that way—"their children's failures"; but in fact it usually is a failure in the classroom, which is as much their responsibility as their pupils. When students fail to respond, it is usually not so much because they can't as because the teacher hasn't offered them something to respond to. (Kohl 1967: 58)

Unfortunately, the more teachers at Harlem School ascribed negative tendencies to the children the more likely these teachers were to base their own teaching on these ascriptions. This precluded an appreciation of any child who was not willing to fit this pattern. But teachers foster such a pattern and then reinforce their perceptions when they bring it about. A whole range of children's possible creative reactions is thus submerged.

> I regret to say that teachers in the United States do not give a place of great importance to either *independence in judgment* or *being courageous*. Independence in judgment and being courageous stands . . . lower than in any of the other six countries for which we have data. In fact, it is far more important to teachers in the United States for their pupils to be courteous than to be courageous. It is also more important that pupils do their work on time, be energetic and industrious, be obedient and popular or well liked among their peers, be receptive to the ideas of others, be versatile, and be

willing to accept judgments of authorities than to be courageous. Such a set of values is more likely to produce pupils who are ripe for brainwashing than pupils who can think creatively. (Torrance 1963: 222)

One must add that such a set of values also produces teachers who cannot think creatively.

> Miss Moyle, an O.P.T. teacher (supplementary teachers who relieve the regular classroom teacher), comes in at 11:00 for social studies. These children are scheduled to study (the syllabus says they *do* study) math, social studies, science, music, and art, although they can't read. Miss Moyle is very amiable with teachers, recently engaged, salt-and-pepper gray in her hair, and happy.
> For a month we had walk-ups and skyscrapers, multiple dwellings, and the subway. "You'd be amazed," Moyle would insist, "how many of the children just don't know what the subway is."
> "But Miss Moyle, all the children go to every borough with their families over the week-end, visiting relatives, staying overnight. The little boys sneak on and ride the subway all day Saturday by themselves. They ride all over New York; they go to Coney Island, Forty-second Street, and get themselves home on the subways."
> Moyle: "Many of them have simply never seen a subway. Many of these children, dwelling in the world's largest metropolitan area, simply grow up without having learned what 'sub-way' means. We're here to teach them about their cultural environment, such as the subway." (Greene and Ryan 1965: 34)

This "innocent" unawareness of teachers is so often turned around and reshaped into an array of myths and distorted allegations about children. Children are seen as "deprived" and "underprivileged," yet it is not always clear what their deprivation or underprivilege is, particularly in relation to classroom performance. Children cannot simply be incapable of learning because inappropriate methods have been employed in teaching them. This cannot be a workable pedagogic position. The belief that they cannot learn is no doubt more potent in fulfilling this suggestion. Perhaps a change in philosophic orientation is needed. In some instances teachers have come to recognize such a necessity.

> A breakthrough in my own thinking about formal education at Blackfish Village came about in the metamorphosis of my original research orientations. I had proposed to investigate what it is about village life that makes Indian pupils so refractive to formal education and why Indian pupils fail in school. As I observed and participated in village life and in the classroom, I realized that posing the query in such terms narrowed the perspective of the search. There is another question to ask one which can be considered an alternative but which is, I think, better regarded as a complement to my original orientation: How do schools fail their . . . pupils? (Wolcott 1967: 131)

A willingness to explore alternatives in facilitating children's learning brings also an immense hope. In so doing, it may be that we discover ways of teaching all children, not only the poor and discriminated against. Certainly this would be better than the present estrangement children and teachers feel in our schools, particularly where ethnic minority children attend. It would allow the development of new theories of instruction, so glaringly missing at the present time (Bruner 1963). A comparative view of education in other settings is also relevant.

If there is anything written clear across the almost infinite diversity of primitive society, it is that the group molds its members toward emotion, toward the experience of crises of realization and of conscience, and toward a profoundly romantic world-view which includes a profoundly romantic view of man in the world . . . Hence, to an extent hardly imaginable in our modern society and state, the ultimate concentration of the primitive group is upon education—upon personality development. Every experience is used to that end, every specialized skill and expression is bent to that end. There results an integration of body-mind and of individual-group which is not automatic, not at the level of conformity and habit, but spontaneous . . . and at the level of freedom. Many readers will resist this statement, and as in most matters that are essential in human life, the proof that it is true cannot be coercive. Modern man does not like any suggestion that he has fallen away from a greater good which he once had. But let once the mind be opened, let once a curious and sympathetic interest be born, and then the data of ethnology yields overwhelming conviction on the statement here made. (Collier 1947: 22–23)

As I continued to look at what was happening at Harlem School, I came to think that it may be possible that a social system can survive and perpetuate itself even though it does not serve to support its individual members. It may likewise be that individuals can behave in ways that offer no substantial psychological supports for that behavior. Filling immediate need does not necessarily bring subsequent satisfaction with it. Teachers at Harlem School might have sought expedient means to meet immediate need to reduce frustration in the classroom, but they could not be happy with the long-range results. They repeatedly expressed ambivalence and annoyance about themselves, and continually they had to force their own reassessment of their role with the children. The children too asked a reassessment.

How would you have us, as we are?
Or sinking neath the load we bear?
Our eyes fixed forward on a star,
Or gazing empty at despair?

Rising or falling? Men or things?
With dragging pace or footsteps fleet?
Strong, willing sinews in your wings,
Or tightening chains about your feet?
(Johnson n.d.)

NOTES

1. Innumerable guidelines for procedure emanated from the school office. The quotation cited is from "Teacher's Responsibilities." It prescribed procedures for maintaining maximum order in the classroom; n.d.
2. Many teachers consistently employed this procedure, though it is not designed as an art lesson in the formal sense. It was an "escape valve" when one did not know what more to do or if one wanted to "take it easy." I might conjecture that this is why sex education is not taught in the public schools, for then children would have to "draw pictures of what they had learned."
3. James Baldwin in "Liberalism and the Negro: A Round-Table Discussion" (1964: 32).

REFERENCES

Baldwin, James, 1967, "Tell Me How Long the Train's Been Gone," *McCall's* 94 (February): 118ff.

Becker, Howard S., 1960, "Notes on the Concept of Commitment," *The American Journal of Sociology* 66 (July): 32–40.

Brown, Claude, 1966, *Manchild in the Promised Land*. New York: The Macmillan Company.

Bruner, Jerome S., 1963, "Needed: A Theory of Instruction," *Educational Leadership* 20 (May): 523–532.

——, 1966, "The Will to Learn," *Commentary* 41 (February), 41–46.

Collier, John, 1947, *Indians of the Americas*. New York: New American Library.

Decter, Midge, 1964, "The Negro and the New York Schools," *Commentary* 38 (September): 25–34.

Geertz, Clifford, 1966, "The Impact of the Concept of Culture on the Concept of Man," *Bulletin of the Atomic Scientists* 22 (April): 2–8.

Greene, Mary Frances, and Orletta Ryan, 1965, *The Schoolchildren*. New York: Pantheon Books, Inc.

Henry, Jules, 1963a, *Culture Against Man*. New York: Random House, Inc.

——. 1963b. "Reading for What?" *Teachers College Record* 65 (October): 35–46.

——, 1965, "White People's Time, Colored People's Time," *Trans-Action* 2 (March–April) 31–34.

Jencks, Christopher, 1966, "Who Should Control Education?," *Dissent* 13 (March–April): 145–163.

Johnson, James Weldon, n.d., mimeographed reprint of poem, no title given.

Kimball, Solon T., 1963, "Cultural Influences Shaping the Role of the Child," in *Education and Culture*, George D. Spindler, ed. New York: Holt, Rinehart and Winston, Inc., pp. 268–283.

——, and James McClellan, 1962, *Education and the New America*. New York: Random House, Inc.

Kohl, Herbert R., 1967a, *Teaching the Unteachable*. New York: A New York Review Book.

——, 1967b, *36 Children*. New York: New American Library.

Kozol, Jonathan, 1967, *Death at an Early Age*. Boston: Houghton Mifflin Company.

"Liberalism and the Negro: A Round-Table Discussion," 1964, *Commentary* 37 (March): 25–42.

Riessman, Frank, 1964, "The Process of Learning," *Current* (June–July): 50–54.

Schickel, Richard, 1964, "P.S. 165," *A Commentary Report*, pp. 3–11.

Thomas, Piri, 1967, *Down These Mean Streets*. New York: Alfred A. Knopf.

Torrance, E. Paul, 1963, "The Creative Personality and the Ideal Pupil," *Teachers College Record* 65 (December): 220–226.

Wolcott, Harry F., 1967, *A Kwakiutl Village and School*. New York: Holt, Rinehart and Winston, Inc.

Zamoff, Richard, 1966, "The Attitudinally Disadvantaged Teacher," *The Urban Review* 1 (December): 875–876.

17 / Realities of the Urban Classroom

G. Alexander Moore

A SECOND-GRADE CLASS

The Background

The class is one that the principal himself warned visitors, with a kind of negative pride, to be one of the "wild" classes. He was not at all reluctant that visitors should witness the problems his school faced. The class is in ill repute throughout the school; several teachers commented on it, one calling it "a zoo." It ranks ninth and lowest of the second-grade classes. There are twenty-four students on roll, fifteen boys and nine girls. They are all in the reading-readiness stage. They are either non-English-speaking or are considered "seriously disturbed" by the administration. Remembering the large turnover of pupils in the school—only 15 percent remained from last year—it should not be surprising to find many pupils entering this school still speaking only Spanish. However, the visitor does not readily imagine why a second-grade class should still be on the kindergarten level and, like the pupils, the observer enters the classroom "somewhat disturbed."

This observation was on a spring day, starting at 9:30 in the morning and continuing till 11:15, or lunchtime. On this day there are only eighteen of the twenty-four students present. Six of these struck the observer as being American Negroes; the remaining students were Hispanos.

Mrs. Auslander, the teacher, is a tall woman in her late forties or early fifties. Her hair is mixed gray and white and her face is deeply lined. One's first impression of her is that of a nervous and harassed woman.

The classroom itself is in the full sense of the word nondescript.

The Morning Session

It is 9:30 and Mrs. Auslander is telling the children to hold their hands up in order that she may inspect them to see if they are clean. Completing this, she tells the children to sing their morning song. "This is the way we wash our hands," the children start singing, and make appropriate motions as they continue through the various verses. Looking around, one notes that the boys have long trousers, not short pants, and the girls are wearing cotton dresses. In general the children appear somewhat unkempt in comparison to other second-grade classes noted in the hall. This is particularly true of the boys.

The Morning News

The song is over and the teacher, attempting to drill them on the days of the week, asks them, "What day is today? What day was yesterday? What day will tomorrow be?" As the children call out the names of the various days, she stops to correct them: "Give your answers in sentences!"

Meanwhile several children are noisily running around the room hitting one another. Others sit in a stupor, apparently quite unaware of their surroundings. In the space of the first ten minutes, the teacher has used physical force and actually hurts the children in an attempt to control them. Yet she has not achieved control of the class, nor does she at any time during the morning. She frequently addresses her noisy, restless class, saying, "When I have everyone's attention and your hands are folded, then I will listen to what you're trying to say." Since this never happens, she never really listens to any of the children during the morning, yet many of them do seem to want to say something to her.

She suddenly turns upon a child who was quietly looking at a book, and says, "Why are you playing with your book?"

Some children in another part of the room then begin to write; the teacher calls out, "We're talking. We're not writing now." In the meantime a few children do give her the proper names of the days; however, most of the class is not paying any attention.

"Take out your notebooks," she calls. "We are going to write our morning news." She turns to the board and prints the number of the school, the class number, and the date.[1] Under this she writes the words "Our News." Underneath this she begins to write sentences: "Today is Friday. . . . There are nine days left in May. . . . It is sunny and warm and clear. . . . We saw a film about flowers." This last is a reference to a film that the class had just seen minutes before in the second-grade weekly assembly which started off this Friday. These sentences are a long time in appearing on the board for she tries to elicit them from the children by such questions as "How many days are left in May?" or "What kind of weather are we having?" The children are not paying any particular attention and though a few replies are called forth, she is left to do most of the work. In any case, the exercise is going on the board for the children to copy down in their notebooks; she tells them to do this sentence by sentence.

Leaving the sentences on the board and giving the children more time to copy them, Mrs. Auslander goes back to the observer and starts a conversation. "This is a discipline class. It is not an ordinary class. I have emotionally disturbed children and mentally retarded children and I can't get perfect attention. I don't try to. I can't ride them all the time. I hope you understand that it is this type of class and will not be too upset by what you see in this classroom." The observer reassured her, saying that we wanted to see the problems presented by this kind of class, and she seemed completely at ease. Indeed she never appeared to feel a threat from any visitors.

At 10:05, Mrs. Auslander walks around the room to see if the children are copying the work from the board in their notebooks. Frequently she approaches a child and asks, "Where is your book?" If the child does not answer, she repeats the question until he or she does. In one case, she repeated it a good six times, each time raising her voice more until she was shouting.

Some children are not copying the work because they do not have pencils, so she tries to persuade other children to lend them one. "George, will you lend a pencil to Lucille?" she asks. George has a small pencil case from which he removes a pencil to lend to Lucille. "What a nice boy you are," she commends George.

While she was looking for a pencil for Lucille, Mrs. Auslander remarked to the observer what a problem she has because the children forget or lose pencils. The observer offered a pencil for Lucille, but Mrs. Auslander protested, saying without lowering her speaking voice, "You'll never get it back." After George has lent his pencil to Lucille, Mrs. Auslander comments aloud to the observer, "You know, George *could* be a very *good* boy."

She returns to the board and attempts to elicit a response to the sentence under discussion. "Does anybody know how many days are left in May?" She sends a child to the front of the room to count the number of days on the May calendar. She tries to engage the rest of the children in counting along with him but only a few children join in.

Suddenly the observer realizes that several children have been out of the room on pass all this time. One boy is returning with his pass and six children have raised their hands to ask for permission to go to the bathroom. They shout, "Teacher, can we leave the room? Can we leave the room?" Whenever anyone wants Mrs. Auslander's attention, she is addressed as "Teacher." Not one student has called her by name yet.

To the students' requests she answers, "Nobody may leave." Nonetheless, in a moment she gives the pass to one of the children, who quickly leaves the room. When he returns, the same commotion begins anew and she hands the pass to another child. The pass is constantly in use.

Another sentence has been left on the board and the children have been told to copy it. Mrs. Auslander then shows the observer some of her children's work. She shoves a handful of papers forward and says they belong to a boy who is almost ten years old. A glance shows that the child has not even been able to begin to copy the work from the board. In a loud voice she comments, "This is the best this child can do." All those sitting in the back of the room must have overheard her, for it is obvious that several children are listening. She shows a second notebook and comments, "Now this girl, she's slow, but she writes very nicely."

There is a momentary lull in the noise. But soon the sounds of voices, shuffling feet, moving chairs, and scuffling children fill the room with a din. A boy comes back with the pass and the noise is diverted to him as others also want to leave the room. The teacher declares, "A girl goes after a boy. You know that after a boy goes, a girl goes." Mrs. Auslander is now in the back of the class. She tells the children to look at their clowns, which are clown posters made by the pupils. The balloons the clowns hold are of litmus paper and change color according to the weather. "Today the balloons are blue. This means that it is a fair and sunny day." Having answered her own question, she returns to the blackboard to write the sentence she was trying to elicit from the children: "It is sunny and warm and clear."

"Now copy that," she calls, and returns to the observer to comment, "I bought pencils for all these children when I first came here and gave each one a small pencil case with pencils in it. But all these children lost their pencils and the only way I have now of solving the pencil problem is to get them to lend pencils to each other because obviously I can't be providing pencils for them all the time."

She spies a child chewing gum. "Empty your mouth and keep it closed when it's empty." She stops and stands in front of a boy who is quietly working at his desk and tells him, "Take your jacket off. Take your jacket off. Take it off." It is a suit jacket.

The boy protests: "I don't want to take it off because I'm afraid something will happen to it."

"The other children trust you. Why shouldn't you trust them?" she retorts, and insists once again that he remove his jacket. "And hang it up. Or would you like to visit Mr. Selby?" The last remark was said with a threatening sound. (Mr. Selby is the name we have given to the principal.) The boy reluctantly gets up, goes over to the closet, takes his jacket off, hangs it up, and stomps back to his desk.

It is 10:19. Mrs. Auslander is telling Carol, a Negro girl, "Get up and stand in the corner and face the wall. Put your hands on your head." The girl obeys, standing in a corner at the back of the room, and immediately begins to cry. In a moment, she takes her hands off her head and stops crying.

A boy who has been given the pass flourishes it. As he leaves the room, he pauses at the door and salutes the class. Once he is gone, the teacher goes to the door and, taking out her key, locks the door from the inside. Some older boys are passing in the hall. They stop at the door, look into the classroom, and make faces through the window.

Mrs. Auslander is standing alongside the boy that she had earlier forced to remove his jacket. She addresses him: "Would you like to stay in Mr. Selby's office all day?" Carol is sucking her thumb in the corner. Disorder reigns.

The teacher pulls Vera, a Hispano girl, over to the observer and introduces her. She explains, "Vera is a C.R.M.D. child."[2] Mrs. Auslander waves the page Vera is working on in front of the observer, who silently notes that the work is very poor. Vera likes the idea of showing her work to the observer and no sooner is she at her seat than she picks up her entire notebook and returns with it. The idea catches on. Other children follow so that the observer soon is surrounded by six or seven children, all anxious to display their work.

Vera came first. One or two of the other children in this impromptu line become eager and attempt to push ahead of her and shove their notebooks in front of her. Vera, who is husky, pushes them back out of the way. Several small fights begin this way with Vera winning. One is lasting more than a few seconds, and the observer puts her hand on the shoulder of Vera's rival and tells her quietly, "I will look at your work but Vera is first." The children wait quietly without pushing. But now Vera is the problem, for as the observer turns the pages of her notebook, Vera turns them back to the first page. The observer explains, "I will have to look at the notebooks of the other children." Vera steps aside docilely to let the others come forward. The observer finds some of the copying work done quite well and some that is incoherent or illegible.

Allen, a Negro boy with crossed eyes, is standing in front of the observer. The observer asks him, "May I look at your book?" He nods eagerly. On the first page there is a note written by the teacher. "Allen has exposed himself in school today. He has many kinds of problems. Take this note home to your mother and have her sign it." A signature below this shows his mother has read it.

A second entry is her reply. "I beat Allen at home for having done this but Allen says he didn't do it but that another boy has done it to him." On the second page there is another note from Mrs. Auslander in ink as her first had been. "Allen did expose himself but I do not want to make an issue of it." All these notes are in the ordinary pages of Allen's class notebook, an article he carries around with him and uses daily. The observer passes quickly on to other pages for fear of embarrassing Allen, who must know what the notes are about. She tries to find a particularly nice comment as she closes his book and hands it back to him.

A group of children still surround her and begin to ask questions. She asks their names and such things as "How long have you been in this school?" All of the children who speak to her do so in English, thus showing some knowledge of it. Mrs. Auslander quickly breaks up the exchange, sending them back to their seats.

To all outward appearances, Mrs. Auslander is spending all of her time pushing the children around, frequently hurting them as she does this. At the moment she is pinching Allen on the arm; he grimaces in pain. Then she shoves him into the corner and he begins to cry. Moments later similar events befall a boy named Edward.

Suddenly Mrs. Auslander makes an attempt at teaching the concept of time. "What time is it?" she calls out. A child begins to pack up his books and arranges his briefcase, perhaps taking her cue. But she turns on him sharply: "What time do you go home? Put your books down. It's not time to go home."

She notices that Carol has left the corner and joined a group that is back lingering near the observer. "So you want me to smack you. Get back in the corner and put your hands on your head." Carol does so and starts sucking her thumb again. A girl near the observer remarked to her, "Carol is our baby because she sucks her thumb." From the front of the class Mrs. Auslander cries shrilly, "Listen, are you going to get into your seats or are you going to stay there?" The children return to their seats.

The observer turns her head to survey the room. Things seem to be getting worse. Fighting occurs frequently among the children. A child will run around the room and hit another child who will then give chase or retaliate later. Edward, who has remained only briefly in the corner to which he was sent, has been feuding with George, the boy who lent a pencil to Lucille.

The teacher pulls a child by the hair. It is short hair on a Negro boy's scalp, and he yells from the pain.

At 10:50, she makes her second concerted effort to get the class quiet by silently doing exercises, expecting them to join in. Earlier, at 10:00, she had done it for a moment with little effect. Standing in the front of the room, she has both hands on her hips. The exercises are simple ones involving placing and removing the hands on the hips while raising one leg and then the other. A few children take them up, but most remain seated with a few children still running around the room. She meets this challenge by going directly to a child's desk and standing in front of it, glaring at the child and continuing the exercise until he gets up and joins in. She says not a word. This technique finally succeeds in getting all the children up and exercising quietly for a few minutes. But as soon as the exercise period ends and the children sit down again, noise begins to fill the air.

At 10:55 Mrs. Auslander releases Carol from her place in the corner, by walking over and asking, "Are you going to do your work, Carol? I'm going to give you one more chance. If you don't do your work, you'll spend the rest of the day standing." Thus Carol went back to her seat for the second time between 10:19 and 10:55, the period she was officially disciplined, save for a few moments of grace during which she had resumed her seat. Although she was supposed to have stood with her hands on her head, she did not do so. Her hands went down to her sides whenever the teacher was not looking.

Angel, a Hispano boy, is becoming particularly obstreperous. He runs around the room and pushes some of the children, an act he has engaged in several times before. Two or three times earlier in the morning the teacher had threatened him with being sent to Mr. Selby's office. At one point she had told the observer, "This boy does not like or trust anybody. He is a problem child." At 11:00 A.M. she makes good her threat, marching out of the room saying, "I'm going to get John." As soon as she is out of the door, the noise in the room drops. Attention seems to be centered on the door. Several of the children "ooh" and "ah." One child says, "Here he comes." Mrs. Auslander enters, accompanied by a tall, slender Negro boy from an older grade. They approach Angel, the small Hispano boy, who is in his seat, clutching his desk for dear life and bawling loudly. The teacher tries to pry him loose but without success. She turns to her companion, "John, would you take him, please."

Angel is wailing louder all the time and babbles, "Leave me alone. Leave me alone." He clings to his desk but John succeeds in prying him loose and drags him screaming from the room. His screams can be heard echoing down the hall.[3]

Mrs. Auslander explains to the observer, "When I use one for an example, the rest behave. It's the only way."

The observer inquires, matter-of-factly, "Where does John take the children when he takes them out?"

"He takes them to Mr. Selby."

If that is so, the observer wonders why there has been so much screaming in the process.

It is 11:00 A.M. and another child is being put in the corner and told, "Put your hands on your head." Mrs. Auslander turns to go through some words on the board. These are part of the vocabulary appearing in the Dick and Jane Series of readers. The list numbers from fifteen to twenty words. She reads each word aloud and the children repeat it in unison. Their task is to copy the words down into their notebooks at the same time. A few do. Her reprimands are constant: "Will you please do your work?" Or again, "Why are you not writing?" To a third, "Do you want to go to Mr. Selby?"

Presently Angel reappears at the door with John on one side of him and a beefy, tough-looking Negro child on the other. They take him over to the teacher and have him apologize to her. He goes to his desk to sit, and he's quiet for at least ten or fifteen minutes.

Two or three of the boys have, of their own accord, gone back to the observer to show her their work. While she glances through their notebooks, she asks them, "Where do the big boys take the children when they take them out of the room?" "To see Mr. Selby," they say.

A cry goes up as the teacher pulls Allen by the ear over to the wastepaper basket where he must spit out his gum. She shouts at several other children, "You want me to get John? Let me see you act up once more and you'll be in trouble." She hustles another boy off to the corner to stand with his hands on his head. Ann, who was already in another corner, is now sucking her thumb.

Lining Up

At 11:50 the children are in line for lunch, which they must eat on an early shift. During the lineup two of the children are continually fighting one another. One of the children fighting has been "teacher's pet" all morning. Several times he seconded her commands to children and mimicked some of her behavior. An example of this would be when he pulled a boy's hair and told him to behave. Now two or three children are hitting him and he begins to cry.

In the midst of this bedlam, a Negro girl approaches the observer and asks her to tie her hood. She turns her face up and the observer ties a bow under her chin. While she is doing this, the teacher comes over and says, "It is ridiculous for this child to be wearing a hood on a warm day. She might get sick if she wears it." Silently the observer ties the bow and the child lines up with the others. Out in the hall, the class is not as noisy. The teacher leads them down the stairs to the cafeteria. At each landing, the class halts before descending the next flight. The noise has been sufficient to bring a man teacher out of his room to see what is going on. He reenters and closes his door with a bang. The children have started out ahead of the teacher and, as they go downstairs, she asks to pass between the two lines in order to get to the head of the class. The children separate and make a passageway for her along the double line. As she goes down the staircase, several children raise their feet as if to kick her.

The Afternoon Session

During the afternoon another person came to observe Mrs. Auslander's class. She came after the lunch period was over and the children were back in their room.

As the new observer came in the door, Mrs. Auslander greeted her, saying, "You see that child over there? She clings all the time. That's all she does, cling." She was referring to a Hispano girl who has a piece of cloth which she is rubbing up and down a steampipe at the side of the room. The new observer next notices a boy sitting in the front of the room, sucking his thumb. The teacher audibly continues her discussion of the class: "This is a class of low intelligence. They have taken all the worst children in this grade and formed this class. I'm a new teacher! What do you think of the fact that I was given a class like this? All of these children are terrible problems."

The observer sees the teacher has a lesson on the board but notes that there is a great deal of activity among the children. One boy is crawling on the floor looking for a nickel. Allen, the Negro youngster with crossed eyes, is sitting in the front of the room, but maintaining constant activity from his seat. Many of the children are hitting one another; a child will get up from his seat, go over to another child for no apparent reason and slap him in the face, or perhaps push him or strike his body before rushing back to his seat. These are all initial impressions made after the first few minutes in the classroom.

One boy, Angel, runs over to Allen, throws him on the floor, and jumps up on his back with both feet. Allen quite natrually screams and yells. The teacher screams too: "Get away from there!" She continues to scream and we learn the names of the two brawlers.

Many children are calling out and shouting to one another across the room. As the observer looks around the room, she sees many children hitting each other on the head with pencils.

Handwriting

The teacher withal is attempting her lesson. She has written the letter *G* on the board and now prints the word goat. Chalk in hand, she turns from the word directly to a child: "Where is your book? Get to work! Why don't you write?" Her face is severe and threatening. Chalk still in hand, she sends a boy to stand in the corner, where he remains for some time before she releases him.

A crack is heard. A child has hit another student and thrown his books on the floor. The teacher ignores this incident, as she does most of its kind. The child directly in front of the observer is striking the child next to him with his pencil, so much so that the observer fears for his eyes. But the teacher takes no notice; she is telling the boy in the corner to put his hands on his head. Allen, who is in the front of the room, is constantly dancing away from the teacher in a boxing step whenever she approaches as if to dodge her. He seems to be engaging in a mock boxing dance but she is not striking him. However, children are, for he seems to be a target for the rest of the class. Yet, he does nothing to resist or protest the constant barrage of attacks he is under; he just dances away from the teacher. The observer spies Edward hitting another boy over the head with a book. At one point or another as many as ten of the eighteen pupils are out of their seats. Some of the children are chasing each other. At times the teacher darts forward to quiet students. One method is to pull a child up by his ear. She does this twice, once to a Negro boy and once to a Hispano boy. Each cries out, and then obeys her momentarily. The ear-pulling is accompanied by the threat, "All right, if you won't be quiet, I will go get John."

Presently Mrs. Auslander leaves the room. Shortly, she is back with John. She stations him at the front of the room where he stands quietly and says, "If you children get bad, you must go to Mr. Selby."

Science

With John watching from the front, the teacher turns her attention to teaching, saying, "The class is going to have a science lesson. I want to show you a good way to pour water." She presents them the idea of a funnel. Her demonstration actually awakes some interest in the children. But, to her annoyance, they are soon shouting answers to her.

Her face and stance grim and tense with annoyance, the teacher takes a piece of paper and dips it into water, asking the children, "Why does water go up in the paper?" The children are listening but have no answer. She answers, "The reason that water goes up is that there are tiny holes in the paper." A number of children are out of their seats to gather around the teacher as she conducts this experiment.

She is saying, "We are going to learn some of the facts about water." John, at this point, is trying to make the children return to their seats. Sometimes he grabs a child and pushes him down into his seat. The boy in the corner begins to move away from there. The teacher calls out sharply, "Get back into that corner quickly." She darts forward and pulls him back by his ear.

Leaving the corner, the teacher passes by the observer and says, "You see what I have to put up with. These children's parents have given me permission to beat them because they do not know what to do with them in order to get them to listen. You see that child there? There is no one at home to talk to her." While she is saying this, Edward, a Hispano youngster (who had been in the corner in the morning), is constantly striking George, a Negro youngster (who had lent his pencil to Lucille).

A child in the front of the room raises his hand to ask to leave the room, but is ignored. Edward is now going around hitting other children; however, each time he hits George, Robert arises and hits him, defending George. The teacher explains to the observer, "Edward really thinks he is helping me. That's why he is hitting other children." Another frequent target for Edward's barrage is Allen.

The teacher points out a boy, Frankie, and says in a normal speaking voice, "His father killed his mother. The boy stays with an aunt and thirteen children. The home background of most of these children is simply terrible. They are all emotionally disturbed. They are really problems. They don't understand normal psychology. They only know brute force."

At this point the observer got up, excused herself, and left hastily. She had been in the room one hour exactly. . . .

Discussion and Comment

Having probably read the foregoing discussion with a sense of mounting shock, one would possibly agree that Mrs. Auslander herself is in a state of culture shock. The way she attends to the lessons, putting written work on the board in the midst of all this bedlam, is reminiscent of the disaster victims who do trivial things such as sweeping off the steps of a flattened house. An anthropologist would also say, on first impression, that she has withdrawn from the children and is living in her own world, meeting the pupils only in terms of punishment.

It must be remembered that it was Mrs. Auslander herself who defined this class as a discipline class. She went further and defined "discipline class," saying it consists of emotionally disturbed and mentally retarded pupils. The term *discipline class* is her own coinage and not official usage. However, the principal had also referred to her class as a wild one, and the assistant principal spoke of it as being one of several "jungle classes." Other teachers in casual conversations with our observers called it a "zoo" or "mental institution." It is to be noted that everybody but Mrs. Auslander refers to the class in terms of wildness, of nondiscipline, while only she is speaking of discipline. The class's reputation is something it has undoubtedly earned during the school year. Already one teacher was seen coming out of his class to investigate what the noise was when this class was out in the hall. Mrs. Auslander herself does not hesitate in reporting and complaining about conditions. She sends some of her pupils to the principal and other times relies on Mr. Levy, the neighboring male teacher, for one or two of his bigger boys to come as impromptu discipline monitors to her class. There is no question then of this class's notoriety.

But the point to be made is that the class just seen is not exactly the same class that Mrs. Auslander confronted at the start. She was given not a "discipline class" nor a "wild class." These terms have developed after she arrived. She was given a difficult class, indisputedly. It is a small class; on the day observed, all this havoc was the work of only eighteen pupils.

Consider how the class was formed. The principal, who formed it, said it consists of non-English-speakers and the "seriously disturbed." Non-English speakers seem to be the majority of students for there are only five Negroes in the class and the rest are Hispanos. The seriously disturbed are those pupils who have come to the unfavorable attention of the school authorities in one way or another. If they are frequently sent to the principal's office for discipline, and complaints are heard often enough about them in supervisory offices, a "record" is started on them. This is a dossier kept in the principal's office which contains anecdotal records by teachers about the behavior of these children. Thus Angel, the small boy dragged from the room by John, has quite a thick record. These are children who, in the first grade, have distinguished themselves unfavorably in behavioral, not academic, terms so that they have been removed from the better classes. To this class were added children with a faulty command of English, their only logical connection with the others being that they too are more difficult to teach than ordinary children. This, then, ought to be one of the most challenging classes in the school; but who has been recruited to teach it?

Although Mrs. Auslander is somewhere near her fiftieth year, and has a grown daughter, she is in the midst of her first year of teaching. She graduated from a local college many years ago and sometime since then had picked up twelve hours of education courses. It is to be remembered that the principal had to recruit an entire staff and as opening day drew near he became "desperate." Mrs. Auslander is not yet licensed or certified. She is a marginal member of her profession and, as such, is getting the least desirable job. It is only natural that a principal would want to reward long-term, capable teachers with good classes. And a principal in this situation would have to offer such classes in order to attract teachers to his school. Mrs. Auslander, his last resort, has had no experience in handling children, and as an older woman would be less likely to be flexible in meeting unexpected problems and less able to withstand the physical wear and tear of strenuous experiences.

The class just seen is *not* the same class that Mrs. Auslander met on her first day. The shock that she is under is not exactly the same shock the reader has just experienced. A number of beginning teachers have told us about their experiences on their first day of teaching. First days are formal affairs. The children come freshly scrubbed and dressed in their best clothes. They are quiet and nervous, and concentrate on the teacher and generally obey her. This is not to say that the first day is without shocks. But they are of a different nature. Thus one teacher was amazed to be unable to elicit any information about special "summertime activities" among her pupils. They did not go to camps or go on vacations or do any of the special things middle-class people associate with summertime. Another girl, eager for her first day of teaching, had prepared a very careful lesson plan, but had to throw it out when she discovered that her charges were reading two years behind grade level. Shocks of this order were in store for Mrs. Auslander on that first day: to find that her charges were not yet reading, and in the second grade to find that many of them were not articulate in English, while others were extremely articulate in drawing attention to themselves, away from her. It is probably this order of shocks that made Mrs. Auslander decide, very early no doubt, that she had a "discipline class." Add to this her anger on the realization that she had the worst class in the grade. Note she is still angry; among her first words said indignantly to the afternoon observer were, "I'm a new teacher. What do you think of the fact that I was given a class like this?"

Imagine what things Mrs. Auslander might have done to cope with this class once she realized that she was going to be assigned it. Since it is the worst class in the grade, she would be quite justified in demanding special consideration from the school authorities. She might have pressured the principle to have siphoned off at least one or two of the worst troublemakers. What's more, this school is richly endowed in specialists. There is a teacher trainer whose aid in particular she might have enlisted. The guidance counselor is responsible for help with the "seriously disturbed" children and the remedial reading teacher also has something to offer a second-grade class that cannot yet read.

But the teacher trainer has said that Mrs. Auslander is not interested in her suggestions; the guidance counselor mentioned that Mrs. Auslander has not referred a single student to her for help. If the reading teacher has been called upon, it is not evident. Yet Mrs. Auslander has sought help from others in the school. How? Her neighbor, Mr. Levy, provides his bigger boys to help with discipline. The principal and one assistant principal regularly receive pupils sent by Mrs. Auslander for discipline. Mrs. Auslander wants help only for discipline. Reading, guidance, teacher training do not seem to interest her.

Since she has defined this as a discipline class, it is necessary to consider the entire problem of social control, or put another way, obedience to orders. This subject has been the object of much sociological inquiry; and, according to the eminent sociologist George Homans,[4] if Mrs. Auslander were controlling her class, she and they would be complying with norms. The norms in this case are most obviously, those of teaching and learning certain amounts of knowledge. And like work norms, these are very well defined in our society. Teachable knowledge is measured in terms of the amount of time within which it is expected to be learned. These norms are national ones and although they are made explicit and formal in law and school system regulations, they are very much like the informal, implicit norms that Homans shows are common to every human group, however small. That is, they are built up over a period of time from the interactions and sentiments of many persons. In this case the process is extremely complex, reflecting the demands of parents, colleges, and the diverse willingness of students to learn. Nonetheless something like a national consensus or norm has been established, commonly indicated by achievement on nationally standardized tests.

It is a marked feature of urban school systems that the bulk of their students (with some remarkable exceptions) some well below the national standards, far enough below to be measured in terms of large amounts of time: six months, one year, two years, etc.

However, sociological analysis shows that norms are rarely complied with exactly anywhere. Some people fall short; others surpass. The important thing is that most people reach a stable level below or above the "normal" goal, and remain there. Thus most teachers will accept a low level of performance if it is steady and if learning progress is made at a rate proportional to the level already demonstrated. Since this process, like industrial work norms, is quite explicit, it is made very obvious to children. They must "get through the grade," "pass tests," "learn their lessons," and so on. The teacher must let them know that there is a norm. Yet Mrs. Auslander, who is so concerned with discipline, has hardly begun to do this.

In both sociological and popular usage the word "norm" has two seemingly opposed meanings, which, however, are in this discussion the same, for it is dealing with the two concepts when they are still one. The first usage is statistical, referring to the items of behavior which are common or average, when they are all counted up, and are therefore "normal." The second usage is evaluative or judgmental and refers to that behavior which is sanctioned, that is, rewarded or punished. It is Homans' contention that the statistical meaning comes first. Once a certain item of behavior—for example, the production of a certain amount of work in a day by a factory worker—is common enough to be average, then people become aware of it. They accept it and reward its presence and punish its absence. It is no longer merely "normal," but is also the norm.

To follow Homans further, his idea of social control is simply that the term "social control" is but another way of saying that leaders and followers fulfill conscious norms or goals. They do so willingly because such behavior is simply the standardization of behavior that grew naturally within certain social situations. That is, when Homans analyzes social control in various small groups, he discovers that it is not anything added. It is nothing separate in itself that can be defined as control. Rather it is just a special way of looking at the ongoing and successful life of any human group. It is all the processes that people have set for themsevles to keep them toeing the line. This may be surprising to anyone who is used to thinking of authority as a thing in itself, usually applied from above, and expressed most clearly in punishment. It might be argued that what Homans is saying applies to small groups, but has nothing to do with impersonal school systems. It is true that school systems are imposed by the constituted authority of a society. It is further true that in urban schools this constituted authority is likely to be very distant from the working- and lower-class population that the schools serve. But nonetheless the classroom is a small group, and if it is going to work successfully, it is reasonable to assume that it will do so as small groups do everywhere. Therefore, it can be stated that pupils are not going to obey authority, or in other words, comply with norms, unless they want to.

Punishment, like authority, is not a thing in itself. It is merely the negative side of the forces that keep people complying with their norms. The positive side is the reward. Indeed, as Homans points out, punishment may bring further distance from the norm, for the victim now adds resentment to whatever forces induced him to fall short to begin with. Homans concludes that punishments have mainly a ritual value: to dramatize the norm, to vindicate those who comply with it and to warn them against deviance. Punishments are for the benefit of decent people, not criminals. Moreover, they seldom fit the crime, usually being far in excess of the magnitude of the offense. Thus they serve as a warning.

Therefore, it might be asked again why Mrs. Auslander considers her group a discipline class. Perhaps, in terms of the whole school, she thinks these children are being punished for being "the worst children in this grade," the children who have been expelled from the other classes. Perhaps in this sense she does consider her class a threat, a warning to all the other pupils and a ritual affirmation of those pupils who are decent enough to comply with the norms and learn their lessons.

In short, Mrs. Auslander has given up any attempt at communicating the standard, official norms of the school system, i.e., lesson content or learning achievements, but she has somehow decided that her duty, or work norm, is punishment. This decision in the statistical sense of the word, is, to say the least, abnormal.

But even so, Mrs. Auslander's concept of a discipline class does not explain the exact conduct of the class. To understand that, it is necessary to know something of what sociologists have to say about good manners. One sociologist, Erving Goffman, having worked in insane asylums where rules of conduct are commonly broken and therefore made more obvious, has written enough about them to give the best analysis of them.[5] Since good manners are so conspicuously absent here in this class, it might first be asked what they are. It would seem that they are not a one-way affair, as they would be if one is thinking simply in terms of a quiet, well-ordered class. Rather they may be analyzed in complementary terms, deference and demeanor, which apply equally to all actors in any situation.

Deference is "the appreciation an individual shows another to that other," while demeanor is that element of an individuals "polite" or "ceremonial" behavior typically seen in his dress, deportment, and bearing, which sets him up to those in his presence as a person having desirable qualities and being worthy of respect. Good demeanor is necessary to establish basic trust in any relationship, however casual: it is that poise of another person that assures a person he will not be in danger by interacting with the other.[6] These terms can further be expressed in terms of mental images. That is, demeanor is the image of himself the individual owes it to others to maintain through his conduct while deference is the image of the individual that others are obliged to express to him in their conduct.[7]

Now, while rules of deference may be asymmetrical and a superordinate person may have rights to certain familiarities or invasions of the metaphorical boundary around the self that the subordinate cannot reciprocate, yet the superordinate still must respect the subordinate and not press too far. Thus, while it may be expected that teachers have the right to touch pupils, particularly in a friendly manner, it would not be expected that the same right be freely exercised by pupils. Nor would teachers be expected to go too far—for example, to accompany the boys to the bathroom to insure good behavior, something observed by the project members in an urban school.

This has been a very sketchy presentation of deference and demeanor, and the article itself is recommended for anybody who might be planning to teach in urban schools. The behavior in the classroom may now be examined in terms of deference. It should be remembered that the teacher, although superordinate, still owes deference to her subordinates.

The first kind of deference can be termed avoidance rituals, "those forms of deference which lead the actor to keep at a distance from the recipient and not to violate the 'ideal sphere' that lies around the recipient.[8] It was noted that the teacher often said detrimental things about the students aloud, in their presence to the observer. She also wrote a personal and shameful note in a pupil's notebook, hardly a private or a discreet place. (In the better ward of Goffman's insane asylum, an important rule was never to refer to past shameful conduct or difficulties in public.)

Presentational rituals are "acts through which the individual makes specific attestations to recipients concerning how he regards them and how he will beat them in the on-coming interaction.[9] "Avoidance rituals specify what is not to be done; presentational rituals specify what is to be done.[10] These include salutations, compliments, invitations, and minor services. There is a singular lack of all of these in the classroom just observed. There is one compliment: "What a nice boy you are," to George, but the teacher takes it back later: "George *could* be a very good boy." There are no salutations. No minor services save once in the distant past— the distribution of pencils by the teacher. Perhaps the children are saying something to her by making the pencil supply one of her major problems, and by using pencils as one of their favorite weapons. Touch, which can be commonly understood as a friendly salutation, when effected in proper ways, is in this class neither avoided, nor presented in a deferential way. Touch here is always an invasion, and usually inflicts pain; the teacher hits, twists ears, pulls children by the ears, pulls hair, and pinches.

The demeanor of the teacher should be considered, in order to see how she has established herself as a person to whom deference is owed. It is doubtful that she has. It is apparent that an image of her as an individual did not come through very sharply in the observation. In the course of the entire day a child was heard to address her by her name only once. The rest of the time she was simply "teacher." She has tried to establish certain rules through which communication may take place between her and the students, but they are ineffective. For instance, she wants them to sit with folded hands, quietly, and then she will listen to what they have to say. But this never happens; therefore she never listens. The children are also to give answers to her questions by raising their hands; since they seldom do, but rather shout out, she seldom acknowledges their answers. The observers say she seems worried and harassed, and when she does begin a lesson about science, she shows annoyance when the students shout their answers. In conclusion, this teacher has utterly failed to establish a demeanor that itself can command deference from the children.

This being so, it is a miracle that the children are not actively aggressive toward the teacher. It is significant that they are not. They are not violating her sacred self in the same way that she violates theirs. The closest they come is by performing what Goffman calls a "ceremonial profanation," which is "the practice of defiling the recipient but in such a way and from such an angle that he retains the right to act as if he had not received the profaning message."[11] Thus, when Mrs. Auslander passes through the double file of children in the hall, many of them ceremonially pretend to kick her behind her back.

It is now possible to assess the behavior of the children themselves. This is not spontaneous "wildness." If these children were left to themselves to play in a custodial area, without Mrs. Auslander, and without the history of the year in this class, it is extremely unlikely that they would behave as they do. Children do not normally run around and hit each other without a reason. Yet this is the most typical item of behavior in the classroom. The only possible conclusion is that the children are imitating Mrs. Auslander. One child in fact does so quite consciously, hitting the children that she has reprimanded. A psychologist would say that they are displacing their hostilities onto each other.

In sum, it can be concluded that what has happened here is that, after her initial shock from the first days, Mrs. Auslander has defined her class as a "discipline class," not a "problem class" or even a "custodial" one. These other definitions might have led to different behavior on her part. As it is, her behavior is entirely positive. She seems to feel that she is here to punish and that is what she does. In effect she has declared war on these children, and they, quite naturally, behave like infant warriors. But they are defensive warriors, they are not fighting back. When Allen does his boxing dance step every time Mrs. Auslander approaches him, he is not offending her but defending himself. He is marking very clearly and quite explicitly the boundaries of his "ideal self" which he expects, quite reasonably, that she is going to invade. Whatever her initial difficulties might have been, and they were probably great and vexing, it is unbelievable that they would necessarily have led to the results that have just been seen. In conclusion it can only be said that social control is not affected by mass punishment, nor are good manners taught by declaring war. . . .

This discussion has given the reader some initiation into the mysteries of urban schoolrooms. It is hoped that it has also given the new teacher the strength to meet the culture shock awaiting any newcomer to these classrooms. Our concept of strength is not that of the rigid fortress, but rather that of the human muscle. Well-conditioned muscles have four distinct and measurable qualities. They can produce force; that is their strength. They can store energy—their muscular endurance. They can shorten—their speed of contraction. They can stretch and recoil—their elasticity. These are all qualities that can grow and improve with use. This conclusion will review both the guideposts which are considered most helpful to the teacher, and the discussions on the observations. Then, finally, two types of persons will be discussed as possible models for the task that awaits new teachers: the anthropologist working with native informants in a strange culture, and the revitalization prophet who converts and changes native peoples.

Newcomers are bound to receive some sort of initiation on entering any urban school system. By this advance initiation any damaging effects of the real one may be obviated, while preparing the teacher to benefit from the new experience. The new teacher must expect to begin with one of the poorer classes. Teachers with training completed and licenses will be less likely to have the most difficult classes. Such teachers must expect to meet their first classes in the midst of the assembly and other standardized routines of the school system. But if they are successful, they will have the satisfaction at the end of the year of being treated by teachers and supervisors as those who have proved themselves and who belong. But, forewarned by this book, it is hoped that they will never interpet "belonging" to mean a timorous dependence upon supervision and routines.

Now to consider strength against culture shock. On the one hand, newcomers will be initiated into a new formal system, the school, with its own norms and personalities in charge. They will be unused to the demands of formal organization except for those they have experienced in a different role, as students. However, supervisors and colleagues alike will share their middle-class culture. On the other hand, the pupils and their neighborhood will share no such thing. Newcomers will be not unlike Americans who go to outposts in unknown countries. Yet it would be incorrect to think of them as missionaries; they cannot "save souls." They can only help to develop people more fully.

The comparison to an outpost is apt, for it is easy to see the many qualities these schools share with fortresses; locked doors and gates, hall patrols, persons marching from point to point. Yet the simile is incomplete and misleading, for schools lack the resources to totally convert their clients into that image. The schools are not total institutions, as, for example, our insane asylums are. They can only succeed by winning the consent of their clients, something which in the last analysis is true even of total institutions. Consent is most easily obtained when persons are approached in their own terms.

One might argue that in the earlier days the school system succeeded in transforming whole generations of immigrants into Americans and that it did so by never considering their native heritage but by ignoring it. This is not so. Rich European heritages still survive in all our ethnic communities today, no matter how American they consider themselves and are considered. Moreover, many of them were never wholly converted to middle-class values, but remain resolutely working class.

Furthermore, today's urban migrants, as shown here, are almost entirely Negroes and Hispanos. These are two groups that are still very close to their ethnic roots. Modern transportation allows Hispanos to return constantly to their homeland and their peasant villages. A history of low-caste status and high visibility due to their race render Negroes different from any other ethnic group in this country. Long years of facing limited opportunity, even for the educated, have caused many Negroes to question the worth of schooling. For both these groups, the simple presentation of American and middle-class values will not be sufficient.

Yet the culture shock of meeting these two groups can be a great aid to a newcomer. It can jolt him out of the theory of Fortress America which some teachers have been shocked into offering as an interpretation of the school system. It can make him search out for himself the realities of the students' life, and from this knowledge prepare a synthesis of their lives and his.

These, then, are some of the guideposts for the newcomers. First they must learn how to assess the school's neighborhood accurately. They have learned not to expect exceptional modern architecture in an urban school; but they can sometimes expect a functional, clean plant, whose extent of modern improvement depends upon the interest of the city government in the school and the area and reflects the power or powerlessness of the local community.

The urban school attempts to segregate children by ability and by classroom behavior, and this segregation starts very early, in the first grade, within a class, and in the second grade class-by-class. The system shuffles children up and down in a rank series, and it is the job of the teacher to push the child as far up as possible.

Infant scene-stealers and precocious rascals exist from the first grade in any class. New teachers must expect such children, and must learn to cope with them without such doubtful aids as attempts to categorize these children as "seriously disturbed." Such categorization seems to rationalize the school's failure to control and direct these children's energies. No one appears to have attempted to control this categorization by seeking well-behaved children with equally disturbed backgrounds.

A new teacher must know that there will be great emphasis on the movement of children through halls under his supervision, and equally great emphasis on daily routines of attendance checking, and on such rituals as opening exercises and weekly assemblies. These activities should not be overemphasized to the detriment of teaching. New teachers should, however, seek ways of utilizing these activities for the benefit of teaching.

Discipline, as this book has tried to make clear by negative examples, is not the same as social control. Discipline per se is not to be glorified or worshiped, but is to be used sparingly, and then largely for ritual effect. Pupils, though of tender years, are human beings with an ideal sphere of dignity around their persons. Even though they are not yet adults, nor perhaps of the same social class, they still deserve deference and courtesy, and they have a right to their privacy. The teacher also must establish a demeanor showing himself as certain to give deference and worthy of receiving it.

Many specialties exist to help teachers and students, and one of the most conspicuous of these is the guidance program. It can be seen as a convenient specialization of supervisory functions: someone has been delegated to take over the testing job. Yet the guidance counselor can also be seen as someone who is, at least potentially, an advocate or spokesman for the child's quasi-political interests.

Successful teaching centers upon the material being taught, while the successful teacher's use of discipline is entirely unapparent. A good teacher can be recognized, respected, and rewarded in the school system by both supervisors and pupils.

A pupil's ethnic background, far from implying a vacuum or emptiness in his previous or nonschool experiences, may indicate a wealth of resources which the teacher might know and draw upon. In many, perhaps most, classrooms the teacher's job ceases to be that of presenting standardized lessons prescribed by the administration in order to fulfill national teaching norms; the problem becomes one of urging the pupils to catch up with these national norms. The pupils can only start this if they want to and are encouraged to want to themselves.

While class control must be unobtrusive, teaching style can vary widely, and the two models that follow may help by suggesting ways to find the style and method that suit individual teachers and their students.

The suggestion of a model does not mean that teachers must "become" some other sort of person. But since the teacher's role is so diverse and uncertain, so dependent upon the situation in relation to pupils and supervisors, other types of persons may hold useful hints for successful classroom behavior.

It is impossible to define the teacher's role in any one way. Many young people enter urban teaching with the ideal of the social worker in mind. The social worker, it seems to them, is the person who is accomplishing much in urban surroundings. But the school provides an easier way of doing the same good work. This ideal is commendable for its compassion; but the social worker is on the whole an inappropriate model for urban teachers. The urban teacher is not there to "cure." He is there to impart knowledge and show the children another world than that of their family, to prepare them for an independent life in modern society. At their best teachers do not solve family problems, nor redress wide social evils, but teach their pupils how to teach themselves. Therapeutic functions are more properly the province of the guidance counselor, who may well have contacts with social workers.

But nonetheless this proper province of the teacher, guiding and inspiring minds to learn within the classroom, is diverse enough to encompass many approaches. Here are two avenues of search for a classroom style.

"Revitalization prophets" are persons anthropologists have come upon throughout the world. Only recently have they been grouped together and given this name. They are initiators of sudden, total changes of the cultural patterns of their own peoples. Classically, the phenomenon was first apparent in North America. Since then it has become very prominent in the South Pacific, and today sophisticated anthropologists are finding it in all the "developing areas."[12] Such leaders arise after long periods of great shock; classically, the shock has been caused by Western domination and the consequent destruction of traditional ways of life. These leaders are persons of great creativity who take elements of their own culture and combine them with Western elements to create a "revitalization code." This code seeks to reform the existing state of affairs completely. Although it often draws on old values, it completely rejects them as they previously stood. The content of such movements varies enormously around the world. Sometimes their net result is disillusioning and negative, preparing the way for yet another revitalization prophet. Thus the Tupi-namba Indians of Brazil are seen setting off on a messianic quest for an earthly paradise in the sixteenth century. Our Plains Indians went into months of frenzied dancing during the ghost dance revivals of the 1880s, which they believed would recall their ancestors to drive out the white man by supernatural means and restore to them their primordial paradise. In other times the "revitalization code," no matter how strange its mythic structure may seem to us, succeeds in imposing a Western, even middle-class value structure upon native peoples. Notable examples of such movements are one led by Handsome Lake among the Seneca Indians of New York State during the late eighteenth century,[13] and another led by Paliau among the Manus of the Admiralty Islands in the 1950s.[14]

Whatever the effect of a single revitalization prophet, taken as a group it is seen they do conform to behavioral and personality types. The name "prophet" is apt. They often present their code after some hallucinatory experience or other traumatic episode. They make great use of ceremonies and rituals, religious or secular, to effect conversions. They have personal, perhaps innate, qualities of great magnetism. By the force of their voice and bodily movement, they can keep great crowds at attention for hours, often arousing them to the well-known excesses of crowd behavior that all mammals are capable of, but that are here necessary in order to achieve hysterical conversions, the most rapid and sometimes the most lasting ones. In short, they have that quality of personal grace that Max Weber has called "charisma." That is, in person as well as through their preachings, they can inspire worship in their followers.

Now, all teachers should not become charismatic prophets or "inspirational" teachers. It is simply that if a school system consciously desires to achieve far-reaching changes in its pupils' ways of life, it also ought to be aware of the social type that has been most effective in achieving such changes. The schools that have just been observed would not take kindly to the more hysterical properties of prophets, even though they afford very fine occasions, as in the assembly, for these properties to be displayed. The example was merely used to suggest that teachers might find it useful to follow further this idea of the prophet as an image of a successful cultural innovator.

The other model proposed is the anthropologist. Anthropologists and school-teachers share one obvious feature in common; to remain professionally effective, they must both continue to learn throughout their adult life. As the tempo of change in modern America quickens, it is clear that all our professionals must learn how to meet new situations. Who can say that in twenty years urban schools will look anything like those shown here?

But the model of the anthropologist is more specifically important to the school-teacher. The teacher need not, of course, acquire the entire body of specialized knowledge that an anthropologist must take years to master. However, there are certain tools of their trade that an urban teacher could use. Anthropologists enter strange cultures with very few preconceptions. First they are taught that they must respect, and if possible, like their new acquaintances. Beyond that there are few rules. Although most anthropologists have some idea of problems they are interested in, they must be ready to abandon them if something more important or more germane to the lives of their people turns up. They know that they can never know beforehand what they may find, and they must be willing to learn from their new acquaintances.

An anthropologist's guidepost for presenting himself and getting information is equally simple. He must present himself for what he is: a student of the ways of others. He also knows that he must accept his own strangeness to his informants, and if he ignores that, they will too. Watchers become exceedingly aware of anything of which one is self-conscious, and it has been seen that the teachers who are most self-conscious about discipline are those that are least successful with social control.

Lastly, an anthropologist also knows that his best informants will also be his friends, with whom there is a real bond. Such ties of friendship do not always come at once, but they always come in the end.[15] Observation and participation are inseparable and, in fact, participation often enhances the value of the new information.

It is hoped that this book has provided the teacher with some helpful guideposts for a lifelong process of what must be first learning before it can be teaching. This, the public, too, must understand if it is to support the schools and teaching profession intelligently. All the parents of whatever background who enroll their children in urban schools face an equally difficult task. Still it is the child and his teacher, not the parent, who will spend five hours or more daily in the confines just explored here. The parent needs guideposts as he watches his child embark on a course, partly charted here, which must seem strange and perilous. Parent and teacher both must be constantly learning afresh in our changing world. Both must learn new knowledge as the subject matter of all the traditional disciplines is broadened by constant research. But both must learn too of the new social situations that face us in the urban classroom. This book is only a partial introduction. The new teacher will have to learn from his pupils in order to teach them. That much is clear. The teacher will also have to learn to present the fruits of his teaching to his superiors in such a way that they will recognize them. But the teacher must seek his own rewards: the right to continue teaching in the way his students show to be best suited for them.[16]

NOTES

1. In this school system this is a standard heading which teachers must teach children to use for written work.
2. C.R.M.D. is an abbreviation for Children with Retarded Mental Development.

3. An observer in another classroom heard the commotion which the teacher in that class tried to shut out by closing the door while she commented, "Tears, tears, and more tears."

4. George C. Homans, *The Human Group* (New York: Harcourt, Brace, 1950), chap. 11, "Social Control," pp. 281-312.

5. Erving Goffman, "The Nature of Deference and Demeanor," *American Anthropologist* 58 (June 1956): 473-502.

6. Ibid., p. 489.

7. Ibid., p. 492.

8. Ibid., p. 481.

9. Ibid., p. 485.

10. Ibid.

11. Ibid., p. 495.

12. Anthony Wallace, *Culture and Personality* (New York: Random House, 1961), "Revitalization Processes," pp. 143-56.

13. Anthony F. C. Wallace, "Handsome Lake and the Great Revival in the West," *American Quarterly*, Summer 1952, pp. 149-65.

14. Margaret Mead, *New Lives for Old: Cultural Transformation, Manus*, 1928-1953 (New York: William Morrow 1956). See also Theodore Schwartz, *The Paliau Movement of the Admiralty Islands*, 1946-54 (Anthropological Papers of the American Museum of Natural History, Vol. 49, Part 2, New York. The American Museum of Natural History, 1962), pp. 211-421.

15. See Karl Menninger's "Love Against Hate," quoted on pp. 57-60 in Marjorie B. Smiley and John Dickhoff, eds., *Prologue to Teaching* (New York: Oxford University Press, 1959), for a discussion of the importance of teacher's love in the classroom. For a discussion of the anthropologist's relationship with those in a foreign culture, see Elenore S. Bowen, *Return to Laughter* (New York: Harper Brothers, 1954; also N36, Garden City, N.Y.: Natural History Library, Anchor Books, 1964).

16. For the question of gaining independence and recognition from supervisors, see Fred E. Katz, "The School is a Complex Social Organization: A Consideration of Patterns of Autonomy," *Harvard Educational Review* 34, no. 3 (Summer 1954): 428-55. For a teaching career successful in our terms, see Sylvia Ashton-Warner, *Teacher* (New York: Simon & Schuster, 1963).

Part IV

Culture, Education, and the Individual

18 / The Transmission of Culture

Solon T. Kimball

If there is any aspect of human knowledge which is uniquely distinctive of education, and which can be claimed as the major prerogative of professional educators, it is to be found in the conditions and processes associated with the transmission of culture.

Ordinarily when we speak of education we have in mind the formally organized enterprise through which the teaching of subject matter and skills is accomplished. Presumably the purpose of this activity is to prepare the young to take their place in the society of adults. But the achievement of physical maturity, the acquisition of knowledge and skills, the development of moral judgment, and the learning of patterns of acceptable behavior are not restricted to the period of institutionalized and formal instruction. Infancy and early childhood furnish crucial experiences for the formation of the emotional and cognitive patterns that the individual will carry into later life. In fact we can hardly expect to understand the consequences of directed teaching unless we know the personal and cultural antecedents which the child brings with him into the classroom.

We are very far from knowing what can and must be known about these early years, in part, because we have not known how to proceed. Study of the psychological aspects of child development has been helpful, but much of our energy has been directed toward accumulating those static data which tests and measurements render. This is not the stuff which reveals to us the intricate interdependencies between individual and environment. They do not lend themselves to a statement of the processes which explain growth and change. Furthermore, those who are wedded to their use are trapped in an intellectual procedure which seeks orderliness through the categorization of the atomistic bits and pieces which they have gathered. There is the temptation to label the results obtained as nonsense since the reality they portray is not that of the world they examine but of the operations which they represent.

Before we attempt to specify the ingredients necessary for a more rewarding approach to this problem, let us make certain that the objective toward which we are moving is clearly understood. If it is our concern to isolate that which is unique to education then we must extend our perspective to include more than is contained within the limits of formal education. In particular we must view formal education as a special aspect of the socialization of the individual. Furthermore, we cannot say that subject matter, or that any one subject, exemplifies that to which we should pay special attention because knowledge is not in itself inherently related to the manner in which it is learned. We can similarly climinate the acquisition of skills as the main point of emphasis, for although skills can be taught, and their acquisition implies learning, these are only part of what the individual acquires in his movement toward adulthood. In essence, what we have been rejecting is a concern with the *consequences* of learning, the results of influences, direct and indirect, which shape the individual in his progression from birth onward. Instead, what we propose is that that which is unique to education is knowledge of the conditions which affect the transmission of culture.

When we come to enumerate what should be subsumed within this area we must include the relationship between teacher and learner; the cultural tradition and social environment within which learning occurs; the organic and psychic capacities of the individual to be modified through experience; and the dynamics of the learning process itself. Although we must examine each of these aspects in some detail we can clarify and place in better perspective the ensuing discussion if at this moment we make brief reference to current learning theory.

The individual has been the focus of almost all of those who have been concerned with learning. This bias is understandable if we view it as stemming from a major theme of Western culture. It is exemplified by the attention given to the great and little in religion, history, and literature and to our interest in explaining their behavior. Traditionally, we have turned to such inner qualities as spirit, wisdom, character, or ambition to give us the key to the forces which have shaped their lives. These explanations are usually of two kinds. On the one hand, they seek a source of external energy such as God or Society for the locus of inspiration, and, on the other, they have turned to an innate force such as the instincts which create a property acquiring economic man as postulated by Adam Smith or the libido-driven patients and disciples of Freud.

In some cultures men are moved by acquisitive desires or by the need for love; but as explanations of pan-human behavior, these suffer from many inadequacies. Some portion of our willingness to accept such schemes can be attributed to our too easy acceptance of motivation as explanatory of the direction which individual human behavior seemingly exhibits. In fact, we would be wiser to treat motivation as a psychological artifact than as a basic human variable. We might with equal cogency argue for the primacy of "guilt" or of "anxiety" or of "fear." These are terms which refer to recognizable emotional states, but we should not confuse the stimuli which evoke behavior and the behavior itself. Which is the motivant?

Those who seek for inner-state explanations of behavior implicitly assume a concreteness in the subject of their inquiry. If something can be treated as an entity, then its qualities or attributes can be made explicit through dissection; and presumably the mechanisms which control its functioning can be made explicit. Unfortunately for those who follow this course, neigher "spirits" nor "instinct" nor "id" nor any of the other postulations lend themselves to the kind of examination applied to substances. My objection, however, does not deny that under certain circumstances it is useful to speak of the needs of the organism, or that the designation of emotional states may have utility, or that cerebration is necessary for comprehension and insight. My objection is of a more fundamental kind. It is that the focus upon the individual has led to an inadequate statement of the problem and that, in consequence, the results of analysis have given us only partial, if not inadequate, answers.

In their search for the mechanisms which explain human behavior and learning, the psychological empiricists have made a great contribution in dispelling some of the metaphysical confusions. If we start with the simple pleasure-pain formulation offered by Jeremy Bentham over a century and a half ago, we can trace to the present the genetic links of a long intellectual and theoretical tradition. Its basic formulation is of utmost simplicity, the famous stimulus-cue-response. The focus is clearly upon the individual, but in its pure form it dispels any necessity to rely upon an ineffable "force," and it takes account of variables external to the individual. Among those we associate with advances in this field are Pavlov, Thorndike, Watson, and Skinner. But pleasure-pain, conditioned reflex, tension reduction, need-fulfillment, or reinforcement are still variations within the more general stimulus-response theory and the question at hand is whether or not this theory is sufficiently inclusive to cover the range of empirical evidence with which we must contend.

The problem is an intricate and difficult one because if its solution depends upon unraveling the intricacies of the human neural system, it is far from certain that we can ever arrive at anything more than an approximate solution. The less complex brains and sensory apparatuses of dogs, rats, and pigeons are better subjects for experimentation, but the transferability to humans of the results obtained is always open to doubt.

There is a second and even more valid reason for doubt, however. If we divide behavior into that which reflects the responses based on conditioning and which we call "training" as one category, and classify behavior which is based upon the arrangement of experience in new combinations and which we label "cognition" as another category, then it becomes clearer why stimulus-response as an inclusive formula seems inadequate. As a simple example which distinguishes between the two, we can take the case of the student who learns by rote the answers to set questions. Irrespective of the complexity of either questions or answers, this type of learning falls within the category of training and offers no essential difference from the patterned behavior which a Pavlov instills in his dogs or a Skinner in his pigeons. However, if a student learns how to utilize experience to frame questions, the answers to which express relationships, then we can say that the intellectual process has broken free of the limitations imposed by set responses to specific stimuli and exemplifies cognition.

The experimental problems formulated by Pavlov or Skinner represent congnitive behavior; and no matter how elaborate or intensive the training they give their animals, the latter can never create an experimental situation in which their erstwhile experimenters become the subjects. This does not deny the importance of training in the development of an orderly intellect. But the neural complexity of man's cortex permits the synthesis of experience into new combinations. Furthermore, immediate stimulus to cerebral activity may be apparent, and set stimuli may yield variable responses. Indeed, this may be what those who write of creative thinking have in mind. It is the process of cognition.

The distinction between behavior based on training and that based on cognition is a useful one, but it still leaves some tough questions unasked and unanswered. As yet, we have hardly touched upon the problem of the response as a function of the stimuli. I prefer to phrase the problem differently although the intent can remain the same. Of what relevance is the relation between an individual and his environment to the learning process? In this formulation the emphasis is directed to relationship and process, and the individual and environment are seen as variables. Specifically, both of the latter are seen as undergoing continuous change of greater or lesser magnitude, hence the consequences of the interdependency between them continuously vary.

This formulation is one which avoids the trap of assigning fixed attributes or qualities to an individual and the danger of accepting an enumeration of these as expressing either process or relationship. Furthermore, I believe that the relationship between the individual and his environment is the crucial problem if we are to understand the transmission of culture as a function of conditions. Among other things, this formulation recognizes the cultural systems as one aspect of the environment.

But there is much more that needs to be examined, and the remainder of this paper will address itself to the task at hand. In the development of the argument we shall range widely over several disciplines for our facts. Physical anthropology will help us to understand the relationship between the individual as an organic being and the culture milieu. We will then turn to some of the findings in the field of culture and personality, and to the problem of cultural perspective. Next, we shall seek an example in the socialization of the child to exemplify the operation of cultural patterning. This, then, brings us to an analysis of the mechanisms of culture and their relation to learning. Finally, we shall attempt a synthesis of the evidence to provide a new formulation of the processes of the transmission of culture.

MAN AS A CULTURE-CREATING ANIMAL

Among the characteristics which distinguishes man from other forms of animal life is his capacity for culture. But we hold a quite erroneous perspective if we separate for analysis and description the physical attributes of *Homo sapiens* and consider them as developing according to biological processes quite apart from the influence of culture. If we did so, we would then attribute to the human organism the inevitable capacity to achieve full physical maturity outside of the environmental influence which human society provides. The evidence does not support any such assumption. Instead, we are forced to accept, in the spheres of both phylogeny and ontogeny, an intricate arrangement of intermeshing influences between the physical and cultural aspects of man. Each helped to shape the other, and the point in time a million or more years ago when this process began can be justifiably called "The Human Revolution."[1]

It is not our purpose nor is it necessary to recount in detail the inferred effects of man's tool-making-and-using pattern of skills, his social groupings, nor the appearance of articulate speech with its system of abstract symbols. What we do need to understand, however, is that man represents a unique form of animal life in the creation of a nonphysical, that is cultural, environment which, in turn, affected the selective process that led to the appearance of modern man.

There are, however, several much commented upon consequences of this evolutionary sequence which need to be mentioned. The human infant at birth, and for a considerable time thereafter, is incapable of survival outside an environment which provides him with nurture. This dependency of the young upon its mother, or other adults, which is not necessarily restricted to man, is necessary because of its physical immaturity. One consequence of the prolonged dependency is that the individual in his progression toward maturity is subject to an intense and continuous period of learning. Thus the extended period of dependency may be seen as a function of the inmense amount of learning which must be acquired in the context of the minimally developed physiological processes which accompany the individual at birth.

The fact that infants do progress from an original immature condition to full cultural and physical maturity is significant. From this fact we can infer that given the conditions of a cultural environment and of the stage of physical and neural development at birth, the infant does possess the capacities for responding to this environment. Furthermore, the fact that this process is successfully achieved in all known varieties of culture establishes that any existent cultural environment is adequate for the human infant.

We must also decide, however, whether or not mere physical nurture, that is, an environment lacking culture, is sufficient for the human infant to achieve full humanity. The evidence upon which we can reach a conclusion is provided from many sources, but the most dramatic instances are those of feral man. Reports of other children who have lived virtually isolated from human contact substantiate the overwhelming importance of the environment in the shaping of the human infant.[2]

The conclusion to which this evidence leads us is that the achievement of full humanity is not an inevitable attribute of the human infant. Minimal physical nurture can ensure the survival of the individual, but other patterned behavior is essentially a function of the environment. When this evidence is joined with that which studies of child development have provided, we feel secure in accepting the almost infinite impressionability of the human neural system, an impressionability the development of which is itself a function of the environment. If this is the case then how, we might ask, is it possible to understand the processes of learning, or the development of the child if we focus our attention upon the subject, and not upon the influences which shape him? Such a procedure ignores the dynamic interplay between subject and his cultural environment and minimizes or even excludes variability within the environment as a significant factor.

When we come to seek an explanation for the failure to take culture into account as a significant variable there are several reasons which come quickly to mind. Most of those who have been doing research in this area have been trained in psychology and are generally unconversant with culture theory. The minimum advantage which flows from acquaintance with anthropological materials is that, through comparison of findings in several cultures, the danger of assuming a universal application is reduced.

Cross-cultural comparisons, however, can be a trap for the unsophisticated. The assumption that apparently similar culture traits or patterns are identical ignores the possibly divergent meaning which each carries in its original context. Some anthropologists are now attempting to overcome this hazard by developing more comprehensive models which are based upon cognitive comparisons in which they utilize linguistic and relational analysis.[3,4] Their approach has not yet been sufficiently tested, however, to judge if it solves difficulties in comparative analysis.

The most relevant contribution thus far has come from those studies in which psychological theory has been combined with the methods of ethnology in the field of culture and personality. The several studies by Mead, Bateson, Linton, Hallowell, Whiting, Hsu, Honigmann, and others have focused attention upon child training practices as a mechanism for the transmission of culture. Although these studies provide great insights into the variability in the patterning of emotions as a function of cultural differences, very little effort has been made thus far either to describe the cognitive environment within which child training operates, or to ascertain how cognitive patterns are acquired or expressed in the child. Until this deficiency has been corrected, it will remain impossible to construct an adequate theoretical model of learning in its relation to culture.[5] Nevertheless, anthropological studies have confirmed the validity of one enormously valuable principle through clarifying the origin and variability of *perspective* and in demonstrating how the cultural perspective provides the screen through which experience is filtered and interpreted.

In its most comprehensive sense, the perspective system is synonymous with world view. This is the system of thought and feeling which explains the operation of the universe. It makes meaningful to man such natural phenomena as the seasonal rhythms of nature, earth, and heaven, and the origin and destiny of life. It provides the rationale for explaining success, failure, and tragedy. It identifies things and their attributes and expresses relationships between them through categorization. In essence, the world view provides the orderly system through which the aspects of experience are identified and interpreted.

Everyday experience easily confirms the point. Where the sheep rancher views the wolf as a predator, the conservationist sees him as one element in a harmonious balance of nature. Where we rely upon knowledge of the physiology of the body for diagnosing and treating illness, the Navaho sees illness as an active intrusion into the body of a spirit; and the removal of the spirit is accomplished through ritual means.

Even within the realms of science, world view may inhibit or advance the understanding of the processes of nature. One of the more dramatic instances is that of the great scientific naturalist, Louis Agassiz, who refused to accept the implications of his own evidence, and that of others, which supported the concept of evolution.[6] Agassiz believed in a Divine Intelligence which through acts of special creation populated the earth with life forms that were immutable and fixed. From time to time this Divinity caused catastrophies which wiped out all life but in a succeeding epoch brought forth new life forms that were divergent from the preceding period. From this a priori conception it was unnecessary and, in fact, impossible to accept any phylogenetic connection between earlier and later species as they were revealed through the succession of geologic strata. Agassiz believed that in his discovery and classification of species he was fashioning the pattern of a great divinely inspired cosmic plan. He even utilized his theory of an Ice Age to support his view of divinely inspired catastrophes.

It seems unnecessary to adduce further examples to establish the point. As a part of each culture is a system of identifying and interpreting the things and events which constitute experience. In fact without the culturally induced perspective, experience is meaningless. Furthermore, we may posit that each such system operates within a framework of logical consistency and that it is possible to extract from the behavior of individuals those rules which explain categorization.

Perspective or world view, then, is more than the specific content of culture. It also contains the unstated premises which order thought and feeling. For those who would attempt to make these explicit, the problem they face is to develop those techniques which expose the structural logic of the culture they examine. Some of those who are working in the symbolic analysis of language, as did Whorf, are attempting to do just this. Their results will eventually be of great assistance in examining the transmission of culture, but in the meantime, we must explore the problem with such knowledge as we possess.

Understanding of perspective and its variability does have direct relevance, however, for our central problem. It alerts us to the fact that we cannot understand the process of learning by a mere recounting of the sequence of stimuli which the individual receives in passing through infancy to adulthood. Stimuli cannot be viewed as bits and pieces which somehow add up to a whole. They come to the subject from a cultural environment in which the perspective has already colored their meaning, and somehow they are received by the subject in the same manner. Otherwise we could not speak of cultural transmission at all, and an individual would present an idiosyncratic personality. Observation readily establishes that this is not the case, but until we know more about the relation of neural and cultural patterning, we cannot know how one may mirror the other. This should not deter us from seeking the consequence of this process as it is manifested in the behavior of the individual, nor from examining the pattern of the culture which has been embedded in a physical base.

CULTURAL PATTERNING AND LEARNING

It would seem that this is an appropriate time to examine what we mean by the patterning of culture and its relation to the socialization of the child. It will be remembered that considerable attention was given to the overwhelming importance of the environment in developing those capacities which make possible the physical, psychic, and cultural maturation of the child. It should also be remembered that variations in environment are reflected in the child's development. This being so, it would seem completely logical that examining the cultural environment itself could make explicit the learning process. This is, of course, what we must do because we must not rule out the possibility that the subject patterns his processes of learning from the influences exerted by those around him.

Although this proposal does not contradict our normal assumption that the infant is already prepared at birth to receive and organize stimuli, it does assert that the pattern of the organization of experience is a variable and is external to the infant in origin. What we insist on is that all the evidence support the view that we cannot look to any innate neural tendency to fashion the impact of the cultural environment in a given direction. The restrictions imposed by the neural system upon the newly arrived, cultureless creature are minimal and give to the infant the capacity to cope with sensory experience of a limited kind only. The higher nervous centers are not yet organized, in fact, they are not fully developed. Only in mythology do we find godlike creatures, not humans, springing fully developed from their progenitors.

In humans, a determinate period must elapse before the child can respond to stimuli on other than a physical basis. Such a proposal does not deny, however, that all the stimuli flowing to the infant from its mother or other persons, as well as the type of physical environment provided for it, are not highly charged with cultural significance. The methods and rhythms of handling, suckling, cleaning, and comforting have been shown in study after study to be culturally variable and presumably significant in personality formation. (This latter supposition would be on much sounder ground if we knew what would happen if we transferred the child to a culturally different environment immediately preceding the appearance of the the sense of self.)

The point I wish to make is that child rearing practices impose upon the infant the necessity of adjusting to a particular set of stimuli and, by implication, to the distinctive cultural patterning which they represent. Specifically, the infant must learn how to learn, an argument advanced by Gregory Bateson some time ago. This line of reasoning adds further support to those who have protested the validity of intelligence tests on the grounds that they are culturally biased, although in this instance the objection is advanced from a different basis. We would argue that the learning process, once acquired, varies from one culture to another, and in each instance organizes experiences differently.

Our understanding of the relation between culture, the mode of its transmission, and learning can be enriched and deepened if we turn now to empirical evidence provided by a study which is relevant to our focus. Most such research has been primarily concerned with the affective aspects of child rearing and the failure to look at cognitive processes represents a real deficiency. With this limitation in mind, I have chosen a study of the Hopi Indians by Dorothy Eggan for illustrative purposes.[7] Her immediate concern is with "the emotional commitment involved in the socialization process." She contends that the Hopi were experts in the use of *affect* in their educational system, and that the results continued to be effective throughout the life span of the individual as a "reconditioning factor." She also argues that the internalized code of right behavior served as an effective social control for a society which lacked institutionalized means of individual restraint and punishment, and also added stability to the personality structure and to the society.

There are many aspects of Hopi life which need to be known if we are to understand the particular form in which their culture has been cast. We should know that the semi-desert environment in which they live imposes a precarious balance upon their ability to gain a livelihood through agriculture and some livestock grazing. The little villages in which they cluster atop the high mesas probably originally provided some protection against enemies, but also permitted them a better position from which to exploit the meager resources of their habitat. They are grouped in maternal clans which regulate the obligations of their members and provide rules of residence and descent. They possess an elaborate calendar of religious observances; the participation in ceremonies is practically obligatory. When their children come to puberty, they are subject to initiation rites. Although this quick summary barely touches the richness and complexity of the cultural life, particularly that related to cosmology, it hopefully contributes some sense of the situation.

The emotional commitment of the Hopi is contained in the concept of the "good heart." It means a heart at peace with itself and one's fellows. There is no worry, unhappiness, envy malice, nor any other disturbing emotion in a good heart. In this state, cooperation, whether in the extended household or in the fields and ceremonies, is selfless and easy. Unfortunately, such a conception of a good heart is also impossible of attainment.[8] But the Hopis also recognized the "bad heart— Kahopi," and when an individual was in this state he was threatedned by imminent retribution manifested in illness or death, or other misfortune. But he might also cause harm to others and even to the group as a whole. One who was not in a proper state of "grace" when ceremonies were performed and prayers offered might prevent rain and cause the crops to fail. For those who attempted to achieve or maintain the "good heart" the *burden* was enormous, not alone an individual one, but affecting the welfare of the universe since they believed that the Hopi way of life had been bestowed when the world began, and only as it was perpetuated could the world continue.

The duality of good and evil, and the sense of burden gain further significance when we add to them the concept of the "wall of Hopiness." We can think of it as a bounded area within which Hopiness prevails and expresses the separation of inside and outside. The tight relationships which bind a kin group might also be conceptualized as the wall which separates one clan from another. It reflects the sharp sense of identity which has been built on a commonalty of origin, residence, and way of life. It would seem that we would be justified in viewing this cultural centripetality as a force of great potency and in harmony with the other concepts.

The origin and meaning of these concepts must be sought in the environment provided by the family, and in participation in religious practices. In the maternally organized household, usually including more than one generation, the infant learns to make distinctions among those who are his caretakers, distinctions which include the terms, obligations and feelings toward those who are in one's kin group, toward the outperson or stranger, and also toward oneself as a reciprocally participating member of a group.

Implicit within these learned distinctions, feelings, and behavior, are the categories, stated and unstated, which the cultural system provides. These include the dichotomy contained within sexual separation, ordination expressed in generations, the polar duality of good and evil, the inside-outside division based on the distinction of the right and familiar versus the strange and uncertain, the categories by which things and qualities are arranged, and a way of perceiving time, space, and process. These distinctions and arrangements constitute the cognitive pattern. They provide the logical framework upon which world view rests, and when combined with the affective overtones which accompanied their acquisition, they provide the perspective within which all experience is seen and interpreted.

It would still be useful, however, to look at some of the devices which shape the child in the image of Hopi culture. Eggan emphasizes that the effect of the teaching effort was to inculcate in the child a sense of interdependence. Even the act of weaning which in many societies is a beginning step in creating independence for the infant, among the Hopi led to a different consequence. Her apt statement follows:

> He [the Hopi infant] was in no way *forced to find satisfactions within himself*; rather these were provided for him, if possible, by his household or clan group. His weaning, then, was from the breast only, and as he was being weaned from the biological mother he was at the same time in a situation which increased his emotional orientation toward the intimate in-group of the extended family which was consistent with the interests of Hopi social structure. Thus, considering weaning in its wider implications, a Hopi was never 'weaned'; it was not intended that he should be. For these numerous caretakers contributed greatly to a small Hopi's faith in his intimate world and conversely without question to a feeling of strangeness and *emotional insecurity* as adults in any world outside of this emotional sphere.[9]

It is quite clear that the instruction was deliberate and persistent. That which was relevant to kinship behavior was learned within the context of the event through patient and unceasing explanation and admonition until by the time the Hopi was an adult his "kinship reaction patterns were so deeply ingrained in his thinking and feeling, and in his workaday life, that they were as much a part of him as sleeping and eating." But any occasion could be utilized for the recitation of stories, adventures, journeys or other experience which could illuminate for the child "what it meant to be a good Hopi from a wide variety of determined teachers who had very definite and *mutually consistent* ideas of what a good Hopi is."

But the base upon which all instruction could be effective had been laid in the earliest years. The simplest acts were responded to from the polar reference of the Hopi definition of the "good heart." Offenders soon learned that their acts would evoke the condemning term "Kahopi" and serious offenses brought forth a stern isolation, the most severe of penalties in a world which rewarded interdependence. The desire to want to learn and to observe right behavior was further reinforced by the use of fear. Children were told that their misdeeds might attract the evil spirits who either harm them or take them away. Thus, in these and other ways an emotional base was laid from which all acts, theirs and those of others, could be judged against the ideal of the "good heart." What we must remember, however, is that irrespective of the physiology of the human neural and glandular systems, their response to each stimulus, to each item of experience, was the consequence of a patterned learning that had its origin in culture.

That which is learned in childhood, however, nowhere completes the education that must be given if the cultural heritage is to be transmitted. In one sense childhood should be viewed as the period of preparation for the important knowledge that is still to come. Among those peoples who practice formal initiation ceremonies, usually at the time of puberty, we have the opportunity to observe the dramatic fashion in which the new learning is conveyed.

The analysis by Hart[10] of the differences between prepubertal and postpubertal education has helped enormously to clarify some of the problems related to learning and the transmission of culture. He argues that in most primitive societies that the educational vehicle and its purposes in those two periods are clearly distinct. Education in the prepubertal period is provided primarily by one's intimates—the members of his family and the associates of his place of residence. He notes the variations, the wide latitude in practices and even laxness in the insistence that learning occurs at a given time or place or under the supervision of designated personnel. It is true, of course, that a basic commonality exists within and between cultures in the practices observed by the nurturant group in bringing the infant to increasing stages of physical independence and in the training of bodily functions, but this constitutes only a small portion of the skills and knowledge that is learned from peers and adults.

Postpubertal education is an entirely different matter. Among those peoples who observe formal initiation ceremonies, and such practices are found among most primitive tribes, the pubescent members of the group are separated from their intimates, oftentimes forcibly, and subjected to periods of formal instruction which may last from several months to several years, depending upon traditional practice. Hart makes the significant observation that the personnel responsible for this period of instruction are different from the intimates of childhood because, among other reasons, the material of education, the manner of its preservation, and the urgency of its acquisition requires a type of relationship and a type of knowledge that the group of intimates could not provide.

Hence, this responsibility is vested in "strangers" who even though they may be known to the initiates represent a different, sometimes hostile, segment of tribal organization. Where such internal divisions do not exist, and intimates carry out the initiation practices, the fiction of strangers is created by the use of masks.

Deeper understanding of the relevance of initiation ceremonies can be gained through a brief excursion into the theory of *rites de passage*.[11] Over a half century ago Van Gennep noted that those occasions on which an individual was in transition from one status or category to another were marked by ceremonies. These included the universal life crises of birth, puberty, marriage, and death, but also included other situations in which changes in behavior or group indentification were involved. In many of these ceremonies there was a ritually enacted simulation of death and of a subsequent rebirth into the new condition. Van Gennep also noted a structural arrangement of the sequences into three phases. The initial phase in which the connections with a current way of life were severed he called *separation*. The individuals, or, in the case of puberty ceremonies, the neophytes, then found themselves in an intermediate stage in which they were neither of one group nor another, they were *not-beings*.[12] This liminal condition was labelled *transition*. In the final stage of *incorporation* the individual returned to the group but into a different social niche and with altered behavior.

From a societal point of view the most significant *rite de passage* is initiation into tribal membership and adulthood at puberty. The ceremony marking this event may be quite brief, but it may also extend over a lengthy time period depending upon the nature of the instruction which must be given. Even among those groups which do not have formal observance of physiological puberty as the point in time for initiation, there are other occasions, or educational devices which serve the same purposes and which incorporate the basic ritual and instructional aspects. The important point is that each society does have ways to *claim* the young.[13]

In those societies in which the origin and operation of the universe is viewed from the perspective of supernatural forces, instruction in and revelation of religious mysteries constitute a major portion of the knowledge which is transmitted during the period of initiation. In contrast, instruction is not in the mundane matters of how to make a living or to build a house, nor even in the private magical practices which accompany so many activities. This useful knowledge is gained elsewhere. In Australian tribes, for example, the neophytes are taught theology— the mythology which explains the origin and meaning of life, the sacred songs and prayers, and the ritual and dances of world-revival ceremonies. Much of this knowledge must be acquired so precisely that, in theory, there is no deviation from generation to generation in ceremonial performance.

Hart interprets postpubertal education as preparation for citizenship and argues that "Citizenship training in these societies ... means exposing the boy under particularly stirring and impressive conditions to the continuity of the cultural tradition, to the awe and majesty of the society itself, emphasizing the subordination of the individual to the group at large and hence the mysteriousness, wonder, and sacredness of the whole individual-society relationship."[14]

If we turn once again to the particulars of Hopi culture, we can exemplify not only the relevance of the analysis but also extend our own perspective. The induced striving to achieve the "good heart" and to learn and follow the Hopi way of life is not an individual goal in our sense of the word. Our perspective could readily equate the individually centered orientation, as it has been described, with the ultimate goal of self-fulfillment which our own culture emphasizes. The similarity is a superficial one and to treat it otherwise would lead us astray.

For the Hopi, self-perfection serves a larger purpose. Their mythology posits a preestablished universal order but in order that this cosmic orderliness be actualized it is necessary to have man's cooperation. In such a formulation we are again witness to the *interdependence* of basic Hopi thought and social behavior. Man is also a necessary aspect of the universe and without his contribution and only through the fulfillment of his part can that which might be exist. The responsibility constitutes a cosmic burden which can only be properly discharged by those whose moral rightness is manifested in the striving for the "good heart." Hence the linkage between the private life of the individual and the public life of the society. Hence also the distinction between the instruction and training received from one's intimates in childhood and the formal education which begins with a first initiation between the ages of six and ten, and a subsequent initiation ceremony eight to ten years later. The learning of the values, mythology, and ceremonies of the society is further extended in the years which follow.

It is true that the initiation ceremony marks the separation of the individual from his childhood and from other children, and his entry into the public and adult world, but it is also much more. When the Katchinas—the gods—are unmasked and the realization breaks through that these are mortal men among whom are some you know, there follows the destruction of the illusion, the loss of childhood innocence, the final separation from childhood, but also the realization of man's part in a great cosmic scheme.

Before we begin the next part of our analysis, it might be well to recapituiate briefly our original objectives and the relevance of the description and analysis to these. The search for an understanding of the conditions affecting the transmission of culture constitutes our primary goal. Toward this end we have, first of all, argued for the validity of the distinction between affective and cognitive learning. The stimulus-response paradigm appears as adequate to explain affective and skill learning although it is not realized through simple, additive repetition. It seems, however, that we must look to some other mechanism to explain cognitive learning. We were also interested in establishing the cultural fashioning of the how and what of learning and to show that the stimulus-response connection is itself a variable of the cultural environment.

We wanted to show next the distinction in the educational approach and personnel for prepubertal and postpubertal education and to relate this to subject matter and objective. In particular, we wanted to draw attention to the fact that the stuff of the deliberate and highly patterned instruction of the postpubertal period was knowledge, although we cannot exclude the influence of the affective context within which it was imparted, nor the affective disposition which the individual carried into the situation from childhood experience.

But the preschool learning includes much more than the organization of instincts and emotions, the ethos, as described by Bateson and Mead.[15] It also includes the acquisition of the tools with which the world can be apprehended symbolically, the facility of language and the patterns of differentiation of things, events, relationships, and processes. These are the intellectual tools which can be used quite apart from any affective predisposition. They constitute the basic sine qua non of intellectual efforts in learning the knowledge or subject matter of formal schooling. The instruction may focus upon mythology and sacred ceremonies as exemplified by initiation rites, or it may be organized in formal courses under the rubrics of mathematics, grammar, logic, and science.

There is, however, a basic similarity in the instructional content of either "bush" school or classroom. In both, there is transmitted not only knowledge and a way of thinking about such, the whole of which we may call world view, but there is also transmitted the criteria by which events may be analyzed and judged. The use of these criteria in the understanding process represent the epitome of cognitive learning. Among the Hopi, for example, everything ranging from simple good fortune to catestrophic drought can be placed in the interpretive reference of individual behavior or of cosmic process. Let it be said now that the problem is not one of testing the validity of such interpretations against our own explanations of the workings of the laws of nature. It is quite certain that each contestant examining a specific event from his own perspective would inevitably be guided by his own rules of evidence, logic, and process in rendering a decision. How else can we understand an Agassiz, a Darwin, a Hopi priest, or a Murngin elder? Nor is the problem of who is right or wrong ours to consider; it leads us astray. The problem is to make explicit the criteria and the mechanisms which explain cognition and ultimately to examine these for their relevance to formal education. It is to that problem that we now turn.

CULTURE AND COGNITION

There are several approaches to the study of the relation between culture and cognition that promise fruitful results, and eventually all of these should be used. The analysis of the internal structure of language, as developed by Whorf,[16] has yielded early rich rewards. His procedure shows that certain thought processes are derived from the structure of the language employed by the speakers. Language may also be examined as a tool in communication or studied semantically as a system of symbols. But its study may also be approached from the more purely cultural perspective in which it is treated as one aspect of culture.

The approach used by social anthropologists introduces a rather different perspective. Their intellectual tradition stems from Comte through Durkheim and Radcliffe-Brown, to those contemporary anthropologists who are seeking the processes of change through study of the structure of human groupings and their relation to other aspects of the environment. From this perspective all symbolism, of which language is a significant part, may be understood as a hypostatization of social reality. Warner utilizes this approach in his analysis of Murngin totemism.[17] Patterning of behavior as a function of culture has been utilized constantly. The specification of these approaches here recognizes their contribution and shows the breadth of the conceptual base from which this analysis proceeds. They will be implicit in much of what follows.

In this paper I have consistently insisted that the learning process must be viewed as an aspect of the cultural milieu. Since culture is transgenerational, we should find in culture those clues which could explain both what and how the child learns. But our effort must also be transcultural if we are to abstract that which has universal relevance. Since it is the screen of cultural perspective through which experience is received, ordered, and acted upon, our problem is to identify those commonalities which encompass all cultures irrespective of their substantive divergences.

There are three such commonalities which I believe to be universally present; namely, the categories of knowledge, the canons of discrimination, and process as a function of relationship between variables.

Each individual who has participated in the full range of cultural experiences appropriate to his sex and status possesses a set of categories which permits him to distinguish and classify individuals, things, qualities, events, and processes. The language which he speaks contains the verbal referents for all such distinctions and may itself be analyzed for grammatical structure. Among such other commonly agreed upon categories are those of order, class, number, shape, time, and space. These *agreed upons*, not just the label they carry, but the basis upon which groupings of similar and dissimilar may be made, are part of the cultural heritage which is transmitted in a multitude of ways, and which makes possible meaningful communication among cultural similars. In our society those who operate from private symbol systems are often institutionalized, or if they are artists, may be considered as avant-garde and tolerated in the hope that they may be expressing something significant.

The social base of such categories is readily apparent in the terminology of any kinship system and in the acquisition of identifying terms and appropriate behavior easily observable in parental teaching of the young. In the acquisition of such knowledge, the child also learns implicitly the more inclusive distinctions based upon sex, age, generation, descent, and sequence through birth order. For example, in the kinship terminology used by Navaho Indians, all those who use the reciprocal term of sister for each other are called "mother" by their children. The extension of the principle contained within this system of categorizing means that you apply the term "sister" to all those who are daughters of the persons you call "mother." The further fact that both classes of persons (mothers and sisters) are sexually taboo excludes them from the group from which one may choose a marriage partner. When categories and the process of categorizing is extended to all experience, we can see how extensive, comprehensive, or orderly is the cultural framework. We should also note its stability since it is embedded in the language, expressed in mythology, and governs the thought processes.

If the categories of knowledge are supraindividual, so also are the canons of discrimination.[18] Here we are concerned with two aspects each one of which must be treated separately, although they are related. The learning of identities is only one step in acquiring a cognitive framework. The individual must also learn the criteria which make identification possible and which permit classification of the item of experience in the larger whole. Not only must each individual learn the basis upon which items are classified, but he must also learn the criteria which permit him to evaluate and hence to respond.

From our knowledge of how cultural interconnections exhibit an internal consistency we can infer that evaluative responses are expressions of a coherent system. Our analysis of Hopi affective patterns supports this view. Our goal, then, is not only to discover the canons which order the system, but also to make explicit the criteria upon which these are based. Being unstated assumptions of behavior, their exposure will not be easy. Knowledge of them cannot be gained by blunt question and answer approaches; they must be pried out through processes of inference utilizing linguistic, mythologic, and behavioral data. Only with the appearance of the conscious questing of the practitioners of science has it been possible for us to even begin to discover these wellsprings of human thought. We cannot assume, however, that they lie buried in the unconscious of the human psyche or that they spring from an assumed inner force. Rather, we shall gain knowledge of them from culture itself. If we accept the supraindividual sources of discrimination and of the canons which govern their use, then we must accept cultural variability in the criteria by which one identifies and evaluates. What is culturally universal is the process by which canons and criteria are transmitted.

This brings us to the consideration of process as the third member of our group of cultural commonalities. We have defined process as a function of change in the relationships among variables. Sometimes these changes may be seen as a consequence of modification in the magnitude or quality of variables, and sometimes they may be due to changes in the conditions within which a system operates. Further elaboration of this terse statement is necessary.

Relatively little attention has been given thus far to the analysis of the internal dynamics of culture as viewed from the internal vantage of a specific cultural perspective. The task would be far from easy, since it would require two sets of intellectual tools. It would require, first, an adequate general theory of social and cultural change; and secondly, a theory of change, or process, viewed from within each culture. Few people would grant that a general theory now exists, although Marxian and Freudian theorists make such claims. Such a theory could be the base from which cultural data would be probed for the purpose of yielding another theory of change specific to the culture under study. It is quite probable that we shall win through to such a model only through the slow, laborious process of inductive empiricism. It is possible, however, to designate some of the data that must be examined and the direction in which we can proceed.

The simplest formulation of what we are seeking is contained in the question, "How do things happen?" Now the mythologies of the various cultures of the world provide an explanation to their members of how the universe came to be. In content these creation myths vary widely. Some specify set stages of development with the appearance of man in a culminating epoch. Others see the tension between natural forces as essential to creation. In some, a transcendental power effectuates a divine plan, or a mythological culture here prepares the way for man and lays down the rules of life. There are some cultures in which their myths express only a feebly developed sense of beginning. The direct comparison of the contextual material of differing cultures has been tried time and again, and does not yield much, but there is another approach which holds great promise.

The difficult problem, of course, is to hit upon a method of analysis that will yield results of a kind we are seeking. If we could examine mythological events of a given people within their context of time, then we might begin to make meaningful the pattern of rhythm and sequence as they see it. If the cycle of birth and death, or the succession of the seasons or of other recurrences are contained in these accounts, then we can compare them to seek for the framework of repetition. But we must also examine the explanations which accompany the descriptions. In these we must search for the relationships which explain emergence, becoming, being, and ending. Hopefully, this approach will yield the principles of process for which we seek.

The activity suggested above, however, is only one phase of our quest. We must subject the ongoing communal life to the same kind of examination, seeking out the time patterning as men join and separate in activities. And finally, we must see what the structure of language reveals. Hopefully, we might some day be able to establish the connections among all of these. The rich rewards garnered by the few who have begun the exploration give great promise.

Let us not forget that the same purposes are to be served in the applicability of this approach to modern science, philosophy, or theology. We must make explicit the pattern of the process by which we interpret events. We seek the processes of nature in the cyclotron, in experiments with substances and animals, and in the observation of plant and animal life in their ecological settings. But we must also make explicit the process by which we achieve results, for this is the essence of education. These are the tools of cognition. In the systems of categorization and discrimination and their associated criteria and in the conceptualization of process, we find cognitive commonalities which are transcultural.

CONCLUSION

If we view the primary function of education as the transmission of culture, then that which is unique to education are the conditions which govern its process. Process is a variable relationship of two systems, the social and cultural environment which prescribes the method and content of education and the individual in whom experience is organized and internalized.

From each segment of the culture comes knowledge of a different sort. Within the family the child is trained in bodily functions, kinship behavior, and household skills. In institutionalized schooling the child is taught by strangers. In both, the child learns body skills, and affective and cognitive behavior, although the emphasis will vary from one to another. Presumably, experience is cumulative, but the differential of the limits for performance between training and cognitive development remains largely unexplored. It is possible that the affective disposition of most persons has been set in early childhood, particularly so if there are no changes in the conditions of life. Certainly one of the conditions which affects the transmission of culture is the nurturant environment of the infant. It is here that the individual is prepared to be culturally acquisitive. Since what happens here is apparently so crucial to what happens later, and because the content and method of education in early childhood is substantially different from that of formal schooling, knowledge of the process of the preparation of the infant for responding to cultural experience is a basic concern in education.

We must turn to the social and cultural environment itself to discover the other applicable conditions. We should distinguish, however, between those which we call operational and those which are conceptual. The former includes all those informal or institutional arrangements which a society provides for instruction. It should also include the organization of the presentation of subject matter and, as a separate category, the relationship between teacher and learner. In essence the operations in cultural transmission subsume the how to do it.

Although the conceptual conditions which affect the transmission of culture are of far greater significance, because in these are found the stuff of full humanity, they have been left largely implicit in educational theory. From these conditions comes the perspective which is reflected in world view. The rules which govern the organization and evaluation of knowledge and explain the processes of change are to be found here. In them are the oftentimes unstated assumptions which make experience meaningful. In them are the guideposts for learning itself.

All of the conditions which affect the transmission of culture constitute a proper, if not exclusive, concern of educators. It is my belief that in the study of the mechanisms of cognition, seen as functions of social and cultural reality, educators can gain that understanding which is essential to the process of education.

NOTES

1. Charles F. Hockett and Robert Ascher, "The Human Revolution," *Current Anthropology* 5, no. 3 (1964): 135-47.
2. Kingsley Davis, *Human Society* (New York: Macmillan, 1949), pp. 204-8.
3. A. Kimball Romney and Ray Goodwin D'Andrade, eds., "Transcultural Studies in Cognition," *American Anthropology*, 66, no. 3, pt. 2 (1964).
4. Anthony Wallace, "Culture and Cognition," *Science* 135 (1962): 351-57.
5. Solon T. Kimball, "Communication Modalities as a Function of Social Relationships," *Transactions of the New York Academy of Sciences* 25, no. 4 (1963): 439-68.
6. Edward Lurie, *Louis Agassiz: A Life in Science* (Chicago: University of Chicago Press, 1960).
7. Dorothy Eggan, "Instruction and Affect in Hopi Cultural Continuity," in *Education and Culture*, ed. George Spindler (New York: Holt, Rinehart & Winston, 1963) pp. 321-50.
8. Ibid., p. 338.
9. Ibid., p. 329.
10. C.W.M. Hart, "Contrasts Between Prepubertal and Postpubertal Education," in Spindler, *Education and Culture*, pp. 400-25.
11. Arnold Van Gennep, *The Rites of Passage* (Chicago: University of Chicago Press, 1960).
12. Victor W. Turner, "Betwixt and Between: the Liminal period in Rites des Passage: Symposium on New Approaches to the Study of Religion," *Proceedings of the 1964 Annual Spring Meeting of the American Ethnological Society* (Seattle: University of Washington Press, 1964), pp. 4-20.
13. Solon T. Kimball and James E. McClellan, Jr., *Education and the New America* (New York: Random House, 1962), chap. 10.
14. Ibid., p. 420.
15. Gregory Bateson and Margaret Mead, *Balinese Character. A Photographic Analysis* (reprinted 1962; New York: New York Academy of Science Special Publication, 1942).
16. Benjamin Lee Whorf, "Language, Thought, and Reality," in *Selected Writings of Benjamin Lee Whorf*, ed. John B. Carroll (Cambridge, Mass.: Technology Press of Massachusetts Institute of Technology, 1942).
17. W. L. Warner, *A Black Civilization* (New York: Harper & Brothers, 1937).
18. Solon T. Kimball, "The External Source of Values" (manuscript, 1964).

19 / Lineal and Nonlineal Codifications of Reality

Dorothy Lee

The following study is concerned with the codification of reality, and more particularly, with the nonlineal apprehension of reality among the people of the Trobriand Islands, in contrast to our own lineal phrasing. Basic to my investigation is the assumption that a member of a given society not only codifies experienced reality through the use of the specific language and other patterned behavior characteristic of his culture, but that he actually grasps reality only as it is presented to him in this code. The assumption is not that reality itself is relative; rather, that it is differently punctuated* and categorized, or that different aspects of it are noticed by, or presented to the participants of different cultures. If reality itself were not absolute, then true communication of course would be impossible. My own position is that there is an absolute reality, and that communication is possible. If then, that which the different codes refer to is ultimately the same, a careful study and analysis of a different code and of the culture to which it belongs, should lead us to concepts which are ultimately comprehensible, when translated into our own code. It may even, eventually, lead us to aspects of reality from which our own code excludes us.

It is a corollary of this assumption that the specific phrasing of reality can be discovered through intensive and detailed analysis of any aspect of culture. My own study was begun with an analysis of linguistic formulation, only because it is in language that I happen to be best able to discover my clues. To show how these clues can be discovered and used as guides to the apprehension of reality, as well as to show what I mean by codification, I shall present at first concrete material in the field of language.

I

That a word is not the reality, not the thing which it represents, has long been a commonplace to all of us. The thing which I hold in my hand as I write, *is* not a pencil; I *call* it a pencil. And it remains the same whether I call it *pencil, molyvi, Bleistift*, or *siwiqoq*. These words are different sound-complexes applied to the same reality; but is the difference merely one of sound-complex? Do they refer to the same *perceived* reality? *Pencil* originally meant little tail; it delimited and named the reality according to form. *Molyvi* means lead and refers to the writing element. *Bleistift* refers both to the form and to the writing-element. *Siwiqoq* means painting-stick and refers to observed function and form. Each culture has phrased the reality differently. To say that *pencil*, for example, applies primarily to form is no idle etymologic statement. When we use this word metaphorically, we refer neither to writing element nor to function, but to form alone; we speak of a pencil of light, or a styptic pencil.

When I used the four words for this object, we all knew what reality was referred to; we knew the meaning of the word. We could visualize the object in my hand, and the words all delimited it in the same way; for example, none of them implied that it was a continuation of my fist. But the student of ethnography often has to deal with words which punctuate reality into different phrasings from the ones with which he is familiar. Let us take, for instance, the words for "brother" and "sister." We go to the islands of Ontong Java to study the kinship system. We ask our in-

*I have taken over this special use of the terms *codification* and *punctuation* from Gregory Bateson.

formant what he calls his sister and he says *ave*; he calls his brother *kainga*. So we equate *ave* with "sister" and *kainga* with "brother." By way of checking our information we ask the sister what she calls her brother; it turns out that for her, *ave* is "brother," not "sister" as we were led to expect; and that it is her sister whom she calls *kainga*. The same reality, the same actual kinship is present there as with us; but we have chosen a different aspect for naming. We are prepared to account for this; we say that both cultures name according to what we would call a certain type of blood relationship; but whereas we make reference to absolute sex, they refer to relative sex. Further inquiry, however, discloses that in this, also, we are wrong. Because in our own culture we name relatives according to formal definition and biologic relationship, we have thought that this formulation represents reality; and we have tried to understand the Ontong Javanese relationship terms according to these distinctions which, we believe, are given in nature. But the Ontong Javanese classifies relatives according to a different aspect of reality, differently punctuated. And because of this, he applies *kainga* as well to a wife's sister and a husband's brother; to a man's brother's wife and a woman's sister's husband, as well as to a number of other individuals. Neither sex nor blood relationship, then, can be basic to this term. The Ontong Javanese name according to their everyday behavior and experience, not according to formal definition. A man shares the ordinary details of his living with his brothers and their wives for a large part of the year; he sleeps in the same large room, he eats with them, he jokes and works around the house with them; the rest of the year he spends with his wife's sisters and their husbands, in the same easy companionship. All these individuals are *kainga* to one another. The *ave*, on the other hand, names a behavior of great strain and propriety; it is based originally upon the relative sex of siblings, yes, but it does not signify biologic fact. It names a social relationship, a behavior, an emotional tone. Ave can never spend their adult life together, except on rare and temporary occasions. They can never be under the same roof alone together, cannot chat at ease together, cannot refer even distantly to sex in the presence of each other, not even to one's sweetheart or spouse; more than that, everyone else must be circumspect when the ave of someone of the group is present. The *ave* relationship also carries special obligations toward a female ave and her children. *Kainga* means a relationship of ease, full of shared living, of informality, gaiety; *ave* names one of formality, prohibition, strain. These two cultures, theirs and our own, have phrased and formulated social reality in completely different ways, and have given their formulation different names. The word is merely the name of this specific cultural phrasing. From this one instance we might formulate the hypothesis—a very tentative one—that among the Ontong Javanese names describe emotive experiences, not observed forms or functions. But we cannot accept this as fact, unless further investigation shows it to be implicit in the rest of their patterned behavior, in their vocabulary and the morphology of their language, in their ritual and their other organized activity.

One more instance, this time from the language of the Wintu Indians of California, will deal with the varying aspect or segmentation of experience which is used as a basis of classification. To begin with, we take the stem *muk*. On the basis of this stem we form the word *mukada*, which means: "I turned the basket bottom up"; we form *mukuhara*, which means: "The turtle is moving along"; and we form *mukurumas*, which means: "automobile." Upon what conceivable principle can an automobile be put in the same category as a turtle and a basket? There is such a principle, however, and it operates also when the Wintu calls the activity of laundering, *to make foam continuously*. According to this principle, he uses the same stem, (*puq* or *poq*) to form words for the following:

puqeda: I just pushed a peg into the ground.
olpuqal: He is sitting on one haunch.
poqorahara: Birds are hopping along.

olpoqoyabe: There are mushrooms growing.
tunpoqoypoqoya: You walked shortskirted, stifflegged ahead of me.

It is difficult for us to discover the common denominator in the different forma-tions from this one stem, or even to believe that there can be one. Yet, when we discover the principle underlying the classification, the categories themselves are understandable. Basic to the classification is the Wintu view of himself as observer; he classifies as an outsider. He passes no judgment on essence, and where we would have used kinesthetic or participatory experience as the basis of naming, he names as an observer only, for the shape of the activity or the object. The turtle and the automobile can thus naturally be grouped together with the inverted baskets. The mushroom standing on its stem, the fist grasping a peg against the ground, the stiff leg topped by a short skirt, or by the body of a bird or of a man resting on a haunch, obviously all belong together in one category. But the progress of a grass-hopper cannot be catagorized with that of a hopping bird. We, who classify on a different basis, apprehend the hop of the two kinesthetically and see it as basically the same in both cases; but the Wintu see the difference in recurrent shape, which is all-important to them, and so name the two by means of completely different stems. Again, when we discover this principle, it is easy to see that from the observer's point of view laundering is the making of a lot of foam; and see why, when beer was introduced, it was named *laundry*.

An exhaustive study of the language and other aspects of Wintu culture shows that this principle is present in all of the Wintu language, as well as in the Wintu's conception of the self, of his place in the universe, in his mythology, and probably in other aspects of his culture.

II

I have discussed at length the diversity of codification of reality in general, be-cause it is the foundation of the specific study which I am about to present. I shall speak of the formulation of experienced reality among the Trobriand Islanders in comparison to our own; I shall speak of the nature of expectancy, of motivation, of satisfaction, as based upon a reality which is differently apprehended and experi-enced in two different societies; which is, in fact, for each, a different reality. The Trobriand Islanders were studied by the late Bronislaw Malinowski, who has given us the rich and circumstantial material about them which has made this study pos-sible. I have given a detailed presentation of some implications of their language elsewhere; but since it was in their language that I first noticed the absence of lineality, which led me to this study, I shall give here a summary of the implications of the language.

A Trobriand word refers to a self-contained concept. What we consider an at-tribute or a predicate, is to the Trobriander an ingredient. Where I would say, for example, "a good gardener," or "The gardener is good," the Trobriand word would include both "gardener" and "goodness"; if the gardener loses the goodness, he has lost a defining ingredient, he is something else, and he is named by means of a com-pletely different word. A *taytu* (a species of yam) contains a certain degree of ripeness, bigness, roundedness, etc.; without one of these defining ingredients, it is something else, perhaps a *bwanawa* or a *yowana*. There are no adjectives in the language; the rare words dealing with qualities are substantivized. The term *to be* does not occur; it is used neither attributively nor existentially, since existence it-self is contained; it is an ingredient of being.

Events and objects are self-contained points in another respect; there is a series of beings, but no becoming. There is no temporal connection between objects. The taytu always remains itself; it does not *become* overripe; overripeness is an ingredient of another, a different being. At some point, the taytu *turns into* a yowana, which contains overripeness. And the yowana, overripe as it is, does not put forth shoots, does not *become* a sprouting yowana. When sprouts appear, it ceases to be itself; in its place appears a *silasata*. Neither is there a temporal connection made—or, according to our own premises, perceived—between events; in fact, temporality is meaningless. There are no tenses, no linguistic distinction between past or present. There is no arrangement of activities or events into means and ends, no causal or teleologic relationships. What we consider a causal relationship in a sequence of connected events, is to the Trobriander an ingredient of a patterned whole. He names this ingredient *u'ula*. A tree has a trunk, u'ula; a house has u'ula, posts; a magical formula has u'ula, the first strophe; an expedition has u'ula, a manager or leader; and a quarrel contains an u'ula, what we would call a cause. There is no purposive *so as to*; no *for the purpose of*; there is no *why* and no *because*. The rarely used *pela* which Malinowski equates with *for*, means primarily *to jump*. In the culture, any deliberately purposive behavior—the kind of behavior to which we accord high status—is despised. There is no automatic relating of any kind in the language. Except for the rarely used verbal it-differents and it-sames, there are no terms of comparison whatever. And we find in an analysis of behavior that the standard for behavior and of evaluation is noncomparative.

These implications of the linguistic material suggest to my mind an absence of axiomatic lineal connection between events or objects in the Trobriand apprehension of reality, and this implication, as I shall attempt to show below, is reinforced in their definition of activity. In our own culture, the line is so basic, that we take it for granted, as given in reality. We see it in visible nature, between material points, and we see it between metaphorical points such as days or acts. It underlies not only your thinking, but also our aesthetic apprehension of the given; it is basic to the emotional climax which has so much value for us, and, in fact, to the meaning of life itself. In our thinking about personality and character, we have assumed the line as axiomatic.

In our academic work, we are constantly acting in terms of an implied line. When we speak of *ap*plying an *at*tribute, for example, we visualize the process as lineal, coming from the outside. If I make a picture of an apple on the board, and want to show that one side is green and the other red, I connect these attributes with a pictured apple by means of lines, as a matter of course; how else would I do it? When I organize my data, I *draw* conclusions *from* them. I *trace* a relationship between my facts. I describe a pattern as a *web* of relationships. Look at a lecturer who makes use of gestures; he is constantly making lineal connections in the air. And a teacher with chalk in hand will be drawing lines on the board whether he be a psychologist, a historian, or a paleontologist.

Preoccupation with social facts merely as self-contained facts is mere antiquarianism. In my field, a student of this sort would be an amateur or a dilettante, not an anthropologist. To be an anthropologist, he can arrange his facts in an upward slanting line, in a *unilinear* or *multilinear course* of development, in *parallel lines* or *converging lines*. Or he may arrange them geographically, with *lines* of *diffusion* connecting them; or schematically, using *concentric circles*. Or at least, he must indicate what his study *leads to*, what new insights we can *draw from* it. To be accorded status, he must use the guiding line as basic.

The line is found or presupposed in most of our scientific work. It is present in the *induction* and the *deduction* of science and logic. It is present in the philosopher's phrasing of means and ends as lineally connected. Our statistical facts are presented lineally as a *graph* or reduced to a normal *curve*. And all of us, I think, would be lost without our diagrams. We *trace* a historical development; we *follow the course* of history and evolution *down to* the present and *up from* the ape; and it is interesting to note, in passing, that whereas both evolution and history are lineal, the first goes up the blackboard, the second goes down. Our psychologists picture motivation as external, connected with the act through a line, or, more recently, entering the organism through a lineal channel and emerging transformed, again lineally, as response. I have seen lineal pictures of nervous impulses and heartbeats, and with them I have seen pictured lineally a second of time. These were photographs, you will say, of existing fact, of reality; a proof that the line is present in reality. But I am not convinced, perhaps due to my ignorance of mechanics, that we have not created our recording instruments in such a way that they have to picture time and motion, light and sound, heartbeats and nerve impulses lineally, on the unquestioned assumption of the line as axiomatic. The line is omnipresent and inescapable, and so we are incapable of questioning the reality of its presence.

When we see a *line* of trees, or a *circle* of stones, we assume the presence of a connecting line which is not actually visible. And we assume it metaphorically when we follow a *line* of thought, a *course* of action or the *direction* of an argument; when we *bridge* a gap in the conversation, or speak of the *span* of life or of teaching a *course;* or lament our *interrupted career.* We make children's embroidery cards and puzzle cards on this assumption; our performance tests and even our tests for sanity often assume that the line is present in nature and, at most, to be discovered or given visual existence.

But is the line present in reality? Malinowski, writing for members of our culture and using idiom which would be comprehensible to them, describes the Trobriand village as follows: "Concentrically with the circular row of yam houses there runs a ring of dwelling huts." He saw, or at any rate, he represented the village as two circles. But in the texts which he recorded, we find that the Trobrianders at no time mention circles or rings or even rows when they refer to their villages. Any word which they use to refer to a village, such as *a* or *this*, is prefixed by the substantival element *kway* which means *bump* or *aggregate of bumps.* This is the element which they use when they refer to a pimple or a bulky rash; or to canoes loaded with yams. In their terms, a village is an aggregate of bumps; are they blind to the circles? Or did Malinowski create the circles himself, out of his cultural axiom?

Again, for us as well as in Malinowski's description of the Trobrianders, which was written necessarily in terms meaningful to us, all effective activity is certainly not a haphazard aggregate of acts, but a lineally planned series of acts leading to an envisioned end. Their gardening with all its specialized activities, both technical and magical, leading to a rich harvest; their *kula* involving the cutting down of trees, the communal dragging of the tree to the beach, the rebuilding or building of large seaworthy canoes, the provisioning, the magical and ceremonial activities involved, surely all these can be carried through only if they are lineally conceived. But the Trobrianders do not describe their activity lineally; they do no dynamic relating of acts; they do not use even so innocuous a connective as *and.* Here is part of a description of the planting of coconut: "Thou-approach-there coconut thou-bring-here-we-plant-coconut thou-go thou-plant our coconut. This-here it-emerge sprout. We-push-away this we-push-away this-other coconut-husk-fiber together sprout it-sit together root." We who are accustomed to seek lineal continuity, cannot help supplying it as we read this; but the continuity is not given in the Trobriand text; and all Trobriand speech, according to Malinowski, is "jerky," given in points, not in connecting lines. The only connective I know of in Trobriand is the *pela* which I mentioned above; a kind of preposition which also means "to jump." I am not maintaining here that the Trobrianders cannot see continuity; rather that lineal connection is not automatically made by them, as a matter of course. At Malinowski's persistent questioning, for example, they did attempt to explain their activities in terms of cause or motivation, by stating possible "results" of uncooperative action. But Malinowski found their answers confused, self-contradictory, inconsistent; their preferred answer was, "It was ordained of old"—pointing to an ingredient value of the act instead of giving an explanation based on lineal connection. And when they were not trying to find answers to leading questions, the Trobrianders made no such connections in their speech. They assumed, for example, that the validity of a magical spell lay, not in its results, not in proof, but in its very being; in the appropriateness of its inheritance, in its place within the patterned activity, in its being performed by the appropriate person, in its realization of its mythical basis. To seek validity through proof was foreign to their thinking, yet they attempted to do so at the ethnographer's request. I should add here that their names for constellations imply that here they see lineal figures; I cannot investigate the significance of this, as I have no contextual material. At any rate, I would like to emphasize that, even if the Trobriander does occasionally supply connecting lines between points, his perception and experience do not automatically fall into a lineal framework.

The fact remains that Trobrianders embark on, what is certainly for us, a series of acts which "must require" planning and purposiveness. They engage in acts of gift-giving and gift-receiving which we can certainly see as an exchange of gifts. When we plot their journeys, we find that they do go from point to point, they do navigate a course, whether they say so or not. Do they merely refrain from giving linguistic expression to something which they actually recognize in nature? On the nonlinguistic level, do they act on an assumption of a lineality which is given no place in their linguistic formulation? I believe that, where valued activity is concerned, the Trobrianders do not act on an assumption of lineality at any level. There is organization or rather coherence in their acts because Trobriand activity is patterned activity. One act within this pattern gives rise to a pre-ordained cluster of acts. Perhaps one might find a parallel in our culture in the making of a sweater. When I embark on knitting one, the ribbing at the bottom does not *cause* the making of the neckline, nor of the sleeves or the armholes; and it is not part of a lineal series of acts. Rather it is an indispensible part of a patterned activity which includes all these other acts. Again, when I choose a dress pattern, the acts involved in the making of the dress are already present for me. They are embedded in the pattern which I have chosen. In this same way, I believe, can be seen the Trobriand insistence that though intercourse is a necessary preliminary to conception, it is not the cause of conception. There are a number of acts in the pattern of procreating; one is intercourse, another the entrance of the spirit of a dead Trobriander into the womb. However, there is a further point here. The Trobrianders, when pressed by the ethnographer or teased by the neighboring Dobuans, showed signs of intense embarrassment, giving the impression that they were trying to maintain unquestioningly a stand in which they had to believe. This, I think, is because pattern is truth and value for them; in fact, acts and being derive value from the embedding pattern.

So the question of perception of line remains. It is because they find value in pattern that the Trobrianders act according to nonlineal pattern; not because they do not perceive lineality.

But all Trobriand activity does not contain value; and when it does not, it assumes lineality, and is utterly despicable. For example, the pattern of sexual intercourse includes the giving of a gift from the boy to the girl; but if a boy gives a gift so as to win the girl's favor, he is despised. Again, the kula pattern includes the eventual reception of a gift from the original recipient; the pattern is such that it keeps the acts physically and temporally completely disparate. In spite of this, however, some men are accused of giving gifts as an inducement to their kula partner to give them a specially good kula gift. Such men are labeled with the vile phrase: he barters. But this means that, unvalued and despised, lineal behavior does exist. In fact, there are villages in the interior whose inhabitants live mainly by bartering manufactured articles for yams. The inhabitants of Omarakana, about whom Malinowski's work and this study are mainly concerned, will barter with them, but consider them pariahs.

This is to say that it is probable that the Trobrianders experience reality in nonlineal pattern because this is the valued reality; and that they are capable of experiencing lineally, when value is absent or destroyed. It is not to say, however, that this, in itself, means that lineality is given, is present in nature, and that pattern is not. Our own insistence on the line, such as a lineal causality, for example, is also often based on unquestioned belief or value. To return to the subject of procreation, the husband in our culture, who has long hoped and tried in vain to beget children, will nevertheless maintain that intercourse causes conception; perhaps with the same stubbornness and embarrassment which the Trobrianders exhibited when maintaining the opposite.

III

The line in our culture not only connects, but it moves. And as we think of a line as moving from point to point, connecting one to the other, so we conceive of roads as *running from* locality *to* locality. A Trobriander does not speak of roads either as connecting two points, or as *running from* point *to* point. His paths are self-contained, named as independent units; they are not *to* and *from*, they are *at*. And he himself is *at*; he has no equivalent for our *to* or *from*. There is, for instance, the myth of Tudava, who goes—in our view—from village to village and from island to island planting and offering yams. The Trobriand texts puts it this way: "Kitava it-shine village already (i.e., completed) he-is-over. 'I-sail I-go Iwa'; Iwa he-anchor he-go ashore . . . He-sail Digumenu . . . They-drive (him off) . . . he-go Kwaywata." Point after point is enumerated, but his sailing from and to is given as a discrete event. In our view, he is actually following a southeasterly course, more or less; but this is not given as course or line, and no directions are even mentioned. In fact, in the several texts referring to journeyings in the Archipelago, no words occur for the cardinal directions. In sailing, the "following" winds are named according to where they are *at*, the place where they strike the canoe, such as wind-striking-the-outrigger-beam; not according to where they *come from*. Otherwise, we find names for the southwest wind (*youyo*), and the northwest wind (*bombatu*), but these are merely substantival names which have nothing to do with direction; names for kinds of wind.

When a member of our society gives an unemotional description of a person, he follows an imaginary line, usually downward: from head to foot, from tip to toe, from hair to chin. The Navaho do the opposite, following a line upward. The Trobriander follows no line, at least none that I can see. "My head boils," says a kula spell; and it goes on to enumerate the parts of the head as follows: nose, occiput, tongue, larynx, speech, mouth. Another spell-casting a protective fog, runs as follows: "I befog the hand, I befog the foot, I befog the head, I befog the shoulders . . ." There is a magic formula where we do recognize a line, but it is one which Malinowski did not record verbatim at the time, but which he put down later from memory; and it is not improbable that his memory edited the formula according to the lineality of his culture. When the Trobriander enumerates the parts of a canoe, he does not follow any recognizable lineal order: "Mist . . . surround me my mast . . . the nose of my canoe . . . my sail . . . my steering oar . . . my canoe-gunwale . . . my canoe-bottom . . . my prow . . . my rib . . . my threading-stick . . . my canoe-side." Malinowski diagrams the garden site as a square piece of land subdivided into squares; the Trobrianders refer to it in the same terms as those which they use in referring to a village—a bulky object or an aggregate of bumps. When the plots in the garden site are apportioned to the gardeners, the named plots are assigned by name, the others by location along each named side of the garden. After this, the inner plots, the "belly" of the garden, are apportioned. Following along a physical rim is a procedure which we find elsewhere also. In a spell naming villages on the main island, there is a long list of villages which lie along the coast northward, then westward around the island, then south. To us, of course, this is lineal order. But we have no indication that the Trobrianders see other than geographical location, point after point, as they move over a physically continuous area; the line as a guide to procedure is not necessarily implied. No terms are used here which might be taken as an implication of continuity; no "along the coast" or "around" or "northward."

IV

When we in our culture deal with events or experiences of the self; we use the line as guide for various reasons, two of which I shall take up here. First, we feel we must arrange events chronologically in a lineal order; how else could our historians discover the causes of a war or a revolution or a defeat? Among the Trobrianders, what corresponds to our history is an aggregate of anecdotes, that is, unconnected points, told without respect to chronological sequence, or development, or causal relationship; with no grammatical distinction made between words referring to past events, or to present or contemplated ones. And in telling an anecdote, they take no care that a temporal sequence should be followed. For instance, they said to Malinowski. "They-eat-taro, they-spew-taro, they-disgusted-taro"; but if time, as we believe, is a moving line, then the revulsion came first in time, the vomiting was the result, coming afterward. Again, they say, "This-here . . . ripes . . . falls-down truly gives-birth . . . sits seed in belly-his"; but certainly the seed is there first, and the birth follows in time, if time is lineal.

Secondly, we arrange events and objects in a sequence which is climactic, in size and intensity, in emotional meaning, or according to some other principle. We often arrange events from earlier to later, not because we are interested in historical causation, but because the present is the climax of our history. But when the Trobriander relates happenings, there is no developmental arrangement, no building up of emotional tone. His stories have no plot, no lineal development, no climax. And when he repeats his garden spell, his list is neither climactic, nor anticlimactic; it sounds merely untidy to us:

> "The belly of my garden lifts
> The belly of my garden rises
> The belly of my garden reclines
> The belly of my garden is-a-bushhen's-nest-in-lifting
> The belly of my garden is-an-anthill
> The belly of my garden lifts-bends
> The belly of my garden is-an-ironwood-tree-in-lifting
> The belly of my garden lies-down
> The belly of my garden burgeons."

When the Trobrianders set out on their great ceremonial kula expedition, they follow a preestablished order. First comes the canoe of the Tolabwaga, an obscure subclan. Next come the canoes of the great chiefs. But this is not climactic; after the great chiefs come the commoners. The order derives meaning not from lineal sequence, but from correspondence with a present, experienced, meaningful pattern, which is the recreation or realization of the mythical pattern; that which has been ordained of old and is forever. Its meaning does not lie in an item-to-item relationship, but in fitness, in the repetition of an established unit.

An ordering of this sort gives members of our society a certain esthetic disphoria except when, through deliberate training, we learn to go beyond our cultural expectation; or, when we are too young to have taken on the phrasings of our culture. When we manipulate objects naively, we arrange them on some climactic lineal principle. Think of a college commencement, with the faculty arranged in order of rank or length of tenure or other mark of importance; with the students arranged according to increasing physical height, from shortest to tallest, actually the one absolutely irrelevant principle as regards the completion of their college education, which is the occasion for the celebration. Even when the sophisticated avoid this principle, they are not unconscious of it; they are deliberately avoiding something which is there.

And our arrangement of history, when we ourselves are personally involved, is mainly climactic. My great grandmother sewed by candle light, my grandmother used a kerosene lamp, my mother did her studying by gaslight, I did it by a naked electric ceiling light, and my children have diffused fluorescent lighting. This is progress; this is the meaningful sequence. To the Trobriander, climax in history is abominable, a denial of all good, since it would imply not only the presence of change, but also that change increases the good; but to him value lies in sameness, in repeated pattern, in the incorporation of all time within the same point. What is good in life is exact identity with all past Trobriand experience, and all mythical experience. There is no boundary between past Trobriand existence and the present; he can indicate that an action is completed, but this does not mean that the action is past; it may be completed and present or timeless. Where we would say "Many years ago" and use the past tense, the Trobriander will say, "In my father's childhood" and use non-temporal verbs; he places the event situationally, not temporally. Past, present, and future are presented linguistically as the same, are present in his existence, and sameness with what we call the past and with myth, represents value to the Trobriander. Where we see a developmental line, the Trobriander sees a point, at most swelling in value. Where we find pleasure and satisfaction in moving away from the point, in change as variety or progress, the Trobriander finds it in the repetition of the known, in maintaining the point; that is, in what we call monotony. Esthetic validity, dignity, and value come to him not through arrangement into a climactic line, but rather in the undisturbed incorporation of the events within their original, nonlineal order. The only history which has meaning for him is that which evokes the value of the point, or which, in the repetition, swells the value of the point. For example, every occasion in which a kula object participates becomes an ingredient of its being and swells its value; all these occasions are enumerated with great satisfaction, but the lineal course of the traveling kula object is not important.

As we see our history climactically, so do we plan future experiences climactically, leading up to future satisfaction or meaning. Who but a very young child would think of starting a meal with strawberry shortcake and ending it with spinach? We have come to identify the end of the meal with the height of satisfaction, and we identify semantically the words dessert and reward, only because of the similarity of their positions in a climactic line. The Trobriand meal has no dessert, no line, no climax. The special bit, the relish, is eaten *with* the staple food; it is not something to "look *forward to*," while disposing of a meaningful staple.

None of the Trobriand activities are fitted into a climactic line. There is no job, no labor, no drudgery which finds its reward outside the act. All work contains its own satisfaction. We cannot speak of S——R here, as all action contains its own immanent "stimulus." The present is not a means to future satisfaction, but good in itself, as the future is also good in itself; neither better nor worse, neither climactic nor anticlimactic, in fact, not lineally connected nor removed. It follows that the present is not evaluated in terms of its place within a course of action leading upward to a worthy end. In our culture, we can rarely evaluate the present in itself. I tell you that Sally is selling notions at Woolworth's, but this in itself means nothing. It acquires some meaning when I add that she has recently graduated from Vassar. However, I go on to tell you that she has been assistant editor of *Vogue*, next a nursemaid, a charwoman, a public school teacher. But this is a mere jumble; it makes no sense and has no meaning, because the series leads to nothing. You cannot relate one job to another, and you are unable to see them discretely simply as part of her being. However, I now add that she is gathering material for a book on the working mother. Now all this falls in line, it makes sense in terms of a career. Now her job is good and it makes her happy, because it is part of a planned climactic line leading to more pay, increased recognition, higher rank. There was a story in a magazine about the college girl who fell in love with the milkman one summer; the reader felt tense until it was discovered that this was just a summer job, that it was only a means for the continuation of the man's education in the Columbia Law School: Our evaluation of happiness and unhappiness is bound with this motion along an envisioned line leading to a desired end. In the fulfillment of this course or career—not in the fulfillment of the self as point—do we find value. Our conception of freedom rests on the principle of noninterference with this moving line, noninterruption of the intended course of action.

It is difficult to tell whether climax is given in experience at all, or whether it is always imposed on the given. At a time when progress and evolution were assumed to be implicit in nature, our musicians and writers gave us climactic works. Nowadays, our more reflective art does not present experience climactically. Then, is emotion itself climactic? Climax, for us, evokes "thrill" or "drama." But we have cultures, like the Tikopia, where life is lived on an even emotive plane without thrill or climax. Experiences which "we know to be" climactic, are described without climax by them. For example, they, as well as the Trobrianders, described intercourse as an aggregate of pleasurable experiences. But Malinowski is disturbed by this; he cannot place the erotic kiss in Trobriand experience, since it has no climactic function. Again, in our culture, childbearing is climactic. Pregnancy is represented by the usual obstetrician as an uncomfortable means to a dramatic end. For most women, all intensity of natural physical experience is nowadays removed from the actual birth itself; but the approach of birth nevertheless is a period of mounting tension, and drama is supplied by the intensive social recognition of the event, the dramatic accumulation of gifts, flowers, telegrams. A pregnancy is not formally announced since, if it does not eventuate in birth, it has failed to achieve its end; and failure to reach the climax brings shame. In its later stages it may be marked with a shower; but the shower looks forward to the birth, it does not celebrate the pregnancy itself. Among the Trobrianders, pregnancy has meaning in itself, as a state of being. At a first pregnancy, there is a long ceremonial involving "preparatory" work on the part of many people, which merely celebrates the pregnancy. It does not anchor the baby, it does not *have as its purpose* a more comfortable time during the pregnancy, it does not *lead to* an easier birth or a healthy baby. It makes the woman's skin white, and makes her be at her most beautiful; yet this *leads to* nothing, since she must not attract men, not even her own husband.

V

Are we then right in accepting without question the presence of a line in reality? Are we in a position to say with assurance that the Trobrianders are wrong and we are right? Much of our present-day thinking, and much of our evaluation, are based on the premise of the line and of the line as good. Students have been refused admittance to college because the autobiographic sketch accompanying their application showed absence of the line; they lacked purposefulness and ability to plan; they were inadequate as to character as well as intellectually. Our conception of personality formation, our stress on the significance of success and failure and of frustration in general, is based on the axiomatically postulated line. How can there be blocking without presupposed lineal motion or effort? If I walk along a path because I like the country, or if it is not important to get to a particular point at a particular time, then the insuperable puddle from the morning's shower is not frustrating; I throw stones into it and watch the ripples, and then choose another path. If the undertaking is of value in itself, a point good in itself, and not because it leads to something, then failure has no symbolic meaning; it merely results in no cake for supper, or less money in the family budget; it is not personally destructive. But failure is devastating in our culture, because it is not failure of the undertaking alone; it is the moving, becoming, lineally conceived self which has failed.

Ethnographers have occasionally remarked that the people whom they studied showed no annoyance when interrupted. Is this an indication of mild temper, or might it be the case that they were not interrupted at all, as there was no expectation of lineal continuity? Such questions are new in anthropology and most ethnographers therefore never thought of recording material which would answer them. However, we do have enough material to make us question the line as basic to all experience; whether it is actually present in given reality or not, it is not always present in experienced reality. We cannot even take it for granted as existing among those members of our society who are not completely or naively steeped in their culture, such as many of our artists, for example. And we should be very careful, in studying other cultures, to avoid the unexamined assumption that their actions are based on the prediction of a lineal reality.

BIBLIOGRAPHY

Lee, Dorothy. "A Primitive System of Values." *Philosophy of Science* 7 (1940): 1355.
Lee, Dorothy. "Being and Value in a Primitive Culture." *Journal of Philosophy* 46 (1949): No. 401.
Malinowski, B. *Argonauts of the Western Pacific.* London, 1922.
Malinowski, B. *The Sexual Life of Savages.* New York, 1929.
Malinowski, B. *Coral Gardens and their Magic.* New York, 1935.

20 / Autonomous Motivation

Dorothy Lee

I

I have called the subject of my paper "autonomous motivation," only because I could find no other term which would communicate what I want to say before I present it at length. I hope to show that where there is full engagement of the individual in his life, he is invited to act, rather than motivated to act. I shall speak of a view of motivation which is gaining ground in recent years; in my own case, it was arrived at through work with non-Western cultures, and it is original only insofar as the journey I made, from departure to arrival, was my own.

In writing my paper I encountered great difficulty, because all the words at hand, and all the concepts they represented, were relevant to a view of motivation which I have found inadequate to cover all the data I encountered. In describing cultural situations which have forced me to reconsider my old view, I have had to use negatives when I was referring to something whose very peculiarity was affirmation. I have had to go against my long training in restrained and measured scholarly prose. The words I sometimes choose are deplorable, because what they refer to—

the uninhibited, the impulseful—is itself unacceptable. But in fact, there were far too few such words available to me. So I have had to describe that which is without limit, in terms which imply limit.

At first I saw such situations only in the non-Western cultures I was studying, perhaps because the entire structure of the society was based on a non-Western assumption of "motivation." I have later come to see that this was true also of the people around me, in my own society; I saw that the official view of motivation, which I had accepted, and the conception of the self which this presupposed, had blurred my vision, with the result that I did not see what was there.

When I first started studying anthropology, I had accepted the notion that man behaved in response to basic needs. Man's activities were presented to me as economic, or as at any rate leading to the satisfaction of needs. When they were religious, even religion was presented to me as a means to an end, usually to an economic end, with pre-imagined, hoped-for results, furnishing the activity literally with an end, a finish. Over the years, the social sciences have provided me with a variety of theories of motivation. Man was motivated to satisfy basic needs, or to reduce tension, or in response to an externally applied stimulus; or he was propelled by some inner drive.

To my mind, all these theories differed only in specifics. Essentially they all viewed man as inert, driven or prodded or otherwise dependent on a furnished motivating power. But what I found when I read about "primitive cultures," contradicted all this. The behavior I saw was often nonutilitarian or even anti-utilitarian; it was often deliberately wasteful of materials and energy, and consciously inefficient—to use a term which has relevance only within my own framework of concepts. For such and similar behavior, the social scientist provided me with motivation—for example, with the desire for prestige. But by this time I was wary of Western explanations. It seemed to me that the Western social scientist actually described how *he* felt, how *he* behaved, with his Western needs for sensible moderation, for weighing the consequences of his action, for the rigid limiting logic, with his admiration for restraint and reasonableness. He said to himself, "If I were a Kwakiutl or a Trobriander, why would I be doing this?" But the fact is that he was not a Kwakiutl. In fact I am not even sure that he told me how he as a person felt in this situation, what propelled him to action. I rather think he told me how he *ought* to feel, in accordance with the theories he held.

At any rate, the data from other societies questioned all this. For instance, I started with the view that man acted to satisfy basic needs, and that when he could not be expected to be acting directly so as to satisfy these needs, then he had to be stimulated in some other way. Reward had to be dangled before him, a stimulus had to prod him, or, later, a drive had to push him; or the discomfort of tension moved him to act to achieve a resolution, or at any rate to reduce the tension. Yet there were the Eskimo who ate when they were hungry and fully satisfied their hunger—acting, I imagine, according to the traditional theory of motivation—but then kept on eating unreasonably for many hours, as long as the food lasted. Why? Conversely, there were the hungry Arapesh, who instead of being properly motivated to work so as to satisfy their hunger, instead of spending time and energy in producing more food so that they would not be continually hungry, wasted the larger part of their time and effort in a variety of undertakings which resulted merely in a virtuosity of nonutilitarian social intercourse.

In fact, in a variety of ways I saw people of other cultures going to absurd lengths of effort, to extremes of behavior completely inexplicable when set within my own reasonable framework of views about human behavior. I found people like the Kwakiutl, who worked outrageously, with vigor and involvement, beyond any crying need to satisfy hunger; people who collected stupendous amounts of oil only to burn it in a gigantic public conflagration, in a fantastic game of trying to unseat their visitors who had come on purpose to engage in this sport. I read

Malinowski's account of the Trobrianders who undertook laborious and fearful expeditions involving the careful working of a variety of magical performances and the observation of greatly depriving taboos; expeditions which meant the cutting down of large trees with stone implements and taking them to the shore without vehicles and without roads; which necessitated the building of seagoing canoes, the collection of provisions, the striking out into witch-infested water; time-consuming, effort-demanding expeditions which brought in no food, no clothing or shelter, nothing but some "ornaments" which in fact did not adorn, as most of them could not or would not be worn; and which would be possessed for probably not more than a year. I could not see these people propelled by any of the basic needs. And what drives could be strong enough to push the Kwakiutl and the Trobrianders into such extremes of exertion? What stimulus was massive enough to result in this response?

Such questions forced me to discard all theories of motivation with which I was acquainted and to see what I could find for myself. The needs and drives and tensions which I had been offered as sources of behavior were too bounded by the limits of our own reason to account for the exorbitant behavior I found. And in fact the whole list of needs and drives was to my mind irrelevant when I tried to see it in connection with this behavior. Hunger does motivate, but meagerly, within limits: its satiation forms a rigid ceiling. Hunger goads me as I goad a reluctant animal which responds up to a point, compelled into moving a required amount. But what explains the running, the skipping, the bounding? Why does my goat leap over the highest "obstacles" in the path instead of taking the easy, effortless way around them as I do—obstacles which obviously invite rather than obstruct through their demand for effort? Why does the Eskimo, after he satisfies hunger, eat food which he has risked his life to get, without thought of tomorrow's hunger? Why did the Trobrianders grow, with such unreasonable exertion, twice as many yams as they needed, doing a great amount of hard work which did not go into increasing or bettering or ensuring the yield, "unnecessary" work, and then have magic made so that these yams should rot undisturbed and uneaten in the yamhouse?

Once I decided that I needed a fresh theory, I saw that people in all the societies which I studied exerted themselves often to unimaginable lengths; but their efforts might or might not result in food or shelter or prestige. It seemed as if the exertion itself expended within a meaningful situation, was sufficient in itself.

When I looked around me in this country, I did not at first glance see such absurdity of exertion. I saw people preferring to ride rather than walk, to push a button rather than light a stove, to turn on an automatic washing machine rather than scrub clothes. I saw people responding to the stimulus of profit, working harder and longer for more pay. Yet I also saw these same people working even harder, beyond profit and beyond pay. I saw women inventing new stitches to make their knitting more engrossing, and demanding of more alertness; and I saw them devising more intricate and laborious cooking to do on their push-button stoves.

All around me, I saw people who work to earn money to buy themselves the opportunity to exert themselves, for no profit beyond any imaginable limit; unreasonably, without calculating risk or effort or profit, in danger to limb and life itself; attempting to climb inaccessible cliffs and peaks, skiing, shooting rapids, swimming beyond the limits of safety. Occasionally they did this in public, perhaps seeking prestige, but much more often they did it in obscurity.

I saw all this most clearly in connection with our own educational process. This happened when my son, a high school freshman, took up tennis. He had been a textbook paradigm of the theory of motivation which I had held. According to his teachers and the school authorities, he was a model student, fulfilling all requirements and meeting all obligations. He carried out all his assignments competently, completing them acceptably on time. In every school situation, he moved until he bumped his head against the ceiling of his goal: the reasonable expectations of his teachers, and of the established requirements for an *A*. His mind was flabby, he was bored and listless. He did not want to get up in the morning, because there was nothing to get up for.

Then he discovered tennis. This had an inviting horizon, a horizon which could never stop him because it retreated as he moved. No contrived incentive had to be furnished, no fixed grade insured a reasonable effort, no defined achievement put an end to his effort. Tennis invited him to unlimited exertion. Now on Sundays he got up at daybreak so as to have a long time at the tennis courts: and without a break for meals, dressed unbecomingly in sweat clothes against the cold drizzle of late winter, paying no heed to discomfort or the passage of time, he played far into exhaustion.

What motivated him? He was certainly not motivated by the need to succeed competitively. I watched him win a junior championship; he was apathetic and sluggish, he was engaged only to a minimum; his opponent did not offer him strong competition. It was a poor game and he did not enjoy it. He was not glad or proud of his "success." Conversely, whenever he could, he chose for himself partners who were bound to defeat him. He chose them because they gave him a good game. What was he seeking? What he was seeking was an opponent—and I use this term in its literal sense of someone who is opposite, who would draw from him the full exercise of all that was in him; one who would evoke him—not push or compel him, to an answering response of exertion beyond known limits. The partners he liked usually defeated him. Yet he chose them, because they invited him to actualize all his capacities—his coordination, his split-second judgment, his foot-work, his skill, his imagination, his planning; all of these focused upon the one instant of hitting the tennis ball. He sought for a partner who would engage his whole being to full commitment.

You will say that all this was because he liked sports, and not books; but I believe this is not the case. He went to his school with a passion for mathematics. He was filled with an urgent inquiry into logic and values and metaphysics; he wanted to know how we know that we know, and what is man. But the school could not recognize urgency, and felt responsible to protect him against the enormity of his own appetite for knowledge and exploration. Besides, they had on hand a system of organized, externally applied motivations for the students, since the filling of school assignments could not be left to the compelling force of basic needs. So they stopped his immoderate appetite by feeding him what was moderate and good for him, what was appropriate for a boy of his age. For his clamorous inquiry they substituted their concept of what an educated man should know, or even the so-called need for achievement, which could be satisfied when one's limited goal had been achieved. If his urgency had been recognized and encouraged, instead of being firmly fenced in; if the view of motivation as depending on needs and drives and external stimulus had not been substituted for the striving of the human spirit, I believe he would have been truly as alive in school as he was on the tennis court. Actually, he himself was aware of the constricting effect of set goals, and chose to go to a college without grades, where his inquiry is gushing freely and tennis has taken second place.

II

Eventually I came to form another view of man's behavior. I saw man as moving rather than motivated, as thrusting forward, striving, aspiring. As I said above, others also have come to this view of man. The biologist Edmund Sinnott means something of this sort when he speaks of the "inner urgencies that guide behavior," and when he says of man: "there come bubbling up in him a host of desires . . . his cravings for beauty, his moral aspirations, his love of his fellows." Another biologist, Ludwig von Bertalanffy, speaks of this when he says, "The organism should not be considered as a responding machine but rather as primary activity. . . . Primary behavior is continuous." Gordon Allport refers to this as "propriate striving," which could distinguish itself from other forms of motivation in that "however beset by conflict, it makes for unification of personality." Abraham Maslow speaks of the value of being fully human, and of the urge of the self to flex its muscles, so to speak; and both he and Kurt Goldstein speak of man as striving toward self-actualization.

What struck me about what I call striving or thrust was that the behavior in which it eventuated was prodigal, exuberant, unpredictable in its reach. I now saw man as spontaneously eager to exert himself to the utmost of his capacities, in his striving to be fully human. And immediately I was appalled at the niggardliness of my terms, and of the concepts which they named. The "utmost" I just used, merely pushes the limit out a little further; the fullest is still limited by what it fills. I can fill my cup to its utmost limit, but that is only to the known lip. If I speak of brimming over, of excess or exorbitance, all my terms refer to concepts which take account of measure and limit. Yet I have to use these terms, though they are in contradiction to what I say. In fact, I believe that lack of limit, infinitude, is a necessary dimension of this propriate striving, thus differentiating it absolutely from motivation, whose quality is finitude and limit. Thus the thrust can be so exuberant as to bring down the criticism of the Western observer who will speak of improvidence, or of the inability to resist one's impulses: or, as a participant, will worry at the childishness of people who cannot be taught rationing, or to realize the necessity for forced marches.

The exuberance of which I speak is most obvious in situations where we ourselves would have been moved to calculation and measure. For instance, among people who are constantly on the brink of starvation, hospitality may be exercised to the point of what we would call madness. Consider, for instance, Thesiger's accounts of the Arabs of the Empty Quarter, whom he visited some ten years ago. There is his description of the occasion when he and his five companions met an encampment of Bedu in this most desolate of deserts. These people had no tent, no blankets, no headdresses, no shirts, nothing but their ragged loincloths to spread over themselves in the freezing cold of the desert night. They had no food except the milk of their camels, and this they pressed on their sudden uninvited guests, brooking no refusal; yet they had had nothing to eat or drink for a day, and would have nothing for another twenty-four hours. This is excessive giving, beyond the limits of common sense or rationality.

For that matter, their entire way of living was beyond the bounds of reason or common sense. Thesiger reports that at this time the oil fields were in need of workers, who would be paid large sums for doing nothing except sit in the shade and guard a dump. Yet these Bedu resisted all invitation—I will not say temptation; it would have tempted *me* in their place, but it obviously was no temptation to them—to this easy way of earning a living. They lived in an appalling discomfort, they went hungry, cold, and exhausted from hard traveling by day and from unrefreshing nights, when sleep was disturbed by the need to move about to get some warmth. They were in constant danger of death from starvation, from thirst, from camel-raiders.

Thesiger speaks of hiring a pack camel, whose owner was ready to walk across the desert with him. This man had worn out the soles of his feet on the journey he had just completed, and was prepared to walk on raw flesh, on the harsh floor of the desert. This is absurd, particularly since he could easily have earned money working in a garden in a village.

These people chose to live this way and no Western explanation can contain the effulgence which gave rise to and supported their choice.

In one form or other, I find this exuberant exertion in most of the cultures I know. There are differences, among the cultures, however. Each culture contains its own definition of what it is to be fully human, has its own areas where man is invited to limitless exertion, and furnishes its own peculiar situations which call forth men's exertion. If to be fully human means to be completely, organically continuous with one's social unit, as it does among the Nyakyusa of Tanganyika, the people will exert themselves in learning and performing meticulously the minutely detailed and intricate practices which, for instance, will make a woman at one with the lineage of her husband, or a newly conceived embryo continuous with the body of its father. If to be a man fully meant to be a gardener, as it did among the Trobrianders whom Malinowski visited, then a man went to all sorts of (to us) unnecessary and inexplicable lengths in performing his gardening.

If, as I believe to be the case in our own culture at present, there is no official recognition of exuberance, then the human spirit burgeons beyond the official stricture. At present, for instance, we do not give sanction to effulgence, to excess, to gushing behavior without calculation or measure or risk. Officially, we ask for the calculable, the graspable. We aspire to a set ceiling. (See, for instance, David Riesman's "The Found Generation" in the Autumn 1956 *American Scholar*.) Full humanness for us means no spilling over, no bursting through the bounds of measure and prediction. Yet, unofficially, outside the recognized structure of our culture the human spirit even in our present-day society does thrust beyond the limits set by the measure, and spills over into activities of absurd exertion and commitment, such as the ones I mentioned above.

Another characteristic of thrust which I found was that it could not come forth in isolation; it existed in an open system of transaction. In every culture I studied, I found that if man was not "motivated," that is if he was not prodded into moving, he had to be invited to thrust forward. Cultural systems, affording man his place in the universal whole, furnished a variety of situations (to use a phrase which I shall have to contradict later) for calling forth man's exertion. I shall speak here of only one such system, which I find in a variety of forms among the Indians and the Eskimo of this continent.

I believe that generally among these people, man was viewed as a collaborator with the rest of nature or the universe in building the world of experience. I have found this to be so, at any rate, among those cultures which have been studied intensively enough to uncover man's view of his place in the universe. For instance, such a view seems to be underlying the verbal structure of the Navaho language. Here we have verbal forms which indicate that rollingness, or flyingness through the air, preexist as potential, or as design, in certain objects. A man does not *cause* a ball to roll, he releases its predisposition to roll, or actualizes the potential to roll, or puts the rollingness into operation. (I am profoundly aware of the inadequacy of all these phrases I have used just now; there are no such concepts in American culture, and all the words with which this culture provides me are inadequate and in fact wrong when I use them to present what I am trying to present.)

Such a picture of man in the universe is clearly presented in the language of the Wintu Indians of California. Here the primary verbal stem refers to a world, a universe, that neither exists nor does not exist. We might say that it refers to the nature of things, a nature which is not realized because the things themselves do not exist, the situations have not come to be and may never come to be. Only at the instant when man experiences these do they come into existence, into history. The experiential or existential stem of the verb is derivative from this other stem. When man speaks with the aid of this stem, he asserts existence through his own experience of it. And it is only through his doing, through, probably, his decisive act or his act of will, that the world to which the primary stem refers can have concrete existence. This dialogue between the idea of the universe or the potential of the universe, and man's experience, runs through the entire verbal system, and perhaps through the entire linguistic structure.

With the Hopi Indians, we find this picture systematically expressed in their "Hopi way." Here there was a preestablished universal order, a design; but it needed man's cooperation to become actualized. The course of the sun was set between winter solstice and summer solstice; but the sun could not move between these two solstices unless man cooperated. The land could not thaw to allow for planting, unless man translated the design into the actuality.

Man's part in all this was to work—both in a technical sense and also in a religious sense through his ceremonials. Through such ceremonials the sun was enabled to move from stage to stage, the corn was enabled to grow along its given cycle of growth. When he cleared the fields, when he dug and planted and weeded, when he sang to the growing corn to make it happy, and when he worked his corn ceremonial, man was cooperating with the corn to enable it to follow its course. To do this a Hopi needed to put himself through a long, in fact an endless educational process. He had to train his body, he had to learn to endure pain and cold and hunger and thirst. He had to learn technical processes, to get detailed knowledge about the corn and its ways, and also he had to grow himself into a person who could carry out the necessary ceremonials. For instance, he had to learn to empty his mind from all dissonance and anxiety, from all evil thoughts. He had to discipline himself strongly, so that he could eventually concentrate on thinking good and peaceful thoughts only. Some men went further than others along this Hopi way. After the training of childhood, which did include punishment, all went eventually along this way without external coercion, in answer to the invitation to bring the design into human history.

This kind of picture of man's share in the universe emerged for the Eskimo, also, in a recent study by Paul Riesman. These people show a gusto for life, that is, for their own way of life, which is difficult for us to comprehend. In fact, Western society was concerned to the point of making an effort to "ease the lot" of the Eskimo, thereby probably destroying the meaning of life for them. And it was easy to see them as people in need of help. Here were people for whom sudden disaster was commonplace, an everyday matter of living; people for whom impending starvation was a reality to be encountered at any time; people who froze to death, murdered or were murdered with apparently slight provocation, were mauled to death by polar bears, fell into crevasses and were killed, overturned in their kayaks and were drowned. Their lives were so full of such hardships that it is incredible that anyone could have endured them, let alone chosen to endure them.

And yet these people have repeatedly been reported as being sorry for the white because he had to live a different kind of life. In fact, some forty years ago, when one of them visited New York and came back to report on its large population, he was thought to be lying because the hearers could not believe that such a large number of people could choose to live this way, when they could have lived in an Eskimo way.

This zest for (Eskimo) life, this readiness to endure hardship and encounter mortal danger, is called forth apparently through the part which a person finds for himself in the universal scheme. The Eskimo is a collaborator with the rest of the universe in creating the Eskimo world of existence.

For the Eskimo the universe is thought, but man only has the capacity to think. Yet man cannot think unless thought enters him, and thought cannot exist unless man thinks it. If I say, then, that thought exists outside man, every one of the words I use is wrong because I use them in the context of my culture where man is complete in himself, the universe is complete in itself, and thought either exists or does not exist. For the Eskimo thought outside man does not have existence, it hovers on the brink of existence; in fact it is not thought, it does not exist, it is not outside, since the universe itself contains man, and man is not man completely without the so-called outside.

Now this incompletion except in mutual collaboration, this interdependence for very existence, furnishes the equivalent of what we call motivation. Man is constantly invited to make actual both the existence of the world and his own existence. At the moment when he thinks, at the moment when he gives existence to the potential thought which is outside him (thought which is potential only insofar as man is ready and striving to give it actuality), at this moment man and the universe come into existence. Thought has now become "a think," to use Paul Riesman's term.

All events come into being in this way through man's collaboration; they have existed as thoughts outside man until man has brought them into history. And if man is to create a strong, full situation, he has to do this with full humanity, he has to meet the universe with all his being strained to its utmost limits or, I should say, beyond any preconceivable limit. Now this in our own culture would be seen as motivation; here it is human striving in response to evocation, which takes the form of a call to create one's world in collaboration. This is what is behind his urge to learn without end, to discipline himself, and to endure without limit.

And in fact, to live his life in the arctic, an Eskimo had to have a high development of skills, of perceptiveness and sensitivity, of alertness. For instance, a man traveling through a dense snowstorm had to know where, in the vast expanse, to dig with his heel to uncover the two-inch track of the sled which went by before the storm. What multitude and variety of perceptions, what wealth of detailed knowledge, went into this one discovery, I cannot imagine, and the ethnographers themselves could not find out. A man had to grow in self-discipline until he could remain motionless at a seal hole for three or four days at a time, "feet planted together, head down, bottom high, forced by the seal's acute hearing to maintain absolute silence," and to do this while fully and passionately engaged, gazing with intensity, alert to the tiniest movement. He had to be ready and able to build an igloo in a blinding and smothering blizzard, imperturbable in the face of what was catastrophic to his white companion, without disorganizing haste, gently prodding the ground with his harpoon to find the proper snow, carefully cutting blocks with precision and speed, trimming lightly and accurately; and then, while his white companion huddled in the igloo in fear and misery, he had to be able to go out again into the blizzard, as a matter of course, to dig up the snow-buried dogs and feed them.

All this was an aspect of collaboration in building the world; it was all part of being Eskimo. When they lived a non-Eskimo life of ease, de Poncins describes the people as apathetic. He speaks about them at the trading post, where they had "warmth, they had biscuits, they had tea. . . . They are dull, sullen, miserable. . . . But open wide the door, fling them into the blizzard and they come to." Now they are Inuk, men-preeminently.

I have not been indulging here in an exercise in cultural relativity. Though it is a view so foreign to our own official culture that our language itself cannot be used to express it, actually this view of man as invited to collaboration has been gaining ground for many years. When Dewey spoke of the transaction between buyer and seller, he was describing something like the Eskimo world. Buyer and seller are not buyer and seller, except insofar as they create each other in the process of transaction. I am not a buyer, unless you are willing to sell to me. Conversely, you can become a seller only insofar as I am ready to buy.

There is a further dimension to this, however. This is something which my son pointed out to me when I told him how I had described his tennis playing in the first part of this paper. He pointed out that he did not "play a game of tennis" against a competitor. There was no game to play. The two partners collaborated to create the game. The effort beyond calculable limit, the training in skills, the development of imagination, the boundless exertion, all these grew naturally out of the striving to help create a good game. And the choice of a strong competitor grew also out of this. If success came, it was welcome, but it was secondary. To be motivated by the need for success in choosing a partner would have been to make the creation of the game itself incidental only.

The game of tennis is one of many situations in our culture which are so structured as to evoke the putting forth of effort, energy, exertion through an invitation to collaborate. Most of these situations, however, are outside the official framework of our society. For many years now, for instance, our artists, our musicians, our writers have been proceeding on this basis. As Koestler puts it: "The artist's aim is to turn his audience into accomplices." And Virginia Woolf, speaking of the author, says to her reader: "Be his fellow worker and accomplice."

III

I have directed my attention to motivation here largely because of the increasing concern in the schools with "underachievement" and with "underdevelopment of the capacity to learn." I have attempted to say in this paper that the theory of motivation which we have applied generally in the schools does motivate, but only up to a limit. If the full capacity of the individual is to be tapped and encouraged toward development, we have to have a new view, to operate on a new basis.

The basis which I have been describing in this paper, the strong invitation to the individual to collaborate in creating his situation—in this case his educational situations—has been progressively eliminated from the schools in this century.

We have seen competition only as competitive success, as leading to a harmful comparative evaluation of the human being; and much of it was exactly this, and was rightly expelled from the school situation. We saw achievement only as a pawn in the winning of conditional love, or as a bid for approval. As such it was undesirable and harmful, and was eliminated, at any rate at the policy-making level. We failed to see achievement as the end product of spontaneously entered exertion and discipline, as the enjoyed performance of carefully learned skills. And we failed to see the necessity for the competitor as collaborator in creating the situations which would call forth this unmeasured exertion, this chosen self-discipline and learning; and, in fact, there were no situations to create, as they were furnished ready-made.

In the beginning of my paper I said that I was not speaking of autonomous motivation. I have tried to show that I speak of striving and thrust instead, and that an individual, if he is to strive with all his capacity, is not completely autonomous: he needs to see himself as collaborating.

21 / Conceptual Styles, Culture Conflict, and Nonverbal Tests of Intelligence

Rosalie A. Cohen

In 1963 a series of studies on the cognitive nature of educational disadvantage was begun at the Learning Research and Development Center at the University of Pittsburgh.[1] A number of studies were completed, and others are still in progress. Some of these investigations have dealt with the generic requirements for pupil performance in school and some with the cognitive framework from which such requirements are derived (Cohen 1967). Others have dealt with comparative language styles of low-income groups and those used as standards in the school (Cohen, Fraenkel, and Brewer 1968) with sources of different conceptual styles in primary-group participation, with the replacement of socioeconomic status with a discriminator among children from low-income homes (Cohen 1967), with the relationship of conceptual styles to ego development (Cohen 1967, 1968a), and with an analysis of programs for the educationally disadvantaged (Cohen 1965). A common thread through all these inquiries was the two-way analysis of the cognitive requirements of the school and their derivative social and psychological behaviors and those learning characteristics brought to the school by children from low-income homes.

Findings from the above body of research helped to isolate specific areas of response difficulties in these tests, which we have identified as areas of culture conflict, and to define and clarify some of the culture-bound characteristics of nonverbal tests of intelligence. In order to outline the pattern of reasoning used by the investigators, some of the findings from the studies are reported briefly below.

In order to operationalize the middle-class orientation of the school the content of the ten most widely used standardized tests of intelligence and achievement were analyzed, and a sample of the researchers who develop and revise these tests were surveyed (Cohen 1967). The object of this inquiry was to identify the generic requirements for achievement that such instruments make of the people to whom they are administered. These types of requirement were isolated: (1) breadth and depth of general information, (2) analytic abstraction, and (3) field articulation (the ability to extract salient information from an embedding context, as in reading comprehension or in the extraction of an arithmetic problem from a word context). Although information growth with growing maturity is taken for granted, development in analytic abstraction and field articulation is often obscured by the information contexts in which the demonstration of these cognitive skills is embedded.

Standardized tests of intelligence and achievement are made up of items that assess both increasing assimilation of concepts and general information and increasing skills in formal analysis and field articulation. The latter skills are measured by items requiring the subject to derive analogies or "logical" sequences. Here is a sample from the Metropolitan Achievement Inventory (ninth-grade level):

Chair: sit; bed:—— (*Chair* is to *sit* as *bed* is to ——.)
Select from the following: *lie; bedroom; night; crib; tired.*

To arrive at the appropriate response (*lie*), the subject must abstract the part of speech required, in addition to other attributes of the choices, in order to complete the logical sequence. Reading-comprehension tests directly measure increasing skills in field articulation, although performance on all subtests requires this skill. Thus, the school requires improvement in analytic abstraction and field articulation skills in increasingly measured amounts of each higher grade level as well as a demonstration of growth in pupils' information repertoires. In general, intelligence tests are weighted toward information components; achievement tests are weighted somewhat on "logical" skills, that is, on skills of analytic abstraction and field articulation.

Analytic-abstraction and field-articulation skills require a specific kind of approach to selecting and organizing information. Individuals differ, however, in what they select as salient information in a given stimulus or situation. They also differ in how they classify and generalize that information. Methods of selecting and processing information can be classified in terms of "cognitive styles" or "styles of cognitive control." Some individuals are "splitters," and others are "lumpers." Some individuals think attributes of a stimulus have significance in themselves; others think they have significance only in reference to some total context (Kagan, Moss, and

Siegal 1963). But the school requires one specific approach to cognitive organization—analytic—so the ability to use it well becomes more critical at higher grade
levels. Pupils with inadequate development of these skills and those who develop a
different cognitive style could be expected not only to be poor achievers early in
their school experience but also to grow worse, comparatively, as they move to
higher grade levels.

Having determined that achievement in school requires increasingly sophisticated
analytic cognitive skills, a second study inquired into the characteristics of other (or
perhaps conflicting) approaches to cognitive organization that might divert, or
handicap the development of, analytic skills (Cohen 1967; Kagan, Moss, and Siegal
1963; Gardner, MS). The literature on cognitive styles suggests that at least one
clear-cut "other" cognitive style has been observed reliably over time. The nonana-
lytic cognitive style is called here "relational," although in literature it is more
commonly called "self-centered" (as opposed to "stimulus-centered" character
of the analytic style). The literature indicates that cognitive styles are independent
of native ability and that they are definable without reference to specific substantive content.

The analytic cognitive style is characterized by a formal or analytic mode of ab-
stracting salient information from a stimulus or situation and by a stimulus-centered
orientation to reality, and it is parts-specific (i.e., parts or attributes of a given
stimulus have meaning in themselves). The relational cognitive style, on the other
hand, requires a descriptive mode of abstraction and is self-centered in its orientation
to reality; only the global characteristics of a stimulus have meaning to its users,
and these only in reference to some total context (Cohen 1967; Kagan, Moss, and
Siegal 1963).

In the literature, it was also possible to identify clear-cut social and psychological
correlates to both analytic and relational cognitive styles. Marked distinctions between individuals using each of these two cognitive styles have been drawn using a
wide variety of tests, as well as through consideration of many of their social and
psychological characteristics. Many school-related learning characteristics, such as
length and intensity of attention, preferences of optional reading material, and the
differential dependence upon primary groups, also distinguish between these two
types of individuals (Cohen 1967; Kagan, Moss, and Siegal 1963) Their language
styles differ as well (Bernstein 1964a: 288–314, 1964b). Appendix A systematizes
these relationships as they have been demonstrated empirically by other investigators.

A new observation that emerged from this study of the literature on cognitive
styles was that not only test criteria but also the overall ideology and learning environment of the school embody requirements for many social and psychological
correlates of the analytic style. This emphasis can be found, for example, in its
cool, impersonal, outer-centered approach to reality organization. Analytic correlates can also be found in the requirements that the pupil learn to sit increasingly
long periods of time, to concentrate alone on impersonal learning stimuli, and to
observe and value organized time-allottment schedules. In order to appreciate fully
the impact of the analytic approach on the school environment, therefore, it is
necessary to consider how many of its impersonal behavioral requirements ensue
subtly from this analytic frame of reference. So discrepant are the analytic and
relational frames of reference that a pupil whose preferred mode of cognitive organization is emphatically relational is unlikely to be rewarded in the school setting
either socially or by grades, regardless of his native abilities and even if his information repertoire and background of experience are adequate. It appears that,
although relational patterns of response have been known to exist, both the cognitive characteristics of this style and its sociobehavioral correlates have been considered deviant and disruptive in the analytically oriented learning environment of the
school.

Although the relationship of the analytic frame of reference to curriculum components has engaged the attention of researchers, possible sources of this and other conceptual styles have escaped systematic exploration. Indeed, the psychological literature suggests that cognitive styles are either predetermined by the nature of the organism or that they are the result of idiosyncratic early experiences that have developed into learning pathways as the result of random trials in problem settings. These explanations do not account for the dominance of relational modes of cognitive organization among individuals from low-income environments[2] and of analytic modes among those of middle-class origins. The absence of normal distributions of these characteristics suggests that such systematic variations may have arisen as a result of different social environments that stimulate, reinforce, and make functional the development of one style of conceptual organization and constrain and inhibit others.

Because low-income environments were known to produce some analytic as well as relational thinks, a search for with-group discriminators was begun. During a year of observation and interview in low-income neighborhoods in and around Pittsburgh, families, young people, indigenous leaders of poverty communities, and sophisticated principals of schools in these districts all were able to identify certain consistent and definably "deviant" characteristics of family and friendship-group organization in these areas, which were validated by observation.

The structure of these important face-to-face groups and the manner in which critical functions were distributed in them appeared to be quite different from typical middle-class methods of primary-group organization. In the family and friendship groups in certain segments of all these low-income districts, regardless of ethnic differences among them, critical functions such as leadership, child care, and the discretionary use of group funds are not assigned to status roles within the group. Instead, critical functions are periodically performed or widely shared by all members of the group; for this reason they came to be called "shared-function" primary groups. A summary of some of their characteristics are compared with those of a simplified formal model in Appendix B, and discursive commentary and further description of their internal dynamics and their articulation with institutional group structures appear in other papers (Cohen 1968b, 1968c). Observation indicated that relational and analytic cognitive styles were intimately associated with shared-function and formal styles of group organization. The manner in which critical functions were distributed in them seemed to parallel closely the observable cognitive functioning of their members. When individuals shifted from one kind of group structure to the other, their modes of group participation, their language styles, and their cognitive styles could be seen to shift appropriately to the extent that their expertise in using other approaches made flexibility possible. It appeared that certain kinds of cognitive styles may have developed by day-to-day participation in related kinds of social groups in which the appropriate language structure and methods of thinking about self, things, and ideas are necessary components of their related styles of group participation and that these approaches themselves may act to facilitate or impede their "carriers" ability to become involved in alternate kinds of groups.

Although our major concern was with the relationships between total primary group configurations and their interarticulation and the development of internally consistent conceptual styles, it was possible to identify comparable methods of group participation and their associated conceptual styles within a single group structure in relatively insulated interaction webs.

Several of the studies that followed made use of multidimensional instruments in an attempt to reduce own-discipline and own-culture bias. They studied the relationships among shared-function and formally organized families and friendship groups, relational and analytic conceptual styles, and school achievement (one case

of formally organized institutional involvement).[3] In order to determine whether
the response styles that appeared on psychological tests were *dominant* modes of
conceptual organization, an effort was made to "triangulate" on mode of conceptual organization through the methods and techniques of several disciplines.[4] Two
psychological instruments were used, two conventional linguistic instruments, and
a seventy-two-item set of attitude scales.[5] A typical outline of an instrument plan
follows in table 21.1 and is elaborated in table 21.2.

This plan was designed to determine the extent to which a given mode of reality
organization is demonstrated persistently—on psychological tests of cognitive style,
in language selections and organization, and in attitudes about one's self and one's
environment. "Conceptual style," then, is a composite construct that incorporates
all three dimensions in each of the two cognitive-skill areas. Dominant patterns of
conceptual organization were then related to dominant styles of family and friendship group participation (determined by the distribution of critical functions in
these two primary groups and producing a longitudinal component, family impact
having occurred earlier in time than that of the friendship group) and to school
achievement (as measured by eighteen subtests of the Project Talent achievement
inventory, covering the areas of general screening, vocabulary, literature, music,
social studies, mathematics, physical science, biological science, scientific attitude,
aeronautics and space, electronics and electricity, mechanics, farming, home eco-

TABLE 21.1. ANTICIPATED RESPONSES IN ANALYTIC AND RELATIONAL APPROACHES CONCEPTUAL SKILLS BY CONCEPTUAL STYLES

| CONCEPTUAL STYLES | CONCEPTUAL SKILLS | |
	MODE OF ABSTRACTION	FIELD ARTICULATION
Analytic	Formal (analytic)	Field independent
Relational	Descriptive	Field dependent

TABLE 21.2. THE TEST BATTERY CONCEPTUAL SKILLS BY TEST SUBROUTINES

| SUBROUTINES | CONCEPTUAL SKILLS | |
	MODE OF ABSTRACTION (ANALYTIC OR RELATIONAL)	FIELD ARTICULATION (FIELD INDEPENDENT OR FIELD DEPENDENT)
Psychological test responses	Sigel test of conceptual style (adaptation)	Witkin graphic figure embedded test (adaptation)
Linguistic characteristics	Synonym set	"Tell-a-Story" test
Social contexts (attitudes)	Guttman I mode of abstraction	Guttman II field embeddedness
	Guttman III[a] difference-variation	Guttman IV[a] luck-achievement

[a]Second-order derivations.

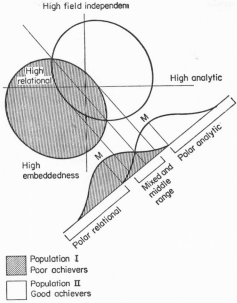

Population I
Poor achievers

Population II
Good achievers

FIGURE 21.1. The construction of response types. Polar relational: participants in both shared-function families and shared-function friendship groups; mixed: one type family, the other type of friendship groups; middle range: (conflict) family and friendship group responsibilities vary by mode of abstraction and field embeddedness; polar analytic: participants in both formally organized families and formally organized friendship groups.

nomics, sports, abstract reasoning, word creativity, and reading comprehension). Norms had been established for the Talent inventory on a 5 percent national sample.

All items relevant to each cognitive skill (mode of abstraction and field articulation) were Guttman scaled, changing nominal data into ordinal data. Through the mechanism of discriminant analysis the pupils conceptual skill scores were ordered on a common baseline, and a neutral point was established. This ordering was related to similar common baselines produced by the pupils' Guttman scaled scores on the shared-function formally organized family and friendship group subroutines and similarly scaled scores on the Project Talent achievement inventory. Some typical analytic and relational responses on these instruments appear in Appendix C. Analysis produced the configuration in figure 21.1.

Achievement appears in figure 21.1 as two normally distributed populations of "good" and "poor" achievers, rather than as a distribution along a single continuum. (IQ is held constant and is discussed in later paragraphs.) The relationships among relational and analytic responses, school achievement, and style of primary-group participation are apparent. From this analysis it was possible to isolate four clear response types represented by: (1) high-relational pupils who were poor achievers and who had been socialized in, and were at the time of testing, participating in shared-function friendship groups; (2) high-analytic pupils who were good achievers and who were socialized in and continue to participate in formally organized primary groups; (3) middle-range relational and analytic pupils who were middle-range achievers and who had been socialized in one type of family and were then participating in the other type of friendship group; and (4) a conflict pattern (high-analytic abstracters but high field dependent) who were middle-range achievers and whose shared-function formal-group style responses were uniquely mixed. Response characteristics of each of these four groups follow as tables 21.3–21.6.

TABLE 21.3. RELATIONAL AND ANALYTIC POLAR RESPONSE
CHARACTERISTICS: PSYCHOLOGICAL, LINGUISTIC, AND
ATTITUDE SUBROUTINES, PRIMARY GROUPS AND ACHIEVEMENT

| TEST SUBROUTINES | RESPONSE CHARACTERISTICS | |
	POLAR ANALYTIC	POLAR RELATIONAL
Psychological, Linguistic, and Attitude		
Psychological Tests		
Sigel test of conceptual style	High analytic scores	High relational scores
Witkin figure embedded test (adaptation)	High graphic field articulation scores	Low graphic field articulation scores
Linguistic Subroutines		
Synonym set (25-word stimulus set)		
Number of words	Average	High
Percent abstracted descriptively	Low	High
"Tell-a-Story" test	Non-ego-centered Nonembedded	Ego-centered Embedded
Content analysis	Subject: "reality" or "achievement"	Subject: "luck" or "fantasy"
Attitude Scales		
Guttman I mode of abstraction	High analytic on all four scales	High relational on all four scales
Guttman II field embeddedness		
Guttman III difference-variation		
Guttman IV luck-achievement		
Response Style	Response style more than 80 percent middle-range responses	High polar response style; more than 20 percent "strongly agree" or "strongly disagree"
Primary Groups		
Family	High Guttman formal family style	High Guttman shared-function family style
Friendship group	High Guttman formal friendship-group style	High Guttman shared-function friendship-group style
Achievement	High achievers	Low achievers

TABLE 21.4. MIDDLE RANGE RESPONSE CHARACTERISTICS[a] I AND II: PSYCHOLOGICAL, LINGUISTIC AND ATTITUDE SUBROUTINES, PRIMARY GROUPS AND ACHIEVEMENT

TEST SUBROUTINES	RESPONSE CHARACTERISTICS	
	MIDDLE RANGE I	MIDDLE RANGE II
Psychological, Linguistic and Attitude		
Psychological Tests		
Sigel test of conceptual style	Middle range	Middle range
Witkin figure embedded test (adaptation)	Middle range	Middle range
Linguistic Subroutines		
Synonym set (25-word stimulus set)		
Number of words	Average	Average
Percent abstracted descriptively	Middle range	Middle range
"Tell-a-Story" test	Non-ego-centered Nonembedded	More ego-centered More embedded
Content analysis	Subject: "reality" or "achievement"	Subject: "luck" or "fantasy"
Attitude Scales		
Guttman I mode of abstraction	Middle range	Middle range
Guttman II field embeddedness	Middle range	Middle range
Guttman III difference-variation	Middle range	Middle range
Guttman IV luck-achievement	Middle range	Middle range
Response Style	More than 80 percent middle range, few polar responses few undecideds	20 percent or more polar responses
Additional observations	Strongly desirous of school achievement, good jobs, etc.	Behavior problems in school gang activities outside of school
Primary Groups[b]		
Family	Shared-function	Formal
Friendship group	Formal	Shared-function
Outstanding characteristics	Movement from shared-function to formal	Movement from formal to shared-function
Achievement	Middle range	Middle range

[a]Outstanding characteristics: Participation in both kinds of primary groups, direction of movement focus.

[b]Family organization was seen as an earlier influence in the lifetime of the individuals tested. In all cases, the direction of movement determined their outstanding behavioral characteristics, i.e., response patterns were more like those of the latter (friendship) groups.

TABLE 21.5. DIRECTION OF MOVEMENT AND RESPONSE
CHARACTERISTICS: NONCHOICE, SINGLE-TYPE
EXPERIENCE AND CHOICE, MIXED EXPERIENCE[a]

EXPERIENCE	DIRECTION OF MOVEMENT	RESPONSE CHARACTERISTICS
Socialization Pattern Nonchoice: single-type experience		
Formal family and formal friendship group	No movement	High analytic conceptual style Relative consistency in test dimensions
Shared-function family and shared-function friend-ship group	No movement	High relational conceptual style Relative consistency in test dimensions
Choice Pattern Choice: mixed experience		
Mixed family and friendship group	from: shared-function family to: formal friendship	Mixed or middle-range response pattern; more like analytic conceptual style; candidates for social mobility
Mixed family and friendship group	from: formal family to: shared-function friendship group	Mixed or middle-range response pattern; more like relational conceptual style; candidates for mass movement, aggressive in groups, etc.

[a]Conflict pattern excepted.

The two polar-response patterns—polar analytic and polar relational—were called "socialization patterns." Pupils with polar-response configurations appeared not to be able to synthesize the expectations for either the alternative kind of group participation or the alternate kind of stimulus analysis. Some pupils, it was hypothesized, had either selected or structured their friendship groups to conform to their conceptual styles.

Among members of the polar-response groups, the relationship of group style to conceptual style was clearly observable in group discussions. Methods of thinking about group process were very similar to methods of approaching test items. For example, it was functional for members of shared-function groups to perceive themselves to have relevance only within the context of their social groups, and they demonstrated on tests of conceptual style that they perceived parts of standardized stimuli to have relevance only when viewed within their given contexts. They did not extract and specialize functions in their primary groups, and they were not led to extract and organize parts of standardized stimuli on tests. The reverse was true of polar-analytic pupils. Style of primary-group participation appeared to have produced a subtle component of learned behavior that could be viewed in both the development of its related conceptual style and in light of its utility in subsequent group process.

It was found that those pupils with mixed analytic and relational responses had had experience in both types of primary groups. The direction of movement was important in predicting future performance, considering that family impact had occurred earlier in time than that of the friendship group. When movement was from shared-function family to formally organized friendship group, the pupils were more like the polar-analytic pupils both in their test scores and in their social and psychological characteristics. When movement was from formal family to shared-function friendship group, however, pupils were more like the polar-relational pupils. Both groups were flexible in their approach to reality organization; they could become more relational or more analytic at will, within the middle range, and they could participate in both kinds of group organization with some medium of success. The middle-range achievement patterns with mixed conceptual style response configurations were called "choice patterns." Identification of the factors that had contributed to the pupils choice when both styles of conceptual organization were possible and both styles of group participation were available was beyond scope of these studies and opened areas for further research.

TABLE 21.6. MIXED RESPONSE CHARACTERISTICS (THE CONFLICT PATTERN): PSYCHOLOGICAL, LINGUISTIC AND ATTITUDE SUBROUTINES, PRIMARY GROUPS AND ACHIEVEMENT[a]

TEST SUBROUTINES	RESPONSE CHARACTERISTICS
Psychological Tests	
Sigel test of conceptual style	High analytic but vacillating responses
Witkin figure embedded test (adaptation)	High embedded
Linguistic Subroutines	
Synonym set	
Number of words	Low
Percent abstracted descriptively	Too low to evaluate
"Tell-a-Story" test	Ego-centered
	Embedded
	Subject: "Fantasy"
Attitudes	
Response style	High in "undecided's" (some as high as ninety percent "undecided" responses)
Primary groups	
Family	Mixed responses
Friendship group	Mixed responses
Achievement	Middle range

[a]Outstanding characteristics: conflict in skills, i.e., high analytic scores and high field dependence scores. Theoretically, high analytic skills should also be accompanied by high field articulation skills. In those cases in which these two scores were in conflict there appeared also to be a conflict in reality organization. These pupils were characterized by vacillating responses, high numbers of "undecided" responses, and high levels of anxiety and suggestibility. Almost 75 percent were girls despite varied ethnic and social-class origins.

The conflict-response group of middle-range achievers was of special interest. When analytic skills were high and field dependence scores also high, pupils demonstrated an apparent conflict in reality organization. Pupils with the conflict pattern were highly suggestible and anxious, told fantasy stories, and could not decide how to respond to attitude statements (for example, they returned to 90 percent "undecided's" on 72-item attitude questionnaires).

Although our major concerns were with the poor participation of the high-relational pupils in the highly analytic school environment, the middle-range achievers—those with mixed skills and those producing a conflict pattern—represented intriguing areas for systematic study. The mixed group, which demonstrated flexibility in their use of relational and analytic approaches to reality organization, was made up of both sexes and varied ethnic origins. The pupils who demonstrated the conflict pattern, however, were 75 percent girls. Since embedded responses covered the gamut from abstract categories, through language behaviors, to expressions of embeddedness in their social environments, it is possible that embeddedness may be a distinctive characteristic of female sex-role learning in this society regardless of social class, native ability, ethnic differences, and the cognitive impact of the school.[6] Demonstration of a unique response configuration among girls lent weight to the belief that identifiable subgroup interaction webs can exist within a single social structure such as the family, which can produce, as a result, demonstrable related conceptual patterning.

From the findings reviewed briefly above conceptual styles had emerged as integrated rule-sets for the selection and organization of sense data. Two definable systems of conceptual organization could be identified and demonstrated, along with several distinctive mixtures, and linked to two different styles of functioning in groups. Within each rule-set certain relationships and patterns of organization are possible and others are not whether they appear in learning materials or in social interaction. These organized systems had apparently been learned in varied contexts, including group process, but as subliminal components of each context. The many different contexts in which a similar system of relationships could be observed by individuals had acted as examples of the system, reinforcing each other. When they had occurred persistently, they had served to define and reinforce the method of organization, as well as to fix the substantive contexts in which they appeared in retrievable memory storage (socialization patterns). Persistence in their use appeared to have determined the degree to which an individual believed them to be valid as well as the extent to which he was attached to related social and psychological behaviors and held to values and beliefs associated with them. When the patterns had not been repeated persistently (choice patterns), they had become relevant to certain contexts only. Both the patterns themselves and the substantive context in which they appeared seemed not to be retrievable except on the denotative level; that is, each context had to be learned separately and not as an example of recurring theme. The necessity for memorizing each context separately was believed to explain in part the characteristic middle-range achievement performance of those pupils with mixed and conflicting conceptual styles.

Methods of selection and conceptual organization, then, are comparatively subtle characteristics of substantive contexts; they are required for successful group participation as well as for structured learning. As such, they are meant to be remembered and transferred to new and unfamiliar situations as well as are the information components in which they are embedded. Indeed, it is the explicit intent of school texts, curricula, and methods to teach the analytic rule-set subliminally in many different contexts; and intelligence and achievement are measured by the school, in part, by how well pupils have learned it. What is less apparent is that the same analytic rule-set is also embedded in formal school organization and in the social settings in which teaching and learning take place. For analytic children the school's formal organization acts as an additional reinforcer of analytic thinking as well as of its related social behaviors. For relational children, however, its impact on conceptual patterning is disorganizing; its climate lacks the cues necessary to understanding, or they are ambiguous; and its requirements for social participation are of low value. When transported to a shared-function environment, both the cognitive requirements of the school and their related social skills are as dysfunctional and disruptive as the relational approach is in the school.

INFORMATION AND CONCEPTUAL SKILLS

The foregoing comment on the relation of conceptual styles to school achievement leaves virtually unanalyzed the information contexts in which styles of reality organization are embedded. It will be remembered that progressive increments in the breadth and depth of the pupils' information repertoires are also required for achievement in school. This third variable accounted for most of the unexplained variance between tested IQ and school achievement. This separate yet hitherto confounded component of the achievement profile, when combined with conceptual style performance, produced the combinations in table 21.7, which were effective predictors of academic performance.

From this analysis it was possible to clarify the circumstances under which information components enter into academic performance as separate from conceptual style, when native ability is held constant.

Although native ability is not related to the preference of a cognitive style, it does apparently, affect the size of a pupil's information repertoire, as well as the level of abstraction attainable with either mode of conceptual organization. In a sample of 500 ninth-grade pupils with a full intelligence range from "barely educable" to "gifted," there were found to be sharp differences between the barely educable and the gifted in the size of the information components of their test scores (Cohen 1968d). There were similar large differences in the levels of abstraction usable by them. Both types of differences appeared on all measures of ability and performance regardless of which conceptual style the pupils used. Native ability, then, may be better defined as the differential ability of individuals to absorb large bodies of information and to reach high levels of abstraction using *either* mode of conceptual organization.

Standardized tests of intelligence and achievement, in their present form, do attempt to identify the relative size of pupils' information repertoires, provided that their frames of understanding overlap or interpenetrate the items used in the test

TABLE 21.7. ORIENTATION TO SCHOOL REQUIREMENTS BY SKILL-INFORMATION COMBINATIONS

SKILL-INFORMATION COMBINATIONS	ORIENTATION TO SCHOOL REQUIREMENTS
High analytic skills, high information	High achievement; high IQ[a]; high success in school
High analytic skills, low information	High achievement; average IQ[a]; anxiety (overachievers)
High relational skills, high information	Low achievement; high IQ[a]; behavior problems (underachievers)
High relational skills, low information	Low achievement; low IQ[a]; complete inability to relate to the school; withdrawal and dropout

[a]Tested IQ

construction, and to measure increments in their ability to use formal analytic methods on higher levels of abstraction. Discrimination in levels of abstraction using relational pathways, however, is not incorporated into their construction plans. Text construction plans also incorporate, as measures of intelligence, some relevant analytic correlates, such as the length of the time frames planned into them for subroutine completion. The time frames, together with information-analytic skill elements, produce their speed-power components. Much of the socialization impact of the school is thus embedded in its cognitive requirements; it may be separated from the information contexts in which it appears. It focuses on the development of social and psychological correlates or derivatives of the analytic approach on all levels of pupil performance, from test application and response characteristics to classroom management and school administration.

DEPRIVATION, CULTURE DIFFERENCE AND CULTURE CONFLICT

Once one has become aware of the stringent analytic requirements for performance in school and of the separate information-cognitive skill requirements of standardized tests, it is no longer appropriate to speak of "deprivation," "culture difference," and "culture conflict" synonymously. "Deprivation" and "culture difference" have to do with the information components of these tests and "culture conflict" with different conceptual styles and their conflicting sociobehavioral correlates.[7]

Within the information components themselves two types of distinctions can be drawn—quantitative and qualitative. The term "deprivation" may be used to refer to the quantitative characteristics of a pupil's information repertoire and "culture difference" to its qualitative characteristics. When there is a relative lack of the number of concepts and experiences on which a pupil has to draw in order to do well in school, he may be said to be deprived. Limited experience with varied environments and limited access to books and other sources of knowledge may limit the amount of information a pupil has to use. Children from low-income environments may be deprived in this way as a result of their position in society. Institutionalized children or those from other environments that present limited stimulation for those who are sensorially limited, such as blind children, may share this disability. "Culture difference," on the other hand, involves qualitatively different kinds of things and events from those usable in school. A slum child may not know what a refrigerator is, for example, but he may know a great deal about rats. The information repertoires of such children may be sizable but different from those required by the school curriculum.

Neither the quantitative nor qualitative characteristics of a pupil's information repertoire should effectively hamper his ability to communicate with the school environment, however, because neither of them implies incompatibility with school requirements. The school curricula are relatively eclectic in the units of information that are acceptable. In addition, there is no known limit to the number of new concepts individuals can learn. It is, therefore, only when incompatibilities exist (whether or not deprivation and culture difference are also present) that "culture conflict" may be said to exist.

Relational and analytic modes of conceptual organization reflect such incompatibilities; that is, many specific kinds of response characteristics can be factored out of each style that can be demonstrated to impede the development of the alternate kind. Some incompatible response characteristics lie on basic levels of learned behavior, such as conditioned perceptual discrimination and audiomotor reactivity. Others are found in lexical choice and language organization and still others in a wide range of interpersonal and social process behaviors and in many derivative values and beliefs. Each context acts as separate reinforcement of the conceptual process that has been used, and each lower-order derivative of each conceptual style suppresses its alternative. It is to selection and classification rule-sets, then, that many mutually incompatible psychological and social behaviors are tied and not to information components per se. Moreover, because of their integrity relational and analytic rule-sets can, to a great extent, both limit and determine the size and nature of an individual's information repertoire when native ability and environmental stimulation are held constant.

In addition to incompatible selection and classification rule-sets, three other areas of mutual incompatibility emerged from a semantic feature analysis of the lexicon of the hard-core poor. The additional three areas of incompatibility were in perceptions of time (as a series of discrete moments, rather than a continuum),[8] of self in social space (in the center of it, rather than in a position relative to others who are passing together at different rates of speed through social space), and in causality (specific causality rather than multiple causality). (Cohen, Fraenkel, and Brewer 1968). Each of the above categories of thought was closely associated with relational and analytic styles along several different dimensions; that is, each reflected a number of rule components in common with its related conceptual style. For example, the analytic mode of abstraction presumes a system of linear components. Similar linear components are found in the perception of time as a continuum or in a linear projection of social space, and they underlie the notion of multiple causality. This linear component does not appear among polar-relational children on tests of cognitive style, in their characteristic language style, nor in the ordering of authority or responsibility in shared-function social groups. Certain common values and beliefs follow from such a common component. For instance, without the assumption of linearity such notions as social mobility, the value of money, improving one's performance, getting ahead, infinity, or heirarchies of any type, all of which presume the linear extension of critical elements, do not have meaning for the relational child. In essence, the requirements for formal abstraction and extraction of components to produce linear continua are not logically possible within the relational rule-set.

Nonverbal Tests of Intelligence

In addition to distinguishing among "deprivation," "culture difference," and "culture conflict," the findings of these investigations also challenge the rationale for the "culture-free" nonverbal tests in current use. It has been most commonly believed that it is the information (direct experience) components of these tests that carry their culture-bound characteristics. Nonverbal tests concentrate on the ability to reason "logically." However, it is in the very nature of these logical sequences that the most culture-bound aspects of the middle-class, or "analytic," way of thinking are carried. Even more critical than either the quantitative and qualitative information components of such tests are the analytic mode of abstraction and the field-articulation requirements they embody. Figure 21.2, taken from the Lorge-Thorndike nonverbal battery on the ninth-grade level, may clarify this point.

The logical sequences in Figure 21.2 are most effectively solved by a parts-specific, stimulus-centered, analytic mode of abstraction. This strategy depends upon

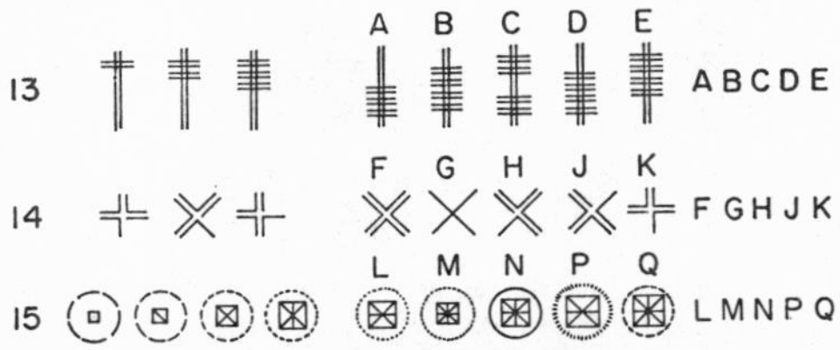

FIGURE 21.2. The pupil is instructed to complete the logical sequences by choosing from the multiple choice items that are presented.

the ability of the subject to extract and relate relevant parts of the stimulus. All contextual information has been removed in advance. When an entire test battery is constructed of items like the above, as nonverbal batteries indeed are, analytic-cognitive skills have been separated explicitly from general-information components. If the essential aspect of "culture conflict" is discrepancy between cognitive modes among pupils, these tests are even more discriminatory than those formed in part to test for information growth. Even the best informed and the most widely experienced relational pupil, regardless of his native ability, would score poorly on such tests.

As a matter of fact, the most intelligent relational pupils score the worst of all. Their ability to reach higher levels of abstractions through relational pathways take them farther away from the higher levels of abstraction reached through analytic pathways. Highly intelligent high-relational pupils were found, in fact, to communicate best with the demands of the school on the concrete level. This was evidenced in our findings in an initial sampling of sixty-six ninth- and tenth-grade pupils of average or better intelligence (Cohen 1967) and in the markedly better scores of high-relational pupils on two achievement subtests of the Project Talent Achievement Inventory.[9] A content analysis of the Talent battery found that the questions on only these two subtests were framed on concrete levels. Although the more intelligent high-relational pupils scored extremely poorly (15th to 20th percentiles) on the other subtests of achievement, they did extremely well (90th to 95th percentiles) on these two sets of concrete problems. It appears, therefore, that given concrete settings with intelligence held constant, high-relational pupils can compete with analytic ones. It is only when high levels of analytic abstraction are required that their ability to compete is inhibited.

Such findings suggest that in addition to the focused analytic cognitive style requirements of nonverbal tests of intelligence, the level of abstraction they require provides an additional area of difficulty for relational pupils. Since contentless figures are almost completely abstract, they tend to focus on the most extreme levels for the use of analytic cognitive skills. Therefore, not only is the *mode* of cognitive organization required for successful performance on nonverbal tests a critical factor in the inability of relational pupils to deal with them, but the *level of abstraction* on which they focus for the demonstration of these skills intensifies the problems they present to relational pupils.

In addition to illuminating the relationship of the pupils to the tests, the two-way analysis that was followed also cast some light on the relationship of relational and analytic pupils to each other. Not only do relational and analytic pupils communicate with each other best on the concrete level, but the greatest gaps in com-

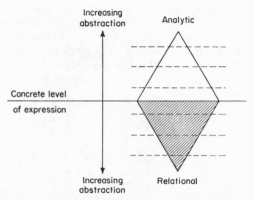

FIGURE 21.3. Dissociating levels of abstractive through analytic and relational pathways.

munication occur between the most intelligent members of the two categories of pupils.

Nonverbal tests of intelligence have not freed themselves, then, of their culture-bound characteristics. Instead, they have focused on one critical aspect of culture—its method of selecting and organizing relevant sense data. Traditional attempts to develop culture-free tests have eliminated their information components in the belief that it is only their substantive experience components that are culture-bound. An additional assumption has been that because they are nonverbal, they are non-structured. The most culture-bound characteristics of these tests, however, are not their information components but the analytic-logical sequences they require. Both in the mode of abstraction these tests require and in the level of abstraction in which the items are couched, nonverbal tests of intelligence are much more discriminatory against relational pupils than are conventional instruments, which test partly for information growth. Since both the size and nature of a pupil's information repertoire and his native ability are apparently unrelated to his conceptual style, the analytic-relational opposition may be defined as a separate area of pupils performance. Pupils may be deprived or culturally different from or in culture conflict with the school. They may represent one or two or all these separate kinds of educational problems. Analytic schemata geared to the definition of learning disabilities and programs designed for one type of educational problem cannot hope to deal with the others as well.

This paper has focused (1) on incompatibility in conceptual styles as a notable indicator of "culture conflict" and on the characteristics that distinguish it from "deprivation" and "culture difference" and (2) on styles of conceptual organization as culture-bound characteristics of nonverbal tests of intelligence. Evidence is also presented of the reciprocal relationships between conceptual styles and styles of primary-group process.

Conceptual styles are composites of two cognitive skills—mode of abstraction and field articulation. Along with information growth, these two cognitive skills have been identified as generic components of learning. Conceptual styles are essentially integrated rule-sets for the selection and organization of sense data. Within each rule-set certain assumptions and relationships are logically possible, and others are not. They are definable without reference to specific substantive content and are not related to native ability. They can be identified in the abstract, in language selection and organization, and in attitudes about one's self and one's environment. Associated with these rule-sets, or derivative from them, are a wide variety of social and psychological characteristics in their carriers.

Although there may be more, two conceptual styles have been identified and demonstrated reliably—relational and analytic styles. Relational and analytic conceptual styles were found to be associated with shared-function and formal primary-group participation, respectively, as socialization settings. So intimate were the relationships between primary-group styles and conceptual styles that among pupils with experience in both types of groups mixed and conflicting conceptual styles could be observed.

The school was defined as a highly analytic environment in all its salient characteristics and requirements. Many children, however, demonstrate a relational approach to reality organization. Relational and analytic conceptual styles were found to be not only different but mutually incompatible. That is, one approach to reality organization could effectively hinder the development of the other; each could affect its carrier's ability to participate effectively in the alternate kind of group process or to deal directly with its cognitive requirements. In practice, it was found that children who had been socialized in shared-function environments could not participate effectively in any aspect of the formal school environment even when native ability and information repertoires were adequate.

The information-cognitive skills requirements for school performances were used to distinguish among the constructs "deprivation," "culture difference," and "culture conflict." "Deprivation" and "culture difference" have to do with the quantitative and qualitative characteristics of the information repertoires of individuals. "Culture conflict" deals with conflicting styles of conceptual organization. Highly relational children in the highly analytic school are thus seen as a case of culture conflict, regardless of whether deprivation and culture difference are also present.

Attention was then directed to nonverbal methods of measuring intelligence and achievement. Nonverbal tests have been designed to reduce their culture basis by drastically reducing their information components. However, they were found instead to deal in a focused fashion with the demonstration of analytic conceptual skills. Rather than freeing themselves of their culture-bound characteristics, they have focused on one critical aspect of it—the analytic mode of selecting and organizing information. When contextual inputs have been held constant, then, nonverbal tests of intelligence are more discriminatory against relational pupils than are the conventional types, which test partly, for information growth.

A number of educational problems may be separated out of the above analysis without challenging the relevance of school curricula to future concerns among children. As in any relatively consistent environment in which there are standardized criteria for performance, in which quantity and quality of inputs are relatively standardized, in which a heterogenous population is found, particularly one in which participation is nonvoluntary, as in the school, pupils may be relatively deprived or culturally different from or in culture conflict with it. One, two, all, or none of these separate kinds of phenomena may be represented. Although, as they are defined here, deprivation and culture difference may be compensated in part through individualization or variation in the input level of the settings in which pupils learn, culture conflict represents an educational problem of some magnitude. Multiple-method learning environments can be devised. However, they will not only require the development of rules of transformation from one rule-set to another, but they can also be foreseen to produce far-reaching effects on school organization, teacher training, curricula, methods, and materials, the impact of which cannot yet be predicted. Moreover, culture conflict—a transactional concept—does not yield to unimodal analysis. If this is true, procedures for more valid measurement of learning potential and the development of more appropriate learning methods and settings are dependent upon the abandonment of assumptions that there is a single method for knowing.

Although the foci of these studies arose out of practical considerations, the issues that have been explored reflect basic science concerns. If such cognitive mechanisms as styles of cognitive control act reciprocably as mediating factors between social-system characteristics and individual-response characteristics, they are seen as important keys not only to effective program development but also to basic behavioral-science research.

NOTES

1. This research and development was performed pursuant to a contract with the U.S. Office of Education, Department of Health, Education, and Welfare under the provisions of the Cooperative Research Program.
2. That conceptual style is not a function of deprivation and income inadequacy, however, is supported by the finding that the relational style also characterizes the old-money upper class. Data for this study are still being analyzed.
3. Relationships among the family, the friendship group, and the school represent a useful analytic configuration for several reasons. First, they are major socializ-

ing agencies. In addition, because the school has been designed to perform socialization functions for society, the relevance of its requirements to other major institutional frameworks is imposing, both in its impact on learning and behavior and through its sorting and selection functions. In this dual role the school acts as a sluice gate to participation in other major societal institutions.

Use of the schools as an arena for study also presented strong methodological advantages. Because of compulsory education laws, at least in urban centers, the public, private, and parochial schools provide the only social setting in which total normal school-age populations are available for study, cutting across all relevant demographic characteristics. The schools also provide a reasonably standardized stimulation "input," environment against which performance could be measured. The availability of longitudinal records on each pupil, record and pupil accessibility, and the contributions of other specialized professional staff, such as physicians, psychologists, and social workers, were other advantages.

4. "Triangulation through the own-cultural bias of observers . . . requires multiple methods focused on the same construct from independent points of observation. This is required because the sense data or meter readings are now understood as the result of a transaction in which both the observer (or meter) and the object of investigation contribute to the form of the data. With a single observation at hand, it is impossible to separate instruments and separate vantage points can be matched as reflecting the same objects, then it is possible to separate out the components in the data due to observer (instrument) and observed. It turns out that this disentangling process requires both multiple observers (methods) and multiple, dissimilar, objects of study," [Campbell 1964: 34-35].

5. Attitude statements about perceptions of time, self, social space, and causality were included but not reported here.

6. Some items on the subroutines of cognitive style also reflected sex differences. In general, females tended to impute process or motivation to perceived relationships. In addition, girls clustered in the middle ranges on all scales and did not reflect the polar variations of the boys. This may be due to similarity in female role expectations despite other demographic variation.

7. The term "culture conflict" is used in subcultural and subgroup contexts without apology on the basis that similar analytic schemata may be used with varied units of analysis.

8. See the description of the "action seekers" in Gans 1962.

9. This achievement inventory developed norms from five percent national sample of high school pupils in public, private, and parochial schools. The instrument and a report of findings appear in Flanagan et al. 1964.

REFERENCES

Bernstein, Basil. "Social Class and Linguistic Development: A Theory of Social Learning." In *Educational, Economy, and Society*, edited by A. H. Halsey, Jean Floud, and C. Arnold Anderson. New York: Free Press of Glencoe, 1964a.

Bernstein, Basil. "Elaborated and Restricted Codes." In *The Ethnography of Communication. American Anthropologist* 66 (1964b): 55-69.

Campbell, Donald T. "Distinguishing Differences of Perception from Failure of Communication in Cross-cultural Studies." In *Cross-cultural Understandings: Epistemology in Anthropology*, edited by F. S. C. Northrup and Helen H. Livingston. New York: Harper & Row, 1964.

Cohen, Rosalie. "The Value Laden Contexts in Programs for the Educationally Disadvantaged." Learning Research and Development Center, University of Pittsburgh, 1965.

Cohen, Rosalie. *Primary Group Structure, Conceptual Styles, and School Achievement*. Monograph, Learning Research and Development Center, University of Pittsburgh. Studies I, II, III, IV, 1967.

Cohen, Rosalie. "Language Styles and Communication Failures in Therapy." Paper read at Fourth International Congress of Group Psychotherapy, Vienna, Austria, 1968a.

Cohen, Rosalie. "Is Formal Role Analysis Generalizable to Low-income Groups?" Paper read at the Midwest Sociological Society annual meetings, Omaha, Nebraska, 1968b.

Cohen, Rosalie. "Formal Role Analysis and the Culture of Poverty." Paper read at the Ohio Valley Sociological Society annual meetings, Detroit, Michigan, 1968c.

Cohen, Rosalie. "1967 Teenage Survey." Unpublished paper, 1968d.

Cohen, Rosalie. "The Relation between Socio-conceptual Styles and Orientation to School Requirements." *Sociology of Education* 41 (1968e): 201-20.

Cohen, Rosalie, Fraenkel, Gerd, and Brewer, John. "The Language of the Hard Core Poor: Implications for Culture Conflict." *Sociology Quarterly* 10 (1968): 19-28.

Gans, Herbert. *The Urban Villagers.* New York: Free Press of Glencoe, 1962.

Flanagan, John C., et al. "The American High School Student." Project Talent, University of Pittsburgh, 1964.

Gardner, Riley. "Cognitive Control Structures and Their Measurement at Preadolescence." In *Programs in Cognitive Development.* Mental Health Grant 05517, Menninger Clinic. MS.

Kagan, Jerome, Moss, Howard A., and Siegel, Irving E. "Psychological Significance of Styles Conceptualization." In *Basic Cognitive Process in Children.* Society for Research in Child Development monograph 86. Chicago: University of Chicago Press, 1963.

Kelly, E. Lowell, and Lingoes, James C. "Data Processing in Psychological Research." In *Computer Application in the Behavioral Sciences*, edited by Harold Borko. Englewood Cliffs, N.J.: Prentice-Hall, 1962.

APPENDIX A
TAXONOMY OF TEST RESPONSE CHARACTERISTICS AND SOCIOBEHAVIORAL CORRELATES OF CONCEPTUAL STYLES[a]

TEST	CONCEPTUAL STYLE	
	ANALYTIC	RELATIONAL
Cognitive style	Mode of abstraction is stimulus centered	Mode of abstraction is self-centered
	sensitivity to parts of objects	sensitivity to global characteristics
	awareness of obscure, abstract nonobvious features	awareness of obvious, sensed features
	many abstractions based on parts of objects and features of these parts	few abstractions—free association stimulated by stimuli
Siegel test of conceptual style	"arms akimbo . . . etc."	"two boys . . . etc."
Sorting ability	many piles	few piles
Figure sort tests / Behavior sorting test / Object sorting test / Photo sorting test	can resort many times drawing new relationships each time	cannot resort—most obvious relationship remains constant
Pettigrew's category width test	groups formed represent minimal conceptual distance from properties of the objects	groups formed represent greater conceptual distance from the properties of the objects

APPENDIX A (*Continued*)

TEST	CONCEPTUAL STYLE	
	ANALYTIC	RELATIONAL
Geometric form drawing test	relative differences are marked by the ratios of the shorter and longer sides [emphasized independence of level of abstraction from conceptual style]	little perception of relative differences
Memory organization	organization of words for commitment to memory based on varied types of relationships	organization of words functional and inferential
Word association	noun-noun sequences; verb-verb sequences	meaning critical inferential sequences recall functionally related words
Psycho-physical judgements requiring selective attention (facilitation-inhibition phenomena), e.g., Embedded Figures Tests, Size Estimation Tests, etc.	good	poor
Perceptual vigilance	high ability to detect changes in monotonous but constantly changing perceptual field over a long period of time	low ability to detect changes in a monotonous constantly changing perceptual field
Serial learning	categorical responses	related words
California test of mental maturity	analytic scores high on nonlanguage sections	analytic scores low on nonlanguage sections
What is learned [parts as whole]	attaches verbal labels to parts as well as wholes of geometric designs	attaches verbal labels only to relevant wholes
Stability of conceptual style after entry into school	stable	creation of more analytic responses and reduction of relational responses
TAT	relatively constricted stories containing much description of the properties of the stimuli and minimal creative thematic material	much creative thematic material, little sensitivity to properties of the stimuli

APPENDIX A (*Continued*)

TEST	CONCEPTUAL STYLE	
	ANALYTIC	RELATIONAL
	stories close to physical properties of the pictures (equivalence ranges close)	(wide equivalence ranges)
Rorschach responses	indistinct perception infrequent	indistinct perceptions frequent
	high stimulus differentiation	minimal stimulus differentiation
	attends to ambiguous projections of stimuli	ignores ambiguous portions of stimulus
	fewer human responses, whole responses, human vs. mammalian animal responses, human movement responses, color responses and extensor vs. flexor responses	project more life and activity into the inkblots
Reaction time	greater—more time is necessary for scanning	less—time required for response to global characteristics is less
	attitude more reflective	response appears impulsive
Verbal content in personal interviews	reluctant to be dependent on family and friends	dependent on their families as adults
	striving for social recognition	less concerned with the acquisition of recognition goals
	concern for intellectual mastery	
	confident in their approach to challenging intellectual tasks	not confident of ability to solve intellectual problems
	motivated to obtain achievement oriented goals	not motivated to achievement goals
	categorization of statements concerning behavior is highly differentiated	categorization of statements concerning behavior has a low degree of differentiation

APPENDIX A (*Continued*)

TEST	CONCEPTUAL STYLE	
	ANALYTIC	**RELATIONAL**
Tolerance for unrealistic experiences [e.g., simulation of the effects of motion when movement is not present]	good	poor
Constricted flexible control	flexible	constricted
Impulse control	good	poor
[e.g., Stroop's Color Word Test]	effective use of primary process learning rapid response	ineffective use of primary process thinking, difficulty in inhibiting irrelevant, overlearned, or highly compelling motoric responses (e.g., reading the words while verbalizing the names of the colors)
Learning-related characteristics:		
Attention span	can sit still long time	short attention span
Concentration depth	deep concentration (stimulus remains constant)	shallow concentration
Distractibility	not easily distracted by nonrelevant sounds and movements	easily distracted
Perceptual vigilance	high perceptual vigilance; notice small changes in moving stimulus	low perceptual vigilance
	can do above task without utilitarian purpose	task considered irrelevant
Intensity of attention	deep	shallow
Related school behaviors	sees teacher as a source of information, not individual	sees teacher as individual
	sees teacher as appendage to a problem	
	persistent in task orientation	easily distracted from task

APPENDIX A (*Continued*)

TEST	CONCEPTUAL STYLE	
	ANALYTIC	RELATIONAL
	confident in approach to intellectual tasks	lacks confidence in ability to solve intellectual problems
	motivated to achievement related goals	not motivated to achievement
Optional reading (content)	reality	fantasy
Preferred classroom illustrations (content)	reality	fantasy, humor
Related personality characteristics	stimulus centered activity does not require an affective response	relationship to descriptive characteristics of people and objects requires an affective response
	requires detachment, concentrated attention	global orientation does not require long or concentrated attention
	learning is nonsocial	learning is a social experience
	belief that relationships are "out there" in the stimulus	belief that significant relationships are a product of self and others
	a faith in processes and natural laws	specific causation need not rest on natural laws
	a willingness to listen attentively, to differentiate subtle meanings in words, a desire to look for reasons and processes, and to take directions and compare results	primary focus on self, not on stimulus
	ambitious	passive
	independent	dependent
	high spontaneous sudomotor reactivity	less labile sudomotor reactivity
	objective	subjective
	confident of control over the environment	sense of powerlessness

APPENDIX A (*Continued*)

TEST	CONCEPTUAL STYLE	
	ANALYTIC	RELATIONAL
	focus on rules of role performance not individual performance	
	confident in new social situations	anxious in new social situations
		acts as though expecting rejection by new associates
	preference for complexity	preference for simplicity
	preference for social distance	preference for social integration
Behavior plasticity	resist the effect of interfering stimuli	more susceptible to modification by immediate perceptual experience
		difficulty in inhibiting reactions to task irrelevant cues
		behavior is more malleable in the face of continual changes in the stimulus field
Sociobehavioral correlates of conceptual style	reflective attitude a tendency to differentiate experience	impulsive less likely to differentiate complex stimulus situation
	ability to resist the effects of distracting stimuli	more reactive to external stimuli
	able to become oblivious of external surroundings	impulsively aggressive
		less likely to withdraw from the group to work on a task
	sedentary	more hyperkinetic
		easily angered by minor frustrations
	capacity for sustained attention	short attention span

APPENDIX A (*Continued*)

TEST	CONCEPTUAL STYLE	
	ANALYTIC	RELATIONAL
		affectionate
		rarely played alone as children
		colorful vocabulary
		easily give up on difficult tasks
Language style		
Lexical; mode of abstraction	analytic abstraction	descriptive abstraction
	words have formal meanings	words have meanings specific to certain contexts; they are concrete with much use of visual and tactile symbols
	[e.g., *money*—coins, cash, currency, etc.; *wine*—port, sherry]	[e.g., *money*—green, bundle, trash, etc.; *wine*—blood, slop, molasses]
		rules for new verbal selections tie actors to action, causes to results, means to ends
		expressions are colorful
		many idiomatic expressions
		low level of generality
Use of synonyms	synonyms used	few synonyms, greatly reduced overlap of semantic ranges
		a great variety of words specific to specific situations or to certain characteristics or functions
Distinctive feature analysis	"token into type" constructions few and used for new developments	"token into type" constructions common for old objects
	depersonalized	personified (reversal)
	euphemisms not very common	euphemisms and reverse euphemisms common

APPENDIX A (*Continued*)

TEST	CONCEPTUAL STYLE	
	ANALYTIC	RELATIONAL
	word choices relate to bundles of features of objects or persons and to prototypical situations	choices relate to individual features of objects or individuals to specific situations
	many forms offered for generalization and comparison	few mechanisms for generalization and comparison
	change not too rapid comparatively	rapid change in signifiers of the language
	outer-centered orientation	self-centered orientation
	meaning is not dependent upon extraverbal context	meaning dependent on time, place, authority, and other social relationships between communicants
	critical analysis of meaning verbalized	meaning embedded; not verbalized
Syntax	elaborated code; grammatically complex	restricted code; grammatically simple
	low predictability	high predictability
	sentences of varied lengths	short sentences
	usually finished; good syntax	often unfinished; poor syntax
	periods at ends of thoughts	simple and repetitive use of conjunctions
	many subordinate clauses	little use of subordinate clauses
	integrity of speech sequence	inability to hold a formal subject through a speech sequence
	informational content has integrity	dislocated informational content
	much use of adjectives and adverbs	rigid and limited use of adjectives and adverbs
	discretionary use of impersonal pronouns	infrequent use of impersonal pronouns

APPENDIX A (*Continued*)

TEST	CONCEPTUAL STYLE	
	ANALYTIC	RELATIONAL
	reinforcement is direct and explicit	sympathetic circulatory for reinforcement (e.g., "you know . . . ," "don't say a word . . . "
General characteristics	verbally explicit	not verbally explicit
	verbal arrangement closely fits specific referents	structure of speech is simple; the extraverbal component is a major channel for the transmission of individual qualifications
	verbal planning promotes a high level of syntactic organization and lexical selection	
	preparation and delivery of explicit meanings is the major function of the code	meanings may be highly condensed
	the code facilitates the transmission and elaboration of the individual's unique experience	speech is impersonal; it is not tailored to fit a given referent
	the condition of the listener is not taken for granted and the speaker is likely to modify his speech in the light of the special conditions and attributes of the listener	the intent of the listener is taken for granted
	code facilitates the verbal construction and exchanges of individualized or personal symbols	the code facilitates the construction and exchange of communal symbols
	induces in speakers a sensitivity to the implications of separateness and differences and points to the possibilities inherent in a complex hierarchy for the organization of experience	

APPENDIX A (*Continued*)

TEST	CONCEPTUAL STYLE	
	ANALYTIC	RELATIONAL
	the ability to switch codes controls ability to switch roles	only single code available
Delivery	frequent pauses (hesitation phenomena) for verbal planning	little hesitation; high fluency
Articulation	clear, cool deliberate	articulatory clues reduced; sloppy; meaning carried in extra verbal channels

APPENDIX B
SOME IMPORTANT DIFFERENTIATING CHARACTERISTICS OF FORMALLY ORGANIZED AND SHARED-FUNCTION FAMILY AND FRIENDSHIP GROUPS

CHARACTERISTICS OF THE GROUP	FORMALLY ORGANIZED	SHARED-FUNCTION
Distribution of critical group functions	Critical functions formally defined and attached to statuses	Widely shared among all members of the group, even children
Interaction patterns	Formally organized and generally understood; relatively constant; attached to status-role coordination	Fluid and changing
Organization of status relationships	Relatively stable; often hierarchically organized	Fluid and shifting; seldom hierarchically organized
Pattern of change in interaction arrangements	Emergent; rationally planned for optimum group efficiency and convenience; change proceeds commonly toward greater specialization of functions	Unplanned and unpredictable; often characterized by disintegration of the organization and restructuring in a fashion similar to the one preceding
Distribution of rewards	Formally set according to analytically abstracted and defined characteristics of the importance of the status and of the position incumbent	Widespread and equal, or snatched through the use of power and thus grossly unequal

APPENDIX B (*Continued*)

CHARACTERISTICS OF THE GROUP	FORMALLY ORGANIZED	SHARED-FUNCTION
Characteristics of leadership function	Leadership often attached to most important status as determined by salient group objectives	Leadership shared along with other group functions, regardless of objectives of the group
Distribution of privilege	Distributed in an orderly fashion; often attached to the hierarchial ordering of statuses	Widely shared or snatched by power and thus grossly unequal in distribution
Reasons for privilege	Privilege attached to occupying an important status	Attached to individual acts of individual persons under idiosyncratic circumstances or to an individual mystique
Generic role expectations	Built around formal functions of each status	Built around identification with total group activities
Scope of role expectations	Necessary expectations are limited to functions defined by specific statuses occupied	Role encompasses all critical functions of the group as well as expectations geared to its sense of group identity
Range of participation in group functions	Intrusions on the functions of other statuses negatively sanctioned	Periodic or continuing participation in all critical group functions positively sanctioned
Status boundaries	Varying degrees of firmness; relationships to each other relatively constant	Loosely held; statuses fluid and shifting in relationship to one another
Latency of role expectations of other statuses	No; individuals are involved in isolated functions assigned to their statuses	Yes; all members ready to act in any capacity at any time
Refusal-to-act privileges	Individual retains the right to refuse to act in any capacity not defined as his job	Individual cannot refuse to act in any critical capacity when called upon to do so

APPENDIX B (*Continued*)

CHARACTERISTICS OF THE GROUP	FORMALLY ORGANIZED	SHARED-FUNCTION
Individual right to challenge group objectives	No, in general, once he has assumed a status; he can leave the status if dissatisfied	Yes
Individual right to challenge current means of attaining group objectives	Variable, depending on the nature of the group	Yes
Use of initiative by individual members	Initiative generally limited to devising new means of performing preset and generally understood functions attached to a status	Permitted both in setting objectives or devising means for attaining them. Either great freedom or great constraint on the use of initiative is positively sanctioned at different points in time
Depth of identification with the group	Casual	Intense
Manner of identification with the group	Marked by commitment to perform a given set of group functions and to the interaction patterns which define the status occupied	Marked by *involvement* in all group functions and in the general sense of group identity
Focus of personal identity	Individual identity partly attached to definable functions which he performs in many groups, and partly to conceptual organizing principles which he uses in coordinating these multiple functions	All group members participate in the development of a joint individual-group identity. Reformulation of the group creates a new sense of individual identity
Sense of individual identity	Yes; individual only *participates* in his groups, he does not feel as one with them ("in" the group, not "of" it)	Only as attached to group identity ("of" the group, not "in" it)

APPENDIX C
SOME TYPICAL ANALYTIC AND RELATIONAL RESPONSES

Illustration A: Sigel Test of Conceptual Style

Pupil is instructed to choose two of the three pictures on each plate that are alike or that go together in some way and to tell why he selected them. Test consists of 19 plates.

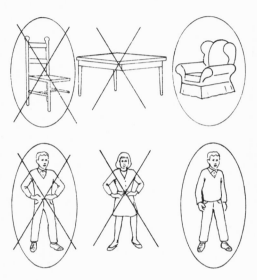

Typical Responses:

Analytic (Xs)—because a leg is missing from each or because they are wood. Characteristics of response: —stimulus centered; —parts specific. *Relational (Os)*—because they look good together, or because they are both chairs. Characteristics of response: —self-centered; —global characteristics of stimulus have meaning.

Analytic (Xs)—because both figures have arms on hips. Characteristics of response: —stimulus centered; —parts specific. *Relational (Os)*—because they look good together, or because they are both boys. Characteristics of response: —self-centered; —global characteristics of stimulus have meaning.

Illustration B: Witkin Test of Graphic Field Articulation (Adaption)

Pupil is instructed to find the simple figures in the complex ones.

High relational pupils have difficulty finding any simple figures in the complex ones. High analytic pupils find from 15–19 out of a possible 22. Test consists of 7 plates.

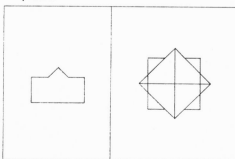

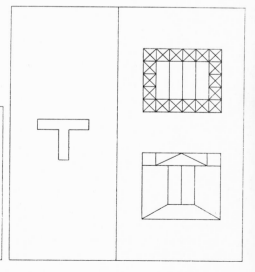

Illustration C: Typical Responses to the Synonym Set

Pupil is instructed to list as many words as he can think of with the same or similar meaning to those used as stimulus items. Test consists of 25 words.

WORDS	ANALYTIC RESPONSES	RELATIONAL RESPONSES
Money	coins, currency medium of exchange, nickels, dimes, etc. (Formal abstraction, i.e., each word has a relatively set meaning which is not dependent upon the circumstances in which it is used. Each set of circumstances is defined in dependent clauses.)	green, trash, bundle, etc. (descriptive abstraction) or bones, berries, etc. (embedded for meaning in the manner in which this money is used) or cabbage, lettuce, etc. (bidimensional: both descriptive and embedded)
Wine	Port, sherry, etc., or selections with alcohol content in common, e.g., beer, whiskey, etc. (formal abstraction)	blood, slop, molasses, etc. (descriptive abstraction)
Fight	struggle, battle, war, etc. (formal abstraction)	27 different selections, each of which is specific to who the combatants are (males, females, or both, whether they are young or old, gangs or individuals etc.); where the fight takes place (e.g., on a street corner, in one's own territory or elsewhere, etc.), and with what weapons (e.g., fists, brickbats, deadly weapons etc.) [e.g., "big red rumble"—a routine fight between gangs, using whole bricks; parts of bricks would use the reference, "little red . . ." etc.] (descriptive abstraction and embedded)

Illustration D: The Attitude Scales

The following are sample items from the scales of descriptive abstraction and field dependence. Pupils were asked to respond to each item on a five point scale from "strongly agree" to "strongly disagree."

Each positive response was scored as indicating a preference for descriptive abstraction in social contexts. Each negative response was scored as a rejection of descriptive abstraction in social contexts. Reverse statement items provided internal reliability checks against negative responses.

A person's outward appearance gives you a good   Descriptive abstraction
idea of what he is like

To be like someone you admire, it is more important to imitate his clothes and mannerisms than to copy what he thinks and believes	Descriptive abstraction
How we use words depends mostly on where, when, and to whom they're spoken	Word embeddedness
I wouldn't want to be rich if my family couldn't be rich too	Family embeddedness
You can't depend on knowing how to act when you get out of your own neighborhood	Neighborhood embeddedness
You just can't trust strangers very much	Group embeddedness

22 / Culture and Memory [1]

Michael Cole and John Gay

This chapter is concerned with a question that has interested Western man ever since the voyages of discovery beginning in the fifteenth century: *Do the bearers of different cultures think differently?*

As interesting and straightforward as the question of cultural differences in cognition may seem, it has proved resistant to scientific inquiry in the general form in which it is usually stated. It is the purpose of this paper to explore the relation between culture and cognition in the hope that we may be able to reformulate this question in ways which suggest empirical and experimental studies and which will have concrete educational implications.

One difficulty with this enterprise is that terms such as thinking, cognition, and culture are defined so variously and often so vaguely that it is very difficult to ascertain whether disagreements are problems of fact, definition or interpretation. For instance, one anthropologist commented, upon hearing about the results of our first research in this area (Gay and Cole 1967):

> The reasoning and thinking processes of different people in different cultures don't differ . . . just their values, beliefs. and ways of classifying differ. (Personal correspondence)

Implicit in such a statement is a definition of thinking that excludes a great deal of what psychologists have traditionally included under that term. Implicit too is a distinction between *what* people think and *how* they think, the "static" and "dynamic" aspects of cognitive behavior. A great deal of what has come to be termed "cognitive anthropology" (Tyler 1969) has been concerned with the *what*, rather than the *how*.

In our own work, we have found it useful to make this distinction between the *content* of cognitive activity and cognitive *processes*. At the very minimum, everyone would agree that Eskimos and Bushmen often think *about* different things simply because of the radically different environments in which they carry on their daily activities. General agreement can also be easily reached on the proposition that Bushmen and Eskimos "think differently" about some things which they experience in common. For instance, both groups think about their families, but have different thoughts (e.g., different "beliefs" or "values") concerning them. These examples seem to characterize the kind of cultural differences in cognitive activity accepted by our anthropological correspondent.

When one turns to consideration of *how* people think, agreement is more difficult to achieve; when the contents of thought are the same, do people operate differently on these contents as the result of training specific to certain cultural settings? At one extreme, it is suggested that there are universal modes of expression, shared by all languages investigated thus far (Greenberg 1963). At the other extreme, each man's approach to problem solving may depend significantly on his personal background and training.

Early interest in these issues was stimulated by the controversial studies of cultural variations in cognitive processes contained in Lévy-Bruhl's treatise on *Primitive Mentality*, in which he drew upon a wealth of informal anthropological and missionary evidence to support his generalization that the thinking of primitive people is governed by different laws than that of their civilized brethren.

Thus we find him reporting:

> These observers (missionaries-authors) have maintained that primitives manifest a decided distaste for reasoning, for what logicians call the "discursive operations of thought"; at the same time they have remarked that this distaste did not arise out of any radical incapability or any inherent defect in their understanding, but was rather to be accounted for by their general methods of thought. (Lévy-Bruhl 1966:21).

Without denying primitives' abilities to function ably and skillfully in many situations, Lévy-Bruhl comes to the conclusion that the laws of mental functioning of primitive peoples are fundamentally different from his own.

> Their mentality, essentially mystic and prelogical as it is, proceeds to other objects, and pursues other paths than our minds do . . . To follow primitive mentality in its course, to unravel its theories, we must, as it were do violence to our own mental habits, and adapt ourselves to theirs. (Lévy-Bruhl 1966: 442)

Lévy-Bruhl's point of view has been roundly and repeatedly criticized by anthropologists and others (beginning with Boas 1911). The most recent and perhaps the most cogent criticism has appeared in two papers by an English anthropologist, Robin Horton (1967a, 1967b). The gist of Horton's argument is that in terms both of its function and its structure, the examples of primitive thought marshalled by Lévy-Bruhl and others are quite consistent with analogous belief systems of Western man. The anthropologist should not be seduced by the seemingly bizarre beliefs of some primitive peoples into thinking that they do not share his thought processes. Horton suggests rather that the anthropologist study human behavior in well defined and limited situations in order to determine what cognitive processes are at work. General conclusions can be drawn only on the basis of a large number of such studies among widely diverse peoples, studies as free as possible from the tacit assumption of Western superiority.

The number of carefully controlled studies of the relation between culture and thinking is as yet quite small. The various attempts which have been made by anthropologists, linguists, and psychologists to solve the general problem of culture and cognition can at best be suggestive only of hypotheses for research. We thus take Horton's advice to heart and consider the cognitive processes of particular groups of people in particular circumstances. In so doing, we can temporarily avoid the difficulty of having to define such lofty terms as culture and cognition, pointing instead to the set of circumstances and operations that interest us. When we have learned enough to account adequately for some limited sets of data, we might feel freer to attack the general problem, armed with some facts. Nevertheless, even with our limited aims there remain serious methodological problems which limit the inferences that can be drawn from our work. It is our hope that an understanding of the difficulties which we have encountered with problems of limited scope will point the way to conducting more ambitious and firmly based research projects.

The particular problem we wish to discuss is the relation between memory and the specific social and intellectual contexts within which it occurs. For many years, Westerners who have lived in traditional, preliterate communities have returned with tales of remarkable feats of memory to complement their tales of "lack of discursive thinking." Lévy-Bruhl cites many examples of a presumed ability to memorize, claiming that "In every case in which their memorizing power, which is really excellent, could relieve them of the effort of thinking and reasoning, they did not fail to make use of it" (Lévy-Bruhl 1966:25). Similar general comments are often made by Westerners who teach in Africa; their students do well with material that can be "learned by rote," but are poor or indifferent students when dealing with subjects in which brute memorization will not work.

In addition to this anecdotal evidence, there is good reason to expect members of a preliterate, traditional society to have developed mnemonic skills different from those of literate, technological societies.

For example, with no written language to mediate recall of every day items, a successful trip to the local market to buy supplies depends on remembering the desired goods. Another example is the emphasis placed on learning the history of the tribe, its traditions, ancestors, taboos, and heroes. History is so much a part of many traditional societies (cf. D'Azevedo 1962, Gay and Cole 1967) that someone who cannot commit large amounts of information to memory is likely to be looked upon as mentally deficient in some way. Thus, D'Azevedo recounts that among the Gola of Liberia "an elder with a poor memory, or 'whose old people told him nothing' is a 'small boy' among the elders and might very well be looked upon with contempt by younger persons" (D'Azevedo 1962:13). Similarly, Elenore Bowen recounts the displeasure and consternation of her Nigerian hosts when she was unable to learn the names of local plants which every six year old in the village had long since committed to memory (Bowen 1964:16).

The generally held belief that mnemonic skills are in some way connected with culture has generated very little research on the question (but see Goody and Watt 1962). Not only have social scientists failed to identify the factors which control the learning of various memory skills, they have as yet failed to document cultural differences in memory at all.

One of the few psychological investigations of memory among African tribal people was carried out by Bartlett and is reported in his famous monograph, *Remembering*. Having heard of the "marvelous word-perfect memory of the Swazi from his childhood up" (1932:248), Bartlett set out to find out when this phenomenal memory manifested itself. First he asked a young boy to carry a message to someone else in the village and found that recall was about on a par with what one would expect of an English child of similar age. Then he tested a cattleherder's memory for a series of transactions involving cattle sold the year before. In this case, Bartlett found that the herder's memory was phenomenally accurate, although he was only peripherally involved in the transaction. Bartlett points out the importance of cattle among the Swazi, and suggests that it is really not so remarkable. The cowherder's feat of memory seems outstanding because what is socially important to him is irrelevant to the Western observer, who therefore finds a good memory for cows and prices unusual. We might expect the Swazi cowherder to be equally astounded should he happen to encounter a Los Angeles ten-year-old trading baseball cards with a friend with the intricate recall of players, teams, batting averages and relative standing, that the successful trader requires. Unfortunately, the many hypotheses that can be generated from this demonstration have never been followed up and tested.

Our own work in the area of memory grew out of our interest in the factors which impede the education of tribal children in the Western-oriented government schools sprinkled around the interior of Liberia (Gay and Cole 1967). Like other observers, we noted the heavy reliance on what appeared to be serial rote learning in the classroom. Students copied exactly what the teacher did, often failing to grasp the principle involved. Rote learning seemed, however, to be coupled with "rote" teaching. Observations of rote learning in the classroom led us to investigate the tendency of African tribal people to learn by rote under various conditions; perhaps the rote learning was learned in the classroom and not at mother's knee!

To move beyond our rather casual observations required us to choose an experimental tool, or set of tools, which would be appropriate for the study of rote learning. Although the term "rote" as applied to classroom behavior is rather vague, it presumably refers to a person's tendency to repeat material in the same order and manner in which it was presented to him.

This description suggests the serial learning task familiar to the psychologist in which material is presented in a certain fixed order and the subject's task is to recall the material in that order using each response term as the stimulus for the next response (Underwood 1966:457). However, we chose not to begin our research with this experimental procedure because the questions it could answer seemed unnecessarily limited; learning such a task can only be carried out in a serial manner since any deviations from the serial order produce incorrect responses. Instead we chose the method of free recall, which gives both more flexibility and more generality.[2]

The free-recall experiment has several features which render it useful for our purposes. First, it is extremely easy to administer. A subject is presented a series of items, one at a time, and is told that he must try to learn them so that he can recall them at a later time. After the last item is presented, a fixed period is given for recall. The list can then be repeated as many times as desired.

Secondly, the subject is free to remember in any manner he chooses; the way in which subjects reorder to-be-learned lists when recalling them in this unconstrained fashion gives important insight into the mechanisms of memory. Bousfield and his associates (Bousfield 1953; Cohen 1963) stimulated interest in this area by demonstrating that when the items to be remembered came from easily identifiable semantic categories, recall tended to be "clustered" so that items from a given semantic category were commonly recalled together. Although there are many questions of fact and theory remaining to be clarified, it is clear from the work of Bousfield and other investigators that North American high school and college students show a strong predilection toward reorganizing material presented for memorization and that success in recall is related to the degree of organization (see the summary article, Tulving 1968).

Given the rather copious experimental literature on organization of free recall as background and the ease of collecting data using the free recall technique we decided to initiate our studies of memory in Liberia with a set of experiments on the factors contributing to the accuracy and organization of free recall.

A few comments need to be made about the experimental context of our studies, although a thorough discussion is beyond the scope of this paper (for more detail see Cole, Gay, Glick, and Sharp 1971).

All of the studies to be reported here were first carried out among the Kpelle tribe in North-Central Liberia. There are approximately 250,000 Kpelle in Liberia, where they are the largest of sixteen major tribes. Approximately the same number live in Guinea, where they are known as the Guerze.

The people live in small towns perhaps ten miles apart of between twenty and

300 huts with between fifty and 1,500 inhabitants. Rice is the basic crop; others merely supplement the diet or the family income. Kpelle land is dense tropical rain forest.

The Kpelle language is related to Mende in Sierra Leone and Malinke in Mali; Kpelle culture shares many features, in particular, a strong secret-society system, with the neighboring West African tribes. There is no traditional form of written Kpelle, but a few Kpelle have learned to read and write their language using a phonetic alphabet.

As a rule, our Kpelle experimentation was done by Kpelle students attending Cuttington College, the base of our operations. Assistants were trained by the authors who were present while many of these data were collected. The experimenter-informants were always consulted as to the proper manner for translating the various instructions from English into Kpelle and were provided with typed versions of the instructions. Experiments were conducted informally in a village house, a local gathering place, or simply on the ground beneath a tree. It was not uncommon for a small crowd to gather nearby to watch the proceedings; participation in the experiments was an amusing diversion for many of the villagers but, where extensive time was required, the subject was "dashed" a can of meat or a quarter. Before beginning a series of experiments in a village, the general purpose of our research was explained to the town chief and the villagers whose cooperation as a group was essential to the success of our work.

The critical first step for this particular set of experiments was the selection of the set of stimulus items which would comprise the to-be-recalled list (hereafter referred to as the input list). Our initial procedure for generating this list was quite simple: we interviewed our experimenter-informants one at a time and asked them what kinds of things were commonly purchased in the local tribal market and small shops. From the set of items generated in this way, we selected a group of twenty items which met the criteria of being known and mentioned by all informants, named by a single generally accepted word in Kpelle, unambiguously identified if shown to a Kpelle person, a member of a familiar nameable category of objects, and easy to present physically. The list of items produced in this manner is presented in table 22.1. With this list in hand we set out to collect data.

The first data we shall present are from ten Kpelle adults who spoke essentially no English. A subject was chosen and the list of words was read to him at a rate of approximately one word every two seconds. The order of presentation was random with the restriction that no two items from the same category appear next to each other. When the list had been completed, ninety seconds were given for the subject to recall the words while the experimenter noted each response on his answer sheet.

The results in terms of the average number of correct responses per trial and the average degree of clustering per trial are given in table 22.2.

The data concerning the number of correct responses per trial are easily interpreted and indicate that there is little, if any, improvement in recall with successive learning trials.[3] The clustering scores require a few words of explanation since our

TABLE 22.1. STIMULUS MATERIALS FOR FREE-RECALL STUDIES

"CLUSTERABLE" LIST			
Orange	Pot	Hoe	Headtie
Banana	Calabash	File	Singlet
Onion	Cup	Knife	Trousers
Potato	Plate	Cutlass	Hat
Coconut	Pan	Hammer	Shirt

TABLE 22.2. RECALL AND ORGANIZATION: ORAL PRESENTATION

	TRIAL				
	1	2	3	4	5
African adults					
Number correct	9.1	9.9	10.0	10.0	10.8
Clustering score	-.53	.04	-.27	.52	.28
College students					
Number correct	12.9	15.9	17.5	18.9	18.7
Clustering score	2.31	3.95	4.16	4.09	4.58

particular scheme for calculating the degree of semantic clustering differs from measures proposed by earlier workers in this field.

Clustering is defined as the tendency of items from a given semantic category to occur next to each other in greater than chance fashion. Using formulas derived from Mood and provided by Wallis and Roberts (1956:569) we were able to calculate a z score which in turn yields the probability of observing the amount of clustering in the output list (see Cole, Frankel, and Sharp 1971 for a discussion of the measurements of clustering). A z score of zero indicates a randomly structured list, a positive z score indicates that there are fewer runs than expected by chance (and hence more clusters).

Returning to an examination of table 22.2, we see that the Kpelle adults' z scores fluctuate around zero with some suggestion that clustering is increasing slightly over trials.

By way of an initial comparison, data for an analogously constructed list run under the same conditions with a group of American college students are included in the bottom half of table 22.2. The Americans remember more, cluster more, and improve more over trials.

The set of observations brings us face to face with the major problem confronting not only this particular bit of research, but all experimental comparisons of the cognitive activity of different cultural groups. What inferences can be made about underlying cognitive processes from the comparison of performances of groups from the two cultures on a particular task? What kinds of experiments can we design involving these groups which will permit us to draw inferences relevant to specific questions and hypotheses?

Let us examine this question with reference to our little "cross-cultural experiment." From the data in table 22.2 what would we want to conclude? Are Americans better memorizers than tribal Africans? Does the lack of clustering indicate that Africans are indeed rote learners? What about the lack of improvement across trials—does this indicate that Africans are slow learners? On the contrary, *we have only demonstrated differences in the way that adult representatives of two cultures recall a set of common nouns.* This conclusion is neither interesting nor profound. What we really wish to know is the particular variables which control the differential performance of the two groups and the way in which these variables relate to particular cultural differences.

We are by no means the first to recognize the difficulties of such experimental comparisons. The area of greatest concern in this regard has been the research on IQ testing, where early interest centered on the use of these tests to make inferences about the genetic components of racial differences. For reasons very similar to the criticisms of the crude use of IQ tests within the United States to make inferences about racial differences (Gottesman 1968), the use of IQ tests in Africa and elsewhere has come under heavy attack (Cryns 1962). More recently, Campbell and his associates (Campbell 1961; Segall, Campbell, and Herskovits 1966) and others (Doob 1958, 1968; Jahoda 1968) have considered the general problem of experimental comparisons. Several safeguards against faulty inference have been suggested by these authors. Campbell put the matter well when he says

> We who are interested in using such [cross-cultural] comparisons for delineating process rather than exhaustively describing single instances must accept this rule: *No comparison of a single pair of natural objects is interpretable* . . . However, if there are multiple indicators which vary in their irrelevant attributes, and if these all agree as to the direction of the difference on the theoretically intended aspects, then the number of tenable rival explanations becomes greatly reduced and the confirmation of theory more nearly certain. (Campbell 1961:344–345)

As we have pointed out elsewhere (Cole, Gay, and Glick 1968), while accepting the importance of Campbell's suggestions we seek, where possible, to supplement them by an additional consideration; *that wherever possible the inferences about differences between cultures with respect to a given psychological process rest on evidence from the pattern of differences within the cultures being compared.* We will attempt to illustrate the application of this principle in the discussion which follows.

If we take seriously the advice we have been giving in the above paragraphs there is little or nothing that we can infer from the "mini-experiment" summarized in table 22.2. Clearly we must greatly expand the range of conditions before we can claim to be on solid ground.

The expansions that we decided to undertake were designed to evaluate two main sets of rival hypotheses concerning the relatively poor performance of Kpelle subjects on the first task we gave them. The first set we will consider relates to the materials to be remembered. We generated the experimental list in a relatively informal fashion. Perhaps we put together a "categorizable" list which contained what *we* believed to be reasonable categories, but which were not, in fact, naturally occurring Kpelle categories, or perhaps the subjects categorized the lists subjectively in ways which differed from our assumed classes. If the list were in fact not categorizable from the Kpelle point of view, we would expect little clustering and poorer recall. (Cofer 1968 reviews the evidence showing that clusterable lists are generally easier to learn than nonclusterable lists although there is as yet no generally accepted theory to account for this phenomenon.) Moreover, if the lists were categorizable in different ways, we would also expect not to identify the classes used by the Kpelle, with the basic techniques we employed to measure clustering.

The second set of hypotheses by which we might explain poor Kpelle performance relates to the conditions under which the experiments were performed. On a relatively trivial level, it might be that the subjects are too frightened to respond appropriately, or they fail to take the task seriously, or they need more trials to show the expected improvements or they fail to understand what is expected of them. On a deeper level, it may be that the context of the experiment or the procedures used may radically affect the outcome.

Let us consider first the set of problems dealing with the nature of Kpelle categories and the reality of the categories on our list. Fortunately for us, the problem of discerning indigenous classifications of the environment has been an active area of research among anthropologists in recent years, and techniques have been developed which seek to reduce, if not eliminate, the bias produced by the ethnographer's own language and culture (cf. Romney and D'Andrade 1964 for a general description of this research and its applications to problems such as those dealt with here). We have borrowed two of these techniques to provide independent checks upon the status of the categories used in the experiment reported above. The first is a relatively structured eliciting technique reported in detail in Metzger and Williams (1963), supplemented by group discussion. We began with the Kpelle word *seng* which roughly has the same meaning as the word "things" in English. Every speaker of English or Kpelle can give many terms which fall within this very general class and can organize these terms into subclasses.

This work, carried out by John Kellemu, a college graduate and member of the Kpelle tribe by birth, used the substitution frame "—— kaa a ——" which can be roughly translated as "—— see as ——." The first term is a member of the class named by the second. Either term may be replaced by a question word. For example in English we might say "A stone is a thing. What else is a thing? A bird is a thing. A bird is what else? A bird is an animal. Or, the sequence might go, "A bird is an animal. What is an example of a bird? A robin is a bird." There are clearly many ways to use this frame sentence to elicit members of particular classes and classes which include particular objects.

The result of these procedures is a tree diagram which divides the universe of material objects into town things and forest things. These two main classes correspond to the two basic features of Kpelle life, the human village community and the non-human surrounding rainforest. Each of these main classes is in turn divided into subclasses determined by their relation to human life (see table 22.3).

This classification of material objects (*seng*) is clearly not the one familiar to a person brought up in the American culture. A comparable American chart might divide things at the highest level into animate and inanimate, with living things divided into animals and plants as the next lower division of the whole tree diagram.

Comparing the categories on the *seng* chart with the recall list, we found reflected in the chart what we took to be categories on the basis of our informal elicitations. We learned in addition that three of the categories were unambiguously located within the more general class of household goods, while the fourth, foods, is doubly classified; it is a type of work under the heading of town things, and a major category under forest things. Although a systematic study of the relation between the horizontal and vertical distance among classes on the *seng* chart as it relates to memory would be a worthwhile project (parts of which we have undertaken, but do not intend to discuss here; see Cole et al. 1971), the evidence generally supports the acceptability of our categorized list.

However, we were not entirely happy with this procedure. For one thing, we suspected that the eliciting procedure might have influenced the kinds of categorization we observed. For instance, Kpelle people will also separate *seng* into "good things" and "bad things" and indeed this sort of response makes good sense to us. But in the case that the elicitor expects some other response, it may be more detailed questioning that will cause the typical informant to switch to the "town-forest" dichotomy. How general, then, are the situations in which the *seng* chart categories are appropriate and rapidly elicited?

To obtain some information on this point, we gathered data on items from the *seng* chart using an eliciting technique which is considerably less structured than that used by Kellemu. For this purpose, we applied a technique used extensively by Stefflre in studies of similarity structures (Stefflre 1969). This eliciting technique is tedious, but extremely simple and nondirective. We will illustrate the procedure using the twenty items from our clusterable list augmented by sixteen items chosen in a manner similar to the original list except that they were intended to be randomly selected with respect to semantic categories. These thirty-six words were read one at a time to the informant whose task was to make up an acceptable sentence using that word. When a sentence was produced in this way for each word, the subject was read each of the sentences with each of the total list of thirty-six words inserted in the place of the original word. The subject was asked to judge for each new sentence if "a Kpelle person would say this." For instance, the subject might use the word "cup" in the sentence "I took the cup off the table." He would

TABLE 22.3. SENG CHART

PERSONS	TOWN THINGS					FOREST THINGS						
	STRUCTURES	HOUSE-HOLD	WORK	TOWN ANIMALS	PLAY	FOOD	TRAPS	TREES	SHRUBS	VINES	EVIL THINGS	EARTH
Children	House	Sleeping things	House-hold goods	Birds	Dancers	Yams		Secondary bush	Wild shrubs	Wild vines	Male society leader	Dirt
Important persons	Shed	Tools	Medi-cine	Walking animals	Dancing equip-ment	Vine fruits	NUMEROUS	High forest	Culti-vated shrubs	Culti-vated vines	Female society leader	Stones
Fine persons	Fence	Cooking utensils	Vehi-cles		Games	Tree fruits		Culti-vated trees			Frighten-ing things	Sand
Workmen	Bench	Clothes	Food		Drums	Liquids					Witches	Mud
Evil persons	Loom		Traps		Horns	Mush-rooms					Genie	
Ways of working	Society fence					Animals					Dwarfs	
Ways of being	Chief's fence										Spirits	

THINGS

then be asked whether or not it made sense for a person to say, "I took the —— off the table" where —— was each of the remaining words of the list. If the substituted word was acceptable in a given sentence, a "1" was inserted in the proper position for that word and sentence in a 36 × 36 matrix. This procedure was carried out with fourteen Kpelle adults, and the fourteen matrices summed to form a matrix whose elements ranged from 0 to ten. This matrix was then processed using a program provided by Stefflre which rearranges the rows and columns in such a manner that words whose distributions of elements in the resultant matrix were most similar were closest to each other. This procedure produces a new list of words which are "clumped" together in terms of the similarity of their distributional characteristics. The results of this analysis are included in table 22.4 as the "Rearranged list," and show clearly that the clusterable items in fact separate themselves from the nonclusterable items. In addition, two of the nonclusterable items fall within or next to a category cluster to which they seem to belong; thus, "bottle" falls within the cluster that we have identified as utensils and "nail" comes next to the category of tools.

The convergence in results for these three widely different ways of arriving at a set of commonly categorized items leads us to be fairly confident that for some contexts at least, the items we used on our memory experiment really are categorized by the Kpelle in the way we originally assumed them to be. Since the eliciting situation is formally quite similar to the free-recall experimental situation we feel moderately safe in assuming that the lack of categorizing observed in our memory data is not the result of using inappropriate materials or of expecting them to be organized in inappropriate ways.

Having thus assured ourselves of the material and linguistic foundation for our Kpelle studies, which is all too often taken for granted in United States-based research we felt free to turn again to the experimental question before us with some assurance that it is in fact a proper question.

Our experimental attack focused on the types of persons, verbal instructions, and material conditions which could reasonably be expected to affect the rate of learning and degree of clustering in the free recall experiment. The first variation involved the nature of the stimulus materials. One point upon which many observers

TABLE 22.4. REARRANGED LIST

Calabash	Potato
Bottle	Onion
Pot	Banana
Pan	Orange
Cup	Coconut
Plate	Cigarette
Box	Nail
Horn	File
Book	Hammer
Trousers	Hoe
Singlet	Knife
Shirt	Cutlass
Headtie	Mat
Hat	Candle
Cotton	Stone
Rope	Battery
Stick	Feather
Grass	Nickel

of African learning seem to agree is the presumed "concreteness" of African thought. For instance, Cryns (1962), who has no use for IQ tests as ordinarily applied, maintained that the "empirical evidence suggesting the prevalence of a concrete way of thinking in the African ... is too substantial to be refuted." Perhaps, then, if we showed the objects named by each of our stimulus words to our subjects, instead of reading them aloud, we would observe greatly augmented recall and clustering. Several studies with Americans have shown increased recall using pictures rather than verbal stimuli (e.g., Scott 1967). Thus, if African mentality is more "concrete" than that of Americans, we should expect not only augmentation, but proportionally greater augmentation than ordinarily observed with Americans.

A second variation involves the clusterability of the lists themselves. As mentioned earlier, American evidence (Cofer 1968) indicates that clusterable lists are easier to learn, in general, than lists chosen so that their members belong to disparate classes. If the Kpelle rely on rote memory rather than the clusterability of the list, then they ought to recall equally well on both lists. We used the list given in table 22.5 as our nonclusterable list. These terms were elicited informally with checks only on their general unrelatedness. When the nonclusterable list is used, of course, no clustering score can be computed.

Another variable which has been found to affect clustering and recall is the arrangement of items in a clusterable list. If the items are *not* randomly arranged as in our original experiment, but rather are presented in a clustered fashion, clustering and recall are enhanced for American college students (Cofer, Bruce, and Reicher 1966).

We chose subjects of different ages and educational levels because we guessed these variables might influence clustering and recall. The three age groups represented are six to eight years, ten to fourteen years and eighteen to fifty years. For the first two age groups educational levels were unschooled, first grade and second to fourth grade. Since it is very rare to find an educated tribal adult, we did not include an educated adult group in our early experiments. At a later stage, we added comparisons which included high schoolers who ranged in age from fifteen to twenty. In general, Kpelle children do not know their ages. Moreover, grade in school very often does not correspond to years in school, since a student is likely to remain in the beginner's half of the first grade until his English comprehension is adequate to continue. These factors should make us generally cautious about overstating the accuracy with which we can relate performance to age and schooling, a fact which complicates our already complicated task of cross-cultural comparison. We ought also to point out that factors such as status and degree of Westernization are likely to co-vary with age and education, leading to further restrictions on any conclusions we might want to draw from the data.

In order to make cross-cultural comparisons we have collected data from children in Southern California who are primarily white, from middle-class homes. Although this population is clearly not optional (a wide range of socioeconomic and ethnic backgrounds should be investigated), it was used because of its availability.

The first two variables we consider are education and the clusterability of the lists. This experiment included four groups of Kpelle children ages ten to fourteen, two

TABLE 22.5. "NON-CLUSTERABLE" LIST

Rope	Grass	Nickel	Orange
Cotton	Horn	Bottle	Pot
Book	Battery	Feather	Knife
Candle	Mat	Nail	Shirt
Stone	Cigarette	Stick	Box

TABLE 22.6. FREE-RECALL RESULTS: EXPERIMENT 1

		TRIAL				
		1	2	3	4	5
African						
Recalled	Clusterable	7.6	8.6	9.0	9.2	9.6
	Nonclusterable	6.6	6.8	6.6	7.8	8.2
	Educated	8.0	9.0	9.0	9.4	9.8
	Illiterate	6.2	7.2	7.6	7.7	8.0
Clustering		-.17	-.14	-.23	-.03	-.08
Position correlation		-.05	-.04	-.02	.00	-.09
American						
Recall	1st Grade	4.8	6.8	6.8	8.0	8.4
	4th Grade	7.4	9.2	9.8	10.8	11.2
	6th Grade	8.6	11.0	11.6	12.8	13.4
	9th Grade	8.8	11.6	13.1	14.6	14.9
	Clusterable	7.6	10.8	11.8	12.2	12.4
	Nonclusterable	7.0	9.1	9.9	10.9	11.6
Clustering	1st Grade	-.69	-.36	.15	.34	.75
	4th Grade	-.35	.48	.16	.43	1.32
	6th Grade	.49	1.17	.89	1.71	1.40
	9th Grade	.46	.83	1.30	2.04	1.98
Position correlation		+.22	-.17	-.31	-.25	-.20

groups being educated and two illiterate, with ten children in each group. One group at each educational level was presented the clusterable list in table 22.1, and the other the nonclusterable list in table 22.5. All other conditions were identical to those described in our initial example; in particular, presentation of the lists was oral. Results of this experiment, as well as results from American groups, are presented in table 22.6.

Looking first at the African data, we see that the clusterable list was more easily learned than the nonclusterable list and the school children were superior to their nonliterate counterparts.[3] None of the groups recalled particularly well and although the improvement across trials was reliable, it was very small in magnitude (about 1.7 items).

No group showed a significant degree of clustering on any trial. The data from the educated and nonliterate groups were homogeneous in this regard, and are thus not reported separately.

For the American school children, too, clusterability of the list produced improved recall although in both relative and absolute terms, the enhancement was *less* than that found among the Kpelle. The *pattern* of American results reported is quite different than the *pattern* for the Kpelle, even where average scores are quite similar. The American children show considerable increases in the recall and clustering scores from the first to the last trial and all American groups exhibit significant clustering by trial 5.

At this point we want to introduce two additional measures of performance indicative of the qualitatively different ways in which items are being recalled in the two cultural settings.

First, let us consider the possibility that the lack of clustering among the Kpelle occurred because they were attempting to learn by rote, i.e., remember the items in the order in which they were presented.

As one measure of "rote learning," we calculated the correlation between word order on the input list and the word order of each subject's output list. A high correlation is indicative of a close correspondence between input and output orders.

It is apparent from a brief consideration of the "Position correlation" measure in table 22.6 that the Kpelle subjects are *not* "rote learning," while the American subjects show a good deal of rote learning on the first trial, but not thereafter.

A second difference in the *way* items are being recalled, and one which helps to explain the negative position correlations observed among the American subjects is apparent in an examination of the performance of the two populations as a function of the serial position of the items.

The American subjects manifest a typical serial position curve (Deese 1957); items very late in the list are best recalled, then items at the beginning and finally the middle items. By contrast the African data are relatively flat with respect to serial position (figure 22.1).

How should we interpret the outcome of this expanded experiment? We have observed some clear differences in the Kpelle subjects' performance as a function of education and the organization of the stimulus materials. However, these differences were generally small in magnitude: accuracy levels characteristic of American subjects were not reached. Moreover, the pattern of results indicates that the African subjects approach the memory task in a different way from their American counterparts. However, this difference cannot easily be attributed to rote memorizing, the traditional hypothesis concerning the nature of such differences, since there is no evidence in our data to confirm this hypothesis.

A second experiment in this series looked once again at the effect of education. This time, however, the clusterable list was used for all groups, half being school children aged ten to fourteen, and the other half nonliterate ten- to fourteen-year-olds. These two populations were subdivided so that half of each group were shown objects to recall, while the other half followed the procedure of the previous experiment in having the words read to them. Each of these subgroups was again divided so that half the subjects were shown the objects (told the words) in the random order used in the initial experiment, while items for the remaining subjects were "blocked" so that all items from a given category occurred together. Thus, education, stimulus materials, and list order were all factors in this experiment.

In this case, education did *not* have an overall effect. The mean number of words per trial recalled by all educated subjects was about the same as that of the uneducated subjects. However, education interacted in an interesting way with the nature of the stimulus materials. Educated subjects performed much better when objects were presented than when words were used (10.8 vs. 9.1), whereas uneducated subjects performed equally well for both modes of presentation (9.6 vs. 9.6). This finding points up the extreme caution that we must use when the magnitude of our effects is small, remember that in the previous experiment a small but consistent advantage accrued to the educated subjects. This same superiority did not occur in the present experiment under the original conditions, but only when objects are used. It is the partially Westernized Kpelle child who benefits from concrete stimuli, not his traditional and nonliterate brother. Moreover, the American child benefits still more than the Kpelle school child from use of objects.

The blocked order of presentation also facilitated recall slightly for the Kpelle, but did not differentiate between nonliterate and educated subjects. Americans likewise showed only slight improvement in recall as a result of blocking.

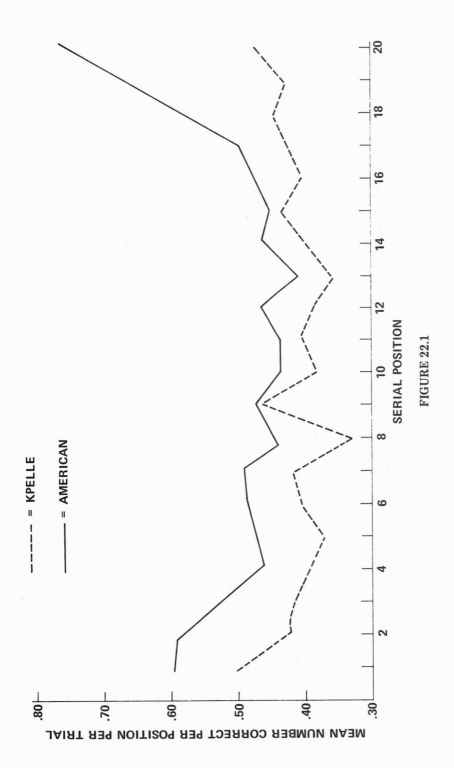

FIGURE 22.1

The degree of clustering observed in the present experiment was consistent with that in the previous experiment in that presentation of words in a random order resulted in a total lack of clustering (.07). However, when the words were presented in a blocked fashion, significant clustering appeared (1.2). Use of objects rather than words enhanced clustering for both the random (.23) and blocked (1.92) methods of presentation. In cases where there is a high clustering score, the organizational hierarchy of terms which emerges when pairs of terms are considered is exactly that of the presumed classes and is quite pronounced, in contrast to the hierarchy derived from the original experiment and reported above.

The same pattern of results was obtained with American school children. Blocking the materials according to classes increased clustering greatly. Presenting objects increased clustering by a wide margin, just as it had increased recall.

In terms of the average magnitude of the effects, the Kpelle children performed very much like American first graders who were 4.8 years younger on the average. However, the pattern of responding was once again not the same. The American children exhibited a strong serial position effect, while the Africans displayed roughly the same accuracy at all serial positions. And again it was the *American* subjects who showed an initial tendency to order their recall according to the order of the to-be-remembered list. The correlations between input and output for the African subjects were always near zero.

What can we conclude on the basis of the experiments reported thus far? We seem to have established that although the Kpelle and American subjects are effected in a similar manner by some standard experimental manipulations, the Kpelle performance remains inferior in quantity recalled, and the *pattern* of responding under different circumstances is quite different. In particular, the Americans seem to take much greater advantage of such presumed aids to learning as organization according to semantic category, physical presence, and privileged position in listing the materials. The assumption that such factors aid learning may in itself be culture-bound. Our experimental manipulations were chosen because they are familiar to Americans, not because of known relevance to the Kpelle.

We therefore must consider possible hypotheses to explain Kpelle performance, both in terms of recall and clustering levels, and in terms of pattern and response. Might there be reasons why our presumed American aids to learning are ineffective, and might there be procedures which the Kpelle find helpful?

A simple alternative is that our African subjects simply don't care—they aren't taking the task seriously. To test this notion we used the same basic subject populations in an experiment designed to give the subject good reason to want to perform well. In addition to being asked to remember as much of the list as possible, each subject was told that he would be given a stone for each correctly recalled word and that the stones could be traded for money at the end of the experiment.

The result of this experiment is easily summarized. Recall averaged 10.1 items when all of the groups were summed (schooled and nonschooled six to eight and ten- to fourteen-year-olds plus a group of nonliterate adults). There were no differences among groups and no changes over trials. Clustering followed the same pattern; it began and ended at a chance level among all groups. These results are different in no significant way from those obtained in the initial experiment.

Similarly, we found that extending the number of trials, promising more money, and using more "traditional" items failed to influence the major pattern of the results.

At this point, we shifted our attention to a consideration of the cues that our subjects were using at the time of recall. We began with a vague notion that the performance of the Kpelle subjects would be improved if the *categories* latent in our clusterable list were somehow signalled by an object in the real world. Thus we arranged a situation in which the objects shown to our subjects were associated with chairs. Perhaps the "concreteness" is not in the to-be-learned material, but in the relation of this material to recall cues.

The experimenter stood behind four chairs, in front of which stood the subject. Behind the experimenter was a table containing the objects to be remembered. These objects were held up one at a time over chairs as the list of items was presented and then the subject was asked to recall the items (but not which chair they were associated with).

The presentation of items followed a different pattern for each of three different groups of ten to fourteen-year-old school children. For one group items from a given category were held over one particular chair on each trial, so that each category was assigned one chair. For the second group, items were assigned at random to the four chairs, with the assignment remaining the same for each trial. For the third group there was only one chair over which the items were held, while the other three chairs were not used.

This variation in procedure produced much greater recall for all three groups than we had previously observed. The average number of items recalled per trial was 14.2, 14.6, and 15.1 for the three groups respectively (this difference was not statistically significant). However, the clustering scores for the three groups varied widely. The group for whom chairs corresponded to categories produced an average clustering score of 2.27, the group having only one chair had a score of $-.27$, and the group having items assigned at random to chairs had a score of $-.59$. This latter group significantly avoided clustering according to the semantic categories, indicating that they might be grouping by chairs (an hypothesis not yet evaluated).

It appears that we have produced greatly augmented recall by our "concrete cuing" procedure. Under the proper circumstances we also produced augmented categorical organization. However, organization according to categories is *not* a necessary condition for improved recall. The chairs in groups two and three are not related to the semantic categories, but nonetheless appear to augment recall. If they do so by augmenting organization, the means of organization remain obscure.

We are presently extending this cuing notion to other populations and other forms of cuing. Particularly important from a pedagogical point of view is the question of whether we can find a means of *verbal* cuing which can augment recall. Can we teach our subjects to remember better using mechanisms less unwieldy than chairs?

An initial attempt to use verbal cues involved a variation on a technique used by Tulving and Pearlstone (1966). Subjects were read the standard clusterable list and recall was measured under five conditions. For the groups cued when the list was introduced on each trial, the experimenter said "I am going to tell you about several things. *These things will be clothing, tools, food, and utensils.* When I tell you these things, listen carefully." The list was then presented in the standard, oral fashion. For groups cued at the time of recall, the list of categories was repeated. If no cuing occurred, the italicized sentence was omitted. The possibilities of cuing or not cuing, prior to presentation (input) or prior to recall (output) resulted in four experimental conditions. In addition, a group of subjects was run for four trials with no cuing at input, but highly constrained cuing at the time of recall. After the list of items was presented to subjects in this group, they were asked to recall the items category by category. For instance, the experimenter would say, "Tell me all the clothing you remember." After the subject had named all the clothing items he could remember, the experimenter would repeat the procedure with each of the other categories. On the fifth trial no cuing was given at all, and these subjects were told simply to remember as many of the items as they could.

Comparison of the first four groups indicated that our unconstrained cuing manipulations had little effect on recall or clustering. There were no significant differences between groups on either measure and performance measures were comparable to those obtained in the standard, oral presentation situation.

The results from the fifth group were quite different from those of the four unconstrained groups. Recall for the first four trials was extremely high, averaging approximately seventeen items per trial. Moreover, recall remained high on trial 5, when 15.2 items were recalled. Clustering was forced to be perfect for the first four trials with this group, but on trial 5 clustering remained high, 2.23, a score comparable to that achieved with the chairs, and comparable to the performance of American school children. It appears that good performance at memory and organization can be induced through sufficiently explicit verbal instruction and training.

This entire experiment was repeated with American school children in the third and sixth grades, and essentially the same results were obtained as with the Kpelle. The first four cuing procedures, at input and output, did not augment clustering or recall. Only when subjects were constrained to recall by category was performance improved, and improved substantially.

Finally, we sought to evaluate recall of our basic terms in a situation as similar as possible to situations in which the Kpelle are likely to be good at remembering things. For this purpose we chose memory for stories, but not just any stories. Instead we constructed several pseudo-Kpelle folkstories built around our twenty clusterable memory terms. The question at issue was whether recall of these terms would reflect the way in which they were embedded in the story.

For example, in one story a young man comes to the chief of a town and asks to marry the chief's daughter. He brings good bridewealth and the chief gives his daughter to the man. However, she soon learns that he is a witch and she wants to let her parents know where the man has taken her. So she leaves clues along the path as she travels to the witchman's farm. As she is going out of the door of her house she drops a banana. At the edge of town she drops a kerchief. As they are crossing the bridge over the river she drops a spoon, and so on. The subject is asked to tell what clues the girl left behind.

A second story involves four men who come to town to ask for the chief's daughter. The first man brings five items of clothing, the second brings five items of food, and third brings five utensils, and the fourth brings five tools. Once the story is told the subject is asked which man ought to get the girl and secondly to tell which things each man brought.

In analyzing the results we found that the structure of the subject's recall was isomorphic to the way in which the to-be-recalled items were structured within the story. If the terms were structured in a linear manner, a high correlation between input and output orders was observed. However, if presentation structure was clustered, so was the structure of recall.

A complete answer to the question of how cultural factors influence memory is clearly not contained in our work, nor do we believe it possible to obtain a complete answer. We can affirm only that we have reached a much better understanding of the situation than that represented by our initial, naive, two-group comparison. In particular, we have seen that good performance at clustering and recall is not simply a function of the materials to be remembered and the persons doing the remembering. Each of our experimental procedures combines an occasion for the exercise of memory as well as with a set of cues facilitating memory. On certain occasions, and with certain cues, the Kpelle are able to recall and organize the material in a way comparable to that which American subjects display on different occasions and with other cues.[4]

The problems that remain are numerous. We have entered upon the study of some of them already, while others are on the agenda for future work. We must find other places within the culture where the cues and occasions we identified help to facilitate cognition. In particular, use of chairs to improve recall, even when clustering itself was at the chance level, may well have spatial organization counterparts in other areas of Kpelle thought.

In the future, our work must be still more closely allied with an analysis of Kpelle (and other) culture which is sufficiently detailed to provide us specific links between cultural patterns and learning. This is the goal we seek, an experimental "ethnology of learning," and it is little closer to our grasp now than when we began.

NOTES

1. An earlier version of this paper was delivered at the American Educational Research Association Meetings in Los Angeles, California, 6 February 1969. The authors wish to thank Fredrick Frankel, John Kellemu, David Lancy, Richard MacFarland, Paul Mulbah, Paul Ricks, and Donald Sharp for their assistance in collecting and analyzing these data. The comments of Robert Calfee, Joseph Glick, William Kessen, George Mandler, and others on the earlier draft of this manuscript are gratefully acknowledged. This research was supported by grant number GS 1221 from the National Science Foundation.
2. Several readers of an earlier version of this paper objected to our model for rote learning. It should be clear that we are using only one of many tasks in which rote learning could be manifested. It should also be clear that we do not use the term "rote" to mean unorganized, since seriation can clearly be an organizational principle.
3. The within-culture comparative statements which follow are based on conclusions from analyses of variance of the data. If a difference is said to exist, statistical evidence placed the reliability of the difference at the .01 level. No formal analyses were made comparing Kpelle American data.
4. For a fuller account of these studies and suggestions for characterizing the nature of the occasions eliciting full recall see Cole et al. 1971.

REFERENCES

Bartlett, F. C. *Remembering.* London: Cambridge University Press, 1932.

Boas, Franz. *The Mind of Primitive Man.* New York: Macmillan, 1911.

Bousfield, W. A. "The Occurrence of Clustering in the Recall of Randomly Arranged Associates." *Journal of General Psychology* 49 (1958): 229-40.

Bowen, Elenore Smith. *Return to Laughter.* New York: Doubleday, 1964.

Campbell, Donald T. "The Mutual Methodological Relevance of Anthropology and Psychology." In *Psychological Anthropology.* F. L. K. Hsu, ed. Homewood, Ill.: Dorsey Press, 1961.

Cofer, C. N. "Does Conceptual Clustering Influence the Amount Retained in Immediate Free Recall?" In *Concepts and the Structure of Memory.* B. Klienmuntz, ed. New York: J. Wiley and Sons, 1968.

Cofer, C. N., D. R. Bruce, and G. M. Reicher. "Clustering in Free Recall as a Function of Certain Methodological Variations." *Journal of Experimental Psychology* 71 (1966): 858-66.

Cohen, B. "Recall of Categorized Word Lists." *Journal of Experimental Psychology* 66 (1963): 227-34.

Cole, Michael, John Gay, and J. Glick. "Some Experimental Studies of Kpelle Quantitative Behavior." *Psychochronomic Monograph Supplements* 2(10) (1968): 173-90.

Cole, Michael, F. Frankel, and D. W. Sharp. "The Development of Free Recall Learning in Children." *Developmental Psychology* 4 (1971): 109-23.

Cryns, A. G. J. "African Intelligence: A Critical Survey of Cross-Cultural Intelligence Research in Africa South of the Sahara." *Journal of Social Psychology* 57 (1962): 283-301.

D'Azevedo, W. "Uses of the Past in Gola Discourse." *Journal of African History* 1 (1962): 11-34.

Deese, J. "Serial Organization in the Recall of Disconnected Items." *Psychological Reports* 3 (1957): 577–82.

Doob, L. "The Use of Different Test Items in Non-literate Societies." *Public Opinion Quarterly* 21 (1958): 499–504.

————, "Just a Few of the Presuppositions and Perplexities Confronting Social Psychological Research in Developing Countries." *Journal of Social Issues* 26 (2) (1968): 71–81.

Gay, John, and Michael Cole. *The New Mathematics and an Old Culture.* New York: Holt, Rinehart and Winston, 1967.

Gottesman, I. I. "Biogenetics of Race and Class." In *Social Class, Race, and Psychological Development.* M. Deutsch, I. Katz, and A. R. Jensen, eds. New York: Holt, Rinehart and Winston, 1968.

Greenberg, Joseph. *Universals of Language.* Cambridge: Massachusetts Institute of Technology Press, 1963.

Horton, R. "African Traditional Thought and Western Science: Part I, From Tradition to Science." *Africa* 37(1) (1967a): 50–71.

————, "African Traditional Thought and Western Science: Part II, The 'Closed' and 'Open' Predicaments." *Africa* 37 (1967b): 155–87.

Jahoda, G. "Some Research Problems in African Education." *Journal of Social Issues* 26(2) (1968): 161–75.

Lévy-Bruhl, L. *Primitive Mentality.* New York: Beacon Press, 1966.

Metzger, Duane, and G. Williams. "A Formal Ethnographic Analysis of Tenejapa Ladino Weddings." *American Anthropologist* 65 (1963): 1076–1101.

Mood, A. M. "The Distribution Theory of Runs." *Annals of Mathematical Statistics* 11 (1940): 367–92.

Romney, A. Kimball, and Roy G. D'Andrade, eds. "Transcultural Studies in Cognition." *American Anthropologist* 66(3, pt. 2) (1964): 1–253.

Scott, K. G. "Clustering with Perceptual and Symbolic Stimuli in Free Recall." *Journal of Verbal Learning* 6 (1967): 864–66.

Segall, M. H., D. T. Campbell, and M. J. Herskovits. *The Influence of Culture on Visual Perception.* Indianapolis: Bobbs-Merrill Co., 1966.

Stefflre, V. *Language and Behavior.* Reading, Massachusetts: Addison-Wesley, 1969.

Tulving, E. "Theoretical Issues in Free Recall." In *Verbal Learning and General Behavior Theory.* T. R. Dixon and D. L. Horton, eds. Englewood Cliffs, N.J.: Prentice-Hall, 1968.

Tulving, E., and Z. Pearlstone. "Availability Versus Accessibility of Information and Memory for Words." *Journal of Verbal Learning and Verbal Behavior* 5 (1966): 381–91.

Tyler, Stephen A., ed. *Cognitive Anthropology.* New York: Holt, Rinehart and Winston, 1969.

Underwood, B. J. *Experimental Psychology.* New York: Appleton-Century-Crofts, 1966.

Wallis, W. A., and H. V. Roberts. *Statistics: A New Approach.* New York: Free Press, 1956.

Part V

Language and Cultural Learning

23 / Language and Socialization

J. A. Cook

From a review of the literature on child rearing it is often assumed that parents and children have only a pedagogical intent in pursuing their daily lives. This gives a rather distorted view of the socialization process. The activity of child rearing does not consist only in following the rules, but also in making the rules fit the activity already performed, or decided upon. The need in socialization research is to look for these organizing principles as the parents define them *and* as the child perceives them. It is possible that what the child acquires from the parent are these general principles *which he can use to generate his own behavior.* The way the child learns language should give us examples of particularly detailed studies of this learning process. Language acquisition may show us in some detail how the mother and child are able reciprocally to negotiate a (nonpedagogical) learning situation, for parents are not in doubt that the child needs to learn language. The child's need for this skill is taken for granted and most parents are able, when necessary, to point to the rules of language (its grammar) as all are competent speakers of *their* native language. The way parents help the child to gain this essential skill shows us something of their ability to socialize the child into other taken-for-granted competencies. For we suggest that parents do not *explicitly* formulate the learning tasks of child rearing but use their own daily lives as an implicit model of social competency for their children. We suggest that a special characteristic of the "rules" of child rearing is that they are only brought into being explicitly, after the fact. After the child had done something the parent thinks is "not right" a rule is seen to be infringed and is given or explained by the parent, but for most of the child's daily life the "rules" remain implicit in the activities. Garfinkel (1967) has suggested that it is the nature of "everyday reasoning" to be guided by general rather than detailed principles. It is often only a recollection that a person "gives a reason" for an action, and his "reason" may not have been the original instigation for the action. We act and reason in everyday life pragmatically to give solutions to practical problems which are sufficient, for the while, to guide our further actions. So far the research on child rearing does not seem to have suggested that the child acquires his knowledge of the social structure in a similar way.

THE CHILD'S ACQUISITION OF LANGUAGE

Studies of child socialization have neglected the linguistic transmission of cultural knowledge; language has been regarded as a transparent medium in which information was given both to the child and to the interviewer, but the way in which the form of the language shapes the information was not entertained. It is in the area of language learning that theories of the child's acquisition of the rule-governed behavior is being shaped. Theories of the acquisition of syntactic rules may provide a parallel model for the child's acquisition of the "rules" of social structure.

We suggest that a study of the way language is used in giving social rules to children and in conducting actual social scenes would give us more information *about the rules themselves*, and the study of the speech in interaction settings with mothers and children can show us how rules guide and constrain actual social performances. For this study we need to know something of the way the child learns language, and the various ways of talking in different social situations, which have been described as the linguistic repertoire of communicative economy of the society (see Gumperz 1964, Hymes 1964). Until recently the child's developing linguistic competence has been evaluated apart from the occasions that give rise to the child's communications. The need for alternative approaches for the study of this and other aspects of the child's social learning is being increasingly raised (see Cazden 1966; Cicourel 1968, 1970; Hymes 1968; Slobin *et al.* 1967). In this section we will review some of the studies of the child's acquisition and use of language.

Two approaches to language development have developed in the last few years: (1) the study of grammatical development of linguistic competence; (2) the study of linguistic usage rules, or communicative competence. In the former approach the investigator focuses on the child's control of the linguistic rules proper, regardless of context; and in the latter the investigator looks at linguistic rules in relation to how they are used in particular communication settings, along with other communication skills (e.g. rules of etiquette, rules of appropriate usage, etc.). By far the greatest amount of work has been concentrated in the area of linguistic rules and has focused largely on the work in Western, middle-class communities. The study of communicative competence is only just beginning and will be reviewed briefly at the end of this section.

The literature on the study of linguistic competence has grown to enormous proportions in recent years; a complete review is outside the scope of this paper (an excellent introductory discussion can be found in Slobin 1971; for other reviews see Brown, Cazden, and Bellugi 1969; Ervin-Tripp 1970), therefore we will focus on some of the main issues emerging from this research which are of special interest. These issues can be discussed from two perspectives: (1) by focusing on stages of the development of language; (2) by looking at the nature of the linguistic rules acquired. Early grammatical development can be divided into the following stages: a babbling stage when the child exercises his voice in almost random fashion, producing an amazing variety of apparently meaningless sounds of syllables (Weir 1962); the one-word stage when the child learns to name structurally similar individual words, whether referring to actions, requests, or objects. The development of grammar proper begins with the two-word or pivot-word stage (Braine 1963). Following this early grammatical stage the child begins to develop the ability to form hierarchically organized constructions and the ability to perform transformations of the type postulated by generative grammarians (Slobin 1971). While there are wide differences in individual learning and in the age at which a particular stage is reached, the sequence of the stages is *universal* and the average age at which these stages emerge is also universally similar (Slobin 1970). There is no evidence to show that social class or cultural differences in any way affect the child's learning of these basic grammatical patterns. It seems that all children by the age of four or five, regardless of how they have been reared, have gained control of the grammatical system of their own native language.

These universal aspects of language-learning processes, when viewed along with other linguistic findings on the universality of grammatical structure, have given rise to the claim by Chomsky and his followers (Chomsky 1968) that linguistic competence, that is the child's knowledge of grammatical rules, is innate; that, in a sense, a child is born with a latent knowledge of grammatical rules and that the socialization process activates this knowledge and gives it cultural substance. This view of the innateness of grammar brings the generative grammarian into direct conflict with followers of the earlier imitative-practice model of language learning. In this latter view the newborn child was seen as a *tabula rasa* who acquired language only by direct imitation of the speech models provided by his family. The search for solutions to this issue has for the first time lead to direct psycholinguistic inquiries into the nature of linguistic rules.

Ervin-Tripp (1964) has examined the research on the imitative models and has shown that there is little evidence that the child directly imitates its parents. Braine (1969) and Ervin-Tripp give the example of children being incapable of correctly repeating an inflectional change and correction after the parent. The child will appear to keep to his "own" rule while at the time adding the parent's version to please the parent.[1] Also, as Cazden (1966) has noted, evidence for the practice model is hard to find because children make mistakes that pass unperceived by the parents. The apparent "randomness" of the parents' correction of the child's speech has often been cited as evidence that the behaviorist view of language learning by imitation alone cannot be an adequate explanation. It has also been noted that children repeatedly hear ungrammatical remarks from their parents but do not appear to imitate these.

A more plausible explanation is that the child employs a *generative model*; that is, from the performances that he experiences he is able to develop a set of rules about language for himself, from which he can produce his own varied, linguistic performances.

These rules are adapted and expanded by the child until most of the utterances the child produces are grammatically acceptable to adults. No research has yet shown how long this process might continue; possibly with considerable slowdown after the of five–seven, it might continue into adulthood. Considerable research has shown the usefulness of this model (for example, Menyuk 1964, Brown and Frazer 1964, Slobin 1966). There is a great deal of evidence available for, as McNeill (1966) has said, "Sentences that cannot be accounted for as adult sentences provide the best evidence that the child knows productive rules." Some research has focused on the way in which the child appears, from his performances, to construct his own rules. Braine (1963) has suggested that the child's basic generative rule might be $S - P + O$, (where P is a pivot class and O is an open class). These classes in the child's speech contain items which are heterogeneous in adult grammars. The *pivot* word always remains in the same position and can be variously conbined to make complete utterances. Weir (1962) gives good examples of this in her research of the "overhead" speech of her two-and-a-half-year-old son. McNeill has shown how Braine's findings can be substantiated in the research of Ervin-Tripp, and Brown and Bellugi. This seems to give some strong evidence for the child's generative-productive capacity.

Other research (for example, see Chomsky 1969, Menyuk 1964, Slobin 1966) has focused on examining in detail how the rules which can be written by the researcher from children's performances can be compared with adult rules, and so how judgments of the child's linguistic competence can be made. The way the child acquires language is assumed to be expressed by the generative model if the rules and the child's performances match. Menyuk (1964) has described the acquisition process as follows: "With a generative model of grammar, it is hypothesized, that the perceiver or child has incorporated both the generative rules of the grammar and a heuristic component, that samples an input sentence and by a series of successive approximations determine which rules were used to generate the sentence." In short, studies of the child's growing linguistic competence look at the child's performance as though the child could select from all possible examples without other (performance, situational) criteria influencing his judgment. Rules are written from the assumption of situationally "unembedded" or context-free performances, and it is assumed that "something like" the rules the linguists write exist "in the head" of the child. These rules can then be used by the child to generate the "infinite" set of possibilities which is linguistic performance. As Menyuk has described "the child uses his set of rules to generate not only the sentences he has heard but all possible examples. In addition his linguistic knowledge is systematically extended without further instruction." The earlier transformationalist arguments have been weakened somewhat by the observation of more recent researchers that although some of the child's sentences may look like adult grammar, their usage is sufficiently limited or context-bound that these rules may not be needed to account for what the child does (Kernan 1969, Bloom 1969). There are indications that Fillmore's case grammar or similar generative semantic approaches to the study of grammar may more efficiently account for the differences between child grammar and adult grammar (Filmore 1968), than simply matching the child rules to adult rules.

The work on grammatical rules reveals another important issue in language acquisition, that the child may be able to comprehend more than he can produce, and thus not reveal his competence by his performance. Frazer, Bellugi and Brown (1963) examined this problem experimentally. They found that children's ability to comprehend and to distinguish between different grammatical statements for similar pictures, an ability to distinguish tense and other inflectional differences, was in advance of their ability to *produce* similar distinctions. McNeill points to the young child's "holophrasistic" speech where single words "stand for" a whole utterance, the meaning of which (or rather the communicative intent) the child knows when an adult misinterprets, but which he is not able to produce linguistically. Brown and Bellugi (1964) point to the problems parents have in deciding which of several alternatives can be the appropriate expansion of the child's "telegram." It appears that along with the child's performance it is necessary to take other features of the speech setting into account. The search for the child's competence in his performance depends upon the researcher's ability to decide upon the "meaning" of the speech. This will probably entail the assumption that the same or similar "ideas" are in the mind of the child as in the mind of the interpreting adult. Slobin (1966) has described the problem of attempting to write a grammar of children's speech:

> Linguistic competence is a model of what is assumed to exist in the mind of the speaker, a model built by the linguist on the basis of his intuitive ability to discriminate well-formed from ill-formed utterances. The plausibility of its existence can only be ascertained by careful study of the actual performance which it is believed to determine.

It may be necessary for the researcher to make assumptions about the child's speech as the parent does, for it may be necessary to consider the meaning of the utterance in order to assess its grammatical acceptability. Thus, in order to write the "rules" of a generative grammar for children's speech the researcher may have to consider the performance as part of a communicative event, but the description of this event will not eventually be a part of the rules or of the theory. The situated dependence of children's speech is shown in Brown and Bellugi's work—the child's telegraphic speech. Parents find many utterances ambiguous or open to several interpretations and so have to turn to the context of the event and personal knowledge of the child to "know what he means." Cazden (1966) suggests that the "everyday" way in which we "work out" what the child means often passes without notice. She says "in discussing optimal sequencing of stimuli, I suggest that if it does occur . . . it must be fortuitously. Expansions by their very nature, provide such sequencing. No one has suggested that the parents expand with any conscious tutorial intention. *It seems simply to be one way of keeping a conversation with a young child going.*" It seems that in order to develop rules for the child's speech competence in terms of its grammaticality, researchers may have to take into account what they know of the language, of the speech situation, of the topic and of the child. This suggests that the rules which are deduced and written for the child's performance may not be as independent of contextual assumptions as the generative model supposes. Several recent experimental investigations in the areas of phonological and semantic development also point to the context-embeddedness of children's speech. Moskowitz (1970), in a review dealing with the acquisition of syllables structure, has shown that when the child first learns sounds these are not learnt in isolation but in syllable sequences, e.g. consonant vowel sequences. The ability to separate particular sounds from surrounding sequences is acquired only at a later stage. Similarly, Stross (1970) demonstrates that children can make what seem to be highly complex semantic distinctions among variants of the same activity, but that such distinctions are always learnt in the context of particular sentences and not in isolation.

Thus it seems that in order to write competence rules the researcher has to make assumptions and trade upon his own knowledge of "social appropriateness." The researcher cannot write rules for a child's grammar unless the "meaning" of the child's utterance is taken into account, and this meaning will be context-dependent. Part of this context-dependent knowledge will be the adult's own conception of the language. As Klima and Bellugi (1966) have commented, "It shall be understood that when we write rules for the children's grammar it is just a rough attempt to give substance to our feelings about, and general observations demonstrating, the regularity in the syntax of children's speech."

We have noted that no matter how "clear" and context-unspecific grammatical descriptive rules appear they will have relied upon, in their construction, features and details which are not now a part of the rules or the theory. Therefore, no matter how detailed these rules are they will not be sufficient for the generation of adequate social performances of appropriate speech acts. An alternative approach has developed using the notion of communicative competence (Gumperz and Hymes 1964). This concept was advanced to deal with some of the objections raised against the type of linguistic research that separates grammar from context and from rules of usage. Although studies of communicative competence may deal with rules of phonology and grammar, they see the acquisition of these features as dependent on, or as developing in response to, the type of communicative tasks that the child's lifestyle requires. Whereas psycholinguistic analysis concentrates on the analysis of words and sentences, the studies of communicative competence focus on interaction sequences seen as exchangers between speakers, i.e. mother-child, child–child, etc. If we look at the interaction sequences rather than mere sentences we have to take account of a number of additional linguistic features of what Hymes has called speech acts (Hymes 1962, Gumperz and Hymes 1972); for example; it becomes necessary to account for intonation contours, paralinguistic features of speech, variations in style etc. Other discourse features to be accounted for are: the child's ability to select words appropriate to his intent or to choose appropriate styles or codes, his control over sequencing rules, that is the rules which govern the assignment of right to speaking (Sacks 1972) and the selection of appropriate content. The study of these features of speaking is still in its beginning but it is clear these features are regulated by "rules" which, like grammatical rules, are not consciously explicit (Gumperz 1970). There is also some evidence to show that acquisition of these sociolinguistic rules is subject to the same problems of overgeneralizations and the generation of structures different from those of adults as syntactic rules.

The studies of communicative competence have gone some way towards remedying the neglect of context in the earlier linguistic studies. Yet, although they have explored the nature of speech events and the regulation of these by sociolinguistic rules, they have not approached the critical question raised in this review, that of the nature of social rules. In the following section we will briefly explore this question.

SUGGESTIONS FOR AN ALTERNATIVE APPROACH

In this section we would like to suggest the direction that an alternative approach should take, towards more contextually specific and detailed studies, which will attempt to show how the "rules" of the society are put into practice in child-rearing situations. We shall look briefly at some of the ethnographic studies which take this kind of approach. The problems that these studies have encountered in giving detailed descriptions of the "rules" of everyday life suggest some of the characteristics of social rules which need to be taken into account. Just as the study of language acquisition provides an insight into the nature of grammatical rules, the study of how the child acquires an understanding of what is necessary for competent membership of a social group can elucidate the nature of social rules. The parents' need to make clear and available to the child the conditions of membership and also provide additional information on these rules, as Cicourel (1968) suggests: "Adult descriptions of the why of everyday life to children provide a rich source of information on adult notions of simplified social structures." Further, the researchers' attempts to discover this information will, as we have already indicated, reveal something of the implicit assumptions and knowledge that the researcher has about the "working" of the social structure, and on which he/she must necessarily rely to make sense of the available information. In this way the researcher can be seen to be in a similar position to the child in having to uncover the "rules" regulating social scenes while also being a practicing member of them.

There exists a large body of literature which has made detailed, descriptive studies of child-rearing practices—the ethnographic studies of anthropology which have studied foreign cultures and the social anthropological and ecological studies that have been made in our own society. We will very briefly comment upon a few of these studies in order to see what problems they may have encountered in making detailed descriptions of socialization practices. The best examples of the social anthropological studies are represented by the work of Beatrice Whiting and colleagues on the "Six cultures" project (1963) and by the British tradition of community studies reviewed in detail by Klein (1965) as *Samples from English Cultures*. The six cultures project attempted to give detailed and comparable accounts of child-rearing practices in six different societies (both rural and urban), in India, Kenya, Japan, the Philippines, Mexico, and the US. The English studies were made for various purposes, but all were concerned with giving detailed accounts of what it would be like to live as a participant, in a mining village, a northern industrial town, as an industrial worker, and in a London single-class (working-class) community. Both sets of studies implicitly contain a theory of the relationship of the individual and his personality to the social system. The explicit aim of the Whiting studies was to explore this relationship through making comparable descriptions of the societies.

Psychological-ecological studies made by Barker and Wright (for example, *One Boy's Day*, 1951) represent a rather different tradition of studies which has not been extended much beyond their own work. Barker and Wright attempted to describe in detail the ongoing behaviour in a community (as in *The Mid-West and Its Children*, 1955) *in the process of its occurrence*. Earlier Bossard (1943, 1945) had suggested a similar attempt could be made from a sociological viewpoint in studying family conversations, but this work also has not been extended much be beyond Bossard and Boll's (1950) studies of family rituals. We will look at some problems that these researchers met in making their descriptions. Their experience will show us how difficult it is to observe social rules in practice, and also to write rules for everyday practices.

We will look at three problems that these studies have raised. *First*, there is the problem of the immense amount of detail that any direct observation of actual situated behavior presents to the researcher. Barker (1963) and colleagues have described the process as the need to select from a continuous "stream of behavior." The studies made by Barker and Wright were attempts to code all the details of any action sequence within different units of behavior. The descriptions that they gave of even a simple sequence, such as a child pulling off his coat and speaking with his mother at the same time, show how complicated is the seemingly simplest action sequence. Anyone familiar with participant observation coding will know that the details available at any moment seem to be "infinite." In a recent paper Gumperz (1970) has discussed some of the difficulties of assigning meanings to conversational data under these conditions where the investigator does not share the speaker's background assumptions. Yet Barker and Wright's work shows, through just a glance at any page of analysis, how mutually *embedded* actions or events are. Talk is embedded in sequences of actions, some of which may need to be known in order to understand the talk itself. The actions may also depend on the accompanying talk for their relevance. The ethnographic researcher is presented with the task of "making sense" and interpreting these contingent events. It has sometimes been noted in ethnographic work that the problem of selection is easier if the researcher is "foreign" to the scene. Whiting commented, in describing the difficulties of an American ethnographer in an American community, "It is difficult for natives to collect ethnographic data which is comparable to that collected by an individual of a different culture." The reason for the value of "strangers" is twofold. A stranger who is not involved in the culture himself is likely to perceive events that are "taken-for-granted" by the native of the culture. But at the same time a stranger is less likely to be aware of the possible "infinite," or at least the multiplicity of meanings that an action can have for a native, and so he is less likely to be overwhelmed by the immensity of detail that a description might need. In this way, by being or attempting to be a stranger to a culture, the ethnographer solves the problem of selection of detail.

The *second* problem raised by these studies is how can the researcher uncover the relevant regularities of rules to which his theoretical perspective guides him? The ethnographer has to give some "shape" to the events which he observes and records in order to be able to find the regularities or details for which he is looking. Dollard (1935), in proposing that socialization studies should use the information contained in life histories as accounts of how a new person is added to the group and becomes an adult through the traditional experiences of "his society," suggests how important is this theoretical "shaping."

> We propose a common sense definition of the life history as a deliberate attempt to define the growth of a person in a cultural milieu and to make theoretical sense of it . . . it is not just an account of a life with events separately identified like beads on a string, although this is the form in which naïve attempts to present a life history usually meet us; if this were true, every man would be a psychologist, because every person can give us data of this type. The material must, in addition be worked up and mastered from some systematic viewpoint.

Dollard's view points out that the researcher uses his theoretical perspective to know what to look for in the field. But members of Whiting's project found that theoretical agreement did not solve the problem of agreement at the level of description of events in the various cultures, as Whiting comments in the introduction to the study, "In spite of the research design, the data are not always comparable, that in the different areas studied some monographs have better coverage than others." In spite of a common theoretical perspective the selection of details from the cultural scenes remained difficult and a matter of each ethnographer's negotiation between the theoretically governed category and the actual, observed events.

This reveals the *third* problem of these studies. Once the researcher becomes aware of his own perspective, of how his categorization acts as a grid or filter through which the data are sifted, this perspective can appear to "get in the way." The researcher becomes aware of the fact that the way in which he fits his observations into the categories is itself a problem. Douglas (1970) touches upon this issue when she points out the difficulty of not finding instances of the expected rituals in culture. She suggests that an ethnographer is tempted to press his data further to find instances that might fit. Once the ethnographer is alerted to his own interpretations, he may also consider how the events can be classified and variously perceived by members. The ethnographer, in spite of his "strangeness" becomes aware of some of the implicit assumptions which he makes in order to achieve his classifications. As Cicourel (1968) suggests, "The researcher has to 'work' to achieve a fit—the source of structural descriptions of members' behaviour by the researcher, is through misleading but self-contained packages of meaning or blue-prints for behaviour. Situational constraints and unfolding contingencies are eliminated or minimized, and normative structure becomes the ethnographic focus." The researcher, in looking for the "clear" or rulelike structure of everyday behaviour which the ethnographer observes, may leave aside much of the "confusing" detail that members actually rely upon to make the rules work. As we noted in the case of writing linguistic rules, researchers "traded upon" details which were neither written into the theory nor the rules of the grammar. In such instances it would not be possible to work back from the descriptive rules to the actual behavioural events. That is what we take Cicourel to mean when he speaks of "misleading but self-contained packages of meaning or blue-prints for behaviour."

It seems that these detailed descriptions of activities may not be used, without controversy, to locate the "social rules," for such rules are not visible without the researchers' interpretation. In order to see how rules are put into practice in everyday settings, it becomes necessary to look at what constitutes the "rule" for members of the society. It is not enough to rely on our observer's judgment. We suggest that it might be necessary to do the reverse of Dollard's directions and look at "every man as a psychologist" and at his own "interpretation or even description of his actions." This is, in fact, what the linguist theoretically attempts to do with the notion of competence. It is noticeable that ethnographic studies which rely strongly on verbal reportage do not consider members' descriptions from what Dollard calls their "naïve standpoint" at face value. If this were done the ethnographer in having to "work" to negotiate a fit between the social rules and the behavior which is said to come under the rules, would discover that members are in fact in a similar position to the ethnographer himself. One ethnographer, Moerman (1970), has described this experience in looking at the working of the marriage and divorce rules in Lue society:

> The proposition that three divorces damage a reputation and that marriage ends gossip are both "true as a rule" in two senses characteristic of social rules. First, counter instances do not disprove them (Helmer and Resher, 1960). Second, a member can use the rules to argue but not, to clinch, the correctness of his judgements about actions, events, and persons . . . To phrase it somewhat differently, in addition to their "et cetera clause" (Garfinkel, 1964) social rules, and members' procedures for subsuming cases under them, have an "unless clause" which members can cite in order to classify a case or to explain their having, "as it turned out" retrospectively, misclassified it.

If we accept Moerman's two principles of social rules it appears that members, ethnographers, and linguists are in the same position of using rules to "account for"

behaviors and events, while at the same time adjusting the accounts of the behaviors or the rules to fit the case at hand.

RULE FOLLOWING AS A SITUATED ACCOMPLISHMENT

If it is the case that we are compelled to negotiate the fit of social rules to social
events, then rule-following becomes a "situated accomplishment." Rule-following
is not simply a matter of applying a rule which is sufficiently detailed to cover all
cases, and so independent of the context in which it is used. How is it we make
social rules work? Previous comments from Clausen (1968) suggest an answer. He
has said,"Most parents do not explicitly formulate the various aims . . . in child-
rearing some of these are so completely taken-for-granted they need not be formulated, others become formulated when what is taken-for-granted proves to be
problematic." If we shift Clausen's perspective slightly and look, not only at the
parents' statements of problems, their statements of "social rules," but also at what
they "take-for-granted," we will see something of the "background expectancies"
that make the rulelike statements workable (Garfinkel 1967). What kind of taken-
for-granted information do members and researchers use? Brown (1965) has suggested one possibility when he describes how child-rearing researchers make the
category "withdrawal of love" fit the data that they are coding, as follows:

> "Withdrawal of love" is a psychologist's phrase. Mothers do not spontane-
> ously report using it and interviewers do not even ask about it. The rating
> had to be made by inference from certain kinds of reported behaviour. Do
> we know what withdrawal of love is like? Mother looks hurt or her voice
> quivers a little. She has less to say than usual, her movements are brusque,
> her jawline shows a certain tension. If something slightly disagreeable
> happens—a cup breaks or the cat gets in her way—she over reacts, bursting
> into tears or a temper. Perhaps you recognize it, not only mothers practice
> it but husbands and wives, sisters and brothers.

What Brown is suggesting is that researchers use their *own* knowledge of everyday
activities to interpret and fill out the member's descriptions. What he seems to
overlook is that we all, as members, trade upon certain taken-for-granted features of
social actions, and that filling out and interpreting other's "accounts" is a member's
problem too. We all solve this problem, for the while and for practical purposes, by
our talk. We ask, probe and reflect during ongoing social action through talk,
which enables us to make our social accounts and inflections visible to the other
participants. We generate social interaction through talk. Cicourel (1968) has
described this process as follows:

> Members use the interpretive procedures and their reflexive features as in-
> structions for negotiating social scenes over time. Members are continually
> giving each other instructions (verbal and non-verbal cues and content) as to
> their intentions, their social character, their biographies and the like . . .
> [these] features provide continuous instructions to participants such that
> members can be said to be programming each other's actions as the scene
> unfolds.

What this perspective is suggesting is that researchers can see how members make
the social rules "work" for themselves by looking *at*, not beyond, the talk that
members offer. Although interpretation of this talk will rely upon certain "interpretive procedures" or "background expectancies" which we all share, we will see
something of *the procedure of practicing social rules in members talk.*

From this perspective we see that social rules can never be *self-explicating*. No matter how much detail they contain, they need to be made to fit the particular circumstances of the activities. Socialization is not a matter of learning the "rules" and applying them, but of developing a set of "interpretive procedures," a set of taken-for-granted assumptions that enables the member to see the rules in the first place. This view is rather different from that proposed in most studies of socialization, where the ability to behave in socially acceptable ways is equated with the ability to "follow the rules," as in this description by Strauss (1953):

> Conceptions of roles and conceptions of rules grow *pari passu*. Built into role conceptions are justifications of motivations for behaviour appropriate or inappropriate for enactment of roles . . . To talk of rules and punishment for rule infraction is just another way of stating role relationships. The young child's inability to grasp the nature or full extent of adult rules means that he is unable to make proper conceptual distinctions, likewise he is unable to grasp the consequences for certain roleplayers of certain acts committed by certain other role players.

We are suggesting here an opposing view to that of Strauss, which Cicourel (1970) has described as:

> The members of a group or tribe or society do not live by social rules or norms or laws that are self-explicative, but must acquire (psychological and) sociological cognitive properties that generate and provide the basis for interpreting rules as guides to social conduct . . . these sociological cognitive properties are essential presuppositions or "interpretive procedures" necessary for the speaker-hearer to make sense of his environment as an emergent, temporally constituted scene.

Cicourel is suggesting that what the child acquires from his socialization experience is a developmental *generative* understanding of the social structure and other activities which enables him to "see" and to take-for-granted what others do. From this generative basis the child can produce his own varied social performances (Cicourel 1968):

> The child cannot be taught to understand and use surface rules unless, like language, he acquires a basis for assigning meaning to his environment; a sense of social structure . . . there are no surface rules for instructing the child on how articulation is to be made . . . Surface rules always require some specification of the particulars which would render rules as appropriate and useful for dealing with actual behavioural displays.

Parents cannot explicitly teach the child how to acquire the generative interpretive procedures, but through showing the child how, for all practical purposes, "surface rules" can be understood and made to work in the child's daily life. The parent is helping the child to develop a "sense of the social structure," of what can be taken-for-granted and what can be discussed and questioned. Therein lies the importance of Bernstein's theory of the parent's explanations and the different models of social control (Bernstein 1964, 1965, 1970). Thus, in acquiring the ways of talk of his social group, the child is acquiring, "for all practical purposes," a way of producing and recognizing "perceivedly normal" or routine behavior in himself and others. Through learning to talk and negotiate social interaction with others the child is learning to apply and to follow rules as a "situated accomplishment."

NOTE

1. The example cited above is also illustrative of the child having his own language rules. The child says, "nobody don't like me"; the mother replies, "No, say nobody likes me." The child replies with his version. This dialogue is repeated eight times until the child says in exasperation "all right, nobody don't likes me."

REFERENCES

Barker, R. (1963), *The Stream of Behaviour.* New York: Appleton-Century-Crofts.

Barker, R. and Wright, H. (1951), *One Boy's Day.* New York: Harper & Row.

Barker, R. and Wright, H. (1955), *The Mid-West and its Children.* New York: Harper & Row.

Bernstein, B. (1964), "Elaborated and restricted codes; their social origins and some consequences," *Ethnography of Communication* (ed.) D. Hymes and J. J. Gumperz, special issue, *American Anthropologist,* 66, no. 2.

Bernstein, B. (1965), "A socio-linguistic approach to social learning," *Survey of the Social Sciences* (ed.) J. Gould. London: Penguin.

Bernstein, B. (1970), "Social class, language and socialization," *Current Trends in Linguistics,* 12, A. Abramson *et al.* (eds). The Hague: Mouton.

Bloom, L. (1969), *Language Development: Form and Function in Emerging Grammars.* Cambridge, Mass.: MIT Press.

Blossard, J. (1943), "Family table talk—an area for sociological study," *Am. Soc. Rev.,* pp. 295-301.

Blossard, J. (1945), "Family modes of expression," *Am. Soc. Rev.,* pp. 226-37.

Blossard, J. and Boll, E. (1950), *Ritual in Family Living.* Philadelphia: University of Pennsylvania Press.

Braine, M. D. S. (1963), "The ontogeny of English phrase structure: the first phase," *Language,* 39, pp. 1-13.

Braine, M. D. S. (1969), "On two types of models of the internalization of grammar," *The ontogenesis of grammar: some facts and several theories* (ed.) D. Slobin (in press).

Brown, R. (1965), "The child's acquisition of morality," *Social Psychology.* New York: Free Press.

Brown, R. and Bellugi, U. (1964), "The processes in the acquisition of syntax," *New Directions in the Study of Language* (ed.) E. Lenneberg. Cambridge, Mass.: MIT Press.

Brown, R., Cazden, C. and Bellugi, U. (1969),"The child's grammar from 1 to 11," *Minnesota Symposia on Child Psychology,* vol. 2 (ed.) J. P. Hill. Minneapolis: University of Minnesota Press.

Brown, R. and Frazer, C. (1964), "The acquisition of syntax," *Child Development Monographs: The Acquisition of Language* (ed.) R. Brown and U. Bellugi, 29, pp. 43-79.

Cazden, C. (1966), "Sub-cultural differences in child language: an inter-disciplinary review," *Merrill Palmer Quarterly,* 12, pp. 185-219.

Chomsky, N. (1968), *Language and Mind.* New York: Harcourt, Brace, Jovanovich.

Chomsky, C. (1969), *The Acquisition of Syntax in Children from 5 to 10.* Cambridge, Mass.: MIT Press.

Cicourel, A. V. (1968), "The acquisition of social structure: towards a developmental sociology of language and meaning," *Understanding Everyday Life* (ed.) J. Douglas. London: Routledge & Kegan Paul.

Cicourel, A. V. (1970), "Generative Semantics and the structure of social interaction," International Days of Sociolinguistics, Lugi Struzo Institute, Rome. To be published in *Current Trends in Linguistics,* vol. 12, (ed.) A. Abramson *et al.* The Hague: Mouton.

Cicourel, A. V. and Boese, R. (1970), "Sign language acquisition and the teaching of deaf children," *The Functions of Language: an anthropological and psychological approach* (ed.) D. Hymes, C. Cazden and V. John.

Clausen, J. (1968), "The history of socialization studies," *Socialization and Society* (ed.) J. Clausen. New York: Little, Brown.

Dollard, J. (1935), *Criteria for the Life History*, Yale University Press.

Douglas, M. (1970), *Natural Symbols: Explorations in Cosmology.* London: Cresset Press.

Ervin-Tripp, S. and Miller, W. (1964), "The development of grammar in child language," *Child Development Monographs: The Acquisition of Language* (ed.) R. Brown and U. Bellugi, 29, pp. 9–34.

Ervin-Tripp, S. (1970), "Structure and process in language acquisition," 21st Annual Round Table: Monograph Series on *Language and Linguistics* (ed.) J. Alatis, Georgetown University, Washington D. C.

Fillmore, C. J. (1968), "The Case for case," *Universals in Linguistic Theory* (ed.) E. Bach and R. T. Harms. New York: Holt, Rinehart & Winston.

Frazer, C., Bellugi, U. and Brown, R. (1963), "Control of grammar in imitation, comprehension and production," *Journal of Verbal Learning and Verbal Behaviour*, 2, pp. 121–35.

Garfinkel, H. (1967), *Studies in Ethnomethodology.* New York: Prentice-Hall.

Gumperz, J. J. (1964), "Linguistic and social interaction in two communities," *The Ethnography of Communication* (ed.) D. Hymes and J. J. Gumperz, op. cit.

Gumperz, J. J. (1970), "Verbal strategies in multilingual communication," Working Paper 36, Language Behaviour Research Laboratory, University of California, Berkeley.

Gumperz, J. J. and Hymes, D. (eds) (1964), *The Ethnography of Communication*, special issue the *American Anthropologist*, no. 2, 66.

Gumperz, J. J. and Hymes, D. (eds) (1972), *Directions in Sociolinguistics.* New York: Holt, Rinehart & Winston.

Hymes, D. (1962), "Ethnography of speaking," in *Anthropology and Human Behaviour* (ed.) T. Gadwin and W. Sturtevant, Anthropological Soc. of Washington.

Hymes, D. (1964), "Introduction: towards ethnographies of communication," in *The Ethnography of Communication* (ed.) D. Hymes and J. J. Gumperz, op. cit.

Hymes, D. (1968), "On communicative competence." *The Proceedings of the CIBA Conference on the Mechanisms of Language Acquisition*, London, May.

Kernan, K. (1969), "Acquisition of language by Samoan children," Working Paper 21, Language Behaviour Research Laboratory, University of California, Berkeley.

Klein, J. (1965), *Samples from English Cultures.* London: Routledge & Kegan Paul.

Klima, E. and Bellugi, U. (1966), "Some syntactic regularities of children's speech," *Psycholinguistic Papers: Proceedings of the Edinburgh Conference* (ed.) J. Lyons and D. Wales, op. cit.

McNeill, D. (1966), "Developmental psycholinguistics," in *The Genesis of Language* (ed.) F. Smith and G. Miller. Cambridge, Mass.: M.I.T. Press.

Menyuk, P. (1964), "Alteration of rules in children's grammar," *Journal of Verbal Learning and Verbal Behaviour*, 3, pp. 486–8.

Moerman, M. (1970), "A little knowledge," *Cognitive Anthropology* (ed.) S. Tyler. New York: Holt, Rinehart & Winston.

Moskowitz, A. (1970), "The acquisition of phonology," Working Paper 34, Language Behaviour Research Laboratory, University of California, Berkeley.

Sacks, H. (1972), "The analysability of children's stories," in *Directions in Sociolinguistics*, (ed.) J. J. Gumperz and D. Hymes, op. cit.

Slobin, D. (1966), "Grammatical transformations and sentence comprehension in childhood and adulthood," *Journal of Verbal Learning and Verbal Behaviour*, 5, pp. 219–27.

Slobin, D. (1970), "Suggested universals in the ontogenesis of grammar," Working Paper 32, Language Behaviour Research Laboratory, University of California, Berkeley.

Slobin, D. (1971), *Psycholinguistics.* Glenview, Ill.: Scott, Foresman.

Slobin, D., Ervin-Tripp, S. *et al.* (1967), "A field manual for cross-cultural study of communicative competence," Language Behaviour Research Laboratory, University of California, Berkeley.

Strauss, A. (1953), "The development of conceptions of rules in children," *Child Development*, 25, pp. 193–208.

Stross, B. (1970), "Language acquisition in Tenejapa Tzeltal children," Working Paper 20, Language Behaviour Research Laboratory, University of California, Berkeley.

Weir, R. (1962), *Language in the Crib.* The Hague: Mouton.

Whiting, B. (1963), *Six Cultures: Studies in Childrearing.* New York: Wiley.

24 / Dialect Differences and Bilingualism

Courtney B. Cazden

No language is spoken in exactly the same way by all its speakers. The most neutral, nonjudgmental label for the different ways in which a language may be spoken is "variety":

> The term variety . . . merely designates a member of a [speech community's] verbal repertoire. Its use implies only that there are other varieties as well. These can be specified by outsiders on the basis of the phonological, lexical, and grammatical differences that they (the varieties) manifest. Their functional allocations, however—as languages or as dialects—are derived only from societal observation of their uses and users rather than from any characteristics of the codes themselves. (Fishman 1970: 23)

A variety may be regional, ethnic or religious, social, functional, occupational, etc., depending on the characteristics of its speakers. The term "dialect" is properly reserved for varieties "that initially and basically represent divergent geographic origins" (Fishman 1970: 22). It is in this sense that it can be applied to the language of many black adults and children in the United States today.

> The first and most obvious generalization about the English of many Negroes is that it shows abundant characteristics of the southern United States. . . . In recent decades, as southern Negroes have surged into northern cities, they have brought along their varieties of southern speech. Since they have largely been forced to live in segregated ghettos, often shut off even more completely from association with whites than in their southern homes, their dialects have been perpetuated and passed on to their northern-born children. What had been geographically distinctive features have been converted into ethnic features. (Burling 1970: 118)

This chapter begins with dialect differences and their implications for education. Because of the social importance of questions about the education of black children, research on dialect differences has concentrated on this group and so this chapter concentrates here too. But similar questions should be asked about children from Appalachia, rural Maine, and elsewhere. The chapter ends with a shorter section on bilingualism.

The notion of a "nonstandard" dialect raises a necessary introductory question about the validity of the concept of "Standard English" (SE). Is there in fact a single variety of English used by educated speakers throughout the country? The answer to this question depends on which aspect of language is being considered. In pronunciation, there is no single standard. Regional variations in "accent" exist and are widely accepted without social stigmatism. Taylor (1971) makes the obviously justified plea that black speakers should be accorded the same courtesy. In syntax, by contrast, a single standard does seem to exist. With certain very minor exceptions, educated speakers around the country follow the same syntactic rules. Exceptions can be found in the case (in the grammatical sense) of pronouns. Linguistic change can be rapid, and utterances like *It is me* and *Who are you talking to?* are becoming acceptable except in the most purist circles (largely English classrooms, I suspect). Another exception in the grammatical case of pronouns is psycholinguistically more interesting. In the special sentence construction where two pronouns are conjoined, one very often hears even the most highly educated speakers utter such "errors" as the following:

> I stepped between she and the police (MC graduate student, October 1967).
> They flew my wife and I to Puerto Rico (college professor, September 1968).
> There's very little difference between they and their South Boston peers (psychologist, October 1968).

These pronoun forms constitute the only widespread instance of syntactic variability among educated speakers that I have found. In the discussion that follows, therefore, I will assume that a standard syntactic form of English does exist, and that style switching for SE speakers uses selection of vocabulary and shifts in pronunciation, as from -ing to -in', for expressive purposes.

BLACK ENGLISH

The most extensive research on black dialectic patterns has been done by William Labov in New York City. He has used a variety of very carefully designed interview techniques to obtain a wide range of linguistic data from adolescent and preadolescent males in central Harlem. We will draw heavily on his findings, as reported in a two-volume monograph (Labov et al. 1968), and numerous articles supplementing them at several points with the work of other researchers.

Although Labov's work has been financed by the U.S. Office of Education because of its importance in providing a knowledge base for decisions about educational practice, it represents more than linguistic research prompted by the demands of social action. It also represents a shift in perspective and methodology within linguistics itself. There is an important contrast between Labov's view of language and that expressed by most other transformational grammarians. For instance, Katz states that "a necessary condition for something to be part of the subject matter of a linguistic theory is that each speaker be able to perform in that regard much as every other does" (Katz 1964: 415). In Labov's sociolinguistic view, however, the multidimensional structure of variation across persons and across settings is an essential feature. Labov is primarily interested in language change and the factors influencing it. His goal is a "socially realistic linguistics"—a description of the structure of social and stylistic variation and an explanation of changes in that structure of social and stylistic variation and an explanation of changes in that structure over time. The shift from the study of language as a homogeneous abstraction to the study of variability as an integral part of any linguistic system can be related to a corresponding contemporary shift in biological theory from typological to population models and concepts. To the typologist, differences among individuals are a kind of troublesome noise in the biological system. The populationist, on the contrary, regards diversity among individuals as the prime observable reality and the source of evolutionary possibilities (Dobzhansky 1967). Labov's findings are extensive. This chapter can report only some of them in a fairly general form, and the reader should consult Labov's own writings for a wealth of rich detail and discussion.

The discussion is organized around eight issues; differences in meaning, differences in superficial form, the asymmetry between comprehension and production, relationships among dialects, dialect switching, dialects versus developmental change, the power of attitudes, and monitoring. Throughout, the labels Standard English (SE) and Black English (BE) will be used, except in quoting from Labov himself, where his label Negro Nonstandard English (NNE) will be retained.

Differences in Meaning

Labov has identified a few forms in BE which probably indicate basic differences in the deep structure of the dialect, in the underlying meaning being expressed.

> One is the use of *be* to indicate generality repeated action, or existential state in sentences such as *He be with us; They be fooling around*. . . . [A distinction which in S.E. is possible only with main verbs—*walks* (habitually) versus *is walking*—but only with the copula. —C. B. C.] Another such element is *done* to indicate an intensive or perfective meaning as in *The bullet done penetrated my body; I done got me a hat.* Both of these are part of an aspectual system which is plainly distinct from tense; there still remains the problem of specifying their use and limitations precisely, and then relating them to the tense system." (Labov and Cohen 1967: 76)

To date, Labov's published research has not included children younger than preadolescents. Henrie's (1969) study is one of the few careful descriptions of the speech of younger black children. Using a story retelling technique, he elicited speech samples from three black California kindergarten children selected as the most extreme BE speakers in their grade. In story retelling, as in sentence imitation tests, meaning is generally preserved, but the form is recoded into the speaker's own language system. (See John, Horner, and Birney 1970 for further description of this research technique.) Henrie found that these children, like Labov's older subjects, frequently used unconjugated *be* to express habitual meaning:

> Story: . . . he was always there
> Child's version: He always be there.

Differences in Superficial Form

Given a certain idea to be expressed, NNE has different transformational rules governing its surface realization. One example is the deletion of the copula *be* in certain specific environments. The following are all examples of NNE (Labov et al. 1968: I, 175–83):

Be deleted:	*Be* appears:
He fast in everything he do.	I'm not no strong drinker.
You out the game.	I was small.
They not caught.	Is he dead?
He gon' try to get up.	Allah *is* God. (emphasis)
	It always somebody tougher than you are.

Labov found that this alternation between the deletion and appearance of *be* is not simply random variation produced by dialect mixtures, but rather a highly structured system. Phonological influences can be specified: for example, *is* and *are* are deleted where *'m* is not because "there are no phonological processes which delete nasals" (Labov et al. 1968: I, 284). An explanation can also be given of the conditions under which *is* and *are* can be deleted:

> One general principle holds without exception: *wherever SE can contract. NNE can delete is and are, and vice-versa; wherever SE cannot contract. NNE cannot delete is and are, and vice-versa.* (Labov et al. 1968: I, 185)

The examples above illustrate these two phonological and syntactic rules.

The rules governing SE contraction, and thereby BE deletion, follow the stress assignment rules provided by N. Chomsky and Halle (1968) and, as Labov points out, provide independent confirmation of the validity of Chomsky and Halle's work.

Question forms constitute another instance. Whereas in mature SE, the inversion transformation is what Labov calls a "categorical rule" that is rarely violated, in NNE it is a "variable rule" with certain probabilities of occurrence and considerable individual variation. So one may hear mature NNE speakers ask—

> So why you didn't go to school?
> What I'm thinking of?
> Why I can't play?

Comprehension and Production

"There is strong evidence of an asymmetry between the rules which NNE speakers use in comprehension and production. When Boot hears *I asked Alvin if he knew . . .* and repeats back instantly *I ax Alvin do he know . . .* it is clear he has understood the abstract meaning" (Labov et al. 1968: I, 320).

The same translation ability was found by Baratz (1969) among third- and fifth-grade lower-class black and lower-middle-class Caucasian children in Washington, and by Garvey and McFarlane (1968) among fifth-grade lower-class black and Caucasian children in Baltimore. Baratz's study is particularly interesting because she gave an imitation test consisting of both SE and NNE sentences to both SE and NNE speakers. For example, with the sentences containing embedded questions—*I asked Tom if he wanted to go to the picture that was playing at the Howard* or *I aks Tom do he wanna go ta the picture that be playin' at the Howard*—both groups repeated more accurately the sentence presented in their own dialect and translated the other one.

Troike (1970) reports the same results with white Appalachian children and contrasts the knowledge of both black and Appalachian children with that of their teachers. Parenthetically, the sentences in Troike's test deserve comment. According to Troike, they come from materials produced by Devine and Associates in Austin, Texas, designed for teaching English to speakers of other languages and later used with speakers of nonstandard English dialects. They are examples of language materials that embody superficial "middle-class values" and little intellectual interest.

Of particular interest is the response of many Negro children and white Appalachian children to the task of repeating a sentence they hear on tape while watching a coordinated colored cartoon filmstrip. Some examples follow (N indicates Negro, A indicates Appalachian white):

Model	*Response*
Mother helps Gloria.	Mother help Gloria. (N)
Gloria has a toothbrush.	Gloria have a toothbrush. (N)
She cleans her teeth with a brush.	Her cleans her teeth with a brush. (N)
David has a brush for his hair.	David has a brush for he hair. (N)
She has soap on her head.	She has soap(t) on hers head. (A)
David and Gloria are clean.	David and Gloria is clean. (A)
They are on their knees.	They are on theirs knees. (A)
The socks are on Gloria's bed.	The socks is on Gloria's bed. (A)
The children go to bed.	The children goes to bed. (A)

These examples show very clearly, I think, that the child has not merely attempted to repeat the stimulus, but has decoded it first and then reencoded it in the form he might have used in framing the sentence as an original utterance. The rapidity with which this is accomplished suggests that the performance is closely akin to that attributed to the coordinate bilingual speaker (and might therefore be considered a type of simultaneous transla-tion). . . . It follows that a difference between the receptive and productive competence of these children must be hypothesized. Thus they are bidialectal, with an asymmetry in their bidialectal performance, since they can pre-sumably both understand and produce the forms of one, "nonstandard," dialect, while understanding, but not producing, the forms of a second, "standard," dialect. . . .

A common complaint from white teachers is that they cannot understand their Negro pupils; from this report I think we may infer that the teachers simply lack the receptive competence which they tacitly expect of their pupils in reverse. Since most students are able to understand their teachers, it should be clear that the dialectal range of their receptive, if not their pro-ductive, competence often exceeds that of their teachers. (Troike 1970: 66–68)

It is generally true that we understand more language than we speak. This is true throughout development. In an experiment by Fraser, Bellugi, and Brown (1963), sentences containing ten grammatical features such as *not* or the passive construction were presented to children in three tasks: imitation; comprehension, demonstrated by pointing to the correct picture; and production, demonstrated by repeating the proper sentence when the experimenter pointed to a picture. For all ten features, the sequence of sentences correct was imitation, comprehension, and then production. As adults, we also understand more words and complex struc-tures than we use in our own speech.

The nature of this comprehension-production asymmetry remains to be explained. Presumably, production somehow makes greater cognitive demands. See McNeill (1968) and other papers in that volume on the general lag between perceiving and performing in cognitive development. In the special case of asymmetry in com-prehending and speaking another dialect, attitudinal influences discussed below may also be important. One may wish to understand members of another group, but not behave like them.

When a special comprehension test of SE forms is designed on the Fraser, Bellugi, and Brown (1963) model, some BE speakers do have difficulty. Torrey (1969) gave 27 Harlem second graders such a test. Comprehension of plurals, possessives, third-person singular verb endings, and contracted *is* was tested by asking the chil-dren to match appropriate pictures to sentences with and without the inflection; for example:

The duck nurse.
The duck's nurse.

Torrey also taped samples of the children's spontaneous speech and evaluated their spontaneous production of these same inflections. She credited a child with an inflection if he supplied it 75 percent of the time it was required. When based on this criterion, the SE forms had a varied status: 26 of the children used plurals; nearly half of the children used possessives and the contracted *is*; only 4 children used the verb ending.

On the comprehension tests, some of Torrey's children did comprehend forms they never were to use spontaneously (the asymmetry described above); but some chil-dren did not comprehend them in this test situation. In interpreting the communi-cative significance of these findings, we must remember that speech is normally sufficiently redundant so that no information is carried by one grammatical mor-pheme alone. In fact, experimenters have a hard time creating test situations in which all normally available contextual cues are removed.

Relationships among Dialects

Dialect differences are less categorical than had been believed, and are more a case of different probabilities of occurrence of particular features in specifiable social and linguistic contexts. One example is the tendency (which all speakers of English share to some extent) to simplify final consonant clusters—for example, to reduce *first* to *firs'*. This simplification depends not only on the social class of the speaker, but also on the formality of informality of the social context, whether the sound represents a separate morpheme such as past tense (*walked*) or not (*first*), and whether the subsequent sound is a consonant (*first thing*) or a vowel (*first of all*).

Figure 24.1 shows the variation among and within individuals for the simplification of *-t* or *-d* (Labov and Cohen 1967: 70). Following is the authors' discussion:

> The percentage of simplification is given for casual speech and careful speech, for clusters followed by words beginning with a consonant K or a juncture # or a vowel, V. The solid lines represent the working class speakers; the dashed lines, the middle class speakers, [all Negro.] On the left, the diagram for monomorphemic clusters first shows small stylistic shift for working

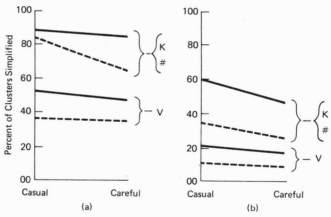

FIGURE 24.1. The Effects of Style, Class, Grammatical Status, and Phonetic Environment on the Simplification of Constant Clusters Ending in *t/d*: Some Preliminary Data from Adults in South Central Harlem. (a) Monomorphemic Clusters [*-t/d = ed*]; (b) Grammatical Clusters [*-t/d = ed*]
Source: Labov and Cohen 1967: 70.

class speakers, with the same slope for clusters before consonants as for clusters before vowels. But the middle class line for clusters before consonants moves sharply upward, approximately the position of the working class in casual speech. Note, however, that there is no such phenomenon for the middle class use of clusters before vowels. Here the percentage of simplification is low and does not rise sharply; we can interpret this lack of parallelism by noting that a pattern of simplification before consonants but not before vowels preserves the underlying forms of the words. If we say *firs' thing* but *first of all*, there is no doubt that the underlying form is *first*.

In the right half of the diagram [where t/d = the past tense *-ed*] the same general pattern can be observed, but at a much lower level. The grammatical status of *-ed* is obviously important to both groups, since the position is lower and the slope of the lines [from casual to careful speech] is greater than for monomorphemic words. Furthermore, the middle class groups show a sharper downward shift than the working class. There is less tendency for the middle class to shift upward in casual speech to approximate the working class norm; that is, even before consonants we find no sharp stylistic increase in simplification. We can argue here that the middle class has a general constraint against the dropping of the grammatical formative *-ed* as a stylistic indicator. In these respects, the middle class group approximates the behavior of white speakers as indicated in other studies. (Labov and Cohen 1967: 69–71)

One implication of this complex relationship among social and linguistic factors is that social-class differences in speech behavior and stylistic shifts within a social class fall on a continuum—a single continuum for the middle-class teacher and her lower-class pupil—rather than into separate categories:

> But members of a speech community are not aware of this. Their experience is limited to (a) a wide range of speech styles among their own family and friends, and (b) the speech of a wide range of social classes in one or two styles. Thus the teacher hears the differences between middle class and working class children in classroom recitation, but does not follow his students home and hear them at their ease among their own friends. He does not realize how similar the students are to him—how they fit into the same sociolinguistic structure which governs his own behavior. Instead, teachers like most of us tend to perceive the speech of others categorically: John always says *dese* and *dose*, but Henry never does. Few teachers are able to perceive that they themselves use the same non-standard forms in their most casual speech; as we will see, almost everyone hears himself as using the norm which guides his speech production in most formal styles. In a word, the differences between speakers are more obvious than their similarities. (Labov 1969)

Dialect Switching

If any individual can speak in more than one dialect, what controls his selection or switching among them? Labov has identified a continuum of speech situations from most casual and excited to most formal. In research in Norway, Blom and Gumperz (in press) identified two forms of switching between a local dialect and standard Norwegian: role switching and metaphorical switching.

Two reports of role switching come from classrooms.

In Norway:

> Teachers report that they use the dialect in order to mark the transition from formal lectures in the standard, without interruption, to open discussion where the students are encouraged to speak freely. . . . there is a clear change in the actors' mutual rights and duties and in the definition of the situation. (Blom and Gumperz, in press)

In the United States, Rainey (1969) studied the style-switching of one Headstart teacher by listening for four indicators of a switch from formal to informal style: *you*→*ya*; *them*→*'em*; *have to* and *got to*→*hafta* and *gotta*; *ing*→*in'* as in *goin'*. In two classroom situations in which the teacher was telling the story of Henny Penny and giving directions for going home, her unmarked style (as identified by the most frequent features) was formal, and she switched into a more informal way of speaking only when inserting personal comments to the children into the ongoing task, presumably in order to lessen the psychological distance between herself and them. In a third situation, when teacher and children together retold the story, the teacher's unmarked style was informal, and she switched to formal features only for the refrain of the story, "The sky is falling and I am going to tell the king."

Metamorphical switching occurs ". . . whenever two or more differently coded social relationships between the same set of individuals are relevant, [and] the use of the dialect or standard to allude to these ties serves to enrich the content of the message" (Blom and Gumperz, in press). For instance, when students who had been close friends in a Norwegian village returned home after attendance at universities in Oslo or Bergen, their conversation on local matters was in dialect, while on topics related to their Pan-Norwegian life as students, they switched to standard Norwegian. The students were not aware of this switching. Blom and Gumperz comment that "code selection may thus seem to be akin to grammatical rules. Both operate below the level of consciousness and may be independent of the speaker's overt intentions."

Even in a seemingly more homogeneous speech community, such code selection occurs. Fisher (1958) discovered switching between -ing and -in' in a semirural New England village. Children from three to ten years old varied their pronunciation, depending on the formality of the setting, changes in mood as they became more relaxed within a single interview, and even (for one boy) the formality or informality of the connotations of specific verbs: *reading, criticizing* versus *swimmin'* and *punchin'*.

Gumperz and Hernandez (in press) show how easily misunderstandings can result if teachers are insensitive to the communicative functions that dialect switching can serve—

> Imagine a child in a classroom situation who in a moment of special excitement shifts to black speech. The teacher may have learned that black speech is systematic and normal for communication in Afro-American homes. Nevertheless, intent as she is upon helping the child to become fully bilingual, she may comment on the child's speech by saying, "We don't speak this way in the classroom," or she may ask the child to rephrase the sentence in standard English. No matter how the teacher expresses herself, the fact that she focuses on the form means that the teacher is not responding to the real meaning of the child's message. The child is most likely to interpret her remark as a rebuff and may feel frustrated in his attempt at establishing a more personal relationship with the teacher. In other words, by imposing her own mono-stylistic communicative norms, the teacher may thwart her students' ability to express themselves fully. An incident from a tape-recorded language session in Black Language Arts will illustrate the point.
>
> *Student (reading from an autobiographical essay)*: This lady didn't have no sense.
> *Teacher*: What would be a standard English alternate for this sentence?
> *Student*: She didn't have any sense. But this lady *she didn't have no sense*.

Dialects Versus Developmental Change

One phenomenon invites misinterpretation: Some features of mature BE coincide in superficial form to stages in the language development of children in a SE-speaking community. This is true of multiple negation (*I don't want none*), omission of the verb *to be* in certain contexts (*He sick*), omission of verb endings (*He go to the store*), and even the relationship between contraction and deletion of the copula. The easy misinterpretation is to say that BE is therefore an immature version of SE.

Brown (in press) has a careful discussion of this phenomenon. He points out that important differences also exist between the two language systems. At a general level, both children and BE speakers exhibit what Labov calls "inherent variability": any one speaker will sometimes supply syntactic features and sometimes omit them in unpredictable ways. But BE also is characterized by "contingent variability" where the probability of features can be predicted from the linguistic and social context. Labov's diagram (figure 24.1) of the simplification of consonant clusters shows one example of contingent variability in pronunciation. This kind of variability has not been found in child language. At a more specific level, children are more apt to delete forms of the verb *be* after noun subjects (perhaps because they temporarily think that *it's* is a variable form of *it*) while BE speakers are more apt to delete *be* after a pronoun (as in *He sick*).

Despite these differences, important similarities exist and "challenge interpretation," in Brown's words. Wolfram (1971) suggests that certain features of a language. may be particularly susceptible to modification in situations like acquisition and dialect differences. But why? And why these particular features? Brown suggests a more specific reason:

> The very fact that we were able to identify large numbers of "obligatory contexts" and score for the presence or absence of required morphemes means that these morphemes when present are often redundant. In the N + N construction the possessive inflection usually redundant; with plural determiners like *some* or *two* the plural inflection on the head noun is redundant. . . . [etc.]. The grammatical morphemes are especially likely to be redundant in fact-to-face conversation between persons having a large fund of common experience which is the situation that obtains for child and parent and for nonliterary adult dialects. It does seem likely to me, therefore, that grammatical morphemes are especially vulnerable to deletion because they are often redundant, and their omission will not result in serious misunderstanding. . . .
>
> The meanings they convey are generally only "modulations" of the meanings carried by content words and by content word order, and these modulations may be less important than names and semantic relations. In sum, it seems probable to me that grammatical morphemes constitute an aspect of English grammar particularly susceptible to misconstruction both in adult dialects and in child speech. We have seen, however, that there is no evidence that the stable misconstructions of particular dialects are "simpler" than the standard construction; as far as is known they are just different. (R. Brown, in press)

The Power of Attitudes

Labov has studied the relation of dialect differences to the attitudes of his informants toward the speech they speak and hear. The power of attitudes to influence speech behavior first came to his attention in his study of the pronunciation of vowels on Martha's Vineyard, an island off the coast of Massachusetts.

> The linguistic variable studied was the centralization of the diphthongs /ay/ and /aw/ in words such as *right*, *ride*, *my*, *about*, and *down*. . . . The overall social significance of this sound change was its association with a positive orientation towards Martha's Vineyard. Those who laid claim to native status as Vineyarders shared the greatest centralization, while those who were excluded from this status, or who abandoned their claims to pursue a career on the mainland, would show no centralization of these vowels. (Labov 1966a: 186–87)

Next, Labov studied (1966c) the role of attitudes in explaining the social stratification of certain phonological features among adults and children on the Lower East Side of New York City. Consider the distribution of the presence (r-1) or absence (r-0) of final and preconsonantal /r/ as in *car* or *cards*: Regardless of their own speech patterns, 100 percent of Labov's informants between 18 and 39 years recognized the r-1 pattern as socially preferred. Only 60 percent of those over 40 did so, presumably because they grew up when r-0 was the general pattern throughout New York City, while "young people below the age of 19 or 20 have not yet acquired full sensitivity to the socially significant dialect features of their community" (Labov 1966c: 421). These judgments express conformity to values imposed by the community, what Labov calls "pressure from above." But many of the very people who deprecate r-0 use the stigmatized form in their own speech. Labov hypothesized the presence of conflicting pressures from below: "the need for self-identification with particular subgroups in the social complex. . . . We observe the process of increased differentiation of language behavior despite close contact of the social groups concerned, and their participation in a relatively uniform set of social norms" (Labov 1966c: 450). In a pluralistic urban society, dialect differences are maintained not out of isolation and ignorance but because of "the need for self-identification with particular subgroups in the social complex" (Labov 1966c: 450).

Labov's later research in Harlem confirms the power of attitudes. How any person—child or adult—speaks depends not only on who he is, but also on how he sees himself vis-a-vis others, on who he wants to be. This is a clear example of affective influences on cognitive learning. From the beginning of the language-learning process, children must pick their models. This is not done consciously. But we have seen before how powerful nonconscious knowledge can be, and attitudes are made up of knowledge plus a strong positive or negative valence. If children didn't pick their models in this sense, there would be no way to explain why black children speak the dialect of their parents or their peers despite hours of exposure to network (usually standard) English over TV.

The power of attitudes to affect language learning is of critical importance for education. When teachers become language planners, powerful social and political values lie behind their decisions and will affect the success of their work.

Monitoring

Finally, and more speculatively, there is the interesting cognitive process which Labov calls "monitoring," the attention that a speaker pays to his own speech. Monitoring must go on at many levels. Consider three: first, the automatic feedback processes present in all speech production whose disruption is evident in the stammering produced under experimental conditions of delayed auditory feedback; second, the largely nonconscious dialect switching described above, away from some unmarked, or neutral form, toward either "monitoring black" or "monitoring white" (Kernan, in press), depending on the impression the speaker wishes to convey; and third, the more deliberate, conscious, stylistic choices of words and syntactic constructions for greater explicitness in the low-context situations.

Is there any relationship among these three processes? Is the third level related at all to either metalinguistic awareness or the use of speech for intrapersonal functions? Is it possible that the more experience children have in conversation where such monitoring is required, the earlier they become aware of their own language, and "listen to themselves" as they solve intellectual tasks? This may seem a far-out idea, but hypotheses are sorely needed to explain how different interpersonal uses of language differentially affect the speaker's disposition to use language as an aid to thought. Perhaps investigation of this process of monitoring could be a start.

IMPLICATIONS FOR EDUCATION

In the Westinghouse study of Head Start effectiveness (Cicirelli et al. 1969) the Head Start children and their equally disadvantaged controls scored below the norms on three subtests of the Illinois Test of Psycholinguistic Abilities. One of the three is the grammatical closure subtest, which taps knowledge of SE morphology by completion items such as

Here is a bed. Here are two——.

In their recommendations, the authors argued that these three subtests correlate with school achievement and that "since grammatical closure tests the ability to respond automatically with proper grammatic form, more intensive training in Standard English appears needed (Cicirelli et al. 1969: I, 249).

Here the basic non sequitur, and a shockingly prevalent one, is the leap from correlation to causation—that, because use of SE correlates with school achievement, it is a causal factor in that achievement and worth teaching for that reason. The same children probably have more dental cavities as well, but no one would claim causality there. Sometimes correlational data can support hypotheses of a causal relationship, as between smoking and cancer, but only where there is independent evidence for postulating an intrinsic connection. What is the evidence that dialect features per se carry any implications for a child's education? This question will be discussed under five headings: cognitive implications, beginning reading, social implications, strategies for nourishing bidialectalism, and the attitudes of teachers and peers.

Cognitive Implications

Differences between BE and SE are small in number and linguistic significance, no matter how socially important they may be. With the exception of a few features such as the special use of *be*, they are all matters of surface structure and affect meaning not at all. There is therefore no reason why a BE-speaking child cannot express any and all ideas in his dialect. A correlation does exist between the speaking of a nonstandard dialect and the size of a child's vocabulary, as the findings of Lesser, Fifer, and Clark (1965) and others suggest. And a small vocabulary can indeed limit educability. But there is no intrinsic connection between them. The correlation exists for historical and sociological reasons of discrimination and poverty. As Burling put it, "One cannot, in other words, characterize a language by its lexicon" (1970: 179).

Children can extend their vocabulary while still retaining BE patterns of grammar. One of the black three-year-olds in my research on expansions (Cazden 1965) showed me how easily this could be done. One of the tutors was Australian, and occasionally dropped an unusual vocabulary item into her conversations. One day she admonished a child for "*treading*" on a toy. The child promptly defended herself in fluent BE: *I ain't tread on nothing*.

A first-grade teacher is upstate New York told me that during a science lesson, one of her children excitedly told her that *The magnet brung the paper clips*. She tried to explain that we say *brought*, but the child kept saying *brung*. Finally she gave up and told the child that scientists have a special word for what magnets do, they *attract*.

Although BE and SE may not be completely mutually intelligible, BE-speaking children have considerable receptive command of SE. It seems unlikely, therefore, that their educability will be seriously affected by misunderstanding the oral language of their teacher or SE-speaking classmates. How dialect differences between BE and SE affect the process of learning to read is a separate question, considered in more detail below. If differences do make a difference there, one solution is to change the initial teaching materials and not try (with little realistic expectation of success) to change the child.

One last question, perhaps the most interesting, is about the possible implications of functional specialization of language varieties. BE is intrinsically usable for the full range of language functions. For example, while in a first grade in a black neighborhood in Philadelphia, I heard BE children use language for advanced communicative purposes. One child examined a Polaroid picture I had taken earlier in the day of another child facing directly into the camera, and commented, *He looking at you*—a sophisticated example of perceptual role-taking. In a sharing time at the end of the morning, another child was reporting to the teacher on how many cars had been accommodated in his block-building garage: *We count them and there was nine*—an unsolicited demonstration of verification. Clearly, these children did not seem cognitively impeded by their dialect. It may be the case, however, that among adults who control more than one dialect, their switching toward SE may be controlled by function as well as by listener and topic. We need more information on this point. But even if such a relationship does exist, the wisest course for education would seem to be concentration on the elaboration of language functions, letting linguistic features come out as they may.

Finally, because the relationship between dialect features and cognition is one of correlation at most, there is no basis for expecting that dialect change, even if successful, would by itself have any corresponding effect on the intellectually more important questions of vocabulary and language use.

Paul Olson, director of the Tri-University project in Elementary Education, reminds us:

> A teacher must possess extraordinary knowledge and humanity if he is to distinguish what the school demands of children simply to symbolize its capacity for authority over them from what it legitimately "demands" or "woos out of them" to equip them for a niche in a technological society. (Olson 1967: 13)

In the area of verbal behavior, Labov (1970) makes a comparable distinction between all the "verbal habits" of middle-class speakers and the "verbal skills" needed for success in school. The two are not identical, and a very important job remains to be done in separating out essential verbal skills.

Beginning Reading

Learning to read is usually judged the single most important task a child faces in school. Whether dialect differences per se interfere in that task is one specific form of general questions about the match or mismatch between some aspect of children's language and the language of their books: How much of a match does, or should, exist?

Baratz and Shuy (1969) published a set of articles urging the design of initial reading materials written in the child's native dialect. The articles focus on differences in production between Black and Standard English, saying less about how differences in comprehension interfere with reading. Since speakers of nonstandard dialects understand more Standard English than they speak, this is an important omission.

Torrey (1969) says of John, a precocious BE-speaking kindergarten boy in Atlanta, Georgia that the types of errors he made in oral reading "suggest that John expected to find in print the things he would normally say." In other words, in the process of oral reading he recoded the written text in his own dialect. For example:

(30a) *Text: When do you go to school?*
(30b) *John's Reading: When you go to school?*

John's response raises a critical question that will be answered only by further investigation of young readers, black and white: A child holds certain expectations about the relation between reading and spoken language; should he expect to find in print what he would normally say? Or is it sufficient that he has heard other people say, and can understand, the kind of things he finds in print?

The first recent books in black dialect were produced during the summer of 1965 by paraprofessionals teaching in the Head Start program—the Child Development

Group of Mississippi (CDGM). One book, entitled *Pond*, from Mt. Peel, Mississippi, reads in part:

> If a toad frog hop up on you and wet on you
> he make a big blister on your feet.

Another book, *Today*, from Holly Springs and Durant, includes:

> We supposed to take a nap but we reading instead.
> My Daddy he helping make a kitchen in the schoolhouse.

Four years later, during 1969, the first sets of readers written in nonstandard dialect became widely available. The Education Study Center (1970) in Washington, D.C., produced one set of these books and a companion set of "control" books with identical content and pictures written in Standard English. The first book, *Ollie* (ESC 1970: 1–3), begins as follows in the two versions:

Here go Ollie.	This is Ollie.
Ollie have a big family.	Ollie has a big family.
He have three sisters.	He has three sisters.
A sister name Brenda. . . .	A sister named Brenda. . . .

These two sets of readers are being used with different children in an attempt to determine whether these initial teaching materials in the child's native dialect aid beginning reading.

The Chicago Board of Education also produced a set (Davis, Gladney, and Leaverton 1968, 1969). In books 1 through 3, each story is presented twice, first in "Everyday Talk" and then "School Talk." Books 4 through 7 are written in two editions, the "Everyday Talk" book and the "School Talk" book. All children may use both versions. Contrasting sentences from books 1 through 3 (Davis, Gladney, and Leaverton 1969: 4) are:

I got a mama.	I have a mama.
My mama she pretty.	My mama she's pretty.
My mama work.	My mama works

It will not be easy to answer the important question about whether such materials do help. It is always hard to isolate aspects of a complex situation and keep all other factors controlled, and this situation is particularly complex. If the purpose of these readers is to provide a match between the oral language of the reader and his initial reading materials, how can we assume or assure such a match, given the range of variability within any black community? Does it matter that the use of such readers will increase racial segregation during reading instruction? What will be the attitudes of children, teachers (black and white), and parents to these materials? What are effective ways to gain acceptance for them at least for an experimental period? These questions, and more, remain. Johnson's (1971) research now in progress at the University of California at Berkeley should begin to provide answers.

Books written in nonstandard dialect are not the only answer to problems of the "match." At least four other alternatives are open: First, one can try to teach standard speech patterns before the child learns to read. So far, there is no evidence of success here. For instance, Rystrom (1968) found that neither oral language nor reading was affected by instruction in Standard English. Second, one can retain SE texts, but let the child give BE readings, as Torrey's pupil John did.

Third, since dialect differences are concentrated in only a few features, one could probably write books that avoid those features entirely. Fourth, Serwer (1969) offers new arguments for using individually dictated stories and experience charts in which the teacher records each child's language as spoken in Standard English spelling. From my experience, however, a teacher trying this method will face more difficult decisions about how to do that recording than Serwer acknowledges.

Finally, one can decide that structural interference is not as important as functional interference, and that efforts to improve reading should be concentrated on content and context. Bernstein speaks to Americans from his English perspective:

> There is nothing, but nothing, in the dialect as such, which prevents a child from internalizing and learning to use universalistic meanings. But if the contexts of learning, the examples, the reading books are not contexts which are triggers for the child's imaginings, are not triggers on the child's curiosity and explorations in his family and community, then the child is not at home in the educational world. If the teacher has to say continuously, "Say it again, darling, I didn't understand you," then in the end the child may say nothing. If the culture of the teacher is to become part of the consciousness of the child, then the culture of the child must first be in the consciousness of the teacher. This may mean that the teacher must be able to understand the child's dialect, rather than deliberately attempting to change it. (Bernstein, in press (a))

In considering content, there is a danger of assuming too narrow a definition of relevance. In a brush-shelter school in Rough Rock, Arizona, I saw a Navajo woman in a lunch line, engrossed in Marjorie Flack's book *The Story about Ping* (Viking, 1933), the tale of a duck on a Yangtze River houseboat. I was told that the book is a favorite with Navajo children. On any superficial criterion, nothing could be more irrelevant to children living on an American desert than life on a Chinese houseboat. Yet, at some deeper level, meaning was caught. V.W. Jones (1970) speaks of "conceptual" relevance rather than "cultural" relevance, and that seems the better term. It can encompass Claudia Kernan's remark (personal communication) that black students in her own high school English class liked Julius Caesar "because Cassius was such a great signifier." Signifying is a special speech style highly developed in the black community in which meaning is "signified" by gesture and innuendo rather than stated explicitly in conventional terms. Evidently, recognition of this speech style helped high school students in Gary, Indiana, relate to ancient Rome. See Bloom, Waite, and Zinet (1970) for a content analysis of children's primers, including newer "multiethnic" ones.

As for context, Labov (1970) believes that cultural and social conflicts are more important than structural interference, and conducted an important study (Labov and Robbins 1969) of the positive correlation between street-gang participation and reading retardation.

Whatever the solution to the problem of the "match," teachers must understand the difference between dialect differences in pronunciation and failures in reading readiness or reading comprehension. If a reading-readiness teacher says, "Whose name begins like *that?*" and a child says "David," it may be because he hasn't learned to attend to beginning sounds in his own speech or it may be because he does not himself produce a *d-th* contrast. Instruction to attend to sounds that the child does in fact make must be distinguished from instruction in the perception and production of phonemic contrasts that are not part of the child's dialect. The former is an educationally beneficial process of making nonconscious behavior a matter of conscious attention; the latter is an attempt at dialect change which is probably necessary only at the level of perception, not production at all.

Once reading has begun, comprehension and not pronunciation must be the critical test. One result of dialect differences in pronunciation is a set of homonyms that are different from the teacher's and may be more numerous than hers. If one has pronounced *during* and *doing* the same way all one's life, learning to read the two words and associate differential meaning with differential spelling is no different from what every English speaker does with *sun* and *son*. And even if children cannot match word to picture correctly when BE homonyms like *six* and *sick* are spoken out of context, they may respond correctly to written sentences in which that contrast in meaning is important—such as *sick cats* versus *six cats* (Paul Melmed, personal communication).

The same contrast between pronunciation and reading comprehension applies to other dialect features. Labov (1970) constructed sentences such as

> When I passed by, I read the posters.

to separate pronunciation of the past tense *-ed* suffix from visual recognition and comprehension of its meaning. If a reader pronounces *read* in the past tense, he must have understood the *-ed* on *pass*, whether the latter was present in his speech or not. Labov found that whereas an adverbial phrase like *last month* did alert adolescent males in Harlem to the past-tense meaning, the *-ed* suffix was much less successful, even in generally capable readers. Instruction in such cases should concentrate on the meaning of the *-ed* suffix, not on its pronunciation.

Social Implications

If being able to speak SE is not an intrinsic requirement for any cognitive process or educational task, then decisions about whether to teach SE must be made on other grounds—on beliefs and values about the nature of the good life, the appropriate role of the school in achieving it, and the relevance for the United States in the 1970s of the Pygmalion effect of language on social mobility.

In applying these criteria, it is necessary to distinguish fact from folklore about what and where liabilities exist for NNE speakers in the world of jobs. Service industries are one source of expanded employment opportunities in the future, and the telephone company is one place where communication is critical. Of the 10,000 operators employed in New York City, 7,000 are black and Puerto Rican. But it is not obvious even here that dialect per se is the main problem.

> One spot check a few weeks ago disclosed some kind of "communication difficulty" in 25% of information calls. Dr. Bray [a psychologist in charge of employment and training] cited a typical example: A woman called information and asked for Korvette's. The information operator, who did not know Korvette's was a department store, asked the woman for "Mr. Korvette's first name." (N.Y. *Times*, 29 Aug. 1969, p. 18)

Such information needs to be continuously brought up to date as social change continues over the years.

But even if all such facts were available, attitudes and values would still be important. In any nonhomogeneous speech community, decisions cannot be avoided about which language varieties to use in which aspects of public life. In his description of language planning in contemporary Norway, Haugen (1968) presents an interesting case of citizen participation in language planning. Language planning is "the activity of preparing a normaltive orthography, grammar and dictionary for the guidance of writers and speakers in a non-homogeneous speech community. In this practical application of linguistic knowledge, we are proceeding beyond descriptive linguistics into an area where judgment must be exercised in the form of choices among available forms" (Haugen 1968: 672–73). In Norway a deliberate attempt is being made to fuse a new national language from two competing, though linguistically very similar, languages. The Norwegian government has appointed numerous committees to investigate and make recommendations. Elected representatives debate matters of language in the Norwegian parliament; and "A system of local option administered through schoolboards has ensured that the voice of the people should be heard and has made these problems part of the daily diet of even the humblest citizen" (Haugen 1968: 677).

In the United States, the same participation by people affected by decisions should take place, but the people most deeply affected are members of minority groups who are grossly underrepresented at all levels of government and educational planning. Protests against this state of affairs continue to increase across the country.

Documentation of the range of attitudes on the goals of oral language education for black children consists of the views of two white linguists (Sledd 1969, Kochman 1969); a newspaper account of a discussion among a group of civil rights workers in Mississippi, including Stokely Carmichael; and a report of research on the attitudes of parents, teachers, and community leaders in Roxbury, Massachusetts (Cazden, Bryant, and Tillman 1970).

Two Linguists

In the U.S.A., we are being told, everybody wants approval—not approval for doing anything worth approving, but approval for doing whatever happens to be approved. Because approval goes to upward mobility, everybody should be upwardly mobile; and because upward mobility is impossible for under-dogs who have not learned middle-dog barking, we must teach it to them for use in their excursions into the middle-dog world. There is no possibility either that the present middle class can be brought to tolerate lower-class English or that upward mobility, as a national aspiration, will be questioned. Those are the pillars on which the state is built, and the compassionate teacher, knowing the ways of his society, will change the color of his students' vowels although he cannot change the color of their skins. (Sledd 1969: 1213)

My first quarrel with such a program is that it does not develop the ability of a person to use language, which I would further define as performance capability in a variety of social contexts on a variety of subject matter. . . . Underlying this approach seems to be a misapplication of Basil Bernstein's terms which falsely equate *restrictive code* and *elaborated code* with, respectively, non-standard dialect and standard dialect. It ought to be noted, as Bernstein uses the term, code is not to be equated with *language*, but *parole*, not with *competence* but *performance*. What is restrictive or elaborated is not in fact, the *code* as sociolinguists use the term, but the message. (Kochman 1969:2.)

Civil Rights Workers, 1965

At the Waveland, Mississippi, language workshop, SNCC field secretary Stokely Carmichael wrote on the left of the blackboard four sentences in the phraseology of common usage by Negroes in Mississippi. They were:

I dig wine.
The peoples wants freedom.
Whereinsoever the policemans goes, they causes troubles.
I wants to reddish to vote.

On the right side of the board, he wrote the equivalents:

> I enjoy drinking cocktails.
> The people want freedom.
> Anywhere the officers of the law go, they cause trouble.
> I want to register to vote.

Jane Stembridge, another SNCC worker recorded the colloquy:

STOKELY: What do you think about these sentences, such as, *The peoples wants freedom?*

ZELMA: It doesn't sound right. *Peoples* isn't right.

STOKELY: Does it mean anything?

MILTON: *People* means everybody. *Peoples* mean everybody in the world.

ALMA: Both sentences are right as long as you understand them.

HENRY: They're both okay, but in a speech class you have to use correct English.

ZELMA: I was taught to use the sentences on the right side.

STOKELY: Does anybody you know use the sentences on the left?

CLASS: Yes.

STOKELY: Are they wrong?

ZELMA: In terms of English they are wrong.

STOKELY: Who decides what is correct English and what is incorrect English?

MILTON: People made rules. People in England, I guess.

STOKELY: You all say some people speak like on the left side of the board. Could they go anywhere and speak that way? Could they go to Harvard?

CLASS: Yes. No. (*Disagreement*)

STOKELY: Does Mr. Turnbow (*a Holmes County farmer, whose idiomatic use of English is legendary. He was the first Negro in the county to attempt to register, after which his house was burned in retaliation and he was arrested for arson*) speak like on the left side?

CLASS: Yes.

STOKELY: Would he be embarrassed?

CLASS: Yes . . . No!

ZELMA: He wouldn't be, but I would. It doesn't sound right.

STOKELY: Suppose someone from Harvard came to Holmes County and said *I want to register to vote.* Would they be embarrassed?

ZELMA: No.

STOKELY: Is it embarrassing at Harvard but not in Holmes County, the way you speak?

MILTON: It's inherited. It's depending on where you are from. The people at Harvard would understand.

STOKELY: Do you think the people at Harvard should forgive you?

MILTON: The people at Harvard should help teach us correct English.

ALMA: Why should we change if we understand what we mean?

SHIRLEY: It is embarrassing.

STOKELY: Which way do teachers speak?

CLASS: On the left, except in class.

STOKELY: If most people speak on the left, why are they trying to change these people?

GLADYS: If you don't talk right, society rejects you. It embarrasses other people if you don't talk right.

HANK: But Mississippi Society, ours, isn't embarrassed by it.

SHIRLEY: But the middle class wouldn't class us with them.

HANK: They won't accept *reddish*. What is *reddish*? It's Negro dialect and it's something you eat.

STOKELY: Will society reject you if you don't speak like on the right side of the board? Gladys said society would reject you.

GLADYS: You might as well face it, man! What we gotta do is go out and become middle class. If you can't speak good English, you don't have a car, or anything.

STOKELY: If society rejects you because you don't speak good English, should you learn to speak good English?

CLASS: Nop.

ALMA: I'm tired of doing what society say. Let society say *reddish* for a while. People ought to just accept each other.

ZELMA: I think we should be speaking just like we always have.

ALMA: If the majority speaks on the left, then a minority must rule society. Why do we have to change to be accepted by the minority group? If I change for society, I wouldn't be free anyway.

(W. A. Price, *National Guardian*, 3 July 1965)

Parents, Teachers, and Community Leaders

If members of any black community were asked about their attitudes toward language education for young children, what would they say? A study was conducted (Cazden, Bryant, and Tillman 1970) in order to tap black attitudes toward language and language education.

Small discussion groups were arranged with preschool parents, preschool teachers, and community leaders in Roxbury, the black community in Boston. All participants in all of the groups were black. Two open-ended questions were asked: How do you feel about the use of Standard English and black dialect? What kind of preschool language education do you want for your children?

In research of this kind, two methodological questions must be raised. What is the status of talk *about* language, and how representative is the group of informants? We are dealing here not with samples of speech, nor even with judgments elicited in direct response to samples of speech. We are dealing instead in metalanguage, talk about language. We make no assumption that what our informants say they do actually matches what they do. Whether a mother does in fact correct her children when they speak "as if they were hit on the end of their tongue with a hammer," or whether she really doesn't "feel ashamed if they don't say the right thing"—these questions have to be investigated directly. The opinions we heard may or may not coincide with the speaker's behavior—in speaking or responding to the speech of others. But it seems reasonable to assume that these opinions do indicate how these individuals would respond if actually asked to participate in decisions about present or proposed school programs.

The people who attended our discussions certainly cannot be considered representative of the entire black community. The parents were unrepresentative first because their children attended preschools; then they were self-selected a second time because they were willing to come to an evening meeting on an educational topic, with only token reimbursement for travel and baby-sitting expenses. Comparable selection factors affected the sample of teachers. The group of community leaders invited to come together for this purpose also undoubtedly did not reflect the entire range of opinions. The group did not include more conservative church leaders, at one end, nor any member of the Black Panthers, at the other end, though we tried to include them. It did include some of the more vocal, articulate, and militant leadership. And we believe it reflected the opinions of the larger group of community leaders who would be most likely to speak out on educational questions whenever there is opportunity to do so.

In other words, in eliciting and reporting verbal statements about language, we only claim to be dealing in what Ferguson calls "myths": "attitudes and beliefs, regardless of their truth value" (Ferguson 1968: 375). In eliciting these myths from selected groups of people, we only claim that they represent those who would speak out if given the chance to make real decisions about preschool education. Since all the discussions were arranged and conducted by Melissa Tillman, a native of Roxbury, we believe that a good atmosphere prevailed in which people did honestly speak their minds.

Parents. Discussions were held with parents of children in two preschools. The schools were picked to provide a possible contrast in degree of influence of Black Power ideology. One school is physically close to the center of Black Power activity in Roxbury, and has been more influenced by it through its personnel and educational program. For example, black artists and musicians have come to share their skills with the children and help build their self-conscious pride in being black. The other school is both physically farther away and less changed in personnel and program over the past few years.

Whether these black parents reject Black English because it originated in the slave experience or appreciate it for its power of expression, they feel it has no place in school. They realize that "most of us have two faces." But since children will learn to speak Black English at home anyway, they believe the job of the school is to teach in, and teach, Standard English. Indications of the linguistic self-hatred which Labov (1966c) found in New York City appear in our protocols, both in a father's association of his own people's current speech with slavery and a mother's description of her children's pronunciation—as if "they were hit on the end of their tongue with a hammer."

Where feelings among black parents are this deep and this negative, any programs that attempt to teach in a nonstandard dialect are likely to encounter strong opposition, even if the goal remains literacy in Standard English. Stewart (1970) narrates events in Philadelphia when the Education Study Center readers were suggested. This does not mean that such attempts should not be made if there is empirical evidence that they increase the likelihood of success with goals the parents do want, such as literacy. But it does mean that full discussion with the parents is essential. Nearly 20 years ago a UNESCO report on the use of vernacular languages in education said:

> Some people in a locality may be unmoved by the benefits to be derived from the use of the mother tongue in education and may be convinced that education in the mother tongue is to their disadvantage. We believe that educationists must carry public opinion with them if their policy is to be effective in the long run, since, in the last resort, the people of a country must always be in a position to express their free choice in the matter of the language in which their children are to be educated: and we urge that the educational authorities should make every effort to take the people into consultation and win their confidence. The problem will lose many of its elements of conflict if the people are confident that the use of languages in the educational system does not favor any section of the population at the expense of others. If the people as a whole will not accept the policy of education in the mother tongue, efforts should be exerted to persuade a group to accept it at least for experimental purposes. We believe that when the people as a whole have had an opportunity of observing the results of education in the mother tongue, they will be convinced that it is sound policy. (UNESCO 1953: 53–54)

Teachers. Discussions were held with teachers and teacher-aides from the same two preschools. Originally we planned to talk with teachers and aides separately, since the aides represent a distinct group in social class background and social mobility. But the resulting groups were so small, and the four aides so silent, that the staff groups were combined. We wondered whether their reluctance to speak may have been at least partly because language was an area of sensitivity in their own lives. It would be important to explore whether this is generally true for this new group of educational personnel. If so, their sensitivity may influence how they respond to children. Adults—whether teachers or parents—who are themselves anxious about language forms may pay more attention to the form of children's speech and less attention to the ideas the children are learning to express.

These teachers express more conflict about language than the parents did. Survival is the main thing, and "lots of times your mouth can help you." Within the black community, survival requires street language. Maybe it's an illusion—a myth with no basis in fact—that survival in relationship with the white community requires Standard English. And maybe we should be paying more attention to language for thinking and for creativity.

Alone among the three groups, some of the teachers referred to black people in the third person: "*their* way of talking," "black people, *they* also change," "*their* black language." Not all the teachers spoke this way. Even in these excerpts, one teacher speaks of the illusion that "*we*" can't make it in this world. Use of the third person may seem an expression of psychological distance, but we cannot be sure of its real meaning to speaker or listeners.

Community leaders. A group of five community leaders assembled by invitation for an evening meeting at Melissa Tillman's apartment in Roxbury.

In their roles as leaders, community leaders are further away from the direct socialization of young children than parents and teachers. Their concern is to reflect the current needs of the group in educational policy, and at the same time to institute those changes that will move the group forward. In comparison to both parents and teachers, and closer to the Mississippi civil rights workers, these leaders were more positive in their evaluation of Black English, and more openly resentful that it is always black people who have to change. "Survival" for them means not only economic survival in a white-dominated society but also psychological survival as a people. Language for intragroup solidarity, for "going home," is as important as language for "making it." And in education, the myth that language education is the way out is not only questioned but rejected. Control over the environment is critical. Language programs without that control are at best false hopes, and at worst insidious racism.

General comments. One of the limitations in this research is that our meta-language is too vague to refer to specific linguistic features. We can't be sure that any two speakers agree about what Black English is, or what features they reject or value. Various features were mentioned as examples during the discussions:

> Words: *Chunk* the ball.
> Idioms: You're a *cool cat*. Momma *broke your face*.
> Syntax: I *gots no* . . . . *Diane, she* . . . . Look at *hims hat*.
> Pronunciation: ". . . hit on the end of the tongue with a hammer."
> Prosodic features: rhythm; speaking "very flat and southern."

Experimental research is necessary to determine which features are most important for identification within and across groups. This information is essential for language planning.

Kochman (in press) distinguishes between two concepts of black dialect: "the linguistic or structuralist concept, which focuses on grammar, and the social or popular concept, which focuses on rhythm, intonation, and pronunciation." He suggests that "Blacks who do not grammatically speak Black dialect still can satisfy the 'ethnicity' of the Black Context by modifying the latter aspects," and cites Malcolm X's speech, Message to the Grass Roots, as an example. This seems to be the style that many national black spokesmen have adopted, and to which the teacher refers when she describes the people seen on TV who get their message across without speaking Standard English. She is probably not referring to people who speak a pure black dialect, but to people who have learned to speak so that their messages contain enough Standard English so that others can understand, but which at the same time signal to blacks their credibility. Effective use of the two dialects in this manner requires the speaker to use both self-consciously. Perhaps this is the skill that parents want their children to acquire.

Discussion by the community leaders of the hustler's use of language is important.

> People who have control of the language are hustlers. You know, they can really make it. You don't have to have any substance in terms of ideas—just rap a good game. In that context, language is very important.

Many researchers have commented on lower-class use of language for expressing group solidarity and contributing to it. Less often stressed is the use of language for social control and manipulation, especially in inter-group confrontations. Kochman summarizes a detailed analysis:

> The purpose for which language in *inter*-group contexts is used suggests that the speaker views those social situations as essentially agonistic, by which I mean that he sees his environment as consisting of a series of transactions which require that he be continually ready to take advantage of a person or defend himself against being victimized. He has absorbed what Horton calls 'street rationality.' (Kochman, in press)

We need to think about how the skills of using language for group solidarity and social manipulation can be exploited in education while we also nourish language for thinking more creatively (in the teacher's words) or "using language as an instrument for the free expression of thought and feeling" (N. Chomsky, n.d., p. 66). As suggested above, questions of language use are separable from questions of dialect. One could in principle use any dialect for any purpose. But because of functional specialization, it may be easier to use black dialect for some purposes and Standard English for others. Again, more information is needed for language planning.

Valentine (1969) suggests that the socialization of black children must be seen as "biculturation." Mitchell discusses some of the complexities of this process:

> Socialization for many Black Americans is a process during which an individual, while acquiring his culture, is also enculturated to its disadvantaged and negatively valued status for the wider culture of which he is also a part. To the extent that an aspect of Black culture is different from some corresponding aspect of Standard Average American culture, even when it enjoys normative status intraculturally, it may become stigmatized for some individuals due to their identification and desire to participate in the wider culture. The bi-cultural status of Black Americans makes the socialization process a time when each individual attempts to find some viable personal reconciliation to cultural patterns, values and attitudes which do not cohere or intersect in any consistent fashion. Some solutions find individuals essentially submerged in things Black, rejecting outside standards and valuations across the board. Others look outward toward the wider culture and still others straddle the two, selecting from either as the needs of the moment require. Language is an important reflector of these various positions. (Mitchell 1969:82–83)

Wolfram and Fasold (1969) suggested that increasing emphasis on racial pride is not yet extended to language. Obviously, changes in the social-political situation in this country will affect the biculturation process, and thereby also alter the language goals that black people hold for their children. Ways must be found to ensure that these changes are reflected in education.

Strategies for Nourishing Bidialectalism

If a decision is made to try to help children become bidialectal, what strategies are most likely to succeed? As Sledd (1969) makes clear, success stories are few. By-and-large, techniques have been adopted from foreign-language instruction, notably drills of all kinds. Even though American education has been largely unsuccessful in foreign-language teaching, we ignore that record and adapt the unsuccessful techniques to teaching a second dialect—and this, despite the fact that bidialectalism is probably harder to achieve than bilingualism.

One reason bidialectalism is harder is that the internal variation already present in many BE speakers' language raises important questions about what that speaker needs to learn. Ervin-Tripp (1971c) presented a full discussion of this point. Assume for the moment that we wish to "teach" a lower-class black speaker to pronounce all final consonants that constitute a separate morpheme, as in *washed*, at least in formal situations. What exactly does the speaker have to "learn": a new linguistic rule, consistent mastery of a skill, or enhanced motivation for accepting a particular norm? Obviously, decisions about curriculum strategies depend on selecting among these alternatives.

A detailed analysis of curriculum attempts to teach SE is outside the scope of this book. Here, only four general questions will be raised—about priorities in linguistic features; timing; selection of staff personnel and peer-group composition; and whether the goal should be changes in oral speech or in writing.

Linguistic Features

If the purpose of teaching Standard English is for its "Pygmalion effect," then educational programs should concentrate on those nonstandard features that are most crucial in eliciting negative reactions. Shuy, Wolfram, and Riley (1967) suggest that one index of such cruciality is the degree of social stratification of the linguistic features. For instance, there are greater social class differences in the use of multiple negation (*He can't hit nobody*) than in pronominal apposition (*The playground, it has all kinds of bars and stuff*). Shuy and his associates suggest that multiple negation is therefore more important in any SE curriculum.

Timing

Separate from questions of *what* to teach and *how* is the question of *when*. How much variation in speech patterns can children of various ages control? Do the assertions that foreign languages are harder to learn after early adolescence apply to learning a second dialect—learn in the sense of automatic production without the excessive strain of careful monitoring? If attitudes play a critical role in dialect-learning, at what age are those attitudes more likely to work *for* oral language instruction rather than against it? In summary, at what age are ability at switching, flexibility of motor control of articulation and grammatical patterns, and attitudes toward SE (as influenced by peer-group identification and/or vocational hopes) at optimal values for second-dialect instruction?

Selection of Adults and Peers

If providing models of Standard English is considered desirable, important questions are raised about school personnel and the composition of the peer group. How much weight should be given to the standardness of the speech patterns of adult staff members, and how much weight to other reasons for including adults indigenous to lower-class communities—such as on-the-job training for parents and future parents, counteraction of home-school alienation, and the participation of male adults in the schools? If family day care, in which one mother cares for several children in her own home, comes under more careful licensing, how much weight should be given to the mother's language in making licensing decisions? Criteria for selecting school personnel is shifting from dependence on formal educational credentials toward reliance on judgments of successful performance. Should there be any performance standards for speech? If so, what should they be?

And what about the composition of the peer group? We want to maximize the benefits from communication among children. How much can be gained in deseg-regated classrooms? Is it worth making a fight against present governmental funding policies, which usually result in preschool groups segregated by social class? So far, research evidence on the effects of heterogeneous classrooms on child language is equivocal. Perhaps children don't naturally interact across racial or social class lines as much as we hope or expect. Perhaps even if they do interact, attitudes influence which "models" are chosen. Perhaps teachers attend to and talk to the most verbal children, rather than the least verbal. We need more research in these classrooms themselves.

Speech or Writing

In other countries, attempts are also being made to teach a standard dialect. In England, one project to develop a language program for children of West Indian origin is directed by Jim Wight at the University of Birmingham. The program is planned for children from seven to nine years old because it is based in part on children's writing. It has two objectives:

> ... to help children to write Standard English—concentrating on the places where the West Indian dialect creates special difficulties for the child; and to improve the oral fluency and general communi-cation skills and confidence of the children. ... (Wight and Norris 1969:2–3)

Only the first objective will be discussed here.

In its approach to Standard English, the Birmingham project takes an interme-diate position between the extremes of "teaching English as a second language" on the one hand, and "leaving their dialect alone" on the other. In addition to the usual distinction between home language (in this case a Caribbean Creole) and school language (Standard English), Wight and Norris separate their goals for oral and written language and concentrate their efforts in trying to help children *write* Standard forms. According to Wight, no matter how you try to disguise it, if you suggest an alternative way of speaking, you are implicitly suggesting that something is wrong with what the child said in the first place. Moreover, written work is where children receive the most criticism for irregular forms. Grammatical deviations may be ignored by listeners, but the same deviations become glaringly obvious in written compositions. In Wight's program, oral drills are used for oral practice in forms needed in writing. "It is intended that these standard forms should be primarily associated in the child's mind with written English" (Wight and Norris 1969:27).

Three additional arguments in favor of practicing SE in written form can be suggested. First, as noted above, Taylor (1971) argues in favor of widening the range of pronunciations acceptable as SE to include Black English pronunciations as we now include all regional variations, thereby limiting SE to matters of gram-matical structure. In print, pronunciation automatically becomes irrelevant. Second, Kernan (in press) found that black high school students more easily accept the need for writing SE while considering as affected their peers' attempts at "proper" speech. Finally, one of the skills that working-class children most need to practice is the explicit communication of ideas without dependence on gestures or concrete referents. Written language imposes exactly that task.

Wight's project (Wight and Norris 1969) is developing some unusual puzzlelike materials for teaching Standard English morphology, such as the following for noun and verb agreement:

The cook	s	run

The cook	run	s

If one adds an *s* to the noun, then the only verb piece that fits is one that cannot itself take an *s*; if the noun is singular, then the matching verb piece has a space that must be filled by an *s*.

At first glance, it may seem inappropriate to use a mnemonic device to teach a linguistic rule. But as Wight pointed out (personal communication), this rule is a completely arbitrary, meaningless part of our language. If the visual shapes of words can aid learning, why not exploit them? Another good feature in the materials is that the original decision is made about the noun: is it plural or singular? Once that decision has been made, the shape of the noun determines the shape, literally, of the verb.

The incidence of nonstandard forms may not be the same in speech and writing, even for one child. De Stefano (in press) made one such comparison for a group of nine- to ten-year-old black children in a Philadelphia summer remedial program. Written compositions were obtained after a walk around the school neighborhood and compared with speech samples from tapes and written notes on the children's talk with peers and teachers. De Stefano found significant differences between the children's language in the two media. For example, verb forms constituted a higher proportion of all nonstandard forms in speech. Most dramatically, omission of the third-person singular *-s* accounted for 45 percent of all nonstandard speech forms, as in *he act nice*, but this form did not occur once in writing. De Stefano (in press) inferred that "it is more a phonological feature of Black English than a deep structural grammatical feature, due to its evidently fairly easy inclusion in writing but with little carryover in speech habits." One cannot conclude from her data that slower, more deliberate nature of the writing process will inevitably produce fewer nonstandard forms. Some items constituted a higher proportion of nonstandard forms in writing than in speech. For example, there were no recorded nonstandard possessive pronouns, but these accounted for 4 percent of the errors in writing, as in *They car* . . . . Perhaps spelling is the source of difficulty here, which in turn may be related to a tendency to drop final consonants in pronunciation. More such research should yield both insight on the status of particular features in a child's language system, and suggestions for curriculum.

Attitudes of Teachers

Previous sections have discussed the direct effects of a child's dialect on his intellectual and social experience. His education will also be affected indirectly through the effect of his speech patterns on his peers and his teachers. We do not know how early black children learn that their speech patterns are stigmatized in the larger society. Given the early age at which they show such responses as preferring white dolls (Porter 1971), we should expect an early realization of sociolinguistic facts of life as well. But children will be affected by the reactions of others, whether or not they are aware of them.

Evidence is accumulating that speech cues are one important source of the expectations teachers build up about their children's success in school. Williams in Chicago (1970, in press), and Shamo in Memphis (1970), found that teachers evaluate children more negatively when their speech has nonstandard pronunciation and syntax. Guskin (1970) found that Michigan teachers-in-training rated black speakers as less likely to succeed academically than white speakers. Seligman, Tucker, and Lambert (in press) found in Montreal that a recorded speech pattern or a child's photograph had more influence on third-grade teachers' ratings than the quality of a child's composition or drawing. Holmes, Holmes, and Friedman (1968) compared the evaluations of a Head Start teacher in Coney Island with observations and IQ tests of the children in her class. The teacher's ratings of her children's intelligence were not correlated with actual intelligence test scores, and they were biased by such actual behaviors as the child's willingness to respond to directions and his general verbal skills.

We do not know how to change such ethnocentric biases. See Campbell (1967) for one analysis of the general problem. Teachers' reactions are deeply founded in their own past experience. Part of that experience is simply living in a discriminatory society; but part is also what they have read and heard from psychologists and educators (for example, Cazden 1966) about "culturally disadvantaged children," as Labov (1970) has rightly pointed out. Although these problems were approached with the best of intentions, our analyses of cultural differences—no matter how accurate—may have contributed to teachers' lowered expectations for children's success, and thereby to self-fulfilling prophecies, by implying a causal relationship—which cannot be substantiated—between those cultural differences and school success. We have, in short, helped to "blame the victim" (Ryan 1971).

How can teachers' perceptions of their children be changed? Perhaps the kinds of "cultural therapy" that anthropologist George Spindler (1969) advocates for teacher education in general could help. Perhaps Bruce Fraser will be successful in his current effects at the Language Research Foundation in Cambridge, Massachusetts, to develop a curriculum for teachers specifically about language—their children's and their own. At some point, there is probably a limit to what words can convey. As Landes says in her report of a teacher-education project in California, "when educators talk more *about* pupils than *with* them and their families, separateness from the objects of discussion forfeits the experiences words should mirror" (1965:64).

Attitudes of linguistic chauvinism may also limit intergroup communication among children themselves. Bouchard (1969) found that on the basis of voice cues alone, middle-class fifth- and sixth-grade children ranked MC white speakers, LC white speakers, and LC black speakers in descending order on personality characteristics such as tall, trustworthy, intelligent, helpful, and friendly. On the other hand, there is current anecdotal evidence that those same features may under some circumstances be highly valued among white peers, especially in adolescence. In either case, educational efforts toward valuing speech differences as one reflection of cultural pluralism should enhance the likelihood of all children learning from each other. O'Neil suggests that "students (urban, suburban, rural) should have understanding of the naturalness of language differences" (1968:15) and tried to teach such a curriculum to Roxbury ninth graders (O'Neil in press). We don't know at what age such efforts would be most effective.

BILINGUALISM

The subject of childhood bilingualism deserves book-length treatment by itself; here it is given only a section at the end of a chapter. Since thorough treatment is impossible, it seemed better not to attempt a halfway job. Therefore, only a few important issues will be raised and sources of further discussion will be suggested. Through the selected references cited, the reader can trace back to most of the important literature. Discussion is organized in three sections: becoming a bilingual child; teaching a second language; and bilingual education.

Becoming a Bilingual Child

Some children learn two languages simultaneously; other children learn them sequentially, one language after another. There are still very few descriptions of either route toward becoming a bilingual child which match in detail and linguistic analysis the studies of first-language acquisition described in this book.

A classic study of simultaneous bilingualism is Leopold's four-volume diary (1939–1947; summarized in Leopold 1953) of his two daughters' learning of English and German in their first two years. In a review article on child language research through 1946, Leopold (1948) cites only three other studies: Geissler 1938, Pavlovitch 1920, Ronjat 1913. Since then, there is at least Burling's (1959) account of the almost simultaneous acquisition by his son Stephen of English and Garo, a nonwestern language in India.

Studies of children who successfully learn a second language when already speaking a first language should be even more relevant for educational planning. Unfortunately, studies of such sequential bilingualism seem, if anything, even rarer. One excellent study is Dato's (1970) syntactic analysis of the acquisition of Spanish by English-speaking children who went with their families to live in Madrid. As Dato points out.

> That children do indeed acquire a second language is borne out in the numerous accounts by parents visiting foreign countries for any extended periods of time.
>
> Although many of the accounts by parents are unfortunately anecdotal, we know that children learn to speak a second language, and that they do so within a relatively short time. If we were to entertain the hypothesis that a second language is learned by a child in a manner not unlike that of acquiring his first language, then we should be able, within a relatively short time, to gain a great deal of insight into second-language learning (Dato 1970:2).

During his first year in Madrid, Dato studied one four-year-old boy; in the second year, he added four more children (5½ to 6½ years old), all of whom were encountering Spanish for the first time. Dato's research techniques were partly derived from Brown's study of Adam, Eve and Sarah, and the analytic framework was that of transformational grammar.

For just the reasons that Dato gives, we need many more studies of natural second-language learning—both simultaneous and sequential—of English-speaking children learning other languages and of child speakers of other languages learning English. See Kelly (1969) for the proceedings of an international conference.

Teaching a Second Language

Becoming a bilingual child in the natural conversational environments described above is as dramatically successful as first-language acquisition. But the record of deliberate attempts to teach a second language in school presents an entirely different picture.

Currently, for social reasons, concern in the United States centers on teaching English to children from minority groups who speak a foreign language. The largest such groups speak Spanish or Navajo. For example, "it is estimated that more than one-sixth of the school-age population of the Southwest is Spanish-speaking [and] in New York City, Puerto Rican children . . . make up nearly one-fourth of the city's total elementary public school enrollment" (John and Horner 1971:1–2). In a recent survey, Spolsky (1970) found that 73 percent of six-year-old Navajo children did not know enough English for success in first grade. See Fishman et al. (1966) for further demographic and historical information. So far we have failed to help these children become bilingual, without or with the latest techniques for "teaching English as a second language," and their dropout rates are high (Campbell 1970). Hope for the future may lie in different methods of teaching a second language, or in bilingual education of which learning English would be one part, or both.

In an important article, Ervin-Tripp challenges the assumptions underlying second-language teaching:

> I think two major changes have taken place in our views of language acquisition in recent years. One is that we now are beginning to see the functions of language in the life of the speaker as of far more importance in its acquisition than we had realized, and the other is that the mechanical view that practice makes perfect has given way under the impact of evidence that speechless children can have well developed language [a reference to a case study by Lenneberg]. (Ervin-Tripp 1970:314)

On the process of language development, two questions have been raised about implications for education: whether adults who are trying to be helpful should attend to a child's meaning or to his superficial forms; and whether sequencing of instruction plays an important role. On these two issues, natural language acquisition and second-language teaching diverge sharply. In the former, as argued earlier in this book, the child is a full participant in conversation from the beginning, adults respond to his intended meaning, and no one attempts to segment, organize, and sequence all that he eventually must learn. In second-language teaching, by contrast, adults attend to how children talk, not what they are trying to say, and assume that "organization of input, plus practice, will have predictable results" (Ervin-Tripp 1971:315). It should be possible to design an educational environment that reactivates the natural language-learning abilities which all children have. Dodson, Price, and Tundo (1968) present a detailed account, including two case histories of individual children, of an infant school in Wales in which Welsh was the medium of conversation in the afternoons, but no "Welsh lessons" were given.

Reactivating language-learning abilities necessarily means harnessing children's motivations as well. Here, as much as in teaching strategies, is where the problems of minority-group children may lie. At least that seems to be the implication of one success story of second-language learning in school. Lambert, Just, and Segalowitz (1971) describe two classes of monolingual English children in Montreal who received their first years of schooling entirely in French. The kindergarten program, which the authors think may be crucial, "conducted almost entirely in French by two very skilled and experienced teachers from Europe, stressed vocabulary development and listening comprehension through art, music and play, and encouraged spontaneous verbal expression in French" (Lambert, Just, and Segalowitz 1971:233). French was the only language used from first grade on.

> The results of the experiment to date indicate that the type of bilingual training offered these children is extremely effective, even more so than was originally expected. The similarity of the findings for two different sets of classes, involving changes in teachers' methods of instruction, and modes of testing and analysis, speaks well for the stability and generality of the effects produced by the experimental program. These effects demonstrate a very high level of skill in both receptive and productive aspects of French, the major language of instruction; a generally excellent command of all aspects of English, the home language of the children; and a high level of skill in a nonlanguage subject matter, mathematics, taught through the foreign language only. (Lambert, Just, and Segalowitz 1971:229-230)

Furthermore, the children transferred what they had learned about reading from French to English with little trouble.

Ervin-Tripp asks the obvious question: Why does being taught in a foreign language work for these Montreal children and fail for Chicano, Puerto Rican, and Navajo children in the United States? In her words, "the differences are social" (1971:314). In commenting on the same contrast, Haugen agrees—

> We need to think in terms of dominant and nondominant, but these are terms we don't like to talk about because they are ultimately political. . . . It makes a great deal of difference whether the schools are teaching the children a language that is nondominant or one that is dominant, because the children are sensitive to the pressure of society through their parents and their peers. I think the opposition of dominant and nondominant is so important that I wonder if Lambert's good results may not be accounted for by the fact that he is teaching the members of a dominant group a nondominant language which has potentialities of dominance, while in Texas or New Mexico we are teaching a dominent language to a nondominant group. This alters the educational picture totally. (Haugen, discussion in Alatis, 1971:310)

The same conclusions about the importance of attitudes was reached by Tax and his colleagues in the Carnegie Corporation Cross Cultural Education Project of the University of Chicago (Tax and Thomas 1969; Walker 1965, 1969) which was concerned not with teaching English but with raising the literacy level of Cherokees in eastern Oklahoma. Cherokee history is particularly interesting because in the nineteenth century they had been 90 percent literate in their native language—using a writing system developed in 1819 by Sequoyah, a Cherokee with no formal education— and they were more literate in English than neighboring white communities in Texas and Arkansas (Walker 1969). Walker suggests what it would take to regain this status:

> It seems clear that the startling decline during the past sixty years of both English and Cherokee literacy in the Cherokee tribe is chiefly a result of the recent scarcity of reading materials in Cherokee and of the fact that learning to read has become associated with coercive instruction, particularly in the context of an alien and threatening school presided over by English speaking teachers and controlled by English speaking superintendents and P.T.A.'s which conceive of Cherokee as a "dying" language and Cherokee school children as "culturally impoverished" candidates for rapid and "inevitable" social assimilation. Indians and whites alike are constantly equating social competence in the school with assimilation into the middle class. . . .
> For the Cherokee community to become literate once again, Cherokees must be convinced that literacy does not imply the death of their society, that education is not a clever device to wean children away from the tribe. This is not a uniquely Cherokee situation. Identical attitudes toward education and the school no doubt can be found in Appalachia, in urban slums, in Afro-Asia, and, indeed, in all societies where the recruitment of individuals into the dominant society threatens the extinction of a functioning social group. (Walker 1965:10)

Bilingual Education

Gaarder defines bilingual education as "a school which uses, concurrently, two languages as mediums of instruction in any portion of the curriculum except the languages themselves" (1967:110). In reality, the term covers a wide range of practices. See John and Horner (1970, 1971) and Gaarder (1971) for reviews of recent programs in this country; G. R. Tucker (1970) for a description of one project in the Philippines; and Dodson, Price, and Tundo (1968), mentioned earlier, about an infant school in Wales.

One important aspect of most bilingual programs is teaching initial literacy in the child's native language. Arguments for doing this have been made for some time. See UNESCO (1953) and Bull's (1955) critical book review, Macnamara (1967) for a general review of the topic, and Modiano (1968) for one comparative study in Mexico. Some arguments for initial literacy in the child's first language apply whatever the first and second languages may be. But similarities and differences between the two should be considered. For instance, because Spanish orthography is simpler than English, it is almost certainly preferable for Spanish-speaking children to learn to read first in Spanish. For speakers of Chinese, on the other hand, the extent of transfer or interference is less certain. C. A. Tucker (1969) suggests that memorizing hundreds of "words" may make it harder to learn to read with an alphabet; according to Kolers, however, "The idea that the skilled reading of even alphabetic languages involves the interpretation of symbol systems implies that the reading of Chinese and the reading of English have more in common than would at first appear" (1970:118). Venezky (1970) reviews research on beginning reading materials for speakers of both nonstandard dialects and other languages.

Too often, "bilingual education" is only a euphemistic name for new means to the old goals of teaching children to speak and read the dominant language, in our case English, as fast as possible. The clue to true bilingual education is whether the concurrent use of two languages continues through the school grades, or whether the non-English language gradually drops out year by year. Many of the strongest advocates of bilingual education see it as far more than a means to such narrow ends. In the preceding quotation, Walker spoke for the goals of increased self-identity for minority people. Others, such as Fishman, stress the goal of a truly multilingual and multicultural society:

> The day is coming when more and more genuine bilingual education, for all who want it, regardless of income, mother tongue or language dominance, will be part of the variegated picture of American education. At that time it will not be a mere euphemism for programs in English as a Second Language which, though unquestionably essential, constitute only one part and one kind of dual language education. It will not be just a promissory note to the poor, nor a left-handed contribution to increasingly vocal and organized (though still exploited and dispossessed) Hispanos and Indians. It will be available to my children and grandchildren, and to yours, because it is too good to keep it from all the people. (Fishman 1970:53)

Obviously, school alone cannot achieve a multilingual society. Their success will depend on sociolinguistic aspects of language use in the community, and they must be evaluated in relation to that social context. That is what Ervin-Tripp and Haugen were saying about the success of Lambert and his associates in Montreal. See Fishman et al. (1968) for the study of one Puerto Rican community in New Jersey. And see O'Huallachain (1970) and Macnamara (1966) on Irish attempts to use bilingual education to revive an "ancestral" language.

But influences do operate in the other direction, too, from school to society as well as from society to school. That is what the Irish government is hoping for. And it is the point of a news item in the (London) *Times Educational Supplement* on the Welsh Language Society's campaign to deface road signs printed only in English. Evidently some teachers had been active in this campaign. After a strong statement on behalf of acts that do not violate public opinion even if they violate the law, the reporter urged the local education committees not to take action against these teachers:

> I should have thought it is ridiculous that children whose mother tongue is Welsh should grow up hearing one set of place names in the tongues of their families but always seeing another, English form on road signs and in official use.
> The same goes for all the words used in public notices and so forth. What sense does it make for an education committee to teach Welsh in its schools (unless it thinks of it as a dead language) and at the same time show no concern for the public status and use of the language. (Thomas, *Times Educational Supplement*, 9 May 1969)

In the United States, too—through its influence on children, teachers, and parents —bilingual education can affect both speech behavior and attitudes toward language outside school as well.

REFERENCES

Alatis, J. E. *Twenty-first annual round table: bilingualism and language contact.* Monograph Series on Languages and Linguistics, No. 23, Washington, D.C.: Georgetown University Press, 1970.

Baratz, J. C., and Shuy, R. W. *Teaching black children to read.* Washington, D.C.: Center for Applied Linguistics, 1969.

Bernstein, B. A socio-linguistic approach to socialization: with some reference to educability. In J. Gumperz & D. Hymes (eds.), *Research in sociolinguistics.* New York: Holt, Rinehart and Winston, in press. (b)

Blom, G. E.; Waite, R. R.; and Zimet, S. G. A motivational content analysis of children's primers. In H. Lavin & J. F. Williams (eds.), *Basic studies in reading.* New York: Basic Books, 1970.

Bouchard, E. L. Psycholinguistic attitude study. Ann Arbor: University of Michigan Center for Research on Language and Language Behavior, Progress Report No. VIII, February 1969.

Brown, R. *A first language.* Cambridge, Mass.: Harvard University Press, in press.

Bull, W. A. The use of vernacular languages in fundamental education. *International Journal of American Linguistics,* 1955, *21,* 288–94; Reprinted in D. Hymes (ed.), *Language in Culture and Society.* New York: Harper & Row, 1964. pp. 527–33.

Burling, R. Language development of a Garo and English-speaking child. *Word,* 1959, *15,* 45–68. (Reprinted in Bar-Adon & Leopold 1971.)

Burling, R. *Man's many voices: language in its cultural context.* New York: Holt, Rinehart and Winston, 1970.

Campbell, D. T. Stereotypes and the perception of group differences. *American Psychologist,* 1967, *22,* 817–29.

Campbell, R. N. English curricula for non-English speakers. In J. E. Alatis (ed.), *Twenty-first annual roundtable: bilingualism and language contact.* Washington, D.C.: Georgetown University Press, 1970.

Cazden, C. B. Environmental assistance to the child's acquisition of grammar. Unpublished doctoral dissertation, Harvard University, 1965.

Cazden, C. B.; Bryant, B. H.; and Tillman, M. A. Making it and going home: the attitudes of Black people toward language education. *Harvard Graduate School of Education Association Bulletin,* Spring 1970, *14,* (3), 4–9.

Chomsky, N. *Form and meaning in natural language.* Amsterdam: North-Holland, n.d.

Chukovsky, K. *From two to five.* Berkeley: University of California Press, 1963.

Cicirelli, V., et. al. The impact of Head Start: an evaluation of the effects of Head Start on children's cognitive and affective development. Vols. I and II. Bladensburg, Md.: Westinghouse Learning Corp., 1969. (Distributed by Clearinghouse for Federal Scientific and Technical Information.)

Dato, D. P.   *American children's acquisition of Spanish syntax in the Madrid environment* (preliminary ed.).   U.S. Department of Health, Education and Welfare, Office of Education, May 1970. (Available from Georgetown University Bookstore, Washington, D.C.)

Davis, O.; Gladney, M.; and Leaverton, L.   *The psycholinguistics reading series, Books 1–7.* Chicago: Board of Education, 1968.

Davis, O.; Gladney, M.; & Leaverton, L.   *The psycholinguistics reading series: a bidialectal approach. Teachers Manual.* Chicago: Board of Education, 1969.

De Stefano, J. S.   Productive language differences in fifth grade Black students' syntactic forms. *Elementary English,* in press.

Dobzhansky, T.   Of flies and men. *American Psychologist,* 1967, *22,* 41–48.

Dodson, C. J.; Price, E.; and Tundo, I.   *Towards bilingualism: studies in language teaching methods.* Cardiff: University of Wales Press, 1968.

Education Study Center *Ollie.* Washington, D.C.: Author. 1970.

Ervin-Tripp, S.   Discourse agreement: how children answer questions. In J. R. Hayes (ed.), *Cognition and the development of language.* New York: Wiley, 1970. Pp. 79–107. (a)

Ervin-Tripp, S.   Structure and process in language acquisition. In J. E. Alatis (ed.), *Twenty-first annual round table: bilingualism and language contact.* Washington, D.C.: Georgetown University Press, 1970. Pp. 313–44. (b)

Ervin-Tripp, S.   Social background and verbal skills. In R. Huxley and E. Ingram (eds.), *Language development: models and methods.* New York: Academic Press, 1971. Pp. 29–39. (a)

Ervin-Tripp, S.   Social dialects in developmental sociolinguistics. In R. Shuy (ed.), *Sociolinguistics: a cross-disciplinary perspective.* Washington, D.C.: Center for Applied Linguistics, 1971. Pp. 35–64. (b)

Ferguson, C. A.   Myths about Arabic. In A. F. C. Wallace (ed.). *Men and cultures.* Philadelphia: University of Pennsylvania Press, 1956. (Reprinted in J. Fishman (ed.) *Readings in the sociology of language.* The Hague: Mouton, 1968, Pp. 375–81.)

Fisher, J. L.   Social influence in the choice of a linguistic variant. *Word,* 1958, *14,* 47–54.   Reprinted in D. Hymes (ed.), *Language in culture and society,* New York: Harper & Row, 1964. Pp. 483–88.

Fishman, J. A.   *Sociolinguistics.*   Rowley, Mass.: Newbury House, 1970.   (a)

Fishman, J. A.   The politics of bilingual education. In J. E. Alatis (ed.), *Twenty-first annual round table: bilingualism and language contact.* Monograph Series on Language and Linguistics, No. 23. Washington, D.C.: Georgetown University Press, 1970. Pp. 47–54. (b)

Fishman, J. A., et al. *Language loyalty in the United States.* The Hague: Mouton, 1966. (Summarized briefly in Fishman 1965.)

Fishman, J. A., et al. *Bilingualism in the barrio.* 2 vols. U.S. Department of Health, Education and Welfare, Office of Education, August 1968.

Fraser, C.; Bellugi, U.; and Brown, R.   Control of grammer in imitation, comprehension and production. *Journal of Verbal Learning and Verbal Behavior,* 1963, *2,* 121–35.

Gaarder, A. B.   Organization of the bilingual school. *Journal of Social Issues,* 1967, *23,* 110–20.

Gaarder, A. B.   The first seventy-six bilingual education projects. In J. E. Alatis (ed.), *Twenty-first annual round table: bilingualism and language contact.* Washington, D. C.: Georgetown University Press, 1971. Pp. 163–75.

Garvey, C., & McFarlane, P. T.   A preliminary study of Standard English speech patterns in the Baltimore city public schools. The Johns Hopkins University Center for the Study of Social Organization of Schools, Report No. 16, 1968.

Geissler, H.   *Zweisprachigkeit deutscher Kinder in Ausland.*   Stuttgart, 1938.

Guskin, J. T.   The social perception of language variations: Black and white teachers' attitudes towards speakers from different racial and social class backgrounds.   Unpublished doctoral dissertation, University of Michigan, 1970.

Haugen, E.   Language planning in modern Norway. *Anthropological Linguistics,* 1959, *1* (3), 8–21. Reprinted in J. Fishman (ed.), *Readings in the sociology of language.* The Hague: Mouton, 1968. Pp. 673–87.

Henrie, S. N., Jr.   A study of verb phrases used by five year old nonstandard Negro English-speaking children.   Unpublished doctoral dissertation, University of California at Berkeley, 1969.

Holmes, M. B.; Holmes, D.; and Friedman, A.   Interaction patterns as a source of error in teacher's evaluations of Head Start children.   Final report to OEO. New York: Associated YM-YWHAs of Greater New York, August 1968.

John, V., and Horner, V. M. Bilingualism and the Spanish-speaking child. In F. Williams (ed.), *Language and poverty: perspectives on a theme*. Chicago:Markham, 1970.

John V., and Horner, V. M. *Early childhood bilingual education*. New York: Modern Language Association, 1971.

John, V.; Horner, V.; and Berney, T. Story re-telling. In H. Levin and J. P. Williams (eds.), *Basic studies in reading*. New York: Harper & Row, 1970. Pp. 246-62.

Johnson, K. A report on research to determine if Black children can read dialect with fewer errors and greater comprehension than standard English dialect. Paper presented at annual meeting of Teachers of English to Speakers of Other Languages, New Orleans, March 1971.

Jones, V. W. The Alaskan reading and language development program. Paper read at meeting of American Educational Research Association, Minneapolis, 1970.

Katz, J. Semi-sentences. In J. Katz and J. Fodor (eds.), *The structure of language*. Englewood Cliffs, N.J.: Prentice-Hall, 1964.

Kelly, L. G. (ed.) *Bilingualism: description and measurement—an international seminar*. Toronto: University of Toronto Press in association with the Canadian National Commission for UNESCO, 1969.

Kernan, C. M. On the status of Black English for native speakers: an assessment of attitudes and values. In C. B. Cazden, V. P. John, and D. Hymes (eds.), *Functions of language in the classroom*. New York: Teachers College Press, in press.

Kochman, T. Social factors in the consideration of teaching standard English. Paper read at convention of Teachers of English to Speakers of Other Languages (TESOL). Chicago: March 1969.

Kochman, T. Black English in the classroom. In C. B. Cazden, D. Hymes, and V. John (eds.), *The functions of language in the classroom*. New York: Teachers College Press, in press.

Kolers, P. A. Three stages of reading. In H. Levin and J. P. Williams (eds.), *Basic studies in reading*. New York: Basic Books, 1970. Pp. 90-118.

Labov, W. The effect of social mobility on linguistic behavior. *Sociological Inquiry*, 1966, *36*, 186-203. (a)

Labov, W. *The social stratification of English in New York City*. Washington, D.C.: Center for Applied Linguistics, 1966. (c)

Labov, W. The logic of non-standard English. *The Florida FL Reporter*, 1969, 7 (1), 60-74. (a)

Labov, W. Some sources of reading problems for Negro speakers of non-standard English. In J. C. Baratz and R. W. Shuy (eds.), *Teaching Black children to read*. Washington, D.C.: Center for Applied Linguistics, 1969. Pp. 29-67. (b)

Labov, W. *The study of non-standard English*. Washington, D.C.: Clearing-house for Linguistics, Center for Applied Linguistics, 1969. (e) (Available from the ERIC Document Reproduction Service.)

Labov, W. The reading of the -*ed* suffix. In H. Levin and J. P. Williams (eds.), *Basic studies in reading*. New York: Basic Books, 1970. Pp. 222-45.

Labov, W. and Cohen, P. Systematic relations of standard and non-standard rules in the grammars of Negro speakers. *Project Literacy Reports* No. 8. Ithaca, N.Y.: Cornell University, 1967. Pp. 66-84.

Labov, W.; Cohen, P.; Robins, C.; and Lewis, J. A study of the non-standard English of Negro and Puerto Rican speakers in New York City. Vol. 1, Phonological and grammatical analysis. Vol. 2. The use of language in the speech community. Final report of Cooperative Research Project No. 3288. Columbia University, 1968. (To be distributed through ERIC.)

Labov, W., and Robins, C. A note on the relation of reading failure to peer-group status in urban ghettos. *The Record—Teachers College*, 1969, 70, 395-405.

Lambert, W. E.; Just, M.; and Segalowitz, N. Some cognitive consequences of following the curricula of the early school grades in a foreign language. In J. E. Alatis (ed.), *Twenty-first round table: bilingualism and language contact*. Washington, D.C.:Georgetown University Press, 1970.

Landes, R. *Culture in American Education*. New York: Wiley, 1965.

Leopold, W. F. *Speech development of a bilingual child: a linguistic record*. 4 vols. Evanston, Ill.: Northwestern University Press, 1939-1947.

Leopold, W. F. The study of child language and infant bilingualism. *Word*, 1948, 4, 1-17. (Reprinted in Bar-Adon & Leopold, 1971.)

Lesser, G. S.; Fifer, G.; and Clark, D. H. Mental abilities of children in different social and cultural groups. *Monograph of Social Research and Child Development*, 1965, *30*, No. 4 (Serial No. 102).

MacNamara, J. *Bilingualism and primary education: a study of the Irish experience*. Edinburgh: Edinburgh University Press, 1966.

MacNamara, J. The effects of instruction in a weaker language. *Journal of Social Issues*, 1967, *23*(2), 121–35.

McNeill, D. Production and perception: the view from language. In D. R. Olson and S. M. Pagliuso (eds.), From perceiving to performing: an aspect of cognitive growth. *Ontario Journal of Educational Research*, 1968, *10*, 181–85.

Mitchell, C. I. Language behavior in a black urban community. Unpublished doctoral dissertation, University of California at Berkeley, 1969.

Modiano, N. National or mother language in beginning reading: a comparative study. *Research in the Teaching of English*, 1968, *1*, 32–43.

O'Huallachain, C. Bilingual education program in Ireland: recent experiences in home and adult support, teacher training, provision of instructional materials. In J. E. Alatis (ed.), *Twenty-first round table: bilingualism and language contact*. Washington, D.C.: Georgetown University Press, 1970. Pp. 178–93.

Olson, P. A. Introduction. *The craft of teaching and the school of teachers*. Report of the first national conference, U.S. Office of Education Tri-University Project in Elementary Education, Denver, September 1967.

O'Neil, W. A. Paul Roberts' rules of order: the misuses of linguistics in the classroom. *The Urban Review*, 1968, *2*(7), 12–16.

O'Neil, W. A. *On the way to M.I.T. one day: essays on linguistics and education*. Englewood Cliffs, N.J.: Prentice-Hall, in press.

Pavlovitch, M. *Le langage enfantin: acquisition du serbe et du francais par un enfant serbe*. Paris, 1920.

Porter, J. D. R. *Black child, white child: the development of racial attitudes*. Cambridge, Mass.: Harvard University Press, 1971.

Rainey, M. Style switching in a Head Start class. University of California at Berkeley, Language and Behavior Research Laboratory, Working Paper No. 16, 1969.

Ronjat, J. *Le dévelopment du langage observé chez un enfant bilingue*. Paris, 1913.

Ryan, W. *Blaming the victim*. New York: Pantheon, 1971.

Rystrom, R. The effects of standard dialect training on Negro first-graders learning to read. Concord, Calif.: Diablo Valley College. Final Report, 1968.

Seligman, C. R.; Tucker, G. R.; and Lambert, W. E. The effects of speech style and other attributes on teachers' attitudes toward pupils. *Language in Society*, in press.

Serwer, B. L. Linguistic support for a method of teaching beginning reading to Black children. *Reading Research Quarterly*, 1969, *14*, 449–67.

Shamo, G. W. The psychological correlates of speech characteristics of sounding "disadvantaged", a southern replication. Paper presented at Annual Convention of American Educational Research Association, Minneapolis, March 1970.

Shuy, R. W.; Wolfram, W. A.; and Riley, W. K. Linguistic correlates of social stratification in Detroit speech. Final report, Cooperative Research Project 6–1347, Wayne State University, 1967. (To be distributed through ERIC.)

Sledd, J. Bi-dialectalism: the linguistics of white supremacy. *English Journal*, 1969, *58*, 1307–1315.

Spolsky, B. Navajo language maintenance: six-year-olds in 1969. *Language Sciences*, No. 13, December 1970, 19–24.

Stewart, W. A. Current issues in the use of Negro dialect in beginning reading texts. *The Florida FL Reporter*, 1970, *8*(1–2), 3–7ff.

Tax, S. and Thomas, R. K. Education "for" American Indians: threat or promise. *The Florida FL Reporter*, 1969, *7*(1), 15–19ff.

Taylor, O. L. Social dialects and the field of speech: response to F. Williams. In R. Shuy (ed.), *Sociolinguistics: a cross-disciplinary perspective*. Washington, D.C.: Center for Applied Linguistics, 1971. Pp. 13–20.

Torrey, J. W. Learning to read without a teacher: a case study. *Elementary English*, 1969, *46*, 550–56. (a)

Torrey, J. W. Teaching Standard English to speakers of other dialects. Paper presented at Second International Congress of Applied Linguistics, Cambridge, England, September 1969. (b)

Tucker, C. A. The Chinese immigrant's language handicap: its extent and its effect. *The Florida FL Reporter*, 1969, *7*(1), 44–45ff.

Tucker, G. R. An alternate days approach to bilingual education. In J. E. Alatis (ed.), *Twenty-first annual round table: bilingualism and language contact*. Washington, D.C.: Georgetown University Press, 1970. Pp. 281–95.

UNESCO. *The use of vernacular languages in education*. Paris: UNESCO, 1953. Pp. 53–54.

Valentine, C. A.   Deficit, difference, and bicultural models of Afro-American behavior. *Harvard Educational Review*, 1971, *41*, 137–57.

Venezky, R. L.   Nonstandard language and reading. *Elementary English*, 1970, *47*, 334–345.

Walker, W.   An experiment in programmed cross-cultural education: the import of the Cherokee primer for the Cherokee community and for the behavioral sciences.   Wesleyan University, Middleton, Connecticut.   Mimeo, March 1965.

Walker, W.   Notes on native writing systems and the design of native literacy programs. *Anthropological Linguistics*, 1969, *11*, 148–65.

Wight, J., and Norris, R. A.   *Teachings of English to West Indian Children*. Report No. 2, University of Birmingham School of Education, 1969.

Williams, F.   Psychological correlates of speech characteristics: on sounding "disadvantaged." *Journal of Speech and Hearing Research*, in press.

Wolfram, W.   Social dialects from a linguistic perspective: assumptions, current research, and future directions.   In R. Shuy (ed.), *Sociolinguistics: a cross-disciplinary perspective*.   Washington, D.C.: Center for Applied Linguistics, in press. 1971. Pp. 86–135.

Wolfram, W. A., and Fasold, R. W.   Toward reading materials for speakers of black English: three linguistically appropriate passages.   In J. C. Baratz & R. W. Shuy (eds.), *Teaching black children to read*.   Washington, D.C.: Center for Applied Linguistics, 1969. Pp. 138–55.

25 / "Teaching" Them Children to Talk

Martha Coonfield Ward

KATHY: Go store Mommy.
MOTHER: Oh, you want to go to the store?
KATHY: Go now.
MOTHER: We can't go now. We have to eat dinner.
KATHY: Eat dinner.

MOTHER: Sing something what Jame Brown just sing.
    What Jame Brown just sing?
    What James Brown just sing, Forry?
CHILD: *(Sings.)*
MOTHER: What else Jame Brown sing? What else he sing? What he sing?
CHILD: Jame Brown say "I'm black and proud."
MOTHER: What he say?
FORTREL: Black and proud! Black and proud!
MOTHER: Jame Brown say what?
CHILD: Black and proud!
MOTHER: And what else he say?

The first tape (recorded by the author) was taken from a white middle-class family; the second from a Rosepoint family. As we shall see from similar conversations, there are differences in the manner in which the Rosepoint mothers and middle-class mothers perceive their role as "teacher." Sometimes this interpretation has subtle linguistic consequences. Children of both types of families acquire language and the ability to communicate within their own communities; but the pattern of their socialization is distinct. This chapter will survey instruction in the mechanics of language itself, instruction in the social context for using language, and the unconscious learning about basic postulates of the culture which result from different forms of instruction.

EXPANSIONS

It has been postulated by some observers that a child approximates well-formed syntax by repeating an utterance or partial utterance of an adult or in turn having his telegraphic speech expanded into an acceptable sentence.

> There is one respect in which parental speech is not random. Quite often adults repeat the speech of small children and, in so doing, change the children's sentences into the nearest well-formed adult equivalent. Brown has called this phenomenon "expansion of child speech" (Brown 1964). It is a kind of imitation in reverse, in which the parent echoes the child and, at the same time, supplies features that are missing from the child's sentence. (McNeill 1966:73)

These expansions were given much attention because they appeared so frequently in the speech of the adults and children studied by Brown and Bellugi (1964); Miller and Ervin (1964); and Braine (1963).

> The mothers of Adam and Eve responded to the speech of their children with expansions about 30 percent of the time . . . A reduced or incomplete English sentence seems to constrain the English-speaking adult to expand it into the nearest properly formed complete sentence. (Brown and Bellugi 1964:144)

A middle-class American adult is seldom able to resist turning "Daddy bye-bye" into "Daddy's gone bye-bye." Frequently, a declarative intonation serves to validate the child's observation, while a rising, "Daddy's gone bye-bye?" serves as a communication check.

Typical child sentences and their expansions follow:

This ring.	This is a round ring.
Donnie all-gone.	Is Donnie all-gone?
It a bus.	Is it a bus?

(Ervin 1966:168)

No native speaker of English could confuse the mother's expansions with the baby's sentences. Not surprisingly, whole grammars of these utterances have been written in an attempt to equate the expansions with linguistic input and output.

If parental expansion of child speech contributed significantly to adult norms of grammar, the situation of the children of Rosepoint would be lamentable. In less than five per cent of the total utterances recorded were reciprocal expansions clearly operative in either child's or parents' speech. The mothers occasionally enhance the pivot structures of the younger children, but not with the same frequency as would a middle-class adult. Three, four, and five morpheme sentences from older children were repeated or expanded with even less frequency. To illustrate: the middle-class mothers of Adam and Eve (Brown's subject-children) would find it difficult, if not impossible, to spend an entire day with two-, three-, and four-year-olds without expanding or repeating a single utterance of the children. To do so is a part of their native speaker's intuition.

The mothers in the present study spend entire days in this manner and suffer not at all from a thwarted instinct. That is not to say that once in a while they do not expand or repeat a child's utterance in the same way as do Adam's or Eve's mother, but rather that such responses occur infrequently and without any evident compulsion.

A closer look at Brown and Bellugi's *Adam* transcripts explains the difference. Below is reproduced a segment of Adam's first record. Adam is at this point twenty-seven months old.

ADAM	MOTHER
See truck, Mommy.	Did you see the truck?
See truck.	No, you didn't see it. There goes one.
No I see truck.	
	Yes, there goes one.
There go one. See a truck. See truck, Mommy. See truck. Truck.	
Put truck, Mommy. Put truck window.	Put the truck where? I think that one's too large to go in the window.

(Brown and Bellugi 1966:135)

Now note their comments on this speech sample.

> The dialogue between mother and child does not read like a transcribed dialogue between two adults . . . The conversation is, in the first place, very much in the here and now. (Brown and Bellugi 1966:134)

Whatever its shortcomings, this little recording is clearly a conversation and a dialogue, but one type specific to mother-child interaction in this subculture.

Compare with the following. The child here is a thirty-six months old, eighth of eight children, and son of a factory worker.

> KENNETH: Mama, look, a train.
> MOTHER: Yeah, Kenneth, I see it.

The child's attempt at initiating this conversation is quite like Adam's method, yet the responses of the mothers differ radically.

> MOTHER: You pissy.
> KENNETH: *(He says nothing; he knows it.)*
> MOTHER: You piss in your pant.
> KENNETH: *(Smiles.)*
> MOTHER: You shame you piss in your pant?
> KENNETH: No.
> MOTHER: You should be.

Kenneth's mother is remarking in a sweet and gentle way; it may be a turn off, but not a put down.

In the next dialogue, a tape recording of a mother and her twenty-eight-month-old son, she initiates the conversation, determines the subject matter and direction. The lack of verbal reciprocity would seem to negate this as a conversation. However, the mother is pleased with its communicative success. The conversation is typical of mother-child interaction in Rosepoint.

MOTHER: Say, Mark, quit it.
           Say, Mark, quit it!
           Say, Mark, quit it!!
(She remarks that children pretend to be deaf when they do not want to listen.)
MOTHER: Mark, oh Mark, come give your mother a kiss.
           Mark, oh Mark, come give your mother a kiss.
           Mark, oh Mark, come give mama a kiss.
(She gets no response at all.)
MOTHER: Oh, nobody to kiss me.
(She tries a new tact.)
MOTHER: Mark, take this belt to Cicero.
(After a long pause, Mark, attracted by her root beer, comes and sits on her lap. She shares her drink with him from the bottle.)
MOTHER: Mark, give me a kiss. He shame to kiss his mother in front of Joan. Mark, you shame to kiss mama in front of Joan?[1] (He still doesn't kiss her.)*

They watch a soap opera together. Later he tries to attract her attention by biting and kissing her.

The fundamental attitude of Kenneth's and Mark's mothers in these conversations is that *children do not function to uphold their end of the conversation.* Neither mother sees any point in training herself or her child to conduct a conversation on such minutiae as trucks and trains. As the taping sessions proved, the mothers were virtual strangers in talking to their children where talk for the sake of talk was required. She responds to questions and requests with as full a measure of love as does Adam's mother. She addresses him with the complete range of affects from rage to admiration, but she will not cater to his verbal whims. Small children learning to talk are not the sort of people with whom Rosepoint adults "engage in dialogue."

If a child has something important to say, his mother will listen, and he had better listen when she decides to tell him something. But for conversation, per se, for the sound of a human voice, she will go visiting, make phone calls, have company, or in sheer desperation talk to an older child (eight or above). She will never find herself politely trapped, as will Adam's mother, by the verbal precocity of a three year old, with whom one cannot honestly discuss an interesting issue.

Adam's mother is committed to talking with him often, an activity which involves expanding and imitating his speech as much as possible. This technique does not necessarily teach him language since children whose parents do not expand their utterances also learn to talk. With or without indirect instruction, the child learns that "no I see truck" becomes "I don't see the truck."

Just as Kenneth and Adam learn two different dialects of English, they also learn two different sociolinguistic dialects. The verbal tricks which Adam learns from his mother will stand him in better stead at middle-class schools than the verbal tricks Kenneth learns from his mother. Kenneth has not learned how to initiate and monopolize a conversation with an adult on a topic of his choosing. Mark has never been awarded for verbal advances; no one expects him to say more than the bare minimum. Boys growing up in Rosepoint do not fill in the bare spaces of time with talk. No one in the community takes seriously the chattering of a child. In fact, as the conversations indicate, the children hold their parent's attention longer *if they say nothing.*

Kenneth and Mark have learned to amuse themselves, to sit very still and listen to adults talk, (timed at three hours on several occasions), and to play happily with siblings and other children for days on end. Their mothers do not exist for the amusement of children.

In an experiment to determine whether expansions of a child's speech would augment grammatical development, Cazden (1965) found that simply replying to what the child had said was just as effective in stimulating speech. Expansions are, it would seem, more helpful to certain groups of parents than to any group of children.

> A difference in the amount of parental expansion, in turn, might depend on the amount of interest parents have in understanding what their children say . . . We might expect that the tendency to expand is greatest among those parents with a conviction that children do have something to say, parents who believe that the behavior of children is worthy of attention, parents who are, in short, subscribers to middle-class values and middle-class child-rearing practices. As a matter of fact, the expansion rate of thirty per cent in Brown's records came from academic parents. (McNeill 1966:75)

CHARACTERISTICS OF ADULTS' SPEECH TO CHILDREN

The mothers of Kenneth and Mark do not imitate or expand the speech of children to any extent. *However, they do expand their own speech to children.* That is the pattern of speaking to children which the mothers of Rosepoint cannot resist. In its most common form the sentence is repeated three times, varying the total intonation pattern by doubling the volume for successive sentences.

> NATALIE: What that is?
> PETER: Hunh?
> NATALIE: What that is? *(louder)*
> PETER: Hunh?
> NATALIE: WHAT THAT IS? *(very loud)*

The possible intervening responses of the children are not necessary to the structure.

> MOTHER: Get out here.
> Get out here!
> Get out here!!

The above form expanded by intonation (louder each time) is primarily used for questions and imperatives. A more complex and interesting form is the mother's expansion of her own speech into paradigms. Ignoring the child's response, she will continue to paraphrase her own utterances systematically, throwing in a few repetitions for good measure.

> NATALIE: Tell the lady your name.
> Tell the lady your name.
> What your name?
> Tell Joan what your name.
> Tell her your name.
> Tell Joan your name.
> LIZ: Tell Joan your name.
> Tell Joan your name.
> NATALIE: Tell her your mama name.
> What your mama name?

Though all of this was directed at eliciting speech from the child, he squeezed in two "Hunh's" and an "I don't know."

A frequently used form of the mother-to-child paradigm follows this rule. The sentence itself remains intact but surrounded by a changing set of form classes.

$$\left\{ \begin{array}{l} \text{Proper Names} \\ \text{Expletives} \\ \text{Directives} \end{array} \right\} + \text{Sentence} + \left\{ \begin{array}{l} \text{Adverbs} \\ \text{Proper Names} \\ \text{Tag Questions} \end{array} \right\}$$

> What does stop on that track out there?
> Hunh, what does stop on that track out there, Anne?
> Anne, what does stop on that track outside?

In the next set of paradigms another type of alternative is offered, that of internal syntactic substitution.

> Come on back sit on *this* chair.
> Come on come on sit on *that* chair.
> Come on Peter sit on *the* chair.

Here the woman runs through the possibilities for an article modifying a singular noun: *this, that, the.* Any word class can be used. The communicative advantage of this expansion form seems to be a wide variety of syntactic and semantic possibilities with a limited number of lexical items. Moreover, she is graphically presenting his range of syntactic choices.

> And where your Daddy just bring you?
> And where your Daddy just bring you?
> And where   he   just bring you??
>   What   he   bring you?
>   What   he   buy you?
>   What   he   buy you?

> Where you all went Sunday?
> Where you all went Sunday?
> Where did you all go Sunday?
> Who brought that sweater to you?
> Who brought that pretty sweater?
> Who brought that pretty sweater?

> What Liz brought you all?
> What Liz brought you Anne?
> What Liz *bought* you?

> What   Scott ate today   for dinner?
> What   you ate   for dinner?
> What did you eat   for dinner?
> What you and Warren have   for dinner?

Sometimes the group of mothers will chime in to complete the paradigm. Women speak in this manner to any children, not just their own.

NATALIE: What your daddy got in his car?
             What your daddy went and put in his car?
CHILD: Soul brother.
LIZ: That what my daddy went and put in his car, eh?

The sentences may be complex with dependent clauses, or they may switch from interrogative to declarative forms. Often the meaning is duplicated and the syntax varied only slightly. A minimal number of lexical items are needed. In the following exchange the same sentence (italicized) is repeated three times, varied somewhat, and accompanied by many extra directions.

1. Come on back here. And let's *talk*. *Come on you all gonna hear you all voice* on that tape recorder, hear, come one.
2. On that tape recorder. *Come on* sit down and *talk* and then *you all gonna hear your voice* on there.
3. Well come see. *Come on*. Sit down there and *say something* and she gonna play it and *you gonna hear your voice*.

This is maximal redundancy. Between (1) and (2) and between (2) and (3) the child says "hunh?" To an outsider, the mother appears to talk at, rather than with the child. But talk she does.

In the event he does not understand or respond to a question with an inverted verb, she may give him a declarative with interrogative intonation or further variations on this theme.

The one sleep with you, what his name?
Who sleep with you?
Who you sleep with?
What your other brother name is?
What the other one name was sleep with you?

Some recurring patterns in this adult–child speech are best described by designating their rhyme schemes. The systematic repetitiveness of the sentences allows such an interpretation. The following might be called an ABA pattern.

NATALIE: I ain't gonna bring them nowhere,
They don't wanna sing
I ain't bringing them nowhere.
I ain't gonna bring you all in the car,
Now if you all don't start talking,
I ain't bring you in the car.

This is a highly stylized threat which points up the rhythmic nature of the language used to children. Such forms exist less often in adults' speech to adults. "Lord have mercy! Jesus have mercy! Have mercy!" is one similar form, though most often abbreviated. Some of the mother–child interactions are constructed like spirituals or folksongs in which the rhythms have an hypnotic effect on the participants. The intellectual content is subordinated to the mode of presentation.

NATALIE: Now tell her what you do all day.
What do you do in the day?
What you do in the day?
What you do in the day?
You play?
Tell her that.
Tell her you play.
Tell her that!
Tell her you play!

If expansions of speech provide the models and the alternatives to facilitate the child's discovery of grammatical features, then these children experience a variety of expanded speech. Not their own but an adult's sentences are expanded. The syntactic models are available in any case. The children of poor factory workers and the children of university graduate students will learn the syntactic rules appropriate to their parents and peers. Along with different dialect, however, they may learn different *sociolects*, or the social uses of language and one's own participation in it.

It is possible that the behavior of the lower-class parent is not simply a function of diminished motivation and interest in the child's communication but might reflect important differences in systems of information exchange characteristic of this group. Linguistic competence, in the usual sense, may not be as useful to the lower-class child as other communication operations. (Chase 1966: 259)

THE CONTRAST OF ADULT-TO-ADULT SPEECH

The expansions of sentences are not the usual manner in which adults address other adults and mature teenagers. Compare the following tape transcript with the mother's speech to children. The interview concerns the mother's reaction to her children's use of unacceptable language. Another woman is present but does not speak in this section of the tape.

INVESTIGATOR: What do you do if one of your kids says a dirty word?
ROSA: Nothing.
INVESTIGATOR: Nothing. Really?
ROSA: Because I had my other two in school, they used to say them.
INVESTIGATOR: What did they say?
ROSA: All sorts of dirty words.
INVESTIGATOR: Did they pick them up from the other children?
ROSA: And maybe from me too. Sometime I get mad but what I like about it, now as soon as they gets old enough to understand that it isn't right, they stop it. And whenever they will hear someone else say one, you know, you heard it so-and-so said bad word. Whereas now they would probably come in off the street, you know, and when they was smaller, they probably repeat it, but now they don't ever come to me and repeat it, or nothing of the kind. You see, as they growing old, is grown, they don't say it, regardless of who they hear say it. Un-hunh, without me having to tell 'em anything. Where I think if you was get on them and brutalize them or beat them it just make them retaliate, get mad or something, they probably would say it just to make you mad. They gotta say it for someone else to hear.
INVESTIGATOR: You know they'll grow out of it then?
ROSA: I know they will, because I have two that have. I think Cicero was even worse than anyone of them. He used to be horrible. And you'll never get Cicero, not even out playing to say bad, using obscene language. And if any of the other kids would say them he will say, oh, he was playing in the front, he don't never come out and say the words. Cause, you know, he say "No I don't know what you saying." But most of the things he do, lots of people think is wrong that I would let, cause I would let him get by with it. But I know my aunt _____ don't love him as much as I do. She never tell them anything. Lots of mothers brutalize their children and really try to chastise them and be hard on them. They have nothing funny, cause those children grew up to hate them and I, we, could see that. They do anything to hurt their mother. I don't know if you call that seeking revenge from their younger days or what.

Compared to this same mother's speech to her children, this segment is free of paralinguistic and marked intonational features. Other differences are easily seen. False starts, communication securing devices such as "you know," and multi-syllabic lexical items such as *brutalize* or *retaliate* are not characteristic of speech to children. She uses tenses other than the present tense. The content, that is, the ideas expressed, is repetitive. For example, the notion that punitive mothers raise children who will grow up to hate them is repeated. This paraphrasing does not resemble the immediate paradigmatic sentence expansions directed to children.

The mean sentence length for adult–child speech is 5.5 words per sentence; the mean sentence length for adult–adult speech is 15.5 words per sentence.[2] This is clearly a substantial differential. The mother is gearing the complexity and length of her sentences to her audience. To her children she uses only a rare relative or subordinate clause ("Now tell her what you do all day"). To the adults she addresses, complex sentences are predominant ("Whereas now they would probably come in off the street, you know, and when they was smaller, they probably repeat it but now they don't ever come to me and repeat it, or nothing of the kind").

This type of language usage is overheard by all children; two preschoolers were present at this taping. However, the above language sample is not aimed directly at children. The mother's idea of speech suitable for interaction with children is carefully regularized, as though she were aware that children need precise, workable models of their language.

CORRECTIONS AND REQUESTS FOR INFORMATION

To correct a child's syntax or pronunciation implies some feeling that there is a standard for language, a common "correct" goal toward which all must move. Furthermore, corrections imply that one knows the reason for using one form rather than another, and that one's social setting furnishes a rationalization for "correctness." This is not the case for all social groups. Some people may value improvisation, content, social appropriateness (for example, Japanese politeness terms), or even quantity above correctness of syntax and pronunciation. Even if such a standard is employed, the task of imparting it may not fall to the parents.

Corrections used by the parents under consideration here always center around the standard of behavior and not around the standards of language. Only one grammatical correction is recorded; none are recorded for pronunciation.

> CHILD: My mama work to Kaiser.
> AUNT: Susie, your mama work at Kaiser. That to New Orlean.

Under these circumstances it is questionable whether the child learned the preposition in question. The following is more typical:

> CHILD: Give me two meat.
> MOTHER: Two meats! You don't never eat what I give you anyway. You leave it on the plate.

"Two meat" and "two meats" are common alternates, though the former is more often heard. Although the mother unconsciously altered the plural morpheme, its correction as such was of no concern to her. The child's behavior patterns in eating are the focus.

When a child asks a question or volunteers a statement, it will be judged on its behavioral import and not on the structure of the language employed. A child's requests for information are not treated as a demand for knowledge (which adults are expected to supply) or as an attempt to open the lines of communication.

Instead, requests are viewed as a behavioral and not a linguistic manifestation of the child. A child actively engaged in seeking information will be treated as a noisy child, not as an inquiring, curious one. As a side effect of being noisy, he may or may not acquire the information he wants.

An insurance adjustor is examining a bedroom damaged by fire.

CHILD: Who that?

FATHER: None of your business!

CHILD: Sarah, what lane you live on?

MOTHER *(laughs):* Child, that funny, what lane do Sarah live on. *(This is an affectionate, pleasant interchange but not an opportunity to distinguish lanes and streets.)*

MOTHER: Kenneth want to ask the questions. Once he get started on them, boy, asking questions.

INVESTIGATOR: What other question does he ask?

MOTHER: Oh boy! What this for? What that for? Most the time, he already know. He say "What are these things?" I tell him, "a horse." "A horse, what that for?" or "What it do?" or something like that. Anything you say, he want to know what it for, what it do. And once he get started . . . And he don't want to talk when it's time to talk. That boy talks so much! OH! I be whip him all the time all the time.

WHO ARE THE TEACHERS?

The mothers do not feel a very heavy responsibility for language instruction. Neither do they expect to gain prestige through the accomplishments of their children. The level of social achievement for preschoolers is very low in this respect. Such children are not expected to exhibit any range of manners, skills, or special knowledge, that is, talents which can be demonstrated for the benefit of admiring friends and relatives. They are responsible only for taking care of themselves and for following orders. By the time they enter school the children are accomplished at child care, household tasks, and sibling relations. They are responsible for their own whereabouts. However, many may not possess the peripheral skills schools regard as important, such as skill in recitation or pencil and paper facility.

Three of the mothers in this study were picked as teachers' aides for the parish Head Start Program. After the orientation session they expressed considerable surprise at what they were told was the pupils' low level of achievement. Some children, they were informed, did not know the names and identity of colors, numbers, shapes, or animals. This, of course (the mothers were convinced), could not apply to their children, since they were certain such skills had been mastered.

As it turns out, it is the special province of older children to impart the type of knowledge that requires drill. Unlike many middle-class mothers, the women of Rosepoint spend no time drilling their children on such cultural content as the sounds cows make ("moo"), or what happened to Humpty-Dumpty. One mother learned a game in Head Start for teaching children to write their names by following the dots made for them on a piece of paper. She came home, taught three of her school-age children who could already write, and they were gradually teaching the preschoolers! To date, none of the younger children can write their names, but the mother is not only convinced that they can, but that she taught them how.

Many simple (and relatively ineffective) learning drills are conducted between older and younger children. The oldest child present is the teacher—a role learned from older children and not from parents or from experience. In the following tape transcript the children are reading a book containing the alphabet and numbers, for example, "C is for Cat. How many cats are there? Three." The three children are brothers and sisters.

GWEN *(eleven years old):* What is this? What is that?

MADELAINE *(four years old):* I got that toy book.

GWEN: That's a notebook.

KENNETH *(three years old):* A popcorn maker.

GWEN: No. What is this—a glass of milk?

(Gwen, as the oldest, is playing the teacher—asking and quizzing. She leaves and Madelaine is the teacher.)

MADELAINE: How many is that?

KENNETH: I don't know.

MADELAINE: That's a two. See that a two. *(It is an eight.)*

KENNETH: A two.

MADELAINE: That's a horse. How much horse they got?

KENNETH: Two. *(Four horses.)*

MADELAINE: Look that one. How many kitten they got?

KENNETH: Cat.

MADELAINE: No, kitten. How many kitten they got?

KENNETH: Two.

MADELAINE: They got three. *(Seven kittens.)* How many? How many? How much kitten they got? Kenneth, how much ducks they got?

KENNETH: Two-oh-oh-oh.

MADELAINE: Look, one-two-three-four-seven—Now that's a three. An' that's a seven. *(None of these answers is correct.)*

Such prodigious activity persuades the mother that her children are learning much. She will never know that the identification was wrong.

INSTRUCTIVE FUNCTIONS

It has sometimes been asserted in the popular press that black mothers do not talk to their children and that that tendency accounts for the observed differences between black and white students in the public schools.

Compare the conversation with Adam to the ones that follow with Kenneth and Mark. There is almost no subject matter which is initiated by children that adults feel is incumbent upon them to pursue. It is the right of adults to select the topic of conversation. Moreover, adults can conduct a satisfying conversation with only the most minimal feedback. A smile, nod, or "hunh?" is all that is required of a child to uphold his end. The subject matter of Adam's conversation is his own choosing and initiation. The mother's participation tends to be non-directive, and control is exercised in a rather subtle manner.

Adam's mother and the mothers of Kenneth and Mark have different assumptions about the proper sentence form in addressing children. These assumptions stem from their beliefs about the nature of children. The middle-class mother will expand her child's telegraphic offering into a short but grammatical sentence appropriate under the circumstances. "Me go" might become "You want to go?," "Yes, we are going now," or "Oh, you went to the store," depending on her evaluation of the situation.

The Rosepoint mother imitates and expands her own utterances. The child is a passive recipient of both the models and the data, as in her child-rearing philosophy he should be. The probable drawback to learning a language under these circumstances is the lack of individualized adjustment to whatever stage of grammatical development the child has reached. The mother's speech is not tailor-made to the child's linguistic maturity. By contrast, Adam's mother renders fuller sentences made to order on the child's own model.

ADAM: There go one.

MOTHER: Yes, there goes one.

Fortrel's mother offers him similar and more sophisticated possibilities. But her paradigms appear to bear little relationship to the structures he may already have mastered.

> FORTREL'S MOTHER: What you ate for dinner?
> What did you eat for dinner?

These differences result from the respective parents' beliefs about their role in language instruction. Fortrel's mother does not view herself as a language instructor nor her child as a budding conversationalist. After all, her child will learn to talk—all children within her experience have. She is concerned about his overt behavior, not his speaking ability.

Few family systems in the world are so constructed that the child is exposed almost exclusively to his mother's speech. The American middle class has this type of isolated, nuclear family. The initial research on language acquisition, perhaps as an artifact of the data, tended to give major emphasis to the role of the mother in language socialization. From information collected from field workers in a symposium on communicative competence (Slobin 1968:9–13), only the Mayan family system, of those considered, exhibited the same characteristics as the American nuclear family. Here, as in the American middle-class home, the mother is the chief source of input. For the Koya of India, the Luo of Kenya and the Polynesians of American Samoa, the most important source of input to children was from peers, siblings, and the members of an extended family (Slobin 1968:9–13). The tendency seems to be that those with control over the children, having caretaking responsibilities, provide the most input.

The situation most analgous to Rosepoint comes from a Negro ghetto in Oakland.

> Most of the speech of mothers to children . . . took the form of imperatives or such questions as *Where are your shoes, Are you hungry*, etc. . . . The artificiality of mother to child conversation beyond what has been mentioned is underscored by many mothers' limitations in eliciting speech from their children at the request of the investigator. Mothers were hard put to engage a child in conversation beyond naming games for younger children and requests for reporting about particular events, such as what went on in nursery school for older children. In other words, they suffered from many of the same limitations as the investigator who was unfamiliar with the children and their attempts to engage their children in conversation were for the most part abortive. (Slobin 1968:12)

If the mother is not the only source of input, who else is? Other adults are not, since either, as in the case of tradesmen, they do not speak to the children, or, as in the case of family friends, they duplicate the mother's type of speech. In view of the above anthropological observations, it is likely that the peer and sibling group are an important source of input. In an extended family with many children whose neighbors are extended families with many children, one primary linguistic resource is probably other children, siblings, and cousins.

This is difficult to demonstrate. The mere presence of an adult investigator ruins the composition and changes the atmosphere of a peer group, particularly preschoolers. Testifying from personal experience, it is extremely hard to spy on the in-group activities of small children and virtually impossible to do so with a tape recorder. The study of peer-group linguistic interaction needs a more controlled setting than a crowded, noisy, rural Louisiana home provides.

Most of what adults and parents in Rosepoint say to children is *administrative speech*—that speech necessary to conduct the business of the day. Administrative speech consists mainly of orders, questions, and short answers. The total amount of speech directly aimed at the child could not possibly account for the complexities of the grammar he is learning. However compensatory peer-group speech may be, it does not approach the adult model. It is probable that the speech of the peer group merely reinforces and imitates what each age grade learns about the adult community model and allows an opportunity for practice.

Meanwhile, for the children of this community the time spent in the presence of adults is spent passively listening. This statement makes no guarantee that the children hear anything; how the language is comprehended and processed is yet a mystery. At any rate, the children spend most of every day within earshot of every type of speech event the community has to offer. This might be called an eavesdropping theory of language learning. Language learning in Rosepoint differs in this respect from that of a community in which a child receives more formal language training in the home but has less chance to observe a wide range of adult behavior.

A THEORETICAL PROBLEM

The verbal reactions of the mothers in Rosepoint present a fascinating theoretical problem. How do children learn their language and its rules in the absence of conscious instruction? Obviously these caretakers do not believe that they are "teaching" children to speak. Teaching here means the formal and observable attempts to impart certain structures, words, or concepts as well as corrections and judgments of the truth value of children's early utterances. In learning philosophies from Dewey to Skinner, great emphasis is placed on the role of verbal instruction and imitations of the parent by the child. In stimulus-response theories the child is rewarded for producing utterances which presumably he has borrowed from his elders. In Rosepoint, however, in a natural setting rather than an experimental one, children imitate adults far less frequently than adults imitate themselves. Furthermore, the parents pay no conscious attention to their role in assisting language learning.

Consider the possibility that children's language comes from their own maturational development and is not just a response to purposive, rewarding speech from adults. This generative, or biologically based theory of language acquisition is described in Lenneberg, (1966, 1967); McNeill (1966); and Lyons and Wales (1966).

According to this theory, language development involves such qualitative features as phonological discrimination (as in the differences between b and p, t and d), syntactic rules (as in "I am," "you are," "he ain't"), and semantic categories (as in "man," "Daddy," "Father," "person"). No differences in the age or speed of acquisition of these features can be found in cultures studied thus far (Lenneberg 1967:138). That is, unless deaf, pathologically diseased, or otherwise seriously handicapped, the average five-year-old has mastered most of the sound system, the syntax, and many of the semantic categories of his language.

A corollary of this theory is that so-called linguistically deprived children do not exist. Certain children lack a familiarity with rhymes, stories, linguistic routines, colors, shapes, numbers, specialized vocabularies, dates, time telling, reading, writing, spelling, approved past tenses or other skills that are the core of formal education; but speak they can. It is a mistake to confuse the set of verbal skills, including notions of "correct grammar," which are measured by a limited set of intelligence and achievement tests with a child's *language*.

Naturally, regular differences in syntax and word forms exist for different experience groups, but the basic process of acquisition is still the same. The process by which one child derives "he do"—"he do not"—"he don't"—"don't he" is the same process that another child uses to derive a chain ending for "doesn't he." It is only the social context that renders "don't he" less acceptable than "doesn't he."

What parent says to her child, "Add an /-s/ to all third-person singular present-tense verbs."? She may correct "he go" to "he goes," but even with this unusual coaching, the child must himself generalize these rules to extend to all words which he has further learned to classify as verbs. The complicated rule systems which a child can generate and the implications of this are also described in Berko (1958), Weir (1962), Menyuk (1964), and Bellugi (1965).

Any theory of language learning would have to explain Rosepoint in which the children appear to receive little formal instruction and even less practice in their emerging skills.

NOTES

1. In the two previous conversations with Kenneth and Mark cited above, the mothers are using a form of appeal to the social oriented feeling of shame rather than to the personal oriented feelings of guilt. For more discussion of the implications of the guilt-shame complex in child rearing, see Benedict (1946:222-23).
2. Mean sentence length is a numerical average calculated on all expansions of adult–child speech recorded in this chapter; the mean sentence length for the adult–adult speech is calculated from the preceding transcript of Rosa's discussion of swearing and blasphemy.

REFERENCES

Bellugi, Ursula, 1965, The development of interrogative structures in children's speech. In K. F. Riegel (ed.), *The Development of Language Functions*, Ann Arbor, Mich.: University of Michigan Center for Human Growth and Development 8, pp. 103-37.

Berko, Jean, 1958, The child's learning of English morphology. *Word* 14: 150-77. Also in S. Saporta (ed.), 1961, *Psycholinguistics: A Book of Readings*, New York: Holt, Rinehart and Winston, Inc., pp. 359-75.

Benedict, Ruth, 1946, *Chrysanthemum and the Sword*. Boston: Houghton Mifflin Company.

Braine, Martin D. S., 1963, The ontogeny of English phrase structure: the first phrase. *Language* 39: 1-13.

Brown, Roger, and Ursula Bellugi, 1964, Three processes in the child's acquisition of syntax. In E. H. Lenneberg (ed.), *New Directions in the Study of Language*, Cambridge, Mass.: MIT Press, pp. 131-62.

Cazden, C. B., 1965, Environmental assistance to the child's acquisition of grammar. Unpublished doctoral dissertation, Harvard University.

Chase, Richard Allen, 1966, Evolutionary aspects of language development and function. In T. Smith and G. Miller (eds.), *The Genesis of Language: A Psycholinguistic Approach*, Cambridge, Mass.: MIT Press, pp. 253-68.

Ervin, Susan M., 1966, Imitation and structural change in children's language. In E. H. Lenneberg (ed.), *New Directions in the Study of Language*, Cambridge, Mass.: MIT Press, pp. 163-89.

Lenneberg, Eric (ed.), *New Directions in the Study of Language*. Cambridge, Mass.: MIT Press.

——, 1967, *Biological Foundations of Language*. New York: John Wiley and Sons, Inc.

Lyon, J., and R. J. Wales, 1966, *Psycholinguistics Papers*. The proceedings of the 1966 Edinburgh Conference. Edinburg University Press.

McNeill, David, 1966, Developmental psycholinguistics. In T. Smith and G. Miller (eds.), *The Genesis of Language: A Psycholinguistics Approach*, Cambridge, Mass.: MIT Press, pp. 15-84.

Menyuk, P., 1964, Syntactic rules used by children from preschool through first grade. Child Developmental Monograph 35:533-46.

Miller, Wick, and Susan M. Ervin, 1964, The development of grammar in child language. In U. Bellugi and R. Brown (eds.), *The Acquisition of Language*, Child Development Monograph 29:9–34.

Slobin, Dan I. (ed.) *et al.*, 1967, *A Field Manual for Cross-Cultural Study of the Acquisition of Communicative Competence.* Berkeley: University of California Press.

———, 1968, Questions of language development in cross-cultural perspective. Manuscript prepared for Symposium "Language learning in cross-cultural perspective," Michigan State University, East Lansing; Sept. 25, 1968.

Weir, Ruth, 1962, *Language in the Crib*. The Hague: Mouton.

Part VI

Educators from an Anthropological Perspective

26 / Teachers and Their Family Cultures

Ruth Landes

The project of reconstructing a family culture through the three latest generations exposed enormous social variety in the origins of teachers despite the teachers' usual middle-class appearances and professional oneness. The ranging differences—of religion, national and regional descents, race, parents' economic class—behind the standard appearance contain unsuspected cultural factors, which are hidden points of behavioral reference heightening an individual educator's troubles with those of other ancestries because they are as unknown as the behavioral standards of minorities at school.

If every individual teacher were securely set by descent from generations of the same American tradition, a strange people or minority might seem less disturbing or threatening. But the teacher who rests heavily on his certificate to symbolize the community's standards, and who must instruct accordingly, is revealed in many of the family analyses as only a first- or second-generation comer. Recent converts take few risks with the authoritative creed, and, at the same time, strive to invalidate a divergent one. On the other hand, old heirs know their latitude: thus, among socially strong and impeccable white southerners are found some of the regional racism's most stubborn foes. Judging from the family studies, educators of subcultural origins feel anxious about conforming to middle-class referents because of the clash with certain ancestral standards, habits, and comforts over which the individual has little conscious control. The clashes and anxieties gave meaning to the educators' reiterated term "frustration." Then suddenly, work on the family cultures appeared to give students the right, as it were, to feel proud of their origins! This was an unexpected consequence of the project. Studying cultural dynamics, individual teachers rediscovered enthusiastically their deep roots in the family's ancestral traditions. It seems that the middle-class demand for adherence to its single standards, or "equality," attacked divergent ancestral loyalties and the personal identities of many teachers trying to earn professional recognition and social comfort from the middle class.

The writer expected that roused family pride and stirred-up sympathies would alert and attune teachers to their minority pupils' similar attachments and needs. They did. Teachers came to recognize the strains placed on a subgroup, on its culture, and its member personalities when defeated by another people and forced into other ways by poverty, prejudice, immigration, and ignorance of the ruling or host society.

Each one who engaged in the research stated in one way or another his new knowledge that culture was a generic function and life condition of all men, a mysterious creation of such power that some culture theorists call it "super-organic." Each one glimpsed the crucial reality that man's culture has taken diverse forms in time and space, and that the historic diversities were corner-stones of existence for the heirs. In the United States, the crucial reality has proved tragic as well for certain groups, notably those of the minority peoples; but the teachers now had firm hold of the idea that, regardless of minority labels, the di-verse cultural or subcultural groups were treasuries of human resource for the heirs, and for other groups—like educators—who understood them.

This family project was planned as instruction and not as therapy; but, as with some experiences, the project cast a healing light on knotty situations in sub-merged areas of students' careers. Each time students resorted for information to relatives, to relics in family trunks, to libraries, and museums, they explained some version of, "This is what life is about! This is how we know we're human!"

Most of the family studies were written with the great feeling we call love. This did not exclude some hostile feelings. Students said, "I left things out because I didn't want to hurt my people," or "I hesitate to read this to the seminar because of what it reveals." One woman, on the contrary, read and wept over her devoted recollections. As director of the Claremont Anthropology and Education program, the writer's view of the supposed omissions was that "what you left out deliberately is immaterial. The purpose is for your report to give a coherent picture of your parental tradition."

The points about which a student declared himself to be privately sensitive, as he felt shame, hate, and pride surge, invariably eluded the listeners when he read his paper aloud. Listeners showed the reader a purblindness similar to that which au-thorities showed regarding sensitivities of minority persons. After this startling ex-perience, and with heightened insight, students now readily guessed how handi-capped and oppressed groups suffered humiliation, anger, and bewilderment—states normally inconceivable to an outsider lacking empathy. One high school adminis-trator concluded discussion of his family culture thus:

> This was an extremely difficult assignment for me. By describing my [Euro-pean Jewish] parents, the lives they spent, the anti-Semitic prejudice to which they, their parents, and grandparents were subjected, I have alluded to factors leaving deep imprints on my own life.
>
> This is the first time that I have ever discussed my background outside the immediate family circle. I guess there are many things one wishes to repress, consciously or unconsciously. While much is unsaid, I believe the major ob-jective of the assignment was attained: namely, that by experiencing a strong resistance to writing about myself, I have sharpened my sensitivity to the deeper feelings, the inner conflicts of other persons with whom I come in daily contact. Yet I had already experienced anti-Semitic prejudice as a child, in school and on the playground; as a student in college; as a member of the Armed Forces during World War II; as an employee on various jobs; and sadly, as a member of the education profession.

A teacher, born and reared in Vienna, described changes in her life brought about by migration to the United States after the Nazi conquest of Austria:

> It was difficult and painful to be uprooted from the culture and country of which one felt a part. It was as hard to grow roots again in a strange soil and learn to become part of the new land. Yet I felt able to retain much of the culture in which I grew up, and still have space left for absorbing the new.
>
> Living most of my life in an authoritarian society only to begin life anew in a democracy is an experience hard to describe. It is almost like learning to walk again after a long illness when one does not quite know what to do with

the new freedom of locomotion. Only slowly one learns to adjust and love freedom. Compared to the rigid social patterns of Europe, the United States is almost classless, for it is really possible to move from one social rank to another. This realization takes time and requires good understanding of how American institutions function.

Meeting and living with people of different racial groups impressed and depressed me in equal measure. I never met a Negro until I was eighteen and never saw an Oriental until I was twenty years old. I was deeply impressed that, according to the Constitution, we were equals in sharing the democratic way. But I was depressed to find segregation of races not very different from the segregation I knew in anti-Semitic Europe. Is it possible that freedom, given to those who never knew it but longed for it, seems of greater value to them than to those having it as a birth right?

Changing cultures may provoke a sense of impossible contrasts. Listening to American-born teachers describe their family cultures, the Austrian-reared teacher exclaimed tartly, "I'm amazed at these long American genealogies! I'm not that interested in my family. I never even met my grandparents, who died early." This view may reflect special aspects of Jewish history, where the people wander under persecution, strongly rooted in an ancient tradition but not for centuries in a geographical terrain until the establishment of the state of Israel in 1948.

This was one of the American genealogies that amazed the former Austrian:

I regard myself as a typical product of the American melting pot. My grandparents and great-grandparents came from five different countries of Western Europe and the British Isles: England, Ireland, Scotland, Holland, and France. It is even possible that the French great-grandmother was part original American.

My paternal grandfather came to this country from Bolwiggie, Scotland, where the family had been weavers. Tradition says he came by steerage when he was fourteen. His name was Alec and in the Civil War he became a drummer boy under Lew Wallace, who wrote Ben Hur. After the war he worked as a carpenter, building depots for the railroad running west. He stopped in Kansas at the then Grasshopper Falls, later renamed Valley Falls, and bought a store. Alec sold his store, moved to a farm, did custom harvesting with a new steam-engine harvester, and later turned building contractor and cabinet maker in Topeka, the state capital.

Alice Ann was of English and Dutch ancestry. Her mother's parents had left Holland for the United States, homesteading and clearing land in Illinois. This was later sold and the family, including six sons and a daughter who became Alice Ann's mother, homesteaded and bought some thousand acres of farm land near Springfield, Missouri. As Dunkards they opposed war; when Missouri pressed men into the Confederate Army they traded their land for cattle and mules, at far below value, and left for Kansas. Heading for a Dunkard settlement north of Kansas, they were asked to settle in the Dunkard community near Valley Falls and Topeka. Later the six boys served in the Union army, one as a doctor. . . .

My father, Clarence, married a girl of English, Irish, French, and possibly Indian ancestry. He learned telegraphy because weak eyes prevented his studying medicine. He was a relief telegrapher for several years in western Kansas and eastern Colorado. My mother, whose family lived in Central Missouri, visited, for her health, some relatives' ranch near Colorado Springs. Here my future parents met and married. My father then went into banking with a friend at Jennings, Kansas. There I was born and lived during the first part of World War I.

Our little community had a rather large Bohemian settlement, which gave a cosmopolitan air. Each year the community held a dinner where families of different racial origins served foods of their countries. I watched the burning of the Kaiser's effigy at night in the public square. . . .

We moved to Topeka, where I first met colored children, at school and play. My home training was that all men are brothers. Two mulatto girls, whose Caucasian father and full-blooded Negro mother were legally married, taught me race prejudice. We used to roller skate down a long hill by the State Fair grounds. At the foot we met two very dark Negro girls, who asked us to skate on to their house. The mulattoes would not let me go and said my parents would disapprove.

After college I married a man of English and German origins. His mother's family had been knighted under Cromwell and with the king's return they left for America. His father's family had left Germany for England, where they remained over two hundred years before any members migrated to America. This family valued time; wasting it was a sin. This is quite a shift from the Celtic love of life I had absorbed from my Scotch-Irish ancestors. . . . We became acquainted with educated Indians. Some of our best friends were proud of their one-eighth, one-sixteenth, or one-thirty-second fraction of Indian blood. Movng to California, we bought a small ranch among Mexican-American neighbors. . . .

Another teacher, born in Hungary and brought to America at the age of four years, described her recollections of culture shifts, vivid after more than thirty years.

My maternal grandfather's family was gentry, being large landowners in Hungary. They traced their land title back over four hundred years, near a little village called Komarom-Szemere. Although untitled, the family was law in town government and society. The estate grew wheat and had large herds of livestock. Until World War II, life there was still somewhat feudal; the same families worked on the estate for generations, and my grandfather's cousin's son operated it. My grandfather was a good landowner, prosperous and beloved; he was the village arbitrator and political figure. He gave his own funds to the village school and other institutions.

My maternal grandmother was a doctor's daughter; she married at sixteen. She ran the household, including my grandfather, unbeknownst to him. Their large manor house was an overnight stop for important travelers in Hungary's agricultural area. In my mother's memory, the travelers even included the Emperor Franz Joseph and his entourage. . . .

The children were educated by governesses until, when my mother was eleven years old, they moved to Budapest for better schooling. My grandfather gave the management of his estate to his cousin and started a wholesale meat business in Budapest, marketing his own cattle. Despite changing to a merchant class, the family lived in style on the estate's wealth. The family's attitude during this period is symbolized in an anecdote about my maternal uncle. His classmates were discussing their fathers' professions of law and medicine. They asked him what his father did. Puzzled, he finally answered, "My father? Why—he's a gentleman."

In contrast, I know little about my paternal antecedents. My parents met by a wartime fluke. Normally they could not have met because of differences in social standing. My father was graduated from Budapest University as a veterinarian. During the First World War he was veterinarian to a Hungarian calvary regiment, with the rank of major. My mother met him and married him against her family's strong disapproval. . . .

My father dreamed of coming to America, feeling he could never succeed in

Hungary. Their final decision to emigrate roused great consternation in my mother's close-knit family in which there had been no mobility because of the estate. My maternal grandmother finally solved the bitter arguments. Quoting the biblical story of Ruth, she stressed the sanctity of marriage vows against her private inclinations.

Thus, we arrived at Pearl River, New York. I remember odd things such as learning that you need not curtsy when you enter a room of adults, that you need not kiss the hand of very old people, that the way to tell girls from boys is *not* that girls wore rings in pierced ears, and that Americans were stupid, understanding neither Hungarian nor German. I remember being puzzled and intrigued at seeing my first colored person....

My father had to be treated with the respect of one whose word was law. He rated with God in my early childhood. Only when I was about ten, and we both collected stamps, did I realize he too was human. I learned that behind his tall frame, military bearing, and deep voice, he was gentle and kind, though still awe-inspiring. He appeared the stern European *pater familias*. Now elderly and ill, he gives himself to his grandsons as he did not to me in my childhood. He feels that somehow he has failed me, from the standpoint of today's American father. But I know that mother and I were the center of his world....

In the rural Long Island of my childhood we were the only foreign family. At home, my parents and I generally spoke Hungarian. They both speak English fluently but in my early teens, I was ashamed of their accent. To overcome this inferiority, I felt I must be spectacular, so I worked to become the best scholar, the best swimmer, and the best basketball player at school.... Now I realize that my early self-consciousness was unfounded. My father was respected in his profession and received honors. Yet I know that he too had some inferiority feelings about his foreign background....

My mother had an easier time making friends because of her superior or more worldly family background, and she turned her accent to good advantage. She brought American friends to our home, unlike my father who always found it difficult to unbend in small talk and social niceties....

After college I worked as a chemist and married an engineer. I made a free choice, with my parent's consent, unlike my mother's free choice with family opposition. To my surprise I received a dowry and much household linen. My mother had collected the linen for years, unsuspected by me....

In my own family we speak English at home, though there are a few words and phrases from German, Hungarian, and Russian because they are untranslatable. However, these languages will be lost to our sons.

I believe we are quite assimilated in our habits and thinking. Our friends are entirely American. I am sympathetic to Hungarian customs, from a highly interested American viewpoint. My husband, born in Moscow, educated in Prague and New York, with an erudite Russian background, is, of course, violently anti-Communist and is perhaps more removed from Russia than I from Hungary.

The most obvious foreign influence is perhaps in my cooking. Much of it is Hungarian, much is American, some is Russian.... Assimilation to another culture is a very difficult and long process but it can be accomplished....

A youthful mother, of Anglo-Russian parentage, married to a Swedish-American teacher and herself teaching high school, interviewed French-Canadian parents who had migrated five months earlier with their children from Trois-Rivières, Quebec, to California. She reported that this Catholic bilingual family felt "a loss of status as a result of the move which one could sense though they did not express it. Parents and their five children all worked hard to be successful in the new situation. They found California different: 'So many autos, so much to do!' The numerous women drivers confounded them. Few women in Trois-Rivières worked outside the home. The husband said he would never approve of his wife's working."

In Quebec the children had attended Catholic school, as did 95 percent of the local school-age group. In California they attended public school.

The interviewer found that "the family is close knit, having few outside activities. The father is undisputed head and the parents supervise their children more closely than do Americans. There is a cheerful camaraderie but no impertinence or belligerence from the children. May this family not become too Americanized!"

This sympathetic attitude contrasted with that of a colleague, a young man who wrote that his father "took a job teaching dumbbell English to underprivileged Mexican children." Neither party was satisfied. In offhand words the father was scorned for his work, the Mexicans for their status.

A mature man, a high school teacher, told of cultural shocks and conflicts, generated by his Mormon upbringing, in his personal life:

One of my earliest recollections is of my [Mormon] parents' emphasis on education. Both parents continually impressed this on us six boys, though my mother only finished eighth grade and my father left school even earlier. Yet both were well read and possessed abundant practical knowledge.

This attitude, it seems to me now, characterized most Mormon families. My grandparents on one side of the family, my great-grandparents on the other, were Mormon pioneers who crossed the plains with followers of Brigham Young.

These pioneers were taught by the Church that "the glory of God is intelliegence," and that "as man is, God once was; and as God is, man may become." So it was the purpose of each life to develop the intellect. It was proclaimed often from the pulpit that the only thing one took on leaving this life was the intellect one developed.

Not all the Mormon attitudes were as positive. Few of the darker races came to Utah in early days, but there developed an intolerance of them despite the church preachment that "all men are brothers in the sight of God." Church *practice* makes it impossible for a Negro to hold authority or "priesthood" in the Mormon Church because the Negro was cursed by God with a dark skin and is an inferior: "the time was not yet ripe when God would forgive him and accept him into His church."

With this background it is particularly difficult for me to accept Negroes as equals. Personal analysis had helped me to realize how ridiculous the attitude is; yet I fear mine is an intellectual rather than an emotional tolerance.

I do not recall ever doubting that mine was the one and only true church until I was well out of high school. For I was born into a Mormon home, in a Mormon town, in a Mormon state, and attended a Mormon university. Certainty of the truth of my beliefs rested on my lack of exposure to other beliefs. There was no other church in our small community; and non-Mormon families could be counted on the fingers of one hand. At the university, I first had opportunity to analyze religion objectively and to examine my own beliefs more scientifically. This is now beneficial to me as a teacher....

It seems to me that, though the Mormon people are part of the greater American culture, they developed patterns peculiar to themselves during their long isolation from the rest of the country.

Another teacher described her parental culture complacently, as though it lifted her above stress: Her middle-class family, she said, "had little opportunity to see how 'others' live. ... My maternal grandmother traces her line back to Miles Standish, though I would never have known without asking because she believes that the only important things are a person's acts.

"There has been no real contact with other races and only limited contact with the Catholic and Jewish religions," she related. "I like to think I am very broad-minded about others' problems. I realize, however, that this is only a rational philosophy about cultural differences. My sole travel has been to West Canada and to Mexico City, though my parents sacrificed lovingly to give me a good education, wide interests, and understanding."

A colleague of similar age and ethnic roots was, on the other hand, strongly alive to the continual stress and change in American life, as exemplified in her family. Her account said:

Paternal grandparents both migrated from England before 1900 and settled in a little town near Vancouver, Canada. After the births of six children, my grandfather died, my grandmother moved to Tacoma, Washington, and later remarried. The second husband also died early, the family was extremely poor . . . and the children began working very young. My father could not even complete elementary school . . . but he and others helped the youngest boy finish college and become a pharmacist.

The family was close and valued homemaking. Traditional recipes were handed from mother to daughter and traditional menus were served on occasions such as Christmas, marriage, showers, births, deaths. Whether from destitution or custom, all members of the family seemed very frugal. . . .

My maternal grandparents migrated from Germany, settling eventually in Seattle, Washington. They produced six children and, when my mother was about ten years old, her mother left home and divorced my grandfather. A housekeeper was brought in. My grandfather, a shoemaker, later married her and four more children resulted. Great friction between stepmother and stepchildren followed, so that most children of the first marriage left home in early adolescence. My mother left at twelve years to do housework with a family; this way she put herself through high scool and studied piano and voice.

My mother felt little affection and happiness in her father's home. The family was run on dictatorial lines, was poor, and was lucky to have the barest necessities.

While a housekeeper my mother took a boat trip to California and met my father, a carpenter, in Los Angeles. He courted her in Los Angeles, they married and built a home there, and remained until after my birth. Then my father moved us back to Washington, hoping to better his prospects. He always felt hampered by lack of education, despite his good mental ability. He was always dissatisfied with manual labor, developed psychosomatic ailments, and still suffers untold misery. He has managed to eke out a living through real estate, occasional jobs, and my mother's occasional employment.

My father long held rather autocratic control over his wife and me, his only child. He did not approve of a wife working outside the home, or having outside interests. Only he could handle money and dole it out. Housework was solely for women.

But through the years his ways changed. My mother came to earn money and control much of the spending. When mother worked, father helped with such house chores as dishwashing. Mother developed outside interests and new friends after they began spending part of each year in Southern California. They had moved far from old family habits until about a year ago when my father's worsening health returned them to his home town of Tacoma. I believe he has an overwhelming desire to live out his days there and be buried in the family plot which the relatives decorate attentively.

As a child I feared my father's anger and tried carefully not to displease him. Though we had poor times during the depression, we were always well dressed and fed. Most of our social life was with my father's family—dining, visiting, and driving together. At times I longed to get away from this close relationship. But now I believe I had considerable freedom—swimming, boating, roaming the woods, playing without someone to organize games or "protect" us. . . .

I was expected to and did graduate from high school, but had no plans for college until my senior year of high school when I got a college scholarship. Besides, we traveled summers with a small carnival, operating concessions, and we decided that all money earned in my concession would be saved for college.

After one and one half years of college and the outbreak of World War II, I married and quit school. We moved to Portland, my husband as a sheet-metal worker for the Oregon Shipbuilding Corporation and I on a job in the transportation office. We both took college extension courses.

A year later my husband was drafted into military services and volunteered for paratroopers; later he was commissioned in the Air Force. George and I lived a very democratic marriage, partly through war and our life with the service, partly through personal ideas. We both believed in equal sharing. An Air Force wife necessarily assumes much responsibility for family affairs, often travels alone, finds a house and job, and develops independence, the first time as far away as the Philippine Islands. In those years we had maids. . . .

When our son was a year old and our daughter nearly four, my husband was killed in a plane crash. It seemed best to bring the children to my parents in California. We soon learned that three generations seldom live happily together. I bought a house for the children and began studying to be a teacher. Teaching seemed the best employment for a mother with two small children.

I taught a year when plans were underfoot for remarriage. Almost three years ago I remarried. We had been acquainted for several years, during which time his wife had passed away. He is much older than I but we seem to have much in common. His one grown daughter, unmarried, opposed our marriage until lately.

Having been single so long, completely independent, and responsible for my children, it was quite an adjustment to marry one a generation older. My husband believes quite autocratically that all family authority is vested in the husband. I believe, more democratically, that husband and wife should plan together and give children some voice, especially about things concerning them. Doubtless we are both modifying our views. However, the children *are* being reared differently from before.

Family ties are now loose compared to the close ones of my childhood. We do not visit our relatives. My children will not have any feeling of family closeness except for our frequent correspondence with grandparents, now in Washington. Nor are the children free to have parties at home, though they may bring friends in casually. Unlike their father and me, they are well provided for financially through their [deceased] father's estate and can afford good medical and dental care, lessons in music and horseback riding, and, eventually, college. I hope that material things are not coming too easily to my children.

A young missionary teacher described explicitly and approvingly the American family values she carried to remote Ethiopia:

In my life philosophy, I recognize beliefs grandma or an uncle taught us children through stories, axioms, and little talks, and which mother taught us when she punished us.

I think our family's first tenet is that *anyone* with ordinary powers can succeed in almost any work is he is willing to struggle. Mother often said, "You can do anything if you want to badly enough." We expected to study, help ourselves financially, and not feel particularly sorry for ourselves. We chose denominational schools, though we could have gone to public schools more cheaply. We all earned board, room, and tuition from the time we were in high school. Even though one sister and her husband are financially able to provide well for their children, they insist that the children work and contribute to their educational costs.

Another family tenet is that each person has his worth, to be valued above material possessions. Often I have heard family stories illustrating the proverb that a good name is to be preferred above riches. My uncles who farm and train horses are as esteemed by the family as my uncles who are college professors and ministers.

We also believe that we should make the world better for having been here, that a life of service brings more satisfaction than abundant material wealth. Our family has three ministers, two nurses, three foreign missionaries, several teachers, a cousin doing cancer research, and an aunt working for retarded children.

Consequently there is little race prejudice in our family. When I asked my mother how this was, she said that her father forbade the children to talk disparagingly of anyone.

When her younger brother ridiculed the humpbacked cloth peddler, a Southern European, my grandfather took this uncle out to the barn for a long talk reinforced with the razor strap. My grandmother and several younger aunts worked in San Francisco's Methodist church; so, in the early 1920's, one aunt wanted to marry a Japanese. She was dissuaded with difficulty, and only by arguments about the hardships for future children. Lack of prejudice allowed the opportunity for a serious friendship. Another aunt married a foreign-born Armenian, and my stepfather is from Holland.

Although several denominations appear in our family, religion always means a personal dynamic relationship with God, a relationship that shows in daily life. I went abroad to teach in our denominational school, feeling I should, and I am content doing the best I can.

One teacher, of Anglo-American Protestant origins, in boyhood acquired a Franco-American Catholic stepfather and a large Franco-American stepfamily settled three generations on California farms. Through charts showing the lineage and social status of his kinfolk, and a lengthy exposition, this young man schematized the culture into which he was introduced by his mother's second marriage and to which he became attached sentimentally though he felt apart otherwise. He thought his sense of cultural separateness was consistent with his mother's choice of a "Frenchman" who was openly rebellious against his own family's French background.

The student's report postulated cultural homogeneity in the immigrant generation.

All were born in Southern France, received some eight years of formal education there, and came to the United States before the age of twenty-one. All males were farmers, all females housewives, all were proficient in their French language, all settled in the same part of Southern California.

The men came as hands on large ranches, the girls came as domestics in ranch homes. Social life centered on the ranch, limiting the pool of potential mates. Those in France often saw to it that an unmarried daughter went to the same ranch as the family friend's unmarried son. This simplified acquaintanceship and courting, and led to semiarranged marriages for all in that generation except E. He was much younger and when he reached marriageable age, conditions had begun to change. Attending high school, he broadened his social circle. His two marriages followed Americanized styles of dating and courting. But he limited his choices to the "French community," subject to traditional chaperonage.

Even in the 1920s and 1930s chaperonage was still required by parents of most French girls. All men of the second generation, that is, the first generation of American-born, rebelled against chaperones, except R. They enjoyed much greater freedom than their fathers. High school was the general rule, and college was for some in this generation. They learned that dating was more fun without the "old people" around to chaperone. Generally, they "wanted to be like the other kids in school." Their parents did not care for this but could do little about it.

The girls found it more difficult to rebel. Hence the men's rebellion greatly reduced the girls' chances of marriage. Two of the girls in this generation therefore married late and one of these marriages had to be arranged. The attractiveness of the French-American girls was not an issue.

All men in the immigrant generation are farmers. By 1915 all owned farms, acquired in one of two ways. Either the men saved enough to purchase land, which was then rather cheap, or the ranch owners gave land to the immigrant workers. In the second generation, only two are farmers, while none are in the third generation. Reasons for the change are more education, rising land values encouraging sale, higher earnings in other occupations, and the young people's attitude that they are "sick and tired" of farming.

Among the immigrant generation, only two had more than eight years of schooling in France. In the United States they had no time for study, often expressing strong regret about this and even becoming fanatics for schooling. All agreed that children and grandchildren were to be better educated, even if this caused the "French community" to disintegrate and the young people to give up the land.

Among the second generation, most felt the same. But this pressure inevitably met second-generation resistance, to the regret now of all. One first-generation father "always wanted a doctor for a son" so he pushed and pulled his Jean in the medical direction without once considering Jean's feelings. Jean is not doing well at medical school and is unhappy, less because he doesn't want to be a doctor than because of the terrific pressure on him to succeed.

The immigrant generation learned English to varying degrees. Justin and Apollonia learned mostly from their sons. Also, when Justin was fifteen, he attended the second grade of school one year to learn English. The poor English proficiency in immigrant parents of two other families accounts for their children's relative proficiency in French, without injuring the children's competence in English. LeRoy's poor French is a consequence of living with his English-speaking mother. Jean understands much French as his mother has spoken this to him during most of his life, but now he hates the sound of it, refuses to answer in French, and wishes his mother "wouldn't do that."

[Family pressures were dramatized by sketching the personalities.] Justin was a tyrant, Apollonia and the boys little more than slaves. Apollonia's role was to bear children and keep house, then work in the fields when she wasn't busy with the first two obligations. For the boys there was nothing but work and study. Justin provided well for the family's material needs, but completely neglected their emotional needs. There were never picnics, trips, other family entertainment, or even after-supper conversations among the family. The home was not happy. The boys were very fond of their mother but towards their father, feelings often reached the point of hate.

[The account ended with a summary.] There are four main areas of change among these families. The areas are marriage, occupation, education, and language proficiency. Changes are discernible in each family and generation. Succeeding generations become less traditionally French in marriage and language. They acquire more schooling, their occupations leave the soil and become diversified; these widen their social contacts, they speak English more and neglect French.

In these areas of change, different degrees of change are also discernible. These seem to be linked to a family "personality" or ethos, by which I mean the family atmosphere of relative happiness and closeness. Justin's family shows the greatest degree of change, or Americanization. To his hard-driven boys, "the French way" became synonymous with "the old Man's way" and so was to be avoided.

A widowed elementary school principal wrote exuberantly of her Scandinavian-American family in Wisconsin, producing a paean to domestic love, stability, and prosperity. "In both the maternal and paternal families," she said, "authority lodged in the father but the goals and means were different. The paternal grandfather exerted quiet, firm pressure; his wife was the mouthpiece. From earliest years, his children conformed. My father felt this strongly and practiced similar ways. There were no harshly spoken directives, but a quiet implying and sensing of direction. Grandfather was a man more of deeds than words; his most effective tool was silence. My father also attained control through directed silence. Silence did not mean consent. My realizations of when to act, and when not to, reflected my father's behavior and his silence or voiced encouragement. He never said no. He never had to. We all knew."

Her maternal grandfather, she said, exerted authority by voice and act, and his wife, fully trained in voiced directives by her father, without kind overtones, understood and accepted her husband's authority. The grandfather did not hesitate to raise his voice. His conduct was above reproach but it included an amount of "do as I say rather than as I do." Children of this line could divert from authority because of their trust in words; that is, they could discuss matters. The paternal line, in contrast, lacked such recourse. Relying on nearly absolute silence the children had no mode of response permitting choice or disagreement.

The principal felt the influence of both family lines. "I could talk to my mother," she said, "but if she felt that my father might uphold her against me, she would say, 'Ask you father.' That was the end of the line; I knew what to expect, though my father was less rigid than *his* father in that he permitted some discussion. I cannot locate the boundary between strict authority and some freedom in my parent's home. I was never terribly afraid. I was confident of the chance for some discussion leading to a calm decision.

"Each family line defined its own goals. The paternal goal was 'a good life,' that is, wealth sufficient for needs but not necessarily more. Most members wanted approval and acceptance. Social status had no great value but unpopularity implied social failure. A 'good life' required conformity to patterned behavior of the class and region, including the standard religious beliefs.

"The maternal family valued land highly, and monetary worth, and cultivation of talents. This meant emphasis on education. The maternal grandmother often said, 'It is nice if you never have to do these things, but it's wonderful to know how if you need to.' So the children were given every opportunity to be prepared for life's demands."

Relatives neighbored one another over a great extent of land, the principal related. Each family had to succeed on its own and contribute to the community by its talents and by returning the body of each deceased member for embalming and burial in the family cemetery. Each bride received a dowry; each deceased received a burial casket—of copper or wood and concrete for a woman, of steel and concrete for a man, materials supposed to defy extinction. At a death there was to be no weeping and also no remarriage. She had supposed these modes of burial and mourning to be general. She felt committed to support all her family traditions. At the time of writing about them she was feeling obligation to return as a teacher to the ancestral community.

She concluded her account: "Mother's family influenced my father greatly. His primary goals remained the same but he also followed his wife's people in acquiring more land, money, prestige in the local community, county, and state than did any of his own family. My mother strongly encouraged him in the goals he adopted from her family.

"I also am continually adding new goals to my life. It is an ever upward struggle and I always question my ability, in the spirit of my paternal line. However, if all one needs are determination and effort, I have not a doubt of succeeding, in the spirit of my maternal line."

A quiet, young teacher described his family culture with details more unusual, even exotic, than are ordinarily attributed to the middle-class public schoolman:

My maternal grandfather, Jacob, was born in Saratdorf, Germany, the youngest of a large family. He appeared to have been the black sheep, leaving home at an early age, traveling around Europe and ending up in Turkey. There he fell in with a band of raiders. When the raiders heard of caravans traveling the desert, they would intercept them, take the goods and sell them in the markets of some Turkish town. After about a year Jacob fell out with the Turks and fled for his life to Siberia. There he brawled and gambled until he met my grandmother.

My maternal grandmother was also born in Germany, in an unknown town. Her parents died when she was very young and she was sent to an aunt and uncle in Siberia. There her aunt made her do the hardest and most distasteful chores. She told me of the times she carried the wash down to the river for scrubbing; there she exchanged gossip and news of friends and relatives.

When girls reached the age of marriage it was then customary to have them seated at a window sewing or quilting until they were noticed as attractive by young men. An interested young man would follow up by approaching the parents to discuss marriage.

When my grandparents were married they moved around Siberia considerably, having inherited a small sum of money. They had four children in quick succession. In 1905 they sailed for the United States on the ship *Missler*. Jacob worked as a farm hand in Colorado, bought farm machinery and land, and they produced six more children. The Depression wiped Jacob out. Now bankrupt, he and the family worked in fruit fields and canneries until he had paid all his debts. Then grandfather again worked as a field hand and turned religious until death. . . .

My paternal great-grandfather was born in Aleksanderthal, Russia, a small village of German descendants. After marrying and having eight children, my great-grandfather came to the United States in 1893. He worked as a railroad section hand in New Jersey, traveled as far west as Wilson, Kansas, then returned to Russia. There my grandfather grew up and married, sailing to the United States in 1901 with his wife and baby daughter.

Working as a section hand on the railroad, he moved his family to Colorado where all worked as farm hands until he staked dry claims to 640 acres of land and acquired other holdings. In 1921 a flood wiped them out. They left to work on California fruit farms and in canneries.

My father was a farm hand until 1941 when he worked at an air force base until after the War. Then he entered a factory. . . . I was the eldest son. I completed college and my two years of military service, I married and now have a year-old son. . . .

The goals of my family, like those of all living from the land, contained the quality of hard work. My father would tell me, "Do the job well the first time so it will not have to be done again." He also said, "For an honest dollar, you must give an honest dollar's work." Actions of my grandparents spoke these points louder than any words.

I believe my father never gave less than the very best to his employers. He worked hard days, and nights he brought home study manuals so as to become even better at his job.

My grandparents and parents believed that hard work would raise us to the middle class. My own goals were to go to college and to become a schoolteacher. Now I have raised them to cover further study and my ambition is to be a *good* teacher. This means hard work in our constantly changing world, but I am extremely satisfied. I enjoy working with students and helping them in their problems.

[Having established the family creed of honest, hard work, he described Americanization in his family.] In Europe, the eldest male of the whole family was the leader. Others obeyed his orders even when the younger men had families. With time in the United States, my family lost some of these ways, and the head of each separate family took control. This lessened authority of parents over grown sons. But my father long continued absolute in his family and would swing from extreme severity to indulgence.

I am less absolute than my father was. I share responsibilities with my wife. Also I find that my parents now share in making their decisions, noticeably more than during my younger days. When our children are old enough to understand rules, I feel that my wife and I should be democratic about establishing rules. Until then, my wife and I will carry out the duties of punishment less severely than in my childhood, for I still resent authority that has not proven itself, such as my father exercised. . . .

My family expected me to be polite and respectful to all my elders. My family taught me about race prejudice. Probably they did it in the reverse of the usual way. In their time, they had been discriminated against as Germans, as had their parents during the First World War. So they would tell me I was as good as anyone. I personally experienced no difficulty but their advice made me aware of racial problems. I came from a town with many Mexicans, where whites opposed Mexicans in snowball fights, soccer games, and otherwise. I remember telling myself, "They're as good as I am" but I went along with the crowd.

My father also stressed my responsibility to admit when I was wrong. Once I threw a rock and hit a friend, so my father ordered, "Go over and say you're sorry." I answered, "Why? Nobody ever does that to me." He insisted, "When a man is wrong, he should always admit it, no matter how it hurts." So I said I was sorry, and from then on tried to make sure I was never in that situation again.

[The elder generations' views of respect, authority, obedience, and integrity included] keeping the family together. My father's father gave each son a portion of land, from his own lands or adjoining ones, to keep the sons from scattering. But when he lost his lands in the 1921 flood, the children sought employment elsewhere and scattered far and wide.

The older generations also took care of their aged. But I would not want my children to support me and my wife. Children feel, as I did, that they must escape parental authority, move away to where they can be free. The same is true of religion. After a rather carefree youth, my maternal grandfather repented and joined the German Congregational Church. My parents were brought up in this church, hearing sermons in German. My grandparents expected everyone to follow their religion and repentance. This somewhat alienated my parents and now I hardly ever attend church without thinking of my grandparents' extreme conduct.

I am the only one in four generations of my family with a high school education and more. But the story is not ended, for there is no ending while the family exists.

Showing major similarities in social forms and conduct to this German-Russian-American account is the brief description given by a young junior high school counselor of Pennsylvania Dutch or German-American antecedents. The social design outlined accompanies these families tenaciously even on far-flung travels, as was shown later by German-American Lutherans long settled in the French Catholic stronghold of New Orleans. The Counselor wrote that arbitrarily starting with the birth of his great-grandparents in Missouri, about 1840, "the husband was the final authority. In the parents' generation there was a shift towards equal cooperation. My own generation shows equal status of husband and wife in family affairs. For the first time, wife and mother work out of the home and experience new satisfactions.

"Formal education reaches higher levels. Grandparents could not have gone beyound the eighth grade, nor did mother. Father finished college, and children continue into graduate study. Women are now expected to have completed high school and to aspire further.

"Religious emphasis is not on church attendance but on total behavior and thought, equated with democracy and with the family's interpretation of the American way. Religious education comes through the church organization rather than through family devotions.

"Family members are no longer close bound, owing to geographical distances. Grandparents and their brothers and sisters reared families within fifty miles of one another, exerting strong reciprocal influences. In the maternal line, parents followed children across the country, keeping the close ties. Ability or readiness of parents to move such distances marks change from the previous generation, to whom a move of one hundred miles seemed impossible. But many obligations persist as taught by older generations. For example, care of older family members is considered necessary; neglect of them is unthinkable. The needs of parents are heeded readily."

A young Greek-American teacher, who had heard no English before entering public school, described the midwestern settlement of Greek immigrants that included his parents.

Over the past half-century the small Greek minority tried to preserve traditions. Families have lived together in great intimacy and know each other only too well. The second generation finds it most difficult to marry within this compact unit. Most have married into other Greek communities of the region.

The immigrants of our community were welded together by the same social and economic forces, the same language, religion, and customs. Their peasant forefathers had lived very frugally, and the immigrants lived similarly. They did not speculate in their American businesses, but expanded slowly. Their personal lives were not spectacular, they did not try to keep up with the Joneses nor make the society columns. Comforts in the Anglo-American home were considered extravagances in the Greek home. Our Greek's first goals were not a new car, new refrigerator, new furniture, or a new house; but rather money for security, the children's education, elevated status, and strengthened identity with the Greek heritage. These four were life's important goals.

Greek culture affected every phase of existence. Within the home, only Greek was spoken; some of the second generation heard English first at grade school. At table, the food was predominantly Greek. Records of Greek music and folk dances often preceded knowledge of American music and dance. *Atlantis*, the Greek-American newspaper, appeared in every home. New Year's Eve, Apokreas or Carnival, Easter, and name days were all festive occasions for the entire group.

Many of these people were vaguely aware of their great heritage. They had heard of Plato, Xenophon, Aristophanes, and Euripides, but had not read them or otherwise understood them. They had been told stories from the *Iliad* and *Odyssey* without distinguishing whether they were history or legend. Though sharply aware of their language, they were vague about Greek civilization's great ideas. They were cognizant of the world's admiration for Greece's past. Therefore why should they embrace all ideas and practices of the adopted land? They sat reluctantly, waiting and observing. . . .

The dozen or so boys who went to war in World War II returned as men. For the first time they had been exposed to completely American surroundings. This second generation now took responsible parts in Greek community affairs. English replaced Greek at all formal meetings, including meetings of the church council, and in the recording of minutes. The younger generation moved into occupations and professions where the elders could not counsel or interfere.

Although today only a few of the immigrants remain, their opinions are heard and rarely opposed vocally. At all social gatherings these men are the first seated, served, and recognized. Sons still ask permission of their fathers to marry and seldom enter marriage without parents' approval. Families are formally introduced when their offspring wish to date. When possible, families contribute materially to establish the newlyweds. The whole community dances at weddings.

Most of the second generation marry in their late twenties. Many marry other Greek-Americans, but some do not, against great parental objection and family heartache. Such pressures often force these young people to leave for other parts. Today a number remain unmarried, victims of rigid tradition, searching for ideals combining their hearts' wishes and their parents' dictates. The marriage barrier crumbles slowly. A few of the elders accept American in-laws. The degree of acceptance seems to depend on the Americans' understanding and tolerance of traditional Greek society, customs, and authoritative elders.

The daily life of second-generation Greek-Americans blends the traditions. Greek is spoken in the presence of elders. American food is served as often as Greek. Gala parties and religious festivals are fewer and less gay. The priest is American born; sermons and Sunday school are in English. An annual formal ball, including Greek folk dances as intermissions, has been started by youth groups. The city's chamber of commerce sponsors "Greek Week," importing a professor of classical Greek to discuss the Greek theatre and also programming youth groups to demonstrate traditional dances, foods, and dress.

More of the youth devote time to play, doing it outside the Greek community, than did their older brothers who had to work in family businesses at comparable ages. However, grandchildren, no longer understanding or speaking Greek, are still named traditionally after grandparents; popular songs of Greece are collected on stereo; young groups study classical Greek literature, and whole families make pilgrimages to Greece.

The era of the elders is ending, but the second generation will carry on the community. There is no ending. Time and the community move on, heedless that the first immigrants had planned to return home to Greece with enough American dollars to buy a farm and start a family there. Today, most of the city's Greek population is middle class and self-employed; there are a few millionaires. No members were ever on a relief roll, there has never been a juvenile delinquent, and there is almost no divorce.

The last illustration of work in family cultures presents our dominant group—the white Anglo-Saxon Protestants of good repute and colonial or American Revolutionary origins. These dominant families are our traditional measure of social accomplishment. The family record to be summarized was assembled during months of effort by a young man teaching high school. The genealogical zeal of successive generations produced oral and printed histories of member families, accounting for every person in lineal and collateral branches. Wherever these kinsmen wandered, they kept in touch. Men and women of the member families contributed actively to their times, founding a university, a major industry, a church, a political movement, having careers in learned professions, in industries, legislatures, judiciaries, commerce, governmental administration, and the military. If the kinsmen had not privately kept in touch, they would have known one another's circumstances through public news and monuments. The student records that none in the family was reputed wealthy, though "comfortably well off"; and none was a social snob, because "the spirit of public service persists through the generations." Some women of earlier times were called "bluestockings" because they taught in university and high school; they were also "such perfect ladies, very formal, sweet and proper."

In the grandparents' generation, a number of men and women failed to marry. Like the bluestockings, "many of the girls educated themselves out of the possibility of marriage; while the men were so committed to public service that they may have lacked the time to get married! Branches of the family tree disappear without male descendants. Thank goodness, my father eventually married to perpetuate the name. He was also the first of his name to leave the Middle West permanently," where ancestors had founded the university and kinsmen still study.

There were no evidences of black sheep. The student's father attributed this to "a solid church background in all generations and to being surrounded by many relatives living within a small geographical range. I am sure this extensive world of my forebears and living relatives, always present in my background, must have weighed on me tremendously as a great debt needing payment, or as a great reputation needing to be sustained, or as a heritage to be fulfilled. Nobody ever said this in so many words. It must have come to me when I was too young even to understand words. It must have been conveyed in attitudes, expressions, and family recollections of dozens of aunts and uncles, great-aunts and great-uncles, and other relatives."

Family records noted that the ancestors migrated "originally from Scotland. In defense of their Presbyterian religion, many fled to northern Ireland in the seventeenth century. Even here they suffered 'civil and religious oppression,' according to the family history, and hence, many moved to America." Aristocracy was not this family's boast, but in America the student's great-great-grandfather, a great-grandson of a Virginia settler, became damned as "that—aristocrat" by those opposing his demands for public education.

The student observed that "the importance of being able to trace the family back to the first American settlers seems to have overwhelmed earlier generations of our family. Our [printed] history is loaded with references to various relatives accepted for membership in the DAR or the Colonial Dames. This seems to have little merit for the present generation." What mattered rather was that the young man, like his predecessors, should earn a living at something he enjoyed. "Accidentally I fell into teaching, after journalism, advertising, radio broadcasting, and management. In this I am happy. I just want to be a teacher! New cars, a big and flashy home, the finest of clothes have *not* been among my goals. The home, car, and clothes we have are fewer and older than those of anybody else I grew up with.

"What we have are four wonderful children. If I sound conservative, I cannot ignore the fact that through all my gentle radicalism goes a paternal strain of conservative Scot and a maternal strain of conservative New England. My radicalism has always been within close bounds."

In this student's long, detailed, and chart-enriched account, expressing an exuberant love of kin—people living and dead—and of the world they patterned, shared, and carefully transmitted, there is a high sense of the family's strong social position. There is not one mention of the great minorities struggling through American history. One would never guess that fateful national issues rested on special social uses of different races, creeds, classes, and nationalities. This omission, no less than the affirmed "spirit of public service," marks a dominant group who, in the words of an English aristocrat, "never meets anyone else." Yet the recorder of this family had been in the American army during the Second World War. He served a little over three years, of which a year or so was spent in India. "There was nothing I liked about it except that I was smart enough—three cheers for my ancestors!—to qualify for the army's college program and so spent six happy months at the university. And there I met the girl I later married."

The student concluded: "I am proud of my forebears, full of a sense of obligation not to let them down, filled by the duty to pass their heritage on to my son. Our family's insistence upon quality in all work, upon devotion to doing the best always, have been practiced and communicated down the generations. My father said that these traits characterized every relative he knew."

All accounts show that pride of family and its ways is not confined to special students, traditions, or families—it is universal. It seems to be an aspect of the psychic quality we call morale, which persuades human beings to go on with the hard business of living, perpetuating, and creating. The concept of the family style of life—its hereditary patterns taught, enacted as life, and transmitted down generations, even centuries—seems to exalt every student's awareness of himself and even of others. Through the systematic communications with persons of his lineage and about them, at distances that lighten pressures and allow conceptualization, the student feels ennobled by an active sense that the family's tradition is his property, and that he holds it as a precious trust. This feeling surprised most students, as a discovery, though it usually did not surprise their kinsmen of older generations.

Perhaps the discovery is surprising only to this century in America, to our epoch of rising social equalities, elevating children of every humble origin, leveling every social diversity to produce a surface of anonymous Americanism. Our creed of Americanism today holds no grand reference to family life but incentives to self-reliant individualism on the one hand, and to joining the army of organization men on the other.

A consequence of the students' work was each one's sudden conviction, by empathy, that the minorities also, even under grinding poverty and humiliation, share similar commitments to their ancestors' traditional past and its future. Occasional Negroes, Mexicans, and others who agreed to serve as informants made it clear that their families also boasted of great persons, achievements, and standards within their own cultural and social realms, even when the group was denigrated by the dominant middle class. Greatness does not rule out meanness in any group, but, on the other hand, its mean status does not erase the group's conviction of worth. And the students found their conviction justified in the minorities' family cultures, whose designs and details captured their imaginations. For these students, the stereotypes about minorities now proved insufficient, and minority persons of all ages and positions became interesting, comprehensible, and worthy fellow humans.

Through all projects a fresh style of thinking was encouraged: to expect tremendous cultural variety in American populations, to ask the meanings of behavior in terms of ancestral family and community traditions, to listen and observe, to question formalistic or stereotyped judgements (like "retarded" or "unmotivated" pupil), and to search for the creativity in each child which might be masked by the educator's own cultural and professional (called at times "subcultural") predilections and by the child's culturally conditioned or class-conditioned disorientation at school. Students were urged to keep abreast of our revoluntionary social changes by reading widely outside of their professional publications, by searching the news media for signposts, and by reading creative writing for invaluable information about man's ways. Conscientious and highly disciplined as a professional group, and considerably overworked by extra tasks, educators had to be urged to trust themselves to look beyond their usual limits. And they did. Some went to extraordinary lengths, as when two women studied a ponderous work on cultural theory and presented a condensation of it as an educators' manual. All took intellectual and professional pleasure in understanding culture's operations affecting schools, including biases of each one's cultural nature, manifest in teacher, pupil, parent, and community.

27 / The Concept of Culture and Its Significance for School Counselors

Eleanor Leacock

The culture concept, central to the field of anthropology, is becoming increasingly familiar in the social service fields. When properly applied, the idea of "culture" can be extremely useful for the understanding of behavior and the breaking down of many barriers to effective communication. However, like most ideas, it can also be distorted, and defeat the very purpose it should serve. This paper will discuss the appropriate use of the culture concept, and indicate the way it can be distorted when incorrectly applied to differences between children from "middle-class," economically well-off homes, and children from economically marginal or insecure homes.

True cultural insight enables us to see behind superficial, socially patterned differences to the full integrity of an individual. It prevents us from misinterpreting behavior different from that to which we are accustomed. To take an example from American Indian culture, people working with Indian children have found that they often do not respond well to teaching techniques that depend on the desire to do better than one's peers on a test, to answer a question more capably, in short to compete successfully. Where Indian societies have retained roots with the past they are still pervaded by a cooperative spirit, and children feel uncomfortable in competitively structured situations, at least insofar as learning is concerned. This is often misinterpreted as a lack of desire to learn, but an awareness of cultural differences reveals that the motivation for learning is present, but that it is being inhibited rather than encouraged by teaching practices foreign to Indian culture.

The persistence of such responses was brought home sharply to me when I assigned oral reports, seminar style, to a college class of bright, argumentative students. One of the girls, who had seldom spoken up in class, asked for permission to write rather than deliver her paper. I was unsuccessful in my attempt to persuade her to try the experience of oral delivery. She later told me that the course had given her insight into her reason for declining, and to the discomfort she had always felt in school. Her father was Indian she said and though there was little of an ongoing Indian community in Connecticut where she was raised, nonetheless the style of American Indian discourse had persisted in her family. For her, discussion should not involve the rapid-fire, essentially competitive argument to which we are accustomed. Instead, it should involve measured, considered statements, and—so difficult for us—attentive listening. Each person should listen patiently to everyone else, and the attempt should be at reaching consensus rather than winning an argument. Therefore, this student had always felt uncomfortable in classrooms, with their built-in competitive atmosphere.

Thus, learning and exchanging knowledge are conceived differently in different cultures. So, too, are traditional styles of behavior between adults and children. Teachers working with Puerto Rican students often find that a child being reprimanded does not look at them or respond to their statements. They may think the child sullen, rebellious, or rude. In the cultural terms of the child, however, he is expressing acquiescence and respect. Understanding this culture difference enables a teacher to see behind socially patterned behavior to a child's actual feelings, and to relate to him as an individual.

MISAPPLICATION OF THE CULTURE CONCEPT

However, the awareness that such differences exist can lead to their exaggeration and misapplication. Such is often the case with the "culture of poverty" described for economically underprivileged and minority communities. Unfortunately, "lower-class culture" is fast becoming a new stereotype behind which the individual is not revealed more fully, but instead is lost. Indeed, the "old-fashioned" but sympathetic and insightful person, who is skeptical of "all this talk about culture," and asserts that what really counts is the individual child, is more correct than those who have gone overboard with distorted expectations for "cultural" differences. Such a person knows intuitively that, although people act and react in terms of learned patterns for behavior, which may differ, nonetheless *all people respond positively to respect and real interest.* The study of man's many and varied cultures indicates that in this regard all human beings are alike. Further, while there are differences among class, religious, national, and racial groups in this country, all are part of a total "American culture."

An example of what can happen when the concept "culture of poverty" is carried too far is described in Estelle Fuch's *Pickets At The Gates* (1966). A principal in a school that had shifted from predominantly white to Negro in the course of several years, wanted to prepare his new teachers, fresh from college, for the children they would be teaching. Drawing from the literature on the "deprived child," he wrote a letter stating that, compared with children from middle-class homes, the schoolchildren would be poor financially, academically, and socially. Many would be on welfare; the school lunch would be the best meal they would get. Their mothers would be so busy with their "broods" that the individual child would be lonely. Often there would be no fathers in the home, and there would be no organized family activities. The children, he continued, would come from noisy atmospheres, and would not hear the quiet voice of the teacher until trained to give attention. They would have received no encouragement to achieve, and socially, economically, and culturally would be poor and not ready for school. This was true, he stated, of poor groups generally; the same characteristics found among our Negro and Puerto Rican families are found in Appalachia, among the hillbillies of the Ozarks, and among Mexican-Americans.

The unfortunate principal continued the letter with specific directives for handling these children and, proud of his efforts, sent a copy to each new teacher and also to the president of the PTA. He was shocked, hurt, and puzzled when irate Negro parents, active PTAers working hard to see that their children got the best education possible, promptly organized a picket line in front of the school, distributed a leaflet describing the principal's insulting attitude toward their children, and demanded his ouster.

The principal had utterly ignored wide variations within the Negro community. Further, by taking all the negative aspects of poverty and grouping them into a composite picture of all the children, he had drawn a picture that could only be false and damaging. It is one thing to say that in a poor community one would expect to find more bitter, angry, and withdrawn children, and greater difficulty mastering school lessons because of the tremendous objective difficulties with which many children are coping. It is quite another to say that children from poor families generally are uninterested in learning—an inference that unfortunately can so easily become a convenient rationale to excuse inadequate teaching and unequal school facilities in low-income areas. Many are the working-class families who aspire to a college education for their children (Purcell 1964). Many also are the hard-working mothers without men at home, facing combined difficulties of bad housing, long hours, low pay, and inadequate community facilities for their children, who nonetheless give them a great deal of love, respect, and encouragement.

Wrenn (1962: 31–32) warns against making premature judgments about family atmosphere based on demographic features alone. He writes:

> . . . whatever the facts about birth rate, family size, and divorce, there are widely varying and deeply held opinions on these topics in any community . . . There is little evidence that a small family or large one per se provides the "best" climate for child growth. Economic capacity to support the children's social and educational needs is a factor, but so also is the love support the child receives, the integrity of the family unit, and the general psychological climate of the home.
>
> Counselors should be knowledgeable about the interrelationship of such family factors and be slow to prejudge the home . . . . A counselor . . . needs to be wary of coming to conclusions about a family which may deviate from his stereotype of a "good" family.

Some literature on "disadvantaged children" begins to sound as if broken homes are the exclusive property of the poor. I have to comment here on the fact that in a parochial nursery school one of my children attended, half of the "white, middle-class, Protestant" children in one grade were from broken homes, several were quite emotionally disturbed, and the mother of one was dying of acute alchoholism. Yet expectations for the children's performance were high, and the children were on the whole living up to them.

CULTURE CONCEPT AS A TOOL

Does this mean the "cultural" dimension should be abandoned entirely by the school counselor who is trying to help the children from working class homes? The answer is no, *if it is used as a tool for reaching and understanding the individual as an individual, not for burying him behind generalizations about a group.* "Culture" refers in part to the general style of interpersonal relations and related attitudes that are traditional in a given society. It does not refer to the infinite variety of ways each individual feels and responds in dealing with his own life circumstances. In addition, the notion of cultural consistency becomes fuzzy when it is applied to class differences in our society. True, any definable group has what can be called a "culture." One can speak of the "culture" of different institutions—hospitals have different "cultures" on the whole from schools, and both from business houses. Within certain general patterns of "school culture," each school develops its own traditions. Once can even speak of a certain "classroom culture," developed during the short lifetime of a common experience shared by a teacher and a group of children.

However, when one talks of anything as general as "working-class culture" or "lower-class culture," one must do so warily, and define what one means. On the one hand, it is part of American "culture" as a whole; on the other, the "working" or "lower" class includes many national, regional, religious, rural-urban, and income variations. Finally, as stated above, one is only referring to certain very general expectations for attitudes and behavior—one is not talking about how the individual incorporates these into his total self.

At present we know more about these general expectations for attitudes and behavior within the so-called middle class than we do for the "working class." Therefore, the best use that can be made of the culture concept is as a tool enabling the counselor to understand his own "values,"—or, as others may see them, biases. He needs as open a mind as possible when attempting to develop rapport with children who are bitter, angry, or withdrawn, and with their families. Conrad Arensberg and Arthur Niehoff (1964), writing a manual for Americans overseas, felt that the basis for giving people insight into other cultures was to given them some understanding of their own unquestioned assumptions about how people should be motivated and how things should be done. They discuss the cluster of attitudes involving time, work, and money, historically based in the Protestant Reformation, and changing with time, but still functioning. Time as a commodity to be apportioned and either "spent well" or "wasted"; work as an activity important for its own sake, as well as a means to an end; money as a measure of personal worth (hence people's embarrassment about revealing their salary)—these tie together in a specifically American pattern based on the assumption that effort leads to success. This pattern was well suited to a frontier country where hard work did indeed lead to financial success for many, and where the many more for whom it did not are forgotten. That effort will succeed is one of the most treasured of American beliefs. For "middle-class" Americans, where it is more or less true, and for those from working class homes who have moved into a higher social status, it is so central a belief that they cannot empathize with those whose experiences have rendered it meaningless. On the whole, they are unable to see life in any other terms and hence are unable to communicate with children to whom the notion that effort will be rewarded has become an empty platitude.

Sensitivity with regard to his own attitudes enables the counselor to put himself in another's place—to *understand* rather than jump to a conclusion. On this basis, he is better able to assess materials he will be using, to evaluate forms of discourse he is employing. Do the filmstrips he is planning to use with a parent group deal realistically with the problems they are facing, or do they take a naïve and superficial approach that will only be a slap in the face? (This would be true of many psychologically oriented films geared to families living in quite comfortable circumstances.) How does the counselor introduce and evaluate test materials? What kinds of questions does he ask children who are in trouble? How meaningful is their experience to the counselor? How are children's problems reinforced by the role defined for them in the classroom? When the world is seen in their terms, do the children who appear unreachable reveal themselves as actually waging a desperate struggle for a sense of identity and self-respect?

Counselors already know the limits of testing and the fact that a child should not be assessed on the basis of test information alone. They also know that children from low income homes will generally do less well than those from middle income homes, even on the Rorschach and other projective tests of personality. Differences in previous educational experience of children, including familiarity with tests, and a bias in constructing and interpreting tests (a matter presently of concern to testing services) are partly responsible.

The problem of motivation is also important, as indicated by a study of the effect upon test scores of money incentives as compared with praise. Klugman (1944) tested a heterogeneous group of children twice, using the revised Stanford-Binet, and the second time offered some of the children money rewards for good scores. Whereas scores on a second testing generally rose somewhat, there was no demonstrable difference between the scores of those white children who were offered a money reward and those who were not. However, the Negro children given money rewards showed definitely better performances than those to whom praise was the only incentive. Now they had something real to work for!

HOW NOT TO WIN FRIENDS

An example of how a "middle-class" cultural bias can hinder communication is afforded unfortunately by an "Inventory" of a "Child's Background of Experience and Interest" in an otherwise fine New York City guide for counseling (Board of Education of New York City 1955-56). The first heading is "Fun at Home," the second, "Reading Fun." The child is asked about favorite activities at home, according to the sample questionnaire, and then, "Do you read aloud? To whom? Does anyone ever read to you? How much of your free time do you spend reading for fun? What kinds of books do you like best? What books have you read this term? How many books do you own?" Anyone who has worked in a low-income neighborhood will recognize that this is hardly the way to establish rapport with a hurt and angry child.

The next topic is "Your Pet," with questions like, "Have you a pet? Who takes care of it?" Then, "Do you take lessons outside of school?" and, "Making and Collecting Things: What things did you make? What things do you want to make soon? What collections have you started?" Only then does the schedule come to less biased topics—helping around the house, friends, radio, TV, movies. The sensitive counselor would know that such questions could only further alienate a child from poor circumstances who is embittered and confused, and has been referred for help.

The consistent bias of school readers with their blond, suburban world that completely negates the existence of urban workers, and especially dark-skinned workers, has become a matter of concern. The presentation of life as a series of amiable and quite vapid incidents where all is "sweetness and light" is unhealthy not only for middle-class children; it has become clear that it is especially hard on underprivileged and minority-group children. Fortunately there are attempts to redress the situation. Illinois has a broad enough guidance program to plan improvements in texts and materials along these lines; Detroit has for some time been addressing itself to this problem; and the Bank Street readers picture urban scenes that include Negroes and Puerto Ricans as well as whites engaged in all manner of activities. However, it takes a long time to change a whole system of textbooks, and it is important for counselors, where it is part of their responsibility, to help introduce more varied materials into classroom libraries. This can be particularly helpful where there is an individualized reading program.

Another instance where the very existence of working-class and minority-group children is denied—but one that lends itself easily to improvements—involves the use of classroom walls. One can still enter classroom after classroom in our public schools without seeing a Negro adult or child pictured on the walls, and this extends to Puerto Ricans, Oriental people, Mexican-Americans. Classroom walls carry a clear message to the children as to what is and is not of value, and here an unhealthy message is being conveyed to children, white as well as nonwhite. Nor is this message fundamentally altered by posting a picture of Frederick Douglass during Brotherhood Month, along with a painting of a Negro and white child happily running hand in hand. A subsidiary message is only being added: pay lip service to the family of man at the appropriate times.

CREATIVE CHILDREN

A final point to develop in relation to cultural bias concerns the question of lost talent and creative children. Sometimes the more creative children are withdrawn, concentrating on their private thoughts, but often they are "difficult" or "rebellious" from a teacher's point of view (Wrenn 1962:55–56): Generally, in handling too large a group it is a temptation for a teacher to value and lean heavily on the more conforming children. Unless she knows how to use the questions raised by more creative children, and feed them into discussions that are meaningful for the class as a whole, creative children become a problem to her.

When a creative child is from a low-income home his difficulties are compounded, and his creativity is more likely to be channelled into unproductive rebellion. We have already mentioned the denial of his very being by classroom materials and exhibits. He is also likely to receive more punishment for transgressions in behavior than is a middle-class child. First discussed by Davis and Dollard in their *Children of Bondage* (1940), this aspect of school life for children was further documented by Hollingshead in his *Elmtown's Youth* (1949). He gives in detail one incident in which a working-class youth was literally driven out of school in the course of an episode stemming from initial lateness, although a worse record of lateness had been ignored in the case of a wealthy boy (Hollingshead 1949:185–198). In *Education and Income* (1961), Patricia Sexton carries the point further, and shows the extent to which differential punishment and other inequities for middle- and low-income children permeate an entire urban school system, and in *The American School* (Sexton, 1967) she summarizes more recent studies of these inequities.

The study of classroom life carried on by the present author under the auspices of the Bank Street College of Education revealed another type of punishment disadvantaged children experience to a greater extent than middle-income children. This is the subtle but pervasive derogation of their personal experiences, which, unfortunately, can be conveyed even by kind and well-meaning teachers. For example, in one classroom an eight-year-old Negro boy talked eagerly and at length about the planes he had seen at the airport. The lesson was on transportation, and one would expect the teacher either to open up the child's account for class discussion, or to question him further. Or she might simply have said, as observed in other classrooms, "How wonderful," or "Good," and asked another question— unimaginative, perhaps, but at least approving. Instead, the teacher asked, "Who took you?" She was clearly puzzled, since children in this neighborhood presumably did not go on trips. Deflated, the child answered, "day care," and the incident was closed. A little enough episode, but when repeated many times in the course of a week, the result would well be what was witnessed in a higher grade in the same school—children listlessly sitting through the day.

When interviewed, the teacher said she felt the "middle-class" content of school readers was desirable since there was nothing in the children's lives on which learning could be built. At least, she said, the readers held up an image of something better (a professional and suburban life,) to which the children could aspire. It never occurred to her—nor does it to most teachers—how undermining this would be to Negro children for whom the "something better" was not only largely unobtainable, but also totally white. Given this, plus the other kinds of denial mentioned, one could only expect a self-respecting Negro child from a low-income environment to meet school personnel with suspicion and growing anger. Many children express this passively through resistance of learning; others, especially those who have been deeply hurt at home as well, are moved to active rebellion.

THE COUNSELOR'S RESPONSIBILITY

It becomes the counselor's responsibility to help reach these children and, whereas one can be depressed at the difficulties of the task, one can, on the other hand, be impressed by how many of them appreciate and respond to the honest concern of a sincere and emphatic counselor. However, to return to the question of creativity, it is sometimes the potentially more creative children, those who in the long run might have more to offer, who give the counselor the hardest time, more consciously challenging him, putting him to the test. Thus a counselor, overburdened though he may be, must be wary of giving up too soon with a very difficult child. But he must deal with the reality of the child's total life situation, and not gloss over problems of inequality and discrimination with a wishful belief that individual effort will necessarily win success. One cannot expect to help a socially disadvantaged child simply to "conform," and this is even more true of a deeply thoughtful and sensitive child. The counselor must instead help him learn that certain forms of rebellion are pointless and self-destructive, whereas other forms are meaningful.

Wrenn writes that the school counselor must be "'radical' in encouraging individualism . . . while at the same time he helps the student see the need for living within present societal expectations. He goes on to say that counselors are often accused of encouraging conformity, and it is indeed their responsibility to help students "learn systematically what is now known, to build a solid foundation of understanding the present." This is not an end in itself, however, but "the *means to the end* [italics his] of creating the new and of being oneself. To understand the present and be dissatisfied with it enough to change it . . . *is to complete the process* [italics his] of which present knowledge and socialization are but introductory steps" (Wrenn 1962:79). Marie Jahoda touches on the same point when she writes of positive mental health as involving "environmental mastery," in the sense that "hard reality" is not seen as "unchangeable and only the individual as modifiable" (Jahoda 1958:60). The individual must see himself as capable (along with others) of modifying environmental factors. In the last analysis, it is only on the basis of such an understanding that socially disadvantaged children really can be reached—precisely because they are *socially* disadvantaged—and this is not only for psychological reasons, but for ethical ones as well.

THE SCHOOL AS A SOCIAL SYSTEM

The concept of culture also has relevance for a totally different aspect of the guidance counselor's functioning, i.e., his role in the school as a social system. Here he has much in common with the applied anthropologist, for both are faced with an impossible task. Both must relate positively and constructively to virtually all members of a social system in order to enable the system to fulfill its functions more adequately. The counselor's role involves helping teachers and children communicate more effectively with each other, likewise teachers and parents, and even parents and children. It also involves smoothing the channels of communication throughout the administrative structure in relation to myriad special services. Above all, his responsibility is to help children relate to schooling more positively, and to encourage their willingness to be taught as the school sees teaching them. Inherent in his role is the implication that he must do this without stepping on any toes, taking his lead from the principal's and teacher's ideas and desires, always being helpful, not threatening or irritating anyone. Nor should he overstep his position with regard to teaching, which is the teacher's responsibility, or individual therapy, which is the school psychologist's province (if there is one), or administration, the task of the principal and his assistants. Yet his contribution to the school as a whole should be substantial.

As to what the science of anthropology has to offer, it is in part to generalize about what the good counselor has already learned from his own experience. As an innovator, he will have learned that many other things besides the intrinsic desirability of an innovation will determine whether or not it will be accepted. He will also have learned not to be unduly discouraged if he meets what seems to him totally unreasonable resistance to an innovation he feels essential. And he will have experienced the fact that success does not automatically lead to encouragement and praise. Insofar as he is socially wise, the counselor—like anyone working in an institution—will know that, while irrationalities vary from school to school, they are characteristic of "bureaucracy" in general. He will know that the better he understands his own institution, and the clearer he is in his own mind about what he wants to accomplish, the readier he will be to develop the most favorable avenues for broadening his program. He will have sized up the "decision-making structure" of his school—the role played by the principle in relation to the older group of teachers, and the influence of the senior teachers as compared with that of new appointees. He will have assessed the sources for support of aspects of his program. He will be wary of being caught between diverse interest groups in the school, and of being forced to decide which to please or displease.

The anthropologist and sociologist rephrase this everyday experience of the counselor in terms of recurrent patterns in the operation of bureaucratized structures. Merton (1964) developed the point that the "manifest" functions of an institution—in this case the education of children—are not the same as the "latent" functions, or the various social and cultural pressures that operate as an institution perpetuates itself and attempts to expand its area of influence and control. For example, the concerns with job security, with promotion, with status and prestige, result in sometimes more hidden, sometimes more open jockeying for position in all institutions.

Furthermore, from a teacher's point of view, record keeping, management problems, and other "custodial" duties are constantly competing with the task of *teaching*, and each day presents the problem of trying to accomplish more than can be done. Any change in routine is thus a burden, unless it clearly and immediately reduces the tasks to be carried out. However, innovation usually involves a greater expenditure of time and energy *now*, with it is to be hoped, reduced time and energy—or at least increased success—later. Further, teachers have all too often had a backlog of experience with unsuccessful innovations. Thus, they are often "unreasonable" from the counselor's point of view, while the counselor may be seen as quite unrealistic from the teacher's point of view.

The wise counselor recognizes that, generally, teachers and administrators, although trying to do the best job they can, respond to all manner of pressures and drives other than those related to the best education for children. If he is really wise, the counselor will be able to assess his own limitations in this regard in the same terms that he assesses those of others. Before assuming their ineptitude or lack of interest, he will look for a "sociological" explanation rather than a more individual one for an existing irrationality, and on this basis seek a way to overcome the obstacle.

REFERENCES

Arensberg, C. M., and Niehoff, A. H. *Introducing Social Change, a Manual for Americans Overseas.* Chicago: Aldine Publishing Company, 1964.
Davis, A. & Dollard, J. *Children of Bondage.* New York: Harper & Row, 1940.
Fuchs, E. *Pickets at the Gates, a Problem in Administration.* New York: Free Press, 1966.
Guidance of Children in Elementary Schools. Curriculum Bulletin, 1955–56, No. 13, Board of Education of the City of New York.
Hollingshead, A. B. *Elmtown's Youth.* New York: Wiley, 1949.
Jahoda, M. *Current Concepts of Positive Mental Health.* New York: Basic Books, 1958.
Klugman, S. F. "The Effect of Money Incentives Versus Praise upon the Reliability and Obtained Scores of the Revised Stanford-Binet Test." *Journal of Psychology* 30 (1944): 255–69.
Merton, R. K. *Social Theory and Social Structure.* New York: Free Press, 1964.
Purcell, T. V. "The Hopes of Negro Workers for Their Children. In *Blue-collar Life*, edited by A. B. Shostak and W. Gomberg. Englewood Cliffs, N.J.: Prentice-Hall, 1964.
Sexton, P. C. *Education and Income, Inequalities of Opportunity in Our Public Schools.* New York: Viking Press, 1961.
Sexton, P. C. *The American-School, a Sociological Analysis.* Englewood Cliffs, N.J.: Prentice-Hall, 1967.
Wrenn, C. G. *The Counselor in a Changing World.* Washington, D.C.: American Personnel and Guidance Association, 1962.

28 / Teachers in Transition
Elizabeth M. Eddy

Each fall thousands of those who once were students become teachers. With their recently acquired certificates of graduation, they enter the classroom in a new position, as those who stand in front of students and direct their activities. These young men and women, equipped with chalk, class records, seating charts, and teaching manuals, are at the starting point of their career. For some, the return to school is an educational homecoming to schools and communities in which they grew up. For others, it is an educational departure as they enter schools far away from family and friends. For all, the moment of reentry into the educational system is filled with hopes and expectations but also fraught with qualms and anxiety about their new role.

The first year of teaching is a hard one. Gone are the days of talking freely with students as peers and joining their discussions about teachers. No longer students but teachers in charge, the newcomers feel the difference and wonder if they can cope with the task ahead. The weight of their new responsibility is heavy. Much must be learned about teaching, the school, the children. The fatigue at the end of the day is incredible. The paperwork is overwhelming. Uncertainty about the ability to establish authority in the classroom makes them tense. The classroom, once so familiar, has new and different dimensions when one must stand in front and face the pupils.

On the surface, it is strange that beginning to teach should be so difficult. The educational system recruits as teachers those who have spent many years as pupils within its ranks. New teachers have usually spent most of their lives in schools not too dissimilar from those in which they begin their careers. First, there have been the elementary, intermediate, and high school years, the selection of the academic classes and the preparation for college. More recently, there have been the college years, the decision to teach, and the formal training in the specialized courses specifically designed to prepare students to remain within the educational system rather than leave it, as will their peers who pursue other occupations. In contrast to trainees for other types of work, who never, or for very limited periods, have a chance to observe experienced workers, those preparing to teach have watched experienced teachers for years and have subtly learned a good deal about what it is that teachers do and how they do it. Even if the student days of observing teachers have resulted in only unconscious learning, there has been the period of formal preparation, including especially the student teaching experience, which is deliberately intended to enable students to make the transition to the role of teacher. Why then should the first year of teaching in any school be the ordeal that it frequently is, and why is it especially difficult in those schools serving the contemporary urban poor?

To answer this question, it is necessary to consider the primary emphasis of the socialization which new teachers have received during their many years as pupils and students, the limitations of past experience as a guideline for the teacher's present conduct, the dissimilarities between the roles of student teacher and actual teacher, and the significant aspects of making a social transition from one position to another in a society. This chapter gives attention to these matters as a prelude to the subsequent chapters, which will be concerned with the socialization of teachers into their new work once they have formally become members of the teaching staff.

THE YEARS OF PARTICIPANT OBSERVATION

Like all roles in society, those of pupil and teacher are ones which must be learned. Essentially, the role of pupil requires behavior appropriate to a subordinate position and a prolonged period of continued dependency on adults in the school. The many years of formal schooling emphasize this dependency and the cultural contrast between the pupil who must obey and the adult who commands. As former pupils, teachers have been conditioned to be submissive doers of the schoolwork initiated by adult teachers. Their learning has been primarily oriented toward the mastery of subject matter and becoming socialized into the student body.

It is true that most new teachers are in the same general type of school environment that they were in as pupils. Now, however, they have a superordinate role which requires that they socialize pupils for subordinate roles. Little in their past experience prepares them for this task, and even the months of student teaching can only partially bridge the gap separating the role of adult as teacher from child as pupil.[1]

Abrupt changes in relationships with others mark the transition from pupil to teacher. These changes are succinctly evident in the fact that while teachers are now formally addressed by students, they have the privilege of calling students by their first names and are at last on a first-name basis with other teachers. Then too, there are the shifts from being the questioned to being the questioner, from being the one who does the work assigned by others to being the one who tells others what to do. Yet teachers quickly discover that there is nothing magical in their new position which automatically insures the desired performance from the children. Authority in the classroom is not conferred together with the provisional license to teach. It must be forged out of human relationships with the class and awarded by pupils themselves.[2] Only the children can truly validate the professional role by doing their lessons and learning the knowledge and skills taught, thereby claiming the professional work as worthwhile.

As college graduates, new teachers have achieved success in the educational system. They have spent their time as pupils largely in the company of peers who have also done schoolwork well. They have fulfilled many, if not all, of their own teachers' expectations. Thus they bring to their new positions specific expectations about the nature of the school and the types of human activities and relationships which are appropriate in the classroom. They may experience a feeling of shock when they meet pupils in the school who do not share their expectations.

In the school in the urban slum, beginning teachers are especially apt to find children who are unlike what they remember themselves as being when they were school children. For these teachers the contrast between what they themselves experienced over a long period and what they encounter in teaching their first classes is particularly sharp, and they quickly recognize that the situation is not one with which they are familiar.[3]

> The most important feeling that I had this week was that Open School Week in this school was very different than it was when I was a child and went to school. When I was younger and we had Open School Week, every single parent came. The room was just filled with parents, and so naturally I expected the same thing. I didn't even think twice about it. I had prepared the children for this. . . . Only four parents came. . . . My feelings when this happened were just to sort of give me another shock and make me a little more aware of how different the environment of these children is from the environment that I and my friends grew up in and went to public school in. I am continually being reminded of this, and this was just one more thing to remind me of it.
>
> In general, I am appalled and can't even conceive of the actions that these kids participate in and the language that they use. I have to remind myself that I have a very different background from theirs, but I keep putting myself in their place. I keep remembering when I was in school, how I wanted to learn, how I was respectful—not that I was a perfect angel, because I wasn't, but I had very good marks, and I received many awards at the end of the junior-high-school career, and I also made the opening speech at graduation. I just can't conceive of how these kids are forever screaming and fighting. . . . This utter lack of respect and the slamming of doors, using filthy words, telling me to drop dead is really the thing that shocked me these past few months. . . .
>
> The assistant principal told me that the school was much better now than when I was there. He meant this with respect to reading and math grades. I disagree with him. Just going through the yearbook, you can see such a vast difference. When I was in the school, there was no such thing as corrective reading. Most of the kids were reading on grade, and we didn't have such problem classes as we do now.

The influence of the past years as pupils in the school is not limited to the acquisition of expectations about the way pupils and parents should respond to the educational effort. Training in techniques of classroom management and teaching also takes place as the pupils observe their teachers:

> The tearing up of exams is an old trick I learned when I was in the eighth grade. I remember I had a teacher who had given us twenty adjectives to memorize. We were then supposed to list them and write a sentence for each one. I was in a good class. It was a bright class. As in all classes, we all had our days, and we were a bit noisy. I remember the teacher administered the test, and still there was some muttering and grumbling going on. He calmly

took the pack of papers, and he tore them up and stacked them in the ash can. He then looked at us and said, "We're going to take the test again, and if you insist on being noisy, I will tear up the papers again, and we will continue doing this until you are absolutely silent." Needless to say, we got the message, and we were very quiet. . . .

The first time I did this was on the first test that I gave all my classes this term. In practically all my math classes, I had to tear up one or two papers just to make the kids realize I meant business. This was mostly for the kids that were noisy or who kept annoying others.

There is one thing I want to stress with them. This is seeing relationships between numbers, which is something I never learned when I was in elementary school, and it always seemed to make math very dull for me. And I remember taking a course in high school where the teacher began at the beginning of the term by doing some very elementary things. He talked about ten and what ten is, and he really made us see what numbers are and what they do. . . . I want to convey some of this to my class.

The examples cited highlight only a few of the things that teachers learn about school while they attend school. They serve to emphasize the basic point that the training of teachers for their formal role begins long before courses in education are taken. For all teachers the prolonged socialization into a dependency role is apt to make the transition into a superordinate role difficult. For beginning teachers in schools in slum or other areas in which pupils are socially and culturally different from those they have known, the educational expectations and techniques acquired during this early training are likely to be inappropriate for large numbers of the children they must now teach.

TRAINING FOR SEPARATION FROM THE STUDENT ROLE

There is not only the failure of the days of pupil observation and experience to bridge the gap between the child-pupil and the adult-teacher. There is also the failure of the education courses and the student teaching experience to adequately prepare teachers for their new positions in the classroom. While this problem is not confined to teachers who begin their careers in slum areas, it is especially acute there, and much attention is now being given to special training of teachers for the children of the urban poor.

In our large cities, the newcomers to the teaching profession have often been most recently taught by those who have themselves attended the local city schools and are capping long and successful careers in the local educational system by teaching those who will succeed them on the lower rungs of the educational hierarchy. Frequently they "have come up the hard way" and are those for whom education has been a means of upward social mobility and who have a deep sense of loyalty to the local public school system. At the same time, they may also be those for whom extended ties of family and ethnic affiliation are highly important, and they may be strongly local in experience and outlook. The way the local school system is operated may be and frequently is upheld as the only known and best way to do things.[4]

Local educational folklore and tradition is passed from one generation to the next, and the local school system becomes one to be guarded against invasion by outsiders though improvement may be sought from trusted insiders. This type of localism is represented in the extreme by the teachers who, after attending a local metropolitan college, begin their teaching career in a school from which they graduated and in which they did their student teaching. An urban school system dominated by those who have literally never left the local schools and who provide the new teacher with careful training in local traditions and practices which have been successful for them is often seriously out of touch with the special needs of the new generation of children in contemporary schools, especially in slum areas. As a consequence, teachers in training may learn considerably more about the perpetuation of educational techniques that have been successful in the past than they do about the innovative techniques needed if present problems are to be resolved.

The formal socialization provided by courses in education is culminated by student teaching, which is intended to facilitate the transition of students from those who think and act like students to those who think and act like teachers. Student teaching is a cooperative venture between the teacher training institution and conveniently located school systems. The students are placed in a particular school or schools on a full- or part-time basis for a period of several months. In the school, they work under the direction of one or more cooperating teachers, with occasional supervisory visits from a faculty member in the training institution.

During this transitional period of student teaching, the students observe and act out the behaviors they are eventually to assume as teachers. Clerical work, lesson planning, practice teaching, classroom management, and other tasks which teachers perform are assigned to them in varying degrees. The students are observed while teaching, evaluations of them are recorded, and suggestions for improvement of teaching techniques are given to them in supervisory conferences. The students nearly always do well enough that the teacher training institution officially states that they are prepared to teach and declares them deserving of a new status in the educational system.

The circumstances under which student teaching eases the transition from the role of student to that of teacher, and the extent to which it does so, are not empirically known. Yet it seems clear that important learnings about the role of teacher do occur during student teaching and that this time may be particularly useful for the transmission of written and oral traditions about teaching from one generation of teachers to the next. As the following examples indicate, the handing down of written materials, teaching techniques, and classroom management procedures provides a means for the communication of the traditions, beliefs, and customs of the more experienced teachers in the school.

> I had Mrs. LaSalle as a cooperating teacher when I student taught in the school, and she gave me a copy of her plan book, and I've been using this as a guide. It just happens to be a very good plan book, and she happens to be an excellent teacher, so I have talked with her, and I'm copying her style of doing it.

> I'm using this method of teaching reading now because when I student taught it was the method the teacher was using, and naturally becuase I don't know any other really. You know, you copy their methods because you're there to learn from these teachers and it worked well with her.

> Last year when I student taught, the teacher gave me a whole bunch of rexographs that she had used, and I took them home. I've been using some of them.

> It's from the school that I developed my methods of teaching—from the student teaching. I watched how the other teachers did it, and the assistant principal told me how she wanted it done.

> It is very important for a teacher to always be on her guard and to be very, very strict the first weeks of school. This is something which many people will tell a young teacher, or this is something that we have heard constantly

while we were student teaching. This is not to smile for the whole first month of school, not even to smile at all, not to let them get away with anything, and to hold on very tight. Only after you have the children disciplined can you begin to let go. . . .

There is one thing I learned about a slow class from my student teaching experience. You absolutely cannot teach a slow class anything until you have complete control of that class. I saw my cooperating teacher take period after period just to tell her class and yell at them that they should be quiet, and that they should really obey the rules of the school. This lecturing really did pay off because the class knew she meant business, and she followed up everything she said, and they worked for her.

I learned from my cooperating teacher that it's a good idea to have everything removed from the desks, because this way they can concentrate on you. If there are any notebooks or papers or pens and pencils, they tend to start playing with them. This way they have nothing to do but keep their hands on their lap or on their desks and look at you.

For those teachers whose first job is in the school where they did student teaching, the student teaching experience provides direct acquaintance with the staff, administrative procedures, and some of the children. Therefore, these teachers presumably have different types of interaction with administrators, peers, and pupils than do those who eventually teach in schools where they have not done student teaching. The evidence is not clear on this point, but the following comments suggest that there are important consequences of returning to a school in which one is already known.

I am quite fortunate in that I student taught in this school last term, and the assistant principal set me up in my room and gave me as many supplies as I thought I needed. . . . He also had me get all my textbooks last year, so that when the children came in I had something to work with.

I had lunch one day this week with the teacher with whom I student taught last year. She is the teacher to whom I would go if I really had a bad problem. She gives me a lot of helpful hints. For instance, I told her that my children were having trouble recognizing the letters of the alphabet, and she told me the best way to do this was to play a game with them, and the game that we would play would be this. . . . She told me a way to approach the problem I was having with mathematics. . . . She constantly asks me how everything is going. Do I have any problem I want to discuss with her? This week I didn't have anything I wanted to discuss with her, but it made me feel very secure that I have her. She's a wonderful person, and she'll help me with anything at any time.

She was my cooperating teacher. We are quite close and friendly. If there are any problems I go to her, and she is sort of taking a protective attitude towards me. I find that she has taken my part in several instances when the administration has gotten a little too demanding.

The man who was my cooperating teacher last term has been a tremendous help this week. He explained all the little details such as attendance books and how attendance cards are made up.

I student taught in this school, and the minute the UFT chairman in my school found out that I had been appointed to this school, she approached me and asked me if I would like to join and, of course, I joined the group.

> Since I student taught in the school, the administration felt that I knew much
> about the school, and so they didn't come to me and give me the help which I
> did need. However, the principal came around to my class the first day . . .
> and told them that I was a very good teacher, mainly because I had been
> trained to teach in their school.

The suggestion has frequently been made that teachers be assigned to the school
in which they did student teaching, or a similar school, as a means of improving
teacher performance in slum areas. On the assumption that student teaching in a
school composed of "middle-class" children does not prepare the teacher to teach
children from the slums, new experimental programs in teacher education emphasize the importance of deliberately arranging student teaching in slum area schools
for those whose first teaching assignment will be there. In some programs there are
special arrangements with the Board of Education so that this may be done.[5] These
programs have yet to be carefully evaluated. However, the preceding comments
indicate that the benefits to future teachers include more than the official rationale
that they have a better understanding of and rapport with the pupils. Indeed, it is
likely that the primary benefits may have more to do with readily establishing or
continuing working relationships with colleagues and administrators to whom one
is already known than with teaching pupils more successfully.

Yet it is evident from some of the observations of beginning teachers that student
teaching in a school in the slum does not necessarily result in a smooth transition to
the teaching role. Although the typical school in these areas is composed primarily
of children who are classified as "slow" and "behind" in school work, there are
nearly always some classes attended by children who are "average" or above in their
abilities. Some student teachers encounter primarily these children and are unaware of the problems presented by the "slow" child until they are assigned their
first classes as beginning teachers.

> I see a vast difference between student teaching and actual teaching. During
> student teaching, you're under the watchful supervision of a trained teacher.
> The classes realize they're rather special and act accordingly. . . . Last year I
> had the academically top eighth-grade class . . . I remember eagerly awaiting
> each day when I was student teaching. . . . Now I look forward to certain
> classes, lunch, and prep periods. I pray that my "time" with the bottom
> seventh-grade class goes by real quickly.

> When I student taught, I taught the average first grade, in which the children
> really learned things. My second-grade class can't do what this first grade
> did, and I am assuming they can do it. I just have to start from the beginning
> and forget that they ever learned anything and just try to build up from the
> first grade through the second grade. Especially since I have non-readers in
> the class, I have to start at the beginning.

Because student teaching is invariably done in classes on the grade level and in
subject areas the teacher is later licensed to teach, actual assignment to other grades
or subjects may be another source of discontinuity between the student teaching
experience and the reality of the first teaching assignment, particularly at the
junior and senior high school level. The problem is well stated by a junior high
school teacher who returned to a school which she had attended and in which she
did student teaching:

> I am a social studies major and having to teach math is something that I
> didn't look forward to. I must admit that I have always hated math . . . I've
> always been very weak in math, and, as a matter of fact, in high school I

flunked every math course I took. . . . When I covered the education sequence in college, I never covered any mathematical subject . . . I never expected to have to teach it.

The dissimilarity between the student teaching and actual teaching experiences entails not only potential differences between schools, grades, and pupils. There are also differences in the responsibility for and relationships with pupils. Student teachers are quite literally neither students nor teachers but persons in the social position of transition, and new teachers are keenly aware of the fact:

> There is a great difference between being a teacher and a student teacher. First of all, when you're a teacher, you have your class for yourself. You start from the beginning in September. These children are all strangers to you. You're a stranger to them. You start on an even basis, and what you build up from there is built between you and your class. When a stranger, which is what a student teacher is, gets up and teaches a lesson, this rapport that the teacher has built up with her class all year long is not there, and the students will react the way they've always reacted to strangers. . . . I always felt when I got up to teach a lesson when I was a student teacher that these children in front of me were strangers, and each lesson was in isolation. As a teacher I feel that I have control, and I care about what they do, how they act in my classroom and with other teachers in other classrooms. This makes my job much more meaningful for me, because I have a set of children that I'm responsible for and that I do care about. . . . This is a feeling a student teacher can never have, because the children do not belong to the student teacher. They belong to the teacher. The teacher starts out with them in September and ends up with them in June. A student teacher is a stranger and will always be a stranger to these pupils.

> The greatest difference between being a teacher and a student teacher is that the amount of responsibility is tremendous. You are certainly given more power, and you're more involved. You no longer are an onlooker, and you miss some of the observations that you get when you just have time to sit in the back of the room looking and watching students. You don't get this any more when you are standing in front of the room. You no longer see what goes on in the back of the room, and you don't see the students from the back. You see them from the front. You don't see them as each individual responding. You see them as one of a group responding. . . . Your conduct is also a little different. You've got to be a little more reserved. You can't be as friendly with some of the students as you may have been when you were a student teacher. You lose some contact with them. When you are a student teacher, students may talk to you a little more freely or discuss the teacher with whom you are working more freely than they do now when you are the teacher. There is a big difference there. You're the teacher in charge now, and you no longer are just an onlooker and maybe one of them in a way.

Upon the completion of the student-teaching experience and the formally prescribed course work, the student is publicly declared by the teacher training institution to be prepared to teach. The formal graduation ceremony and the awarding of the college degree symbolically express the end of the student role and the beginning of a new role. These "strangers" and "outsiders" now have to be incorporated into their new role as teachers. They have observed and learned much about teaching during the long transitional years as students, yet it remains to be fully accepted as teachers by those in the schools to which they will go.

When the summer vacation is over and the fall brings the traditional opening of school, these young men and women will struggle hard for social and personal identity in their new positions. Their success in achieving this identity will depend largely upon those who greet them in the school and attempt to incorporate them into their professional roles. Administrators, fellow teachers, pupils, and others will all play a part in the humdrum activities of the first year of teaching, which, no matter how tedious or difficult, will provide the means for incorporation or rejection of the newcomers.

Many of those who begin teaching in slum areas will encounter special problems due to their orientation toward norms of scholastic achievement, academic progress, and pupil behavior; for such norms are often incongruent with the needs of pupils who are still in the process of urbanization and are unfamiliar or unable to cope with the demands of the school as they are currently presented.[6] Moreover, the professional training of beginning teachers has usually prepared them to teach pupils who respond to the formal education system sufficiently well to do at least average work and to behave in ways acceptable to the school; but it has seldom prepared them to teach pupils who have a history of school failure or underachievement and, in some instances, of disruptive classroom behavior. As a consequence, the successful transition of teachers in these schools is especially difficult and may be pathologic when it does occur.[7] To better understand what is involved and to provide the theoretical background for subsequent chapters, it is necessary now to turn to a general consideration of what it means to be in a process of social transition.

THE SIGNIFICANCE OF SOCIAL TRANSITION

It has been noted that as new teachers complete their formal training and embark upon their professional careers they make a transition from child-pupil to adult-teacher within the educational system. Important changes in relationships to others, status, activities, and procedures accompany this transition. From the subordinate position of pupils who are dependent on teachers, the beginning teachers must move into the superordinate position of those who plan the work that pupils do and socialize them into their dependent roles in the school. The appropriate relationship with teachers is now that of a colleague and peer, although they still maintain a subordinate relationship to school administrators.

New teachers are not unique in experiencing social transition. All individuals experience changes in status and relationships to others in their societies as they move through the universal life cycle of birth, childhood, adolescence, adulthood, and death. These changes have long been of interest to anthropologists and other scholars who have noted that the critical turning points in the life cycle are often accompanied by ceremonial activities, such as weddings, funerals, and initiation ceremonies, which give ritual expression to the transition of the individual from one social position to another.

A half century ago, the French scholar van Gennep first called attention to the universality of these ceremonies in his classic cross-cultural study.[8] Calling them *rites de passage*, van Gennep noted that most of these rituals have three components—separation, transition, and incorporation—and provide a symbolic expression of the actual changes in the relationships of the individuals to others in their society. Examples drawn from the familiar ceremony of a wedding in our own society will serve to make more explicit the connection between critical alterations in one's social relationships and the rites symbolizing them.

In all societies, the marriage of one individual to another is usually accompanied by a marked reduction or even cessation of interaction between the individual and the groups with which he was formerly identified. In American society, for example, it is common for the young man or woman who marries to leave his or her own family and place of residence and to establish a separate home and family. In our religious and civil ceremonies the act of the father or other close relative giving the bride away may be viewed as symbolic of separation from or decreased interaction with her own family as a result of marriage. Similarly, the bachelor dinner and the bridal shower are ceremonial expressions of the alterations in relationships to peers of one's own sex which will come about as a consequence of marriage.

As the individual begins to make the transition from the status of being single to that of being married, he is in a critical state. He has severed his former relationships with others, but has not yet become a part of the new group into which he is moving. He is neither fish nor fowl. He has lost his former status but has not yet acquired a new one. During this phase the individual begins to learn about the behavior which will be expected in his new status. Symbolically, the wedding ceremony takes note of this phase by providing for the couple to pledge their troth publicly to each other and repeat the mutual responsibilities involved in marriage.

The incorporation of the individual into his new status as a married person concludes the social movement which the act of marriage implies. In this phase the person begins to interact again with the members of his community, but in his new position. Again, the marriage rites symbolize the new behavior and position of the individual in his relationships to others. The officiating clergyman pronounces the couple man and wife and acts on behalf of both the church and the state in officially announcing the couple as married and having a new position in society and a changed relationship with others.

From the insights of van Gennep and others who have subsequently concerned themselves with rites of passage, it is clear that these ceremonies have a profound significance for individual and social identification. Of the three phases, that of transition is the time most laden with insecurity and anxiety for the individual and for those associated with him. Separated from former meaningful relationships, these are the moments, weeks, months, or even years when the individual is most in danger of losing all significant connections with others as a result of his own action or that of others. Consider, for example, the loss of individual and social identity for the bride who is left at the altar or for the bridegroom who leaves her there.

The successful movement from a period of transition requires the incorporation of the individual into the new group and status. In primitive societies, this often meant a reintroduction into a community from whence one came, but with a change of status, activities, and associates. In modern societies, it increasingly means an incorporation by those who cannot be counted as family, friends, and associates. The young couple who, shortly after marriage and honeymoon, leave to establish themselves in the husband's new work location is but one illustration of the greater social discontinuity of our society in contrast to primitive societies or even small-town America. It is important also to note that even though persons may be physically intermingled with members of the new group and may struggle for individual and social identification, this cannot be realized unless others accept them.

Historically, an analysis of rites of passage has been primarily used to provide an understanding of the individual's life crises as they affect his relationships to his family in his passage from birth to death.[9] Yet similar rites occur when individuals are inducted into religious groups, fraternal organizations, political office, occupational groups, gangs, and institutions.[10] In these latter types of situations, the terms *ritual* and *rite* are not to be understood in the restricted sense of the formal aspects of a religious service, although these would be included. Rather, the terms are used in the broader sense of "any social behavior performed for the sake of expressing a certain meaning or meanings of importance to the group concerned."[11] It is in this sense that *ritual* or *rite* is used in this article in considering the induction of the beginning teacher into the school during the first semester of teaching.

Those familiar with the contemporary educational system may well wonder what relevance the rites of passage of primitive tribes or even modern societies have to those who enter the teaching profession. Certainly new teachers are not participants in dramatic ceremonies, which with song and dance symbolically express the end of student days and the beginning of the teaching career. On the contrary, when they refer to "being given a song and dance" at all, they are referring in a derogatory way to being required to participate in activities they find dull and uninspiring.

In contrast to the colorful ceremonies described in anthropological literature, the arrival of the new professional to take up duties in the school appears a humdrum affair, and, in fact, it is. That this event is not dramatized, however, does not detract in any way from its importance or lessen the trauma of the new teacher. By providing a universal cultural and social analogue, an understanding of rites of passage can lead to a new perception of what happens to beginning teachers and also perhaps a new insight into how badly they are inducted into their professional careers.

As noted earlier, new teachers are essentially persons in transition. Within the school, they are gradually but firmly taught the responsibilities and activities appropriate to their new role. Several groups in the school, including administrators, specialists, fellow teachers, and pupils, attempt to reach out and claim the newcomers as teachers, and the transition period is marked by a number of ceremonial activities which ritually express the several phases of this period, as well as the meaning of teaching. Beginning with the initial formal orientation to the school, the beginners undergo an intensive formal and informal training period in which the culture of the school, with its long history, is transmitted to them, so that they, in turn, may become bearers of it for succeeding generations of pupils and eventually for other new teachers.

NOTES

1. Ruth Benedict has noted that dominance-submission, "where like does not respond to like, but where one type of behavior stimulates the opposite response," is one of the most prominent ways in which behavior is patterned in American culture. It is one of the central cultural themes which the school transmits to the child. See Ruth Benedict, "Continuities and Discontinuities in Cultural Conditioning," in *Personality in Nature, Society, and Culture*, ed. Clyde Kluckhohn and Henry A. Murray (New York: Alfred A. Knopf, 1948), pp. 414–23.
2. See Chester I. Barnard, "A Definition of Authority," in *Reader in Bureaucracy*, ed. Robert K. Merton, Ailsa P. Gray, Barbara Hockey, Hanan C. Selvin (Glencoe, Ill.: Free Press, 1952): "If a directive communication is accepted by one to whom it is addressed, its authority for him is confirmed or established. It is admitted as the basis of action. Disobedience of such a communication is a denial of its authority for him. Therefore, under this definition the decision as to whether an order has authority or not lies with the persons to whom it is addressed, and does not reside in 'persons of authority' or those who issue these orders" (p. 180).
3. The twenty-two teachers were not specifically questioned on this point, however, in response to other questions, the effects of the past days as a student were spontaneously mentioned. All quotations from teachers used in this and later chapters are taken from the reports of the twenty-two teachers and have been edited to preserve the anonymity of all schools and persons.
4. The degree of localism that may pervade an urban school system is well illustrated by the New York City schools. A recent report indicates that perhaps as many as 90 percent of this system's teachers are graduates of colleges or universities located in the New York City area. Sixty percent of the teachers are graduates of the City University. "For all intents and purposes, all of the promotional ranks in the system are filled by people who began as teachers in the system and who have moved up the ladder." Mayor's Advisory Panel on De-

centralization of the New York City Schools, *Reconnection for Learning* (New York, 1957), p. 45.

5. For a description of one of these programs, see Vernon E. Hasbrich, "Teachers for Big-City Schools," in *Education in Depressed Areas*, ed. A. Harry Passow (New York: Teachers College Press, 1963), pp. 243-61.

6. A description of some of the problems presented to school pupils by the present organizational structure of schools in slum areas is presented in Elizabeth M. Eddy, *Walk the White Line: A Profile of Urban Education* (Garden City, N.Y.: Doubleday Anchor Books, 1967, and New York: Frederick A. Praeger, 1967).

7. Howard S. Becker, "The Career of the Chicago Public School-Teacher," *The American Journal of Sociology 57* (1952): 470-77.

8. Arnold van Gennep, *The Rites of Passage* (Chicago: University of Chicago Press, 1960). For a discussion of van Gennep's contribution to theory and methodology in anthropology, see Solon T. Kimball's biographical sketch of him in the *Encyclopedia of the Social Sciences*. See also Frank W. Young, *Initiation Ceremonies* (Indianapolis: Bobbs-Merrill, 1965); Eliot D. Chapple and Carleton S. Coon, *Principles of Anthropology* (New York: Henry Holt, 1942).

9. See W. Lloyd Warner, *A Black Civilization* (rev. ed., New York: Harper & Bros., 1958), and *The Living and the Dead: A Study of the Symbolic Life of Americans* (New Haven: Yale University Press, 1959).

10. See Everett C. Hughes, "Social Change and Status Protest: An Essay on the Marginal Man," *Phylon 10* (1949): 60-65; Howard S. Becker, Blanche Geer, Everett C. Hughes, and Anselm L. Strauss, *Boys in White* (Chicago: University of Chicago Press, 1961); Erving Goffman, *Asylums* (Garden City, N.Y.: Doubleday Anchor Books, 1961); Elizabeth M. Eddy, "Rites of Passage in a Total Institution." *Human Organization 23* (1964): 67-75; Herbert A. Bloch and Arthur Niederhoffer, *The Gang* (New York: Philosophical Library, 1958): Chapple and Coon, *Principles of Anthropology*.

11. Warner, *The Living and the Dead*, p. 104.

29 / Schools and Teachers Union Interaction

John Singleton

THE STRUCTURE OF THE UNION

Just as the Japan Teachers Union (JTU) includes about 90 percent of Japanese elementary and middle school teachers in its organization, so does it encompass many of the professional activities of teachers. Other than the governmental administrative organizations and their programs, the JTU and related teachers union activities account for the greatest part of the professional activity of Japanese teachers.

It is, perhaps, a unique feature of Japanese education that there is a clearly separable administrative and professional community in direct contact with the schools. Though there are many professional activities carried out under the auspices of the administrative community, the teachers union is a clearly separate entity with which the teachers are identified and within which there is a good deal of professional as well as union activity. Partly due to the national controversy between the JTU and the Ministry of Education, there is usually a clear distinction between union-related and professional administrative activities. This is true, even in the prefecture of Nichū, where there is a unique practice of combining administrative support with one union-sponsored activity, the annual educational research meeting.

The JTU is organized with four levels of union associations. At the top, there is The *Nippon Kyōshokuin Kumiai* (Japan Teachers Union) which is usually called *Nikkyōso*. The executive offices of the national JTU are located in Tokyo in an old brick building called the *Kyōikukaikan* (education hall). Five stories high, it is usually draped with one or more long white streamers on which are printed the union's current slogans. Also located in the building are the offices of the high school teachers union which is a separate and weaker union whose membership includes only about one third of all high school teachers.

A weekly newspaper and a monthly journal published by the central office are used for direct communication with the JTU membership. At Nichū school, these periodicals came directly to the school and were available in the teachers' room.

An annual nationwide educational research meeting for teacher members is sponsored by the JTU and always receives much attention. The Ministry of Education began, during the period of this study, to sponsor a smaller competitive research meeting for teachers.

The JTU finances its own research organization, the Peoples Education Research Institute, which publishes regular reports of its own educational research in a variety of forms. As might be expected, the problems chosen for study are generally within the area of union concern. The Ministry of Education finances a National Institute of Educational Research, in addition to its own research section. Thus the Ministry and the JTU have parallel and competitive research organizations.

During the period of this study, no Nichū teacher was observed to have had direct personal contact with the central JTU office. It is likely, however, that some teachers went to meetings where national JTU officers were present.

The second level of JTU organization consists of the prefectural unions. Each prefecture has its own union organization with a headquarters staff maintaining union affairs. The relative strength or enthusiasm of the prefectural unions varies greatly and seems to be related to a number of factors. Tokyo, a prefecture in itself, has one of the strongest union organizations. Several outlying rural prefectures also have the reputation of being especially strong in union support.

The prefecture which included Nippon City, however, was known for the weak union spirit of its teachers. During the period of this study, no major teachers union demonstration was observed in the prefecture or recorded in the local newspapers; though demonstrations and activities elsewhere were noted.

The prefectural teachers union had its central office in the capital city of the prefecture about three blocks from the prefectural Board of Education office. Located in a small, two-story "education hall" which it shared with the high school teachers union, a full-time executive staff ran the affairs of the union's prefectural branch.

The current chairman of the prefectural union had formerly been principal of a large elementary school. The vice-chairman had come from his job as head teacher of an elementary school. One of the other prefectural officers had been a head teacher before election to his current job. However, it was indicated that the number of principals and head teachers entering prefectural union offices in recent years had declined.

At the time of this study, there were several features of prefectural teachers union organizations that varied from one prefecture to the next. One was the degree of participation by principals and head teachers in union affairs. In the Tokyo teachers union, for instance, principals and head teachers no longer participated. In the prefecture concerned in this study, principals and head teachers were still active participants in union affairs. The question of whether they could or should continue this role in union affairs was under active discussion. The Ministry of Education was applying pressure to the school administrators to leave the union.

A second differentiating feature of prefectural teachers union organization was the occurrence in some prefectures of two separate organizations, one representing the JTU and the other carrying on as a prefectural teachers union. Such a separation of offices was not established in Nichū's prefecture. The union officials interviewed by the author were careful to explain their feeling of complete support for the JTU and would not indicate any areas of possible conflict between local and national goals.

Third, some prefectures were able to support full-time employees at local branch offices of the teachers union. In this prefecture, there were no such employees, or local branch offices, though one prefecture visited by the author has an "education hall" and local office in each region.

The next level of teachers union organization is called the *shibu* (local branch). In the prefecture of Nichū there were more than twenty *shibu* organized on a regional basis that covered the prefecture completely. Nichū school was included in the Nippon City *shibu*. Though each *shibu* had a formal organization, specialized sections, and a regular program of meetings, it had no physical office facilities in this prefecture.

Once a year, each *shibu* would hold a general membership meeting with elections of local officials. The executive committee of the *shibu* would meet monthly to carry out the business of the union.

Important sections of the *shibu* which maintained their own slate of officers and program of meetings in addition to the regular *shibu* activities were the women's division, the youth division, and the school clerks' division. All female teachers were members of the women's division and all male teachers less than thirty-five years old were included in the youth division. The school clerks, though union members, did not participate in the *shibu* general meeting. Rather, the school clerks held an annual prefecture-wide meeting.

Principals and head teachers monopolized the top elective positions in the different *shibu* of Nichū's prefecture. Only one *shibu* chairman was not a school principal. In Nippon City, an elementary school principal was elected chairman during the period of this study, replacing a middle school principal in the job.

Both the principal and the head teacher of Nichū had served in various union offices, though they were not holding a union office during the period of this study. When the author first questioned a Nichū teacher-representative to the general committee of the *shibu* about the way to arrange for observation of the meeting, he was referred to the Nichū head teacher and principal. Though they indicated some initial reluctance, the principal tried to resolve the question by a direct phone call to the *shibu* chairman. When he found that the chairman was out of town, he took it upon himself to issue an invitation to the meeting, after a short consultation with some of the teachers. He explained, "Last year it would have been a problem, but this year it should be all right. The Nippon City teachers union is weak. The principals and head teachers are included here—but that is a problem, too."

A fourth level of union organization was the *bunkai* (chapter) which included all teachers in one school. Each *bunkai* was expected to elect representatives to the *shibu* general committee and the *shibu* executive committee. The executive committee representative was most important because he formed the major communication link between the teachers and the union organization.

ANNUAL MEETING OF THE NIPPON CITY *SHIBU*

On the first Saturday in June, shortly after the opening of the school year, the annual meeting of the Nippon City branch of the prefectural teachers union was scheduled. The mimeographed program describing the order and content of business indicated that the meeting was planned to last from one thirty to five o'clock in the afternoon. In this manner, the meeting did not infringe upon the official forty-four-hour, five-and-a-half-day working week of the teachers. It was the only meeting of any kind during the year at which all of the Nippon City teachers were expected to assemble. Of 403 members of the *shibu*, the official attendance count showed 268 actually present with 80 proxies received. This allowed the meeting to fulfill the union requirements that two-thirds of the membership must be present (physically or by proxy) to constitute an official quorum for the conduct of union business.

The meeting was held in a centrally located Nippon City elementary school assembly hall. In attendance, as invited guests, in addition to the teachers and a curious American researcher, were the vice-chairman of the prefectural teachers union, a Socialist member of the Nippon City Assembly, and the Nippon City superintendent of education. None of the city or prefectural *shidō shuji* were at the meeting. The teachers sat in sections of the assembly hall assigned to their school. Union officials and committee members sat on the stage in front of the hall. The three invited guests sat at a table at one side of the front of the hall.

As the meeting opened, three men were chosen, ostensibly without prior notice, to chair the meeting in rotation. The Nichū head teacher was the first one so chosen and left his seat in the Nichū section of the hall to take over the meeting. He called the meeting to order and the chairman from the previous year, principal of the Nippon City Yonchū Middle School, gave his opening greetings. He mentioned several union problems of national scope, among which were the nationwide achievement testing program being carried out by the Ministry of Education and the question of inclusion of principals in the union. The chairman's short talk was followed by an introduction of new teachers in each of the schools represented. This completed the opening formalities of the meeting.

First on the agenda was a report of the previous year's activities of the *shibu*. Some time was spent describing the problems that arose out of the transfer to another school, without prior consultation or notice, of two Tokai Elementary School teachers. Union activists with the local reputation of being Communists, they had protested their transfer publicly at the previous annual meeting of the *shibu*. Their case had been taken to court by the union. In spite of this action, the two teachers had not been returned to the Tokai school.

Descriptions of the struggles against the merit rating system for teachers, the nationwide achievement examinations, and the present salary scale for teachers formed the body of the report. The concluding statement described the research reports and activities of the *shibu*, some of which had been included in the national JTU-sponsored research meeting.

Questions from the floor were related to the achievement testing problem. One teacher wanted to know how long the local board of education's promise would hold to not use the test results in evaluation of teachers. Another added his doubts about the construction of the tests.

The official program for the coming year, given in a series of five slogans, was then proposed. Mild applause was the signal for approval of the program as stated. No opposition was expressed to the slogans which represented the major concerns of the JTU in the political and economic sphere.

One young teacher rose from the floor of the meeting to propose a resolution, addressed to the Nippon City Assembly, opposing the scheduled installation of a missile-launching base near Nippon City. The presiding officer ruled him out of order because he had not brought up his proposal before the opening of the business session. The *shibu* chairman, however, intervened to propose that a vote be taken on whether the proposed resolution should be discussed at the meeting. The chairman asked, "Who is against discussion of this problem?" When only two people stood up to signify their opposition, the discussion began. After some confused parliamentary procedure, mild applause signaled the passing of the resolution.

An older Nichū teacher said later that he did not feel the resolution represented the feelings of the majority of the teachers. He attributed its passage to a few "young red hot-heads." He felt that the older teachers really agreed with the national government on this issue.

A good deal of time was taken up on budgetary reports and proposals. When the officers proposed an increase in *shibu* dues, two men and a woman stood up to say why they approved of the increase. A Nichū teacher commented fatalistically, "It is gradually getting more difficult to express any opposition." As before, mild applause was used to signal approval of the proposed budget, including the raise in dues.

An important item of business that raised a good deal of discussion was a proposed revision of the *shibu* constitution. The major effect of the revision was to change the system of election of *shibu* officers so that they might be elected earlier in the year at local school *bunkai* meetings, rather than waiting for the annual general meeting. Several younger teachers expressed vehement opposition to the proposed revision. One of them, a teacher involved in the previous year's personnel transfer problem previously described, complained that the principals would be able to dominate the elections if they were held in the local schools. Only at the general meeting did he feel free of the influence of his principal. The statements of the younger teachers in opposition were vehement and vigorous. Occasionally, one of them would call out *dōkan* (expression of approval) loudly at one of the other teachers' points. But the majority of teachers remained uninvolved in the discussion. One elementary school principal did stand up to express his opinion that the *bantai* (opposition) arguments were "feeble."

Then the chairman requested that speakers in favor of revision make their views known. Three teachers, in turn, were ruled out of order when they rose to express more opposition arguments.

Finally a vote was called for on the revision of the constitution. For the first time, hands were raised to cast a vote and the votes were counted carefully. The results of the vote were not clear and seemed ambiguous. The chairman called for a second vote, but was vigorously opposed by the younger teachers. The chairman had to retract his proposal for a recount and announced that although a majority of those present had voted in favor of the revision, the necessary two-thirds vote for a constitutional revision had not been reached. Thus the small group of young radical teachers, as they were generally regarded, won a small victory in the meeting.

When it came time to vote for the next year's officers, an elaborate ballot box and voting booth apparatus was erected on the stage in front of the hall. The teachers lined up and had their names checked as they received a ballot. Despite the physical trappings, however, they had only one slate of nominated officers from which to choose. Their vote was merely a "yes" or "no" in the case of each candidate selected by the nominating committee. A good deal of time was taken up with the voting and the counting of ballots after the ballots had been marked. John B. Cornell, an anthropologist who studied a *buraku* election of local officials in a rural community, noted a similar type of process. "The formal selection, though done by ballot, is merely part of the form that since the war has come to be regarded as democratic procedure" (1962: 38).

A Nichū teacher later told the author that it was not always the case, however, that there was a single slate of nominees on the ballot for union officials. The previous year, one of the young teachers involved in the school transfer problem mentioned above, had opposed the Yonchū principal in the election and had drawn quite a few votes.

During the ballot-counting, the vice-chairman of the prefectural teachers union was called on for a speech. He presented two proposals to the teachers, one related to a union mutual aid fund and the other to the disposition of money awarded to the teachers for back pay which had been secured by a union court action. In each case he received informal approval by the meeting without discussion. He then spoke of the different national JTU struggles. Immediately following his speech, the Nippon City superintendent of education was called on to give his greetings. He spoke in general terms for a brief ten minutes.

It was then the turn of the Socialist City Assembly member to talk to the group. He ranged over a variety of political questions and included some references to the coming Diet election. His electioneering caused some amusement among the teachers.

After some time, the ballots were counted and the results announced. The slate of officers nominated had been accepted. There was a short speech from the new *shibu* chairman and concluding greetings from the outgoing chairman and vice-chairman before the meeting finally came to a close, later than the previously announced closing hour.

By comparison with the public clamor on the national level between the JTU and the Ministry of Education, the *shibu* meeting was meek and gentle. There had been perfunctory approval of slogans supporting the national JTU platform. One political issue had been raised relating to the missile base installations in Nippon City. The inclusion in the union activities of principals and the invitation to the city superintendent of education to the meeting gave an appearance of professional more than trade union organization. The discussion relating to the proposed revision of the *shibu* constitution was the single incident that cast a union orientation into the meeting. During the discussion the idea was expressed that principals and teachers were representing opposing sides in a labor-management model of school organization. Such feelings were evidently held by a minority of the teachers at the meeting, though they were able to block the proposed constitutional changes.

SHIBU COMMITTEES AND SECTIONS

Two *shibu* committees have already been mentioned. The general committee is composed of representatives from each *bunkai*, with the number of representatives being proportional to the number of teachers in the *bunkai*, on the basis of one representative for every ten teachers. This makes a total of forty-three representatives on the general committee, including two representatives from each of the two *shibu* section organizations described below. This committee met rarely. Some announcements generated by meetings of the general committee were made during Nichū daily teachers' meeting periods.

The second committee, called the executive committee, has one representative from each *bunkai* and section and includes the elected officers of the *shibu*. It meets monthly and is responsible for carrying on the business of the *shibu* between the annual meetings. The executive committee is particularly responsible for communication from the higher levels of union organization to the teachers and for the organization of activities initiated either locally or from above. At Nichū during the daily teachers' meetings before school, the executive committee representative would occasionally announce the decisions of the committee and carry out union-initiated activities.

The first meeting of both the executive and general committees was combined. It occurred six days after the general meeting of the *shibu*. Major items of business included the selection of twenty Nippon City representatives to the general meeting of prefectural teachers union scheduled for the following week, and representatives for standing committees of the prefectural union.

One of the activities carried out by the executive committee during the period of this study was a conference of union representatives with the Nippon City superintendent of education. The meeting was requested by the union for the purpose of protesting against the nationwide achievement testing program of the Ministry.

They secured a promise from the superintendent that the test results would not be used for the evaluation of teachers, which was the committee's major concern.

Two sections of the *shibu* cut across *bunkai* divisions to enlist all the women teachers in the women's section and all of the male teachers under thirty-five years of age in the youth section. These sections maintained separate organizations and held annual meetings as well as sponsoring some special activities. These sections were affiliated, in turn, with the women's and youth sections of the prefectural teachers' union.

Female teachers at Nichū were not especially active in the Nippon City *shibu* women's section. The youngest Nichū teacher, a home economics specialist, was the Nichū representative to the committee of the women's section which met on a monthly basis. Like the *shibu*, itself, there was an annual meeting for all the female teachers and a committee to carry on the affairs of the section at another time. One of the older Nichū female teachers described the activities, other than the annual meeting, as including institutes for the study of laws relating to women's rights as teachers and workers, sessions for cooking and sewing lessons, and the promotion of meetings bringing mothers and female teachers together for discussion of educational problems.

The youth section of the *shibu* had a local reputation of being the most radical and active of the teachers union activities. This was, in part, a reflection of the national reputation of the younger teachers in the union.

Several of the Nichū teachers were active in the youth section. During the annual meeting, a radical leadership group was deposed from power in favor of a more moderate group.

Organized like the *shibu* and the women's section, the annual meeting was a time for business relating to the program for the year and the election of officers. About one hundred and twenty teachers came to meet in the cramped library of the Itchū Middle School on a Thursday afternoon about four weeks after the *shibu's* annual meeting. Two older officers of the *shibu*, formerly active in the youth section, attended as observers for the *shibu*.

Less formally organized than the *shibu's* annual meeting, the program was similar. Reports of past and proposed activities, finances, and slogans were much the same. In the mimeographed program, activities of the past year were listed under five sections: (1) protection of peace, independence, and democracy, (2) protection of democratic education, (3) protection of livelihood and rights, (4) enlargement of freedom for union activities, and (5) miscellaneous.

Under the first section, stress was laid on activities of youth division members in the anti-atomic bomb testing movement. "Protection of democratic action" had been supported by opposition to the nationwide achievement tests and participation in regional research and study meetings.

In his concluding remarks on activities of the past year, the chairman was critical of teacher participation in youth division activities. He felt that the meetings of the general committee had been very poor, and that the youth division programs were insufficiently active. He blamed this on the fact that members were so busy in their work as teachers and in carrying out their school responsibilities. He also mentioned, though, a lack of spirit among the members of the youth section's committee and a lack of spirited guidance from the youth division officers. These comments reflected his own position as a union activist.

When the time came for election of new officers, there was, again, a single slate of nominees. The same collapsible ballot box and voting booths that had been set up for the *shibu* general meeting were used and the teachers lined up to cast their ballots.

The election results that were announced indicated, however, that the entire slate of officers had been rejected. This left the chairman obviously confused on how to proceed. Since it was already past the scheduled closing time of the meeting, someone suggested that it be adjourned. Another person suggested that a committee be appointed to nominate a new slate of officers. Amidst some confusion, such a committee was appointed and it retired from the room to consider the problem. After some time during which there was no programed activity for the general meeting, the committee returned to announce its nominations. Instead of going through the balloting procedure once more, the new slate of officers was elected by acclamation and the meeting adjourned after a brief greeting from the new chairman.

Until this meeting, the leadership of the youth section had been dominated by representatives of the radical "anti-mainstream" faction of the JTU. The Nichū teacher who was elected vice-chairman of the youth division, in the second slate of nominees, explained, "The anti-mainstream factions of the JTU were in control of the Nippon City youth section. There were all kinds of communist-style movements and opposition to educational officials. This year we decided to stand up. Up to now, 5 or 6 members dominated 120 members of the youth division. But we are not a principals' union. We are not going to be used by the principals. But then we are not a real labor union, either."

As it happened, the slate of nominees, first proposed during the meeting had been drawn up by the youth division officers. Rather than enter a second slate of candidates in direct opposition to the first slate, the moderate dissenters had decided to vote against the officer's slate and then put up their own candidates for election.

The second slate of candidates had, in fact, been chosen far in advance of the meeting, with the candidates informally agreeing to serve, if elected. Communication among the teachers had been sufficiently good to let them know that a second slate was available so that they would vote against the first slate. This activity had apparently gone on without the knowledge of the former youth division leaders so that they were truly surprised to find themselves out of power after the election.

One of the moderate candidates had actually been selected for inclusion in the first slate of nominees, but had withdrawn his name several weeks before the general meeting when he was told of the formation of a second slate of nominees. He was then elected in the second slate.

Two of the four nominees in the first slate were the two Tokai teachers who had been transferred the preceding year without their consent and had caused the *shibu* meeting that year the troubles described previously.

The underlying structure of such meetings in Japanese society is obviously well organized. The outward form of a nominating committee, chosen ostensibly on the spur of the moment, conceals the fact that candidates have been effectively elected by a different procedure earlier. Another example of this procedure has already been given in the description of the Nichū PTA election of officers.

That the union organization also fulfills a social function was evident in the sponsorship of an annual *bōnenkai* (year-end party) for youth section members on Christmas day at a local restaurant. Strictly an occasion for drinking *sake* and renewing friendships, the young teachers looked forward to the occasion.

During the winter vacation, one of the Nichū teachers mentioned above participated in a two-day "labor course" sponsored by the youth section of the prefectural teachers union. According to his description the meeting included people who are very extreme in union affairs. He said that the youth section of the prefectural union had the same problems of leadership as the Nippon City youth section. The prefectural union had not, however, ousted the radical leadership.

Much emphasis is placed on research and study for teachers in both their union and nonunion activities. A large annual educational research meeting is sponsored on a nationwide basis by the JTU as the culmination of research activities at the prefectural and local levels. Most prefectures, too, have a teachers' union-sponsored annual meeting for reports of educational research conducted within the prefecture during the previous year.

At the local level, the teachers' union *shibu* organized "research circles" to bring together teachers interested in study and research related to specific topics. At Nichū school, the *shibu* executive committee representative made an announcement in July about the planning meeting for local research circles which would be held the following week. Each school was to send several representatives to the central meeting for the *shibu* which would discuss topics to be prepared for the annual prefectural educational research meeting in November.

One of the Nichū representatives to the *shibu* general committee went to represent the Nichū teachers. There were no *shidō shuji*, or school principals, in attendance at the meeting. Discussion centered on the preparation of research reports that would be taken to both the prefectural and national educational research meetings.

According to the general schedule for research activities outlined on the program for the planning meeting, the months of April to August were to be used for research activity and writing of reports at the local schools. September and October were to be used for research circle activities and discussion of the individual reports. The prefectural research meeting was scheduled for the second week in November, on a Saturday and Sunday, to give many teachers the opportunity to attend.

In spite of the lack of organization or enthusiasm at the Nippon City planning meeting, the prefectural educational research meeting did not reflect this spirit. Although the organization of the prefectural meeting was atypical for Japan, it represented a most interesting pattern of cooperation between union and administrative educational groups.

The meetings attended by the author, many of the Nichū teachers, and more than a thousand of the prefecture's elementary and middle school teachers were held on the campus of the prefectural university's school of education. It was called the "Seventh Annual Educational Research Assembly" of the "Prefectural Educational Research Federation." Official sponsorship of the meeting was not listed on the printed program though one assumed that it was to be the prefectural level meeting in preparation for the national research meeting sponsored publicly by the JTU.

In the early postwar years, two prefectural-level educational research meetings had been held annually. One was sponsored by the prefectural university's school of education and was a continuation of similar prewar meetings organized by the prefectural normal school which was the predecessor of the school of education. The second annual meeting had been sponsored by the prefectural teachers union. At the request of the teachers, a combined educational research meeting was organized through the cooperation of the union and the school of education to eliminate the duplication of educational research reports that had been occurring. Because the prefectural education office had cooperated earlier in the university-sponsored research meetings, they continued to cooperate with the new prefectural research organization in spite of the union affiliation. This cooperation consisted mainly of inclusion of the prefectural education office's guidance section staff of *shidō shuji* in the program as advisers for each of the separate research sections. Thus official sponsorship of the meetings rested with the university and the union, but the education office was included in the planning and conduct of the meetings.

In the year of this study, the Ministry of Education had announced a new plan for a nationwide research organization, covertly designed to compete with the JTU's nationwide organization of educational research by classroom teachers. The new plan did not call for prefectural research meetings, however, and so did not interfere with the conduct of the university and union-sponsored meeting in the prefecture of this study.

Thus professional research activities were an important element of teachers union activities at all levels, though particularly at the prefectural and national level of organization. In general, they complemented, rather than conflicted with, the study and research activities organized by the administrative community at the local level. In this area of union activity, the union was cast much more in the pattern of a professional educators' association than a labor union.

UNION ACTIVITY WITHIN NICHŪ

Union-related activities observed in Nichū school by the author were mainly extensions of activities initiated at higher levels of the union. Only one formal teachers union *bunkai* meeting was observed, though more may have been held. The major intrusion of union matters into the school occurred when announcements were made about union business during the regular teachers' meeting before or after school in the teachers' room.

Early in the school year, three teachers were elected to teachers union *bunkai* positions. The election took place during a Nichū teachers' meeting. The three teachers elected were to represent the *bunkai* on the *shibu* committees, two on the general committee and one on the executive committee.

Six days before the national achievement tests were scheduled to be administered, a formal Nichū *bunkai* meeting was called in the afternoon after classes. Though the meeting was not listed among the week's activities on the head teacher's blackboard, the word had been passed to the teachers. The representative to the *shibu* executive committee chaired the meeting which was held in the teacher's room in a fashion similar to all Nichū teachers' meetings. He moved from his own desk to the principal's desk at the head of the room to call the meeting to order. Later the principal came in and pulled a chair to one side of the desk for himself.

The first item of business was a report from one of the Nichū teachers who served as representative on the *shibu* general committee. He presented a list of five problems that had been discussed at a meeting of his committee, one of which was the problem of the nationwide achievement tests. The conference of the *shibu* representatives with the Nippon City superintendent of education was mentioned in this report. Then the Nichū teachers were asked to express their opinions.

Much in the manner of everyday Nichū teachers' meetings, the teachers were sitting at their desks, correcting students' homework or carrying out other small chores, without giving the impression that they were paying much attention to the discussion at hand. A few teachers, however, did express their opinions. One older teacher expressed a strong concern for the way in which the test results would be used. Another teacher, answering his arguments, said, "When you get to be a principal, your opinion will change." Most of the teachers laughed at this, but it did start a tangential discussion of the role of the principal and head teacher. An older teacher, classmate of the principal, turned to both the principal and head teacher and said, "It really must be difficult for you."

Going back to the discussion about the achievement tests, the chairman asked what conclusions should be drawn from the *bunkai* discussion. The *shibu* general committee representative replied, "After all, we are all employees, so we cannot do much but submit a petition."

At the end of the meeting, a petition opposing the achievement tests was passed around for the teachers' signatures by the chairman.

Less than an hour and a half after the opening of the meeting, the chairman brought it to a close. The major accomplishment was the signing of the anti-achievement test petition.

After the achievement tests had been carried out with the full cooperation of the Nichū teachers, the *shibu* executive committee representative reported at a teachers' meeting that the committee was collecting criticisms of the test and would like each *bunkai* to hold a special meeting to make their criticisms. Because Nichū teachers had a very busy schedule, however, he suggested that the teachers speak to him individually about their criticisms and he would then relay them to the committee.

Several months later on their way to attend the prefectural educational research meeting, the executive committee representative and several other teachers from different Nippon City schools were discussing union activities with the author. An example that was given of the lack of activity in the Nippon City teachers union *shibu* referred to the call for local school meetings in opposition to the achievement tests. According to the teachers, the JTU central office had called the meetings and specified that they all be held at 9 A.M. on a given day. The prefectural teachers union office thought this was an inconvenient time and so suggested that the meetings be held at 1 P.M. in the prefecture of Nippon City. The Nippon City *shibu*, however, thought this timing inconvenient too, and suggested meetings at 3 P.M. By the time the call for the meetings had reached the individual schools, there was a great deal of variation—and Nichū had not even held a formal meeting.

During the period of this study, a national election for members of the Diet's House of Councillors was held. The House of Councillors has 250 members of whom 150 are elected from the prefectures and 100 are elected from the nation at large. Each voter is allowed to vote for one prefectural candidate and one national candidate. One of the candidates running at large in the election was the JTU national chairman, Takeshi Kobayashi. Though officially a candidate of the Socialist party, he based his successful campaign on his teachers union affiliation, and used teachers union channels of communication to promote his election.

About a month before the election, the Nichū *shibu* executive committee representative announced at an early morning teachers' meeting that the campaign for Kobayashi's election had been discussed by the committee. He passed out to the teachers several campaign leaflets which were imprinted with the name of an organization called the "Japanese Federation of Democratic Education and Government." Though the name of the JTU did not appear, Kobayashi's positions with the union were given in the biographical data on the leaflets.

Also passed out were some postcards endorsing Kobayashi's candidacy. The teachers were asked to address the postcards to a friend and to sign their names. They were then collected by the executive committee representative to arrange for postage and mailing. All the teachers appeared to sign the cards.

In November the executive committee representative introduced a new teachers union project to the teachers at the regular before-school teachers' meeting. This time, the union was interested in a survey which would show the number of hours actually worked by teachers over and above the regular working day. Forms were passed out to each teacher on which they could record overtime work performed at school in one column and homework in a second column. The starting date of the survey was clearly specified, though no ending date appeared to be set. The form allowed space for three weeks of reporting.

The representative explained that the purpose of the survey was to show that there was a shortage of teachers and that the present pay was insufficient. "After all, in a usual company the people only work until 4:30 and then they are through," he said.

The above examples are representative of the conduct of union business within the school. The teachers and principal never objected to the conduct of such business during school hours or teaching meetings. Union activities had a professional aura and were considered appropriate for discussion and concern in regular school gatherings.

INFORMAL TEACHER ACTIVITIES

Not all the organized activities for Nichū teachers were strictly professional. Similar in pattern to the organized recreational activities of other employed groups, particularly in white-collar occupations, there were plans for group recreational activities which would include all of the teachers. At the end of each of the three school terms during the year, it was general practice to organize a "meeting for reflection." When first invited to such a meeting, the author assumed that it would include some form of professional evaluation of the school term just completed. His suspicions were aroused, however, by the location of the meeting at one of the restaurants near the center of Nippon City.

The occasion turned out to be a full-scale party with beer and food for all. Local Nichū District merchants and the PTA chairman donated some of the food and drink which was appropriately acknowledged by the principal at the start of the party. There were no formalities beyond the first toast led by the principal. As time wore on, the men's shirts came off and they began to sing. The female teachers and school-lunch cook retreated to one end of the room and talked together. At different times, two of the younger male teachers were asleep on the floor. When one of the younger male teachers began an argument with an older teacher that could not be amicably setlled, the party came to a close "because the next party was waiting to get into the room." The argument was not treated seriously, rather, it was the signal that the party had gone on long enough. Each teacher warned the others to be careful on their way home, and they left the restaurant.

At a second such party, the higher PTA officers were invited to join with the teachers in their celebration of the end of the second term. The officials came and were included as full members of the group. The party at the end of the year, after the graduation ceremony, was sponsored by the PTA and the teachers were invited guests.

During the summer vacation, a good deal of planning and anticipation went into a trip by the Nichū teachers to a local resort. Spending only one night and two days there, it was noteworthy to the American researcher that wives and husbands were not included in such an affair. Since the teachers worked together as a group, they were the ones who went together on their vacation trip.

REFERENCES

Cornell, John B., "Buraka Social Organization and Community Life," in Bernard S. Silberman (ed.), *Japanese Character and Culture: A Book of Selected Readings.* Tucson: University of Arizona Press, 1962, pp. 36–67.

30 / Maintaining the System: The Socialization of a Principal

Harry Wolcott

This essay deals with processes by which the schools manage to maintain stable cultural systems in spite of the constant change of personnel assigned to their relatively few statuses. The underlying thesis here is that schools, like other cultural systems, are perpetuated through the processes of socializing new members into the statuses which must be occupied. Considering the benign image usually associated with the nation's elementary schools, the processes of socialization occurring in them are at times surprisingly severe, not only for the ever-changing pupil population but also for adult members of more permanent tenure. Since this study focuses on the principalship, attention is drawn to the ways in which a principal is socialized into teaching and administrative roles.[1]

Although I have chosen first to explore how a principal is socialized, I do not mean to create the impression of a neat sequence in which an individual is completely socialized before he himself can act as a socializer. In varying degrees, these processes occurred concomitantly for Ed Bell as the study progressed, although several years had passed since he had experienced the more intense periods of socialization associated with induction into either teaching or administrative roles. Ed's socialization as a professional educator continued not only through the subtleties of daily interactions with his many "others," but also through such direct means as a periodic evaluation conference for each principal held at the central office. . .

BECOMING A PRINCIPAL

Any impatience Ed once felt about whether he would ever become a principal in the district had dissipated long ago. Ed laughed at his own impatience in recalling how close he had come to leaving the district after his third year at the time he got his first "break" to assume a principalship.

Now, nine years later, as Ed watched the large number of other sometimes-impatient young men obviously anxious to become principals, he occasionally wondered just how he happened to be selected at all, or at least how he had been promoted when he was still relatively a newcomer in the district. "But maybe there just weren't as many fellows available then. And of course, I had Tom Nice supporting me. Tom made quite a bit out of my having prior administrative experience back in Kansas. I didn't really have so much experience as a principal there, but it helped me get to where I *could* get some."

Ed's initial administrative assignment in the Columbia School District was to assume a full-time principalship for the remainder of the school year. A substitute teacher was hired to take the responsibility for his fifth-grade class. Ed's administrative appointment was clearly portrayed to him as a temporary one, but at the end of that year he was assigned to serve as the principal of two small schools elsewhere in the district. Again the temporary nature of the appointment was emphasized, a fact which Ed interpreted as a lack of satisfaction with his administrative style by the central office. "I thought I might end up back in the classroom," he recalled. Instead, he was reassigned at the end of that year as the supervising principal of another elementary school. That assignment was not qualified with the tentative status of a "temporary" appointment.

Whenever Ed talked about becoming an administrator in the district he mentioned how fortunate he had been to receive his initial teaching assignment at Tom Nice's school: "He's the easiest principal in the district to work with." Other principals spoke similarly of how they happened to get their first administrative assignments, typically relating highly personal experiences in which some combination of help from their building principal plus sheer "good luck" accounted for their "break" into administration. As one principal stated:

> I don't think the promotions are based on seniority or on merit. I think it's just luck, catching someone's ear, or being at the right place at the right time. There were other guys who had been around longer than me when they asked me to take my first job as an acting principal.

In their efforts to describe the forces which contribute to upward mobility, social scientists have identified various modes by which new statuses are attained. Two concepts suggested by R. H. Turner[2] (1960), "sponsored mobility" and "contest mobility," seem particularly useful in describing the processes by which teachers become principals. However, I have treated the two modes, sponsored and contest mobility, as complementary rather than as contrasting modes as originally suggested by Turner. To cast these two complementary modes in the jargon of the professional literature of education, I refer to them as "sponsorship" and "GASing." I shall deal first with the concept of sponsorship because it is probably the more crucial of the two processes in becoming a principal generally and it was certainly the more crucial force in Ed's initial promotion.

Sponsorship

In sponsored mobility, as defined by Turner (1960: 856), elite recruits (for example, teachers desirous of becoming principals) are chosen by established elites or their agents (for example, the superintendent, or those to whom he delegates his authority). Elite status is *given* by those in authority rather than *taken* through effort and strategy on the part of the recruits themselves. Sponsorship appeared to have been a key factor in the process by which many of the principals in the district had achieved their administrative status. Sponsorship also provided a way for describing the roles they in turn played in encouraging other promising young men to be "thinking about administration" and in their active support of certain candidates.

Not all sponsors are equally effective, and, as a study of sponsorship in the school superintendency showed (Rose 1969), the people who act as sponsors are themselves not always aware of their roles or of their impact. Among the elementary school principals in the Columbia School District, some were consciously and even aggressively engrossed as sponsors, while others may have had more actual impact. One of Ed's younger cohorts consciously and deliberately pursued the role of sponsor. He explained that he had never realized the extent to which the role of principal required him to be a politician, but since the job seemed to necessitate it, he found himself engaging in politics more and more. He described how he had conspired with one teacher at his school to get the young man an administrative position. Their strategy was for each of them to take every opportunity to keep the sponsoree's name "in the fore" by having him named on committees and by giving him assignments that would constantly increase his visibility to central office personnel and school board members. The principal noted, by way of contrast, that Ed Bell hadn't needed to pursue such an aggressive strategy in order to get a principalship: "Ed had just been there when someone was needed."

If Ed did happen to be at the right place at the right time, that was not the only factor working in his favor. Regardless of what his actual responsibilities as an administrator in Kansas had been, he was recognized in the Columbia School District as an experienced principal who would inevitably receive an administrative assignment there sometime in the future. Promotions to principalships in the larger school districts throughout the country are more often made from within the district than from the outside (see Elkins 1950; Fleming 1967; McDowell 1954), a policy that was unwritten but nonetheless generally adhered to within the Columbia schools. Thus it was virtually essential for Ed to "work up through the ranks."

Assessing his chances for a principalship after spending almost three years in the district, Ed became discouraged. In the continuing financial press of earning an adequate income for his family, he considered moving to a better-paying district to gain an immediate improvement in salary rather than wait out the opportunity of an administrative assignment in Columbia. At that point Ed's principal, Tom Nice, performed two aspects of the sponsor function, while Ed himself had become resigned, at least temporarily, to remaining a classroom teacher. Tom worked officially to encourage consideration of Ed as an administrative candidate at the central office while he also personally encouraged Ed to complete formal course requirements for the administrative credential at the local university.

Tom's sponsorship did not terminate when Ed became a principal. Ed frequently turned to Tom for guidance while finishing out the year in the school where Tom had been principal, and he had continued to call upon him for advice ever since. The same factors which prompted the initial sponsorship had continued to keep their relationship intact, including shared feelings about the importance of elementary school education as well as similarities in ages and commitments to active participation in their respective churches. The fact that Ed and Tom worked and lived in the same part of town facilitated opportunities for communication between them concerning common professional problems as well as frequent arrangements for travelling together to professional meetings. In more recent years, as Ed became thoroughly entrenched as an administrator *within* the district, Tom's sponsorship and personal encouragement had led to Ed's increased activity and influence within the professional associations of principals. With the help of two other senior principals, Tom had actively campaigned on Ed's behalf and had contributed personal funds for printing costs to see Ed elected president of the county and subsequently of the regional principals' associations. Tom expressed personal satisfaction in watching Ed assume responsibilities "beyond the walls of his own school building." In our first meeting Tom explained, out of Ed's hearing, how pleased he was to see Ed becoming "even more involved" in the work of the principalship, by which he meant Ed's recently acquired role as an officer in the principals' organizations.

Although Ed remained in the role of sponsoree vis-à-vis Tom Nice, he also assumed the role of sponsor vis-à-vis certain younger men interested in administrative careers in elementary schools. He had consciously attempted to assist one young male teacher formerly on the Taft faculty to obtain an administrative position. Ed described "mixed feelings" about helping (sponsoring) his former teacher in his bid for a principalship. On the one hand, Ed confessed, he wanted to see capable young men remain in the classroom; on the other hand, he did not want to "stand in the way." Other principals who perceived themselves as sponsors of specific candidates acknowledged facing a similar dilemma and their inevitable and selfless resolution of it. Sponsoring principals did not publicly assume the credit for the successful achievements of their sponsorees. Among his colleagues Ed publicly assumed credit only for "not standing in the way" of the young man. He did make it known, however, that he had announced his intention to help his teacher in obtaining an administrative position "when the opportunity occurred." Although Ed and his sponsoree had not subsequently maintained the close relationship that Ed continued to hold with his own sponsor—perhaps because none of the factors which facilitated the frequent interaction between Ed and Tom (age, church activity, geographical proximity of their schools and homes) was shared between Ed and the younger man—they did attempt at least a brief exchange of greetings at every meeting which brought all principals together. Ed enjoyed hearing reports of the younger man's success as a principal, and he reminded anyone who might not have known or recalled it that the man's prior assignment had been at Taft.

GASing

There is some indication in the literature that career decisions about becoming an administrator are made early and that teachers who intend to "move up" exhibit different behaviors and a different orientation toward the authority system of a school and district from the very onset of their entry into teaching. In a study of socialization into the principalship based on interviews with eighteen recently appointed elementary school principals in California, Ron Blood noted:

The bulk of the principals interviewed were actively engaged in the process of becoming a principal from a very early date. Even the *first* year of teaching, for many, is characterized by a strong focus on the system as a whole and on the principalship specifically. The candidates engage in a pattern which at once serves to get the attention of superiors and provides access to the work-world of the principal. (Blood 1966: 71)

The candidate who aspires to the principalship has already tacitly demonstrated that he recognizes and accepts the authority system of the school. The process of socialization into teaching tends to assure that candidates who survive can live with the educational hierarchy. Advancing up the "ladder" requires more than simply acquiescing to the system, however. One must actively demonstrate willingness and aptitude for assuming greater responsibility. In the parlance of educational administration, such people are sometimes referred to as GASers.

GASing behavior, or *Getting the Attention of Superiors*,[3] describes a style of teacher behavior characteristic of the teacher seeking to move up and out of the classroom. GASing refers particularly to a teacher's taking additional school-related but nonteaching assignments as a strategy to increase his visibility from among the teacher group at large. The consequence of being a successful GASer is that one becomes known to those people who are in a position to make or directly influence promotions or to lend indirect support as sponsors.

In the Columbia School District, seriously considered candidates for principalships were known personally or at least known about, by more principals and central office personnel. No system of examinations existed in the district. Even the technicality of filing a formal notice with the Director of Personnel expressing a wish to be considered as a candidate was not essential for individuals known to be interested in the appointments.

The GASing syndrome appeared to be quite familiar to principals and to would-be principals alike, although the term itself was not used in the district. To what extent Ed had employed such tactics in order to win the initial support of the principal and the eventual support of the central office was never discussed. In Ed's recounting, it was Tom Nice's support which got him the appointment rather than his own effort, although the extent of their shared values, coupled with a possible lack of assertiveness on Ed's part, may have presented Tom with the kind of candidate he preferred to support. Ed and his colleagues recognized and discussed the GASing behavior exhibited by aspiring candidates among the district's elementary school teachers. Ed was appointed to a Principal Selection Committee to recommend to the superintendent and school board the "best people" among the eligible candidates for three principalships opening up the following fall (Wolcott n.d.). During the deliberations of the committee, comments were frequently made indicating a sensitivity toward the amount of GASing behavior each candidate had engaged in as well as an assessment of whether the extent of GASing was appropriate for the particular candidate. For example, Ed's assessment of one candidate, a young man who had attained considerable visibility and was suspected of seeking too much power in the internal organization of the school district, was, "I see too many people ahead of him myself." Ed had stated a similar opinion in more detail a few months earlier after attending a meeting in which that teacher had taken a domineering role:

He's already a resource teacher, and I think this is only his third year in the district. This fellow just doesn't want to wait his turn, that's all. He's trying to get in good with Boggs [the superintendent]. It's not that there is actually a seniority system in selecting principals, but there are a lot of qualified fellows who have been around longer than he has.

Of another candidate apparently not in high favor, one principal's assessment hinted that too little talent in personal dynamics had been exhibited: "I worked closely with him on that big evaluation project. He wasn't loud and forceful, but he did do a good job." Still other candidates were perceived as having tried too hard. The written recommendation of one woman principal reviewed by the selection committee warned that the candidate had done "too much of the business of the local teachers' association" when he should have been attending to his responsibilities as the school's resource teacher. Another woman principal expressed concern about a candidate from her staff: "I think his one big problem is relating to people because he tends to want to move too fast."

Some candidates had apparently managed to exhibit the appropriate degree of GASing. Ed offered this appraisal in support of a candidate whom he felt would be an excellent principal: "He has dealt with some difficult situations very well as the committee chairman in the Teachers Association. He has a real ability to make his leadership felt." The other members of the committee joined in unanimous agreement regarding the candidate in question, capped by an endorsement from the Director of Elementary Education, "I used to think of him as a guy who just 'went along,' but I see him differently now." From the candidate's point of view, her comments could be interpreted as the successful culmination to all his efforts as a GASer, not only to getting the attention of superiors, but to getting that attention to the proper extent and for the right reasons.

Formal Academic Preparation

Complaints about formal graduate studies in "ed-admin" are legion among practicing school administrators. Their complaints provide them with a common bond regardless of differences in the region of the country in which they work, where they pursued their administrative courses, or the types of schools or districts to which they are presently assigned. Often they categorically dismiss all their "professional" training (for teaching as well as for school administration), creating an epithet out of the whole comprehensive field in which they have pursued their studies, "Education courses, aggh!" Less frequently, someone who has experienced both the study and practice of school administration makes his grievances explicit, a sport which appears to be open to all public school personnel and is not unknown among their professors (see the criticism of the preparation programs issued by the 1960 yearbook commission of the American Association of School Administrators,[4] or suggested in a title like Andrew W. Halpin's "Administrative Theory: The Fumbled Torch" [Halpin 1970]).

During a taped interview made at Taft School, Mr. Adam, the one teacher on Ed's faculty who had experienced both the theory and practice of school administration, volunteered this opinion on administration courses:

> I don't think of administration as being a separate function. For instance, when I think of the presidency of the United States, I can't think of the courses that either Lyndon Johnson or Jack Kennedy or Eisenhower ought to have taken in order to assume those jobs. I can't think of any real courses that I've had in administration, although I've had the three basic elementary administration courses, the three basic secondary administration courses, three basic school district administrative courses, and then the junior college administrative courses. To me it was a dickens of a lot of repetition. Many of the people who taught me were teaching according to what they had learned 20 years before. Good people are apt to do good jobs, they're apt to assume the responsibilities, and they are apt to be flexible enough to find out what they need to know in a hurry.

Ed's own experience as a graduate student in educational administration had been neither bitter nor rewarding. It was simply a fact of life that he had to take sufficient courses to earn an administrative credential if he hoped and planned eventually to become a full-time principal (State law required that the administrator of any school of eight or more teachers hold a valid administrative credential.) Ed had left Kansas as soon as he completed the formal course work for a bachelor's degree, and he realized that he needed to begin the accumulation of units toward a master's degree and administrative credential at once, particularly since his opportunities to take courses were limited to evenings and summer sessions.

Ed's perception of himself was that he was "not much of a student." "I'd rather be doing things and be up and about. And I'm a very slow reader." He found his graduate courses generally disappointing and his major professor in his graduate program "less than no help as an adviser and never prepared as a teacher." Like most of his colleagues, Ed's program at the university terminated immediately upon satisfying the necessary course-work requirements for the degree and credential. The requirements for the master's degree in school administration and the elementary school administrative credential were virtually synonymous, and no thesis was required. Although the degree and credential represented the ultimate pay-off in his graduate studies, the accumulation of course hours beyond his bachelor's degree also had an immediate, practical value, since the school district followed the usual pattern of placing its professional employees at higher increments in the salary schedule with the accumulation of additional hours of study.

Even when he attained the master's degree, Ed's formal education was not completed. A "professional growth" policy of long standing in the district, and widely followed across the nation, not only encouraged continuing course work for professional employees through salary increments but actually required such study ("or equivalent travel or work") as a prerequisite for professional advancement. The requirement could be met in part by participating in in-service workshops and programs offered by the school district and by receiving credit for taking extra assignments (for example, serving on a curriculum project). Not more than eight years could elapse without actually enrolling in course work offering university credit. Ed did not relish having to take more courses, but he had let the requirement slip by so long that he received a terse reminder from the central office that he had to acquire more "hours." He reacted, "It's true I haven't gotten campus credit for quite a while, but I've been involved in workshops 'up to here'!" Administering the summer school at Taft precluded an opportunity for him to meet the requirement by attending a university summer session, and neither his inclination nor his daily schedule led him to consider enrolling in a late afternoon or evening university class except as a last resort. Ed was spared from this dilemma when the university literally came to the doorstep of Taft School with a course especially designed for intern teachers but open to any teachers who wished to enroll.

The proximity of the university, the constant exposure to at least a selected segment of its faculty in education, and the continual press for pursuing additional in-service and graduate studies left Ed with an unsettling career question faced by many elementary school principals in similar circumstances: Should he go on for a doctorate? The question seemed to be in the back of the minds of several of Ed's colleagues, particularly the younger ones. A few persons in the administrative hierarchy held a degree at the doctoral level, including the four key central office administrators—Superintendent, Assistant Superintendent, and Directors of Elementary and Secondary Education—as well as others like the Director of Counselling and Guidance, and the Director of Buildings and Grounds. So also did some academic department heads in the high schools. None of the principals held a doctorate, although a few had completed the course requirements for the degree or had accumulated a number of graduate course hours. Ed's ambivalence about the doctorate had seemingly been settled against pursuing such a course himself. "I've thought about it, but I just don't see what good it would do me," he explained. In support of that position, he liked to cite the example of the teacher he had helped sponsor into administration: "Did you know that he completed all of his doctoral program except the dissertation? Yet he has told me he never wants to go back where he can't work with kids. I think he's satisfied where he is, now that he is in administration and getting a better salary than he was as a teacher."

The tangible evidence of Ed's graduate program in school administration was contained in textbooks numbering 7 among a total of 33 books, pamphlets, and journal copies on a shelf in his office that constituted his professional library. Among the 7 titles were several widely read authors in curriculum, supervision, and school administration in the late fifties: Baldwin (1955); Burton and Brueckner (1955); Elsbree and McNally (1951); Hanna, Potter, and Hagamann (1955); Kyte (1952); Smith, Stanley, and Shores (1957); and Spears (1951).[5] Shelved next to these "classics" was a rather uneven assortment of professional pamphlets and single copies of professional journals (for example, *Elementary School Journal, Child-hood Education*, three yearbooks of the Association for Supervision and Curriculum Development), a copy of *Webster's New Secondary School Dictionary*, one children's library book (*Island of the Blue Dolphins*), and a paperback copy of what was probably the most widely read book among teachers in the 1960s, Jerome Bruner's *The Process of Education* (1961).[6] Since half of the 16 dated pamphlets were from the year 1964, the collection looked suspiciously as though it had last been reviewed during that year or earlier; only one book, the ASCD yearbook for 1965, contained a copyright date more recent than 1964 when I inventoried the library shelf in March 1967. I know of no occasion when Ed so much as glanced toward any of the materials on the shelf (nor candidly am I able to think of any occasion when his library shelf would have contained reference material to which he would have needed to refer).

Ed was not alone in feeling that his formal course work in administration was rather unrelated to his actual work as a school principal. In the national study of elementary school principals (DESP 1968: 28), principals were asked, "What type of experience or preparation has contributed most to your success as a principal?" Less than two percent of the total sample of principals gave credit to their college preparation as the major source contributing to their success (see table 30.1).

TABLE 30.1. PREPARATION OR EXPERIENCE CONTRIBUTING MOST TO SUCCESS AS A PRINCIPAL

TYPE OF EXPERIENCE	TOTAL SAMPLE (IN PERCENTAGES)	SUPERVISING PRINCIPALS (IN PERCENTAGES)
As classroom teacher	40.9	38.8
College education	1.9	1.6
On-the-job as a principal	41.5	41.9
As an intern	1.8	2.0
As an assistant principal	7.1	8.3
In-service programs of school systems	1.5	1.6
By self-study and research	3.7	4.0
Other	1.6	1.8
Total	100.0	100.0
Number	2,304	1,882

Source: The Elementary School Principalship in 1968 (DESP 1968: 29). Copyright 1968, National Association of Elementary School Principals, NEA. All rights reserved. Used by permission.

Perhaps understandably, the major type of experience identified in this regard was on-the-job experience as a principal (41.5 percent of the total sample), particularly among the more experienced principals in the sample. It is less easy to understand why an equally large proportion of the sample (40.9 percent—composed largely of principals with less than five years' experience), indicated that their *experience as classroom teachers* contributed most to their success. Classroom teaching may indeed be necessary in order to validate one's claim to, and authority in, the principalship, but it is questionable how classroom teaching contributed to "success" in administration. However, except for 10 percent of the principals who reported that they had first served as assistant principals, vice principals, or interns, respondents were faced with a forced choice between two alternative answers regarding the source of their success—either that their college program contributed most or that their classroom teaching contributed most. Their responses may have been based more on their disregard for the first alternative than on their endorsement of the second one.

Principals not only eschew their formal training, they also look for evidence in support of their intuitive disregard for its utility. A research "finding" popular among the principals in the district and cited by them in discussions of the university's contribution to their administrative problems was that "the worst principals are the ones who have had the most courses." The source of this gleefully touted finding is elusive, but, as one study notes, even more modest findings "should give all professors of school administration cause for concern" (Hemphill et al. 1962: 340–41):

> The finding of essentially no relationship between amount of academic preparation and performance on the various tasks in school administration that were investigated is consistent throughout. There is no evidence that the principal with a lengthier preparation does a more effective job of school administration, from any point of view from which one may examine the data.[7]

Higher Education and the Principalship: Some Paradoxes

In spite of a strong element of ritual in the perennial complaining about their programs of graduate studies, the professional lives of principals are intricately linked with colleges and universities both in their own individual careers and in the complex relationships between the nation's schools and its institutions of higher learning. Colleges and universities perform functions which are at once critical and paradoxical for school administrators. Three of these functions, and the problems associated with them, are discussed under the headings Screening, Sponsoring, and Source of Knowledge.

The essential paradox of the principal-university relationship has already been presented implicitly in the discussion of the preceding pages: although the central objective of their professional lives is to promote the educational attainment of the pupils who attend their schools, principals hold their own formal education, and particularly their most recent experiences with it at its "highest" levels, in low esteem. Their endorsement of the efficacy of education is for education's potential contribution to others. Like Ed, they have generally found their graduate studies in ed-admin disappointing and irrelevant. For the most part they have pursued their studies as a necessary evil leading to pragmatic objectives like improving their salaries or satisfying credential requirements rather than in a quest for knowledge.

Screening One function which higher education serves for schools, a major one in terms of the magnitude of the educational establishment, is to help with the screening of personnel who are either moving *into* or moving upward *within* the permanent cadre of school personnel. These two facets of the screening function affect the principalship in different ways. In the first circumstance, school administrators are consumers who have become highly dependent on having screening services performed for them. At the same time, a would-be principal's career requires a typically prolonged period in which he himself is again subjected to scrutiny within the halls of academe. In the latter regard, principals are more inclined to perceive the screening function performed by college faculties as a hurdle or obstacle rather than as a contribution to their careers. As Ed noted,

> The people at the university are just like medical doctors. Once they get in, they want to make it as tough as they can on the next guy. They aren't all like that, but a lot are.

When it came to making assessments of others, particularly in filling staff vacancies, Ed, and his colleagues did not appear hesitant about relying on academic achievement as a criterion measure, even though they were critical of teacher-training and graduate education programs. It is hardly surprising that they did depend to a great extent on formal academic performance as recorded in official transcripts and letters of recommendation. Usually they had little other evidence on which to make judgments, particularly if they were not able to observe a candidate teaching or to conduct a personal interview. Furthermore, public school systems place a high regard on academic achievement in awarding status and determining salaries. Certificated personnel (i.e., persons who have met formal educational requirements for teaching, counselling, school administration, and so forth) are clearly distinguished from noncertificated ones; Ed sometimes used "qualified" as a synonym for "certificated" in referring to his professional staff. Central office personnel who held a doctorate degree were formally addressed as "doctor" by those lower in the hierarchy (for example, principals) and frequently referred to each other in the same manner. As noted earlier, professional salaries in school districts also recognize minute increments in hours of graduate study beyond the bachelors' and masters' degrees in awarding salary increases.

Ed demonstrated a deference toward people whose formal academic achievements surpassed his own. He showed a preference for teacher candidates whose academic records were substantial in quantity or outstanding in quality. At least one teacher felt that Ed exhibited a blind faith in relying on college transcripts as a criterion for the selection of new staff and that he had failed to recognize how he had been fooled by academic accomplishment several times before. She volunteered these comments during a taped interview.

> Ed has a tendency to look at some wonderful record of courses the person has taken and be a little overwhelmed by it. Just the other day he was wondering about my student teacher, and he asked my feeling about hiring him for a position next year that has recently opened up in the staff. I said I thought he would be fine and told him why. And he said, "Well, I have two or three possibilities that I have in mind that I would request before I would consider him," and he went on to tell me the glowing record that their files had.
>
> The next day I said to him, "You know, we've been fooled three times in this building by glowing records and lots and lots of university work and extra credits and this type of thing." In one case it was in guidance and counselling, and in the other it was with a husband and with a new program that was being carried out at the university. Ed thought this would be a wonderful opportunity to get some feedback about the counselling program before we had full time counselling here. Well, it just didn't work that way at all. I have the feeling that maybe some of these younger teachers that we see fit into the philosophy of our building of what we're trying to do here work out

better in the long run. We shouldn't be too overwhelmed by these wonderful records.

The paradox of screening lies in the dilemma of disavowing the utility and significance of one's own formal preparation but relying on, and having to rely on, the success that others have had with essentially the same system as a measure of their ability. Ed went beyond merely recognizing educational achievement; some of his staff felt he was awed by it.

Sponsoring. A corollary of the screening function occurs because school districts relinquish, as they must, part of the responsibility for identifying, training, and validating candidates moving upward within their own hierarchies. The function of relegating to colleges and universities a considerable portion of the burden of screening and evaluating teaching personnel and those hoping to debut as administrators is performed at the cost of making candidates visible outside the district. Faculty members of schools of education serve as sponsors and recruiters for positions outside the closed ranks of individual school districts. Occasionally they recruit personnel into their own ranks from the public schools.

Those principals in the study who had friends (or felt that they had friends) among faculty members at nearby universities frequently mentioned the personal help or attachment they felt to certain professors in spite of any lack of affection they may have felt for the institutions. They availed themselves of opportunities that arose at professional meetings or during visits on campus to make or renew acquaintances with college faculty. The frequency with which certain professors were invited or suggested as speakers, guests, or consultants among local principals acting in their various organizational roles suggested that some professors may have been perceived as "collective" sponsors or as contact men for the group at large.[8]

This aspect of the principal-university-school district triad necessitated light treading among principals. University contacts provided a valuable resource for any principal or would-be principal anticipating a move to another district or planning to pursue further studies, so at least the younger principals tended not to be outspoken critics of programs or professors.[9] On the other hand, principals did not expect their colleagues to become too closely identified with university personnel in educational administration, since that behavior could signal an intention of moving up or out. This relationship was further complicated by the fact that principals often lacked adequate information for making accurate assessments of the status and power which university faculty members wielded in their own institutions. Opportunities for contacts with senior faculty in the course of a school day were exceedingly rare. Those university personnel whose work regularly took them into schools appeared generally to be of low status—or, in the case of doctoral students recruited for supervising student teachers, no status at all—on their own campus, such as new young faculty or old-timers who had not achieved recognition and full-time campus responsibilities for their academic or administrative prowess. Thus the principals individually and collectively tended to defer to faculty who were not necessarily in a position to help them, and in so doing inadvertently contributed to maintaining the status quo in their very efforts to change it.

Source of knowledge. School districts generate much of the authority necessary for their own operation, but they do not generate the knowledge that they impart. Knowledge is provided by sources outside schools. Business and industry serve as sources of knowledge for some aspects of technology, but universities are the traditional sources for at least two major categories of knowledge consumed by schools: society's formally accumulated wisdom, which provides the content for *what* is taught, and the accumulated wisdom for *how* it is taught, the institutionalization of education through the operation of schools. Included in the latter domain is the accumulated wisdom, or what some educators refer to as the "knowledge base," of the administration of education. There is a large body of literature on the administration of education. But it does not speak with the level of specificity sought nor necessarily deal with the kinds of problems confronted by the school man faced with a need for immediate decisions. He lives in a time and a society where knowledge is held in high esteem and where scientific research is the process by which the store of knowledge is increased. Yet the daily operation of the school appears little dependent upon any tangible "knowledge base," and for the ultimate questions which American educators have posed (from classic and rhetorical ones like "What knowledge is of most worth?" or "Dare the schools build a new social order?" to Ed's concern for a question like "How does the teacher really know there is any learning going on?") the answers that administrators seek are not to be found.

To reduce the discrepancy between what they felt they did know and what they felt others expected them to know, the principals tended to draw upon the accepted *source* of knowledge rather than on knowledge itself. That source is "research." Pressed by a subordinate for the rationale behind an opinion or decision, Ed often resorted to an answer frequently employed by other principals as well: "I think you will find that studies have shown . . . ," or, in a dialogue quoted earlier. "Research proves you're wrong," without ever making the referent more specific. Among their peers, research findings cited by one principal were sometimes contraverted with a claimed knowledge of contrary findings cited by another: "I've seen studies that showed exactly the opposite." The impact of the power of "research" diminished as one used it with those higher in the hierarchy, for unless a claimed reference to research supported a higher-up's point of view, he could always mollify the claim by a remark ambiguous in its sincerity but clear in intent, "I'd like to see those findings . . . someday."

Comments made by principals revealed the ambivalent feelings they held toward the accumulated wisdom of their profession and toward those closer to the sources of knowledge than they felt themselves to be. Ed expressed his opinion about the university as a fountainhead of ideas:

> I wish someone related to teacher education on campus would sit down with me and say, "Let's brainstorm how we can work together to get the best involvement of classroom teachers in the business of training teachers." We should put more time, effort, and even money into getting classroom teachers closer to the university program. Maybe once the university was the fountainhead of ideas and training for the public schools, but not any more. I'd like to tell that to the dean or the head of the teacher education program. We compromise too much with the university. We just let them take over. We *say* the classroom teacher is so central. We should *do* something about it.

The aspects of "research" with which principals were in most frequent touch—talking with doctoral candidates about their research programs, or overseeing brief research forays made by university researchers into their schools and classrooms—did little to dispel ambivalence about the ultimate value of the work or entice them to become serious consumers of research findings. Ed inquired routinely about ongoing "research" projects, as in the following brief dialogue with a doctoral student who was also supervising student teachers at Taft, but the research he heard about did not pertain to the problems he faced:

ED: What are you going to do your thesis on?
DOCTORAL STUDENT: I'm going to study "student satisfaction"—the problems of students who transfer from one high school to another.
ED: Sounds real interesting.
DOCTORAL STUDENT: Well, it's a topic, anyway.

Comments recorded during the study, such as the divergent attitudes revealed in the following two remarks, express something of the disparity between the research efforts which principals actually observed firsthand and the status assigned to those most closely identified with the research mystique:

> A lot of this research is just some guy coming out on a doctoral program and asking kids about apples and writing it up.

> Bob Gardner ought to be qualified. He has a Ph.D. in elementary education.

Most references to research were verbal and informal. Therefore they did not require the precision that might have been required for written statements. During the preparation of the series of position papers in the course of the summer administrative workshop, the principals exercised caution and restraint in their written references to or inferences about research by beginning their statements with terms like "We believe . . ." or, "Experience has shown. . . ."

The position paper which Ed and his group prepared contained a statement which began, "We believe that research indicates that. . . ." When that paper was subjected to collective review, one principal read that sentence aloud and commented, "That looks like a tremendous weasel statement to me." The chairman of Ed's group could not restrain a smile as he explained, "We thought if we stated it any stronger, we'd have to cite the studies."

Thus in their process of becoming, principals learn to eschew the formal system of education even as they come to realize that in their chosen careers they can never excape its influence. At the same time, it is their steadfast belief in the importance of formal education for others that gives them their highest professional purpose.

REMAINING A PRINCIPAL

In recent decades the role of the elementary school principal has tended to become more of a career position in its own right and less of a "steppingstone" to secondary school administration. In the national survey, over half of the supervising elementary school principals (57 percent of 1,873 persons responding) reported that in the principalship they had achieved their career goal (DESP 1968: 16). Among the minority of principals who reported that the principalship was not their final goal, far more indicated career objectives immediately related to elementary school education, such as supervisors and directors of elementary education (43 percent), than indicated aspirations to administrative roles like the school superintendency (25 percent) or the secondary school principalship (6 percent); the remainder expressed goals ranging from getting out of the field of education altogether (4 percent) or becoming college teachers (16 percent) to returning to full-time teaching (3 percent) (DESP 1968: 17).[10]

The meaning of the term "career" as used by school principals differs from the meaning assigned the term in some sociological contexts (see Gouldner's [1959] cosmopolitans and locals) and even in the way the term has been applied to the school superintendency (see the "place-bound" and "career-bound" typologies suggested by Carlson 1962, 1972). In the latter case, "career" orientation is presented as the alternative to being place-bound. That is, career commitment for a school superintendent implies a willingness to change districts in order to keep moving "up." In the principalship, at least among Ed's colleagues, career commitment was generally taken to mean a commitment to the position of elementary school principal and to one's school district as well. Ed's assessment of the situation nationally was that there were more career principals than persons using the principalship as a step up; among his fellow principals he knew of only one person who might possibly have his sights set elsewhere. The principals in the Columbia School District shared a perception of their administrative group as relatively stable, one which lacked the internal strife that could result if some principals were trying to push their way ahead of others either directly via obtaining a position in the central office or indirectly via studying for a doctorate. As one principal expressed it, "The principals in this district are free-wheelers. They've arrived."

Whether or not they were conscious of their efforts to maintain group equilibrium, the members of a committee of principals assigned to serve as a preliminary selection committee screening potential candidates for principalships were successful in eliminating applicants whom they suspected might "use" the district rather than commit themselves to it (see Wolcott 1973). Their stated objective in this regard was a consideration for the long-range interests of the district, rather than in the preservation of the status quo in their own group. As one principal explained:

> I would have ranked one candidate higher, but I think of the elementary principalship as a career. He's a stronger candidate than some of the others, but I just don't think he's going to stay—he'll stay about four or five years and use us as a steppingstone.

The real world is replete with examples in which there is a marked difference between the behavior necessary to achieve a new status (such as president, spouse, parent, professor) and the behavior appropriate to maintaining that status once it is achieved (see Benedict 1938). The principalship appears to be no exception. GASing behavior, getting the attention of superiors so that one would be identified as someone special, was precisely the kind of behavior a career-oriented principal wished to avoid once he had achieved his administrative niche. Virtually no advantage accrued to a principal for having his school in the limelight if the principal himself was already established in his career position. If getting the attention of superiors was due to special programs or successes, principals found that the glory of recognition was quickly eroded by the demands of increased visitors, observers, and specialists anxious to introduce other new programs or criticize existing ones.

The alternate way for a principal and school to gain the attention of supervisors was even less desirable—to have attention drawn to the school because someone else's attention, particularly some dissatisfied person or faction in the community, was focused there already. The way to "live and let live" was to run a competent and efficient school program, one that would keep such a wide and disparate group of "customers" (employees, parents, pupils, voters, the school board, university professors, special interest groups) satisfied at best or, at worst, not so dissatisfied that they would organize and stir up trouble. That there would be individual malcontents was generally acknowledged; one parent with children at Taft School had lodged so many complaints over the years, and the complaints had been so well circulated among administrators, that Ed was routinely asked, "How's *that* parent of yours?" Given the inevitable variations among the schools' many customers, principals are less inclined to try to achieve greatness and more inclined to watch instead for signs of any mounting level of discontent. I believe that Ed's effort and anxiety in his work as a principal were to a considerable extent aimed at preventing an event which never occurred during the study: a phone call from the superintendent asking or telling him what was wrong at Taft School. We cannot ignore the significance of such nonevents in the organization of human behavior, events which have sufficiently undesirable consequences that individuals act so as to assure that certain things will *not* happen. Once one had achieved the position of principal, getting the attention of superiors had little potential for contributing toward remaining in that position.

The term "autonomy" was often heard when principals in the district discussed their role or compared the principalship within the district with what they knew or had heard of the position in other school districts. Their feeling was that they enjoyed as much or more freedom to run their schools as other principals throughout the state. The principals who had visited schools in other states felt that their state was above average nationally in the degree of autonomy principals exercised in their schools. Ed once explained to me, "Most of us don't want to give up our autonomy for the sake of conformity. I'm high on that list."

Candidates appearing before the principal selection committee provided further views on autonomy. The following exchange occurred with a candidate who was a principal in an outlying district:

> CANDIDATE: I guess I'm just the kind of an administrator who likes autonomy.
> INTERVIEWING PRINCIPAL: Why do you say you like autonomy?
> CANDIDATE: I like to be an individual—just like you do.
> ANOTHER INTERVIEWING PRINCIPAL (ED BELL): Do you like your teachers to be individuals, too?
> CANDIDATE: Yes! As a matter of fact, I encourage it.

Another candidate had been a vice-principal in the Midwest before accepting a position as a teacher in the district:

> INTERVIEWING PRINCIPAL: How did your previous school district compare with this one?
> CANDIDATE: The principals here have a little more autonomy in the selection of staff.
> INTERVIEWER: Is this autonomy a good thing?
> CANDIDATE: I think this situation is good.
> ANOTHER INTERVIEWING PRINCIPAL: Why do you?
> CANDIDATE: So a staff can develop in abilities to the maximum. For example, maybe one staff can do more with flexibility than another.

It is difficult to discern from these comments the extend to which autonomy meant anything beyond the absence of a feeling that the central office was breathing down each principal's neck or that the overt indications of a rigid and oppressive hierarchy were absent (see Waller's classic description of the school: "despotism in a state of perilous equilibrium" 1932: 10). In any case, the way which principals achieve "autonomy" appears to be universally recognized and practiced: keep to a minimum the dissatisfaction that might threaten it. A researcher conducting a study made of the principal's role in a metropolitan school system several years ago concluded, "When fewer complaints are relayed to the principal's superiors by parents, interested citizens in the school's subdistrict, and teachers, the principal finds that his autonomy increases with his individual school" (McDowell 1954: 370). There are several strategies which principals employ for keeping complaints to a minimum. The one attributed most often to schoolmen is to do nothing that is controversial. Ed often explained any hesitancy about making change because he was "afraid to rock the boat too much." That was not his only strategy, however. He had discovered another strategy which usually had been successful: "Now we just go ahead with the program without making a big issue. We used to announce it, but then everybody started shooting at it." The case in point was related to introducing some aspects of sex education into the curriculum at Taft, but the procedure had more general application.

In the strictest sense, every aspect of the principal's role, every encounter an individual makes while occupying it, every nuance he acquires in his almost lifetime socialization into role occupancy in the school organization contributes something to the sum total of what a principal must be or become in order to remain a principal (see Blood 1966). In the remainder of this section, attention is drawn to two especially influential categories of socializers affecting the role of the principal, central office personnel representing the formal authority of the hierarchy, and peer group influence exhibited by fellow principals.

It is important to realize, however, that in a role as public, ubiquitous, and visible as that of the school principal, virtually anyone may exert some influence toward the continuing process of his socialization, whether it is the dropout who lashes out at the injustice of a former principal, a voter who declares himself opposed to a school tax election because he feels the district's administrators are overpaid, a reporter whose newspaper account makes a principal's comments seem inane, or the anxieties which principals themselves generate in acute self-consciousness about their role. No matter who "starts shooting" first, principals feel that they are the ones who inevitably get caught in the crossfire.

Central Office Personnel as Socializers

Persons at the top of the school district's administrative hierarchy did not merely sit idly in their offices waiting for emergencies. They took many opportunities to remind principals of their obligation to keep them informed of real and potential sources of trouble. The first reminder from the central office about the preparation of teacher evaluations which would be due later in the year provided a very explicit example in this regard: "Please keep us informed all along instead of waiting till it is too late to salvage someone."

Whether Ed was better or worse than most principals in the district about keeping the central office informed I do not know, but it was my impression that he was fairly candid once he made up his mind to let "downtown" know about a budding problem. His preferred professional confidant in the central office was his immediate superior, Dr. Goddard, the Director of Elementary Education. He referred to her telephone number as the "hot line." Although her telephone may have been the hot line to him, his alternatives to it were even hotter: the telephones of the Assistant Superintendent and the Superintendent. In some cases the Director of Personnel had authority to hear a problem and make a decision on it, but Ed's preference was to restrict his discussion of problems to the two administrators who were immediately "over" him (Director of Elementary Education; Assistant Superintendent), and they were the people he called for problems of any consequence. I have no record of his calling the Superintendent or of the Superintendent calling him, although calls were sometimes exchanged between Taft School and the Superintendent's office (i.e., his secretary) concerning the preparation of reports requested specifically by the Superintendent.

Ed's personal feelings about each of these four administrators also influenced his choice of who to call, particularly in this preference for working with Carolyn Goddard. The following excerpts from comments made throughout the course of the field work leave little doubt about Ed's personal feelings:

Of Dr. Carolyn Goddard:

> Isn't that Carolyn something! Even when I might want to react angrily to something, she reacts pleasantly and finds something positive that can be said. And she is always stimulating, and always encouraging of new ideas—even if they aren't any good.

Of Dr. Floyd Prince, the Assistant Superintendent:

> He and I have never gotten along too well. . . . I think he wanted this place [Taft School] to be a showplace. He wanted to put a more sophisticated guy out here. But, then, he could have.
> Floyd doesn't think the elementary school principalship is very important.

Of Dr. Samuel Boggs, the Superintendent:

> I've never known how he felt toward me. Maybe he wasn't sure of what I was doing. And maybe I'm just wondering for nothing. I guess I don't know exactly how he feels. . . . He's the only official I worry about, and I'm not sure just how worried I am about him.
>
> I guess it sounds like I'm anti-central office. Well, maybe I am. I do respect Sam, although I don't particularly like him. He is interested in new ideas. He knows what is going on across the nation. That's where he's so different from Floyd. Floyd is so conservative. . . . We've been riding the crest ever since Sam came here.
>
> I think Boggs is a pretty smart guy. Oh, there's a bit of farmer in him, but he's pretty alert. I just get sort of tired listening to all his talk at times.

Of the Director of Personnel:

> He's next to nothing. If he wasn't Sam's man [the Superintendent had brought the personnel director with him from another district] he'd have been bagged long ago. . . . He doesn't know what's going on in the schools.

Information filtered to the central office (and back) via myriad formal and informal channels. The superintendent explained, "Information just comes to us, in all sorts of ways." Those scholars who look to the "communication problem" in schools and school districts perpetuate a myth in the belief that the remedy to school malfunction is so simple as merely to get school people talking to each other. There are indeed problems in assuring that the messages intended are the ones received, but no one can ignore that information is constantly being exchanged in schools and that for most purposes the channels of communication are exceedingly effective, even when the content of the messages is not especially welcome (see Smith 1968).

Ostensibly to foster the "upward" so well as to facilitate the "downward" flow of information, administrators in the central office had established several regularly recurring meetings in which key personnel met with groups of administrators. Such groups were usually divided on the basis of geographical boundaries or school levels. Monthly "area" meetings held by the superintendent at each high school were attended by the high school principal and principals of the junior high and elementary "feeder" schools. The stated purpose of these meetings was to "keep lines of communication open," but the superintendent had a reputation for dominating any conversation, and the principals looked upon the meetings as a two-hour monologue with compulsory attendance: "It's the same every time. That guy never says a damn thing." The monthly meetings of all elementary principals held by the Director of Elementary Education seemed to allow for a fairly easy flow of information both "up" and "down" of those items of interest to the elementary principals collectively. These formal meetings also provided informal opportunities for exchanging information with members of the central office staff.

One special event of the year in terms of principal-central office interaction was a formal "principal's evaluation" conference held between members of the central office staff and each school administrator midway through the school year. A form letter sent to all elementary principals by Dr. Goddard stated that the evaluation conferences were being held "in accordance with the school board request." Ed did not express undue concern when he received the notice. He recalled a similar evaluation procedure three years earlier:

> It was favorable. I expect this one to go even better. They did say something about losing my temper, which is still a problem. Also, Floyd said I was too dependent on one member of my staff. I didn't agree but I didn't argue.

Ed's conference was scheduled for 8:30 A.M. in Dr. Goddard's office on a Tuesday in February. Ed accepted the appointment hour given to him, although the time chosen happened to be when he would otherwise have attended the guidance committee meeting at his own school, the meeting which he described as the most important one he directed.

Ed's evaluation conference provides an excellent source of information regarding his continuing socialization as an administrator by central office personnel. An account of the meeting is provided here in some detail, although it is not presented verbatim. Those present at the meeting were Ed, Dr. Goddard, Dr. Prince (the Assistant Superintendent), and myself.

ED'S EVALUATION CONFERENCE AT THE CENTRAL OFFICE

Ed and I arrived at the central office about ten minutes before the time scheduled for his appointment. Ed suggested we walk through the halls while we waited. As we walked, the idea occurred to him of stopping at the personnel office to ask which substitute had been sent out in place of a Taft teacher who had "phoned in sick." Ed was still early for his appointment when he arrived at the office of the Director of Elementary Education, but she bade us come in and be seated while we waited for the Assistant Superintendent to arrive. Until he arrived, she continued working at her desk. Ed and I visited. As soon as Dr. Prince arrived, he, Dr. Goddard, and Ed arranged themselves around a small table; I sat some distance away to facilitate note taking and to minimize the distraction of an outsider. After the meeting Ed said that he had not felt restricted by my presence, and he doubted that it had restricted the others.

Dr. Goddard (turning to Ed and indicating the beginning of the conference): We'll let you start and we'll just chime in. What is the emphasis in your school?

Ed: The emphasis at Taft School is toward the individual child. Our philosophy is in the direction of the nongraded school, although we aren't in a position to offer this. I think this year is an all-time high. The children are feeling a greater responsibility for their own education, that it's up to them. We're there to help.

Dr. Goddard: How do you work with your Instructional Materials Center [IMC]? Is it always manned?

Ed: Yes, our teacher aide is always there. And Bob Mason, our resource teacher, is there sometimes. I'm still not satisfied with the amount of materials.

Dr. Goddard: Is there any place where youngsters can work in the library?

Ed: Not much. We do have a conference room in the new wing. Ideally, we need to make Room 7 into an IMC. I'm not satisfied with it as it is. It's too far from the resource teacher.[11]

Dr. Goddard: Bob [Mason] isn't really too interested in instructional materials, is he?

Ed: Oh, yes. He has a good working relationship.

Dr. Goddard: Does the intern program fragment the staff?

Ed: Somewhat. Our in-service training program plus having intern teachers have kept us pretty close to how much teachers can do.

Dr. Goddard: If you were going to plan this year over again, would you still have the in-service program?

Dr. Prince: Who actually made the decision about having the in-service program?

Ed: Well, the whole staff. I made the final decision.

Dr. Prince: How committed does the staff feel?

Ed: They are committed to it. At least, all but a couple. Wally Adam hasn't come; neither has our new teacher we added during the year.

Dr. Prince: How is Wally doing?

Ed: He'll finish his dissertation this summer.

Dr. Goddard: Does he still resist authority?

Ed: Yes. The people around him are not always comfortable and neither am I. But he is a very stimulating person to have on a faculty. He has a very effective way of working with parents, and he has many supporters. Last month he had the father of one of his sixth-graders come in to help with math. I hadn't seen that particular father around before, and I haven't seen him since.

Dr. Goddard: Wally is just one of these offhand people. He doesn't fit in and he doesn't want to.

Dr. Prince: As far as his working with children, do you have any problem with him?

Ed: No. If anything, he overdoes it.

Dr. Prince: Is his class bedlam?

Ed: No, it depends on what they are doing. When he's ready to go, they are with him. But he doesn't expect children to sit around like puppets.

Dr. Prince: And they don't! Well, it proves that there is more than one way to teach.

Ed: I guess you could say he's not much on the "housekeeping" chores.

Dr. Goddard: I've never observed a particular problem there. Maybe it has only been when I wasn't there. How is Sally Jensen doing with her first grade? Is she holding up all right?

Ed: Yes. I finally had to step in and say "no" to her. The social studies consultant wanted her to work one afternoon a week helping to develop more curriculum materials.

Dr. Prince: While we're talking about staff, do you have any other staff problems?

Ed: Yes, I do.

Dr. Prince: Well, let's discuss them.

Ed: Alma [Skirmish]. I've already talked to Carolyn about her. You might say she's a little selfish. She puts other things ahead of school.

Dr. Prince (apparently aware of the problem): She knows our calendar. She better take some other kind of work if she wants to attend conferences with her husband.

Ed: She also had a little trouble with Santa.

Dr. Goddard (to Dr. Prince): She told them there wasn't any Santa.

Dr. Prince: Oh, no, she couldn't have.

Ed: Well, they asked her a direct question. She is a *good* classroom teacher. She just makes some errors in judgment.

Dr. Prince: Who else is a problem on the staff?

Ed: Margaret Elder. She has wonderful rapport with kids, but the children in her class just aren't making the progress the other children are.

Dr. Prince: How experienced is she?

Ed: She's an older person, with lots of experience. She's the kind of person I just can't get to know. She's very pleasant, but she seems aloof. I just haven't gotten to know much about her.

Dr. Goddard: I'm interested in your comment that she's aloof. She seems quite talkative.

Ed: She's friendly enough, but she doesn't say something like, "I wish I knew how to do such and such."

Dr. Goddard: I wonder if Margaret and your other new sixth-grade teacher could develop some plans for teaching cooperatively. Maybe the two of them could work together. And they could also work with the intern supervisor—if she could do anything in a calm way.

Ed: But the intern supervisor doesn't do anything in a calm way. I had a long session with her and Ellwood New last night until quarter of six. It was the same kind of problem she had with one of the interns last year, although I thought it was his fault at the time. I'm really worried about her intensity, overwhelming *fellows*, especially.[12]

Dr. Prince (to Dr. Goddard): Maybe you ought to have a heart-to-heart talk with her. There are so many things it could be.

Ed: I've said to her, "You don't have to prove yourself. You don't have to work so terribly hard at it to prove yourself to me."

Dr. Goddard: I thought that maybe interviewing interns would be a specific kind of job that she could do. Something's not right.

Dr. Prince: Has she really told you what's bugging her?

Ed: No. I thought it was that mother-in-law situation, but after that changed the problem was still there.

Dr. Prince: I know that she's had some tough problems in her personal life. Maybe you need to sit down and have a long talk with her. Do you think you could have that kind of a talk with her? [Ed nodded in the affirmative.] Some women just shouldn't work with men. I can say that here in front of Carolyn.

    We're running out of time. I'd like to ask about "community." What are you doing to encourage community relations?

Ed: We used to have a parent committee, but they depended on me too much to provide everything for them. So we don't have that. We have a very active PTA right now. They just had their big pancake breakfast last Saturday—from 6:15 to 11:00 A.M. They made over one hundred twenty dollars.

    I think the community feels free to come and ask. But they don't as much as I'd like.

Dr. Prince: What does the Taft community need that your school could provide?

Ed: The building is used a great deal. There are about thirty-five activities a week. The community is a bedroom community. The fathers and mothers both work in many cases. They don't have time to do much with kids.

Dr. Goddard: These parents, more than others, may need to know that kids elsewhere have the same problems as theirs.

Ed: I think this community is quite upwardly mobile. These parents are trying to go beyond their backgrounds. Many are living beyond their means, on a prayer and a promise.

Dr. Goddard: Maybe in your community you could use ideas about child rearing. Put them in the Newsletter or something like that. Maybe these are the kinds of things we should be getting for parents.

Ed: I'm sure many people look at the Taft School community as one with pretty high expectations.

Dr. Goddard: Like along El Dorado Drive, where the Princes [the Assistant Superintendent's brother, one of the developers of the El Dorado area] live.

Dr. Prince: And also the von Brockmeiers. And Dr. Meheren [a former school board member]. What has concerned me there is the condition of vandalism in that whole junior high area. Not just Taft School—I see some of it in the Jefferson area—Norm Olds has some of it. I wonder if parents are aware of what their kids do.

Ed: I'm wondering if the kids at East High have somewhat lower goals and whether the vandalism reflects this.

Dr. Prince: I'm not so sure—maybe West High has more problems, but we don't see it because of the scholars at West. For example, I know of one family whose kid went to West High. That family had tried to keep the reins on their kid from when he first entered school. Then suddenly they got a call from the police to come get their boy at the police station.

Ed: I'm interested in the feedback you people get about how the schools are doing. I had a talk with John Robinson, an active PTA father at Taft, on just how he felt about schools. He told me quite frankly.

Dr. Goddard: The little feedback I get is that this is a restless time. I don't think it's done [getting parental feedback] through PTA—but more in informal activities, like coming in to help in a class, or coming to have lunch.

Ed: I think I have an advantage there in having such a good counsellor. She moves slowly but surely, but she is making headway.

Dr. Goddard: You give a somewhat austere impression. There is a certain dignity about you, but people need to see your smile. Sometimes when I come into the building you seem so formal, but I know you aren't that way.

Ed: I know what's underneath. But you have a point there.

Dr. Goddard: You may find yourself getting irritated on a little point that may not matter in the long run.

Ed: I appreciate your saying that.

Dr. Prince: Maybe they need to know you have empathy with them.

[Dr. Prince departed, explaining that he needed to make a telephone call, and that he would leave Dr. Goddard to review with Ed a rating sheet which they had prepared earlier. Dr. Goddard explained to Ed that he had been rated higher in "staff relations" than in "community relations."]

Dr. Goddard: You run a smooth ship there.

Ed: That's not one of my goals.

Dr. Goddard: No, but you are effecting change, and it is comfortable. The general overall evaluation of you would be good. Now this may or may not be true: getting new ideas for meeting educational problems is not your forte, but when it comes to putting ideas of others into practice, you are effective.

Ed: What you say is true. I'm not particularly an idea man. This is why I like to have people around like the intern supervisor, or Sally Jensen, or some of those university supervisors and bright graduate students. This is why I want people to feel comfortable in my school.

Dr. Goddard: I think you have organized it so everyone's ideas can get out.

Ed: Yes. I know of easier ways to run a school, but I want ideas to get out.

Dr. Goddard: If you personally can relax a little more, then do it.

Ed: I think I feel more relaxed in the building than in these other places where you see me.

Dr. Goddard (smiling reassuringly): I think you've done a good enough job so you can feel comfortable at school and not worry.

Dr. Goddard stood to signal the end of the conference. Ed also stood, and they proceeded to the door together. In the outer office another principal was awaiting an evaluation conference. Ed stopped in the hall for a drink of water before we left the building and walked out to his car.

As we rode back to Taft School, Ed commented on the conference. He said he felt the meeting had gone well and that in general his evaluation had been favorable, just as he predicted it would be. "But I thought I'd come out on the check sheet better than I did." He described his difficulty in determining what the ranking meant, since he was given no comparative information about how the other principals had been rated:

> I suppose that people like Angeline or Norman [two of the principals with reputations for being highly organized] come out the highest on the evaluations. In some ways I run circles around them, but these ways don't show. For example, the other morning when we were riding to that meeting with Norman, he was telling me how on that morning one of his teachers had come to him in tears because of the number of memos she had received from him the day before.

Recognizing that some of the misgivings he had about the way he had been evaluated were probably the same misgivings teachers at Taft might be expressing about his evaluations of them, Ed concluded philosophically, "These conferences are a good experience for those of us who have to evaluate teachers."

The secretary, the counsellor, and several teachers were having a morning coffee break when we arrived back at the school. A teacher who had not seen Ed during his brief visit at school earlier that morning joked about his easy job getting to school so late in the day. Several others laughed good-naturedly to share the joke. "Go easy, girls! I've just been evaluated," he countered. In the brief pause that ensued, he added as an afterthought, "But I came out pretty well."

One of the tasks awaiting Ed's return to school that morning was to investigate a complaint turned in by a school bus driver about a fifth-grade boy who had broken a bus rule. Ed's talk with the boy was very straightforward: "Do you want to ride the bus?" "Have you been in trouble with the driver before?" "What happened?" (He had changed seats while the bus was moving; he thought it was about to stop.) "I'll sign this citation and put a note on it that you are not going to cause any future problems." The boy returned to his classroom as matter-of-factly as he had conducted himself during their brief exchange. Apparently musing on his interview earlier that morning. Ed turned to me and said, "I think Carolyn would be surprised to know how unafraid the kids are of me. And how unafraid the teachers feel that the kids are."[13]

Ed did not refer again to his evaluation conference in my presence, and I remained in doubt about whether he really felt he had come out "pretty well" or, in terms of the successful year he perceived this one to be, if he was disappointed in the tone of the evaluation. The fact that each staff member with whom I held a taped interview in the days following Ed's conference brought up the subject of his evaluation suggests that he did continue thinking and talking about it and that, on further reflection, he had felt some misgivings. It was characteristic of Ed not to turn such thoughts inward but to let others know how he felt.

Mrs. Wendy, the school counselor, gave this account of Ed's conference:

> He said he was going to be evaluated last week by some people down at the main office. When he came back, he said of course he wasn't evaluated as high as he would have liked to have been. But I think this is good, I think that we all need to set our goals high and then if we don't achieve them we shouldn't feel that we are inadequate. I don't think he is really that disappointed. I think he was just thinking about himself in terms of how he saw himself.

Mr. New, an intern teacher, explained:

> Ed told me that he didn't do too well on the evaluation that Dr. Prince gave him a few weeks ago. Or at least he didn't feel that he was satisfied with the wording of the evaluation. He didn't have to tell me that. But he was just being honest with me. We were taling about *my* evaluation—I think that is how it came up.

Some attempt was evident among the principals to make light of the evaluation conferences both in anticipating them and in subsequently referring to them. For example, a principal who had the earliest conference scheduled one morning later told Ed and others that he "got the first ride on the donkey" that day. However, I was not privy to any discussions or joking references by the principals regarding the *content* of their individual evaluations, nor were the conferences themselves taken lightly. The principals responded to their individual summoning as directed, even ignoring prerogatives which some of them exercised in other settings, such as arriving late for meetings. The Director of Elementary Education reviewed the conferences with satisfaction: "Everyone has kept on time, and we've not run over by more than ten minutes."

Living Within the Hierarchy

The evaluation conferences served to emphasize the formal hierarchical nature of the school district's organization, but there were other ways, both intended and inadvertent, by which principals were reminded constantly of their station in the professional hierarchy. The policies, directives, regulations, and traditions which a school district develops are designed to clarify lines of authority and responsibility and to introduce consistency into the system. Principals have lived with such procedures all their professional lives. No principal in this study was ever heard making a categorical rejection of policies and directives, and many, perhaps most, of the tasks which they performed in compliance with decisions made by others were accepted as being "all in a day's work." At times ultimatums which were handed down or requests which were made were received stoically or accepted as challenges. But there were other policies, directives, and procedures which rankled, perhaps because they encroached on "autonomy" or served as too candid reminders of restraints on the power invested in the principalship. Often the specific instances of this sort were minor, and an observer could not assess their cumulative effect.[14] Other practices were singled out as whipping boys, providing the principals collectively with evidence of what was "wrong" with their position. A few such practices are described here.

One policy that threatened the feeling of autonomy required principals to have permission from the central office if they were going to be away from the school district on school business during the day. Permission was to be obtained *in advance* and *in writing* and was to be signed by Dr. Goddard or Dr. Prince as well as the Director of Personnel. With Ed's sometimes helter-skelter organization, the occasions when he complied fully with the policy and had his official away-on-school-business form filed in the personnel office before the absence itself were the exception rather than the rule. At the beginning of the drive to one out-of-district meeting, Ed boasted in jest: "I *already* have permission for today's trip." If he did not have a completed permission form on file, he was careful to notify the Director of Elementary Education or, in her absence, the Assistant Superintendent, before actually leaving the district for any extended period of time. I heard of no cases in which permission was denied or in which any principal made a request that tested the limits in which it might have been, although midway through the study the superintendent did announce a new policy of allowing a maximum of one day of professional leave to attend meetings for each fifty school days. Thus actually securing permission was a routine matter. It was, however, the bureaucratic and paternalistic kind of routine which characterized the way persons at each successive step throughout the hierarchy customarily handled the group below it. Like a pupil raising his hand for permission to go to the toilet, the demeaning aspect was not the nature of the request (which is typically, but not invariably, honored in schools) but that the request had to be made at all.

Another whipping boy among the principals did not affect them all, but those who *were* affected by it did not attempt to hide their sense of annoyance at the picayune logic that had worked it out. By starting summer school before the district's elementary administrators had completed the regular service stipulated in their annual contracts, the district found itself paying some administrators for summer employment while they still had three full days of service remaining on their ten-month contracts. The resolution of the problem was that principals who were employed in the summer program were asked to prepare a written statement describing how they planned to "repay" the district *in time* for the 24 working hours covered by the overlapping contracts (8 hour day × 3 days). The principals were assured by Dr. Goddard that any way of working out the problem would be acceptable and that no one was going to "check up" on them in carrying out their commitment. Ed submitted a plan for remaining at his school each afternoon from the official termination of the summer school day at 2:30 P.M. until 5:00 P.M. for the number of days required to make up the time. Most of his colleagues followed the same procedure. By the time the summer school actually opened, the principals involved had ample time to work up strong feelings against being required to make up extra hours. The story was circulated that Dr. Goddard had become so annoyed during a telephone discussion on the topic with one of the principals that she had hung up on him midway in their conversation, a behavior that seemed almost unbelievable to the collectivity of principals who admired her remarkable composure. ("They're still good friends, though," Ed hastened to explain.)

The matter of "repaying" time to the district remained a sore point reviewed intermittently in private conversations for months. Almost a year later I recorded an incident where a principal gently goaded the Director of Elementary Education by declaring that if a new program she proposed was going to keep him at his school later in the day than other principals he wanted to be paid for it. "Or else," he suggested, "you could still use it to make up that week we were dubbed [docked?] if we held summer school." The following summer Dr. Goddard anticipated the recurrence of the problem and issued a memorandum early in June acknowledging the "nitty little problem of overlapping duty periods." At that time she polled each principal to learn whether he "had plans to work later in the summer" to complete the duties of his regular assignments.

From the point of view of the central office, neither of these procedures was probably intended as more than an attempt at organizational efficiency. In fact, however, such measures had a net effect of severely detracting from the image of the principal as an autonomous leader of his school, emphasizing instead his place as a functionary in the hierarchy of the system. That it was even thinkable on behalf of the central office personnel that they should have proposed, albeit gently and even "permissively," that each summer school principal remain an extra two and a half hours "on duty" at his deserted school building until he had accumulated 24 extra hours of duty, epitomized to the principals how oblivious central office personnel were to their actual work week. Having heard the facts themselves, they mused whether those personnel, and specifically the Director of Elementary Education, were really serious about the proposal. Lacking any way of knowing for sure, each principal made his own separate peace. Ed hedged both ways; he felt no qualms about leaving early after the long hours he had put in all year at school, yet he did not wish to go back on his word. Since he lived near his school, he sometimes meandered home after summer school, changed clothes, and returned to school to putter around or "do some filing." But the "nitty little problem" of the total hours he spent at school and the apparent lack of appreciation for the fact was not easily dismissed:

> I have some ideas for helping out with our many problems. But I won't do anything until they tell me from downtown that I don't have to spend every daylight hour in this building, and until they give me some help. Unless I give up my family and just do this job day and night.

The hierarchy was reinforced through formal procedures as well as informal ones. "Voluntary" contributions solicited from school employees provide an instance of the former. Attaining the financial quota for the community's annual United Appeal Fund produced a situation in which formal statements had always assured that the amount of an individual's contribution was "a personal and individual matter," and those were the words that appeared in the letter sent from the central office to all school district employees. At the same time, if the quotas assigned to the school district and distributed among the schools failed to be met, past experience suggested that additional encouragement could be expected. Three principals compared strategies for collecting the money:

First Principal: I told my teachers that with $11.50 from each teacher, $20 from the principal, $5.00 from the custodian and secretary, and $1 from all the other employees—do you know that some of our assistant cooks only make $600 a year—we can make our quota.

Second Principal: The resource teacher [a GASer] and I just make up the difference in our quota each year.

Ed Bell: I put mine in first. I don't intend to make up any deficits.

After the drive began, Ed was queried by principal Norm Olds about whether he had subsequently received any special word regarding the amount contributed at Taft School:

Norman: Say, did you get a letter from Sam on United Appeal?

Ed: No. Not yet, anyway.

Norman: The quota for my school was $290. When they called on a survey from downtown some time ago, my secretary said, "Oh, I think we have collected around $200." So I got a *personal* note from Sam. Not a form letter. It said, "Norm, don't you think we could do a little better?" Well, when it gets to that point . . .

Ed: When I get so that's my only contribution, I'll start thinking differently.

Norman: I wrote across the note, "Collections are now $260" and I sent it back. On the other hand, I know a guy at the bank who has cut down his *monthly* contribution from $10 to $9. That's still more than some teachers give for the *year.*

Ed: Those boys in business and industry are really under pressure from their bosses.

Norman (turning to me): Not that this isn't a good thing, Harry. . . .

Three months later, the teacher appointed to take charge of the United Appeal "Campaign" for the school asked Ed if she could make an announcement about it during a Taft faculty meeting:

Teacher: We were $28 short on United Appeal. We thought that if every teacher gave another dollar, we'd almost make it.

Ed: Has Dr. Boggs called you?

Teacher: No.

Ed: He didn't call me, either. I understand he *did* call some of the principals.

Contributions (totaling about $18,000) the following year put the district "well over the established quota" during the course of the initial drive for funds. A notice in the monthly *Superintendent's Bulletin* commended all personnel: "This is a very positive indication of appreciation shown by school district employees for the improved benefits that have been provided for the current school year budget."

Peers as Socializers

The major emphasis for the continuing socialization of principals into and by the hierarchical structure of the Columbia School District occurred via formal modes. The socialization which occurred among the principals themselves, by contrast, was carried out predominantly by informal means.

The "conventional wisdom" of the elementary principalship, in contrast to its formal body of knowledge, is carried about in the minds of its successful and experienced practitioners. It is transmitted verbally and, for the most part, informally, to succeeding generations. It is an oral literature. Younger men turn to their more experienced colleagues when they wish to draw upon the accumulated wisdom of years of practical experience. Like teachers, school administrators derive satisfaction from a shared perception that no one can really understand what it is like to be a principal until he has been there himself.

An accumulated wisdom based on years of personal experience lends itself to an oral literature for many reasons. For one, the average principal appears not to be an avid reader, and thus an oral tradition is more expedient than a written one. Certainly the average principal is not a writer, so those considered to be in the know are unlikely to have the time or inclination to make their knowledge a matter of written record. Those who manage to get some part of it written down typically are outsiders, students of administration rather than practicing administrators. An oral tradition allows for essential slippage between one man's experience and another man's problem, for no two administrative problems are exactly alike. The elusiveness of an oral tradition provides some minor protection for the principal from critical attack by outsiders, including those among his daily contacts—teachers and parents alike—whose numbers invariably include individuals who feel they could administer a school twice as effectivley with half the effort.

An accumulated body of wisdom presided over by the elders may also provide a certain amount of satisfaction and comfort as a younger man envisions himself coming to hold a more exalted rank among his peers as he accumulates years of service. The senior principals in the group were treated with deference by the younger members. To illustrate: as the principals were gathering for an evening meeting of the local principal's association, one young and recently appointed principal encountered Norman Olds, a senior principal, and the following diologue ensured:

Young Principal: Good evening, Mr. Olds.
Senior Principal: Let's just use "Norm."
Young Principal: Oh, it's just out of habit, I guess. I've been calling you that for a long time.
Senior Principal: I know. But it doesn't sound right. You even did it at a meeting in front of a lot of teachers the other evening.

A useful distinction can be made between the different kinds of information which school principals control and use. Major attention has been given to the task requirements of their work, both in terms of the limited "knowledge base" of school administration and the extent to which the real "know-how" for survival, the wisdom of the role, is transmitted orally. Complementary to the accumulated wisdom or "know-how" of the principalship is an aspect which might be called, "know-who." By reason of their long tenure in the school district, the senior principals controlled a great deal of interpersonal information about their superordinates, their peers, and other long-time employees. They could unfold a complex interpersonal professional network, with the name, rank, and professional history of each of their cohorts. The extent and complexity of the network bore resemblance to the extensive kinship systems which anthropologists have often collected from informants during field studies. Principals knew who among their junior peers had formerly served their senior ones, whose careers had been blocked or enhanced by present and former central office personnel, how each person had come through the ranks, and even what his likely prospects were for the future. The principals perceived and talked about committees, schools, and offices in the central administration building in terms of who occupied them. They referred to a school as often by the name of its principal as by the name assigned to the building. They out-guessed, second-guessed, and critiqued personnel changes and new appointments. Whenever a new committee was formed, their interest was directed to its constituents rather than its purposes.

Ed Bell was accumulating this body of information, both by living it and through hearing stories recounted or questions answered by his "elders." In turn, he could recount some parts to those principals who were junior to him. Such knowledge of how people had come "through the ranks" was not only of passing interest. It was useful in dealing with peers and with central office personnel, and it could prove invaluable in knowing how to work with administrators in other districts, professors of education, and personnel in the State Department of Education, particularly in identifying the extent of their experience in and their commitment to the elementary school principalship. For example, the Director of Elementary Education in a neighboring school district was esteemed among principals throughout the region for his commitment to the principalship: "He's real popular. He came up through the ranks. He was very popular as an elementary principal." This man had continued a close association with the principal group after becoming a central-office administrator. He was an active member of their associations. Wherever he appeared away from his district on school business he was always accompanied by several of the elementary principals with whom he worked.[15]

Principals in Ed's district contrasted the background of that administrator with their own Dr. Goddard. She had served as an elementary curriculum consultant and supervisor but had never been a supervising principal of an elementary school. Perhaps because of her personable nature and remarkable poise, she seemed well accepted by the elementary principals. Ed often commented enthusiastically on his appreciation of the way she performed in her administrative role, and even one of his more pessimistically-inclined colleagues conceded, "She has only been a head teacher before, not a principal. But none of the administrators objects to her." Because the principals accepted her personally, they interpreted her lack of experience in her favor: "She *knows* she hasn't been a principal before, so she doesn't tell us how to go about our work. Customarily, lack of experience at the elementary school level was heralded as the central cause of problems between principals and the typical central office administrator or superintendent. One principal noted, "I *never have* worked with a superintendent who really understands the role of the elementary school administrator."

If there was one obvious means by which principals exerted some audible degree of social control over their colleagues, it was in their institutionalized use of humor. I do not mean by this that principals are especially humorous men in terms of great wit or an uncanny knack for seeing the "funny side" of every situation. Rather, like most schoolmen, principals appreciated and encouraged the efforts of those among them who helped to keep school business from becoming unnecessarily serious and pedestrian. The light vein of give-and-take banter which they maintained while discussing school affairs, particularly in meetings restricted to themselves and Dr. Goddard, sometimes served as a screen for venting pent-up feelings of tedium or of opprobrium at too blatantly authoritarian statements made by colleagues or central office personnel.

Ed Bell was certainly not a humorist, but neither was he humorless. He liked to laugh—or at least to smile broadly. Like the majority of principals, he enjoyed hearing a good joke or an account of a humorous incident, and he enjoyed holding the attention of others with a joke or a true experience from his own youth or from his years as an educator.[16]

In the form of joke-telling, principal humor simultaneously reached its perigee and apogee at professional meetings of sufficient attendance to warrant enlisting someone—not necessarily from within their own ranks—to act as the emcee of a formal program. On such occasions the jokes seemed designed for one purpose only: "keep'em laughing." The principals applauded the efforts of every program chairman to accomplish that goal even if the number or quality of jokes proved to be a test of audience patience. The pattern of beginning county, regional, and state meetings with "a few jokes" seemed less related to the purposes of those organizations than to a patent formula for surefire public speaking success learned long ago in elocution classes and never examined since; start off with an attention-getting device to make sure you have your audience with you. Perhaps schoolmen fall back on such a formula in dealing with their colleagues in voluntary associations because under more routine circumstances most audiences a principal addresses in the course of his daily work are captive ones. For his all-call announcements over the office intercom or his comments at faculty meetings, attention need not be diverted from the business immediately at hand.

Some patterned humor was a consequence of the fact that principals frequently found themselves among professional colleagues with whom they were not sufficiently well acquainted to be able to engage easily in personal conversations. Their greetings and informal introductions often included joking references to incidents where a colleague had achieved an administrative coup or to humorous circumstances shared in common. For example, the meetings of the principals were usually of long duration and the termination of a meeting inevitably saw a rush on the nearest men's lavatory. This situation provoked an equally inevitable set of comments by those present on the uniformity imposed on them from within ("That meeting ended just in time") or, as a result of school architecture, from without ("That's a nice bunch of backs, there"). Occasionally jokes were made at the expense of someone higher in the hierarchy: "Say, who's been writing to Dr. Boggs here on the wall?"

The serious functions carried out in the guise of humor accomplished such purposes as maintaining uniformity in the amount of time and effort expended at particular tasks, giving or testing information about the limits of acceptable behavior, or bringing some individual or part of the group back into line. The maintenance of uniformity of effort worked two ways. Through joking about how they were progressing in the preparation of reports, meeting deadlines, and so forth, the principals had some idea of the range of behavior deemed appropriate by their peers. At the same time, the chronic "rate busters" and early-birds could become, or even volunteer themselves to be, the butt of mild joking which relieved some of the tension which might otherwise have developed. Certain principals, for example, were felt to be almost too adept in getting what they wanted for their schools, especially in "scrounging" equipment and materials from the central office. An exchange of banter such as the following provided an opportunity for a socializing note of constraint on the part of one administrator and an acknowledgement by another that he was pressing the limits of acceptable behavior:

First Principal: Did you get those tiles this year?
Second Principal (Tom Nice): Yes.
First Principal: You son-of-a-gun. How did you get them?
Second Principal: Well, I've worn out one pair of pants just from walking on my knees every time I'm at the central office.

Exchanging information about the expectations of professional behavior was effectively accomplished through humor. For example, most principals subscribed to the idea that it was desirable to know the names of all the children in their school. Whether an individual principal could actually achieve this, however, depended on external factors like school size as well as on personal adroitness in learning names. Ed was not particularly good at remembering names except for those children who were highly visible from the office's point of view. He claimed to have known each child by name when the school was smaller, but he had not been able to keep track of all the pupils in recent years. Bill St. Clair, at a neighboring school, claimed to know the names of all of his students. A principal of a new and rapidly growing school mentioned one day that he had enrolled his 630th pupil, and he and Ed chided Bill that if he had a school of that size he would not be able to keep up any longer. Tom Nice overheard the conversation and added that although *he* could not remember all the names of the children at his school he did have a secretary who knew them. The principal of the large school chuckled at Tom's announcement and made a joke of the secretary's behavior: You see, that's all she does. No reports or anything. She just sits there all day long memorizing names."

Although the major socializing influence of Ed's peers seemed to be in the direction of keeping principals "in tow," the normal structure of their professional organizations did provide a channel for politically mobile career-oriented principals who wished to remain in their present professional role and still achieve greater visibility and power. Two routes "up and out" of the principalship have already been described, one via a direct promotion into central office administration based on success within one's own district, the other via academic success and outside help in obtaining a new administrative position or a post at a college or university. A third alternative was also possible. A principal could become active by seeking offices in his own professional organizations. In recent years, with the sponsorship and encouragement of Tom Nice and others, Ed had pursued this latter alternative. His views were mixed about whether to maintain so active a role in the principals' associations. Early in the study, he said:

> You might call me a reluctant participant. I think you have to do something to help these organizations or else keep your mouth shut. Eventually, I'll probably get involved at the state level.

After four straight years in office, and recognizing some major differences between politicking among acquaintances at the regional association and as a stranger in the rest of the state, Ed was not so sure that he wanted to seek office beyond the regional organization. Whether or not he actually does so will probably depend a great deal on the kind of encouragement he gets from his peers in this region.

NOTES

1. The term "enculturation" appears frequently in anthropological accounts, sometimes used interchangeably with socialization, sometimes subsuming it, and at other times being subsumed by it. The two terms are perhaps best employed as complementary aspects in the process of humanizing individuals, socialization drawing attention to learning how to behave and enculturation drawing attention to the process of acquiring a world view (see Leis 1972: 4-5). I believe that calling attention to these complementary dimensions is a signal contribution from anthropology to the study of human behavior. Nevertheless, I have here employed only the term socialization, since it has wide currency among social scientists and educators, particularly in the context of learning specific role behavior.
2. Turner treated sponsored and contest mobility as contrasting, ideal types by which one could compare upward mobility in American and English systems of education, rather than as complementary aspects of the same process. Although the context to which he applied his examination was in formal educational sys-

tems, his analysis dealt with upward mobility of students rather than with upward mobility among the permanent school cadre as in the present study.

3. The term GASing appeared in a study of teacher mobility in New York City
reported by Dan Griffiths (Griffiths et al. 1963). Griffiths points out that in a
huge metropolitan school district like New York City which used to hold competitive examinations for administrative appointments, it was not the examination which created the pool of potential appointees, as might be assumed; rather,
it was the GASing behavior of aspirants. "The examination system validates the
GASers; it does not create a pool from which promotions are made" (p. 33).

4. "The programs appear to be bookish to the ultimate. . . . The mediocrity of programs of preparation comes from the sterility of the methods reported. Instruction is classroom bound; administration is talked about rather than observed,
felt, and in these and other ways actually experienced" (AASA 1960: 83).

5. Alfred Baldwin, *Behavior and Development in Childhood* (New York: Dryden
Press, 1955); William H. Burton and Leo J. Brueckner, *Supervision, A Social
Process* (New York: Appleton-Century-Crofts, 1955); Willard S. Ellsbree and
Harold J. McNally, *Elementary School Administration and Supervision* (New
York: American Book Company, 1951); LaVonne A. Hanna, Gladys L. Potter,
and Neva Hagamann, *Unit Teaching in the Elementary School* (New York:
Rinehart Publishing Company, 1955); George C. Kyte, *The Principal at Work*
(Boston: Ginn and Company, 1952); B. Othanel Smith, William O. Stanley,
and J. Harland Shores, *Fundamentals of Curriculum Development* (New York:
World Book Company, 1957); Harold Spears, *Principles of Teaching* (New
York: Prentice-Hall, 1951).

6. Jerome Bruner, *The Process of Education* (Cambridge, Mass.: Harvard University Press, 1961).

7. Lest I am unwittingly perpetuating this "finding," let me add that the authors
of the study did *not* accept the explanation that nothing taught in programs of
preparation is relevant to being a school principal. In fact, they reportedly did
find professional knowledge reflected in the performance of principals. They
suggested that their finding of zero correlations between amount of formal education and performance on certain administrative tasks was related to the
variable "years of preparation." That variable was obtained by adding *all* the
years of post-high school education, rather than allowing for more discrete
analyses of special components like graduate preparations in professional education (Hemphill et al. 1962: 341).

8. From the point of view of university faculty, to be perceived as a faculty
"patron saint" may have been ego gratifying but it was also threateningly time-
consuming. One professor of education confided after an evening presentation
to the principal's association: "I just didn't have the time to prepare for my
talk this evening. I took out the material only this afternoon. But you could
be out doing this kind of thing all the time and at the university they wouldn't
give you any credit for it."

9. For example, one principal enrolled in a doctoral program had a student teacher
at his school whom he felt would benefit by an additional term of student
teaching experience. The young lady's university adviser felt otherwise, and his
opinion was never challenged. "That same professor happens to be *my* adviser
on the doctoral program," the principal explained, "so I don't want to go
against him."

10. Dissatisfaction with the position of *teaching principal* as contrasted with *supervising principal* is suggested by comparing the ratio of respondents in each
group who reported that their ultimate goal was to get back into classroom
teaching in the elementary school: 26 percent of the teaching principals versus
3 percent of the supervising principals.

11. I failed to recognize the significance of this comment at the time. Ed was
beginning to lobby for a major improvement he wanted at Taft School. Two
years later Room 7 had been converted into an IMC.

12. En route to the central office that morning, Ed had discussed recent friction
developing between the intern supervisor and the male intern teacher, Ellwood
New. "She doesn't seem to know enough to lay off when someone has had
enough. She has to keep going until *everything* is settled."

13. In my field notes I recorded by personal feeling about Ed's reaction to his
evaluation:

   I guess this charge of being *formidable* bothered him. Personally I think it is
   probably a fair observation. What Ed confuses is his wish to be a good pal
   under most circumstances and his frequently overbearing approach with a few

kids when things go wrong. Maybe this is linked to C. Goddard's and F. Prince's suggestion this morning that he not let occasional little things bother him.

14. For example, the head librarian of the school district once telephoned Ed about a book order he had submitted for additional reading materials for "slow readers" at Taft School. She informed him that one of the books on his order could be purchased but it would have to be placed in the professional library of the school rather than be put on the open shelves. The restricted volume was *Little Black Sambo*.

15. At the same time, outsiders generally felt that his close association with the principals resulted in tight controls over their actions, and that the elementary schools in that district were virtually administered as a single unit from the central office.

16. Ed's most often told story at school was the apocryphal one about an exasperated rural school teacher who finally decided to write a note home concerning the unpleasant odor of one of her pupils. She wrote: "Johnny smells bad. Could you please do something about it." The next day she received a note in reply, "Don't smell him. Larn him!"

REFERENCES

American Association of School Administrators, 1960, *Professional Administrators for America's Schools*. Thirty-eighth yearbook, American Association of School Administrators, National Education Association, Washington, D.C.

Benedict, Ruth, 1938, "Continuities and Discontinuities in Cultural Conditioning," *Psychiatry* 1:161–167.

Blood, Ronald E., 1966, "The Function of Experience in Professional Preparation, Teaching and the Principalship." Unpublished Ph.D. dissertation, Claremont Graduate School, Claremont, Calif.

Carlson, Richard O., 1962, *Executive Succession and Organizational Change—Place-bound and Career-bound Superintendents of Schools*. University of Chicago, Midwest Administration Center, Chicago, Ill.

———, 1972, *School Superintendents: Careers and Performance*. Columbus, Oh.: Merrill.

Department of Elementary School Principals (DESP), 1958, "The Elementary School Principalship—A Research Study." *The National Elementary Principal*, 37th Yearbook of the Department of Elementary School Principals, National Education Association, Washington, D.C.

Elkins, Benjamin, 1950, "Status, Problems, and Practices of Beginning Elementary School Principals." Unpublished Ph.D. dissertation, School of Education, Northwestern University, Evanston, Ill.

Fleming, Emett Eugene, 1967, "Innovation Related to the Tenure, Succession and Orientation of the Elementary Principal." Unpublished doctoral dissertation, Northwestern University, Evanston, Ill.

Gouldner, Alvin W., 1959, "Organizational Analysis." In Robert K. Merton, Leonard Broom, and Leonard S. Cottrell, Jr., eds., *Sociology Today*. New York: Basic Books.

Griffiths, Daniel E., John S. Benben, Samuel Goldman, Laurence Iannaccone, and Wayne J. McFarland, 1963, "Teacher Mobility in New York City: A Study of the Recruitment, Selection, Appointment, and Promotion of Teachers in the New York City Public Schools." New York University, School of Education, Center for School Services, New York. Lithographed.

Halpin, Andrew W., 1970, "Administrative Theory: The Fumbled Torch." In Arthur M. Kroll, ed., *Issues in American Education*. New York: Oxford.

Hemphill, John K., Daniel E. Griffiths, and Norman Frederiksen, 1962, *Administrative Performance and Personality*. Bureau of Publications, Teachers College, Columbia University, New York.

Leis, Philip E., 1972, *Enculturation and Socialization in an Ijaw Village*. New York: Holt, Rinehart and Winston.

McDowell, Harold D., 1954, "The Principal's Role in a Metropolitan School System: Its Functions and Variations." Unpublished doctoral dissertation, University of Chicago, Department of Sociology, Chicago, Ill.

Rose, Robert Louis, 1969, "Career Sponsorship in the School Superintendency." Unpublished doctoral dissertation, College of Education, University of Oregon, Eugene.

Smith, Alfred G., 1968, "Communication and Inter-cultural Conflict." In Carl E. Larson and Francis E. X. Dance, eds., *Perspectives on Communication.* Milwaukee: University of Wisconsin Press.

Waller, Willard, 1932, *The Sociology of Teaching.* New York: Wiley. Science Edition Printing, 1965.

Wolcott, Harry F., 1973, *The Elementary School Principal: Notes from a Field Study.* In George D. Spindler, ed., *Education and Cultural Process: Approaches to the Anthropology of Education.* New York: Holt, Rinehart and Winston.